Steps to Writing an Argument

The cover of this book makes a visual argument about sustainability. Use these steps to develop your own arguments about this or other topics in the book.

Step 1 Find a Topic

Read your assignment and determine what type of argument is called for (see pages 25–26).

Find a topic that interests you by reading, talking, and exploring (see pages 23–34).

Step 2 Make a Claim and Support It with Good Reasons

Make a claim designed to change readers' views or persuade them to take action.

List your main points and think about the order of those points.

Step 3 Think About What's at Stake

What exactly is the problem or issue, what causes it, and who is most affected?

Has anyone tried to do anything about it? If so, why haven't they succeeded?

Step 4 Analyze Your Potential Readers

Who are your readers?

How familiar will they be with what you are arguing?

Which claims are they most likely to accept and which will they disagree with?

Step 5 Write a Draft

Introduction

Set out the issue or problem, and give some background if necessary.

Argue for the seriousness of the issue or problem.

Give your thesis in one sentence.

Body

Present and interpret your evidence and its significance.

Keep your focus narrow and make your structure clear to your readers.

If you are proposing a solution to a problem, state your solution and its benefits.

Take a few minutes to think about other views on your issue or problem.

Conclusion

Leave your readers with somethin̶ ̶ ̶ ̶ ̶ ̶ ̶ ̶ ̶ ̶ ̶ ̶ ̶ ̶

Issue a call to action—if your read̶ ̶ ̶ ̶ ̶ ̶ ̶ ̶ ̶ ̶ ̶ take action.

Step 6 Revise, Edit, Proofr̶ ̶ ̶ ̶

For detailed instructions, see Chap̶ ̶ ̶

For a checklist to use to evaluate your draft, see pages 48–49.

Detailed Contents

PART 2

Analyzing Arguments

PART 3

Writing Arguments

PART 4

Designing and Presenting Arguments

PART 5

Researching Arguments

PART 6

Contemporary Arguments

PART 7   Handbook   661

Alternate Contents: Selections by Types of Arguments

Narrative Arguments

Proposal Arguments

Rebuttal Arguments

Visual Arguments

Preface

Nothing students learn in college will prove to be more important to them than the ability to create an effective argument.

As a student you are already aware that campus life is itself filled with arguments. There are hot-button public issues that engage the academic community—binge drinking, for example, or making the university more environmentally sustainable, or how to improve campus housing or study-abroad opportunities. Meanwhile, in the classroom and in research programs, you and your peers will present arguments on current controversies such as climate change and economic policy as well as on scholarly topics such as the structure of the human brain, the cultural achievements of ancient Egypt, or the means of determining the material composition of the planet Mercury.

After college, you will continue to need to communicate effectively your ideas and points of view. Your livelihood and your successful engagement in the life of your community will depend on it. Sometimes as a citizen you will be moved to register your views on how to improve your local school system or enhance local development; or as a member of a neighborhood group or a civic organization, you will be suggesting ways of making a positive difference. And certainly in the workplace you will often be making arguments to support your recommendations and to refute the flawed recommendations of others.

What This Book Offers You

For a number of years we have studied arguments, taught students how to argue, and listened to others talk and write about the art of persuasion. Although there is no simple recipe for cooking up effective arguments, we've discovered there are definite strategies and tactics that writers can rely on in any situation to ensure that their ideas are considered seriously. However, we also know that regardless of the value of its content, a text will be ineffective if it cannot present its ideas in a way that is engaging, easy to use, and comprehensive. It has been our aim to create such a text in *Good Reasons with Contemporary Arguments and Handbook*.

One-stop guide to everything you need to know. Because you need to have instruction, examples, and writing help at your fingertips, this text combines **three books in one**: an accessible brief guide to argument (**Parts 1–5**), a topically organized anthology of readings (**Part 6**), and a handbook (**Part 7**)—everything you need in a course on argument in one book.

Lively, nontechnical language. We've pointedly avoided technical jargon in order to explain concepts and techniques as clearly as possible. Explanations, examples, captions, and exercises are all written with the goal of keeping language straightforward and accessible.

Emphasis on attractive design and visual arguments. *Good Reasons with Contemporary Arguments and Handbook* is notable for its two chapters that guide students through the process of understanding arguments that are written and /or visual. In addition, the book itself demonstrates the value of visual argument in its attractive design that is liberally illustrated with graphics, photos, and other visuals.

Annotated student writing samples and numerous other examples. In line with our philosophy of showing rather than telling, chapters covering types of arguments include annotated student essays as well as annotated professional essays illustrating six basic types of arguments: definition, causal, evaluation, narrative, rebuttal, and proposal arguments.

Fresh, timely readings—including academic readings—on current issues. These readings demonstrate how complex conversations develop around important issues of interest to students today. Readings span a wide range of material from canonical essays to contemporary journal articles. We've also taken care to select readings that give different points of view on an issue.

Resources for grammar and punctuation. We know that concise, stylistically fluent, and correct writing is essential to making an effective argument. Toward that end, we have included a handbook of grammar and mechanics that covers essential topics and is designed for easy use.

Key Features

In *Good Reasons with Contemporary Arguments and Handbook* you'll find the following specific key features.

Parts 1–5: Guide to Argument

- **Concise explanation and illustration of how to read, analyze, and write arguments,** including an introduction to why people write arguments and to how to find "good reasons" to support your own arguments (Chapters 1–4); two chapters on rhetorical analysis (Chapters 5 and 6) that enable you to understand (and write about) written and visual arguments with confidence; and instruction, with accessible examples, in six common types of argument (Chapters 8–13).

- **"Steps to Writing" guides** that provide a handy visual overview for drafting, developing, and revising each type of argument covered in *Good Reasons with Contemporary Arguments and Handbook,* helping you to review and apply the concepts and strategies presented (Chapters 8–13).

- **Coverage of designing and presenting multimodal arguments that reflects a focus on new media and online texts.** Chapters 14 and 15 cover the principles of visual argument, and examples demonstrate the ways writers are using new forms of digital and multimodal rhetoric to create and deliver arguments to their audiences.

- **Eight sample student arguments, with explanatory annotations,** that provide working models you can use to develop and revise every type of argument covered in *Good Reasons with Contemporary Arguments and Handbook.*

- **Seven professional selections that exemplify the different types of argument,** accompanied by explanatory annotations.

- **Detailed guidance on how to gather information from library and Internet sources and how to document those sources in a way that builds credibility and trust.** The coverage (Chapters 16–19) includes how to use database sources. Numerous examples throughout the book illustrate those explanations.

- **In-depth treatment of how to evaluate and cite online sources in MLA or APA style** in Chapters 20 and 21.

- **Learning objectives** (Chapters 1–21) to guide what you learn from this book in specific terms.

Part 6: Anthology of Readings

- **Seventy-seven engaging professional readings** (in addition to the selections in Parts 2 and 3) that address significant current issues and illustrate effective persuasive techniques for each type of argument to inspire you to mount your own arguments. Included are **sixteen examples of academic arguments** (readings with citations) on topics such as sustainability, the effects of videogames, and the costs of higher education.

- **An "Issue in Focus" section** in each chapter that brings together readings with different points of view on a specific contemporary issue.

Part 7: Handbook

- **Detailed handbook on grammar and mechanics,** including Common Errors boxes that offer guidance on how to recognize, understand, and correct the most frequent errors.

- **A separate handbook glossary and index,** as well as a Revision Guide of commonly used proofreading and editing symbols and a list of Common Errors boxes.

Resources for Teachers and Students

Instructor's Manual

The **Instructor's Manual** that accompanies this text was revised by Brian Neff, of The Pennsylvania State University, and is designed to be useful for new and experienced instructors alike. The Instructor's Manual briefly discusses the ins and outs of teaching the material in each text chapter as well as the handbook topics. Also provided are in-class exercises, homework assignments, discussion questions for each reading selection, and model paper assignments and syllabi. This Instructor's Manual will make your work as a teacher a bit easier. Teaching argumentation and composition becomes a process that has genuine—and often surprising—rewards.

Pearson MyLabs

The Pearson English MyLabs empower students to improve their skills in writing, grammar, research, and documentation with market-leading instruction, multimedia tutorials, exercises, and assessment tools. Students can use the MyLab on their own, benefiting from self-paced diagnostics and extra practice in content knowledge and writing skills. Instructors can use MyLabs in ways that best complement their courses and teaching styles. They can work more efficiently and more closely with students by creating their own assignments and using time-saving administrative and assessment tools. To learn more, visit www.pearsonhighered.com/englishmylabs or ask your Pearson representative.

CourseSmart eTextbook

Good Reasons with Contemporary Arguments and Handbook is also available as a CourseSmart eTextbook. This is an exciting new choice for students, who can subscribe to the same content online and search the text, make notes online, print out reading assignments that incorporate lecture notes, and bookmark important passages for later review. For more information, or to subscribe to the CourseSmart eTextbook, visit www.coursesmart.com.

Acknowledgments

We are much indebted to the work of many outstanding scholars of argument and to our colleagues who teach argument at Texas and at Penn State. In particular, we thank the following reviewers for sharing their expertise: Kamala Balasubramanian, Grossmont College; Greg Barnhisel, Duquesne University; Andrea Deacon, University of Wisconsin-Stout; Jean S. Filetti, Christopher Newport University; Wendy Goodwin, Miami Dade College; Timothy S. Layton, St. Louis Community

College at Florissant Valley; Amisha Patel, Arizona State University; Jeff Pruchnic, Wayne State University; and Jeff Wylie, Maysville Community and Technical College. We are also grateful to the many students we've taught in our own classes, who have given us opportunities to test these materials in class and who have taught us a great deal about the nature of argument. Special thanks go the students whose work is included in this edition.

We have greatly benefited from working with Brad Potthoff, senior editor, and Michael Greer and Linda Stern, development editors, whose talent and creativity continue to impress us and who contribute much to both the vision and the details of *Good Reasons with Contemporary Arguments and Handbook*. They are the best, and we much enjoyed working with them on this and other books. Laura Newcomer provided expert assistance in locating potential selections for Part 6. Special thanks go to Brian C. Neff for preparing the Instructor's Manual. Lindsay Bethoney at PreMediaGlobal and Eric Jorgensen at Pearson Longman did splendid work in preparing our book for publication. We were quite fortunate to again have Elsa van Bergen as our copyeditor, who has no peer in our experience. Finally, we thank our families, who make it all possible.

Lester Faigley

Jack Selzer

Reading and Discovering Arguments

PART 1

1 | Making an Effective Argument

MadV's *The Message* consists of a series of extremely short videos from YouTube members of words written on hands, similar to the one shown here.

What Exactly Is an Argument?

One of the best-known celebrities on YouTube is an anonymous video director who wears a Guy Fawkes mask and uses the name MadV. In November 2006 he posted a short video in which he held up his hand with the words "One World" written on his palm and invited viewers to take a stand by uploading a video to YouTube. They responded by the thousands, writing short messages written on their palms. MadV then compiled many of the responses in a 4-minute video titled *The Message* and posted it on YouTube.

MadV's project has been praised as a celebration of the values of the YouTube community. The common theme that we all should try to love and better understand other people is one that few oppose. Yet the video also raises the question of how any of the goals might be achieved. One hand reads "Stop Bigotry." We see a great deal of hatred in written responses to many YouTube videos. Slogans like "Open Mind," "Be Colorblind," "Love Is Stronger," "No more racism," and "Yup One World" seem inadequate for the scope of the problem.

Like the ink-on-hand messages, bumper stickers usually consist of unilateral statements ("Be Green," "Save the Whales," or "Share the Road") but provide no supporting evidence or reasons for why anyone should do what they say. People committed to a particular cause or belief often assume that their reasons are self-evident, and that everyone thinks the same way. These writers know they can count on certain words and phrases to produce predictable responses.

In college courses, in public life, and in professional careers, however, written arguments cannot be reduced to signs or slogans. Writers of effective arguments do not assume that everyone thinks the same way or holds the same beliefs. They attempt to change people's minds by convincing them of the validity of new ideas or the superiority of a particular course of action. Writers of such arguments not only offer evidence and reasons to support their position but also examine the assumptions on which an argument is based, address opposing arguments, and anticipate their readers' objections.

Extended written arguments make more demands on their readers than most other kinds of writing. Like bumper stickers, these arguments often appeal to our emotions. But they typically do much more.

- They expand our knowledge with the depth of their analysis.
- They lead us through a complex set of claims by providing networks of logical relationships and appropriate evidence.
- They build on what has been written previously by providing trails of sources.

Finally, they cause us to reflect on what we read, in a process that we will shortly describe as critical reading.

Finding Good Reasons

Who's Using up Earth's Resources?

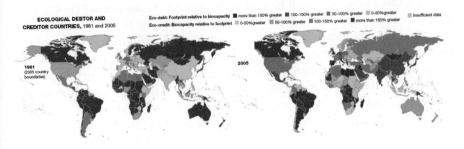

ECOLOGICAL DEBTOR AND CREDITOR COUNTRIES, 1961 and 2005

In the *Living Planet Report* for 2008, the World Wildlife Fund compared the ecological footprints from 1961 and 2005 for each country on Earth. The ecological footprint of a country is determined by its population, the amount of food, timber, and other resources consumed by its average citizen, the area required to produce food, fishing grounds, and the area required to absorb CO_2 emissions minus the amount absorbed by oceans.

Countries fall into four categories: ecological debtor nations (which consume more resources than they can produce), ecological creditor nations (which produce more than they consume), and two categories of ecologically balanced nations, where production and consumption are relatively balanced. In this map you can see that the United States, Mexico, Western Europe, China, India, Pakistan, Japan, and the nations of the Middle East have become ecological debtors with footprints more than 50 percent of their biocapacity—what they are able to produce. Nations such as Canada, Russia, Australia, New Zealand, and most nations in South America are ecological creditors, with footprints less than 50 percent of their biocapacity. In its entirety, the *Living Planet Report* makes the argument that nations should live in balance with what their land, rivers, lakes, and seas can support.

Write about it

1. What might be some of the causes of the differences among the ecological footprints of nations?

2. What is likely to happen in the future when some nations have enough resources (such as clean water and food) and others lack them?

3. Does the map succeed as an argument on its own? Does it contain any of the features of written arguments listed on pages 5–6?

Writing Arguments in College

Writing in college varies considerably from course to course. A lab report for a biology course looks quite different from a paper in your English class, just as a classroom observation in an education course differs from a case study report in an accounting class.

Nevertheless, much of the writing you will do in college will consist of arguments. Some common expectations about arguments in college writing extend across disciplines. For example, you could be assigned to write a proposal for a downtown light-rail system in a number of different classes—civil engineering, urban planning, government, or management. The emphasis of such a proposal would change depending on the course. In all cases, however, the proposal would require a complex argument in which you describe the problem that the light-rail system would improve, make a specific proposal that addresses the problem, explain the benefits of the system, estimate the cost, identify funding sources, assess alternatives to your plan, and anticipate possible opposition. It's a lot to think about.

Setting out a specific proposal or claim supported by reasons and evidence is at the heart of most college writing, no matter what the course. Some expectations of arguments (such as including a thesis statement) may be familiar to you, but others (such as the emphasis on finding alternative ways of thinking about a subject and finding facts that might run counter to your conclusions) may be unfamiliar.

WRITTEN ARGUMENTS . . .	WRITERS ARE EXPECTED TO . . .
State explicit claims	Make a claim that isn't obvious. The main claim is often called a **thesis.** (see pages 40–41)
Support claims with reasons	Express reasons in a **because clause** after the claim (We should do something *because* _____). (see pages 25–26)
Base reasons on evidence	Provide evidence for reasons in the form of facts, statistics, testimony from reliable sources, and direct observations. (see pages 37–38)
Consider opposing positions	Help readers understand why there are disagreements about issues by accurately representing differing views. (see pages 29–31)
Analyze with insight	Provide in-depth analysis of what they read and view. (see Chapters 5 and 6)

(continued)

WRITTEN ARGUMENTS...	WRITERS ARE EXPECTED TO...
Investigate complexity	Explore the complexity of a subject by asking "Have you thought about this?" or "What if you discard the usual way of thinking about a subject and take the opposite point of view?" (see pages 34–36)
Organize information clearly	Make the main ideas evident to readers and to indicate which parts are subordinate to others. (see pages 44–45)
Signal relationships of parts	Indicate logical relationships clearly so that readers can follow an argument without getting lost. (see page 51)
Document sources carefully	Provide the sources of information so that readers can consult the same sources the writer used. (see Chapters 20 and 21)

How can you argue responsibly?

In Washington, D.C., cars with diplomatic license plates are often parked illegally. Their drivers know they will not be towed or ticketed. People who abuse the diplomatic privilege are announcing, "I'm not playing by the rules."

When you begin an argument by saying "in my opinion," you are making a similar announcement. First, the phrase is redundant. A reader assumes that if you make a claim in writing, you believe that claim. More important, a claim is rarely *only* your opinion. Most beliefs and assumptions are shared by many people. If a claim truly is only your opinion, it can be easily dismissed. If your position is likely to be held by at least a few other people, however, then a responsible reader must consider your position seriously. You argue responsibly when you set out the reasons for making a claim and offer facts to support those reasons. You argue responsibly when you allow readers to examine your evidence by documenting the sources you have consulted. Finally, you argue responsibly when you acknowledge that other people may have positions different from yours.

How can you argue respectfully?

Our culture is competitive, and our goal often is to win. Professional athletes, top trial lawyers, or candidates for president of the United States either win big or lose. But most of us live in a world in which our opponents don't go away when the game is over.

Most of us have to deal with people who disagree with us at times but continue to work and live in our communities. The idea of winning in such situations can only be temporary. Soon enough, we will need the support of those who were on the other side of the most recent issue. You can probably think of times when a friendly argument resulted in a better understanding of all peoples' views. And probably you can think of a time when an argument created hard feelings that lasted for years.

Usually, listeners and readers are more willing to consider your argument seriously if you cast yourself as a respectful partner rather than as a competitor. Put forth your arguments in the spirit of mutual support and negotiation—in the interest of finding the *best* way, not "my way." How can you be the person that your reader will want to join rather than resist? Here are a few suggestions for both your written arguments and for discussing controversial issues.

- **Try to think of yourself as engaged not so much in winning over your audience as in courting your audience's cooperation.** Argue vigorously, but not so vigorously that opposing views are vanquished or silenced. Remember that your goal is to invite a response that creates a dialogue and continuing partnership.

- **Show that you understand and genuinely respect your listener's or reader's position even if you think the position is ultimately wrong.** Remember to argue against opponents' positions, not against the opponents themselves. Arguing respectfully often means representing an opponent's position in terms that he or she would accept. Look for ground that you already share with your opponent, and search for even more. See yourself as a mediator. Consider that neither you nor the other person has arrived at a best solution. Then carry on in the hope that dialogue will lead to an even better course of action than the one you now recommend. Expect and assume the best of your listener or reader, and deliver your best.

- **Cultivate a sense of humor and a distinctive voice.** Many textbooks about argument emphasize using a reasonable voice. But a reasonable voice doesn't have to be a dull one. Humor is a legitimate tool of argument. Although playing an issue strictly for laughs risks not being taken seriously, nothing creates a sense of goodwill quite as much as tasteful humor. A sense of humor can be especially welcome when the stakes are high, sides have been chosen, and tempers are flaring.

Arguments as Turns in a Conversation

Consider your argument as just one move in a larger process that might end up helping you. Most times we argue because we think we have something to offer. In the process of researching what has been said and written on a particular issue, however, often your own view is expanded and you find an opportunity to add your voice to the ongoing conversation.

A Case Study: The Microcredit Debate

Two women financed by microcredit sell scarves in Quito, Ecuador.

World Bank researchers reported in 2009 that 1.4 billion people—over 20 percent of the 6.7 billion people on earth—live below the extreme poverty line of $1.25 a day, with 6 million children starving to death every year. One cause of continuing extreme poverty is the inability of poor people to borrow money because they have no cash income or assets. Banks have seldom made loans to very poor people, who have had to turn to moneylenders that charge high interest rates sometimes exceeding 100 percent a month.

In 1976, Muhammad Yunus observed that poor women in Bangladesh who made bamboo furniture could not profit from their labor because they had to borrow money at high interest rates to buy bamboo. Yunus loaned $27 to forty-two women out of his pocket. They repaid him at an interest rate of two cents per loan. The success of the experiment eventually led to Yunus securing a loan from the government to create a bank to make loans to poor people. The Grameen Bank (Village Bank) became a model for other microfinancing projects in Bangladesh, serving 7 million people, 94 percent of whom are women. For his work with the Grameen initiative, Yunus received the Nobel Peace Prize in 2006.

Microcredit now has many supporters, including Hollywood stars like Natalie Portman and Michael Douglas, companies like Benetton and Sam's Club, and former

President Bill Clinton. But the success in Bangladesh has not been replicated in many other poor countries. Many critics point to the shortcomings of microcredit. This debate can be better understood if you consider the different points of view on microcredit to be different voices in a conversation.

Microcredit is the best way to lift people out of extreme poverty.

But in many countries microcredit lenders still charge high interest rates, creating a new generation of loan sharks.

Microcredit is aimed at individuals and doesn't create businesses that can hire workers in steady jobs.

Much of the money lent in microcredit is used to supplement the family income, not create new businesses.

Poor countries typically do not have qualified staff to manage microcredit institutions.

Rather than focusing exclusively on microcredit, poor countries should give citizens access to cheap savings accounts, insurance, and money transfer services.

Now it's your turn to add to the conversation.

The conversation about microcredit has led others to put new ideas on the table.

Mapping a conversation like the debate about microcredit often can help you identify how you can add to the conversation. What can you add to what's been said?

Some people claim that _____.

Other people respond that _____.

Still others claim that _____.

I agree with X's and Y's points, but I maintain that _____

because _____.

Think About Your Credibility

A few writers begin with instant credibility because of what they have accomplished. If you're a tennis player, likely you will pay attention to advice from Serena Williams. If you're interested in future trends in computers and entertainment, you'll listen to the forecasts of Ji Lee, who has served as Creative Director at both Google and Facebook, or Bill Gates. But if you are like most of the rest of us, you don't have instant credibility and so you must build it through your communication itself.

Think about how you want your readers to see you

To get your readers to take you seriously, you must convince them that they can trust you. You need to get them to see you as

> **Concerned.** Readers want you to be committed to what you are writing about. They also expect you to be concerned with them as readers. After all, if you don't care about them, why should they read what you write?
>
> **Well informed.** Many people ramble on about any subject without knowing anything about it. If they are family members, you have to suffer their opinions, but it is not enjoyable. College writing requires that you do your homework on a subject.
>
> **Fair.** Many writers look at only one side of an issue. Readers respect objectivity and an unbiased approach.
>
> **Ethical.** Many writers use only the facts that support their positions and often distort facts and sources. Critical readers often notice what is being left out. Don't try to conceal what doesn't support your position.

Take, for example, the topic of genetically modified (GM) food, which is highly controversial in Japan and Europe and has become increasingly controversial in the United States. The central issue is whether genetically modified food is safe, but the effects on ecosystems, the gene flow into crops that are not genetically engineered, and the control of our food supply by a handful of corporations are also major issues. Because most people in the United States know little about genetically modified food, you will gain credibility by presenting a balanced overview of each of these issues.

Build your credibility

Know what's at stake. What you are writing about should matter to your readers. If its importance is not evident, it's your job to explain why your readers should consider it important.

LESS EFFECTIVE:
We should be concerned about two-thirds of Central and South America's 110 brightly colored harlequin frog species becoming extinct in the last twenty years. (*The loss of any species is unfortunate, but the writer gives us no other reason for concern.*)

MORE EFFECTIVE:
The rapid decline of amphibians worldwide due to global warming may be the advance warning of the loss of cold-weather species such as polar bears, penguins, and reindeer.

Have your readers in mind. If you are writing about a specialized subject that your readers don't know much about, take the time to explain key concepts.

LESS EFFECTIVE:
Reduction in the value of a debt security, especially a bond, results from a rise in interest rates. Conversely, a decline in interest rates results in an increase in the value of a debt security, especially bonds. (*The basic idea is here, but it is not expressed clearly, especially if the reader is not familiar with investing.*)

MORE EFFECTIVE:
Bond prices move inversely to interest rates. When interest rates go up, bond prices go down, and when interest rates go down, bond prices go up.

Think about alternative solutions and points of view. Readers appreciate a writer's ability to see a subject from multiple perspectives.

LESS EFFECTIVE:
We will reduce greenhouse gas and global warming only if we greatly increase wind-generated electricity. (*Wind power is an alternative energy source, but it is expensive and many people don't want windmills in scenic areas. The writer also doesn't mention using energy more efficiently.*)

MORE EFFECTIVE:
If the world is serious about limiting carbon emissions to reduce global warming, then along with increasing efficient energy use, all non-carbon-emitting energy sources must be considered, including nuclear power. Nuclear power now produces about 20 percent of U.S. electricity with no emissions--the equivalent of taking 58 million passenger cars off the road.

Be honest. Readers also appreciate writers who admit what they aren't sure about. Leaving readers with unanswered questions can lead them to think further about your subject.

LESS EFFECTIVE:

The decline in violent crime during the 1990s was due to putting more people in jail with longer sentences.

MORE EFFECTIVE:

Exactly what caused the decline in violent crime during the 1990s remains uncertain. Politicians point to longer sentences for criminals, but the decrease in the population most likely to commit crimes—the 16-to-35 age group—may have been a contributing factor.

Write well. Nothing impresses readers more than graceful, fluent writing that is clear, direct, and forceful. Even if readers don't agree with you in the end, they still will appreciate your writing ability.

LESS EFFECTIVE:

Nobody can live today without taking some risks, even very rich people. After all, we don't know what we're breathing in the air. A lot of food has chemicals and hormones in it. There's a big hole in the ozone, so more people will get skin cancer. And a lot of people have sexually transmitted diseases these days. (The impact of the point is lost with unfocused writing.)

MORE EFFECTIVE:

We live in a world of risks beyond our control to the extent that it difficult to think of anything that is risk free down to the most basic human acts--sex in an era of AIDS, eating in an era of genetically altered food, walking outside in an ozone-depleted atmosphere, drinking water and breathing air laden with chemicals whose effects we do not understand.

For additional writing resources that will help you master the objectives of this chapter, go to your **MyLab**.

2 | Reading Arguments

QUICK TAKE

In this chapter you will learn to

1. Recognize that controversies often involve many nuanced positions (see below)
2. Read an argument critically (see page 14)
3. Use mapping to understand the structure of an argument (see page 17)
4. Identify and define fallacies of logic, emotion, and language (see pages 16–17)

Explore Controversies

People in general agree on broad goals for their society: clean water, abundant healthy food, efficient transportation, good schools, full employment, affordable health care, safe cities and neighborhoods, and peace with others near and far. People in general, however, often disagree on how to define and achieve these goals. Controversies surround major issues and causes.

Often controversies are portrayed in the media as pro and con or even take on political labels. But if you read and listen carefully to what people have to say about a particular issue, you usually find a range of different positions on the issue, and you often discover nuances and complexities in the reasons people offer for their positions.

Find controversies

Online subject directories can help you identify the differing views on a large, general topic. Try the subject index of your library's online catalog. You'll likely find subtopics listed under large topics. Also, your library's Web site may have a link to the *Opposing Viewpoints* database.

One of the best Web subject directories for finding arguments is Yahoo's *Issues and Causes* directory. This directory provides subtopics for major issues and provides links to the Web sites of organizations interested in particular issues.

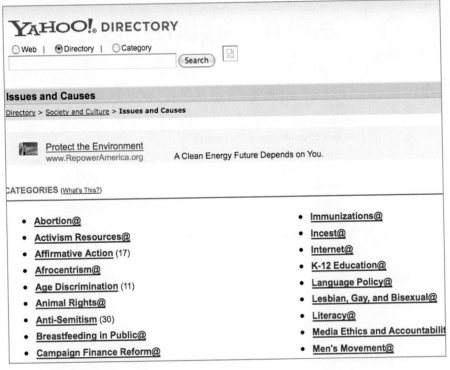

Yahoo! *Issues and Causes* directory (dir.yahoo.com/Society_and_Culture/Issues_and_Causes/)

Read Critically

After you survey the landscape of a particular issue, turn to careful reading of individual arguments, one at a time.

Before you begin reading, ask these questions

- Where did the argument first appear? Was it published in a book, newspaper, magazine, or electronic source? Many items in library databases and on the Web were published somewhere else first.
- Who wrote this argument? What do you know about the author?
- What does the title suggest that the argument might be about?

Read the argument once without making notes to gain a sense of the content

- When you finish, write one sentence that sums up the argument.

Finding Good Reasons

Everyone A Writer

You**Tube**   [Search | Browse | Upload]

Are we producing reality?
thepoasm   27 videos ⌄   Subscribe

▶ ◀)) 1:09 / 6:14   ⤻ ⤢

Video blogs, known as vlogs, became a popular genre on YouTube.

Before the Internet was invented, readers had to make some effort to respond to writers by writing to them directly, sending a letter to the editor, or even scribbling or spray-painting a response. The Internet has changed the interaction between writers and readers by allowing readers to respond easily to writers and, in turn, turning readers into writers. Look, for example, at Amazon.com. An incredible amount of writing surrounds any best-selling book—often an author's Web site and blog, newspaper reviews, and over a hundred readers' reviews. Or read a political, sports, culture, fashion, or parenting blog and the comments by readers of those blogs. Think about how the Internet has changed the relationship between readers and writers.

To find a blog that interests you, use a blog search engine such as *Bloglines* (www.bloglines.com), *Google Blog Search* (blogsearch.google.com), *IceRocket* (blogs.icerocket.com), or *Technorati* (www.technorati.com).

Write about it

1. Using a blog search engine or an online newspaper, find a blog by an author, politician, or news columnist. Answer as many of the questions for critical reading on page 16 as you can.

2. Write a summary of the blog entry.

3. What kinds of reasons do blog writers give for their responses to what they read?

4. How are blogs and online book reviews like or unlike traditional book reviews in print?

Read the argument a second and third time and make notes

- Go back through the text and underline the author's thesis.
- Do your sentence and the author's thesis match? If not, look at the text again and either adjust your sentence or check if you underlined the correct sentence.
- How is the argument organized? How are the major points arranged?
- What reasons or evidence does the writer offer in support of the thesis?
- How does the writer conclude the argument? Does the conclusion follow from the evidence presented?
- Who is the intended audience? What does the writer assume the readers know and believe?
- Do you detect a bias in the writer's position?
- Where do the writer's facts come from? Does the writer give the sources? Are the sources reliable?
- Does the writer acknowledge other views and unfavorable evidence? Does the writer deal fairly with the views of others?
- If there are images or graphics, are they well integrated and clearly labeled?

Annotate what you read

- **Mark major points and key concepts.** Sometimes major points are indicated by headings, but often you will need to locate them.
- **Connect with your experience.** Think about your own experiences and how they match up or don't match up with what you are reading.
- **Connect passages.** Notice how ideas connect to each other. Draw lines and arrows. If an idea connects to something from a few pages earlier, write a note in the margin with the page number.
- **Ask questions.** Note anything that puzzles you, including words you don't know and need to look up.

Map a controversy

Read broadly about an issue and identify three or more sources that offer different points of view on that issue. The sources may approach the issue from different angles or raise different questions instead of simply stating differing positions on the issue. Draw a map that represents the different views. The map on the next page shows some of the different positions on sustainable agriculture.

Map of different issues about sustainable agriculture

Recognize Fallacies

Recognizing where good reasons go off track is one of the most important aspects of critical reading. What passes as political discourse is often filled with claims that lack evidence or substitute emotions for evidence. Such faulty reasoning often contains one or more **logical fallacies**. For example, politicians know that the public is outraged when the price of gasoline goes up, and they try to score political points by accusing oil companies of price gouging. It sounds good to angry voters—and it may well be true—but unless the politician defines what *price gouging* means and provides evidence that oil companies are guilty, the argument has no more validity than children calling each other bad names on the playground.

Following are some of the more common fallacies.

Fallacies of logic

- **Begging the question** *Politicians are inherently dishonest because no honest person would run for public office.* The fallacy of begging the question occurs when the claim is restated and passed off as evidence.

- **Either-or** *Either we eliminate the regulation of businesses or else profits will suffer.* The either-or fallacy suggests that there are only two choices in a complex situation. Rarely, if ever, is this the case. Consider, for example, the case of Enron, which was unregulated but went bankrupt.

- **False analogies** *Japan quit fighting in 1945 when we dropped nuclear bombs on Hiroshima and Nagasaki. We should use nuclear weapons against other countries.* Analogies always depend on the degree of resemblance of one situation to another. In this case, the analogy fails to recognize that circumstances today are very different from those in 1945. Many countries now possess nuclear weapons, and we know their use could harm the entire world.

- **Hasty generalization** *We have been in a drought for three years; that's a sure sign of climate change.* A hasty generalization is a broad claim made on the basis of a few occurrences. Climate cycles occur regularly over spans of a few years. Climate trends, however, must be observed over centuries.

- **Non sequitur** *A university that can raise a billion dollars from alumni should not have to raise tuition.* A non sequitur (a Latin term meaning "it does not follow") ties together two unrelated ideas. In this case, the argument fails to recognize that the money for capital campaigns is often donated for special purposes such as athletic facilities and is not part of a university's general revenue.

- **Oversimplification** *No one would run stop signs if we had a mandatory death penalty for doing it.* This claim may be true, but the argument would be unacceptable to most citizens. More complex, if less definitive, solutions are called for.

- **Post hoc fallacy** *The stock market goes down when the AFC wins the Super Bowl in even years.* The *post hoc* fallacy (from the Latin *post hoc, ergo propter hoc,* which means "after this, therefore because of this") assumes that events that follow in time have a causal relationship.

- **Rationalization** *I could have finished my paper on time if my printer had been working.* People frequently come up with excuses and weak explanations for their own and others' behavior. These excuses often avoid actual causes.

- **Slippery slope** *We shouldn't grant citizenship to illegal immigrants now living in the United States because no one will want to obey our laws.* The slippery slope fallacy maintains that one thing inevitably will cause something else to happen.

Fallacies of emotion and language

- **Bandwagon appeals** *It doesn't matter if I copy a paper off the Web because everyone else does.* This argument suggests that everyone is doing it, so why shouldn't you? But on close examination, it may be that everyone really isn't doing it—and in any case, it may not be the right thing to do.

- **Name-calling** *Every candidate running for office in this election is either a left-wing radical or a right-wing ideologue.* Name calling is frequent in politics and among competing groups. People level accusations using names such as radical, tax-and-spend liberal, racist, fascist, ultra-conservative extremist. Unless these terms are carefully defined, they are meaningless.
- **Polarization** *Feminists are all man haters.* Like name-calling, polarization exaggerates positions and groups by representing them as extreme and divisive.
- **Straw man** *Environmentalists won't be satisfied until not a single human being is allowed to enter a national park.* A straw man argument is a diversionary tactic that sets up another's position in a way that can be easily rejected. In fact, only a small percentage of environmentalists would make an argument even close to this one.

Note fallacies while you read

Marta Ramos noted a fallacy in James McWilliams's argument against locavorism. You can read her rebuttal argument on pages 180–183.

Consider fruit and vegetable production in New York. The Empire State is naturally equipped to grow a wide variety of fruits, including pears, cherries, strawberries, and some peaches. But none of these compare to its ability to grow apples and grapes, which dominate production (accounting for 94 percent of all fruit grown).

At current levels of fruit production, apples are the only crop that could currently feed New Yorkers at a level that meets the U.S. Recommended Dietary Allowances. Every other fruit that the state produces is not being harvested at a level to provide all New Yorkers with an adequate supply. Other fruits such as bananas and oranges are not produced at all because conditions are unfavorable for growing them.

What does this situation mean in terms of feeding the state with the state's own produce?

In a nutshell, <u>it means citizens would have to give up tropical fruits altogether</u>; rarely indulge in a pear, peach, or basket of strawberries; and gorge on grapes and apples—most of them in processed form (either as juice, in a can, or as concentrate).

—James E. McWilliams. *Just Food: Where Locavores Get It Wrong and How We Can Truly Eat Responsibly.* New York: Little, Brown, 2009. 44.

McWilliams makes a straw man argument. Locavores prioritize locally produced food but don't argue that it's only what people should eat.

Map and Summarize Arguments

When you finish annotating a reading, you might want to map it.

Draw a map

Marta Ramos drew a map of James McWilliams's argument.

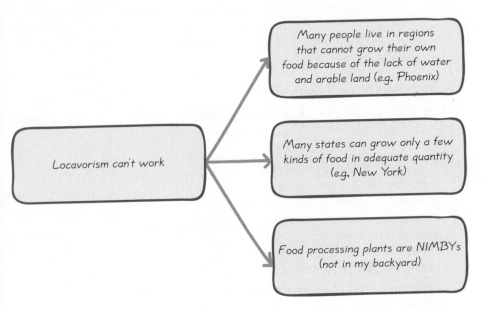

Map of the argument in James McWilliams's *Just Food*

Write a summary

A summary should be concise but thorough representation of the source.

- Begin your summary with the writer's name, the title of the argument, and the main point.
- Then report the key ideas. Represent the author's argument in condensed form as accurately as you can, quoting exact words for key points (see pages 253–254 for how to quote and integrate an author's words into your summary).
- Your aim is to give your readers an understanding of what the author is arguing for. Withhold judgment even if you think the author is dead wrong. Do not insert your opinions and comments. Stick to what the author is saying and what position the author is advocating.
- Usually summaries are no longer than 150 words. If your summary is longer than 150 words, delete excess words without eliminating key ideas.

McWilliams, James. *Just Food: Where Locavores Get It Wrong and How We Can Truly Eat Responsibly.* New York: Little Brown, 2009. Print.

Summary

In *Just Food,* James McWilliams argues that locavorism—the development of local food-supply systems—is an impractical goal. He offers three reasons why locavorism is not achievable. First, many people live in regions where they cannot grow their own food because of lack of water and arable land (for example, Phoenix). Second, many states can grow only a few kinds of food in adequate quantity (for example, New York), thus restricting food choices and limiting consumption to processed fruits and vegetables for much of the year. Third, many people will not like food processing plants near their homes.

For additional writing resources that will help you master the objectives of this chapter, go to your **MyLab.**

3 | Finding Arguments

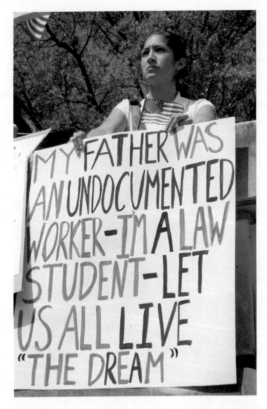

Slogans are meant to persuade, but technically they are not arguments because they lack reasons. Nevertheless, you can often supply a reason for a claim made on a sign. What reason might the demonstrator give to support her claim LET US ALL LIVE "THE DREAM"?

Find Arguments in Everyday Conversations

Let's look at an example of a conversation. When the pain in his abdomen didn't go away, Jeff knew he had torn something while carrying his friend's heavy speakers up a flight of stairs. He went to the student health center and called his friend Maria when he returned home.

JEFF: I have good news and bad news. The pain is a minor hernia that can be repaired with day surgery. The bad news is that the fee we pay for the health center doesn't cover hospital visits. We should have health coverage.

MARIA: Jeff, you didn't buy the extra insurance. Why should you get it for nothing?

JEFF: Because health coverage is a right.

MARIA: No it's not. Everyone doesn't have health insurance.

JEFF: Well, in some other countries like Canada, Germany, and Britain, they do.

MARIA: Yes, and people who live in those countries pay a bundle in taxes for the government-provided insurance.

JEFF: It's not fair in this country because some people have health insurance and others don't.

MARIA: Jeff, face the facts. You could have bought the extra insurance. Instead you chose to buy a new car.

JEFF: It would be better if the university provided health insurance because students could graduate in four years. I'm going to have to get a second job and drop out for a semester to pay for the surgery.

MARIA: Neat idea, but who's going to pay to insure every student?

JEFF: OK, all students should be required to pay for health insurance as part of their general fee. Most students are healthy, and it wouldn't cost that much more.

In this discussion, Jeff starts out by making a **claim** that students should have health coverage. Maria immediately asks him why students should not have to pay for health insurance. She wants a **reason** to accept his claim.

Distinguishing arguments from other kinds of persuasion

Scholars who study argument maintain that an argument must have a claim and one or more reasons to support that claim. Something less might be persuasive, but it isn't an argument.

A bumper sticker that says NO TOLL ROADS is a claim, but it is not an argument because the statement lacks a reason. Many reasons support an argument against building toll roads.

- We don't need new roads but should build light-rail instead.
- We should raise the gas tax to pay for new roads.
- We should use gas tax revenue only for roads rather than using it for other purposes.

When a claim has a reason attached, then it becomes an argument.

The basics of arguments

A reason is typically offered in a **because clause**, a statement that begins with the word *because* and that provides a supporting reason for the claim. Jeff's first attempt is to argue that students should have health insurance *because* health insurance is a right.

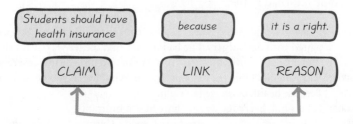

The word *because* signals a link between the reason and the claim. Every argument that is more than a shouting match or a simple assertion has to have one or more reasons. Just having a reason for a claim, however, doesn't mean that the audience will be convinced. When Jeff tells Maria that students have a right to health insurance, Maria replies that students don't have that right. Maria will accept Jeff's claim only if she accepts that his reason supports his claim. Maria challenges Jeff's links and keeps asking "So what?" For her, Jeff's reasons are not good reasons.

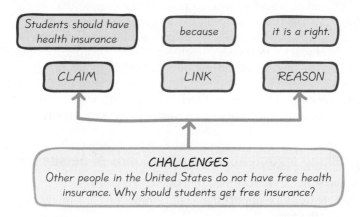

By the end of this short discussion, Jeff has begun to build an argument. He has had to come up with another claim to support his main claim: All students should be required to pay for health insurance as part of their general fee. If he is to convince Maria, he will probably have to provide a series of claims that she will accept as linked to his primary claim. He will also need to find evidence to support these claims.

Benjamin Franklin observed, "So convenient a thing it is to be a rational creature, since it enables us to find or make a reason for every thing one has a mind to do." It is not hard to think of reasons. What *is* difficult is to convince your audience that your reasons are good reasons. In a conversation, you get immediate feedback that tells you whether your listener agrees or disagrees. When you are writing, you usually don't have someone you can question immediately. Consequently, you have to (1) be more specific about what you are claiming, (2) connect with the values you hold in common with your readers, and (3) anticipate what questions and objections your readers might have, if you are going to convince someone who doesn't agree with you or know what you know already.

When you write an argument, imagine a reader like Maria who is going to listen carefully to what you have to say but who is not going to agree with you automatically. Readers like Maria will expect the following.

- A **claim** that is interesting and makes them want to find out more about what you have to say
- At least one **good reason** that makes your claim worth taking seriously
- Some **evidence** that the good reason or reasons are valid
- Some acknowledgment of the **opposing views** and **limitations** of the claim

The remainder of this chapter will guide you through the process of finding a topic, making a claim, finding good reasons and evidence, and anticipating objections to your claim.

Find a Topic

When your instructor gives you a writing assignment, look closely at what you are asked to do. Assignments typically contain a great deal of information, and you have to sort through that information. First, circle all the instructions about the length, the due date, the format, the grading criteria, and anything else about the production and conventions of the assignment. This information is important to you, but it doesn't tell you what the paper is supposed to be about.

Read your assignment carefully

Often your assignment will contain key words such as *analyze, define, evaluate,* or *propose* that will assist you in determining what direction to take. *Analyze* can mean several things. Your instructor might want you to analyze a piece of writing (see Chapter 5), an image (see Chapter 6), or the causes of something (see Chapter 9). *Define* usually means writing a **definition argument**, in which you argue for a definition based on the criteria you set out (see Chapter 8). *Evaluate* indicates an **evaluation argument**, in which you argue that something is good, bad, the best, or the worst in its class according to criteria that you set out (see Chapter 10). An assignment that contains the instructions *Write about an issue using your personal experience* indicates a **narrative argument** (see Chapter 11), while one that says *Take a position in regard to a reading* might lead you to write a **rebuttal argument** (see Chapter 12). *Propose* means that you should identify a particular problem and explain why your solution is the best one in a **proposal argument** (see Chapter 13).

What Is Not Arguable

- **Statements of fact.** Most facts can be verified by doing research. But even simple facts can sometimes be argued. For example, Mount Everest is usually acknowledged to be the highest mountain in the world at 29,028 feet above sea level. But if the total height of a mountain from base to summit is the measure, then the volcano Mauna Loa in Hawaii is the highest mountain in the world. Although the top of Mauna Loa is 13,667 feet above sea level, the summit is 31,784 above the ocean floor. Thus the "fact" that Mount Everest is the highest mountain on the earth depends on a definition of *highest*. You could argue for this definition.

- **Claims of personal taste.** Your favorite food and your favorite color are examples of personal taste. If you hate fresh tomatoes, no one can convince you that you actually like them. But many claims of personal taste turn out to be value judgments using arguable criteria. For example, if you think that *Alien* is the best science-fiction movie ever made, you can argue that claim using evaluative criteria that other people can consider as good reasons (see Chapter 10). Indeed, you might not even like science fiction and still argue that *Alien* is the best science-fiction movie ever.

- **Statements of belief or faith.** If someone accepts a claim as a matter of religious belief, then for that person, the claim is true and cannot be refuted. Of course, people still make arguments about the existence of God and which religion reflects the will of God. Whenever an audience will not consider an idea, it's possible but very difficult to construct an argument. Many people claim to have evidence that UFOs exist, but most people refuse to acknowledge that evidence as even being possibly factual.

If you remain unclear about the purpose of the assignment after reading it carefully, talk with your instructor.

Thinking about what interests you

Your assignment may specify the topic you are to write about. If your assignment gives you a wide range of options and you don't know what to write about, look first at the materials for your course: the readings, your lecture notes, and discussion boards. Think about what subjects came up in class discussion.

If you need to look outside class for a topic, think about what interests you. Subjects we argue about often find us. There are enough of them in daily life. We're late for work or class because the traffic is heavy or the bus doesn't run on time. We can't find a place to park when we get to school or work. We have to negotiate through various bureaucracies for almost anything we do—making an

Finding Good Reasons

Are Traffic Enforcement Cameras Invading Your Privacy?

Cameras that photograph the license plates and drivers of vehicles who run red lights, speed, or ride illegally in high-occupancy-vehicle (HOV) and bus lanes are currently in use in many U.S. cities and states. Cameras aimed at catching speeders, already common in Europe, are beginning to be installed in U.S. cities as well. Traffic cameras have become money machines for some communities, but they also have provoked intense public opposition and even vandalism—people have spray painted and shot cameras in attempts to disable them.

Write about it

1. How do you feel about using cameras to catch red-light runners? Speeders? Illegal drivers in HOV and bus lanes? People who don't pay parking tickets? Make a list of as many possible topics as you can think of about the use of cameras to scan license plates.

2. Select one of the possible topics. Write it at the top of a sheet of paper, and then write nonstop for five minutes. Don't worry about correctness. If you get stuck, write the same sentence again.

3. When you finish, read what you have written and circle key ideas.

4. Put each key idea on a sticky note. If you think of other ideas, write them on separate sticky notes. Then look at your sticky notes. Put a star on the central idea. Put the ideas that are related next to each other. You now have the beginning of an idea map.

appointment to see a doctor, getting a course added or dropped, or correcting a mistake on a bill. Most of the time we grumble and let it go at that. But sometimes we stick with a subject. Neighborhood groups in cities and towns have been especially effective in getting something done by writing about it—for example, stopping a new road from being built, getting better police and fire protection, and getting a vacant lot turned into a park.

Listing and analyzing issues

A good way to get started is to list possible issues to write about. Make a list of questions that can be answered "YES, because . . ." or "NO, because . . ." Think about issues that affect your campus, your community, the nation, and the world. Which issues interest you? About which issues could you make a contribution to the larger discussion?

Campus

- Should students be required to pay fees for access to computers on campus?
- Should smoking be banned on campus?
- Should varsity athletes get paid for playing sports that bring in revenue?
- Should admissions decisions be based exclusively on academic achievement?
- Should knowledge of a foreign language be required for all degree plans?
- Should your college or university have a computer literacy requirement?
- Is there any way to curb the dangerous drinking habits of many students on your campus?

Community

- Should people who ride bicycles and motorcycles be required to wear helmets?
- Should high schools be allowed to search students for drugs at any time?
- Should high schools distribute condoms?
- Should bilingual education programs be eliminated?
- Should bike lanes be built throughout your community to encourage more people to ride bicycles?
- Should more tax dollars be shifted from building highways to funding public transportation?

Nation/World

- Should driving while talking on a cell phone be banned?
- Should capital punishment be abolished?
- Should the Internet be censored?
- Should the government be allowed to monitor all phone calls and all e-mail to combat terrorism?
- Should handguns be outlawed?
- Should beef and poultry be free of growth hormones?
- Should a law be passed requiring that the parents of teenagers who have abortions be informed?
- Should people who are terminally ill be allowed to end their lives?
- Should the United States punish nations with poor human rights records?

Narrowing a list

1. Put a check beside the issues that look most interesting to write about or the ones that mean the most to you.
2. Put a question mark beside the issues that you don't know very much about. If you choose one of these issues, you will probably have to do in-depth research—by talking to people, by using the Internet, or by going to the library.
3. Select the two or three issues that look most promising. For each issue, make another list:

   - Who is most interested in this issue?
   - Whom or what does this issue affect?
   - What are the pros and cons of this issue? Make two columns. At the top of the left one, write "YES, because." At the top of the right one, write "NO, because."
   - What has been written about this issue? How can you find out what has been written?

Explore Your Topic

When you identify a potential topic, make a quick exploration of that topic, much as you would walk through a house or an apartment you are thinking about renting for a quick look. One way of exploring is to visualize the topic by making a map.

If you live in a state on the coast that has a high potential for wind energy, you might argue that your state should provide financial incentives for generating more electricity from the wind. Perhaps it seems like a no-brainer to you because wind power consumes no fuel and causes no air pollution. The only energy required is for the manufacture and transportation of the wind turbines and transmission lines. But your state and other coastal states have not exploited potential wind energy for three reasons:

1. **Aesthetics.** Some people think wind turbines are ugly.
2. **Hazard to wildlife.** A few poorly located wind turbines have killed birds and bats.
3. **Cost.** Wind power costs differ, but wind energy is generally more expensive than electricity produced by burning coal.

To convince other people that your proposal is a good one, you will have to answer these objections.

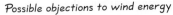

Possible objections to wind energy

The first two objections are relatively easy to address. Locating wind farms 10 kilometers offshore keeps them out of sight of land and away from most migrating birds and all bats. The third objection, higher cost, is more difficult. One strategy is to argue that the overall costs of wind energy and energy produced by burning coal are comparable if environmental costs are included. You can analyze the advantages and disadvantages of each by drawing maps.

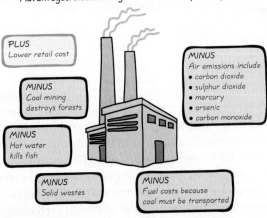

Advantages/disadvantages of coal-fired power plants

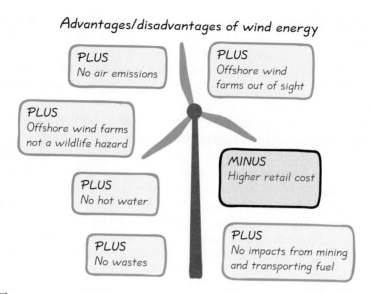

Advantages/disadvantages of wind energy

PLUS
No air emissions

PLUS
Offshore wind
farms out of sight

PLUS
Offshore wind farms
not a wildlife hazard

MINUS
Higher retail cost

PLUS
No hot water

PLUS
No wastes

PLUS
No impacts from mining
and transporting fuel

These maps can help you organize an argument for providing financial incentives for wind energy.

Read About Your Topic

Much college writing draws on and responds to sources—books, articles, reports, and other material written by other people. Every significant issue discussed in today's world has an extensive history of discussion involving many people and various points of view. Before you formulate a claim about a significant issue, you need to become familiar with the conversation that's already happening by reading widely about it.

One of the most controversial and talked-about subjects in recent years is the outsourcing of white-collar and manufacturing jobs to low-wage nations. Since 2000 an estimated 400,000 to 500,000 American jobs each year have gone to cheap overseas labor markets. The Internet has made this migration of jobs possible, allowing companies to outsource not only low-skilled jobs but highly skilled jobs in fields such as software development, data storage, and even examining X-rays and MRI scans.

You may have read about this or another complex and controversial topic in one of your courses. Just as in a conversation with several people who hold different views, you may agree with some people, disagree with some, and with others agree with some of their ideas up to a point but then disagree.

Fox Business Network news anchor Lou Dobbs has been sharply critical of outsourcing. In *Exporting America: Why Corporate Greed Is Shipping American Jobs Overseas* (2006), Dobbs blames large corporations for putting profits ahead of the good of the nation. He accuses both Republicans and Democrats of ignoring the effects of a massive trade deficit and the largest national debt in American history, which Dobbs claims will eventually destroy the American way of life.

Thomas Friedman, columnist for the *New York Times*, takes a different viewpoint on outsourcing in *The World Is Flat: A Brief History of the Twenty-first Century* (2006). By *flat*, Friedman means that the nations of the world are connected like never before through the Internet and the lowering of trade barriers, putting every nation in direct competition with all the others. Friedman believes that outsourcing is not only unstoppable, but also desirable. He argues that Americans need to adapt to the new reality and rethink our system of education, or else we will be left hopelessly behind. (For a fuller account of Friedman's views, see pages 424–429.)

If you decide to write an argument about the issue of outsourcing, you might use either Dobbs's or Friedman's book as your starting point in making a claim. You could begin by taking on the role of **skeptic,** disagreeing with the author; the role of **contributor,** agreeing with the author and adding another point; or the role of the **analyst,** finding some points to agree with while disagreeing with others.

The skeptic: Disagreeing with a source

It's easy to disagree by simply saying an idea is dumb, but readers expect you to be persuasive about why you disagree and to offer reasons to support your views.

X claims that ————————, but this view is mistaken because
————————.

Example claim: Arguing against outsourcing resulting from free trade policies

Thomas Friedman claims that the world is "flat," giving a sense of a level playing field for all, but it is absurd to think that the millions of starving children in the world have opportunities similar to those in affluent countries who pay $100 for basketball shoes made by the starving children.

Example claim: Arguing in favor of outsourcing resulting from free trade policies

Lou Dobbs is a patriotic American who recognizes the suffering of manufacturing workers in industries like steel and automobiles, but he neglects that the major cause of the loss of manufacturing jobs in the United States and China alike is increased productivity—the 40 hours of labor necessary to produce a car just a few years ago has now been reduced to 15.

The contributor: Agreeing with a source with an additional point

Sources should not make your argument for you. With sources that support your position, indicate exactly how they fit into your argument with an additional point.

I agree with _____ and will make the additional point that
_____.

Example claim: Arguing against outsourcing resulting from free trade policies

Lou Dobbs's outcry against the outsourcing of American jobs also has a related argument: We are dependent not only on foreign oil, but also on foreign clothing, foreign electronics, foreign tools, foreign toys, foreign cars and trucks—indeed, just about everything—which is quickly eroding the world leadership of the United States.

Example claim: Arguing in favor of outsourcing resulting from free trade policies

Thomas Friedman's claim that the Internet enables everyone to become an entrepreneur is demonstrated by thousands of Americans, including my aunt, who could retire early because she developed an income stream by buying jeans and children's clothes at garage sales and selling them to people around the world on eBay.

The analyst: Agreeing and disagreeing simultaneously with a source

Incorporating sources is not a matter of simply agreeing or disagreeing with them. Often you will agree with a source up to a point, but you will come to a different conclusion. Or you may agree with the conclusions, but not agree with the reasons put forth.

I agree with _____ up to a point, but I disagree with the
conclusion _____ because _____.

Example claim: Qualifying the argument against outsourcing resulting from free-trade policies

Lou Dobbs accurately blames our government for giving multinational corporations tax breaks for exporting jobs rather than regulating the loss of millions of jobs, but the real problem lies in the enormous appetite of Americans for inexpensive consumer products like HD televisions that is supported by borrowing money from overseas to the point that our dollar has plummeted in value.

Example claim: Qualifying the argument in favor of outsourcing resulting from free-trade policies

Thomas Friedman's central claim that the world is being "flattened" by global-ization and there is not much we can do to stop it is essentially correct, but he neglects the social costs of globalization around the world, where the ban-ner of free trade has been the justification for devastating the environment, destroying workers' rights and the rights of indigenous peoples, and ignoring laws passed by representative governments.

Find Good Reasons

Get in the habit of asking these questions every time you are asked to write an argument.

Can you argue by definition?

Probably the most powerful kind of good reason is an argument from definition. You can think of a definition as a simple statement: _____ *is a* _____. You use these statements all the time. When you need a course to fulfill your social-science requirement, you look at the list of courses that are defined as social-science courses. You find out that the anthropology class you want to take is one of them. It's just as important when _____ *is not a* _____. Suppose you are taking College Algebra, which is a math course taught by the math department, yet it doesn't count for the math requirement. The reason it doesn't count is because College Algebra is not defined as a college-level math class. So you have to enroll next semester in Calculus I.

Many definitions are not nearly as clear-cut as the math requirement. If you want to argue that figure skaters are athletes, you will need to define what an athlete is. You start thinking. An athlete competes in an activity, but that definition alone is too broad, since many competitions do not require physical activity. Thus, an ath-lete must participate in a competitive physical activity and must train for it. But that definition is still not quite narrow enough, because soldiers also train for competi-tive physical activity. You decide to add that the activity must be a sport and that it must require special competence and precision. Your *because* clause turns out as fol-lows: *Figure skaters are athletes because true athletes train for and compete in physical sporting competitions that require special competence and precision.*

If you can get your audience to accept your definitions, you've gone a long way toward convincing them of the validity of your claim. That is why the most controversial issues in our culture—abortion, affirmative action, gay rights, pornography, women's rights, privacy rights, gun control, the death penalty—are argued from definition. Is abortion a crime or a medical procedure? Is pornography protected by the First Amendment, or is it a violation of women's rights? Is the death penalty just or cruel and inhuman? You can see from these examples that definitions often rely on deeply held beliefs.

Because people have strong beliefs about controversial issues, they often don't care about the practical consequences. Arguing that it is much cheaper to execute prisoners who have been convicted of first-degree murder than to keep them in prison for life does not convince those who believe that it is morally wrong to kill. (See Chapter 8.)

Can you argue from value?

A special kind of argument from definition, one that often implies consequences, is the argument from value. You can support your claim with a "because clause" (or several of them) that includes a sense of evaluation. Arguments from value follow from claims like _____ *is a good* _____, or _____ *is not a good* _____.

Evaluation arguments usually proceed from the presentation of certain criteria. These criteria come from the definitions of good and bad, of poor and not so poor, that prevail in a given case. A great burger fulfills certain criteria; so does an outstanding movie, an excellent class, or the best laptop in your price range. Sometimes the criteria are straightforward, as in the burger example. A great burger has to have tasty meat—tender and without gristle, fresh, never frozen—a fresh bun that is the right size, and your favorite condiments.

But if you are buying a laptop computer and want to play the latest games along with your school tasks, you need to do some homework. For realistic graphics the best laptop will have a fast chip, preferably a dual core system. It will be equipped with a wireless modem, so you have access to the Internet at wireless hot spots. The battery life should last several hours, the hard drive should be large enough for your needs, the construction should be sturdy, and the warranty should cover the computer for at least three years. The keys for evaluation arguments are finding the appropriate criteria and convincing your readers that those criteria are the right criteria (see Chapter 10).

Can you argue from consequence?

Another powerful source of good reasons comes from considering the possible consequences of your position: Can you sketch out the good things that will follow from your position? Can you establish that certain bad things will be avoided if your position is adopted? If so, you will have other good reasons to use.

Causal arguments take the basic form of _____ *causes* _____ (or _____ *does not cause* _____). Very often, causal arguments are more complicated, taking the form _____ *causes* _____ *which, in turn, causes* _____ and so on. In one famous example, environmentalist Rachel Carson in *Silent Spring* makes powerful arguments from consequence. Rachel Carson's primary claim is that *DDT should not be sprayed on a massive scale because it will poison animals and people.* The key to her argument is the causal chain that explains how animals and people are poisoned. Carson describes how nothing exists alone in nature. When a potato field is sprayed with DDT, some of that poison is absorbed by the skin of the potatoes and some washes into the groundwater, where it contaminates drinking water. Other poisonous residue is absorbed into streams, where it is ingested by insect larvae, which in turn are eaten by fish. Fish are eaten by other fish, which are then eaten by waterfowl and people. At each stage, the poisons become more concentrated. (See Chapter 9 for additional examples of causal arguments.)

Proposal arguments are future-oriented arguments from consequence. In a proposal argument, you cannot stop with naming good reasons; you also have to show that these consequences would follow from the idea or course of action that you are arguing. For example, if you are proposing designated lanes for bicycles on the streets of your city, you must argue that they will encourage more people to ride bicycles to work and school, reducing air pollution and traffic congestion for everyone. (See Chapter 13.)

Can you counter objections to your position?

Another good way to find convincing good reasons is to think about possible objections to your position. If you can imagine how your audience might counter or respond to your argument, you will probably include in your argument precisely the points that will address your readers' particular needs and objections. If you are successful, your readers will be convinced that you are right. You've no doubt had the experience of mentally saying to a writer in the course of your reading, "Yeah, but what about this other idea?"—only to have the writer address precisely this objection.

You can impress your readers if you've thought about why anyone would oppose your position and exactly how that opposition would be expressed. If you are writing a proposal argument for a computer literacy requirement for all high school graduates, you might think about why anyone would object, since computers are critical for our jobs and lives. What will the practical objections be? What about philosophical ones? Why hasn't such a requirement been put in place already? By asking such questions in your own arguments, you are likely to develop robust because clauses.

Sometimes, writers pose rhetorical questions. You might say, "But won't paying for computers for all students make my taxes go up?" Stating objections explicitly can be effective if you make the objections as those of a reasonable person with an alternative point of view. But if the objections you state are ridiculous ones, then you risk being accused of setting up a **straw man**—that is, making the position opposing your own so simplistic that no one would likely identify with it. (See Chapter 12.)

Find Evidence to Support Good Reasons

Good reasons are essential ingredients of good arguments, but they don't do the job alone. You must support or verify good reasons with evidence. Evidence consists of hard data, examples, personal experiences, episodes, or tabulations of episodes (known as statistics) that are seen as relevant to the good reasons you are putting forward. Thus, a writer of arguments puts forward not only claims and good reasons but also evidence that those good reasons are true.

How much supporting evidence should you supply? How much evidence is enough? As is usual in the case of rhetoric, the best answer is, "It depends." If a reader is likely to find one of your good reasons hard to believe, then you should be aggressive in offering support. You should present detailed evidence in a patient and painstaking way. As one presenting an argument you have a responsibility not just to *state* a case but to *make* a case with evidence. Arguments that are unsuccessful tend to fail not because of a shortage of good reasons; more often, they fail because the reader doesn't agree that there is enough evidence to support the good reason that is being presented.

If your good reason isn't especially controversial, you probably should not belabor it. Think of your own experiences as a reader. How often do you recall saying to yourself, as you read a passage or listened to a speaker, "OK! OK! I get the point! Don't keep piling up all of this evidence for me because I don't want it or need it." However, such a reaction is rare, isn't it? By contrast, how often do you recall muttering under your breath, "How can you say that? What evidence do you have to back it up?" When in doubt, err on the side of offering too much evidence. It's an error that is seldom made and not often criticized.

When a writer doesn't provide satisfactory evidence to support a because clause, readers might feel that there has been a failure in the reasoning process. In fact, in your previous courses in writing and speaking, you may have learned about various fallacies associated with faulty arguments (pages 17–19).

Strictly speaking, there is nothing false about these so-called logical fallacies. The fallacies most often refer to failures in providing evidence; when you don't provide enough good evidence to convince your audience, you might be accused of committing a fallacy in reasoning. You will usually avoid such accusations if the evidence that you cite is both *relevant* and *sufficient*.

Relevance refers to the appropriateness of the evidence to the case at hand. Some kinds of evidence are seen as more relevant than others for particular audiences. On the one hand, in science and industry, personal testimony is seen as having limited relevance, while experimental procedures and controlled observations have far more credibility. Compare someone who defends the use of a particular piece of computer software because "it worked for me" with someone who defends it because "according to a journal article published last month, 84 percent of the users of the software were satisfied or very satisfied with it." On the other hand, in writing to the general public on controversial issues such as gun control, personal experience is often considered more relevant than other kinds of data.

Sufficiency refers to the amount of evidence cited. Sometimes a single piece of evidence or a single instance will carry the day if it is especially compelling in some way—if it represents the situation well or makes a point that isn't particularly controversial. More often, people expect more than one piece of evidence if they are to be convinced of something. Convincing readers that they should approve a statewide computer literacy requirement for all high school graduates will require much more evidence than the story of a single graduate who succeeded with her computer skills. You will likely need statistical evidence for such a broad proposal.

If you anticipate that your audience might not accept your evidence, face the situation squarely. First, think carefully about the argument you are presenting. If you cannot cite adequate evidence for your assertions, perhaps those assertions must be modified or qualified in some way. If you remain convinced of your assertions, then think about doing more research to come up with additional evidence.

For additional writing resources that will help you master the objectives of this chapter, go to your **MyLab**.

4 | Drafting and Revising Arguments

QUICK TAKE

In this chapter you will learn to

1. State, focus, and evaluate your thesis (see page 40)
2. Appraise your readers' knowledge and attitudes (see page 43)
3. Organize your argument using a formal or working outline (see pages 44–45)
4. Write a title, an introduction, and a strong conclusion (see pages 46–47)
5. Use specific strategies in preparation for revision (see pages 48–49)
6. Respond to the writing of others (pages 50–51)
7. Edit and proofread carefully (page 51)

People frequently revise things that they own. What objects have you revised?

State and Evaluate Your Thesis

Once you have identified a topic and have a good sense of how to develop it, the next critical step is to write a **working thesis**. Your **thesis** states your main claim. Much writing that you will do in college and later in your career will require an explicit thesis, usually placed near the beginning.

Focusing your thesis

The thesis can make or break your paper. If the thesis is too broad, you cannot do justice to the argument. Who wouldn't wish for fewer traffic accidents, better medical care, more effective schools, or a cleaner environment? Simple solutions for these complex problems are unlikely.

Stating something that is obvious to everyone isn't an arguable thesis. Don't settle for easy answers. When a topic is too broad, a predictable thesis often results. Narrow your focus and concentrate on the areas where you have the most questions. Those are likely the areas where your readers will have the most questions too.

The opposite problem is less common: a thesis that is too narrow. If your thesis simply states a commonly known fact, then it is too narrow. For example, the growth rate of the population in the United States has doubled since 1970 because of increased immigration. The U.S. Census Bureau provides reasonably accurate statistical information, so this claim is not arguable. But the policies that allow increased immigration and the effects of a larger population—more crowding and higher costs of health care, education, and transportation—are arguable.

> **Not arguable:** The population of the United States grew faster in the 1990s than in any previous decade because Congress increased the rate of legal immigration and the government stopped enforcing most laws against illegal immigration in the interior of the country.
>
> **Arguable:** Allowing a high rate of immigration helps the United States deal with the problems of an increasingly aging society and helps provide funding for millions of Social Security recipients.
>
> **Arguable:** The increase in the number of visas to foreign workers in technology industries is the major cause of unemployment in those industries.

Evaluating your thesis

Once you have a working thesis, ask these questions.

- Is it arguable?
- Is it specific?
- Is it manageable given your length and time requirements?
- Is it interesting to your intended readers?

Example 1

Sample thesis

> *We should take action to resolve the serious traffic problem in our city.*

Is it arguable? The thesis is arguable, but it lacks a focus.

Is it specific? The thesis is too broad.

Is it manageable? Transportation is a complex issue. New highways and rail systems are expensive and take many years to build. Furthermore, citizens don't want new roads running through their neighborhoods.

Is it interesting? The topic has the potential to be interesting if the writer can propose a specific solution to a problem that everyone in the city recognizes.

When a thesis is too broad, it needs to be revised to address a specific aspect of an issue. Make the big topic smaller.

Revised thesis

> *The existing freight railway that runs through the center of the city should be converted to a passenger railway because this is the cheapest and quickest way to decrease traffic congestion downtown.*

Example 2

Sample thesis

> *Over 60 percent of Americans play computer games on a regular basis.*

Is it arguable? The thesis states a commonly acknowledged fact. It is not arguable.

Is it specific? The thesis is too narrow.

Is it manageable? A known fact is stated in the thesis, so there is little to research. Several surveys report this finding.

Is it interesting? The popularity of video games is well established. Nearly everyone is aware of the trend.

There's nothing original or interesting about stating that Americans love computer games. Think about what is controversial. One debatable topic is how computer games affect children.

Revised thesis

> *Computer games are valuable because they improve children's visual attention skills, literacy skills, and computer literacy skills.*

Finding Good Reasons

Should Driving While Talking Be Banned?

In a movement to improve driving safety, California, Connecticut, the District of Columbia, New Jersey, New York, Oregon, Utah, and Washington have passed laws banning the use of handheld cell phones while driving except for emergency workers and people making 911 calls. Several other states have banned cell phones while driving for drivers aged 18 and younger.

Proponents of the ban point to a National Highway Traffic Safety Administration study, reporting that approximately 25 to 30 percent of motor vehicle crashes—about 1.2 million accidents each year—are caused by driver distraction. Opponents of the ban argue that anything that distracts the driver—eating potato chips, talking with passengers, spilled coffee—can cause an accident. The answer, they say, is driver education.

Write about it

1. Write a thesis arguing in support of a ban on cell phones while driving, against a ban, or in support of a more limited position such as banning cell-phone use for drivers 18 and under.

2. Think about the audience that would likely oppose your position. For example, if you support a ban on talking while driving, think about the likely responses of high school students, salespeople who spend much of their workdays driving from place to place, and workers who receive assignments by phone. What good reasons would convince readers who hold an opposing view?

3. What reasons would people who oppose your position likely offer in response? What counterarguments could you give to answer these objections?

Think About Your Readers

Thinking about your readers doesn't mean telling them what they might want to hear. Instead, imagine yourself in a dialogue with your readers. What questions will they likely have? How might you address any potential objections?

Understanding what your readers know—and do not know

Your readers' knowledge of your subject is critical to the success of your argument. If they are not familiar with the necessary background information, they probably won't understand your argument fully. If you know that your readers will be unfamiliar with your subject, you have to supply background information before attempting to convince them of your position. A good tactic is to tie your new information to what your readers already know. Comparisons and analogies can be very helpful in linking old and new information.

Understanding your readers' attitudes toward you

To get your readers to take you seriously, you must convince them that they can trust you. You need to get them to see you as

- **Concerned:** Readers want you to be committed to your subject. They also expect you to be concerned about them. After all, if you don't care about them, why should they read what you write?
- **Well informed:** Many people ramble on about any subject without knowing anything about it. College writing requires that you do your homework on a subject.
- **Fair:** Many writers look at only one side of an issue. Readers respect objectivity and an unbiased approach.
- **Ethical:** Many writers use only the facts that support their positions and often distort facts and sources. Critical readers often notice what is being left out. Don't try to conceal what doesn't support your position.

Understanding your readers' attitudes toward your subject

People have prior attitudes about controversial issues. You must take these attitudes into consideration as you write or speak. Imagine, for instance, that you are preparing an argument for a guest editorial in your college newspaper. You are advocating that your state government should provide parents with choices between public and private schools. You plan to argue that the tax dollars that now automatically go to public schools should go to private schools if parents so choose. You have evidence that the sophomore-to-senior dropout rate in private schools is less than half the rate in public schools. Furthermore, students from private schools attend college at nearly twice the rate of public-school graduates. You intend to argue that one of the reasons private schools are more successful is that they spend more money on instruction and less on administration. And you believe that school choice speaks to the American desire for personal freedom.

Not everyone on your campus will agree with your position. How might the faculty at your college or university feel about this issue? How about the administrators, the staff, other students, and interested community members who read the student newspaper? What are their attitudes toward public funding of private schools? How are you going to deal with the objection that many students in private schools do better in school because they come from more affluent families?

Even when you write about a much less controversial subject, you must think carefully about your audience's attitudes toward what you have to say or to write. Sometimes your audience may share your attitudes; other times, your audience may be neutral. At still other times, your audience will have attitudes that differ sharply from your own. Anticipate these various attitudes and act accordingly. If these attitudes are different from yours, you will have to work hard to counter them without insulting your audience.

Organize Your Argument

Asking a series of questions can generate a list of good reasons, but even if you have plenty, you still have to decide which ones to use and in what order to present them. Thinking about your readers' knowledge, attitudes, and values will help you to decide which reasons to present to your audience.

Writing plans often take the form of outlines, either formal outlines or working outlines. A **formal outline** typically begins with the thesis statement, which anchors the entire outline.

Managing the Risks of Nanotechnology While Reaping the Rewards

THESIS: The revolutionary potential of nanotechnology has arrived in an explosion of consumer products, yet our federal government has yet to recognize the potential risks or to fund research to reduce those risks.

I. Nanotechnology now is in many consumer products.

   A. The promise of nanotechnology to revolutionize medicine, energy production, and communication is years in the future, but consumer products are here now.

   B. Nanotechnology is now in clothing, food, sports equipment, medicines, electronics, and cars.

    C.   Experts predict that 15 percent of manufactured products worldwide will contain nanotechnology in 2014.

    D.   The question that hasn't been asked: Is nanotechnology safe?

II.   Americans have little awareness of nanotechnology.

    A.   Companies have stopped mentioning and advertising nanotechnology.

    B.   Companies and the insurance industry paid $250 billion in asbestos claims in the United States alone.

    C.   Companies fear exposure to lawsuits if nanotechnology is found to be toxic.

A **working outline** is a sketch of how you will arrange the major sections.

Managing the Risks of Nanotechnology While Reaping the Rewards

SECTION 1: Begin by defining nanotechnology—manipulating particles between 1 and 100 nanometers (nanometer is a billionth of a meter). Describe the rapid spread of nanotechnology in consumer products including clothing, food, sports equipment, medicines, electronics, and cars. State projection of 15 percent of global manufactured goods containing nanotechnology in 2014.

SECTION 2: Most Americans know nothing about nanotechnology. Companies have stopped advertising that their products contain nanotechnology because of fear of potential lawsuits. Asbestos, once thought safe, now is known to be toxic and has cost companies $250 billion in lawsuits in the United States alone.

SECTION 3: Relatively little research has been done on the safety of nanotechnology. No testing is required for new products because the materials are common, but materials behave differently at nano-scale (example—aluminum normally inert but combustible at nano-scale).

SECTION 4: Nanoparticles are highly mobile and can cross the blood-brain barrier and through the placenta. They are toxic in brains of fish and may collect in lungs.

SECTION 5: Urge that the federal government develop a master plan for identifying and reducing potential risks of nanotechnology and provide sufficient funding to carry out the plan.

Write an Engaging Title and Introduction

Many writers don't think much about titles, but they are very important. A good title makes the reader want to see what you have to say. Be as specific as you can in your title, and if possible, suggest your stance.

Get off to a fast start in your introduction. Convince your reader to keep reading. Cut to the chase. Think about how you can get your readers interested. Consider using one of the following.

- State your thesis concisely.
- Provide a hard-hitting fact.
- Ask a question.
- Give a vivid description of a problem.
- Discuss a contradiction or paradox.
- Describe a scenario.

Managing the Risks of Nanotechnology While Reaping the Rewards

The revolutionary potential of nanotechnology for medicine, energy production, and communication is now at the research and development stage, but the future has arrived in consumer products. Nanotechnology has given us products we hardly could have imagined just a few years ago: socks that never stink; pants that repel water yet keep you cool; eyeglasses that won't scratch; "smart" foods that add nutrition and reduce cholesterol; DVDs that are incredibly lifelike; bandages that speed healing; tennis balls that last longer; golf balls that fly straighter; pharmaceuticals that selectively deliver drugs; various digital devices like palm pilots, digital cameras, and cell phones that have longer battery lives and more vivid displays; and cars that are lighter, stronger, and more fuel efficient. These miracle products are now possible because scientists have learned how to manipulate nano-scale particles from 1 to 100 nanometers (a nanometer is a billionth of a meter; a human hair is about 100,000 nanometers in width). Experts estimate that 15 percent of all consumer products will contain nanotechnology by 2014. In the rush to create new consumer products, however, one question has not been asked: Is nanotechnology safe for those who use the products and the workers who are exposed to nanoparticles daily?

Write a Strong Conclusion

Restating your thesis usually isn't the best way to finish a paper. Conclusions that offer only a summary bore readers. The worst endings say something like "in my paper I've said this." Effective conclusions are interesting and provocative, leaving readers with something to think about. Give your readers something to take away besides a straight summary. Try one of these approaches.

- Issue a call to action.
- Discuss the implications.
- Make recommendations.
- Project into the future.
- Tell an anecdote that illustrates a key point.

The potential risks of nanotechnology are reasonably well known. Among the more obvious research questions are the following:
- How hazardous are nanoparticles for workers who have daily exposure?
- What happens to nanoparticles when they are poured down the drain and eventually enter streams, lakes, and oceans?
- How readily do nanoparticles penetrate the skin?
- What happens when nanoparticles enter the brain?
- What effect do airborne nanoparticles have on the lungs?

Nanotechnology promises untold benefits beyond consumer goods in the fields of medicine, energy production, and communication, but these benefits can be realized only if nanotechnology is safe. The federal National Nanotechnology Initiative spent over $1.7 billion in 2009 on nanotechnology science and engineering research, but it budgeted only $74 million on environmental, health, and safety research in 2009. The federal government needs to create a master plan for risk research and to increase spending at least tenfold to ensure sufficient funding to carry out the plan.

When you finish your conclusion, read your introduction again. The main claim in your conclusion should be closely related to the main subject, question, or claim in your introduction. If they do not match, revise the subject, question, or claim in the introduction to match the conclusion. Your thinking evolves and develops as you write, and often your introduction needs some adjusting if you wrote it first.

Evaluate Your Draft

To review and evaluate your draft, pretend you are someone who is either uninformed about your subject or informed but likely to disagree with you. If possible, think of an actual person and imagine yourself as that person.

Read your draft aloud all the way through. When you read aloud, you often hear clunky phrases and catch errors, but just put checks in the margins so you can return to them later. You don't want to get bogged down with the little stuff. What you are after in this stage is an overall sense of how well you accomplished what you set out to do.

Use the questions in the box on the next two pages to evaluate your draft. Note any places where you might make improvements. When you finish, make a list of your goals for the revision. You may have to write another draft before you move to the next stage.

Checklist for evaluating your draft

Does your paper or project meet the assignment?

- Look again at your assignment, especially at key words such as *define, analyze causes, evaluate,* and *propose.* Does your paper or project do what the assignment requires? If not, how can you change it?

- Look again at the assignment for specific guidelines including length, format, and amount of research. Does your work meet these guidelines?

Can you better focus your thesis and your supporting reasons?

- You may have started out with a large topic and ended up writing about one aspect of it. Can you make your thesis even more precise?

- Can you find the exact location where you link each reason to your thesis?

Are your main points adequately developed?

- Can you explain your reasons in more detail?

- Can you add evidence to better support your main points?

- Do you provide enough background on your topic?

Is your organization effective?

- Is the order of your main points clear? (You may want to make a quick outline of your draft if you have not done so already.)

- Are there any abrupt shifts or gaps?

- Are there sections or paragraphs that should be rearranged?

Are your key terms adequately defined?

- What are your key terms?

- Can you define these terms more precisely?

Do you consider other points of view?

- Where do you acknowledge views besides your own? If you don't acknowledge other views, where can you add them?

- How can you make your discussion of opposing views more acceptable to readers who hold those views?

Do you represent yourself effectively?

- Forget for the moment that you wrote what you are reading. What is your impression of the writer?

- Is the tone of the writing appropriate for the subject?

- Are the sentences clear and properly emphatic?

- Did you choose words that convey the right connotations?

Can you improve your title and introduction?

- Can you make your title more specific and indicate your stance?

- Can you think of a way to start faster and to get your readers interested in what you have to say?

Can you improve your conclusion?

- Can you think of an example that sums up your position?

- Can you discuss an implication of your argument that will make your readers think more about the subject?

- If you are writing a proposal, can you end with a call for action?

Can you improve your visual presentation?

- Is the type style easy to read and consistent?

- Would headings and subheadings help to mark the major sections of your argument?

- If you have statistical data, do you use charts?

- Would illustrations, maps, or other graphics help to explain your main points?

Respond to the Writing of Others

Your instructor may ask you to respond to the drafts of your classmates. Responding to other people's writing requires the same careful attention you give to your own draft. To write a helpful response, you should go through the draft more than once.

First reading

Read at your normal rate the first time through without stopping. When you finish you should have a clear sense of what the writer is trying to accomplish. Try writing the following:

- **Main idea and purpose:** Write a sentence that summarizes what you think is the writer's main idea in the draft.
- **Purpose:** Write a sentence that states what you think the writer is trying to accomplish in the draft.

Second reading

In your second reading, you should be most concerned with the content, organization, and completeness of the draft. Make notes in pencil as you read.

- **Introduction:** Does the writer's first paragraph effectively introduce the topic and engage your interest?
- **Thesis:** What exactly is the writer's thesis? Is it clear? Note in the margin where you think the thesis is located.
- **Focus:** Does the writer maintain focus on the thesis? Note any places where the writer seems to wander off to another topic.
- **Organization:** Are the sections and paragraphs arranged effectively? Do any paragraphs seem to be out of place? Can you suggest a better order for the paragraphs?
- **Completeness:** Are there sections or paragraphs that lack key information or adequate development? Where do you want to know more?
- **Conclusion:** Does the last paragraph wrap up the discussion effectively?
- **Sources:** Are outside sources cited accurately? Are quotations used correctly and worked into the fabric of the draft?

Third reading

In your third reading, turn your attention to matters of audience, style, and tone.

- **Audience:** Who are the writer's intended readers? What does the writer assume the audience knows and believes?

- **Style:** Is the writer's style engaging? How would you describe the writer's voice?
- **Tone:** Is the tone appropriate for the writer's purpose and audience? Is the tone consistent throughout the draft? Are there places where another word or phrase might work better?

When you have finished the third reading, write a short paragraph on each bulleted item above. Refer to specific paragraphs in the draft by number. Then end by answering these two questions:

- What does the writer do especially well in the draft?
- What one or two things would most improve the draft in a revision?

Edit and Proofread Carefully

When you finish revising, you are ready for one final careful reading with the goals of improving your style and eliminating errors.

Edit for style

- **Check connections between sentences and paragraphs.** Notice how your sentences flow within each paragraph and from paragraph to paragraph. If you need to signal the relationship from one sentence or paragraph to the next, use a transitional word or phrase (e.g., *in addition, moreover, similarly, however, nevertheless*).

- **Check your sentences.** Often you will pick up problems with individual sentences by reading aloud. If you notice that a sentence doesn't sound right, think about how you might rephrase it. If a sentence seems too long, consider breaking it into two or more sentences. If you notice a string of short sentences that sound choppy, consider combining them.

- **Eliminate wordiness.** Look for wordy expressions such as *because of the fact that* and *at this point in time*, which can easily be shortened to *because* and *now*. Reduce unnecessary repetition such as *attractive in appearance* or *visible to the eye* to *attractive* and *visible*. Remove unnecessary words like *very, really,* and *totally*. See how many words you can remove without losing the meaning. Choose words with the right concreteness, the right level of formality, and the right connotation.

- **Use active verbs.** Make your style more lively by replacing forms of *be* (*is, are, was, were*) or verbs ending in *–ing* with active verbs. Sentences that begin with *There is (are)* and *It is* can often be rewritten with active verbs.

Proofread carefully

In your final pass through your text, eliminate as many errors as you can. To become an effective proofreader, you have to learn to slow down. Some writers find that moving from word to word with a pencil slows them down enough to find errors. Others read backwards to force them to concentrate on each word.

- **Know what your spelling checker can and can't do.**
  Spelling checkers are the greatest invention since peanut butter. They turn up many typos and misspellings that are hard to catch. But spelling checkers do not catch wrong words (*to much* for *too much*), missing endings (*three dog*), and other similar errors.

  You can get one-on-one help in developing your ideas, focusing your topic, and revising your paper or project at your writing center.

- **Check for grammar and punctuation.** Nothing hurts your credibility more than leaving errors in what you write. Many job application letters get tossed in the reject pile because of a single, glaring error. Readers probably shouldn't make such harsh judgments when they find errors, but often they do. Keep a grammar handbook bookmarked on or beside your computer, and use it when you are uncertain about what is correct.

For additional writing resources that will help you master the objectives of this chapter, go to your **MyLab**.

Analyzing Arguments

PART

2

5 | Analyzing Written Arguments

What Is Rhetorical Analysis?

To many people, the term *rhetoric* means speech or writing that is highly ornamental or deceptive or manipulative. You might hear someone say, "That politician is just using a bunch of rhetoric" or "The rhetoric of that advertisement is very deceptive." But the term *rhetoric* is also used in a positive or neutral sense to describe human communication; for instance, *Silent Spring* is one of the most influential pieces of environmental rhetoric ever written. As a subject of study, rhetoric is usually associated with effective communication, following Aristotle's classic definition of rhetoric as "the art of finding in any given case the available means of persuasion."

Rhetoric is not just a means of *producing* effective communication but also a way of *understanding* communication. The two aspects mutually support one another: becoming a better writer makes you a better interpreter, and becoming a better interpreter makes you a better writer.

Rhetorical analysis can be defined as an effort to understand how people attempt to influence others through language and more broadly every kind of important symbolic action—not only speeches, articles, and books, but also architecture, movies, television shows, memorials, Web sites, advertisements, photos and other images, dance, and popular songs. It might be helpful to think of rhetorical analysis as the kind of critical reading discussed in Chapter 2. Critical reading—rhetorical analysis, that is—involves studying carefully any kind of persuasive action in order to understand it better and to appreciate the tactics involved.

Build a Rhetorical Analysis

Rhetorical analysis examines how an idea is shaped and presented to an audience in a particular form for a specific purpose. There are many approaches to rhetorical analysis and there is no one "correct" way to do it. Generally, though, approaches to rhetorical analysis can be placed between two broad extremes—not mutually exclusive categories but extremes at the ends of a continuum.

At one end of the continuum are analyses that concentrate more on texts than on contexts. They typically use rhetorical concepts to analyze the features of texts. Let's call this approach **textual analysis**. At the other extreme are approaches that emphasize **context** over text. These focus on reconstructing the cultural environment, or context, that existed when a particular rhetorical event took place. That reconstruction provides clues about the persuasive tactics and appeals. Those who undertake **contextual analysis**—as we'll call this second approach—regard particular rhetorical acts as parts of larger communicative chains, or "conversations." Now let's examine these two approaches in detail.

Analyze the Rhetorical Features

Just as expert teachers in every field of endeavor—from baseball to biology—devise vocabularies to facilitate specialized study, rhetoricians too have developed a set of key concepts to describe rhetorical activities. A fundamental concept in rhetoric is audience. But there are many others. Classical rhetoricians in the tradition of Aristotle, Quintilian, and Cicero developed a range of terms around what they called the canons of rhetoric in order to describe some of the actions of communicators: *inventio* (invention—the finding or creation of information for persuasive acts, and the planning of strategies), *dispostio* (arrangement), *elocutio* (style), *memoria* (the recollection of rhetorical resources that one might call upon, as well as the memorization of what has been invented and arranged), and *pronuntiatio* (delivery). These five canons generally describe the actions of any persuader, from preliminary planning to final delivery.

Over the years, as written discourse gained in prestige against oral discourse, four canons (excepting *memoria*) led to the development of concepts and terms useful for rhetorical analysis. Terms like *ethos, pathos,* and *logos,* all associated with invention, account for features of texts related to the trustworthiness and credibility of the writer or speaker (ethos), for the persuasive good reasons in an argument that derive from a community's mostly deeply held values (pathos), and for the good reasons that emerge from intellectual reasoning (logos). Fundamental to the classical approach to rhetoric is the concept of *decorum,* or "appropriateness": Everything within a persuasive act can be understood as reflecting a central rhetorical goal that governs consistent choices according to occasion and audience.

An example will make textual rhetorical analysis clearer. If you have not done so already, read "The Border Patrol State" by Leslie Marmon Silko in Chapter 11 (pp. 160–166). In the pages that follow, we use the concepts of classical rhetoric to better understand this essay.

Silko's purpose and argument

What is the purpose of Silko's essay? She wrote the essay well over a decade ago, but you probably find it to be interesting and readable still because it concerns the perennial American issue of civil rights. Silko's essay is especially relevant in light of recent debates concerning the Arizona immigration bill and surrounding controversies about the enforcement of state and federal immigration laws. In this case, Silko takes issue with practices associated with the Border Patrol of the Immigration and Naturalization Service (INS). She feels they are reenacting

The statue of Castor stands at the entrance of the Piazza del Campidoglio in Rome. A textual analysis focuses on the statue itself. The size and realism of the statue makes it a masterpiece of classical Roman sculpture.

the long subjugation of native peoples by the white majority. Silko proposes that the power of the Border Patrol be sharply reduced so that the exploitation of her people might be curtailed, and she supports that thesis with an essay that describes and condemns the Border Patrol's tactics.

Essentially Silko's argument comes down to two good reasons: the Border Patrol must be reformed because "the Immigration and Naturalization Service and Border Patrol have implemented policies that interfere with the rights of U.S. citizens to travel freely within our borders" (para. 8), and because efforts to restrict immigration are ineffective and doomed to fail ("It is no use; borders haven't worked, and they won't work," para. 16). Silko's essay amounts to an evaluation of the Border Patrol's activities, an evaluation that finds those activities lacking on ethical and practical grounds.

Silko's use of logos, pathos, and ethos

Logos

When Silko condemns the unethical actions of the Border Patrol early in the essay, she combines ample evidence with other appeals, including our sense of what is legal, constitutional, fair, and honorable. When she explains the futility of trying to

A contextual analysis focuses on the surroundings and history of the statue. According to legend, Castor (left of staircase) and his twin brother Pollux (right of staircase), the mythical sons of Leda, assisted Romans in an early battle. Romans built a large temple in the Forum to honor them. The statues were discovered in the sixteenth century and in 1583 were brought to stand at the top of the Cordonata, a staircase designed by Michelangelo as part of a renovation of the Piazza del Campidoglio commissioned by Pope Paul III Farnese in 1536.

stop immigration, she appeals again to her readers' reasonableness: Constructing walls across the border with Mexico is foolish because "border entrepreneurs have already used blowtorches to cut passageways through the fence" (para. 15), because "a mass migration is already under way" (para. 16), and because "The Americas are Indian country, and the 'Indian problem' is not about to go away" (para. 17).

The bulk of "The Border Patrol State" amounts to an argument by example. The single case—Silko's personal experience, as a Native American, with the border police—stands for many such cases. This case study persuades as other case studies and narratives do—by serving as a representative example that stands for the treatment of many Native Americans.

Pathos

The logical appeals in Silko's essay are reinforced by her emotional appeals.

- The Border Patrol is constructing an "Iron Curtain" that is as destructive of human rights as the Iron Curtain that the Soviet Union constructed around Eastern Europe after World War II (para. 15).

- "Proud" and "patriotic" Native Americans are being harassed: "old Bill Pratt used to ride his horse 300 miles overland . . . every summer to work as a fire lookout" (para. 1).
- Border police terrify American citizens in a way that is chillingly reminiscent of "the report of Argentine police and military officers who became addicted to interrogation, torture, and murder" (paras. 3–5).

The essay's most emotional moment may be when Silko describes how the Border Patrol dog, trained to find illegal drugs and other contraband, including human contraband, seems to sympathize with her and those she is championing: "I saw immediately from the expression in her eyes that the dog hated them" (para. 6); "The dog refused to accuse us: She had an innate dignity that did not permit her to serve the murderous impulses of those men" (para. 7). Clearly the good reasons in "The Border Patrol State" appeal in a mutually supportive way to both the reason and the emotions of Silko's audience. She appeals to the whole person.

Ethos

Why do we take Silko's word about the stories she tells? It is because she establishes her *ethos*, or trustworthiness, early in the essay. Silko reminds her readers that she is a respected, published author who has been on a book tour to publicize her novel *Almanac of the Dead* (para. 3). She buttresses her trustworthiness in other ways too:

- She quotes widely, if unobtrusively, from books and reports to establish that she has studied the issues thoroughly. Note how much she displays her knowledge of INS policies in paragraph 9, for instance.
- She tells not only of her own encounters with the border police (experiences that are a source of great credibility), but also of the encounters of others whom she lists, name after careful name, in order that we might trust her account.
- She demonstrates knowledge of history and geography.
- She connects herself to America generally by linking herself to traditional American values such as freedom (para. 1), ethnic pride, tolerance, and even a love of dogs.

This essay, because of its anti-authoritarian strain, might seem to display politically progressive attitudes at times, but overall, Silko comes off as hard-working, honest, educated, even patriotic. And definitely credible.

Silko's arrangement

Silko arranges her essay appropriately as well. In general the essay follows a traditional pattern. She begins with a long concrete introductory story that hooks the reader and leads to her thesis in paragraph 8. Next, in the body of her essay, she supports her thesis by evaluating the unethical nature of INS policies. She cites their violation of constitutional protections, their similarity to tactics used in nations that are notorious for violating the rights of citizens, and their fundamental immorality. She also emphasizes how those policies are racist in nature (paras. 11–13).

After completing her moral evaluation of INS policy, she turns to the practical difficulties of halting immigration in paragraph 14. The North American Free Trade Agreement (NAFTA) permits the free flow of goods, and even drugs are impossible to stop, so how can people be stopped from crossing borders? Efforts to seal borders are "pathetic" in their ineffectiveness (para. 15). These points lay the groundwork for Silko's surprising and stirring conclusions: "The great human migration within the Americas cannot be stopped; human beings are natural forces of the earth, just as rivers and winds are natural forces" (para. 16); "the Americas are Indian country, and the 'Indian problem' is not about to go away" (para. 17). The mythic "return of the Aztlan" is on display in the box cars that go by as the essay closes. In short, this essay unfolds in a conventional way: it has a standard beginning, middle, and end.

Silko's style

What about Silko's style? How is it appropriate to her purposes? Take a look at paragraphs 3 and 4. You will notice that nearly all of the fourteen sentences in these paragraphs are simple in structure. There are only five sentences that use any form of subordination (clauses that begin with *when*, *that*, or *if*). Many of the sentences consist either of one clause or of two clauses joined by simple coordination (connection with conjunctions such as *and* or *but* or a semicolon). Several of the sentences and clauses are unusually short. Furthermore, in these paragraphs Silko never uses metaphors or other sorts of poetic language. Her choice of words is as simple as her sentences. It all reminds you of the daily newspaper, doesn't it? Silko chooses a style similar to one used in newspaper reporting—simple, straightforward, unadorned—because she wants her readers to accept her narrative as credible and trustworthy. Her tone and voice reinforce her ethos.

There is more to say about the rhetorical choices that Silko made in crafting "The Border Patrol State," but this analysis is enough to illustrate our main point. Textual rhetorical analysis employs rhetorical terminology—in this case, terms borrowed from classical rhetoric such as ethos, pathos, logos, arrangement, style, and tone—as a way of helping us to understand how a writer makes choices to achieve certain effects. And textual analysis cooperates with contextual analysis.

Analyze the Rhetorical Context
Communication as conversation

Notice that in the previous discussion the fact that Leslie Marmon Silko's "The Border Patrol State" was originally published in the magazine *The Nation* did not matter too much. Nor did it matter when the essay was published (October 17, 1994), who exactly read it, what their reaction was, or what other people were saying at the time. Textual analysis can proceed as if the item under consideration "speaks for all time," as if it is a museum piece unaffected by time and space. There's nothing wrong with museums, of course; they permit people to observe and appreciate objects in an important way. But museums often fail to reproduce an artwork's original context and cultural meaning. In that sense museums can diminish understanding as much as they contribute to it. Contextual rhetorical analysis is an attempt to understand communications through the lens of their environments, examining the setting or scene out of which any communication emerges.

Similar to textual analysis, contextual analysis may be conducted in any number of ways. But contextual rhetorical analysis always proceeds from a description of the **rhetorical situation** that motivated the event in question. It demands an appreciation of the social circumstances that call rhetorical events into being and that orchestrate the course of those events. It regards communications as anything but self-contained:

- Each communication is considered as a response to other communications and to other social practices.
- Communications, and social practices more generally, are considered to reflect the attitudes and values of the communities that sustain them.
- Analysts seek evidence of how those other communications and social practices are reflected in texts.

Rhetorical analysis from a contextualist perspective understands individual pieces as parts of ongoing conversations.

The challenge is to reconstruct the conversation surrounding a specific piece of writing or speaking. Sometimes it is easy to do so. You may have appropriate background information on the topic, as well as a feel for what is behind what people are writing or saying about it. People who have strong feelings about the environment, stem cell research, same-sex marriage, or any number of other current issues are well informed about the arguments that are converging around those topics.

But other times it takes some research to reconstruct the conversations and social practices related to a particular issue. If the issue is current, you need to see how the debate is conducted in current magazines, newspapers, talk shows, movies and TV shows, Web sites, and so forth. If the issue is from an earlier time, you must do archival research into historical collections of newspapers, magazines, books, letters, and other documentary sources. Archival research usually involves libraries, special research collections, or film and television archives where it is possible to learn quite a bit about context.

An example will clarify how contextual analysis works to open up an argument to analysis. Let's return to a discussion of Silko's "The Border Patrol State" on pages 160–166. It will take a bit of research to reconstruct some of the "conversations" that Silko is participating in, but the result will be an enhanced understanding of the essay as well as an appreciation for how you might do a contextual rhetorical analysis.

Silko's life and works

You can begin by learning more about Silko herself. The essay provides some facts about her (e.g., that she is a Native American writer of note who is from the Southwest). The headnote on page 160 gives additional information (that her writing usually develops out of Native American traditions and tales). You can learn more about Silko using the Internet and your library's Web site. Silko's credibility, her ethos, is established not just by her textual decisions but also by her prior reputation, especially for readers of *The Nation* who would recognize and appreciate her accomplishments.

Perhaps the most relevant information on the Web is about *Almanac of the Dead*, the novel Silko refers to in paragraph 3. The novel, set mainly in Tucson, involves a Native American woman psychic who is in the process of transcribing the lost histories of her dead ancestors into "an almanac of the dead"—a history of her people. This history is written from the point of view of the conquered, not the conqueror. "The Border Patrol State," it seems, is an essay version of *Almanac of the Dead* in that Silko protests what has been lost—and what is still being lost—in the clash between white and Native American cultures. It is a protest against the tactics of the border police. Or is it?

The context of publication

Through a consideration of the conversations swirling around it, contextual analysis actually suggests that "The Border Patrol State" is just as much about immigration policy as it is about the civil rights of Native Americans. The article first appeared in *The Nation*, a respected, politically progressive magazine that has been appearing weekly for decades. Published in New York City, it is a magazine of public opinion that covers theater, film, music, fiction, and other arts; politics and public affairs; and contemporary culture. If you want to know what left-leaning people are thinking about an issue, *The Nation* is a good magazine to consult. You can imagine that Silko's essay therefore reached an audience of sympathetic readers—people who would be receptive to her message. They would be inclined to sympathize with Silko's complaints and to heed her call for a less repressive Border Patrol.

What is more interesting is that Silko's essay appeared on October 17, 1994, in a special issue of *The Nation* devoted to "The Immigration Wars," a phrase prominent on the magazine's cover. Silko's essay was one of several articles that appeared under that banner, an indication that Silko's argument is not just about the violation of the civil rights of Native Americans but also about the larger issue of immigration policy. "The Border Patrol State" appeared after David Cole's "Five Myths about Immigration," Elizabeth Kadetsky's "Bashing Illegals in California," Peter Kwong's "China's Human Traffickers," two editorials about immigration policy, and short columns on immigration by *Nation* regulars Katha Pollitt, Aryeh Neier, and the late Christopher Hitchens. Together the articles in this issue mounted a sustained argument in favor of a liberal immigration policy.

The larger conversation

Why did *The Nation* entitle its issue "The Immigration Wars"? Immigration was a huge controversy in October 1994, just before the 1994 elections. When the 1965 Immigration Act was amended in 1990, the already strong flow of immigrants to the United States became a flood. While many previous immigrants came to the United States from Europe, most recent immigrants have come from Asia, Latin America, the Caribbean islands, and Africa. While earlier immigrants typically passed through Ellis Island and past the Statue of Liberty that welcomed them, most recent immigrants in 1994 were coming to Florida, Texas, and California. The arrival of all those new immigrants revived old fears that have been in the air for decades (that they take away jobs from native-born Americans, that they undermine national values by resisting assimilation and clinging to their own cultures, that they reduce standards of living by putting stress on education and social-welfare budgets). Many people countered those fears by pointing out that immigrants create jobs and wealth, enhance the vitality of American culture, become among the proudest of Americans, and contribute to the tax base of their communities. But those counterarguments were undermined when a tide of illegal immigrants—up to 500,000 per year—was arriving at the time Silko was writing.

The Immigration Wars were verbal wars. In the 1994 election, Republicans had united under the banner of a "Contract with America." Some 300 Republican congressional candidates, drawn together by conservative leader Newt Gingrich, agreed to run on a common platform in an ultimately successful effort to gain control of the House of Representatives. Among a number of initiatives, the Contract with America proposed changes in laws in order to curtail immigration, to reduce illegal immigration, and to deny benefits such as health care, social services, and education to illegal residents.

The Contract with America offered support for California's Proposition 187, another important 1994 proposal. This so-called "Save Our State" initiative was designed to "prevent California's estimated 1.7 million undocumented immigrants from partaking of every form of public welfare including nonemergency medical care, prenatal clinics and public schools," as Kadetsky explained in her essay in *The Nation*. The Republican Contract with America and California's Proposition 187 together constituted the nation's leading domestic issue in October 1994. The war of words about the issue was evident in the magazines, books, newspapers, talk shows, barber shops, and hair salons of America—much as it is today.

Silko's political goals

In this context, it is easy to see that Silko's essay is against more than the Border Patrol. It is an argument in favor of relatively unrestricted immigration, especially for Mexicans and Native Americans. Moreover, it is a direct refutation of the Contract with America and Proposition 187. Proposition 187 states "that [the People of California] have suffered and are suffering economic hardship caused by the presence of illegal aliens in this state, that they have suffered and are suffering personal injury and damage caused by the criminal conduct of illegal aliens, [and] that they have a right to the protection of their government from any person or persons entering this country illegally."

Silko turns the claim around. It is the Border Patrol that is behaving illegally. It is the Border Patrol that is creating economic hardship. It is the border police that are inflicting personal injury and damage through criminal conduct. Finally, it is the U.S. government that is acting illegally by ignoring the treaty of Guadalupe Hidalgo, which "recognizes the right of the Tohano O'Odom (Papago) people to move freely across the U.S.-Mexico border without documents," as Silko writes in a footnote. Writing just before the election of 1994 and in the midst of a spirited national debate, Silko had specific political goals in mind. A contextual analysis of "The Border Patrol State" reveals that the essay is, at least in part, an eloquent refutation of the Contract with America and Proposition 187—two items that are not even named explicitly in the essay!

We could do more contextual analysis here. There is no need to belabor the point, however; our purpose has been simply to illustrate that contextual analysis of a piece of rhetoric can enrich our understanding.

Write a Rhetorical Analysis

Effective rhetorical analysis, as we have seen, can be textual or contextual in nature. But we should emphasize again that these two approaches to rhetorical analysis are not mutually exclusive. Indeed, many if not most analysts operate between these two extremes; they consider the details of the text, but they also attend to the particulars of context. Textual analysis and contextual analysis inevitably complement each other. Getting at what is at stake in "The Border Patrol State" or any other sophisticated argument takes patience and intelligence. Rhetorical analysis, as a way of understanding how people argue, is both enlightening and challenging.

Try to use elements of both kinds of analysis whenever you want to understand a rhetorical event more fully. Rhetoric is "inside" texts, but it is also "outside" them. Specific rhetorical performances are an irreducible mixture of text and context, and so interpretation and analysis of those performances must account for both text and context. Remember, however, the limitations of your analysis. Realize that your analysis will always be somewhat partial and incomplete, ready to be deepened, corrected, modified, and extended by the insights of others. Rhetorical analysis can itself be part of an unending conversation—a way of learning and teaching within a community.

Steps to Writing a Rhetorical Analysis

Step 1 Select an Argument to Analyze

Find an argument to analyze—a speech or sermon, an op-ed in a newspaper, an ad in a magazine designed for a particular audience, or a commentary on a talk show.

Examples

- Editorial pages of newspapers (but not letters to the editor unless you can find a long and detailed letter)
- Opinion features in magazines such as *Time, Newsweek,* and *U.S. News & World Report*
- Magazines that take political positions such as *National Review, Mother Jones, New Republic, Nation,* and *Slate*
- Web sites of activist organizations (but not blog or newsgroup postings unless they are long and detailed)

Step 2 Analyze the Context

Who is the author?

Through research in the library or on the Web, learn all you can about the author.

- How does the argument you are analyzing repeat arguments previously made by the author?
- What motivated the author to write? What is the author's purpose for writing this argument?

Who is the audience?

Through research, learn all you can about the publication and the audience.

- Who is the anticipated audience?
- How do the occasion and forum for writing affect the argument?

What is the larger conversation?

Through research, find out what else was being said about the subject of your selection. Track down any references made in the text you are examining.

- When did the argument appear?
- What other concurrent pieces of "cultural conversation" (e.g., TV shows, other articles, speeches, Web sites) does the item you are analyzing respond to or "answer"?

Step 3 Analyze the Text

Summarize the argument

- What is the main claim?

- What reasons are given in support of the claim?
- How is the argument organized? What are the components, and why are they presented in that order?

What is the medium and genre?

- What is the medium? A newspaper? a scholarly journal? a Web site?
- What is the genre? An editorial? an essay? a speech? an advertisement? What expectations does the audience have about this genre?

What appeals are used?

- Analyze the ethos. How does the writer represent himself or herself? Does the writer have any credentials as an authority on the topic? Do you trust the writer?
- Analyze the logos. Where do you find facts and evidence in the argument? What kinds of facts and evidence does the writer present? Direct observation? statistics? interviews? surveys? quotations from authorities?
- Analyze the pathos. Does the writer attempt to invoke an emotional response? Where do you find appeals to shared values?

How would you characterize the style?

- Is the style formal, informal, satirical, or something else?
- Are any metaphors used?

Step 4 Write a Draft

Introduction

- Describe briefly the argument you are analyzing, including where it was published, how long it is, and who wrote it.
- If the argument is about an issue unfamiliar to your readers, supply the necessary background.

Body

- Analyze the context, following Step 2.
- Analyze the text, following Step 3.

Conclusion

- Do more than simply summarize what you have said. You might, for example, end with an example that typifies the argument.
- You don't have to end by either agreeing or disagreeing with the writer. Your task in this assignment is to analyze the strategies the writer uses.

Step 5 Revise, Edit, Proofread

For detailed instructions, see Chapter 4.
For a checklist to evaluate your draft, see pages 48–49.

Barbara Jordan

Statement on the Articles of Impeachment

Barbara Jordan (1936–1996) grew up in Houston and received a law degree from Boston University in 1959. Working on John F. Kennedy's 1960 presidential campaign stirred an interest in politics, and Jordon became the first African American woman elected to the Texas State Senate in 1966. In 1972 she was elected to the United States House of Representatives and thus became the first African American woman from the South ever to serve in Congress. Jordan was appointed to the House Judiciary Committee. Soon she was in the national spotlight when that committee considered articles of impeachment against President Richard Nixon, who had illegally covered up a burglary of Democratic Party headquarters during the 1972 election. When Nixon's criminal acts reached to the Judiciary Committee, Jordan's opening speech on July 24, 1974, set the tone for the debate and established her reputation as a moral beacon for the nation. Nixon resigned as president on August 9, 1974, when it was evident that he would be impeached.

Thank you, Mr. Chairman.

Mr. Chairman, I join my colleague Mr. Rangel in thanking you for giving the junior members of this committee the glorious opportunity of sharing the pain of this inquiry. Mr. Chairman, you are a strong man and it has not been easy, but we have tried as best we can to give you as much assistance as possible.

2 Earlier today, we heard the beginning of the Preamble to the Constitution of the United States: "We, the people." It's a very eloquent beginning. But when that document was completed on the seventeenth of September in 1787, I was not included in that "We, the people." I felt somehow for many years that George Washington and Alexander Hamilton just left me out by mistake. But through the process of amendment, interpretation, and court decision, I have finally been included in "We, the people."

3 Today I am an inquisitor. Any hyperbole would not be fictional and would not overstate the solemnness that I feel right now. My faith in the Constitution is whole; it is complete; it is total. And I am not going to sit here and be an idle spectator to the diminution, the subversion, the destruction, of the Constitution.

4   "Who can so properly be the inquisitors for the nation as the representatives of the nation themselves?" "The subjects of its jurisdiction are those offenses which proceed from the misconduct of public men." And that's what we're talking about. In other words, [the jurisdiction comes] from the abuse or violation of some public trust.

5   It is wrong, I suggest, it is a misreading of the Constitution for any member here to assert that for a member to vote for an article of impeachment means that that member must be convinced that the President should be removed from office. The Constitution doesn't say that. The powers relating to impeachment are an essential check in the hands of the body of the legislature against and upon the encroachments of the executive. [By creating] the division between the two branches of the legislature, the House and the Senate, assigning to the one the right to accuse and to the other the right to judge, the framers of this Constitution were very astute. They did not make the accusers and the judgers the same person.

6   We know the nature of impeachment. We've been talking about it awhile now. It is chiefly designed for the President and his high ministers to somehow be called into account. It is designed to "bridle" the executive if he engages in excesses. "It is designed as a method of national inquest into the conduct of public men." The framers confided in the Congress the power, if need be, to remove the President in order to strike a delicate balance between a President swollen with power and grown tyrannical, and preservation of the independence of the executive.

7   The nature of impeachment: [it is] a narrowly channeled exception to the separation-of-powers maxim. The Federal Convention of 1787 said that. It limited impeachment to high crimes and misdemeanors and discounted and opposed the term *maladministration*. "It is to be used only for great misdemeanors," so it was said in the North Carolina ratification convention. And in the Virginia ratification convention: "We do not trust our liberty to a particular branch. We need one branch to check the other."

8   "No one need be afraid"—the North Carolina ratification convention—"No one need be afraid that officers who commit oppression will pass with immunity." "Prosecutions of impeachments will seldom fail to agitate the passions of the whole community," said Hamilton in the Federalist Papers, number 65. "We divide into parties more or less friendly or inimical to the accused." I do not mean political parties in that sense.

9   The drawing of political lines goes to the motivation behind impeachment; but impeachment must proceed within the confines of the constitutional term "high crime[s] and misdemeanors." Of the impeachment process, it was Woodrow Wilson who said that "Nothing short of the grossest offenses against the plain law of the land will suffice to give them speed and effectiveness. Indignation so great as to overgrow party interest may secure a conviction; but nothing else can."

10   Common sense would be revolted if we engaged upon this process for petty reasons. Congress has a lot to do: Appropriations, Tax Reform, Health Insurance, Campaign Finance Reform, Housing, Environmental Protection, Energy Sufficiency, Mass Transportation. Pettiness cannot be allowed to stand in the face of such overwhelming problems. So today we are not being petty. We are trying to be big, because the task we have before us is a big one.

11   This morning, in a discussion of the evidence, we were told that the evidence which purports to support the allegations of misuse of the CIA by the President is thin.

We're told that that evidence is insufficient. What that recital of the evidence this morning did not include is what the President did know on June the 23rd, 1972.

12   The President did know that it was Republican money, that it was money from the Committee for the Re-Election of the President, which was found in the possession of one of the burglars arrested on June the 17th. What the President did know on the 23rd of June was the prior activities of E. Howard Hunt, which included his participation in the break-in of Daniel Ellsberg's psychiatrist, which included Howard Hunt's participation in the Dita Beard ITT affair, which included Howard Hunt's fabrication of cables designed to discredit the Kennedy Administration.

13   We were further cautioned today that perhaps these proceedings ought to be delayed because certainly there would be new evidence forthcoming from the President of the United States. There has not even been an obfuscated indication that this committee would receive any additional materials from the President. The committee subpoena is outstanding, and if the President wants to supply that material, the committee sits here. The fact is that only yesterday, the American people waited with great anxiety for eight hours, not knowing whether their President would obey an order of the Supreme Court of the United States.

14   At this point, I would like to juxtapose a few of the impeachment criteria with some of the actions the President has engaged in. Impeachment criteria: James Madison, from the Virginia ratification convention: "If the President be connected in any suspicious manner with any person and there be grounds to believe that he will shelter him, he may be impeached."

15   We have heard time and time again that the evidence reflects the payment to defendants of money. The President had knowledge that these funds were being paid and these were funds collected for the 1972 presidential campaign. We know that the President met with Mr. Henry Petersen 27 times to discuss matters related to Watergate, and immediately thereafter met with the very persons who were implicated in the information Mr. Petersen was receiving. The words are: "If the President is connected in any suspicious manner with any person and there be grounds to believe that he will shelter that person, he may be impeached."

16   Justice Story: "Impeachment is intended for occasional and extraordinary cases where a superior power acting for the whole people is put into operation to protect their rights and rescue their liberties from violations." We know about the Huston plan. We know about the break-in of the psychiatrist's office. We know that there was absolute complete direction on September 3rd when the President indicated that a surreptitious entry had been made in Dr. Fielding's office, after having met with Mr. Ehrlichman and Mr. Young. "Protect their rights." "Rescue their liberties from violation."

17   The Carolina ratification convention impeachment criteria: those are impeachable "who behave amiss or betray their public trust." Beginning shortly after the Watergate break-in and continuing to the present time, the President has engaged in a series of public statements and actions designed to thwart the lawful investigation by government prosecutors. Moreover, the President has made public announcements and assertions bearing on the Watergate case, which the evidence will show he knew to be false. These assertions, false assertions, impeachable, those who misbehave. Those who "behave amiss or betray the public trust."

18   James Madison again at the Constitutional Convention: "A President is impeach-able if he attempts to subvert the Constitution." The Constitution charges the President with the task of taking care that the laws be faithfully executed, and yet the President has counseled his aides to commit perjury, willfully disregard the secrecy of grand jury proceedings, conceal surreptitious entry, attempt to compromise a federal judge, while publicly displaying his cooperation with the processes of criminal justice. "A President is impeachable if he attempts to subvert the Constitution."

19   If the impeachment provision in the Constitution of the United States will not reach the offenses charged here, then perhaps that 18th-century Constitution should be abandoned to a 20th-century paper shredder.

20   Has the President committed offenses, and planned, and directed, and acqui-esced in a course of conduct which the Constitution will not tolerate? That's the ques-tion. We know that. We know the question. We should now forthwith proceed to answer the question. It is reason, and not passion, which must guide our deliberations, guide our debate, and guide our decision.

21   I yield back the balance of my time, Mr. Chairman.

Sample Student Rhetorical Analysis

T. Jonathan Jackson

Dr. Netaji

English 1102

11 October 2010

An Argument of Reason and Passion: Barbara Jordan's

"Statement on the Articles of Impeachment"

Barbara Jordan's July 24, 1974 speech before the U.S. House Judiciary Committee helped convince the House of Representatives, and the American public, that President Richard Nixon should be impeached. Nixon was under investigation for his role in the cover-up of the Watergate scandal. He knew about the burglary of Democratic Party headquarters, but denied having any knowledge of it and illegally shielded those responsible. Jordan used her speech to argue that the president should be impeached because his actions threatened the Constitution and the people of the United States; however, Jordan never explicitly states this position in her speech. Instead, she establishes her credibility and then uses logic to set out the evidence against the president. •————

> Jonathan Jackson provides background information in the first paragraph and his thesis at the end.

In one sense, the audience of Jordan's speech consisted of the other 34 members of the House Judiciary Committee, gathered together to decide whether or not to recommend impeachment. And yet Jordan was not speaking just to a committee meeting; her speech was very public. The Senate Watergate hearings had been televised during the months before her speech, and millions of Americans watched sensational testimony by a host of witnesses. The Senate hearings produced charges that Nixon authorized break-ins at Democratic campaign headquarters in Washington during the 1972 election and that the White House was involved in many political dirty tricks and improprieties.

But the accusations remained only accusations—and Americans remained deeply divided about them—until it was discovered that Nixon had himself collected possible hard evidence: he had taped many conversations in the Oval Office, tapes that could support or refute the charges against the president. Nixon engaged in a protracted legal battle to keep the tapes from being disclosed, on the grounds that they were private conversations protected under "executive privilege," and he released only partial and edited transcripts. Finally on July 24, 1974, the courts ruled that Nixon had to turn all his remaining tapes over. That same day, knowing that hard evidence was now at hand, the House Judiciary Committee immediately went into session to vote whether to impeach Nixon. Each member of the committee was given fifteen minutes for an opening statement.

Nixon was a Republican and Jordan, like the majority of the committee, was a Democrat. Jordan had to convince her audience she was not biased against the president simply because of her party affiliation. Jordan was also new to Congress, relatively unknown outside of Texas, and a low-ranking member of the committee. Consequently, she had to establish her ethos to the committee as well as to the television audience. She had to present herself as fair, knowledgeable, and intellectually mature.

> Jackson observes that Jordan had a formidable assignment in establishing her ethos in a short speech.

At the heart of Jordan's argument is her faith in the Constitution. She begins her speech from a personal perspective, pointing out that the Constitution is not perfect because it originally excluded African Americans like her. But now that the Constitution recognizes her as a citizen, Jordan says, her faith in it "is whole, it is complete, it is total." She even implies that, as a citizen, she has a moral duty to protect the Constitution, saying, "I am not going to sit here and be an idle spectator to the diminution, the subversion, the destruction of the Constitution." Jordan's emotional connection to the Constitution shows the audience that she is motivated by a love of her country, not by party loyalty. She establishes herself as someone fighting to defend and protect American values.

> Jackson analyzes how Jordan's fervent allegiance to the Constitution made her appear unbiased.

Jordan describes the Constitution as the accepted authority on the laws related to impeachment. She shows the audience how the Constitution gives her the authority to act as an "inquisitor," or judge. She depicts the Constitution and the American people as potential victims, and the president as the potential criminal. She warns of the need to remove "a President swollen with power and grown tyrannical."

Jackson 3

The appeals to pathos and ethos in the opening of the speech establish Jordan's motivations and credibility, allowing her to next lay out her logical arguments. Jordan proceeds to explain how the Constitution defines impeachment, and she fleshes out this brief definition with evidence from several state Constitutional Conventions. She also quotes Supreme Court Justice Joseph Story. Using evidence from the North Carolina and Virginia Constitutional Conventions, Jordan shows that impeachment was intended only for "great misdemeanors," and that the branches of government were intended to act as a check upon one another.

Next Jordan uses quotations from James Madison, Justice Story, and others to define impeachable offenses. For each offense, Jordan provides an example of an act that President Nixon was known to have committed, and she shows how his actions meet the definition of impeachable offenses. She compares Nixon's meetings with Watergate suspects to Madison's statement that "if the President is connected in any suspicious manner with any person and there be grounds to believe that he will shelter that person, he may be impeached." She pairs Justice Story's statement that impeachment should "protect [citizens'] rights and rescue their liberties from violation" with Nixon's knowledge of the burglary of a private psychiatrist's office. She links Nixon's attempts to bribe a judge and thwart grand jury proceedings with Madison's statement that "a President is impeachable if he attempts to subvert the Constitution."

> Jordan uses quotations from respected figures in American history to apply to Nixon's misdeeds.

> Jordan had to confront a legal issue: Were the actions of President Nixon serious enough to justify impeachment?

Throughout this section, Jordan repeats the historical quotes before and after her descriptions of the president's acts. This repetition makes the connections stronger and more memorable for the audience. Jordan also contrasts the formal, high-toned language of the Founders and the Constitution with descriptions that make President Nixon's actions sound sordid and petty: He knew about money "found in the possession of one of the burglars arrested on June the 17th," about "the break-in of Daniel Ellsberg's psychiatrist," about "the fabrication of cables designed to discredit the Kennedy Administration." Words like "burglars," "arrested," "break-in," and "fabrication," sound like evidence in a criminal trial. These words are not the kind of language Americans want to hear describing the actions of their president.

Jackson 4

Jordan then adds another emotional appeal, implying that the Constitution is literally under attack. "If the impeachment provisions will not reach the offenses charged here," she says, "then perhaps that 18th-century Constitution should be abandoned to a 20th-century paper shredder." This dramatic image encourages the audience to imagine President Nixon shredding the Constitution just as he had destroyed other evidence implicating him in the Watergate scandal. It implies that if the president is not stopped, he will commit further abuses of power. Jordan also makes the American people responsible for this possible outcome, saying that "we" may as well shred the Constitution if it cannot be used to impeach Nixon. This emotional appeal has the effect of shaming those who say they cannot or should not vote for impeachment.

> Jackson notes that the metaphor of the paper shredder adds emotional force.

Jordan concludes her speech not by calling for impeachment, but by calling for an answer to the question, "Has the President committed offenses, and planned, and directed, and acquiesced in a course of conduct which the Constitution will not tolerate?" It almost seems like Jordan is being humble and trying not to judge by not stating her position outright. However, the reverse is true: Jordan doesn't state her position because she doesn't need to. The evidence she presented led Congress and the American public inescapably to one conclusion: President Nixon had committed impeachable offenses. Just two week later, Nixon resigned from office. Jordan had made her point.

> In his conclusion Jackson points out how Jordan shifts the focus to her audience in her conclusion.

Jackson 5

Works Cited

Jordan, Barbara. "Statement on the Articles of Impeachment." *American Rhetoric: Top 100 Speeches*. American Rhetoric, 25 July 1974. Web. 25 Sept. 2010.

For additional writing resources that will help you master the objectives of this chapter, go to your **MyLab**.

6 | Analyzing Visual and Multimedia Arguments

What Is a Visual Argument?

We live in a world flooded with images. They pull on us, compete for our attention, push us to do things. But how often do we think about how they work?

Can there be an argument without words?

Arguments in written language are visual in one sense: we use our eyes to read the words on the page. But without words, can there be a visual argument? Certainly some visual symbols take on conventional meanings. Signs in airports or other public places, for example, are designed to communicate with speakers of many languages.

Some visual symbols even make explicit claims. A one-way street sign says that drivers should travel only in the one direction. But are such signs arguments? In Chapter 3 we point out that scholars of argument do not believe that everything *is* an argument. Most scholars define an argument as a claim supported by one or more reasons. A one-way sign has a claim: all drivers should go in the same direction. But is there a reason? We all know an unstated reason the sign carries: drivers who go the wrong way violate the law and risk a substantial fine (plus they risk a head-on collision with other drivers).

Visual arguments require viewer participation

The *Deepwater Horizon* oil spill (also known as the BP oil spill) was the largest off-shore oil spill in the history of the United States. Caused by an explosion on April 20, 2010, the spill dumped millions of gallons of oil every day for months in spite of efforts to contain it. People around the world were reminded of the spill when they turned on their televisions and saw video of the oil gushing from the well, and nearly everyone was outraged.

People interpreted the oil flowing from the pipe quite differently, inferring multiple *because* clauses. Citizens were angry for different reasons.

The *Deepwater Horizon* oil spill was a disaster because

- eleven workers were killed and seventeen were injured.
- enormous harm was done to Gulf wetlands, birds, fish, turtles, marine mammals, and other animals.
- the tourism industry suffered another major blow just five years after Hurricane Katrina.
- the fishing and shrimping industries suffered huge losses.

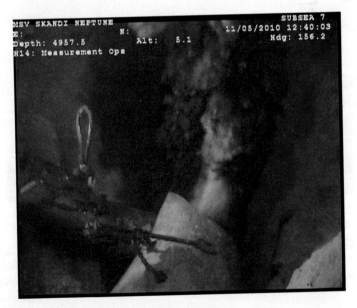

The main oil leak from the *Deepwater Horizon* wellhead.

A photo of this booth at the Taste of Chicago sent on Twitter enraged people in New Orleans.

- President Obama declared a moratorium on deep-water drilling, threatening the loss of jobs.
- BP and its partners were negligent in drilling the well.
- the spill was an unfortunate act of God like Hurricane Katrina.

Differing interpretations of visual arguments extended beyond the spill itself. A news producer in Chicago took a photo of a booth at the Taste of Chicago festival and sent it to a friend in New Orleans, who sent it to a food writer, who posted it on Twitter. The mayor of New Orleans called it "disgraceful."

Talks shows in both Chicago and New Orleans ranted for a few days about the other city. One comment was perhaps telling about the source of the rage: a menu disclaimer would have been acceptable, but a prominent visual argument, even in text form, was hitting below the belt.

What Is a Multimedia Argument?

Multimedia describes the use of multiple content forms including text, voice and music audio, video, still images, animation, and interactivity. Multimedia goes far back in human history (texts and images were combined at the beginnings of writing), but digital technologies and the Web have made multimedia the fabric of our daily lives. But what exactly are multimedia arguments?

For example, games provide intense multimedia experiences, but are they arguments? Game designers such as Jane McGonigal believe they are arguments. McGonigal maintains that games make people more powerful because they connect them into larger wholes.

Images from Michael Wesch's *A Vision of Students Today*

Thousands of multimedia arguments have been posted on YouTube. One frequently viewed video is Michael Wesch's *A Vision of Students Today*, posted in October 2007. Wesch's point is that today's education is ill-suited for most students. He enlisted his students to make the point with text and video.

Analyze Visual Evidence

Videos without narration, images, and graphics seldom make arguments on their own, but they are frequently used to support arguments.

Evaluate photographs and videos as evidence

Almost from the beginnings of photography, negatives were manipulated but realistic results required a high skill level. In the digital era anyone can alter photographs. Perhaps there's nothing wrong with using Photoshop to add absent relatives to family photographs or remove ex-boyfriends and ex-girlfriends. But where do you draw the line? Not only do many videos on YouTube use outright deception, but newsmagazines and networks have also been found guilty of these practices.

Ask questions about what you view.

- Who created the image or video? What bias might the creator have?
- Who published the image or video? What bias might the publisher have?
- Who is the intended audience? For example, political videos often assume that the viewers hold the same political views as the creators.
- What is being shown, and what is not being shown? For example, a video ad promoting tourism for the Gulf of Mexico will look very different from a video showing sources of pollution.
- Who is being represented, and who is not being represented? Who gets left out is as important as who gets included.

The ease of cropping digital photographs reveals an important truth about photography: a photograph represents reality from a particular viewpoint. A high-resolution picture of a crowd can be divided into many smaller images that each say something different about the event. The act of pointing the camera in one direction and not in another shapes how photographic evidence will be interpreted. (See the examples on page 80.)

Evaluate charts and graphs

Statistical information is frequently used as evidence in arguments. The problem with giving many statistics in sentence form, however, is that readers shortly lose track of the numbers. Charts and graphs present statistics visually, allowing readers to take in trends and relationships at a glance.

A photographer's choices about who and what to photograph shapes how we see an event.

However, charts and graphs can also be misleading. For example, a chart that compares the amounts of calories in competing brands of cereal might list one with 70 calories and another with 80 calories. If the chart begins at zero, the difference looks small. But if the chart starts at 60, the brand with 80 calories appears to have twice the calories of the brand with 70. Furthermore, the chart is worthless if the data is inaccurate or comes from an unreliable source. Creators of charts and graphs have an ethical obligation to present data as fairly and accurately as possible and to provide the sources of the data.

Ask these questions when you are analyzing charts and graphs

- Is the type of chart appropriate for the information presented?

 Bar and column charts make comparisons in particular categories. If two or more charts are compared, the scales should be consistent.

 Line graphs plot variables on a vertical and a horizontal axis. They are useful for showing proportional trends over time.

 Pie charts show the proportion of parts in terms of the whole. Segments must add up to 100 percent of the whole.

- Does the chart have a clear purpose?
- Does the title indicate the purpose?
- What do the units represent (dollars, people, voters, percentages, and so on)?
- What is the source of the data?
- Is there any distortion of information?

Evaluate informational graphics

Informational graphics more sophisticated than standard pie and bar charts have become a popular means of conveying information. Many are interactive, allowing viewers of a Web site to select the information they want displayed. These information graphics are a form of narrative argument, and the stories they tell have a rhetorical purpose. (See the examples on page 82.)

Build a Visual Analysis

It's one thing to construct a visual argument yourself; it's another thing to analyze visual arguments that are made by someone else. Fortunately, analyzing arguments made up of images and graphics is largely a matter of following the same strategies for rhetorical analysis that are outlined in Chapter 5—except that you must analyze images instead of (or in addition to) words. To put it another way, when you analyze

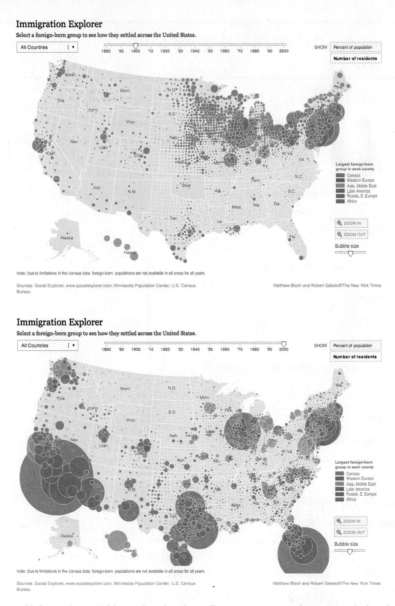

This set of information graphics on immigration tells a story. In 1900 the great majority of immigrants were from Western and Eastern Europe and Russia, and the majority settled in the Northeast and Midwest. In 2000 most immigrants came from Latin America, and they settled in Florida, Texas, and the West Coast along with the metropolitan areas of Chicago and New York City.

a visual argument, think about the image itself as well as its relationship to other images (and discourses). The arguments implied by visual images, like the arguments made through text alone, are carried both by the context and by the image.

Ad for Hofstra University, 1989

Analyze context

A critical analysis of a visual image, like the analyses of written arguments that we discuss in the previous chapter, must include a consideration of context. Consider, for example, the above advertisement for Hofstra University. The context for the ad is not difficult to uncover through a bit of research. The ad appeared in 1989 and 1990 when Hofstra, located on Long Island 25 miles from New York City, was celebrating its fiftieth anniversary and hoping to use the occasion to enhance its esteem. At the time, Hofstra enjoyed a good reputation for its professional programs, particularly in education and business (which one-third of the 7,500 students were majoring in). However, it was not as highly regarded in the core science and humanities disciplines that are often associated with institutional prestige. In addition, Hofstra was quite well known in the New York metropolitan area—half its students were commuting to school rather than living in dormitories—but it was not attracting many students from outside the region, and its campus life was consequently regarded as mediocre. Its student body was generally well prepared, hardworking, and capable, but its most outstanding applicants were too often choosing other universities.

Feeling that its performance was exceeding its reputation and that it was capable of attracting a more diverse and talented student body, Hofstra developed a national ad campaign designed to change the opinions of prospective students and their parents, as well as the general public. It placed the ads—the ad reproduced here is one of a series—in several magazines and newspapers in order to persuade people that Hofstra was an outstanding university not just in the professions but in all fields, and that the opportunities available to its students were varied and valuable.

Analyze visual and textual elements

Ads make arguments, and the message of the Hofstra ad is something like this: "Hofstra is a prestigious, high-quality institution that brings out the best in students because of its facilities, its academic reputation, its student body, and the strength of its faculty and academic programs." The text of the Hofstra ad expresses that argument specifically: "The best" and "we teach success" are prominently displayed; the size of the print visually reinforces the message; and the fine print supports the main thesis by mentioning Hofstra's facilities (the large library with "a collection [of volumes] larger than that of 95% of American universities," the "television facility . . . with broadcast quality production capability"); its reputation (its ranking in *Barron's Guide to the Most Prestigious Colleges* and its "professionally accredited programs"); and its faculty and students. The ad works by offering good reasons and supporting arguments that are based on logical reasoning and evidence, as well as appeals to our most fervently held values. By placing the ad in prestigious publications, Hofstra enhanced its credibility even further.

In this chapter, however, we are emphasizing visuals in arguments. What kind of argument is made and supported by the image of the young girl with the flute? The photo of the girl is black and white, so that it can be printed easily and inexpensively in newspapers and magazines. But the black and white format also contributes a sense of reality and truthfulness, in the manner of black and white photos or documentary films. (Color images, on the other hand, can imply flashiness or commercialism.) Even in black and white, the image is quite arresting. In the context of an ad for Hofstra, the image is particularly intriguing. The girl is young—does she seem about ten or twelve years of age?—and her readiness for distinguished performance suggests that she is a prodigy, a genius—in other words, the kind of person that Hofstra attracts and sustains. The ad implies that you might encounter her on the Hofstra campus sometime: if she is not a student at Hofstra now, she soon will be. Come to Hofstra, and you too can acquire the traits associated with excellence and success.

The girl is dressed up for some kind of musical performance, and the details of her costume imply that the performance is of a high order: it is not just any costume, but one associated with professional performances of the most rarefied kind, a concert that calls for only the best musicians. The delicacy and refinement of the girl are implied by the posture of her fingers, the highly polished flute that she holds with an upright carriage, and the meticulousness of her tie, shirt, and coat. The girl's expression suggests that she is serious, sober, disciplined, but comfortable—the kind of student (and faculty member) that Hofstra features. (The layout and consistent print style used in the ad reinforce that impression: by offering a balanced and harmonious placement of elements and by sticking to the same type style throughout, the ad stands for the values of balance, harmony, consistency, and order.) The girl is modest and unpretentious in expression, yet she looks directly at the viewer with supreme self-confidence. Her age suggests innocence, yet her face proclaims ambition; her age and the quasi-masculine costume (note that she wears neither a ring nor earrings) give her a sexual innocence that is in keeping with the contemplative life. Come to Hofstra, the image proclaims, and you will meet people who are sober and graceful, self-disciplined and confident, ambitious without being arrogant. The ad is supporting its thesis with good reasons implied by its central image—good reasons that we identified with logos and pathos in the previous chapter.

Speaking of pathos, what do you make of the fact that the girl is Asian? On one hand, the Asian girl's demeanor reinforces cultural stereotypes. Delicate, small, sober, controlled, even humorless, she embodies characteristics that recall other Asian American icons (particularly women), especially icons of success through discipline and hard work. On the other hand, the girl speaks to the Asian community. It is as if she is on the verge of saying, "Come and join me at Hofstra, where you too can reach the highest achievement. And read the copy below me to learn more about what Hofstra has to offer." In this way the girl participates in Hofstra's ambition to attract highly qualified, highly motivated, and high-performing minority students—as well as any other high-performing student, regardless of ethnicity or gender, who values hard work, academic distinction, and the postponement of sensual gratification in return for long-term success.

If she is Asian, the girl is also thoroughly American. She appears not to be an international student but an American of immigrant stock. Her costume, her controlled black hair, and her unmarked face and fingers identify her as achieving the American dream of material success, physical health and well being, and class advancement. If her parents or grandparents came to New York or California as immigrants, they (and she) are now naturalized—100 percent American, completely successful. The social class element to the image is unmistakable: the entire ad speaks of Hofstra's ambition to be among the best, to achieve an elite status. When the ad appeared in 1989, Hofstra was attracting few of the nation's elite students. The girl signals a change. She displays the university's aspiration to become among the nation's elite—those who enjoy material success as well as the leisure, education, and sophistication to appreciate the finest music. That ambition is reinforced by the university's emblem in the lower right-hand corner of the ad. It resembles a coat of arms and is associated with royalty. Hofstra may be a community that is strong in the professions, but it also values the arts.

No doubt there are other aspects of the image that work to articulate and to support the complex argument of the ad. There is more to be said about this ad, and you may disagree with some of the points we have offered. But consider this: By 2009, twenty years after the ad was run, Hofstra's total enrollment had climbed above 12,000, with 7,500 undergraduates. Its admissions were more selective, its student body was more diverse and less regional in character, its graduation rate had improved, its sports teams had achieved national visibility, and its minority student population had grown. Many factors contributed to the university's advancement, but it seems likely that this ad was one of them.

Write a Visual Analysis

Like rhetorical analysis, effective visual analysis takes into account the context of the image as well as its visual elements and any surrounding text. When you analyze a visual image, look carefully at its details and thoroughly consider its context. What visual elements grab your attention first, and how do other details reinforce that impression—what is most important and less important? How do color and style influence impressions? How does the image direct the viewer's eyes and reinforce what is important? What is the relationship between the image and any text that might accompany it? Consider the shapes, colors, and details of the image, as well as how the elements of the image connect with different arguments and audiences.

Consider also what you know or can learn about the context of an image and the design and text that surround it. Try to determine why and when it was created, who created it, where it appeared, and the target audience. Think about how the context of its creation and publication affected its intended audience. What elements have you seen before? Which elements remind you of other visuals?

Sample Student Visual Analysis

Discussion board posts are a frequent assignment in writing classes. Usually they are short essays, no more than 300 words. Sources of any information still need to be cited.

The assignment for this post was to find and analyze an example of a visual metaphor.

Thread: "Use Only What You Need": The Denver Water Conservation
Campaign
Author: Chrissy Yao
Posted Date: March 1, 2010 1:12 PM

Partial bus bench from Denver Water's conservation campaign

In 2006, Denver Water, the city's oldest water utility, launched
a ten-year water conservation plan based on using water efficiently
("Conservation"). Denver Water teamed up with the Sukle Advertising firm
and produced the "Use Only What You Need" campaign to help alleviate
the water crisis that the city was enduring (Samuel). The campaign uses
billboard advertising, magazine ads, and even stripped-down cars to
impart messages of water conservation and efficiency. •————

> Yao describes the ad campaign which uses the partial bus bench.

Clever visual metaphors are at the heart of the campaign. One
example is a park bench with available seating only for one individual.
The words, "USE ONLY WHAT YOU NEED," are stenciled in on the back of
the bench. The bench, which can actually be used for sitting, conveys the
idea that if only one person were using the bench, that would only need
a small area to sit on, not the whole thing. The bench makes concrete
the concept of water conservation.

> Yao analyzes the visual metaphor.

The innovative ad campaign that uses objects in addition to traditional
advertising has proven successful. The simplicity and minimalist style
of the ads made a convincing argument about using resources sparingly.
The average water consumption of Denver dropped between 18% and 21%
annually from 2006 to 2009.

Works Cited

"Conservation." *Denver Water*. Denver Water, 2010. Web. 23 Feb. 2010.

Samuel, Frederick. "Denver Water." *Ad Goodness*. N.p., 16 Nov. 2006.
    Web. 24 Feb. 2010.

For additional writing resources that will help you master the objectives of this chapter, go to your **MyLab**.

Writing Arguments

PART

3

7 | Putting Good Reasons into Action

QUICK TAKE

In this chapter you will learn to

1. Identify approaches you can use to achieve a specific purpose (see below)
2. Use different kinds of arguments to achieve your purpose (see page 92)

Find a Purpose for Writing an Argument

Imagine that you bought a new car in June and you are taking some of your friends to your favorite lake over the Fourth of July weekend. You have a great time until, as you are heading home, a drunk driver—a repeat offender—swerves into your lane and totals your new car. You and your friends are lucky not to be hurt, but you're outraged because you believe that repeat offenders should be prevented from driving, even if that means putting them in jail. You also remember going to another state that had sobriety checkpoints on holiday weekends. If such a check-point had been in place in your state, you might still be driving your new car. You live in a town that encourages citizens to contribute to the local newspaper, and you think you could get a guest editorial published. The question is, how do you want to write the editorial?

- You could tell your story about how a repeat drunk driver endangered the lives of you and your friends.
- You could define driving while intoxicated (DWI) as a more legally culpable crime.
- You could compare the treatment of drunk drivers in your state with the treatment of drunk drivers in another state.
- You could cite statistics that alcohol-related accidents killed 10,288 people in 2010.
- You could evaluate the present drunk-driving laws as insufficiently just or less than totally successful.

- You could propose taking vehicles away from repeat drunk drivers and forcing them to serve mandatory sentences.
- You could argue that your community should have sobriety checkpoints at times when drunk drivers are likely to be on the road.
- You could do several of the above.

Finding Good Reasons

What Do We Mean by Diversity?

Colleges and universities talk a great deal about diversity nowadays, but what exactly do they mean by *diversity*? If diversity is connected with people, do they mean diversity of races and ethnicities? Is it diversity of nations and cultures represented among the students? Should the numbers of students of different races, ethnicities, or family income levels be roughly equal to the population of the state where the school is located? Is a campus diverse if about 60 percent of the students are women and 40 percent men, as many campuses now are? Or if diversity is connected with ideas, what makes for a diverse intellectual experience on a college campus?

Write about it

1. Formulate your own definition of what diversity means on a college campus (see Chapter 8).
2. Evaluate diversity on your campus according to your definition. Is your campus good or bad in its diversity (see Chapter 10)?
3. What are the effects of having a diverse campus, however you define diversity (see Chapter 9)? What happens if a campus isn't diverse?
4. If you consider diversity desirable, write a proposal that would increase diversity on your campus, whether it's interacting with people of different backgrounds or encountering a variety of ideas (see Chapter 13). Or if you think too much emphasis is being placed on diversity, write a rebuttal argument against proponents of diversity (see Chapter 12).

Get Started Writing About Complex Issues

You're not going to have much space in the newspaper, so you decide to argue for sobriety checkpoints. You know that they are controversial. One of your friends who was in the car with you said that the checkpoints are unconstitutional because they involve search without cause. However, after doing some research to find out whether checkpoints are defined as legal or illegal, you learn that on June 14, 1990, the U.S. Supreme Court upheld the constitutionality of using checkpoints as a deterrent and enforcement tool against drunk drivers.

But you still want to know whether most people would agree with your friend that sobriety checkpoints are an invasion of privacy. You find opinion polls and surveys going back to the 1980s that show that 70 to 80 percent of those polled support sobriety checkpoints. You also realize that you can argue by analogy that security checkpoints for alcohol are similar in many ways to airport security checkpoints that protect passengers. You decide you will finish by making an argument from consequence. If people who go to the lake with plans to drink know in advance that there will be checkpoints, they will find a designated driver or some other means of safe transportation, and everyone else will also be a lot safer.

The point of this example is that people very rarely set out to define something in an argument for the sake of definition, to compare for the sake of comparison, or to adopt any of the other ways of structuring an argument. Instead, they have a purpose in mind, and they use the kinds of arguments that are discussed in Chapters 8–13—most often in combination—as means to an end. Most arguments use multiple approaches and multiple sources of good reasons.

For additional writing resources that will help you master the objectives of this chapter, go to your **MyLab**.

8 | Definition Arguments

QUICK TAKE

In this chapter you will learn to

1. Use definition arguments that set out criteria and then argue that something meets or doesn't meet those criteria (see page 94)

2. Recognize formal definitions, operational definitions, and definitions by example (page 94)

3. Analyze a specific extended-definition argument (see pages 96–98)

4. Write an effective definition argument (pages 100–101)

Graffiti dates back to the ancient Egyptian, Greek, Roman, and Mayan civilizations. Is graffiti vandalism? Or is it art? The debate has gone on for three decades. In the 1980s New York City's subways were covered with graffiti. Many New Yorkers believe that removing graffiti from subway cars was a first step toward the much-celebrated social and economic recovery of the city. For them graffiti was a sign that the subways were not safe. But at the same time, Martha Cooper and Henry Chalfant released a book titled *Subway Art*—a picture book—that celebrated graffiti-covered subways as an art form. Should we appreciate graffiti as the people's art. Or should graffiti be removed as quickly as possible, as a destructive eyesore?

Understand How Definition Arguments Work

Definition arguments set out criteria and then argue that whatever is being defined meets or does not meet those criteria.

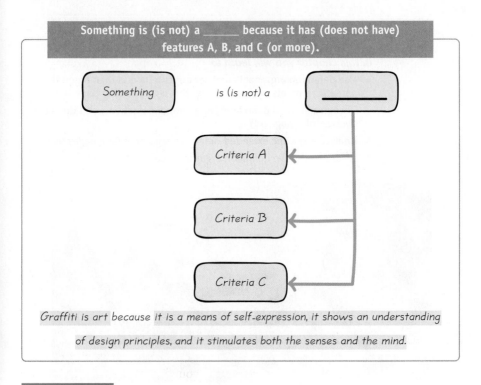

Something is (is not) a _____ because it has (does not have) features A, B, and C (or more).

Something   is (is not) a   _____

Criteria A

Criteria B

Criteria C

Graffiti is art because it is a means of self-expression, it shows an understanding of design principles, and it stimulates both the senses and the mind.

Recognize Kinds of Definitions

Rarely do you get far into an argument without having to define something. Imagine that you are writing an argument about the decades-old and largely ineffective "war on drugs" in the United States. We all know that the war on drugs is being waged against drugs that are illegal, like cocaine and marijuana, and not against the legal drugs produced by the multibillion-dollar drug industry. Our society classifies drugs into two categories: "good" drugs, which are legal, and "bad" drugs, which are illegal.

How exactly does our society arrive at these definitions? Drugs would be relatively easy to define as good or bad if the difference could be defined at the molecular level. Bad drugs would contain certain molecules that define them as bad. The history of drug use in the United States, however, tells us that it is not so simple. In the twentieth century alcohol was on the list of illegal drugs for over a decade, while opium was considered a good drug and was distributed in many patent medicines by pharmaceutical companies. Similarly, LSD and MDMA (methylenedioxymethamphetamine, known better by its street name *ecstasy*) were developed by the pharmaceutical industry but later made illegal. In a few states marijuana is now legal for medicinal use.

If drugs cannot be classified as good or bad by their molecular structure, then perhaps society classifies them by their effects. It might be reasonable to assume that addictive drugs are illegal, but that's not the case. Nicotine is highly addictive and is a legal drug, as are many prescription medicines. Drugs taken for the purpose of pleasure are not necessarily illegal (think of alcohol and Viagra), nor are drugs that alter consciousness or change personality (such as Prozac).

How a drug is defined as legal or illegal apparently is determined by example. The nationwide effort to stop Americans from drinking alcohol during the first decades of the twentieth century led to the passage of the Eighteenth Amendment and the ban on sales of alcohol from 1920 to 1933, known as Prohibition. Those who argued for Prohibition used examples of drunkenness, especially among the poor, to show how alcohol broke up families and left mothers and children penniless in the street. Those who opposed Prohibition initially pointed to the consumption of beer and wine in many cultural traditions. Later they raised examples of the bad effects of Prohibition—the rise of organized crime, the increase in alcohol abuse, and the general disregard for laws.

When you make a definition argument, it's important to think about what kind of definition you will use. Descriptions of three types follow.

Formal definitions

Formal definitions typically categorize an item into the next-higher classification and provide criteria that distinguish the item from other items within that classification. Most dictionary definitions are formal definitions. For example, fish are cold-blooded aquatic vertebrates that have jaws, fins, and scales and are distinguished from other cold-blooded aquatic vertebrates (such as sea snakes) by the presence of gills. If you can construct a formal definition with a specific classification and differentiating criteria that your audience will accept, then likely you will have a strong argument. The key is to get your audience to agree to your classification and criteria. Often your argument will amount to revising your audience's view of the classification or criteria (or both). For instance, imagine that you want to change your audience's view of contemporary universities. You might construct a thesis statement something like this: "While most people still think of universities as institutions of higher learning [classification] that prepare people for citizenship and the workplace [differentiating criteria], they are actually nothing more than big businesses" [revised classification].

Operational definitions

Many concepts cannot be easily defined by formal definitions. Researchers in the natural and social sciences must construct **operational definitions** that they use for their research. For example, researchers who study binge drinking among college students define a binge as five or more drinks in one sitting for a man, and four or more drinks for a woman. Some people think this standard is too low and should be raised to six to eight drinks to distinguish true problem drinkers from the general college population. No matter what the number, researchers must argue that the particular definition is one that suits the concept.

Definitions from example

Many human qualities such as honesty, courage, creativity, deceit, and love must be defined by examples that the audience accepts as representative of the concept. Few would not call the firefighters who entered the World Trade Center on September 11, 2001, courageous. Most people would describe someone with a diagnosis of terminal cancer who refuses to feel self-pity as courageous. But what about a student who declines to go to a concert with her friends so she can study for an exam? Her behavior might be admirable, but most people would hesitate to call it courageous. The key to arguing a **definition from example** is that the examples must strike the audience as typical of the concept, even if the situation is unusual.

Build a Definition Argument

Because definition arguments are so powerful, they are found at the center of some of the most important debates in American history. Definition arguments were at the heart of the abolition of slavery, for example, and many of the major arguments of the civil rights movement were based on definitions. Martin Luther King, Jr.'s, "Letter from Birmingham Jail" is one eloquent example.

King was jailed in April 1963 for leading a series of peaceful protests in Birmingham, Alabama. While he was being held in solitary confinement, Rev. King wrote a letter to eight white Birmingham clergymen. These religious leaders had issued a statement urging an end to the protests in their city. King argued that it was necessary to act now rather than wait for change. His purpose in writing the argument was to win acceptance for the protests and protestors and to make his audience see that the anti-segregationists were not agitators and rabble-rousers,

U.S. National Guard troops block off Beale Street in Memphis, Tennessee, as striking sanitation workers wearing placards reading "I AM A MAN" pass by on March 29, 1968. Rev. Martin Luther King, Jr., returned to Memphis to lead the march and was assassinated a week later on April 4.

but citizens acting responsibly to correct a grave injustice. A critical part of King's argument is his definition of "just" and "unjust" laws.

Supporters of segregation in Birmingham had obtained a court order forbidding further protests, and the eight white clergymen urged King and his supporters to obey the courts. Our society generally assumes that laws, and the courts that enforce them, should be obeyed. King, however, argues that there are two categories of laws, and that citizens must treat one category differently from the other. Morally just laws, King argues, should be obeyed, but unjust ones should not. By distinguishing two different kinds of laws, King creates a rationale for obeying some laws and disobeying others. He then completes his definitional argument by showing how segregation laws fit the definition of "unjust." Once his audience accepts his placement of segregation laws in the "unjust" category, they must also accept that King and his fellow protestors were right to break those laws.

King maintains in his letter that people have a moral responsibility to obey just laws, and, by the same logic, "a moral responsibility to disobey unjust laws." His argument rests on the clear moral and legal criteria he uses to define just and unjust laws. Without these criteria, people could simply disobey any law they chose, which is what King's detractors accused him of advocating. King had to show that he was in fact acting on principle, and that he and his supporters wanted to establish justice, not cause chaos.

Here's how King makes the distinction between just and unjust laws:

> A just law is a man-made code that squares with the moral law of God. An unjust law is a code that is out of harmony with the moral law. . . . Any law that uplifts human personality is just. Any law that degrades human personality is unjust. All segregation statutes are unjust because segregation distorts the soul and damages the personality. It gives the segregator a false sense of superiority and the segregated a false sense of inferiority.

According to King, a just law meets the criteria of being consistent with moral law and uplifting human personality. An unjust law does not meet these criteria. Instead, it is out of harmony with moral law and damages human personality. King's claim that

> "All segregation laws are unjust because segregation distorts the soul and damages the personality"

uses the structure described at the beginning of this chapter:

Something is (or is not) a ___ because it has (does not have) features A, B, and C.

Building an extended definition argument like King's is a two-step process. First, you have to establish the criteria for the categories you wish to define. In King's letter, consistency with moral law and uplifting of the human spirit are set forth as criteria for a just law. King provides arguments from St. Thomas Aquinas, a religious authority likely to carry significant weight with Birmingham clergymen and others who will read the letter.

Second, you must convince your audience that the particular case in question meets or doesn't meet the criteria. King cannot simply state that segregation laws are unjust; he must provide evidence showing how they fail to meet the criteria for a just law. Specifically, he notes the segregation "gives the segregator a false sense of superiority and the segregated a false sense of inferiority." These false senses of self are a distortion or degradation of the human personality.

Sometimes definition arguments have to argue for the relevance of the criteria. King, in fact, spent a great deal of his letter laying out and defending his criteria for just and unjust laws. While he addressed his letter to clergymen, he knew that it would find a wider audience. Therefore, he did not rely solely on criteria linked to moral law, or to the "law of God." People who were not especially religious might not be convinced by those parts of his argument. King presents two additional criteria for just laws that he knows will appeal to those who value the democratic process. He argues that "an unjust law is a code that a numerical or power majority group compels a minority group to obey but does not make binding on itself." In other words, a just law is the law for everyone. It is fairly easy to show how segregation laws fail to meet this criterion. These laws commonly prevented African Americans from using certain facilities reserved for whites, for example, but did not compel whites to stay out of African American seating areas on buses.

King also argues that a just law is a law created by representatives of the people the law will affect. He shows how segregation laws fail to match this criterion by pointing out that many African Americans had been denied the right to vote in Alabama. Consequently, the legislature that passed the segregation laws was not democratically elected.

When you build a definition argument, often you must put much effort into identifying and explaining your criteria. You must convince your readers that your criteria are the best ones for what you are defining and that they apply to the case you are arguing.

King's Extended Definition Argument

After establishing criteria for two kinds of laws, *just* and *unjust*, King argues that citizens must respond differently to laws that are unjust, by disobeying them. He then shows how the special case of *segregation laws* meets the criteria for unjust laws. If readers accept his argument, they will agree that segregation laws belong in the category of unjust laws, and therefore must be disobeyed.

Criteria for Just Laws	Criteria for Unjust Laws	Segregation Laws
Consistent with moral law	Not consistent with moral law	✓
Uplift human personality	Damage human personality	✓
Must be obeyed by all people	Must be obeyed by some people, but not others	✓
Made by democratically elected Representatives	Not made by democratically elected representatives	✓
Appropriate Response to Just Laws: All citizens should obey them.	Appropriate Response to Unjust Laws: All citizens should disobey them.	

Finding Good Reasons

What Is Parody?

Jon Stewart's *The Daily Show* depends on parody as a staple form of comedy.

Downfall, a German film released in 2004 about Hitler's last days, has been used for hundreds of popular YouTube parodies. Most parodies use the same scene of a defeated Hitler, played by Bruno Ganz, unleashing a furious speech to his staff in German with YouTubers adding English subtitles on topics as varied as the plot of *Avatar*, the upgrade to Windows 7, Apple's iPad, academic grant reviews, and the failure of various sports teams to win big games.

The owner of the rights to the film, Constantin Films, demanded that YouTube take down the parodies in April 2010, and YouTube complied. Critics of the move complained that Constantin Films used YouTube's Content ID filter to determine what is acceptable rather than the fair use provisions of copyright law. They argue that fair-use law allows a film clip, a paragraph from an article, or a short piece of music to be adapted if the purpose is to create commentary or satire.

Write about it

1. Which of the following criteria do you think must be present for a work to be considered a parody? Are there any criteria you might change or add?
   - the work criticizes a previous work
   - the work copies the same structure, details, or style of the previous work
   - the connections to the previous work are clear to the audience
   - the work is humorous
   - the title is a play on the previous work
   - the work is presented in either a print, visual, or musical medium

2. Do the various uses of the *Downfall* clip meet the criteria above? Would you define them as parodies? Why or why not?

Steps to Writing a Definition Argument

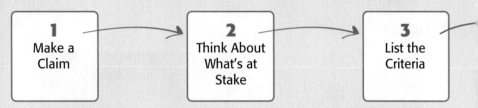

1	2	3
Make a Claim	Think About What's at Stake	List the Criteria

Step 1 Make a Claim

Make a definitional claim on a controversial issue that focuses on a key term.

Template

> _____ is (or is not) a _____ because it has (or does not have) features A, B, and C (or more).

Examples

- Hate speech (or pornography, literature, films, and so on) is (or is not) free speech protected by the First Amendment because it has (or does not have) these features.

- Hunting (or using animals for cosmetics testing, keeping animals in zoos, wearing furs, and so on) is (or is not) cruelty to animals because it has (or does not have) these features.

Step 2 Think About What's at Stake

- Does nearly everyone agree with you? If so, then your claim probably isn't interesting or important. If you can think of people who disagree, then something is at stake.

- Who argues the opposite of your claim?

- Why or how do they benefit from a different definition?

Step 3 List the Criteria

- Which criteria are necessary for _____ to be a _____?

- Which are the most important?

- Does your case in point meet all the criteria?

Step 4 Analyze Your Potential Readers

- Who are your readers?
- How does the definitional claim you are making affect them?
- How familiar are they with the issue, concept, or controversy that you're writing about?
- Which criteria are they most likely to accept with little explanation, and which will they disagree with?

Step 5 Write a Draft

Introduction

- Set out the issue, concept, or controversy.
- Give the background that your intended readers need.

Body

- Set out your criteria and argue for the appropriateness of the criteria.
- Anticipate where readers might question either your criteria or how they apply to your subject.
- Address opposing viewpoints by acknowledging how their definitions differ and by showing why your definition is better.

Conclusion

- Do more than simply summarize. You can, for example, go into more detail about what is at stake or the implications of your definition.

Step 6 Revise, Edit, Proofread

- For detailed instructions, see Chapter 4.
- For a checklist to use to evaluate your draft, see pages 48–49.

Michael Pollan

Eat Food: Food Defined

Michael Pollan is a journalism professor at the University of California, Berkeley, and the author of *In Defense of Food: An Eater's Manifesto* (2008), from which this excerpt is taken. *In Defense of Food* received many prizes and was named one of the ten best books of the year by the *New York Times* and the *Washington Post*. Pollan is also the author of *Second Nature* (1991), *A Place of My Own* (1997), *The Botany of Desire: A Plant's Eye View of the World* (2001), *The Omnivore's Dilemma: A Natural History of Four Meals* (2006), and *Food Rules* (2010). He is also a contributing writer for the *New York Times Magazine*.

Pollan asks why Americans worry so much about nutrition and yet seem so unhealthy. The title, *In Defense of Food*, is one of the many paradoxes that Pollan examines in the book. After all, why should food need defending if it is plentiful and we eat so much of it? Pollan argues that the answer lies in how we define food.

Pollan begins by asking, Why does food need to be defined?

The first time I heard the advice to "just eat food" it was in a speech by Joan Gussow, and it completely baffled me. Of course you should eat food—what else is there to eat? But Gussow, who grows much of her own food on a flood-prone finger of land jutting into the Hudson River, refuses to dignify most of the products for sale in the supermarket with that title. "In the thirty-four years I've been in the field of nutrition," she said in the same speech, "I have watched real food disappear from large areas of the supermarket and from much of the rest of the eating world." Taking food's place on the shelves has been an unending stream of foodlike substitutes, some seventeen thousand new ones every year—"products constructed largely around commerce and hope, supported by frighteningly little actual knowledge." Ordinary food is still out there, however, still being grown and even occasionally sold in the supermarket, and this ordinary food is what we should eat.

Pollan claims that everything that pretends to be food really isn't food, thus establishing the need for a definition.

2   But given our current state of confusion and given the thousands of products calling themselves food, this is more easily said than done. So consider these related rules of thumb. Each proposes a different sort of map to the contemporary food landscape, but all should take you to more or less the same place.

Don't eat anything your great grandmother wouldn't recognize as food.

3   Why your great grandmother? Because at this point your mother and possibly even your grandmother is as confused as the rest of us; to be safe we need to go back at least a couple generations, to a time before the advent of most modern foods. So depending on your age (and your grandmother), you may need to

go back to your great- or even great-great grandmother. Some nutritionists recommend going back even further. John Yudkin, a British nutritionist whose early alarms about the dangers of refined carbohydrates were overlooked in the 1960s and 1970s, once advised, "Just don't eat anything your Neolithic ancestors wouldn't have recognized and you'll be OK."

Pollan's first criterion of what is food offers a simple concept.

4   What would shopping this way mean in the supermarket? Well, imagine your great grandmother at your side as you roll down the aisles. You're standing together in front of the dairy case. She picks up a package of Go-Gurt Portable Yogurt tubes—and has no idea what this could possibly be. Is it a food or a toothpaste? And how, exactly, do you introduce it into your body? You could tell her it's just yogurt in a squirtable form, yet if she read the ingredients label she would have every reason to doubt that that was in fact the case. Sure, there's some yogurt in there, but there are also a dozen other things that aren't remotely yogurt like, ingredients she would probably fail to recognize as foods of any kind, including high-fructose corn syrup, modified corn starch, kosher gelatin, carrageenan, tri-calcium phosphate, natural and artificial flavors, vitamins, and so forth. (And there's a whole other list of ingredients for the "berry bubblegum bash" flavoring, containing everything but berries or bubblegum.) How did yogurt, which in your great grandmother's day consisted simply of milk inoculated with a bacterial culture, ever get to be so complicated? Is a product like Go-Gurt Portable Yogurt still a whole food? A food of any kind? Or is it just a food product?

Another way of defining food is to define what isn't food, but what Pollan calls "food products."

5   There are in fact hundreds of foodish products in the supermarket that your ancestors simply wouldn't recognize as food: breakfast cereal bars transected by bright white veins representing, but in reality having nothing to do with, milk; "protein waters" and "nondairy creamer"; cheeselike food-stuffs equally innocent of any bovine contribution; cakelike cylinders (with creamlike fillings) called Twinkies that never grow stale. Don't eat anything incapable of rotting is another personal policy you might consider adopting.

6   There are many reasons to avoid eating such complicated food products beyond the various chemical additives and corn and soy derivatives they contain. One of the problems with the products of food science is that, as Joan Gussow has pointed out, they lie to your body; their artificial colors and flavors and synthetic sweeteners and novel fats confound the senses we rely on to assess new foods and prepare our bodies to deal with them. Foods that lie leave us with little choice but to eat by the numbers, consulting labels rather than our senses.

7   It's true that foods have long been processed in order to preserve them, as when we pickle or ferment or smoke, but industrial processing aims to do much more than extend shelf life. Today foods are processed in ways specifically designed to sell us more food by pushing our evolutionary buttons—our inborn preferences

for sweetness and fat and salt. These qualities are difficult to find in nature but cheap and easy for the food scientist to deploy, with the result that processing induces us to consume much more of these ecological rarities than is good for us. "Tastes great, less filling!" could be the motto for most processed foods, which are far more energy dense than most whole foods: They contain much less water, fiber, and micronutrients, and generally much more sugar and fat, making them at the same time, to coin a marketing slogan, "More fattening, less nutritious!"

8   The great grandma rule will help keep many of these products out of your cart. But not all of them. Because thanks to the FDA's willingness, post–1973, to let food makers freely alter the identity of "traditional foods that everyone knows" without having to call them imitations, your great grandmother could easily be fooled into thinking that that loaf of bread or wedge of cheese is in fact a loaf of bread or a wedge of cheese. This is why we need a slightly more detailed personal policy to capture these imitation foods; to wit:

Avoid food products containing ingredients that are a) unfamiliar set, b) unpronounceable, c) more than five in number, or that include d) high-fructose corn syrup.

What food is can also be defined by what it isn't, hence a list of criteria for what isn't food.

9   None of these characteristics, not even the last one, is necessarily harmful in and of itself, but all of them are reliable markers for foods that have been highly processed to the point where they may no longer be what they purport to be. They have crossed over from foods to food products.

10   Consider a loaf of bread, one of the "traditional foods that everyone knows" specifically singled out for protection in the 1938 imitation rule. As your grandmother could tell you, bread is traditionally made using a remarkably small number of familiar ingredients: flour, yeast, water, and a pinch of salt will do it. But industrial bread— even industrial whole-grain bread—has become a far more complicated product of modern food science (not to mention commerce and hope). Here's the complete ingredients list for Sara Lee's Soft & Smooth Whole Grain White Bread. (Wait a minute—isn't "Whole Grain White Bread" a contradiction in terms? Evidently not any more.)

Pollan points out that the language used for food products is as convoluted as the ingredients.

> Enriched bleached flour [wheat flour, malted barley flour, niacin, iron, thiamin mononitrate (vitamin B), riboflavin (vitamin B_2), folic acid], water, whole grains [whole wheat flour, brown rice flour (rice flour, rice bran)], high fructose corn syrup [hello!], whey, wheat gluten, yeast, cellulose. Contains 2% or less of each of the following: honey, calcium sulfate, vegetable oil (soybean and/or cottonseed oils), salt, butter (cream, salt), dough conditioners (may contain one or more of the following: mono- and diglycerides, ethoxylated mono- and diglycerides, ascorbic acid, enzymes, azodicarbonamide),

guar gum, calcium propionate (preservative), distilled vinegar, yeast nutrients (monocalcium phosphate, calcium sulfate, ammonium sulfate), corn starch, natural flavor, beta-carotene (color), vitamin D_3, soy lecithin, soy flour.

11   There are many things you could say about this intricate loaf of "bread," but note first that even if it managed to slip by your great grandmother (because it is a loaf of bread, or at least is called one and strongly resembles one), the product fails every test proposed under rule number two: It's got unfamiliar ingredients (monoglycerides I've heard of before, but ethoxylated monoglycerides?); unpronounceable ingredients (try "azodicarbonamide"); it exceeds the maximum of five ingredients (by roughly thirty-six); and it contains high-fructose corn syrup. Sorry, Sara Lee, but your Soft & Smooth Whole Grain White Bread is not food and if not for the indulgence of the FDA could not even be labeled "bread."

12   Sara Lee's Soft & Smooth Whole Grain White Bread could serve as a monument to the age of nutritionism. It embodies the latest nutritional wisdom from science and government (which in its most recent food pyramid recommends that at least half our consumption of grain come from whole grains) but leavens that wisdom with the commercial recognition that American eaters (and American children in particular) have come to prefer their wheat highly refined—which is to say, cottony soft, snowy white, and exceptionally sweet on the tongue. In its marketing materials, Sara Lee treats this clash of interests as some sort of Gordian knot—it speaks in terms of an ambitious quest to build a "no compromise" loaf— which only the most sophisticated food science could possibly cut.

13   And so it has, with the invention of whole-grain white bread. Because the small percentage of whole grains in the bread would render it that much less sweet than, say, all-white Wonder Bread—which scarcely waits to be chewed before transforming itself into glucose—the food scientists have added high-fructose corn syrup and honey to to make up the difference; to overcome the problematic heft and toothsomeness of a real whole grain bread, they've deployed "dough conditioners," including guar gum and the aforementioned azodicarbonamide, to simulate the texture of supermarket white bread. By incorporating certain varieties of albino wheat, they've managed to maintain that deathly but apparently appealing Wonder Bread pallor.

14   Who would have thought Wonder Bread would ever become an ideal of aesthetic and gustatory perfection to which bakers would actually aspire—Sara Lee's Mona Lisa?

15   Very often food science's efforts to make traditional foods more nutritious make them much more complicated, but not necessarily any better for you. To make dairy products low fat, it's not enough to remove the fat. You then have to go to great lengths to

preserve the body or creamy texture by working in all kinds of food additives. In the case of low-fat or skim milk that usually means adding powdered milk. But powdered milk contains oxidized cholesterol, which scientists believe is much worse for your arteries than ordinary cholesterol, so food makers sometimes compensate by adding antioxidants, further complicating what had been a simple one-ingredient whole food. Also, removing the fat makes it that much harder for your body to absorb the fat-soluble vitamins that are one of the reasons to drink milk in the first place.

16   All this heroic and occasionally counterproductive food science has been undertaken in the name of our health—so that Sara Lee can add to its plastic wrapper the magic words "good source of whole grain" or a food company can ballyhoo the even more magic words "low fat." Which brings us to a related food policy that may at first sound counterintuitive to a health-conscious eater:

Avoid Food Products That Make Health Claims.

17   For a food product to make health claims on its package it must first have a package, so right off the bat it's more likely to be a processed than a whole food. Generally speaking, it is only the big food companies that have the wherewithal to secure FDA-approved health claims for their products and there trumpet them to the world. Recently, however, some of the tonier fruits and nuts have begun boasting about their health-enhancing properties, and there will surely be more as each crop council scrounges together the money to commission its own scientific study. Because all plants contain antioxidants, all these studies are guaranteed to find something on which to base a health oriented marketing campaign.

18   But for the most part it is the products of food science that make the boldest health claims, and these are often founded on incomplete and often erroneous science—the dubious fruits of nutritionism. Don't forget that trans-fat-rich margarine, one of the first industrial foods to claim it was healthier than the traditional food it replaced, turned out to give people heart attacks. Since that debacle, the FDA, under tremendous pressure from industry, has made it only easier for food companies to make increasingly doubtful health claims, such as the one Frito-Lay now puts on some of its chips—that eating them is somehow good for your heart. If you bother to read the health claims closely (as food marketers make sure consumers seldom do), you will find that there is often considerably less to them than meets the eye.

19   Consider a recent "qualified" health claim approved by the FDA for (don't laugh) corn oil. ("Qualified" is a whole new category of health claim, introduced in 2002 at the behest of industry.) Corn oil, you may recall, is particularly high in the omega-6 fatty acids we're already consuming far too many of.

Very limited and preliminary scientific evidence suggests that eating about one tablespoon (16 grams) of corn oil daily may reduce the risk of heart disease due to the unsaturated fat content in corn oil.

20   The tablespoon is a particularly rich touch, conjuring images of moms administering medicine, or perhaps cod-liver oil, to their children. But what the FDA gives with one hand, it takes away with the other. Here's the small-print "qualification" of this already notably diffident health claim:

[The] FDA concludes that there is little scientific evidence supporting this claim.

To achieve this possible benefit, corn oil is to replace a similar amount of saturated fat and not increase the total number of calories you eat in a day.

Close reading of labels undercuts health claims of food products.

21   This little masterpiece of pseudoscientific bureaucratese was extracted from the FDA by the manufacturer of Mazola corn oil. It would appear that "qualified" is an official FDA euphemism for "all but meaningless." Though someone might have let the consumer in on this game: The FDA's own research indicates that consumers have no idea what to make of qualified health claims (how would they?), and its rules allow companies to promote the claims pretty much any way they want—they can use really big type for the claim, for example, and then print the disclaimers in teeny-tiny type. No doubt we can look forward to a qualified health claim for high-fructose corn syrup, a tablespoon of which probably does contribute to your health—as long as it replaces a comparable amount of, say, poison in your diet and doesn't increase the total number of calories you eat in a day.

22   When corn oil and chips and sugary breakfast cereals can all boast being good for your heart, health claims have become hopelessly corrupt. The American Heart Association currently bestows (for a fee) its heart-healthy seal of approval on Lucky Charms, Cocoa Puffs, and Trix cereals, Yoo-hoo lite chocolate drink, and Healthy Choice's Premium Caramel Swirl Ice Cream Sandwich—this at a time when scientists are coming to recognize that dietary sugar probably plays a more important role in heart disease than dietary fat. Meanwhile, the genuinely heart-healthy whole foods in the produce section, lacking the financial and polit-ical clout of the packaged goods a few aisles over, are mute. But don't take the silence of the yams as a sign that they have noth-ing valuable to say about health.

Pollan adds a playful touch by echoing the title of a popu-lar movie to make a point.

Sample Student Definition Argument

Conley 1

Patrice Conley

Professor Douglas

English 101

15 Nov. 2010

Flagrant Foul: The NCAA's Definition of Student Athletes as Amateurs

Every year, thousands of student athletes across America sign the National Collegiate Athletic Association's Form 08-3a, the "Student-Athlete" form, waiving their right to receive payment for the use of their name and image (McCann). The form defines student athletes as amateurs, who cannot receive payment for playing their sports. While their schools and coaches may make millions of dollars in salaries and endorsement deals and are the highest-paid public employees in many states, student athletes can never earn a single penny from their college athletic careers.

Make no mistake: college athletics are big business. The most visible college sports—big-time men's football and basketball—generate staggering sums of money. For example, the twelve universities in the Southeastern Conference receive $205 million each year from CBS and ESPN for the right to broadcast its football games (Smith and Ourand). Even more money comes in from video games, clothing, and similar licenses. In 2010, the *New York Times* reported, "the NCAA's licensing deals are estimated at more than $4 billion" per year (Thamel). While the staggering executive pay at big corporations has brought public outrage, coaches' salaries are even more outlandish. Kentucky basketball coach, John Calipari, is paid over $4 million a year for a basketball program that makes about $35-40 million a year, more than 10% of the entire revenue. Tom Van Riper observes that no corporate CEO commands this large a share of the profits. He notes that if Steve Ballmer, the CEO at Microsoft, had Calipari's deal, Ballmer would make over $6 billion a year.

How can colleges allow advertisers, arena operators, concession owners, athletic gear manufacturers, retailers, game companies, and media moguls, along with coaches and university officials, to make millions and pay the stars of the show nothing? The answer is that colleges define

Patrice Conley sets out the definition she is attempting to rectify: amateurs are athletes who aren't paid.

Conley identifies what's at stake.

Conley disputes the definition that college sport are amateur sports.

The huge salaries paid to college coaches are comparable to those in professional sports.

Conley argues that colleges use the definition of athletes as amateurs to refuse to pay them.

athletes as amateurs. Not only are student athletes not paid for playing their sport, they cannot receive gifts and are not allowed to endorse products, which may be a violation of their right to free speech. The NCAA, an organization of colleges and schools, forces student athletes to sign away their rights because, it says, it is protecting the students. If student athletes could accept money from anyone, the NCAA argues, they might be exploited, cheated, or even bribed. Taking money out of the equation is supposed to let students focus on academics and preserve the amateur status of college sports.

The definition of amateur arose in the nineteenth century in Britain, when team sports became popular. Middle-class and upper-class students in college had ample time to play their sports while working-class athletes had only a half-day off (no sports were played on Sundays in that era). Teams began to pay top working-class sportsmen for the time they had to take off from work. Middle-class and upper-class sportsmen didn't want to play against the working-class teams, so they made the distinction between amateurs and professionals. The definition of amateur crossed the Atlantic to the United States, where college sports became popular in the 1880s. But it was not long until the hypocrisy of amateurism undermined the ideal. Top football programs like Yale had slush funds to pay athletes, and others used ringers—players who weren't students—and even players from other schools (Zimbalist 7). The Olympic Games maintained the amateur-professional distinction until 1988, but it was long evident that Communist bloc nations were paying athletes to train full-time and Western nations were paying athletes through endorsement contracts. The only Olympic sport that now requires amateur status is boxing. The college sports empire in the United States run by the NCAA is the last bastion of amateurism for sports that draw audiences large enough to be televised.

Conley shows in this paragraph how the definition of college athletes as unpaid amateurs is based on outdated notions.

Conley argues that everyone else has discarded that old idea of amateurism as unpaid," so why won't the NCAA discard it?

Colleges might be able to defend the policy of amateurism if they extended this definition to all students. A fair policy is one that treats all students the same. A fair policy doesn't result in some students getting paid for professional work, while other students do not. Consider the students in the Butler School of Music at the University of Texas at

Conley 3

Austin, for example. Many student musicians perform at the professional level. Does the school prevent them from earning money for their musical performances? No. In fact, the school runs a referral service that connects its students with people and businesses who want to hire professional musicians. The university even advises its students on how to negotiate a contract and get paid for their performance ("Welcome").

> Comparisons show that colleges do not apply the definition of amateur consistently.

Likewise, why are student actors and actresses allowed to earn money from their work and images, while student athletes are not? Think about actress Emma Watson, who enrolled at Brown University in Rhode Island. Can you imagine the university officials at Brown telling Watson that she would have to make the next two *Harry Potter* films for free, instead of for the $5 million she has been offered? Can you imagine Brown University telling Watson that all the revenue from Harry Potter merchandise bearing her likeness would have to be paid directly to the university for the rest of her life? They would if Watson were an athlete instead of an actress.

> Do you think this analogy is effective?

In fact, compared to musicians and actors, student athletes have an even greater need to earn money while they are still in college. Athletes' professional careers are likely to be much shorter than musicians' or actors'. College may be the only time some athletes have the opportunity to capitalize on their success. (Indeed, rather than focusing student athletes on their academic careers, the NCAA policy sometimes forces students to leave college early, so they can earn a living before their peak playing years are over.) Student athletes often leave school with permanent injuries and no medical insurance or job prospects, whereas student musicians and actors rarely suffer career-ending injuries on the job.

Student athletes are prevented from profiting from their name and image. The NCAA says this rule preserves their standing as amateurs and protects them from the celebrity and media frenzy surrounding professional sports stars. Search for a "Tim Tebow Jersey" online, and you can buy officially branded Florida Gators shirts, ranging in price from $34.99 to $349.99 (autographed by Tebow). The NCAA, the University of Florida, Nike, and the other parties involved in the production and sale of these products get around the problem of using an amateur's name by using his team number instead. Tebow's name doesn't appear anywhere on the jerseys—just his number, 15. Yet all these jerseys are identified as

Conley 4

"Official Tim Tebow Gators merchandise," and they are certainly bought
by fans of Tebow rather than by people who just happen to like the
number 15. Nobody is saying how much money these jerseys have made
for Nike, or for the NCAA. What we do know for sure is the amount Tim
Tebow has made off the jerseys: nothing.

Defenders of the current system argue that student athletes on
scholarships are paid with free tuition, free room and board, free books, and
tutoring help. The total package can be the equivalent of $120,000 over
four years. For those student athletes who are motivated to take advantage
of the opportunity, the lifetime benefits can be enormous. Unfortunately,
too few student athletes do take advantage of the opportunity. Seldom does
a major college football and men's basketball program have graduation rates
at or close to overall student body. A study by the University of North
Carolina's College Sports Research Institute released in 2010 accuses the
NCAA of playing fast and loose with graduation rates by counting part-time
students in statistics for the general student body, making graduation rates
for athletes look better in a comparison. Student athletes must be full-time
students, thus they should be compared to other full-time students. The
North Carolina Institute reports that 54.8% of major college (Football Bowl
Subdivision) football players at 117 schools graduated within six years,
compared to 73.7% of other full-time students. The gap between basketball
players was even greater, with 44.6% of athletes graduating compared to
75.7% of the general student body (Zaiger). For the handful of talented
athletes who can play in the National Football League or the National
Basketball Association, college sports provide training for their future
lucrative, although short-lived, profession. But as the NCAA itself points out
in its ads, the great majority of student athletes "go pro in something other
than sports." For the 55% of college basketball players who fail to graduate,
the supposed $120,000 package is an air ball.

The NCAA would be wise to return to the older definition of *amateur*,
which comes from Latin through old French, meaning "lover of." It doesn't
necessarily have to have anything to do with money. Whether it's a jazz
performer or a dancer or an athlete, an amateur ought to be considered
someone in love with an activity—someone who cares deeply about the
activity, studies the activity in depth, and practices in order to be highly

example of
Tebow
strates how
definition of
ateur works
inst college
etes.

ley gives
lence that
ercuts the
ument that
ege athletes
compen-
d with a
ege degree.

clever use
air ball"
forces
ley's argu-
nt that the
AA's defini-
of amateur
utdated and
air.

ley
cludes with
main claim.
proposes a
v definition
mateur, one
would
nit salaries
royalties
o to the
ege athlete.

proficient. NBA players, Olympians, college athletes, high school players, and even bird watchers, star gazers, and open-source programmers: they're all amateurs. If they are lucky enough to be paid, so be it.

Works Cited

McCann, Michael. "NCAA Faces Unspecified Damages, Changes in Latest Anti-Trust Case." *SI.com*. Time, Inc., 21 July 2009. Web. 3 Nov. 2010.

National Collegiate Athletic Association. Advertisement. *NCAA.org*. NCAA, 13 Mar. 2007. Web. 3 Nov. 2010.

Smith, Michael, and John Ourand. "ESPN Pays $2.25B for SEC Rights." *SportsBusiness Journal*. Smith and Street, 25 Aug. 2008. Web. 1 Nov. 2010.

Thamel, Pete. "N.C.A.A. Fails to Stop Licensing Lawsuit." *New York Times*. New York Times, 8 Feb. 2010. Web. 1 Nov. 2010.

Van Riper, Thomas. "The Highest-Paid College Basketball Coaches." *Forbes.com*. Forbes, 8 Mar. 2010. Web. 3 Nov. 2010.

"Welcome to the Music Referral Service." *Butler School of Music*. Univ. of Texas at Austin, n.d. Web. 5 Nov. 2010.

Zaiger, Alan Scher. "Study: NCAA Graduation Rate Comparisons Flawed." *ABC News*. ABC News, 20 Apr. 2010. Web. 1 Nov. 2010.

Zimbalist, Andrew. *Unpaid Professionals: Commercialism and Conflict in Big-Time College Sports*. Princeton UP, 2001. Print.

For additional writing resources that will help you master the objectives of this chapter, go to your **MyLab**.

9 | Causal Arguments

QUICK TAKE

In this chapter you will learn to

1. Identify the three basic forms of causal arguments (see page 114)
2. Explain the four methods used to identify causes (see page 115)
3. Analyze a specific causal argument (see pages 117–119)
4. Write an effective causal argument (see pages 120–121)

Each year, we hear that American students are falling behind their international peers. Different groups argue that the solution lies in investing more in funding for additional teacher training, or smaller classrooms, or more technology in the classroom. Yet America invests billions more in education than some nations whose students surpass American students in achievement rankings. Still others have suggested that America's problem lies in a wide-scale cultural shift that has created an American student who is less motivated than those of the past. How can America's schools become world leaders again?

Understand How Causal Arguments Work

Causal claims can take three basic forms:

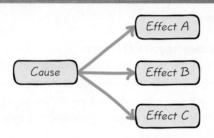

1. One cause leads to one or more effects.

The invention of the telegraph led to the commodities market, the establishment of standard time zones, and news reporting as we know it today.

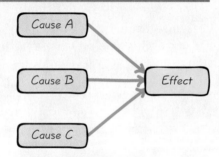

2. One effect has several causes.

Hurricanes are becoming more financially destructive to the United States because of the greater intensity of recent storms, an increase in the commercial and residential development of coastal areas, and a reluctance to enforce certain construction standards in coastal residential areas.

3. A series of events form a chain, where one event causes another, which then causes a third, and so on.

Making the HPV vaccination mandatory for adolescent girls will make unprotected sex seem safer, leading to greater promiscuity, ultimately resulting in more teenage pregnancies.

Find Causes

The causal claim is at the center of the causal argument. Writing a clear claim about cause and effect can be difficult because if a cause is worth writing about, it is likely to be complex. Obvious cases of cause and effect (staying out in the sun too long without skin protection causes sunburn) usually do not require written arguments because everyone is convinced that the causal relationship exists. Many of the causal claims that most people now accept without question—smoking causes cancer, shifting plates on the Earth's crust cause earthquakes, DDT causes eggshell thinning in bald eagles—were "settled" only after long and complex arguments.

The philosopher John Stuart Mill devised four ways for an investigator to go about finding causes.

- **The Common Factor Method.** Sometimes causes can be identified because two or more similar events share a common factor. The common factor may be the cause. For example, if two people in two different states both develop a rare disease, and both of them recently traveled to Madagascar, they were probably exposed to the illness while there.

- **The Single Difference Method.** Causes can often be identified when two situations or events have different outcomes. If there is a single difference in the two scenarios, that difference may be the cause. At the 1998 Winter Olympics in Nagano, Japan, the speed skating team from the Netherlands introduced a technological innovation to the sport— clap skates, which improve skaters' performance by keeping the skate blade in contact with the ice longer. Racing against the best skaters in the world, the Dutch on their clap skates won eleven of thirty medals, five of which were gold. By the 2002 Winter Olympics, all speed skaters had switched over to the new skates, and the medal count was much more evenly distributed. That year the United States, the Netherlands, and Germany each won three gold medals, and a total of eight medals apiece. Clap skates were the most likely cause of the Netherlands' dominance four years earlier.

- **Concomitant Variation.** Some causes are discovered by observing a shared pattern of variation in a possible cause and possible effect. For example, scientists noticed that peaks in the 11-year sunspot cycle match disruptions in high-frequency radio transmission on earth, leading them to conclude that the solar activity somehow causes the disruptions.

- **Process of Elimination.** Another way to establish causation is to identify all the possible causes of something, and then test them one by one to eliminate those that can't be the cause. When an electrical appliance stops working, electricians often trace the problem this way, by checking switches one at a time to see if current can flow across them. The switch that doesn't show a continuous flow of current is the one that needs replacing.

A frequent error of people looking for cause and effect is to mistake correlation for causation. Just because one event happens after or at the same time as another one, you cannot assume that the first one caused the second. Sometimes it's just a coincidence. For example, you may observe that every time the mail carrier comes to your door, your dog barks at him, and then the mail carrier leaves. You might assume that your dog's barking causes the mail carrier to leave (your dog is probably convinced of this). However, the more likely cause is that the carrier has finished delivering your mail, so he goes on to the next house. Using Mills's methods will help you avoid mistaking correlation for causation in your own causal arguments.

To understand how you might use Mills's methods of identifying causes, suppose you want to research the cause of the increase in legalized lotteries in the United States. You research the history of lotteries in order to look for possible causes. You would discover that lotteries go back to colonial times, but were controversial because they were run by private companies that sometimes failed to pay the winners. Laws against lotteries were passed in 1840, but after the Civil War, the defeated states of the Confederacy needed money to rebuild bridges, buildings, and schools. Southerners ran lotteries and sold tickets throughout the nation. But once again, these lotteries were run by private companies, and some of them simply took people's money without paying out winnings. Eventually, lotteries were banned again.

In 1964, New Hampshire became the first state to authorize a lottery to fund the state's educational system. Soon other states, realizing that their citizens were spending their money on lottery tickets from New Hampshire, established lotteries of their own. During the 1980s, states began approving other forms of state-run gambling such as keno and video poker. By 1993 only Hawaii and Utah had no legalized gambling of any kind.

Knowing this background, you can begin using Mills's methods to look for the causes of lotteries' recent popularity. Using the common factor method, you consider what current lotteries have in common with earlier lotteries. That factor is easy to identify: It's economic. The early colonies and later the states have turned to lotteries again and again as a way of raising money without raising taxes. But, you wonder, why have lotteries spread so quickly since 1964, and raised so little concern? The single difference method shows you the likely reason: Lotteries in the past were run by private companies, and inevitably someone took off with the money instead of paying it out. Today's lotteries are operated by state agencies or contracted under state control. While they are not immune to scandal, they are much more closely monitored than lotteries in the past.

Mills's other methods might also lead you to potential causes. If you find, for example, that lotteries grow in popularity in the aftermath of wars, this concomitant variation might lead you to suspect that the economic damage of war can be one cause of lotteries' popularity. This in turn might suggest inflation caused by the Vietnam War as a possible contributing cause to the rise of state lotteries in the 1960s and 1970s. The process of elimination could also lead you to some probable causes for lotteries' popularity, although for such a complex topic, it would be time-consuming. You might begin by making a list of all the reasons you could think of: Perhaps people these days are more economically secure, and don't mind risking a few dollars on lottery tickets? Or maybe people are more desperate now, and lotteries represent one of the few ways they can accumulate wealth? Each of these possibilities would require research into history, economics, and psychology, but this might lead you to some interesting conclusions about the complex forces contributing to today's extensive lottery system.

Build a Causal Argument

Effective causal arguments move beyond the obvious to get at underlying causes. One great causal mystery today is global warming. Scientists generally agree that the average surface temperature on Earth has gone up by 1.3 degrees Fahrenheit or 0.7 degrees Celsius over the last hundred years, and that the amount of carbon dioxide in the atmosphere has increased by 25 percent since 1960. But the causes of those phenomena are disputed. Some people argue that the rise in temperature is caused by natural climate variations, and that the increase in carbon dioxide has little or nothing to do with it. Others argue that the rise in carbon dioxide traps heat in the atmosphere and has increased the earth's temperature. They argue further that the increased carbon dioxide is the result of human activity, especially the burning of fossil fuels and the destruction of tropical forests. The debate over global warming continues because the causation at work is not simple or easy to prove.

There are many events that may be caused by global warming, and they are more dramatically evident in arctic and subarctic regions. The decade from January 2000 to December 2009 is the warmest decade since modern temperature records began in the 1880s. Arctic sea ice shrank by 14 percent—an area the size of Texas—from 2004 to 2005, and Greenland's massive ice sheet has been thinning by more than 3 feet a year.

Many scientists consider these phenomena to be effects of global warming. They argue that a single cause—the rise in the Earth's temperature—has led to many dire effects, and will lead to more. If you wanted to make an argument along these lines, you would need to construct a causal chain:

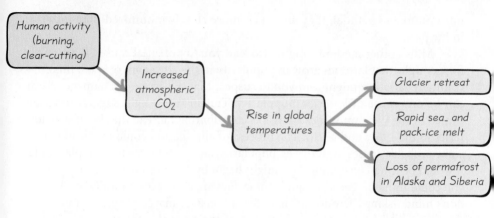

At each step, you would need to show the links between an event and its consequences, and you would need to convince readers that that link is real, not mere coincidence. You might find common factors, single differences, or concomitant variation that supports each causal link. You would also need to use a process of elimination to show that other possible causes are not in fact involved in your causal chain.

Some climate scientists have doubts about all these causal links. While the observable events—the loss of sea ice, glacier retreat, and so on—may be caused by human activity, they may be caused instead by naturally recurring cycles.

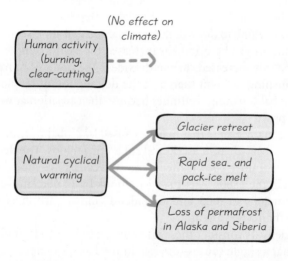

Or the effects could be caused partly by natural cycles and partly by humans.

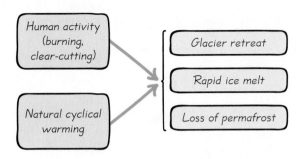

It is difficult to say for certain because much of the detailed data about the great melt in the north goes back only to the early 1990s—not long enough to rule out short-term climate cycles. However, computer models suggest a very low probability that such rapid change could occur naturally. So even if we are in a natural, short-term warming cycle, we still must ask if human activities are contributing to the documented warming, and making it even worse.

Identifying the causes of global warming is important because if we do not know the real causes, we cannot make the necessary changes to stop, reduce, or reverse it. If global warming continues unabated, the economic and human costs will be disastrous. But efforts to stop it are expensive and politically risky. Thus correctly establishing the causes of global warming is a crucial first step in solving the problem.

Glaciers in many parts of the world are melting at rates faster than scientists thought possible just a few years ago. Even major oil companies have acknowledged that global warming is real. Yet the American public has taken little notice of world climate change—perhaps because it's difficult to get excited about the mean temperature rising a few degrees and the sea level rising a few feet. What would get Americans thinking seriously about global warming?

Steps to Writing a Causal Argument

Step 1 Make a Claim

Make a causal claim on a controversial trend, event, or phenomenon.

Template

> SOMETHING does (or does not) cause SOMETHING ELSE.

–or–

> SOMETHING causes SOMETHING ELSE, which, in turn, causes SOMETHING ELSE.

Examples

- One-parent families (or television violence, bad diet, and so on) are (or are not) the cause of emotional and behavioral problems in children.
- Firearms control laws (or right-to-carry-handgun laws) reduce (or increase) violent crimes.
- Putting grade school children into competitive sports teaches them how to succeed in later life (or puts undue emphasis on winning and teaches many who are slower to mature to have a negative self-image).

Step 2 What's at Stake in Your Claim?

- If the cause is obvious to everyone, then it probably isn't worth writing about.

Step 3 Think of Possible Causes

- Which are the immediate causes?
- Which are the background causes?
- Which are the hidden causes?
- Which are the causes that most people have not recognized?

Step 4 Analyze Your Potential Readers

- Who are your readers?
- How familiar will they be with the trend, event, or phenomenon that you're writing about?
- What are they likely to know and not know?
- How likely are they to accept your causal explanation?
- What alternative explanation might they argue for?

Step 5 Write a Draft

Introduction

- Describe the controversial trend, event, or phenomenon.
- Give the background that your intended readers will need.

Body

- Explain the cause or chain of causation of a trend, event, or phenomenon that is unfamiliar to your readers.
- Set out the causes that have been offered and reject them one by one. Then you can present the cause that you think is most important.
- Treat a series of causes one by one, analyzing the importance of each.

Conclusion

- Do more than simply summarize. Consider describing additional effects beyond those that have been noted previously.

Step 6 Revise, Edit, Proofread

- For detailed instructions, see Chapter 4.
- For a checklist to use to evaluate your draft, see pages 48–49.

Finding Good Reasons

Why Are Americans Gaining Weight?

Eric Schlosser, author of *Fast Food Nation* (2001), chows down on a grilled cheese sandwich, fries, and a soda. *Fast Food Nation* traces the rise of fast-food restaurants against the background of American culture based on the automobile. Schlosser claims that one of the effects of fast food is the increase in the number of overweight Americans.

There is no doubt that Americans have grown larger. A 2004 survey of Americans published in *JAMA: The Journal of the American Medical Association* found that nearly one-third (32.5 percent) of adults are obese and two-thirds (66.3 percent) are overweight. An especially disturbing aspect of this trend is that children are increasingly obese. The Center for Disease Control and Prevention reports that the percentage of obese children aged 6 to 11 almost quadrupled from 4 percent in 1974 to 15 percent in 2000, and the percentage of obese children aged 12 to 19 increased from 6 percent in 1974 to 15 percent in 2000.

Write about it

To what extent do you think fast food is the cause of the trend toward excess weight? To what extent do you think lifestyle changes and the content of food are causes? In addition to the amount of fast food Americans consume, consider the following:

- more sedentary lifestyle with more driving and less walking
- more time spent watching television, using computers, and playing video games
- introduction of high-fructose corn syrup in many foods, from ketchup and peanut butter to chocolate milk and yogurt
- inadequate physical education and reduced outdoor recess periods in schools
- more food advertising directed at children

Emily Raine

Why Should I Be Nice to You? Coffee Shops and the Politics of Good Service

Emily Raine recently received a master's degree in communication studies at McGill University in Montreal. She writes about graffiti and street art. This article appeared in the online journal *Bad Subjects* in 2005.

In this article, Raine explains why work in a coffee chain is worse than work in other kinds of service jobs. She also outlines the causes for what she sees as a destructive dynamic in the coffee chain culture and provides a possible alternative.

> "There is no more precious commodity than the relationship of trust and confidence a company has with its employees."
> — *Starbucks Coffee Company chairman Howard Schultz*

I actually like to serve. I'm not sure if this comes from some innate inclination to mother and fuss over strangers, or if it's because the movement and sociability of service work provides a much-needed antidote to the solitude of academic research, but I've always found something about service industry work satisfying. I've done the gamut of service jobs, from fine dining to cocktail waitressing to hip euro-bistro counter work, and the only job where I've ever felt truly whipped was working as a barista at one of the now-ubiquitous specialty coffee chains, those bastions of jazz and public solitude that have spread through urban landscapes over the last ten years or so. The pay was poor, the shifts long and oddly dispersed, the work boring and monotonous, the managers demanding, and the customers regularly displayed that unique spleen that emerges in even the most pleasant people before they've had the morning's first coffee. I often felt like an aproned Coke machine, such was the effect my sparkling personality had on the clientele. And yet, some combination of service professionalism, fear of termination and an imperative to be "nice" allowed me to suck it up, smile and continue to provide that intangible trait that the industry holds above all else, good service.

Raine establishes a credible, ethical stance in her introduction.

2   Good service in coffee shops doesn't amount to much. Unlike table service, where interaction with customers spans a minimum of half an hour, the average contact with a café customer lasts less than ten seconds. Consider how specialty cafés are laid

Even before identifying the effect that she intends to analyze, Raine identifies the cause—an efficient but impersonal assembly-line approach to service.

out: the customer service counter is arranged in a long line that clients move along to "use" the café. The linear coffee bar resembles an assembly line, and indeed, café labor is heavily grounded in the rationalism of Fordist manufacturing principles, which had already been tested for use in hospitality services by fast food chains. Each of the café workers is assigned a specific stage in the service process to perform exclusively, such as taking orders, using the cash registers, or handing clients cups of brewed coffee.

3   The specialization of tasks increases the speed of transactions and limits the duration of any one employee's interaction with the clientele. This means that in a given visit a customer might order from one worker, receive food from the next, then brewed coffee or tea from yet another, then pay a cashier before proceeding down the line of the counter, finishing the trip at the espresso machine which is always situated at its end. Ultimately, each of the café's products is processed and served by a different employee, who repeats the same preparation task for hours and attends to each customer only as they receive that one product.

Raine argues that the assembly-line service model precludes real interaction with customers.

4   Needless to say, the productive work in cafés is dreary and repetitive. Further, this style of service severely curtails interaction with the clientele, and the very brevity of each transaction precludes much chance for authentic friendliness or conversation—even asking about someone's day would slow the entire operation. The one aspect of service work that can be unpredictable—people—becomes redundant, and interaction with customers is reduced to a fatiguing eight-hour-long smile and the repetition of sentiments that allude to good service, such as injunctions to enjoy their purchases or to have a nice day. Rather than friendly exchanges with customers, barista workers' good service is reduced to a quick rictus in the customer's direction between a great deal of friendly interaction with the espresso machine.

Do you agree with this description of a typical coffee shop?

5   As the hospitality industry really took off in the sixties, good service became one of the trademarks of its advertising claims, a way for brands to distinguish themselves from the rest of the pack. One needn't think too hard to come up with a litany of service slogans that holler the good graces of their personnel—at Starbucks where the baristas make the magic, at Pacific Southwest Airlines where smiles aren't just painted on, or at McDonald's where smiles are free. Employee friendliness emerged as one of the chief distinguishing brand features of personal services, which means that the workers themselves become an aspect of the product for sale.

6   Our notions of good service revolve around a series of platitudes about professionalism—we're at your service, with a smile,

where the customer's always right—each bragging the centrality of the customer to everything "we" do. Such claims imply an easy and equal exchange between two parties: the "we" that gladly serves and the "you" that happily receives. There is, however, always a third party involved in the service exchange, and that's whoever has hired the server, the body that ultimately decides just what the dimensions of good service will be.

This "third party"—management, ownership—is the ultimate cause of the phenomenon under discussion.

7 Like most employees, a service worker sells labor to an employer at a set rate, often minimum wage, and the employer sells the product of that labor, the service itself, at market values. In many hospitality services, where gratuities make up the majority of employment revenue, the worker directly benefits from giving good service, which of course translates to good tips. But for the vast majority of service staff, and particularly those employed in venues yielding little or no gratuities—fast food outlets, café chains, cleaning and maintenance operations—this promises many workers little more than a unilateral imperative to be perpetually bright and amenable.

8 The vast majority of service personnel do not spontaneously produce an unaffected display of cheer and good will continuously for the duration of a shift. When a company markets its products on servers' friendliness, they must then monitor and control employees' friendliness, so good service is defined and enforced from above. Particularly in chains, which are premised upon their consistent reproduction of the same experience in numerous locations, organizations are obliged to impose systems to manage employees' interaction with their customers. In some chains, namely the fast food giants such as McDonald's and Burger King, employee banter is scripted into cash registers, so that as soon as a customer orders, workers are cued to offer, "would you like a dessert with that?" (an offer of dubious benefit to the customer) and to wish them a nice day. Ultimately, this has allowed corporations to be able to assimilate "good service"—or, friendly workers—into their overall brand image.

Does your experience as a customer (or worker) at fast food chains match this description?

9 While cafés genuflect toward the notion of good service, their layouts and management styles preclude much possibility of creating the warmth that this would entail. Good service is, of course, important, but not if it interferes with throughput. What's more, these cafés have been at the forefront of a new wave of organizations that not only market themselves on service quality but also describe employees' job satisfaction as the seed from which this flowers.

10 Perhaps the most glaring example of this is Starbucks, where cheerful young workers are displayed behind elevated

counters as they banter back and forth, calling out fancy Italian drink names and creating theatre out of their productive labor. Starbucks' corporate literature gushes not only about the good service its customers will receive, but about the great joy that its "partners" take in providing it, given the company's unique ability to "provide a great work environment and treat each other with respect and dignity," and where its partners are "emotionally and intellectually committed to Starbucks success." In the epigraph to this essay, Starbucks' chairman even describes the company's relationship with its workers as a commodity. Not only does Starbucks offer good service, but it attempts to guarantee something even better: good service provided by employees that are genuinely happy to give it.

The creation of this new kind of worker is in effect a public relations gimmick.

11   Starbucks has branded a new kind of worker, the happy, wholesome, perfume-free barista. The company offers unusual benefits for service workers, including stock options, health insurance, dental plans and other perks such as product discounts and giveaways. Further, they do so very, very publicly, and the company's promotional materials are filled with moving accounts of workers who never dreamed that corporate America could care so much. With the other hand, though, the company has smashed unionization drives in New York, Vancouver and at its Seattle roaster; it schedules workers at oddly timed shifts that never quite add up to full-time hours; the company pays only nominally more than minimum wage, and their staffs are still unable to subsist schlepping lattes alone.

12   Starbucks is not alone in marketing itself as an enlightened employer. When General Motors introduced its Saturn line, the new brand was promoted almost entirely on the company's good relations with its staff. The company's advertising spots often featured pictures of and quotes from the union contract, describing their unique partnership between manufacturer, workers and union, which allowed blue-collar personnel to have a say in everything from automobile designs to what would be served for lunch. The company rightly guessed that this strategy would go over well with liberal consumers concerned about the ethics of their purchases. Better yet, Saturn could market its cars based on workers' happiness whether personnel were satisfied or not, because very few consumers would ever have the chance to interact with them.

13   At the specialty coffee chains, however, consumers *have* to talk to employees, yet nobody ever really asks. The café service counter runs like a smooth piece of machinery, and I found that most people preferred to pretend that they were interacting with an appliance. In such short transactions, it is exceedingly difficult

for customers to remember the humanity of each of the four to seven people they might interact with to get their coffees. Even fast food counters have one server who processes each customer's order, yet in cafés the workers just become another gadget in the well-oiled café machine. This is a definite downside for the employees—clients are much ruder to café staff than in any other sector of the industry I ever worked in. I found that people were more likely to be annoyed than touched by any reference to my having a personality, and it took no small amount of thought on my part to realize why.

14   Barista workers are hired to represent an abstract category of worker, not to act as individuals. Because of the service system marked by short customer interaction periods and a homogenous staff, the services rendered are linked in the consumer imagination to the company and not to any one individual worker. Workers' assimilation into the company image makes employees in chain service as branded as the products they serve. The chain gang, the workers who hold these eminently collegiate after-school jobs, are proscribed sales scripts and drilled on customer service scenarios to standardize interactions with customers. The company issues protocols for hair length, color and maintenance, visible piercings and tattoos as well as personal hygiene and acceptable odorific products. Workers are made more interchangeable by the use of uniforms, which, of course, serve to make the staff just that. The organization is a constant intermediary in every transaction, interjecting its presence in every detail of the service experience, and this standardization amounts to an absorption of individuals' personalities into the corporate image.

Raine spells out her thesis in this paragraph.

15   Many of the measures that chains take to secure the homogeneity of their employees do not strike us as particularly alarming, likely because similar restrictions have been in place for several hundred years. Good service today has inherited many of the trappings of the good servant of yore, including prohibitions against eating, drinking, sitting or relaxing in front the served, entering and exiting through back doors, and wearing uniforms to visually mark workers' status. These measures almost completely efface the social identities of staff during work hours, providing few clues to workers' status in their free time. Contact between service workers and their customers is thus limited to purely functional relations, so that the public only see them as workers, as makers of quality coffee, and never as possible peers.

16   Maintaining such divisions is integral to good service because this display of class distinctions ultimately underlies our

notions of service quality. Good service means not only serving well, but also allowing customers to feel justified in issuing orders, to feel okay about being served—which, in turn, requires demonstrations of class difference and the smiles that suggest servers' comfort with having a subordinate role in the service exchange.

17   Unlike the penguin-suited household servant staffs whose class status was clearly defined, service industry workers today often have much more in common from a class perspective with those that they serve. This not only creates an imperative for them to wear their class otherness on their sleeves, as it were, but also to accept their subordinate role to those they serve by being unshakably tractable and polite.

18   Faith Popcorn has rather famously referred to the four-dollar latte as a "small indulgence," noting that while this is a lot to pay for a glass of hot milk, it is quite inexpensive for the feeling of luxury that can accompany it. In this service climate, the class status of the server and the served—anyone who can justify spending this much on a coffee—is blurry, indeed. Coffee shops that market themselves on employee satisfaction assert the same happy servant that allows politically conscientious consumers, who are in many cases the workers' own age and class peers, to feel justified in receiving good service. Good service—as both an apparent affirmation of subordinate classes' desire to serve and as an enforced one-sided politeness—reproduces the class distinctions that have historically characterized servant-served relationships so that these are perpetuated within the contemporary service market.

Raine begins to shift attention to the customers' role in coffee shop culture.

19   The specialty coffee companies are large corporations, and for the twenty-somethings who stock their counters, barista work is too temporary to bother fighting the system. Mostly, people simply quit. Dissatisfied workers are stuck with engaging in tactics that will change nothing but allow them to make the best of their lot. These include minor infractions such as taking liberties with the uniforms or grabbing little bits of company time for their own pleasure, what Michel de Certeau calls *la perruque* and the companies themselves call "time theft." As my time in the chain gang wore on, I developed my own tactic, the only one I found that jostled the customers out of their complacency and allowed me to be a barista and a person.

20   There is no easy way to serve without being a servant, and I have always found that the best way to do so is to show my actual emotions rather than affecting a smooth display of interminable patience and good will. For café customers, bettering baristas' lots can be as simple as asking about their day,

addressing them by name—any little gesture to show that you noticed the person behind the service that they can provide. My tactic as a worker is equally simple, but it is simultaneously an assertion of individual identity at work, a refusal of the class distinctions that characterize the service environment and a rebuttal to the companies that would promote my satisfaction with their system: be rude. Not arbitrarily rude, of course—customers are people, too, and nobody gains anything by spreading bad will. But on those occasions when customer or management behavior warranted a zinging comeback, I would give it.

21   Rudeness, when it is demanded, undermines companies' claims on workers' personal warmth and allows them to retain their individuality by expressing genuine rather than affected feelings in at-work interpersonal exchanges. It is a refusal of the class distinctions that underlie consumers' unilateral prerogative of rudeness and servers' unilateral imperative to be nice. It runs contrary to everything that we have been taught, not only about service but about interrelating with others. But this seems to be the only method of asserting one's person-hood in the service environment, where workers' personalities are all too easily reduced to a space-time, conflated with the drinks they serve. Baristas of the world, if you want to avoid becoming a green-aproned coffee dispensary, you're just going to have to tell people off about it.

Were you expecting this "solution" to the situation Raine presents?

Raine reveals her specific audience, "baristias of the world," only at the end of her argument.

Sample Student Causal Argument

Armadi Tansal

Professor Stewart

English 115

29 October 2012

Modern Warfare: Video Games' Link to Real-World Violence

"John" is a nineteen-year-old college student who gets decent grades. He comes from a typical upper-middle-class family and plans to get his MBA after he graduates. John is also my friend, which is why I'm not using his real name.

John has been playing moderately violent video games since he was nine years old. I started playing video and console games around that age too, and I played a lot in junior high, but John plays more than anyone I know. John says that over the past year he has played video games at least four hours every day, and "sometimes all day and night on the weekends." I have personally witnessed John play *Call of Duty: Modern Warfare 2* for six hours straight, with breaks only to use the bathroom or eat something.

I've never seen John act violently, and he's never been in trouble with the law. But new research on violent video games suggests that John's gaming habit puts him at risk for violent or aggressive behavior. Dr. Craig Anderson, a psychologist at the University of Iowa, says "the active role required by video games . . . may make violent video games even more hazardous than violent television or cinema." When people like John play these games, they get used to being rewarded for violent behavior. For example, in the multiplayer version of *Modern Warfare 2*, if the player gets a five-kill streak, he can call in a Predator missile strike. If you kill 25 people in a row, you can call in a tactical nuclear strike. Missile strikes help you advance toward the mission goals more quickly, so the more people you kill, the faster you'll win.

Along with *Modern Warfare 2*, John plays games like *Left 4 Dead*, *Halo*, and *Grand Theft Auto*. All these games are rated M for Mature, which according to the Entertainment Software Rating Board means they "may contain intense violence, blood and gore, sexual content and/or strong

> Armadi Tansal establishes a personal relationship to his subject and audience.

Tansal 2

language." Some M-rated games, like *Grand Theft Auto,* feature random violence, where players can run amok in a city, beat up and kill people, and smash stuff for no reason. In others, like *Modern Warfare 2,* the violence takes place in the context of military action. To do well in all of these games, you have to commit acts of violence. But does acting violently in games make you more violent in real life?

> Tansal identifies the causal question at the heart of his argument.

Anderson says studies show that "violent video games are significantly associated with: increased aggressive behavior, thoughts, and affect [feelings]; increased physiological arousal; and decreased prosocial (helping) behavior." He also claims that "high levels of violent video game exposure have been linked to delinquency, fighting at school and during free play periods, and violent criminal behavior (e.g., self-reported assault, robbery)."

> Direct quotations from published sources build credibility.

Being "associated with" and "linked to" violent behavior doesn't necessarily mean video games cause such behavior. Many people have argued that the links Anderson sees are coincidental, or that any effects video games might have on behavior are so slight that we shouldn't worry about them. Christopher Ferguson and John Kilburn, professors of Criminal Justice at Texas A&M International University, feel that the existing research does not support Anderson's claims. In a report published in the *Journal of Pediatrics,* they point out that in past studies, "the closer aggression measures got to actual violent behavior, the weaker the effects seen" (762).

> Tansal is careful not to accept the easy answer that video games cause everyone to be more violent.

From what I can tell, John doesn't have any more violent thoughts and feelings than most men his age. When I asked him if he thought the games had made him more violent or aggressive in real life, he said, "I'm actually less violent now. When we were kids we used to play 'war' with fake guns and sticks, chasing each other around the neighborhood and fighting commando-style. We didn't really fight but sometimes kids got banged up. No one ever gets hurt playing a video game."

Anderson admits that "a healthy, normal, nonviolent child or adolescent who has no other risk factors for high aggression or violence is not going to become a school shooter simply because they play five hours or 10 hours a week of these violent video games" (qtd. in St. George). But just because violent video games don't turn all players into mass murderers, that doesn't mean they have no effect on a player's

Tansal 3

behavior and personality. For example, my friend John doesn't get into fights or rob people, but he doesn't display a lot of prosocial "helping" behaviors either. He spends most of his free time gaming, so he doesn't get out of his apartment much. Also, the friends he does have mostly play video games with him.

Even though the games restrict his interactions with other humans and condition him to behave violently onscreen, John is probably not at high risk of becoming violent in real life. But according to researchers, this low risk of becoming violent is because none of the dozens of other risk factors associated with violent behavior are present in his life (Anderson et al. 160). If John was a high school dropout, came from a broken home, or abused alcohol and other drugs, his game playing might be more likely to contribute to violent behavior.

Anderson contends that violent video games are a "causal risk factor" for violence and aggression—not that they cause violent aggression. In other words, the games are a small piece of a much larger problem. People like my friend John are not likely to become violent because of the video games they play. But Anderson's research indicates that some people do. Although there is no simple way to tell who those people are, we should include video games as a possible risk factor when we think about who is likely to become violent.

Even if the risk contributed by violent video games is slight for each individual, the total impact of the games on violence in society could be huge. *Call of Duty: Modern Warfare 2* is the third-best-selling video game in the United States (Orry). Its creator, Activision Blizzard, had $1.3 billion dollars in sales in the just first three months of 2010 (Pham). Millions of people play this game, and games like it, and they aren't all as well-adjusted as John. If video games contribute to violent tendencies in only a small fraction of players, they could still have a terrible impact.

Tansal 4

Works Cited

Anderson, Craig. "Violent Video Games: Myths, Facts, and Unanswered Questions." *Psychological Science Agenda* 16.5 (2003): n. pag. Web. 6 Oct. 2010.

Anderson, Craig, et al. "Violent Video Game Effects on Aggression, Empathy, and Prosocial Behavior in Eastern and Western Countries." *Psychological Bulletin* 136 (2010): 151-73. Print.

Entertainment Software Rating Board. *Game Ratings and Descriptor Guide*. Entertainment Software Association, n.d. Web. 7 Oct. 2010.

Ferguson, Christopher J., and John Kilburn. "The Public Health Risks of Media Violence: A Meta-Analytic Review." *Journal of Pediatrics* 154.5 (2009): 759-63. Print.

John (pseudonym). Personal interview. 4 Oct. 2010.

Orry, James. "*Modern Warfare 2* the 3rd Best-Selling Game in the US." *Videogamer.com*. Pro-G Media Ltd., 12 Mar. 2010. Web. 6 Oct. 2010.

Pham, Alex. "Call of Duty: Modern Warfare 2 Propels Revenue, Profit for Activision Blizzard." *Los Angeles Times*. Los Angeles Times, 6 May 2010. Web. 7 Oct. 2010.

St. George, Donna. "Study Links Violent Video Games, Hostility." *Washington Post*. Washington Post, 3 Nov. 2008. Web. 5 Oct. 2010.

For additional writing resources that will help you master the objectives of this chapter, go to your **MyLab**.

10 | Evaluation Arguments

QUICK TAKE

In this chapter you will learn to

1. Use evaluation arguments to set out criteria and then judge something to be good or bad according to those criteria (see page 135)
2. Recognize evaluation arguments based on practical, aesthetic, and ethical criteria (see pages 136–137)
3. Analyze a specific evaluation argument (see pages 137–138)
4. Write an effective evaluation argument (see pages 140–141)

By some estimates, as many as five million animals are killed in shelters each year. Are "no-kill" shelters a good idea? Advocates of no-kill shelters argue that alternatives to euthanizing animals can be created by working to increase adoption demand for shelter animals. No-kill shelters also work to promote spaying and neutering to decrease the number of animals sent to shelters in the first place. Others argue that the term "no-kill" is divisive because it implies that some shelters are "kill" shelters and suggests that many shelter workers are cruel or uncaring. Are no-kill shelters an effective solution? What kind of evaluations would support or oppose the concept of the "no-kill" shelter? How can evaluation arguments be used to support more humane treatment of shelter animals?

People make evaluations all the time. Newspapers, magazines, and television have picked up on this love of evaluation by running "best of" polls. They ask their readers to vote on the best Chinese restaurant, the best pizza, the best local band, the best coffeehouse, the best dance club, the best neighborhood park, the best swimming hole, the best bike ride (scenic or challenging), the best volleyball court, the best place to get married, and so on. If you ask one of your friends who voted in a "best" poll why she picked a particular restaurant as the best of its kind, she might respond by saying simply, "I like it." But if you ask her why she likes it, she might start offering good reasons such as these: the food is tasty, the service prompt, the prices fair, and the atmosphere comfortable. It's really not a mystery why these polls are often quite predictable or why the same restaurants tend to win year after year. Many people think that evaluations are matters of personal taste, but when we begin probing the reasons, we often discover that different people use similar criteria to make evaluations.

The key to convincing other people that your judgment is sound is establishing the criteria you will use to make your evaluation. Sometimes it will be necessary to argue for the validity of the criteria that you think your readers should consider. If your readers accept your criteria, it's likely they will agree with your conclusions.

Understand How Evaluation Arguments Work

Evaluation arguments set out criteria and then judge something to be good or bad (or better, or best) according to those criteria.

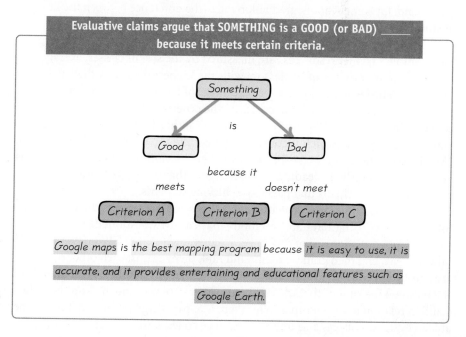

Recognize Kinds of Evaluations

Arguments of evaluation are structured much like arguments of definition. Recall that the criteria in arguments of definition are set out in *because* clauses:

SOMETHING is a ____ because it meets certain criteria.

Evaluative claims argue that

SOMETHING is a GOOD (or BAD) ____ because it meets certain criteria.

While people often agree about general criteria, they sometimes disagree about the relevance and appropriateness of specific criteria in an evaluation. Take as an example the question of which colleges are good schools. Until twenty years ago, most of the information that people used to evaluate a college came from the college itself. You could find out the price of tuition and what courses were offered, but other information was difficult to find, and it was hard to compare one college with another.

In 1983 the magazine *U.S. News & World Report* began ranking U.S. colleges and universities from a consumer's perspective. These rankings have remained controversial ever since. *U.S. News* evaluates schools using a complex set of criteria. Twenty-five percent of a school's ranking is based on a survey in which officials at each college rate the quality of schools in the same category as their own school. The results of this survey reflect the school's reputation among administrators. The remaining 75 percent is based on six kinds of statistical data. These measure retention of students, faculty resources, student selectivity, financial resources, alumni giving, and, for some schools, graduation rates (the difference between the number of students expected to graduate and the number who actually do).

U.S. News chooses specific types of information to look at in each category. For example, "faculty resources" are measured by the size of classes, average faculty pay, the percentage of professors with the highest degree in their field, the overall student-faculty ratio, and the percentage of faculty who are full-time.

Many college officials have criticized the criteria *U.S. News* uses to evaluate colleges. In an August 1998 *U.S. News* article, Gerhard Casper, the president of Stanford University (which is consistently near the top of the rankings), writes, "Much about these rankings—particularly their specious formulas and spurious precision—is utterly misleading." Casper argues that using graduation rates as a criterion rewards schools that pass low-achieving students.

U.S. News replies in its defense that colleges and universities themselves do a lot of ranking, using data and methods that can be questioned. Schools rank students for admission, using SAT or ACT scores, high school GPA, class rank, and other factors, and then grade students and rank them against each other once they are enrolled in college. Schools also evaluate their faculty and take great interest in the national ranking of their departments. They care very much about how they stand in relation to one another. Why, then, *U.S. News* argues, shouldn't people be able to evaluate colleges and universities, since colleges and universities are in the business of evaluating people?

The magazine and the colleges have very different ideas about what constitute fair and relevant criteria for evaluating a college. But the *U.S. News* college rankings generate a tremendous amount of income for the magazine, suggesting that students and their parents agree with the criteria, and use them to help make their own decisions about college.

Some evaluation arguments rely more heavily on certain types of criteria than others. For example, a movie review (_____ is a good movie) is likely to focus most closely on aesthetic considerations: engaging characters, an exciting story, beautiful cinematography. Ethical considerations may be relevant—say, if the film is exceptionally violent, or celebrates antisocial behavior—but usually don't predominate in a movie review. Practical considerations will probably be least important, since anyone reading a movie review is presumably willing to spend the price of admission to see a film. Use aesthetic, moral, and practical criteria for deciding how good or bad a person, a place, an artifact, or a policy is.

Build an Evaluation Argument

Although evaluation arguments seem very similar to definition arguments, there is a key difference. Definition arguments seek to place something in the correct category by observing its qualities. They hinge on our judgments about similarity and difference. Evaluation arguments focus instead on what we value. Because of this, the criteria you choose when making an evaluation argument are very important. If your criteria do not appeal to the values of your audience, your readers will not feel that your evaluation is accurate.

Suppose that a city task force on downtown revitalization has a plan to demolish the oldest commercial building in your city. Your neighborhood association wants to preserve the building, perhaps by turning it into a museum. To persuade officials to do this, you must show that your plan for preservation is a good one, while the taskforce's plan for demolition is a bad one. You might argue that a museum would attract visitors to the downtown area, bringing in revenue. You might argue that the elaborately carved stone facade of the building is a rare example of a disappearing craft. Or you might argue that it is only fair to preserve the oldest commercial building in town, since the city's oldest house and other historic buildings have been saved.

Each of these arguments uses different criteria. The argument that a museum will bring in money is based on practical considerations. The argument about the rare and beautiful stonework on the building is based on aesthetic (artistic) considerations. The argument that an old commercial building deserves the same treatment as other old buildings is based on fairness, or ethical concerns. Depending on your audience, you might use all three kinds of criteria, or you might focus more on one or two kinds. If your city is in the middle of a budget crisis, it might be wise to stress the practical, economic benefits of a museum. If several City Council members are architects or amateur historians, your argument

Windmills produce energy without pollution and reduce dependence on foreign oil. Do you agree or disagree with people who do not want windmills built near them because they find them ugly?

might focus on the aesthetic criteria. You have to make assumptions about what your audience will value most as they consider your evaluation.

Evaluative arguments can look at just one case in isolation, but often they make comparisons. You could construct an argument about the fate of the old building that only describes your plan and its benefits. Or, you might also directly address the demolition proposal, showing how it lacks those benefits. Then your argument might be structured like this:

Finding Good Reasons

What's The Best Alternative Fuel?

Biodiesel is an alternative fuel source that is made from vegetable oil (or animal fats) and alcohol. While biodiesel can be used alone, it is often mixed with petroleum diesel. Blends of up to 20 percent biodiesel can be used in a standard diesel engine without modifications—meaning that many cars on the road today would be capable of using biodiesel if it were to become widely available.

But is biodiesel a realistic solution to the world's dependence on fossil fuels? Many think yes. Proponents point to the reduction in greenhouse gas emissions and the lower dependence on foreign oil that would accompany wide-scale biodiesel adoption. Detractors point to millions of acres of land, which would typically be used for food production, that would be converted to fuel production, inevitably causing shortages and an overall rise in food prices.

Write about it

1. One way to assess a complicated issue like alternative fuel technologies is to evaluate each technology against a set of common criteria. Which of the following criteria are useful for evaluating fuel-efficient cars? Why are they useful?
   - cost of development and production
   - sticker price of cars using the technology
   - how long it takes for cars to reach the market
   - efficiency and reliability of cars using the technology
   - environmental impact
   - convenience of refueling and maintenance
   - driver's aesthetic experience

2. Are any of the above criteria more important than the others? If so, how would you rank them? Why? Are there any criteria you would add?

Steps to Writing an Evaluation Argument

| **1** Make a Claim | **2** Write About What's at Stake | **3** List the Criteria |

Step 1 Make a Claim

Make an evaluative claim based on criteria.

Template

> SOMETHING is good (bad, the best, the worst) if measured by certain criteria (practicality, aesthetics, ethics).

Examples

- A book or movie review.
- An evaluation of a controversial aspect of sports (e.g., the current system of determining who is champion in Division I college football by a system of bowls and polls) or a sports event (e.g., this year's WNBA playoffs) or a team.
- An evaluation of the effectiveness of a social policy or law such as restrictions on newly licensed drivers, current gun control laws, or environmental regulation.

Step 2 Think About What's at Stake

- Does nearly everyone agree with you? Then your claim probably isn't interesting or important. If you can think of people who disagree, then something is at stake.
- Who argues the opposite of your claim?
- Why do they make a different evaluation?

Step 3 List the Criteria

- Which criteria make something either good or bad?
- Which criteria are the most important?
- Which criteria are fairly obvious, and which will you have to argue for?

Step 4 Analyze Your Potential Readers

- Who are your readers?
- How familiar will they be with what you are evaluating?
- Which criteria are they most likely to accept with little explanation, and which will they disagree with?

Step 5 Write a Draft

Introduction

- Introduce the person, group, institution, event, or object that you are going to evaluate. You might want to announce your stance at this point or wait until the concluding section.
- Give the background that your intended readers will need.

Body

- Describe each criterion and then analyze how well what you are evaluating meets that criterion.
- If you are making an evaluation according to the effects someone or something produces, describe each effect in detail.
- Anticipate where readers might question either your criteria or how they apply to your subject.
- Address opposing viewpoints by acknowledging how their evaluations might differ and by showing why your evaluation is better.

Conclusion

- If you have not yet announced your stance, conclude that, on the basis of the criteria you set out or the effects you have analyzed, something is good (bad, the best, the worst).
- If you have made your stance clear from the beginning, end with a compelling example or analogy.

Step 6 Revise, Edit, Proofread

- For detailed instructions, see Chapter 4.
- For a checklist to use to evaluate your draft, see pages 48–49.

P. J.
O'Rourke

The End of the Affair

P. J. O'Rourke is a humorist and satirist who follows in the tradition of the New Journalism where there is no pretense of objectivity and the biases of the writer are in the foreground. Even those who don't agree with his libertarian conservative political views still find him funny, like Bill Maher, who invites O'Rourke on his HBO show. O'Rourke was editor-in-chief of the satirical *National Lampoon* magazine and worked at *Rolling Stone* from 1986 to 2001. The titles of his book suggest his sense of humor: *Modern Manners: An Etiquette Book for Rude People* (1983), *The Bachelor's Home Companion: A Practical Guide to Keeping House like a Pig* (1987), *Holidays in Hell* (1988), *Parliament of Whores: A Lone Humorist Attempts to Explain the Entire U.S. Government* (1991), *Give War a Chance: Eyewitness Accounts of Mankind's Struggle against Tyranny, Injustice, and Alcohol-free Beer* (1992), and *Peace Kills: America's Fun New Imperialism* (2004). O'Rourke's humor is infused with outrage over the influence of government in ordinary life, which you will find in this evaluation argument, published in the *Wall Street Journal* in 2009.

O'Rourke begins by announcing that he is from an older generation. What does he gain and lose from this strategy?

2

The phrase "bankrupt General Motors," which we expect to hear uttered on Monday, leaves Americans my age in economic shock. The words are as melodramatic as "Mom's nude photos." And, indeed, if we want to understand what doomed the American automobile, we should give up on economics and turn to melodrama.

Politicians, journalists, financial analysts and other purveyors of banality have been looking at cars as if a convertible were a business. Fire the MBAs and hire a poet. The fate of Detroit isn't a matter of financial crisis, foreign competition, corporate greed, union intransigence, energy costs or measuring the shoe size of the footprints in the carbon. It's a tragic romance—unleashed passions, titanic clashes, lost love and wild horses. Foremost are the horses. Cars can't be comprehended without them. A hundred and some years ago Rudyard Kipling wrote "The Ballad of the King's Jest," in which an Afghan tribesman avers: Four things greater than all things are—Women and Horses and Power and War.

Note how his favored criteria—romance, passion, horses—have to do with aesthetics, not practical issues like safety or environmental impact.

3

Insert another "power" after the horse and the verse was as true in the suburbs of my 1950s boyhood as it was in the Khyber Pass.

4

Horsepower is not a quaint leftover of linguistics or a vague metaphoric anachronism. James Watt, father of the steam engine and progenitor of the industrial revolution, lacked a measurement for the movement of weight over distance in time—what we call energy. (What we call energy wasn't even an intellectual concept in the late 18th century—in case you think the recent collapse of global capitalism was history's most transformative moment.) Mr. Watt did research using draft animals and found that, under optimal conditions, a dray horse could lift 33,000 pounds one foot off the ground in one minute. Mr. Watt—the eponymous watt not yet existing—called this unit of energy "1 horse-power."

Note how this paragraph establishes O'Rourke's expertise, his credibility.

5   In 1970 a Pontiac GTO (may the brand name rest in peace) had horsepower to the number of 370. In the time of one minute, for the space of one foot, it could move 12,210,000 pounds. And it could move those pounds down every foot of every mile of all the roads to the ends of the earth for every minute of every hour until the driver nodded off at the wheel. Forty years ago the pimply kid down the block, using $3,500 in saved-up soda-jerking money, procured might and main beyond the wildest dreams of Genghis Khan, whose hordes went forth to pillage mounted upon less oomph than is in a modern leaf blower.

O'Rourke's favored criteria—status and being cool—have nothing to do with practicality and everything to do with aesthetics.

6   Horses and horsepower alike are about status and being cool. A knight in ancient Rome was bluntly called "guy on

horseback," Equesitis. Chevalier means the same, as does Cavalier. Lose the capitalization and the dictionary says, "insouciant and debonair; marked by a lofty disregard of others' interests, rights, or feelings; high-handed and arrogant and supercilious." How cool is that? Then there are cowboys—always cool—and the U.S. cavalry that coolly comes to their rescue plus the proverbially cool-handed "Man on Horseback" to whom we turn in troubled times.

O'Rourke uses predominantly male references. Do you think he was writing only for men?

7   Early witnesses to the automobile urged motorists to get a horse. But that, in effect, was what the automobile would do—get a horse for everybody. Once the Model T was introduced in 1908 we all became Sir Lancelot, gained a seat at the Round Table and were privileged to joust for the favors of fair maidens (at drive-in movies). The pride and prestige of a noble mount was vouchsafed to the common man. And woman, too. No one ever tried to persuade ladies to drive sidesaddle with both legs hanging out the car door.

More "status" and "being cool."

8   For the purpose of ennobling us schlubs, the car is better than the horse in every way. Even more advantageous than cost, convenience and not getting kicked and smelly is how much easier it is to drive than to ride. I speak with feeling on this subject, having taken up riding when I was nearly 60 and having begun to drive when I was so small that my cousin Tommy had to lie on the transmission hump and operate the accelerator and the brake with his hands.

"Schlub" is Yiddish slang for an unattractive person. Why does O'Rourke use this term?

9   After the grown-ups had gone to bed, Tommy and I shifted the Buick into neutral, pushed it down the driveway and out of earshot, started the engine and toured the neighborhood. The sheer difficulty of horsemanship can be illustrated by what happened to Tommy and me next. Nothing. We maneuvered the car home, turned it off and rolled it back up the driveway. (We were raised in the blessedly flat Midwest.) During our foray the Buick's speedometer reached 30. But 30 miles per hour is a full gallop on a horse. Delete what you've seen of horse riding in movies. Possibly a kid who'd never been on a horse could ride at a gallop without killing himself. Possibly one of the Jonas Brothers could land an F-14 on a carrier deck.

Cars in the 1950s and 1960s represented the triumph of aesthetics over practical issues like gas mileage and safety.

10   Thus cars usurped the place of horses in our hearts. Once we'd caught a glimpse of a well-turned Goodyear, checked out the curves of the bodywork and gaped at that swell pair of headlights, well, the old gray mare was not what she used to be. We embarked upon life in the fast lane with our new paramour. It was a great love story of man and machine. The road to the future was paved with bliss.

11   Then we got married and moved to the suburbs. Being away from central cities meant Americans had to spend more of their

time driving. Over the years away got farther away. Eventually this meant that Americans had to spend all of their time driving. The play date was 40 miles from the Chuck E. Cheese. The swim meet was 40 miles from the cello lesson. The Montessori was 40 miles from the math coach. Mom's job was 40 miles from Dad's job and the three-car garage was 40 miles from both.

12   The car ceased to be object of desire and equipment for adventure and turned into office, rec room, communications hub, breakfast nook and recycling bin—a motorized cup holder. Americans, the richest people on Earth, were stuck in the confines of their crossover SUVs, squeezed into less space than tech-support call-center employees in a Mumbai cubicle farm. Never mind the six-bedroom, eight-bath, pseudo-Tudor with cathedral-ceilinged great room and 1,000-bottle controlled-climate wine cellar. That was a day's walk away.

13   We became sick and tired of our cars and even angry at them. Pointy-headed busybodies of the environmentalist, new urbanist, utopian communitarian ilk blamed the victim. They claimed the car had forced us to live in widely scattered settlements in the great wasteland of big-box stores and the Olive Garden. If we would all just get on our Schwinns or hop a trolley, they said, America could become an archipelago of cozy gulags on the Portland, Oregon, model with everyone nestled together in the most sustainably carbon-neutral, diverse and ecologically unimpactful way.

14   But cars didn't shape our existence; cars let us escape with our lives. We're way the heck out here in Valley Bottom Heights and Trout Antler Estates because we were at war with the cities. We fought rotten public schools, idiot municipal bureaucracies, corrupt political machines, rampant criminality and the pointy-headed busybodies. Cars gave us our dragoons and hussars, lent us speed and mobility, let us scout the terrain and probe the enemy's lines. And thanks to our cars, when we lost the cities we weren't forced to surrender, we were able to retreat.

15   But our poor cars paid the price. They were flashing swords beaten into dull plowshares. Cars became appliances. Or worse. Nobody's ticked off at the dryer or the dishwasher, much less the fridge. We recognize these as labor-saving devices. The car, on the other hand, seems to create labor. We hold the car responsible for all the dreary errands to which it needs to be steered. Hell, a golf cart's more fun. You can ride around in a golf cart with a six-pack, safe from breathalyzers, chasing Canada geese on the fairways and taking swings at gophers with a mashie.

16   We've lost our love for cars and forgotten our debt to them and meanwhile the pointy-headed busybodies have been exacting their revenge. We escaped the poke of their noses once, when we lived downtown, but we won't be able to peel out so fast the next time. In the name of safety, emissions control and fuel economy, the simple mechanical elegance of the automobile has been rendered ponderous, cumbersome and incomprehensible. One might as well pry the back off an iPod as pop the hood on a contemporary motor vehicle. An aging shade-tree mechanic like myself stares aghast and sits back down in the shade. Or would if the car weren't squawking at me like a rehearsal for divorce. You left the key in. You left the door open. You left the lights on. You left your dirty socks in the middle of the bedroom floor.

17   I don't believe the pointy-heads give a damn about climate change or gas mileage, much less about whether I survive a head-on with one of their tax-sucking mass-transit projects. All they want to is to make me hate my car. How proud and handsome would Bucephalas look, or Traveler or Rachel Alexandra, with seat and shoulder belts, air bags, 5-mph bumpers and a maze of pollution-control equipment under the tail?

18   And there's the end of the American automobile industry. When it comes to dull, practical, ugly things that bore and annoy me, Japanese things cost less and the cup holders are more conveniently located.

19   The American automobile is—that is, was—never a product of Japanese-style industrialism. America's steel, coal, beer, beaver pelts and PCs may have come from our business plutocracy, but American cars have been manufactured mostly by romantic fools. David Buick, Ransom E. Olds, Louis Chevrolet, Robert and Louis Hupp of the Hupmobile, the Dodge brothers, the Studebaker brothers, the Packard brothers, the Duesenberg brothers, Charles W. Nash, E. L. Cord, John North Willys, Preston Tucker and William H. Murphy, whose Cadillac cars were designed by the young Henry Ford, all went broke making cars. The man who founded General Motors in 1908, William Crapo (really) Durant, went broke twice. Henry Ford, of course, did not go broke, nor was he a romantic, but judging by his opinions he certainly was a fool.

20   America's romantic foolishness with cars is finished, however, or nearly so. In the far boondocks a few good old boys haven't got the memo and still tear up the back roads. Doubtless the Obama administration's Department of Transportation is even now calculating a way to tap federal stimulus funds for mandatory OnStar installations to locate and subdue these reprobates.

Is O'Rourke himself one of those good old boys?

21   Among certain youths—often first-generation Americans—there remains a vestigial fondness for Chevelle low-riders or Honda "tuners." The pointy-headed busybodies have yet to enfold these youngsters in the iron-clad conformity of cultural diversity's embrace. Soon the kids will be expressing their creative energy in a more constructive way, planting bok choy in community gardens and decorating homeless shelters with murals of Che.

22   I myself have something old-school under a tarp in the basement garage. I bet when my will has been probated, some child of mine will yank the dust cover and use the proceeds of the eBay sale to buy a mountain bike. Four things greater than all things are, and I'm pretty sure one of them isn't bicycles. There are those of us who have had the good fortune to meet with strength and beauty, with majestic force in which we were willing to trust our lives. Then a day comes, that strength and beauty fails, and a man does what a man has to do. I'm going downstairs to put a bullet in a V-8.

Sample Student Evaluation Argument

Giddens 1

Rashaun Giddens

Professor Chen

English 1302

21 April 2009

Stop Loss or "Loss of Trust"

Looking back on my high school career, my social and extracurricular lives were filled with countless highs: hanging out with my friends, prom, and varsity track to name a few. My academic career, however, was a bit shakier. So busy with what I saw then as the important things in life, I often procrastinated or altogether avoided my schoolwork. My senior year, the recruiter from the U.S. Army Reserves spoke at a school assembly. He asked that we as seniors consider the prospect of becoming "weekend warriors." In the wake of September 11, we could help protect our country and simultaneously work toward paying for a college education, which seemed like a great idea to many students. For those who could not otherwise afford college, the prospect of receiving a higher education in return for patriotism and some good hard work sounded fair enough. My life, however, took a different turn. When I received my track scholarship, I decided to head off to college right away. Many of my friends, however, heeded the call to service. So far, their realities have been far from the lives that were pitched to them; rather, this was the beginning of a path to broken dreams and broken promises.

My cousin, moved to action by a charismatic recruiter, an Army announcement of fifteen-month active tours, and the prospect of a paid college education, chose to join the United States Army Reserves. The Army, suffering from a recruitment shortfall, had recently announced a policy that would allow recruits to serve in active duty for a mere fifteen months. For serving for just over a year, my cousin could do his national duty and put himself on a path to self-improvement. The recruiter did not, however, highlight the fine print to this new program. No one told my cousin that he could be called back to active duty for up to eight years under the government's "stop loss" policy. Further, no one told him that just one day after the Army announced the incentive program, an

Note how the introduction creates a connection with the audience; while anyone can be persuaded by this essay, Giddens is especially addressing people around his own age.

Here the Giddens names the specific issue, "stop loss," and indicates some of what is at stake.

Giddens 2

appeals court ruled that the Army could, under stop loss, compel soldiers to remain beyond the initial eight-year obligation (Wickham).

The stop loss policy forces thousands of soldiers to serve beyond their volunteer enlistment contracts. The all-volunteer Army—on which the government prides itself—is slowly developing into a disgruntled mass of men and women being held against their will. These men and women wanted to serve their countries and their families, and they signed what they believed were binding agreements with a trustworthy employer—the United States government—only to find that their government didn't bargain in good faith.

> "Against their will" raises an ethical issue.

> Giddens announces the point he will defend and that his argument will be based in part on ethical considerations.

As far back as the Civil War, the government needed incentives to retain its troops. (Although we all want freedom, few actually want to put our own lives on the line in the pursuit of that goal.) Both the Union and the Confederacy needed to make tough decisions to maintain strong armed forces when soldiers' contracts were expiring. The Union chose to offer financial incentives to keep its young men in uniform, while the Confederacy instituted a series of (not so) "voluntary" reenlistment policies (Robertson). During World War II all soldiers were forced to remain active until they reached a designated number of points. Vietnam saw the last stage of a mandatory draft, with soldiers serving one-year tours (Hockstader). Today's military relies on stop loss, making soldiers stay in the military after their commitment ends. Congress first gave the military the authority to retain soldiers after the Vietnam War when new volunteers were too few to replace departing soldiers. In November 2002, the Pentagon gave stop loss orders for Reserve and National Guard units activated to fight terrorism (Robertson).

> The research in this paragraph builds Giddens's credibility. He has done his homework.

> The definition of "stop loss" is embedded in the larger argument.

This policy is neither forthcoming, safe, nor compassionate toward those most directly impacted—the soldiers and their families. As the United States became more and more entrenched in the conflicts in Iraq and later in Afghanistan, the military was stretched thinner and thinner. By 2004, approximately 40% of those serving in Iraq and Afghanistan came from the ranks of the part-time soldiers: the Reserves and the National Guard (Gerard). While these individuals did know that their countries could call if they enlisted, they continue to bear an inordinate burden of actual combat time, and this new policy continues

> This specific thesis defines the three criteria that the essay will discuss, in order.

Giddens 3

Giddens presents his first criterion in this paragraph: the "stop loss" policy is not forthcoming.

to create situations further removed from the job for which they enlisted. Recruiters often pitch the military—including the Reserves and the Guard—to young, impressionable, and often underprivileged kids. I have experienced this pitch firsthand and have seen the eyes of my classmates as the recruiter promised them a better and richer tomorrow. Seeing a golden opportunity for self-respect and achievement, young men and women sign on the dotted line. Today, other young men and women are buying a bill of goods. These recruits—and those who came before them—deserve to have an honest relationship with the government they protect. As policymakers tout the all-volunteer Army, those who serve find their rights threatened.

Giddens argues that if the policy is not forthcoming, it isn't fair.

The military claims to teach soldiers respect and honor. Is misleading your employees honest?

Giddens introduces his second criterion—the "stop loss" policy isn't safe.

Aside from being less than forthright, stop loss may be putting our soldiers in harm's way. The policy forces these soldiers to suffer the strain of combat for extended periods of time. Because of the way the policy works, troops may learn of tour extensions mere hours before they had planned to return stateside to lower-stress positions and their loved ones. These troops need to be ready, alert, and equipped with a morale which allows them to fight effectively. Stop loss instead forces these soldiers—often those trained for short stints—to work beyond their experience and training. This policy may prove to overextend, both emotionally and physically, our fighting men and women. As they repeatedly suffer disappointment because of changes in their orders and delays of departure, morale is likely to drop.

This second criterion, safety, is based on practicality—on the policy's negative consequences.

Based on reports from families, this practice has been devastating to their soldiers. Nancy Durst, wife of United States Reservist Staff Sergeant Scott Durst, told *Talk of the Nation*'s Neal Conan that the military detained her husband's unit just thirty minutes before it was to board the bus scheduled to deliver it to a stateside flight. The unit was later informed that tours had been extended for another four months (Durst). War breeds stress, but how can soldiers be expected to function at an optimal level when forced to suffer disappointments at the hands of their own government?

Finally, this policy simply runs contrary to the current administration's stated interest in the preservation of family and the bolstering of small businesses. First (and most obviously), this less-than-forthright policy keeps families separated. Husbands, wives, and children find themselves separated for longer periods of time, left with uncertainty and ambiguity for comfort. How does this aid in preserving the family? Second, when the government deploys reservists, soldiers often take a severe pay cut. Forced to leave their regular jobs, soldiers—and their families—must survive on an often much smaller government wage. Stop loss extends tours of duty and consequently the economic struggles of the families in question. Third, the policy has proven detrimental to the small-business owner. Men and women have used their military experience, discipline, and training to further themselves economically. The United States prides itself on the power of the small businessman; however, individuals such as Chief Warrant Officer Ronald Eagle have been hurt by this policy. After twenty years of service, Eagle was set to retire from the Army and focus on his aircraft-maintenance business. Instead, the Army has indefinitely moved his retirement date. As a consequence, Eagle has taken a $45,000 pay cut and wonders whether his business will survive his hiatus (Hockstader). Is this the way the government and military fight to preserve the family—emotionally and economically?

Because American men and women risk their lives in the name of bettering those of Iraqis and Afghans, the military should think about how their policy affects the lives of their soldiers and those back home. While the stop loss policy does allow the armed forces to build a larger active force without the public backlash (and political suicide) of instituting the draft, this policy comes at a cost. Those who have chosen to serve their country—whether for the training, educational possibilities, economic support, or expression of patriotism—are being bamboozled.

Watch the television commercials that, even now, tout training and part-time service. Read the stories of those serving and the families left behind. The sales pitch and the real picture do not match. The United States is undeniably one of the strongest nations in the world and a bastion of freedom. For these very reasons, the armed forces and the United States government, which represents all citizens, must find a way to lead this war (or conflict or crusade) honestly. If we have to pay soldiers double what they currently make in order to get them to reenlist,

---

Giddens's third criterion maintains that the policy hurts families and small businesses.

Giddens raises the practical consequences on individual soldiers.

This third criterion is not just a matter of impracticality; it's also a matter of fairness.

Giddens sums up what is at stake.

Giddens 5

> Giddens ends by emphasizing the ethical issue because ethical consideration typically are the strongest ones to include in an evaluation argument.

we should do so. Even a draft would at least be aboveboard and honest. But we cannot continue to trick people into risking their lives for our national security. Our country must show the honor and respect deserved by those who fight, and stop loss undeniably dishonors and shows disrespect to our soldiers. The military must take a cue from its own advertising and "be all they can be." Be honest.

Giddens 6

Works Cited

Durst, Nancy. Interview with Neal Conan. *Talk of the Nation*. Natl. Public Radio. WNYC, New York. 19 Apr. 2004. Radio.

Gerard, Philip. "When the Cry Was 'Over the Hill in October.'" *Charleston Gazette* 16 May 2004: 1E. *LexisNexis Academic*. Web. 6 Apr. 2009.

Hockstader, Lee. "Army Stops Many Soldiers from Quitting; Orders Extend Enlistments to Curtail Troop Shortages." *WashingtonPost* 29 Dec. 2003: A01. *LexisNexis Academic*. Web. 8 Apr. 2009.

Robertson, John. "The Folly of Stop Loss." *Pittsburgh Post-Gazette* 19 Dec. 2004: J1. *LexisNexis Academic*. Web. 7 Apr. 2009.

Wickham, DeWayne. "A 15-Month Enlistment? Check Army's Fine Print." *USA Today* 17 May 2005: 13A. *LexisNexis Academic*. Web. 6 Apr. 2009.

For additional writing resources that will help you master the objectives of this chapter, go to your **MyLab**.

11 | Narrative Arguments

In this chapter you will learn to

1. Explain how narrative arguments rely on stories rather than statistics (see page 154)
2. Recognize the kinds of narrative arguments (see page 154)
3. Analyze a specific narrative argument (see page 156)
4. Write an effective narrative argument (see pages 158–159)

Charity: water understands the persuasive power of personal stories. Their online campaign features narratives like the story of Louis Mackenzie, a young boy who lost his father in the January 2010 earthquake in Haiti. "I cried and cried and cried when my mom told me he died," the text reads. As many organizations have learned, people often feel more compelled to donate money when they read personal stories like Louis's than when they are barraged with abstract numbers and statistics. Why are such stories effective as arguments? What makes some stories more compelling than others? © 2010 Charitywater.org. Used with permission.

Understand How Narrative Arguments Work

A single, detailed personal story sometimes makes a stronger case than large-scale statistical evidence. The Annenberg Public Policy Center reported that an estimated 1.6 million of 17 million U.S. college students gambled online in 2005, but it was the story of Greg Hogan that made the problem real for many Americans. Hogan, the son of a Baptist minister, was an extraordinarily talented musician, who played onstage twice at Carnegie Hall by age 13. He chose to attend Lehigh University in Pennsylvania, where he was a member of the orchestra and class president. At Lehigh he also acquired an addiction to online poker. He lost $7,500, much of which he borrowed from fraternity brothers. To pay them back, he robbed a bank, only to be arrested a few hours later. Eventually he received a long prison sentence. Hogan's story helped to influence Congress to pass the Unlawful Internet Gambling Enforcement Act, which requires financial institutions to stop money transfers to gambling sites.

Successful narrative arguments typically don't have a thesis statement but instead tell a compelling story. From the experience of one individual, readers infer a claim and the good reasons that support the claim.

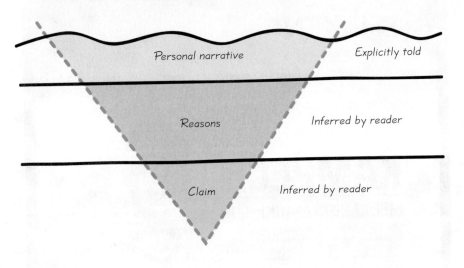

Personal narrative — Explicitly told

Reasons — Inferred by reader

Claim — Inferred by reader

Recognize Kinds of Narrative Arguments

Using narrative to make an argument is part of human nature. As far back as we have records, we find people telling stories and singing songs that argue for change. During periods of history where explicit arguments are dangerous to make, stories allow people to safely criticize authority or imagine how life could be different. The history of folk music is a continuous recycling of old tunes, phrases, and narratives to engage new political situations. Anti-war ballads popular in Ireland in the 1840s were sung in the 1960s by Americans protesting their country's involvement in Vietnam. All the popular narrative genres—short stories, novels, movies, and theater—have been used as ways to make arguments for change.

Singer/songwriter Shawn Colvin is one of many contemporary folk, blues, rock, and rap artists who continue the tradition of making narrative arguments in their songs. Can you think of a song that makes a narrative argument?

Narrative arguments allow readers to fill in the good reasons, and come to their own conclusions. The personal connection readers can feel with the writer of a narrative argument makes this strategy a compelling means of persuasion. Moreover, because the writer usually refrains from making an outright claim, people reading narrative arguments are more likely to feel that they are "making up their own minds" rather than being reluctantly persuaded.

Narrative arguments can be representative anecdotes or they can be longer accounts of particular events that express larger ideas. One such story is George Orwell's account of a hanging in Burma (the country now known as Myanmar) while he was a British colonial administrator in the late 1920s. In "A Hanging," first published in 1931, Orwell narrates the story of an execution of a nameless prisoner who was convicted of a nameless crime. Everyone present quietly and dispassionately performs his job—the prison guards, the hangman, the superintendent, and even the prisoner, who offers no resistance when he is bound and led to the gallows. All is totally routine until a very small incident makes Orwell realize what is happening:

> It was about forty yards to the gallows. I watched the bare brown back of the prisoner marching in front of me. He walked clumsily with his bound arms, but quite steadily, with that bobbing gait of the Indian who never straightens his knees. At each step his muscles slid neatly into place, the lock of hair on

his scalp danced up and down, his feet printed themselves on the wet gravel. And once, in spite of the men who gripped him by each shoulder, he stepped slightly aside to avoid a puddle on the path.

It is curious, but till that moment I had never realized what it means to destroy a healthy, conscious man. When I saw the prisoner step aside to avoid the puddle, I saw the mystery, the unspeakable wrongness, of cutting a life short when it is in full tide. This man was not dying, he was alive just as we were alive. All the organs of his body were working—bowels digesting food, skin renewing itself, nails growing, tissues forming—all toiling away in solemn foolery. His nails would still be growing when he stood on the drop, when he was falling through the air with a tenth of a second to live. His eyes saw the yellow gravel and the grey walls, and his brain still remembered, foresaw, reasoned—reasoned even about puddles. He and we were a party of men walking together, seeing, hearing, feeling, understanding the same world; and in two minutes, with a sudden snap, one of us would be gone—one mind less, one world less.

Orwell's narrative leads to a dramatic moment of recognition, which gives this story its lasting power. His sudden realization of what execution means to both the prisoner and his executioners is a powerful argument to reconsider the morality of the death penalty.

Build a Narrative Argument

Because storytelling is such a familiar activity, it is easy for writers to get carried away with their narratives, and lose sight of the point they are trying to make. Readers find narrative compelling, but not if the narrative is long-winded, full of unnecessary detail, or has no obvious point. Furthermore, readers are quickly put off if they feel they are being given a lecture.

There are two keys to making effective narrative arguments: establishing that the narrative is truthful, and showing its relevance to a wider problem or question. Writing from personal experience can increase the impact of your argument, but that impact diminishes greatly if readers doubt you are telling the truth. And while the story you tell may be true, it is important that it also be representative—something that has happened to many other people, or something that could happen to your readers. Narrative arguments are useful for illustrating how people are affected by particular issues or events, but they are more effective if you have evidence that goes beyond a single incident.

One rule of thumb that you can keep in mind when building a narrative argument is to start out with as much detail and as many events as you can recall, then revise and edit heavily. It's hard to select the best details and events for your argument until you have written them all down, and often the process of writing and remembering will bring up new details that you had forgotten, or hadn't seen the relevance of before. Once you can see the big picture you have painted with your narrative, it is easier to see what your readers do not need, and remove it. This strategy brings your story, and your argument, into sharper focus.

Finding Good Reasons

Can A Story Make An Argument?

This photo shows a lone polar bear standing atop a small ice floe in the Arctic Ocean. The National Wildlife Federation describes the plight of the polar bear, struggling to survive in the face of a changing climate.

As climate change melts sea ice, the U.S. Geological Survey projects that two-thirds of polar bears will disappear by 2050. This dramatic decline of polar all bears is occurring in our lifetime, which is but a minuscule fraction of the time polar bears have roamed the vast Arctic seas. The retreat of ice has implications beyond the obvious habitat loss. The larger gap of open water between the ice and land also contributes to rougher wave conditions, making the bears' swim from shore to sea ice more hazardous. Exacerbating the problems of the loss of hunting areas, the shrinking polar ice cap will also cause a decline in polar bears' prey—seals. The polar bear is the proverbial "canary in the coal mine" of the serious threat global warming poses to wildlife species around the world, unless we take immediate and significant action to reduce global warming pollution.
National Wildlife Federation, Polar Bear Basics (Factsheet)

Write about it

1. What argument might the National Wildlife Federation be making about the state of climate change? What details reveal this argument?

2. Why might the National Wildlife Federation have chosen the polar bear to personify the effects of climate change? What other types of animals would have made good choices? Poor choices?

3. How does the National Wildlife Federation's account of climate change differ from other accounts that you have heard? What is the other side of this issue? Does this story change your thinking about climate change? Why or why not?

Steps to Writing a Narrative Argument

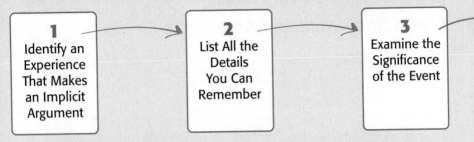

1
Identify an Experience That Makes an Implicit Argument

2
List All the Details You Can Remember

3
Examine the Significance of the Event

Step 1 Identify an Experience That Makes an Implicit Argument

Think about experiences that made you realize that something is wrong or that things need to be changed. The experience does not have to be one that leads to a moral lesson at the end, but it should be one that makes your readers think.

Examples

- Being accused of and perhaps even arrested and hauled to jail for something you didn't do or for standing up for something you believed in.
- Moving from a well-financed suburban school to a much poorer rural or urban school in the same state.
- Experiencing stereotyping or prejudice in any way—for the way you look, the way you act, your age, your gender, your race, or your sexual orientation.

Step 2 List All the Details You Can Remember

- When did it happen?
- How old were you?
- Why were you there?
- Who else was there?
- Where did it happen? If the place is important, describe what it looked like.
- What did it all sound like? smell like? taste like?

Step 3 Examine the Significance of the Event

- How did you feel about the experience when it happened?
- How did it affect you then?
- How do you feel about the experience now?
- What long-term effects has it had on your life?

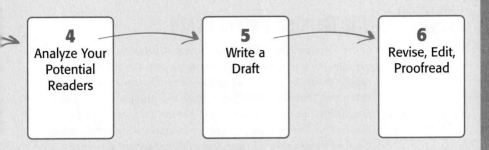

Step 4 Analyze Your Potential Readers

- Who are your readers?
- How much will your readers know about the background of the experience you are describing?
- Would anything similar ever likely have happened to them?
- How likely are they to agree with your feelings about the experience?

Step 5 Write a Draft

- You might need to give some background first, but if you have a compelling story, often it's best to launch right in.
- You might want to tell the story as it happened (chronological order), or you might want to begin with a striking incident and then go back to tell how it happened (flashback).
- You might want to reflect on your experience at the end, but you want your story to do most of the work. Avoid drawing a simple moral lesson. Your readers should share your feelings if you tell your story well.

Step 6 Revise, Edit, Proofread

- For detailed instructions, see Chapter 4.
- For a checklist to use to evaluate your draft, see pages 48–49.

Leslie Marmon Silko

The Border Patrol State

Leslie Marmon Silko (1948–) was born in Albuquerque and graduated from the University of New Mexico. She has received much critical acclaim for her writings about Native Americans. Her first novel, *Ceremony* (1977), describes the struggles of a veteran returning home after World War II to civilian life on a New Mexico reservation. Her incorporation of Indian storytelling techniques in *Ceremony* drew strong praise. One critic called her "the most accomplished Indian writer of her generation." She has since published two more novels, *Almanac of the Dead* (1991) and *Gardens in the Dunes* (1999); a collection of essays, *Yellow Woman* and a *Beauty of the Spirit: Essays on Native American Life Today* (1996); two volumes of poems and stories; and many shorter works. Silko's talents as a storyteller are evident in this essay, which first appeared in the magazine *The Nation* in 1994.

I used to travel the highways of New Mexico and Arizona with a wonderful sensation of absolute freedom as I cruised down the open road and across the vast desert plateaus. On the Laguna Pueblo reservation, where I was raised, the people were patriotic despite the way the U.S. government had treated Native Americans. As proud citizens, we grew up believing the freedom to travel was our inalienable right, a right that some Native Americans had been denied in the early twentieth century. Our cousin, old Bill Pratt, used to ride his horse 300 miles overland from Laguna, New Mexico, to Prescott, Arizona, every summer to work as a fire lookout.

2   In school in the 1950s, we were taught that our right to travel from state to state without special papers or threat of detainment was a right that citizens under communist and totalitarian governments did not possess. That wide open highway told us we were U.S. citizens; we were free. . . .

3   Not so long ago, my companion Gus and I were driving south from Albuquerque, returning to Tucson after a book promotion for the paperback edition of my novel *Almanac of the Dead*. I had settled back and gone to sleep while Gus drove, but I was awakened when I felt the car slowing to a stop. It was nearly midnight on New Mexico State Road 26, a dark, lonely stretch of two-lane highway between Hatch and Deming. When I sat up, I saw the headlights and emergency flashers of six vehicles—Border Patrol cars and a van were blocking both lanes of the highway. Gus

Silko establishes freedom of travel as a fundamental human, as well as American, right—an important assumption underlying her argument.

stopped the car and rolled down the window to ask what was wrong. But the closest Border Patrolman and his companion did not reply; instead, the first agent ordered us to "step out of the car." Gus asked why, but his question seemed to set them off. Two more Border Patrol agents immediately approached our car, and one of them snapped, "Are you looking for trouble?" as if he would relish it.

Specific details paint a vivid picture of the experience and establish credibility.

4   I will never forget that night beside the highway. There was an awful feeling of menace and violence straining to break loose. It was clear that the uniformed men would be only too happy to drag us out of the car if we did not speedily comply with their request (asking a question is tantamount to resistance, it seems). So we stepped out of the car and they motioned for us to stand on the shoulder of the road. The night was very dark, and no other traffic had come down the road since we had been stopped. All I could think about was a book I had read—*Nunca Mas*—the official report of a human rights commission that investigated and certified more than 12,000 "disappearances" during Argentina's "dirty war" in the late 1970s.

5   The weird anger of these Border Patrolmen made me think about descriptions in the report of Argentine police and military officers who became addicted to interrogation, torture and the murder that followed. When the military and police ran out of political suspects to torture and kill, they resorted to the random abduction of citizens off the streets. I thought how easy it would be for the Border Patrol to shoot us and leave our bodies and car beside the highway, like so many bodies found in these parts and ascribed to "drug runners."

Silko connects her experience with border patrol to more extreme incidents to establish the potential danger inherent in these searches.

6   Two other Border Patrolmen stood by the white van. The one who had asked if we were looking for trouble ordered his partner to "get the dog," and from the back of the van another patrolman brought a small female German shepherd on a leash. The dog apparently did not heel well enough to suit him, and the handler jerked the leash. They opened the doors of our car and pulled the dog's head into it, but I saw immediately from the expression in her eyes that the dog hated them, and that she would not serve them. When she showed no interest in the inside of the car, they brought her around back to the trunk, near where we were standing. They half-dragged her up into the trunk, but still she did not indicate any stowed-away human beings or illegal drugs.

7   The mood got uglier; the officers seemed outraged that the dog could not find any contraband, and they dragged her over to us and commanded her to sniff our legs and feet. To my relief, the

strange violence the Border Patrol agents had focused on us now seemed shifted to the dog. I no longer felt so strongly that we would be murdered. We exchanged looks—the dog and I. She was afraid of what they might do, just as I was. The dog's handler jerked the leash sharply as she sniffed us, as if to make her perform better, but the dog refused to accuse us: She had an innate dignity that did not permit her to serve the murderous impulses of those men. I can't forget the expression in the dog's eyes; it was as if she were embarrassed to be associated with them. I had a small amount of medicinal marijuana in my purse that night, but she refused to expose me. I am not partial to dogs, but I will always remember the small German shepherd that night.

Silko implicitly asks, If even the dog recognizes the border patrol's barbarity, how can any reasonable person defend their actions?

8   Unfortunately, what happened to me is an everyday occurrence here now. Since the 1980s, on top of greatly expanding border checkpoints, the Immigration and Naturalization Service and the Border Patrol have implemented policies that interfere with the rights of U.S. citizens to travel freely within our borders. I.N.S. agents now patrol all interstate highways and roads that lead to or from the U.S.–Mexico border in Texas, New Mexico, Arizona and California. Now, when you drive east from Tucson on Interstate 10 toward El Paso, you encounter an I.N.S. check station outside Las Cruces, New Mexico. When you drive north from Las Cruces up Interstate 25, two miles north of the town of Truth or Consequences, the highway is blocked with orange emergency barriers, and all traffic is diverted into a two-lane Border Patrol checkpoint—ninety-five miles north of the U.S.–Mexico border.

9   I was detained once at Truth or Consequences, despite my and my companion's Arizona driver's licenses. Two men, both Chicanos, were detained at the same time, despite the fact that they too presented ID and spoke English without the thick Texas accents of the Border Patrol agents. While we were stopped, we watched as other vehicles—whose occupants were white—were waved through the checkpoint. White people traveling with brown people, however, can expect to be stopped on suspicion they work with the sanctuary movement, which shelters refugees. White people who appear to be clergy, those who wear ethnic clothing or jewelry and women with very long hair or very short hair (they could be nuns) are also frequently detained; white men with beards or men with long hair are likely to be detained, too, because Border Patrol agents have "profiles" of "those sorts" of white people who may help political refugees. (Most of the political refugees from Guatemala and El Salvador are Native American or mestizo because the indigenous people of the Americas have continued to resist efforts by invaders to displace them from their

ancestral lands.) Alleged increases in illegal immigration by people of Asian ancestry mean that the Border Patrol now routinely detains anyone who appears to be Asian or part Asian, as well.

Have you ever crossed an international border? What experiences have you had?

10   Once your car is diverted from the Interstate Highway into the checkpoint area, you are under the control of the Border Patrol, which in practical terms exercises a power that no highway patrol or city patrolman possesses: They are willing to detain anyone, for no apparent reason. Other law-enforcement officers need a shred of probable cause in order to detain someone. On the books, so does the Border Patrol; but on the road, it's another matter. They'll order you to stop your car and step out; then they'll ask you to open the trunk. If you ask why or request a search warrant, you'll be told that they'll have to have a dog sniff the car before they can request a search warrant, and the dog might not get there for two or three hours. The search warrant might require an hour or two past that. They make it clear that if you force them to obtain a search warrant for the car, they will make you submit to a strip search as well.

11   Traveling in the open, though, the sense of violation can be even worse. Never mind high-profile cases like that of former Border Patrol agent Michael Elmer, acquitted of murder by claiming self-defense, despite admitting that as an officer he shot an "illegal" immigrant in the back and then hid the body, which remained undiscovered until another Border Patrolman reported the event. (Last month, Elmer was convicted of reckless endangerment in a separate incident, for shooting at least ten rounds from his M-16 too close to a group of immigrants as they were crossing illegally into Nogales in March 1992.) Or that in El Paso a high school football coach driving a vanload of players in full uniform was pulled over on the freeway and a Border Patrol agent put a cocked revolver to his head. (The football coach was Mexican-American, as were most of the players in his van; the incident eventually caused a federal judge to issue a restraining order against the Border Patrol.) We've a mountain of personal experiences like that which never make the newspapers. A history professor at U.C.L.A. told me she had been traveling by train from Los Angeles to Albuquerque twice a month doing research. On each of her trips, she had noticed that the Border Patrol agents were at the station in Albuquerque scrutinizing the passengers. Since she is six feet tall and of Irish and German ancestry, she was not particularly concerned. Then one day when she stepped off the train in Albuquerque, two Border Patrolmen accosted her, wanting to know what she was doing, and why she was traveling between Los Angeles and Albuquerque twice a month. She

In paragraphs 11 and 12, Silko offers additional stories to exemplify the unnerving nature of these searches.

presented identification and an explanation deemed "suitable" by the agents, and was allowed to go about her business.

12   Just the other day, I mentioned to a friend that I was writing this article and he told me about his 73-year-old father, who is half Chinese and who had set out alone by car from Tucson to Albuquerque the week before. His father had become confused by road construction and missed a turnoff from Interstate 10 to Interstate 25; when he turned around and circled back, he missed the turnoff a second time. But when he looped back for yet another try, Border Patrol agents stopped him and forced him to open his trunk. After they satisfied themselves that he was not smuggling Chinese immigrants, they sent him on his way. He was so rattled by the event that he had to be driven home by his daughter.

13   This is the police state that has developed in the southwestern United States since the 1980s. No person, no citizen, is free to travel without the scrutiny of the Border Patrol. In the city of South Tucson, where 80 percent of the respondents were Chicano or Mexicano, a joint research project by the University of Wisconsin and the University of Arizona recently concluded that one out of every five people there had been detained, mistreated verbally or nonverbally, or questioned by I.N.S. agents in the past two years.

Silko uses statistics from a research study conducted by respected universities as evidence for her claim.

14   Manifest Destiny may lack its old grandeur of theft and blood—"lock the door" is what it means now, with racism a trump card to be played again and again, shamelessly, by both major political parties. "Immigration," like "street crime" and "welfare fraud," is a political euphemism that refers to people of color. Politicians and media people talk about "illegal aliens" to dehumanize and demonize undocumented immigrants, who are for the most part people of color. Even in the days of Spanish and Mexican rule, no attempts were made to interfere with the flow of people and goods from south to north and north to south. It is the U.S. government that has continually attempted to sever contact between the tribal people north of the border and those to the south.[1]

Having established the injustice of U.S. methods for defending its borders, Silko changes her focus to question the idea of borders themselves.

15   Now that the "Iron Curtain" is gone, it is ironic that the U.S. government and its Border Patrol are constructing a steel wall ten feet high to span sections of the border with Mexico. While politicians and multinational corporations extol the virtues of NAFTA and "free trade" (in goods, not flesh), the ominous curtain is already up in a six-mile section at the border crossing at Mexicali; two miles are being erected but are not yet finished at Naco; and at Nogales, sixty miles south of Tucson, the steel wall has been

all rubber-stamped and awaits construction likely to begin in March. Like the pathetic multimillion-dollar "antidrug" border surveillance balloons that were continually deflated by high winds and made only a couple of meager interceptions before they blew away, the fence along the border is a theatrical prop, a bit of pork for contractors. Border entrepreneurs have already used blowtorches to cut passageways through the fence to collect "tolls," and are doing a brisk business. Back in Washington, the I.N.S. announces a $300 million computer contract to modernize its record-keeping and Congress passes a crime bill that shunts $255 million to the I.N.S. for 1995, $181 million earmarked for border control, which is to include 700 new partners for the men who stopped Gus and me in our travels, and the history professor, and my friend's father, and as many as they could from South Tucson.

Silko extends her thesis further.

16   It is no use; borders haven't worked, and they won't work, not now, as the indigenous people of the Americas reassert their kinship and solidarity with one another. A mass migration is already under way; its roots are not simply economic. The Uto–Aztecan languages are spoken as far north as Taos Pueblo near the Colorado border, all the way south to Mexico City. Before the arrival of the Europeans, the indigenous communities throughout this region not only conducted commerce, the people shared cosmologies, and oral narratives about the Maize Mothers, the Twin Brothers and their Grandmother, Spider Woman, as well as Quetzalcoatl the benevolent snake. The great human migration within the Americas cannot be stopped; human beings are natural forces of the Earth, just as rivers and winds are natural forces.

17   Deep down the issue is simple: The so-called "Indian Wars" from the days of Sitting Bull and Red Cloud have never really ended in the Americas. The Indian people of southern Mexico, of Guatemala and those left in El Salvador, too, are still fighting for their lives and for their land against the "cavalry" patrols sent out by the governments of those lands. The Americas are Indian country, and the "Indian problem" is not about to go away.

18   One evening at sundown, we were stopped in traffic at a railroad crossing in downtown Tucson while a freight train passed us, slowly gaining speed as it headed north to Phoenix. In the twilight I saw the most amazing sight: Dozens of human beings, mostly young men, were riding the train; everywhere, on flat cars, inside open boxcars, perched on top of boxcars, hanging off ladders on tank cars and between boxcars. I couldn't count fast

Silko concludes with another story as evidence for her thesis that people cannot be bound by artificial borders.

enough, but I saw fifty or sixty people headed north. They were dark young men, Indian and mestizo; they were smiling and a few of them waved at us in our cars. I was reminded of the ancient story of Aztlán, told by the Aztecs but known in other Uto–Aztecan communities as well. Aztlán is the beautiful land to the north, the origin place of the Aztec people. I don't remember how or why the people left Aztlán to journey farther south, but the old story says that one day, they will return.

1. The Treaty of Guadalupe Hidalgo, signed in 1848, recognizes the right of the Tohano O'Odom (Papago) people to move freely across the U.S.-Mexico border without documents. A treaty with Canada grants similar rights to those of the Iroquois nation in traversing the U.S.-Canada border.

For additional writing resources that will help you master the objectives of this chapter, go to your **MyLab**.

12 | Rebuttal Arguments

Whaling is an ancient form of hunting that greatly expanded in the nineteenth century due to a worldwide demand for whale oil. By 1986 the worldwide whale populations were so seriously depleted that the International Whaling Committee banned commercial whaling to allow whale populations to replenish. Limited whaling continues for scientific research, but environmental organizations such as Greenpeace insist that "science" is a guise for the continuation of commercial whaling. Greenpeace protests all whaling vigorously—both by peaceful means and by open ocean confrontations with whaling vessels. Could their protests at sea be considered a rebuttal argument?

Understand How Rebuttal Arguments Work

There are two basic approaches to rebutting an argument: you can refute the argument, or you can counterargue. In the first case, **refutation**, you demonstrate the shortcomings of the argument you wish to discredit, and you may or may not offer a positive claim of your own. In the second case, **counterargument**, you focus on the strengths of the position you support, and spend little time on the specifics of the argument you are countering. There can be substantial overlap between these two tactics, and good rebuttal arguments often employ both refutation and counterargument.

Because they focus on the shortcomings in the opposition's argument, a refutation argument often takes much of its structure from the argument being refuted.

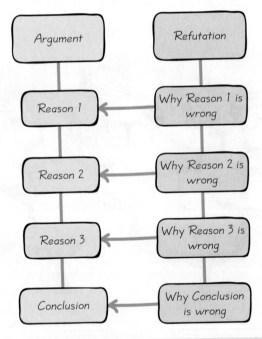

Many college students believe that using technology to "multitask" makes them more productive, believing that studying, texting a friend, and listening to music all at once is an efficient use of their time. But research shows that engaging in multiple tasks is distracting, interferes with memory, and makes it difficult to switch from one task to another, making multitaskers less productive than people focusing on one task at a time.

Counterarguments more often take up ideas the opposing claims has not addressed at all, or they take a very different approach to the problem. By largely ignoring the specifics of the argument being countered, they make the implicit claim that the counterargument is superior.

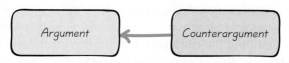

Those who argue for tariffs on goods from China claim that tariffs will protect American manufacturing jobs, but tariffs are a bad idea because they would increase prices on clothing, furniture, toys, and other consumer goods for everyone, and would cause the loss of retailing jobs as well.

Recognize Kinds of Rebuttal Arguments

Refutation

A refutation can either challenge the assumptions underlying a claim, or it can question the evidence supporting a claim. Until about five hundred years ago, people believed that the sky, and everything in it, moved, while the Earth remained still. They observed the stars moving from west to east in a regular, circular motion, and concluded that all the heavenly bodies orbited around an axis between Earth and Polaris, the northern star. This theory, however, did not explain the movement of the planets. If you watch the path of Mars over several nights, for example, you will notice that it moves, like the stars, from east to west. But occasionally, it will appear to move backward, from west to east, before reversing itself and resuming an east-to-west course. This phenomenon is called retrograde motion, and it is exhibited by all the planets in our solar system. In fact, our word *planet* derives from the Greek term *planetes*, meaning "wanderer." The ancient Greeks assumed that the planets and stars orbited the Earth, but that the planets sometimes wandered from their paths.

In the second century CE, the Greek astronomer Ptolemy made precise and detailed observations of the planets and created a model to predict their retrograde motion. In his treatise, the *Almagest*, he theorized that Mars and the other "wanderers" periodically deviated from their path around the Earth, making small circles, or epicycles, before moving on again. It was a complicated system, but it predicted the movements of the planets very accurately, and so it went unchallenged for over a thousand years.

In the early sixteenth century, the Polish astronomer Nicolaus Copernicus recognized that Ptolemy's observations could be explained more simply if the Earth and other planets circled the Sun. Copernicus's theory, later confirmed by the German astronomer Johannes Kepler, eventually replaced the Ptolemaic model of the solar system as the accepted explanation for observed planetary motion.

Copernicus did not question Ptolemy's evidence—the data he had collected showing where the stars and planets appear in the sky to an Earth-bound observer. Instead, he questioned Ptolemy's central assumption that Earth is the center of the solar system. Because evidence of the planet's retrograde motion had been observed by people over such a long period of time, it was unlikely to be wrong. Instead, it was the theory Ptolemy constructed to explain his data that was incorrect.

But sometimes evidence is wrong. Sometimes, too, evidence is incomplete or not representative, and sometimes counterevidence can be found. People who are bent on persuading others may leave out information that weakens their case, or employ evidence in questionable ways to try to bolster their claims. Dermatologists argue that indoor tanning is harmful to people's health because it exposes them to ultraviolet radiation, a known cause of cancer. The tanning industry, not surprisingly, disagrees, arguing that indoor tanning is safer than outdoor tanning because it assures safe levels of UV radiation exposure. While sunbathers often get sunburned, indoor tanners only get safe levels of radiation. This is an intriguing claim, but the AMA has discovered that in fact people who use tanning beds *do* get burned—as many of 50 percent of them. The tanning industry also claims indoor tanning provides people with a "protective" tan that reduces the amount of harmful UV radiation they absorb when they do go out in the sun. Doctors counter this claim by pointing out that a "base tan" provides only as much protection as a sunblock with a Sun Protection Factor, or SPF, of 3, and that the minimum recommended SPF for sunscreen is 15. The protection offered by an indoor tan is minimal at best. Both sides continue to argue over what evidence is valid, and accurate, when assessing the safety of indoor tanning.

Counterargument

Another way to rebut is to counterargue. In a counterargument, you might acknowledge an opposing point of view, but you might not consider it in detail. Rather, you put the main effort into your own argument. A counterarguer, in effect, says, "I hear your argument. But there is more to it than that. Now listen while I explain why another position is stronger." Counterargument is an effective way of persuading audiences, but sometimes it is used as a way to avoid addressing opposing views honestly. People's tendency to be persuaded by counterargument also makes them susceptible to red herrings, when an irrelevant but dramatic detail is put forward as if it were important, or *ad hominem* attacks, where someone makes spurious accusations about an opponent instead of engaging in real debate.

The counterarguer depends on the wisdom of his or her audience members to hear all sides of an issue and make up their own minds about the merits of the case. In the following short poem, Wilfred Owen, a veteran of the horrors of World War I trench warfare, offers a counterargument to those who argue that war is noble, to those who believe along with the poet Horace that "dulce et decorum est pro patria mori"—that it is sweet and fitting to die for one's country. This poem gains in popularity whenever there is an unpopular war for it rebuts the belief that it is noble to die for one's country in modern warfare.

Dulce Et Decorum Est

Bent double, like old beggars under sacks,
Knock-kneed, coughing like hags, we cursed through sludge,
Till on the haunting flares we turned our backs
And towards our distant rest began to trudge.
Men marched asleep. Many had lost their boots
But limped on, blood-shod. All went lame; all blind;
Drunk with fatigue; deaf even to the hoots
Of tired, outstripped Five-Nines that dropped behind.

Gas! Gas! Quick, boys! — An ecstasy of fumbling,
Fitting the clumsy helmets just in time;
But someone still was yelling out and stumbling,
And flound'ring like a man in fire or lime . . .
Dim, through the misty panes and thick green light,
As under a green sea, I saw him drowning.
In all my dreams, before my helpless sight,
He plunges at me, guttering, choking, drowning.

If in some smothering dreams you too could pace
Behind the wagon that we flung him in,
And watch the white eyes writhing in his face,
His hanging face, like a devil's sick of sin;
If you could hear, at every jolt, the blood
Come gargling from the froth-corrupted lungs,
Obscene as cancer, bitter as the cud
Of vile, incurable sores on innocent tongues,
My friend, you would not tell with such high zest
To children ardent for some desperate glory,
The old Lie: Dulce et Decorum est
Pro patria mori.

Owen does not summarize the argument in favor of being willing to die for one's country and then refute that argument point by point. Rather, his poem presents an opposing argument, supported by a narrative of the speaker's experience in a poison-gas attack, that he hopes will more than counterbalance what he calls "the old Lie." Owen simply ignores the reasons people give for being willing to die for one's country and argues instead that there are good reasons not to do so. And he hopes that the evidence he summons for his position will outweigh for his audience (addressed as "My friend,") the evidence in support of the other side.

Rebuttal arguments frequently offer both refutation and counterargument. Like attorneys engaged in a trial, people writing rebuttals must make their own cases based on good reasons and hard evidence, but they also do what they can to undermine their opponent's case. In the end the jury—the audience—decides.

Build a Rebuttal Argument

As you prepare to rebut an argument, look closely at what your opponent says. What exactly are the claims? What is the evidence? What are the assumptions? What do you disagree with? Are there parts you agree with? Are there assumptions you share? Do you agree that the evidence is accurate?

Knowing where you agree with someone helps you focus your rebuttal on differences. Having points of agreement can also help you build credibility with your audience, if you acknowledge that your opponent makes some logical points, or makes reasonable assumptions.

Consider using counterargument if you generally agree with a claim but do not think it goes far enough, if you feel an argument proposes the wrong solution to a problem, or if you think that, while accurate, it misses the "big picture." Counterargument lets you frame your own, stronger take on the question at hand without spending a lot of time trying to find flaws in the opposing position when there may not be many in it.

If you do have serious objections to an argument, plan to refute it, and start by looking for the most important differences in your respective positions. What are the biggest "red flags" in the argument you disagree with? What are the weakest points of your opponent's argument? What are the strongest points of your own? You will probably want to highlight these differences in your rebuttal. You may find many problems with evidence and logic, in which case you will probably want to prioritize them. You do not necessarily need to point out the flaws in every single element of an argument. Direct your audience to the ones that matter the most.

You can also use counterargument in combination with refutation, first showing why an existing argument is wrong, and then offering an alternative. This is one of the more common forms of rebuttal. As you examine your opponent's claims and evidence, look closely for fallacies and faulty logic (see pages 17–19). How do these distort the problem or lead the audience to mistaken conclusions? Pointing them out to your readers will strengthen your position.

Look too at sources. Check your opponent's facts. Scrutinize the experts he or she relies on. And consider the purpose and motivation behind arguments you rebut. Groups funded by major industries, political parties, and special interest groups may have hidden or not-so-hidden agendas driving the arguments they make. Pointing these out to your readers can strengthen your own position.

Finding Good Reasons

Can The Web Be Trusted for Research?

Foxtrot *copyright* © *2006 Bill Amend. Reprinted with permission of Universal Uclick. All rights reserved.*

Most Web users are familiar with the huge and immensely popular *Wikipedia*, the online encyclopedia. What makes *Wikipedia* so different from traditional, print encyclopedias is that entries can be contributed or edited by anyone.

In 2007, Jimmy Wales, president of Wikimedia and one of its founders, debated the legitimacy of *Wikipedia* with Dale Hoiberg, editor-in-chief of *Encyclopedia Britannica.* Hoiberg's main criticism of *Wikipedia* is that its structure—an open-source wiki without the formal editorial control that shapes traditional, print encyclopedias—allows for inaccurate entries.

In response, Wales argues that *Britannica* and newspapers also contain errors, but *Wikipedia* has the advantage that they are easily corrected. Furthermore, he asserts that *Wikipedia*'s policy of using volunteer administrators to delete irrelevant entries and requiring authors of entries to cite reliable, published sources ensures quality. Nonetheless, some universities including UCLA and the University of Pennsylvania along with many instructors strongly discourage and even ban students from citing *Wikipedia* in their work. (*Wikipedia* also cautions against using its entries as a primary source for serious research.) For an article critical of Wikipedia as a reliable source, see the essay by John Seigenthaler on pages 629–630.

Write about it

1. If your college decided to ban the use of *Wikipedia* as a reference because it lacked the authority of a traditional encyclopedia, would you want to challenge it? Why or why not?

2. If you chose to challenge the college's policy, how would you do so? Would it be effective to refute the college's claims point by point, noting fallacies in logic and reasoning? Would it be effective to build a counterargument in which you examine the assumptions on which the college's claims are based? Which strategy would you choose, and why?

Steps to Writing a Rebuttal Argument

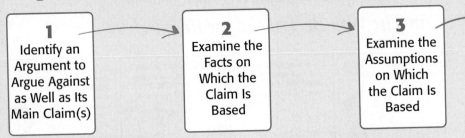

1 Identify an Argument to Argue Against as Well as Its Main Claim(s) → **2** Examine the Facts on Which the Claim Is Based → **3** Examine the Assumptions on Which the Claim Is Based

Step 1 Identify an Argument to Argue Against as Well as Its Main Claim(s)

- What exactly are you arguing against?
- Are there secondary claims attached to the main claim?
- Include a fair summary of your opponent's position in your finished rebuttal.

Examples

- Arguing against raising taxes for the purpose of building a new sports stadium (examine how proponents claim that a new sports facility will benefit the local economy)
- Arguing for raising the minimum wage (examine how opponents claim that a higher minimum wage isn't necessary and negatively affects small-business owners)

Step 2 Examine the Facts on Which the Claim Is Based

- Are the facts accurate, current, and representative?
- Is there another body of facts that you can present as counterevidence?
- If the author uses statistics, can the statistics be interpreted differently?
- If the author quotes from sources, how reliable are those sources?
- Are the sources treated fairly, or are quotations taken out of context?

Step 3 Examine the Assumptions on Which the Claim Is Based

- What are the primary and secondary assumptions of the claim you are rejecting?
- How are those assumptions flawed?
- Does the author resort to name-calling, use faulty reasoning, or ignore key facts (see pages 17–19)?

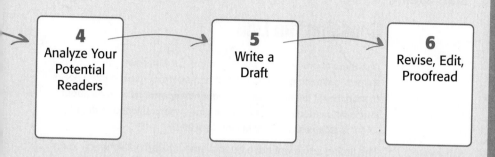

Step 4 Analyze Your Potential Readers

- To what extent do your potential readers support the claim that you are rejecting?
- If they strongly support that claim, how might you appeal to them to change their minds?
- What common assumptions and beliefs do you share with them?

Step 5 Write a Draft

Introduction

Identify the issue and the argument you are rejecting.

- Provide background if the issue is unfamiliar to most of your readers.
- Give a quick summary of the competing positions even if the issue is familiar to your readers.
- Make your aim clear in your thesis statement.

Body

Take on the argument that you are rejecting. Consider questioning the evidence that is used to support the argument by doing one or more of the following.

- Challenge the facts and the currency and relevance of examples.
- Present counterevidence and countertestimony.
- Challenge the credibility of sources cited.
- Question the way in which statistical evidence is presented and interpreted.
- Argue that quotations are taken out of context.

Conclusion

- Conclude on a firm note by underscoring your objections.
- Consider closing with a counterargument or counterproposal.

Step 6 Revise, Edit, Proofread

- For detailed instructions, see Chapter 4.
- For a checklist to use to evaluate your draft, see pages 48–49.

Dan Stein

Crossing the Line

Dan Stein is president of the Federation for American Immigration Reform, a Washington D.C.–based nonprofit organization that seeks to stop illegal immigration. He frequently speaks and writes about immigration issues. "Crossing the Line" was published in the *Los Angeles Business Journal* in February 2007.

Stein uses a fact from a respected polling agency to bolster his assumption that the majority of Americans strongly oppose illegal immigration.

The timing could not have been worse for Bank of America to announce that it would begin issuing credit cards to illegal aliens in Los Angeles. News of Bank of America's decision was published in the *Wall Street Journal* on February 13, the same day that a new Harris Poll revealed that Americans perceive the two greatest threats to their security to be illegal immigration and the outsourcing of American jobs.

2   Even more than the prospect of the Iranians or the North Koreans with nukes, Americans believe that their security is threatened by millions of people pouring across our borders and by corporations that appear willing to sell out the interests of American workers. In one decision, Bank of America managed to pluck two raw nerves by appearing to encourage illegal immigration, while sending the message that it would not let any national interest stand in the way of it making a buck.

3

Stein connects his argument to other issues his audience is likely to relate to.

The Bank of America decision and the overwhelming negative public reaction to it illustrates the growing disconnect between the elite and everyone else in this country. To the elite—including the current occupant of the White House—the traditional idea of the nation has become a bothersome anachronism. To the extent that the entity known as the United States has any relevance at all to them, it is to secure their ability to conduct business and maximize their corporate bottom lines. Concepts of patriotism and loyalty are marketing tools and nothing more.

4   To Bank of America and other large corporations, illegal immigrants are a source of low wage labor and an untapped customer market. It matters not that illegal immigrants are breaking the laws of the United States, taking jobs from and driving down wages for middle class workers, burdening schools (not the ones the children of Bank of America executives attend, of course) and other vital public services. What matters to the banking industry is that the estimated 12 to 15 million illegal aliens living in the United States have purchasing power and that there is money to be made off of serving them.

5   It is true that Bank of America did not create the illegal immigration crisis in the United States, although banking industry decisions to allow illegal aliens to open bank accounts, take out home mortgages and now obtain credit cards has certainly added to the problem. But the fact that the federal government has done little to resolve the problem of illegal immigration does not mean that banks and other business interests have an unfettered right to profit from illegal immigration. Bank of America did not create the illegal drug problem in the United States, but that does not entitle it to market services to the drug cartels, even though it would be enormously profitable to do so.

Stein alludes to the drug industry to assert that corporations' obligation to respect the laws of the country trump their obligation to make a profit.

OVERTLY DISCRIMINATORY

6   The plan to issue credit cards to illegal aliens is also overtly discriminatory, giving a new meaning to their corporate slogan: "Bank of America, Higher Standards" (for some). While American citizens and legal U.S. residents are held to one standard in order to obtain credit, illegal aliens will be held to a lower standard. The plastic that any of us tote around in our wallets required us to open our entire lives to our creditors and to provide verification of our identities and credit-worthiness. In their hunger to make money off of illegal aliens Bank of America is prepared to accept easily counterfeited Mexican matricula cards as proof of identity, and maintaining a checking account for three months as a credit history.

7   Bank of America has obviously felt the sting of a public backlash, as evidenced by their sudden reluctance to discuss it in the media. Some people have gone so far as to pull their accounts out of Bank of America. But given the consolidation of the banking industry generally, and the fact that a handful of banks have a corner on the credit card market, it will require government action to stop financial institutions from pursuing profits in blatant disregard of the law and the public interest.

Stein uses refutation heavily in his rebuttal, never straying too far from the issue: the legality and morality of Bank of America's new policy.

8   Existing federal law clearly prohibits "encouraging or inducing unauthorized aliens to enter the United States, and engaging in a conspiracy or aiding and abetting" people who violate U.S. immigration laws. Products and services specifically marketed to illegal aliens, intended to make it easier to live and work in the U.S. illegally, violate the spirit if not the letter of the law.

9   To Bank of America, illegal aliens are just customers and the United States nothing more than a market. To the American people, illegal immigration and corporate greed are seen as serious threats to their security. Bank of America has provided the proof that both are inexorably intertwined.

Stein summarizes his thesis in the conclusion.

Gregory
Rodriguez

Illegal Immigrants—They're Money

Gregory Rodriguez is a Los Angeles–based Irvine Senior Fellow at the New America Foundation, a nonpartisan think tank in Washington, D.C. He has written widely about issues of national identity, social cohesion, assimilation, race relations, religion, immigration, demographics, and social and political trends. He published "Illegal Immigrants—They're Money," a rebuttal to Dan Stein's article about the Bank of America, as a column in the *Los Angeles Times* on March 4, 2007.

Dan Stein, the premier American nativist and president of the Federation for American Immigration Reform, is shocked, shocked. He's mad at Bank of America for issuing credit cards to illegal immigrants. He says that to Bank of America "and other large corporations, illegal immigrants are a source of low-wage labor and an untapped customer market." You bet they are, and that's the American way.

In paragraphs 2 and 3, Rodriguez defines his vision of the realities of the American dream.

2   Sure, I'm proud to be a citizen of a nation that portrays itself as a refuge for the "tired," "the poor" and the "huddled masses yearning to breathe free." But let's face it, Emma Lazarus, the poet who wrote those words, may have laid it on a bit thick. The truth, no less beautiful in its way, is a little more crass and self-serving. But it wouldn't have sounded nearly as poetic to say, "bring us your able-bodied, poor, hardworking masses yearning for a chance to climb out of poverty, establish a credit history and. . . ." We all love to rhapsodize about immigrants' embrace of the American dream, but it's more like a hard-nosed American deal—you come here, you work your tail off under grueling conditions, and you can try your damnedest to better your lot over time.

3   In their generational struggle for acceptance and security, from outsider to insider and, dare I say, from exploited to exploiter, immigrants could avail themselves of those inalienable rights that stand at the core of our national political philosophy—life, liberty and the pursuit of happiness.

Rodriguez makes a transition to his thesis by pointing out that illegal immigration is a recent construct.

4   But that, of course, was before the invention of illegal immigration.

5   Until the early 1900s, pretty much anybody who wasn't diseased, a criminal, a prostitute, a pauper, an anarchist or a Chinese laborer could gain entrance to the U.S. Between 1880 and 1914, only 1% of a total of 25 million European immigrants were excluded from this country. But after transatlantic crossings had already been halted by World War I, Congress buckled to anti-foreign sentiment and closed the proverbial Golden Door by passing a series of restrictionist laws in 1917, 1921 and 1924.

6   Yet even as the historical front door of the nation was being closed, business interests were busy prying open a new side-door. Only three months after the passage of the Immigration Act of 1917, which required all newcomers to pass a literacy test and pay a head tax, the U.S. Secretary of Commerce waived the regulations for Mexican workers. Thus began America's dishonorable relationship with Mexican immigrant labor.

7   For the next several decades, Mexican workers were brought in when the economy expanded and kicked out when times got bad. They were recruited in the 1920s, only to be deported in the 1930s. They were brought in again during the labor shortage in the 1940s. By the 1950s, one branch of the government recruited Mexican workers, under the illusion that they were "temporary," while another sought to keep them out.

Rodriquez establishes a longstanding tradition of fairweather treatment of Mexican immigrants by U.S. policy.

8   The *piece de resistance* in the creation of the illegal immigrant is the Immigration Act of 1965. Although touted as a great piece of liberal legislation that ended discriminatory immigration barriers, it imposed an annual cap on migrants from the Western Hemisphere that was 40% less than the number that had been arriving yearly before 1965. A decade later, Congress placed a 20,000 limit per country in this hemisphere.

9   In other words, after importing millions of Mexicans over the decades, particularly during the bracero guest-worker program from 1942 to 1963, and establishing well-trod routes to employment north of the border, the U.S. drastically reduced the number of visas available to Mexicans. This reduction, of course, coincided with a rapid rise in Mexico's population. And guess what? When jobs were available on this side of the border, Mexicans just kept coming, whether they had papers or not.

10   Clearly, today as ever, mass migration to the U.S. is being driven by economic need—the immigrants' and our economy's. But the hard-nosed American deal has become unfair because, on top of the handicaps we have always imposed on new arrivals, we've added a rather brutal one—criminal status. Good luck with that pursuit of happiness as you engage in backbreaking labor when your place in society is summed up with that one cutting word, "illegal."

Rodriguez asserts his thesis in this paragraph.

11   No, I'm not advocating open borders. Nor do I believe that immigrants should be guaranteed anything but a chance to achieve their end of the nation's cruel bargain. For hardworking illegal immigrants who've established roots here, we should uphold our end of the bargain and give them a chance to achieve their piece of the American dream. Bank of America is not wrong to give illegal immigrants the tools with which to compete legitimately in the marketplace. We as a nation are wrong for treating all these people as illegitimate.

Rodriquez addresses Stein only briefly in the introduction and here in the conclusion. Why?

Sample Student Rebuttal Argument

Marta Ramos

Professor Jacobs

English 1010

30 April 2012

Oversimplifying the Locavore Ethic

James McWilliams's argument in his book *Just Food* is based on an overly simplistic understanding of the locavore ethic. His claim, that eating locally is an unrealistic goal, fails to take into account the flexibility of locavorism, the ways consumer food preferences drive the free market system, and the realities of food processing infrastructure.

McWilliams's criticism of locavorism would make sense if, as he implies, locavores were a single-minded group of people demanding the complete conversion of the agricultural systems to uniform, regimented local production and consumption. In fact, there is no reason that locavorism has to completely replace the existing agricultural system, and hardly any locavores advocate this. Locavorism, the practice of eating food that is grown locally and in season, is not an all-or-nothing policy. It is a direction in which individuals and communities can move. Locavores.com, a Web site run by the chef Jessica Prentice, who coined the term "locavore," spells out local-eating strategies:

> If not LOCALLY PRODUCED, then ORGANIC.
>
> If not ORGANIC, then FAMILY FARM.
>
> If not FAMILY FARM, then LOCAL BUSINESS.
>
> If not LOCAL BUSINESS, then TERROIR—foods famous for the region they are grown in. ("Guidelines")

This hierarchy of food sources prefers local sources over distant ones, and prioritizes local farms and businesses to receive local food dollars. Eating locally, according to Locavores, represents "A step toward regional food self reliance" ("Top"). Given the political instability of many areas of the world that grow our food and the way energy costs can drastically affect food prices, it makes sense to reduce our dependence on distant food sources. As Jennifer Maiser, one of the founders of the locavore movement, puts it,

---

Ramos identifies the source that she will refute and the source's claim in the first paragraph.

Ramos defines the term "locavore" and asserts that McWilliams misunderstands the movement.

Ramos uses a direct quotation from a respected voice in the locavore community to build credibility.

Locavores are people who pay attention to where their food comes from and commit to eating local food as much as possible. The great thing about eating local is that it's not an all-or-nothing venture. Any small step you take helps the environment, protects your family's health and supports small farmers in your area.

The goal is not to end completely our importation of food.

McWilliams cites Phoenix as an example of why locavorism won't work. Certainly cities like Phoenix, which lacks the water to grow much food, will always rely on external supply chains to feed their populations. But the obstacles to local eating in Phoenix should not prevent residents of San Francisco, Sarasota, or Charleston from eating locally grown foods. Locavorism doesn't have to work everywhere to be beneficial.

In addition to misrepresenting locavorism's goals, McWilliams illogically claims that it cannot meet people's food needs. "At current levels of fruit production," he warns, "apples are the only crop that could currently feed New Yorkers at a level that meets the U.S. Recommended Dietary Allowances" (44). McWilliams is wrong when he claims that if New Yorkers ate locally grown fruits, they could "rarely indulge in a pear, peach, or basket of strawberries" (44). That might be the case if New York farmers continued to grow nothing but apples and grapes. But if some of those crops were replaced with other fruits, New York could have a very diverse supply of produce that would come reasonably close to meeting the nutritional needs of its citizens. In fact, if committed locavores seek out locally grown strawberries, peaches, and pears, and are willing to pay more money for them than they do for apples, local farmers will have sound economic reasons for replacing some of their aging apple trees with peach and pear trees. McWilliams makes locavorism sound impractical because he tries to imagine it working within current agricultural realities. In fact, locavores seek to change the way food is produced and consumed. Moreover, locavorism works toward this change not, as McWilliams suggests, by advocating laws that restrict food producers but by encouraging consumers to vote with their wallets.

McWilliams's argument about New York also rests on the peculiar assumption that every person in the state has to eat the same fruits in

In her refutation Ramos addresses McWilliams's argument point by point.

Ramos quotes McWilliams and then disproves the quoted claim.

Ramos 3

the same amounts in order for locavorism to work. He points out that except for apples and grapes, "every other fruit the state produces is not being harvested at a level to provide all New Yorkers with an adequate supply" (44). McWilliams implies that if you can't grow enough of a crop to supply every single person in the state, there is no point in growing it; however, the goal of locavorism is choice, not total local supply of all food, a fact McWilliams seems to willfully ignore.

> Ramos questions McWilliams's assumptions and finds them lacking.

Finally, McWilliams claims that the cost and inconvenience of processing food locally will prevent communities from moving toward local eating. He notes that "whereas the conventional system of production and distribution has in place a series of large-scale processing centers capable of handling these tasks in a handful of isolated locations," smaller communities do not (45). There are two problems with this argument. First, many of the "processing centers" McWilliams is thinking of *aren't* capable of handling the task of food production. The National Resources Defense Council reports that "from 1995 to 1998, 1,000 spills or pollution incidents occurred at livestock feedlots in 10 states and 200 manure-related fish kills resulted in the death of 13 million fish" ("Facts"). In 2009, Fairbank Farms recalled over half a million pounds of ground beef after nineteen people were hospitalized and two died from E. coli bacteria in the meat (United States). Also in 2009, the King Nut Companies of Solon, Ohio, sickened over 400 people, including three who died, by producing and distributing peanut butter infected with salmonella ("Virginia"). Large-scale processing plants are not a solution to our food security needs. They are part of the problem.

> Ramos addresses the claim that she takes greatest issue with last. She then gives it further emphasis by providing two distinct counterarguments.

Second, the cost of changing the country's food-processing system from large-scale to small-scale is not as prohibitive as McWilliams makes it sound. Factories age. Machines wear out and have to be replaced. Food production facilities are replaced all the time. Newer facilities could easily be built on a smaller, more regional scale. In fact, given the cost of recalls and lawsuits when tainted food is distributed over a large area, food producers have good reason to think about smaller, more localized production and distribution.

McWilliams either does not understand locavorism or understands it and prefers to misrepresent its goals and methods. His arguments in favor of our current food production system ignore both the very real benefits of local eating, and the considerable cost of the existing system.

> Ramos closes with an appeal to the benefits of locavorism.

Ramos 4

Works Cited

"Facts about Pollution from Livestock Farms." *Natural Resources Defense Council*. Natural Resources Defense Council, 15 July 2005. Web. 7 Apr. 2010.

"Guidelines for Eating Well." *Locavores*. Locavores, 3 June 2009. Web. 9 Apr. 2010.

Maiser, Jennifer. "10 Steps to Becoming a Locavore." *PBS: NOW*. Jump Start Productions, 2 Nov. 2007. Web. 8 Apr. 2010.

McWilliams, James E. *Just Food: Where Locavores Get It Wrong and How We Can Truly Eat Responsibly*. New York: Little, Brown, 2009.

"Top Twelve Reasons to Eat Locally." *Locavores*. Locavores, 3 June 2009. Web. 9 Apr. 2010.

United States. Dept. of Health and Human Services. "Multistate Outbreak of E. coli 0157:H7 Infections Associated with Beef from Fairbanks Farms." *Centers for Disease Control and Prevention*. Dept. of Health and Human Services, 24 Nov. 2009. Web. 8 Apr. 2010.

"Virginia, Minnesota Confirms Salmonella Deaths Related to Tainted Peanut Butter." *Fox News*. Fox News Network, 13 Jan. 2009. Web. 10 Apr. 2010.

For additional writing resources that will help you master the objectives of this chapter, go to your **MyLab**.

13 | Proposal Arguments

QUICK TAKE

In this chapter you will learn to

1. Explain how proposal arguments work (see page 185)
2. Recognize how a proposal argument identifies a problem and states a solution that readers find fair, effective, and practical (see page 185)
3. Analyze a specific proposal argument (see page 186)
4. Write an effective proposal argument (see pages 188–189)

The San Francisco Bicycle Coalition, "dedicated to creating safer streets and more livable communities," is an organization whose primary goal is to build a citywide bike network in San Francisco. The success of the coalition's efforts to increase bicycle ridership for commuters created its own problem: Caltrain commuter trains ran out of room for bicycles, and riders were "bumped" because the trains' bike storage cars were filled to capacity. The coalition crafted a new proposal called Bikes On Board to persuade Caltrain to add more bike storage capacity on its trains. The coalition's proposal encourages riders to report "bumps" in order to document exactly how many times cyclists are denied rides on trains due to limited bike storage. This well-defined proposal forms part of a larger campaign and organizational mission encompassing environmental, economic, and personal fitness issues. What local issues inspire you to propose action? How would you go about crafting a proposal argument to promote interest in a cause or solution?

Understand How Proposal Arguments Work

Proposal arguments make the case that someone should do something: "The federal government should raise grazing fees on public lands." "The student union should renovate the old swimming pool in Butler Gymnasium." "All parents should secure their children in booster seats when driving, even for short distances." Proposals can also argue that something should *not* be done, or that people should stop doing something: "The plan to extend Highway 45 is a waste of tax dollars and citizens should not vote for it." "Don't drink and drive."

The challenge for writers of proposal arguments is to convince readers to take action. It's easy for readers to agree that something should be done, as long as they don't have to do it. It's much harder to get readers involved with the situation or convince them to spend their time or money trying to carry out the proposal. A successful proposal argument conveys a sense of urgency to motivate readers, and describes definite actions they should take.

The key to a successful proposal is using good reasons to convince readers that if they act, something positive will happen (or something negative will be avoided). If your readers believe that taking action will benefit them, they are more likely to help bring about what you propose.

Proposal arguments take the form shown here:

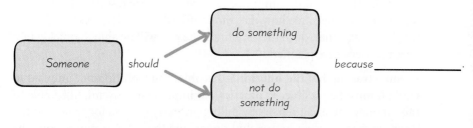

We should *convert existing train tracks in the downtown areas to a light-rail system and build a new freight track around the city* because we need to relieve traffic and parking congestion downtown.

Recognize Components of Proposal Arguments

Most successful proposals have four major components.

- **Identifying and defining the problem.** Sometimes, your audience is already fully aware of the problem you want to solve. If your city frequently tears up streets and then leaves them for months without fixing them, you shouldn't have to spend much time convincing citizens that streets should be repaired more quickly. But if you raise a problem unfamiliar to your readers, first you will have to convince them that the problem is real. Citizens will not see the need to replace miles of plumbing lines running under the streets, for example, unless you convince them that the pipes are old and corroded and are a risk to everyone's safety. You will also need to define the scope of the problem— does every single pipe need to be replaced, or only those more than forty years old? Is this a job for the city, or do federal clean water regulations mean that other government officials must be involved? The clearer you are about what must be done, and by whom, the stronger your argument will be.

- **Stating a proposed solution.** A strong proposal offers a clear, definite statement of exactly what you are proposing. Vague statements that "Something must be done!" may get readers stirred up about the issue, but are unlikely to lead to constructive action. A detailed proposal also adds credibility to your argument, showing that you are concerned enough to think through the nuts and bolts of the changes to be made. You can state your proposed solution near the beginning of your argument (it's in effect your thesis statement), or introduce it later—for example, after you have considered and rejected other possible solutions.

- **Convincing readers that the proposed solution is well considered and fair.** Once your readers agree that a problem exists and a solution should be found, you have to convince them that your solution is the best one. You have to supply good reasons to favor your proposal. Perhaps you want your city to fire the planning committee members who are responsible for street repair. You will need to show that those officials are indeed responsible for the delays, and that, once they are fired, the city will be able to quickly hire new, more effective planners.

- **Demonstrating that the solution is feasible.** Your solution not only has to work; it must be feasible, or practical, to implement. You might be able to raise money for street repairs by billing property owners for repairs to the streets in front of their houses, but opposition to such a proposal would be fierce. Most Americans will object to making individuals responsible for road repair costs when roads are used by all drivers.

You may also have to show how your proposal is better than other possible actions that could be taken. Perhaps others believe your city should hire private contractors to repair the streets more quickly, or reward work crews who finish quickly with extra pay or days off. If there are multiple proposed solutions, all perceived as equally good, then there is no clear course of action for your audience to work for. Very often, that means nothing will happen. Take a clear stand.

Build a Proposal Argument

At this moment, you might not think that you feel strongly enough about anything to write a proposal argument. But if you write a list of things that make you mad or at least a little annoyed, then you have a start toward writing a proposal argument. Some things on your list are not going to produce proposal arguments that many people would want to read. If your roommate is a slob, you might be able to write a proposal for that person to start cleaning up more, but who else would be interested? Similarly, it might be annoying to you that where you live is too far from the ocean, but it is hard to imagine making a serious proposal to move your city closer to the coast. Short of those extremes, however, are many things that might make you think, "Why hasn't someone done something about this?" If you believe that others have something to gain if a problem is solved, or at least that the situation can be made a little better, then you might be able to develop a good proposal argument.

For instance, suppose you are living off campus, and you buy a student parking sticker when you register for courses so that you can park in the student lot. However, you quickly find out that there are too many cars and trucks for the number of available spaces, and unless you get to campus by 8:00 A.M., you aren't going to find a place to park in your assigned lot. The situation makes you angry because you believe that if you pay for a sticker, you should have a reasonable chance of finding a place to park. You see that there are unfilled lots reserved for faculty and staff next to the student parking lot, and you wonder why more spaces aren't allotted to students. You decide to write to the president of your college. You want her to direct parking and traffic services to give more spaces to students or else to build a parking garage that will accommodate more vehicles.

When you start talking to other students on campus, however, you begin to realize that the problem may be more complex than your first view of it. Your college has taken the position that if fewer students drive to campus, there will be less traffic on and around your campus. The administration wants more students to ride shuttle buses, to form car pools, or to bicycle to campus instead of driving alone. You also find out that faculty and staff members pay ten times as much as students for their parking permits, so they pay a very high premium for a guaranteed space—much too high for most students. If the president of your college is your primary audience, you first have to argue that a problem really exists. You have to convince the president that many students have no choice but to drive if they are to attend classes. You, for example, are willing to ride the shuttle buses, but they don't run often enough for you to make your classes, get back to your car that you left at home, and then drive to your job.

Next, you have to argue that your solution will solve the problem. An eight-story parking garage might be adequate to park all the cars of students who want to drive, but parking garages are very expensive to build. Even if a parking garage is the best solution, the question remains: who is going to pay for it? Many problems in life could be solved if you had access to unlimited resources, but very few people—or organizations—have such resources at their command. It's not enough to propose a solution that can resolve the problem. You have to be able to argue for the feasibility of your solution. If you want to argue that a parking garage is the solution to the parking problem on your campus, then you must also propose how to finance the garage.

Steps to Writing a Proposal Argument

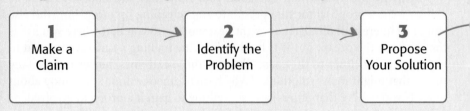

Step 1 Make a Claim

Make a proposal claim advocating a specific change or course of action.

Template

> We should (or should not) do SOMETHING.

Examples

- Redesigning the process of registering for courses, getting e-mail, or making appointments to be more efficient.
- Creating bicycle lanes to make cycling safer and to reduce traffic.
- Streamlining the rules for recycling newspapers, bottles, and cans to encourage increased participation.

Step 2 Identify the Problem

- What exactly is the problem, what causes it, and who is most affected?
- Has anyone tried to do anything about it? If so, why haven't they succeeded?
- What is likely to happen in the future if the problem isn't solved?

Step 3 Propose Your Solution

State your solution as specifically as you can, and support it with good reasons.

- What exactly do you want to achieve?
- What good consequences will follow if your proposal is adopted?
- How exactly will your solution work? Can it be accomplished quickly, or will it have to be phased in over a few years?
- Has anything like it been tried elsewhere? If so, what happened?
- If your solution costs money, how do you propose to pay for it?

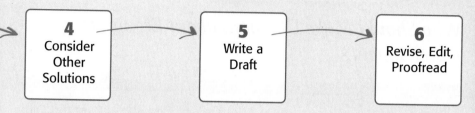

Step 4 Consider Other Solutions

- What other solutions have been or might be proposed for this problem, including doing nothing?
- Why is your solution better?

Step 5 Write a Draft

Introduction

- Set out the issue or problem, perhaps by telling about your experience or the experience of someone you know.
- Argue for the seriousness of the problem.
- Give some background about the problem if necessary.
- State your proposal as your thesis.

Body

- Present your solution. Consider setting out your solution first, explaining how it will work, discussing other possible solutions, and arguing that yours is better. Or consider discussing other possible solutions first, arguing that they don't solve the problem or are not feasible, and then presenting your solution.
- Make clear the goals of your solution. Many solutions cannot solve problems completely.
- Describe in detail the steps in implementing your solution and how they will solve the problem you have identified.
- Explain the positive consequences that will follow from your proposal. What good things will happen, and what bad things will be avoided, if your advice is taken?

Conclusion

- Issue a call to action—if your readers agree with you, they will want to take action.
- Restate and emphasize exactly what readers need to do to solve the problem.

Step 6 Revise, Edit, Proofread

- For detailed instructions, see Chapter 4.
- For a checklist to use to evaluate your draft, see pages 48–49.

Finding Good Reasons

Who Should Make Decisions about Economic Development?

Cape Cod, Massachusetts, is a peninsula that expands from the southern portion of Massachusetts into the Atlantic Ocean. Famous for its beautiful shoreline, Cape Cod is a popular destination for summer vacationers. The Cape Wind Project is a proposed 24-square-mile offshore wind farm that would be built beginning a little less than 5 miles off of the Cape's southern coast. Proponents of the plan cite the benefits of clean energy. Strong opposition, however, has been voiced by the Alliance to Protect Nantucket Sound, which claims that the proposed wind farm will not only destroy property values, but also irrevocably damage the Cape's priceless views, threaten the vital tourist industry, dislocate necessary shipping lanes, disrupt fish populations, and pose a hazard to birds. The Cape Wind Project has brought a prolonged battle in Massachusetts courts that no doubt will continue with a series of appeals.

Write about it

1. If you were the spokesperson for the Cape Wind Project, what reasons would you give to the Massachusetts State Courts to persuade them to begin construction of the wind farm?

2. If you were the spokesperson for the Alliance to Protect Nantucket Sound, what reasons would you give to the Massachusetts State Courts to persuade them to block the construction of the wind farm?

3. If you were a judge on the Massachusetts State Bench, what reasons might you expect to hear from these two groups? Draft a proposal that would win your vote.

Glenn
Loury

A Nation of Jailers

Glenn Loury is Merton P. Stoltz Professor of the Social Sciences at Brown University and a guest on many television and radio news programs. He is the author of *One by One, From the Inside Out: Essays and Reviews on Race and Responsibility in America* (1995), *Anatomy of Racial Inequality* (2001), *Ethnicity, Social Mobility and Public Policy: Comparing the US and the UK* (2005), and over two hundred essays and reviews on racial inequality and social policy.

Instead of immediately announcing his thesis, Loury asks the big question: what is our ideal vision of society?

The most challenging problems of social policy in the modern world are never merely technical. In order properly to decide how we should govern ourselves, we must take up questions of social ethics and human values. What manner of people are we Americans? What vision would we affirm, and what example would we set, before the rest of the world? What kind of society would we bequeath to our children? How shall we live? Inevitably, queries such as these lurk just beneath the surface of the great policy debates of the day. So, those who would enter into public argument about what ails our common life need make no apology for speaking in such terms.

In paragraph 2, Loury narrows the focus to the massive-scale imprisonment of poor Americans.

2   It is precisely in these terms that I wish to discuss a preeminent moral challenge for our time — that imprisonment on a massive scale has become one of the central aspects of our nation's social policy toward the poor, powerfully impairing the lives of some of the most marginal of our fellow citizens, especially the poorly educated black and Hispanic men who reside in large numbers in our great urban centers.

3   The bare facts of this matter — concerning both the scale of incarceration and its racial disparity — have been much remarked upon of late. Simply put, we have become a nation of jailers and, arguably, racist jailers at that. The past four decades have witnessed a truly historic expansion, and transformation, of penal institutions in the United States — at every level of government, and in all regions of the country. We have, by any measure, become a vastly more punitive society. Measured in constant dollars and taking account of all levels of government, spending on corrections and law enforcement in the United States has more than quadrupled over the last quarter century. As a result, the American prison system has grown into a leviathan unmatched in human history. This development should be deeply troubling to anyone who professes to love liberty.

4   Here, as in other areas of social policy, the United States is a stark international outlier, sitting at the most rightward end of

the political spectrum: We imprison at a far higher rate than the other industrial democracies — higher, indeed, than either Russia or China, and vastly higher than any of the countries of Western Europe. According to the International Centre for Prison Studies in London, there were in 2005 some 9 million prisoners in the world; more than 2 million were being held in the United States. With approximately one twentieth of the world's population, America had nearly one fourth of the world's inmates. At more than 700 per 100,000 residents, the U.S. incarceration rate was far greater than our nearest competitors (the Bahamas, Belarus, and Russia, which each have a rate of about 500 per 100,000.) Other industrial societies, some of them with big crime problems of their own, were less punitive than we by an order of magnitude: the United States incarcerated at 6.2 times the rate of Canada, 7.8 times the rate of France, and 12.3 times the rate of Japan.

Comparisons with other nations make a strong argument that the United States has an incarceration problem.

5   The demographic profile of the inmate population has also been much discussed. In this, too, the U.S. is an international outlier. African Americans and Hispanics, who taken together are about one fourth of the population, account for about two thirds of state prison inmates. Roughly one third of state prisoners were locked up for committing violent offenses, with the remainder being property and drug offenders. Nine in ten are male, and most are impoverished. Inmates in state institutions average fewer than eleven years of schooling.

6   The extent of racial disparity in imprisonment rates exceeds that to be found in any other arena of American social life: at eight to one, the black to white ratio of male incarceration rates dwarfs the two to one ratio of unemployment rates, the three to one non-marital child bearing ratio, the two to one ratio of infant mortality rates and the one to five ratio of net worth. More black male high school dropouts are in prison than belong to unions or are enrolled in any state or federal social welfare programs. The brute fact of the matter is that the primary contact between black American young adult men and their government is via the police and the penal apparatus. Coercion is the most salient feature of their encounters with the state. According to estimates compiled by sociologist Bruce Western, nearly 60% of black male dropouts born between 1965 and 1969 had spent at least one year in prison before reaching the age of 35.

Statistics show the degree to which the problem applies to black men.

7   For these men, and the families and communities with which they are associated, the adverse effects of incarceration will extend beyond their stays behind bars. My point is that this is not merely law enforcement policy. It is social policy writ large. And no other country in the world does it quite like we do.

8   This is far more than a technical issue — entailing more, that is, than the task of finding the most efficient crime control policies. Consider, for instance, that it is not possible to conduct a cost-benefit analysis of our nation's world-historic prison buildup over the past 35 years without implicitly specifying how the costs imposed on the persons imprisoned, and their families, are to be reckoned. Of course, this has not stopped analysts from pronouncing on the purported net benefits to "society" of greater incarceration without addressing that question! Still, how — or, indeed, whether — to weigh the costs born by law-breakers — that is, how (or whether) to acknowledge their humanity — remains a fundamental and difficult question of social ethics. Political discourses in the United States have given insufficient weight to the collateral damage imposed by punishment policies on the offenders themselves, and on those who are knitted together with offenders in networks of social and psychic affiliation.

Loury asserts that imprisonment policies cause far greater costs than simply keeping criminals in jail.

9   Whether or not one agrees, two things should be clear: social scientists can have no answers for the question of what weight to put on a "thug's," or his family's, well-being; and a morally defensible public policy to deal with criminal offenders cannot be promulgated without addressing that question. To know whether or not our criminal justice policies comport with our deepest values, we must ask how much additional cost borne by the offending class is justifiable per marginal unit of security, or of peace of mind, for the rest of us. This question is barely being asked, let alone answered, in the contemporary debate.

10   Nor is it merely the scope of the mass imprisonment state that has expanded so impressively in the United States. The ideas underlying the doing of criminal justice — the superstructure of justifications and rationalizations — have also undergone a sea change. Rehabilitation is a dead letter; retribution is the thing. The function of imprisonment is not to reform or redirect offenders. Rather, it is to keep *them* away from *us*. "The prison," writes sociologist David Garland, "is used today as a kind of reservation, a quarantine zone in which purportedly dangerous individuals are segregated in the name of public safety." We have elaborated what are, in effect, a "string of work camps and prisons strung across a vast country housing millions of people drawn mainly from classes and racial groups that are seen as politically and economically problematic." We have, in other words, marched quite a long way down the punitive road, in the name of securing public safety and meting out to criminals their just deserts.

11   And we should be ashamed of ourselves for having done so. Consider a striking feature of this policy development, one that is

crucial to this moral assessment: the ways in which we now deal with criminal offenders in the United States have evolved in recent decades in order to serve expressive and not only instrumental ends. We have wanted to "send a message," and have done so with a vengeance. Yet in the process we have also, in effect, provided an answer for the question: who is to blame for the maladies that beset our troubled civilization? That is, we have constructed a narrative, created scapegoats, assuaged our fears, and indulged our need to feel virtuous about ourselves. We have met the enemy and the enemy, in the now familiar caricature, is *them* — a bunch of anomic, menacing, morally deviant "thugs." In the midst of this dramaturgy — unavoidably so in America — lurks a potent racial subplot.

> Loury introduces a personal narrative argument to give a concrete example to the statistics he has provided.

12   This issue is personal for me. As a black American male, a baby-boomer born and raised on Chicago's South Side, I can identify with the plight of the urban poor because I have lived among them. I am related to them by the bonds of social and psychic affiliation. As it happens, I have myself passed through the courtroom, and the jailhouse, on my way along life's journey. I have sat in the visitor's room at a state prison; I have known, personally and intimately, men and women who lived their entire lives with one foot to either side of the law. Whenever I step to a lectern to speak about the growth of imprisonment in our society, I envision voiceless and despairing people who would have me speak on their behalf. Of course, personal biography can carry no authority to compel agreement about public policy. Still, I prefer candor to the false pretense of clinical detachment and scientific objectivity. I am not running for high office; I need not pretend to a cool neutrality that I do not possess. While I recognize that these revelations will discredit me in some quarters, this is a fate I can live with.

13   So, my racial identity is not irrelevant to my discussion of the subject at hand. But, then, neither is it irrelevant that among the millions now in custody and under state supervision are to be found a vastly disproportionate number of the black and the brown. There is no need to justify injecting race into this discourse, for prisons are the most race-conscious public institutions that we have. No big city police officer is "colorblind" nor, arguably, can any afford to be. Crime and punishment in America have a color — just turn on a television, or open a magazine, or listen carefully to the rhetoric of a political campaign — and you will see what I mean. The fact is that, in this society as in any other, order is maintained by the threat and the use of force. We enjoy our good lives because we are shielded by the forces of law and order upon which we rely to keep the unruly at bay. Yet, in this society to an extent unlike virtually any other, those bearing the

heavy burden of order-enforcement belong, in numbers far exceeding their presence in the population at large, to racially defined and historically marginalized groups. Why should this be so? And how can those charged with the supervision of our penal apparatus sleep well at night knowing that it is so?

14   This punitive turn in the nation's social policy is intimately connected, I would maintain, with public rhetoric about responsibility, dependency, social hygiene, and the reclamation of public order. And such rhetoric, in turn, can be fully grasped only when viewed against the backdrop of America's often ugly and violent racial history: There is a reason why our inclination toward forgiveness and the extension of a second chance to those who have violated our behavioral strictures is so stunted, and why our mainstream political discourses are so bereft of self-examination and searching social criticism. An historical resonance between the stigma of race and the stigma of prison has served to keep alive in our public culture the subordinating social meanings that have always been associated with blackness. Many historians and political scientists — though, of course, not all — agree that the shifting character of race relations over the course of the nineteenth and twentieth centuries helps to explain why the United States is exceptional among democratic industrial societies in the severity of its punitive policy and the paucity of its social-welfare institutions. Put directly and without benefit of euphemism, the racially disparate incidence of punishment in the United States is a morally troubling residual effect of the nation's history of enslavement, disenfranchisement, segregation, and discrimination. It is not merely the accidental accretion of neutral state action, applied to a racially divergent social flux. It is an abhorrent expression of who we Americans are as a people, even now, at the dawn of the twenty-first century.

In this paragraph, Loury makes a causal argument: the present situation is the result of a history of racism in the United States.

15   My recitation of the brutal facts about punishment in today's America may sound to some like a primal scream at this monstrous social machine that is grinding poor black communities to dust. And I confess that these facts do at times leave me inclined to cry out in despair. But my argument is intended to be moral, not existential, and its principal thesis is this: we law-abiding, middle-class Americans have made collective decisions on social and incarceration policy questions, and we benefit from those decisions. That is, we benefit from a system of suffering, rooted in state violence, meted out at our behest. Put differently our society — the society we together have made — first tolerates crime-promoting conditions in our sprawling urban ghettos, and then goes on to act out rituals of punishment against them as some awful form of human sacrifice.

After expressing anger Loury returns to a reasoned argument about public policy.

16   It is a central reality of our time that a wide racial gap has opened up in cognitive skills, the extent of law-abidingness, stabil-

ity of family relations, and attachment to the work force. This is the basis, many would hold, for the racial gap in imprisonment. Yet I maintain that this gap in human development is, as a historical matter, rooted in political, economic, social, and cultural factors peculiar to this society and reflective of its unlovely racial history. That is to say, *it is a societal, not communal or personal, achievement.* At the level of the individual case we must, of course, act as if this were not so. There could be no law, and so no civilization, absent the imputation to persons of responsibility for their wrongful acts. But the sum of a million cases, each one rightly judged fairly on its individual merits, may nevertheless constitute a great historic wrong. This is, in my view, now the case in regards to the race and social class disparities that characterize the very punitive policy that we have directed at lawbreakers. And yet, the state does not only deal with individual cases. It also makes policies in the aggregate, and the consequences of these policies are more or less knowable. It is in the making of such aggregate policy judgments that questions of social responsibility arise.

17   This situation raises a moral problem that we cannot avoid. We cannot pretend that there are more important problems in our society, or that this circumstance is the necessary solution to other, more pressing problems — unless we are also prepared to say that we have turned our backs on the ideal of equality for all citizens and abandoned the principles of justice. We ought to be asking ourselves two questions: Just what manner of people are we Americans? And in light of this, what are our obligations to our fellow citizens — even those who break our laws?

18   Without trying to make a full-fledged philosophical argument here, I nevertheless wish to gesture — in the spirit of the philosopher John Rawls — toward some answers to these questions. I will not set forth a policy manifesto at this time. What I aim to do is suggest, in a general way, how we ought to be thinking differently about this problem. Specifically, given our nation's history and political culture, I think that there are severe limits to the applicability in this circumstance of a pure ethic of personal responsibility, as the basis for distributing the negative good of punishment in contemporary America. I urge that we shift the boundary toward greater acknowledgment of social responsibility in our punishment policy discourse — even for wrongful acts freely chosen by individual persons. In suggesting this, I am not so much making a "root causes" argument — he did the crime, but only because he had no choice — as I am arguing that the society at large is implicated in his choices because we have acquiesced in structural arrangements which work to our benefit and his detriment, and yet which shape his consciousness and sense of identity in such a way that

Loury returns to the question that he set out in the opening paragraph: what is our collective vision of the ideal society?

the choices he makes. We condemn those choices, but they are nevertheless compelling to him. I am interested in the moral implications of what the sociologist Loïc Wacquant has called the "double-sided production of urban marginality." I approach this problem of moral judgment by emphasizing that closed and bounded social structures — like racially homogeneous urban ghettos — create contexts where "pathological" and "dysfunctional" cultural forms emerge, but these forms are not intrinsic to the people caught in these structures. Neither are they independent of the behavior of the people who stand outside of them.

19   Several years ago, I took time to read some of the nonfiction writings of the great nineteenth-century Russian novelist Leo Tolstoy. Toward the end of his life he had become an eccentric pacifist and radical Christian social critic. I was stunned at the force of his arguments. What struck me most was Tolstoy's provocative claim that the core of Christianity lies in Jesus' Sermon on the Mount: You see that fellow over there committing some terrible sin? Well, if you have ever lusted, or allowed jealousy, or envy or hatred to enter your own heart, then you are to be equally condemned! This, Tolstoy claims, is the central teaching of the Christian faith: we're all in the same fix.

Loury makes a surprising move by appealing to the teachings of Jesus.

20   Now, without invoking any religious authority, I nevertheless want to suggest that there is a grain of truth in this religious sentiment that is relevant to the problem at hand: That is, while the behavioral pathologies and cultural threats that we see in society — the moral erosions "out there" — the crime, drug addiction, sexually transmitted disease, idleness, violence and all manner of deviance — while these are worrisome, nevertheless, our moral crusade against these evils can take on a pathological dimension of its own. We can become self-righteous, legalistic, ungenerous, stiff-necked, and hypocritical. We can fail to see the beam in our own eye. We can neglect to raise questions of social justice. We can blind ourselves to the close relationship that actually exists between, on the one hand, behavioral pathology in the so-called urban underclass of our country and, on the other hand, society-wide factors — like our greed-driven economy, our worship of the self, our endemic culture of materialism, our vacuous political discourses, our declining civic engagement, and our aversion to sacrificing private gain on behalf of much needed social investments. We can fail to see, in other words, that the problems of the so-called underclass — to which we have reacted with a massive, coercive mobilization — are but an expression, at the bottom of the social hierarchy, of a more profound and widespread moral deviance — one involving all of us.

21   Taking this position does not make me a moral relativist. I merely hold that, when thinking about the lives of the disadvantaged in our society, the fundamental premise that should guide us is that we are all in this together. *Those* people languishing in the corners of our society are *our* people — they are *us* – whatever may be their race, creed, or country of origin, whether they be the crack-addicted, the HIV-infected, the mentally ill homeless, the juvenile drug sellers, or worse. Whatever the malady, and whatever the offense, we're all in the same fix. We're all in this thing together.

22   Just look at what we have wrought. We Americans have established what, to many an outside observer, looks like a system of racial caste in the center of our great cities. I refer here to millions of stigmatized, feared, and invisible people. The extent of disparity in the opportunity to achieve their full human potential, as between the children of the middle class and the children of the disadvantaged — a disparity that one takes for granted in America — is virtually unrivaled elsewhere in the industrial, advanced, civilized, free world.

23   Yet too many Americans have concluded, in effect, that those languishing at the margins of our society are simply reaping what they have sown. Their suffering is seen as having nothing to do with us — as not being evidence of systemic failures that can be corrected through collective action. Thus, as I noted, we have given up on the ideal of rehabilitating criminals, and have settled for simply warehousing them. Thus we accept — despite much rhetoric to the contrary — that it is virtually impossible effectively to educate the children of the poor. Despite the best efforts of good people and progressive institutions — despite the encouraging signs of moral engagement with these issues that I have seen in my students over the years, and that give me hope — despite these things, it remains the case that, speaking of the country as a whole, there is no broadly based demand for reform, no sense of moral outrage, no anguished self-criticism, no public reflection in the face of this massive, collective failure.

The main work of the essay is getting readers to acknowledge the problem. If the problem is recognized, then various solutions will follow.

24   The core of the problem is that the socially marginal are not seen as belonging to the same general public body as the rest of us. It therefore becomes impossible to do just about anything with them. At least implicitly, our political community acts as though some are different from the rest and, because of their culture — because of their bad values, their self-destructive behavior, their malfeasance, their criminality, their lack of responsibility, their unwillingness to engage in hard work — they *deserve* their fate.

25   But this is quite wrongheaded. What we Americans fail to recognize — not merely as individuals, I stress, but as a political

community — is that these ghetto enclaves and marginal spaces of our cities, which are the source of most prison inmates, are products of our own making: Precisely because we do not want those people near us, we have structured the space in our urban environment so as to keep *them* away from *us*. Then, when they fester in their isolation and their marginality, we hypocritically point a finger, saying in effect: "Look at those people. They threaten to the civilized body. They must therefore be expelled, imprisoned, controlled." It is not *we* who must take social responsibility to reform our institutions but, rather, it is *they* who need to take personal responsibility for their wrongful acts. It is not we who must set our *collective* affairs aright, but they who must get their *individual* acts together. This posture, I suggest, is inconsistent with the attainment of a just distribution of benefits and burdens in society.

26   Civic inclusion has been the historical imperative in Western political life for 150 years. And yet — despite our self-declared status as a light unto the nations, as a beacon of hope to freedom-loving peoples everywhere — despite these lofty proclamations, which were belied by images from the rooftops in flooded New Orleans in September 2005, and are contradicted by our overcrowded prisons — the fact is that this historical project of civic inclusion is woefully incomplete in these United States.

27   At every step of the way, reactionary political forces have declared the futility of pursuing civic inclusion. Yet, in every instance, these forces have been proven wrong. At one time or another, they have derided the inclusion of women, landless peasants, former serfs and slaves, or immigrants more fully in the civic body. Extending to them the franchise, educating their children, providing health and social welfare to them has always been controversial. But this has been the direction in which the self-declared "civilized" and wealthy nations have been steadily moving since Bismarck, since the revolutions of 1848 and 1870, since the American Civil War with its Reconstruction Amendments, since the Progressive Era and through the New Deal on to the Great Society. This is why we have a progressive federal income tax and an estate tax in this country, why we feed, clothe and house the needy, why we (used to) worry about investing in our cities' infrastructure, and in the human capital of our people. What the brutal facts about punishment in today's America show is that *this American project of civic inclusion remains incomplete*. Nowhere is that incompleteness more evident than in the prisons and jails of America. And this as yet unfulfilled promise of American democracy reveals a yawning chasm between an ugly and uniquely American reality, and our nation's exalted image of herself.

Loury proposes that if Americans would embrace the ideals of the United States, the conditions that lead to massive-scale imprisonment would change.

Sample Student Proposal Argument

Lee 1

Kim Lee

Professor Patel

RHE 306

31 March 2009

Let's Make It a Real Melting Pot with Presidential Hopes for All

The image the United States likes to advertise is a country that embraces diversity and creates a land of equal opportunity for all. As the Statue of Liberty cries out, "give me your tired, your poor, your huddled masses yearning to breathe free," American politicians gleefully evoke such images to frame the United States as a bastion for all things good, fair, and equal. As a proud American, however, I must nonetheless high-light one of the cracks in this façade of equality. Imagine that an infertile couple decides to adopt an orphaned child from China. They follow all of the legal processes deemed necessary by both countries. They fly abroad and bring home their (once parentless) six-month-old baby boy. They raise and nurture him, and while teaching him to embrace his ethnicity, they also teach him to love Captain Crunch, baseball, and *The Three Stooges*. He grows and eventually attends an ethnically diverse American public school. One day his fifth-grade teacher tells the class that anyone can grow up to be president. To clarify her point, she turns to the boy, knowing his background, and states, "No, you could not be president, Stu, but you could still be a senator. That's something to aspire to!" How do Stu's parents explain this rule to this American-raised child? This scenario will become increasingly common, yet as the Constitution currently reads, only "natural-born" citizens may run for the offices of president and vice president. Neither these children nor the thousands of hardworking Americans who chose to make America their official homeland may aspire to the highest political position in the land. While the huddled masses may enter, it appears they must retain a second-class citizen ranking.

The "natural-born" stipulation regarding the presidency stems from the self-same meeting of minds that brought the American people the

> Lee sets out the problem with a concrete scenario.

Lee 2

Electoral College. During the Constitutional Convention of 1787, the
Congress formulated the regulatory measures associated with the office of
the president. A letter sent from John Jay to George Washington during
this period reads as follows:

> "Permit me to hint," Jay wrote, "whether it would not be wise
> and seasonable to provide a strong check to the admission of
> foreigners into the administration of our national government;
> and to declare expressly that the Commander in Chief of the
> American army shall not be given to, nor devolve on, any but a
> natural-born citizen." (Mathews A1)

Shortly thereafter, Article II, Section I, Clause V, of the Constitution
declared that "No Person except a natural born Citizen, or a Citizen of the
United States at the time of the Adoption of this Constitution, shall be
eligible to the Office of President." Jill A. Pryor states in the *Yale Law
Journal* that "some writers have suggested that Jay was responding to
rumors that foreign princes might be asked to assume the presidency"
(881). Many cite disastrous examples of foreign rule in the eighteenth
century as the impetus for the "natural-born" clause. For example, in
1772—only fifteen years prior to the adoption of the statute—Poland
had been divided up by Prussia, Russia, and Austria (Kasindorf). Perhaps
an element of self-preservation and not ethnocentrism led to the
questionable stipulation. Nonetheless, in the twenty-first century this
clause reeks of xenophobia.

> Lee gives the historical background of the "natural-born" restriction.

The Fourteenth Amendment clarified the difference between "natural-born"
and "native-born" citizens by spelling out the citizenship status of
children born to American parents outside of the United States (Ginsberg
929). This clause qualifies individuals such as Senator John McCain—born
in Panama—for presidency. This change, however, is not adequate. I propose
that the United States abolish the natural-born clause and replace it with
a stipulation that allows naturalized citizens to run for president. This
amendment would state that a candidate must have been naturalized and
must have lived in residence in the United States for a period of at least
twenty-five years. The present time is ideal for this change. This amendment
could simultaneously honor the spirit of the Constitution, protect and ensure

> Lee states her proposal in this paragraph.

the interests of the United States, promote an international image of inclusiveness, and grant heretofore-withheld rights to thousands of legal and loyal United States citizens.

In our push for change, we must make clear the importance of this amendment. It would not provide special rights for would-be terrorists. To the contrary, it would fulfill the longtime promises of the nation. The United States claims to allow all people to blend into the great stew of citizenship. It has already suffered embarrassment and international cries of ethnic bias as a result of political moves such as Japanese American internment and the Guantanamo Bay detention center. This amendment can help mend the national image as every American takes one more step toward equality. Naturalized citizens have been contributing to the United States for centuries. Many nameless Mexican, Irish, and Asian Americans sweated and toiled to build the American railroads. The public has welcomed naturalized Americans such as Bob Hope, Albert Pujols, and Peter Jennings into their hearts and living rooms. Individuals such as German-born Henry Kissinger and Czechoslovakian-born Madeleine Albright have held high posts in the American government and have served as respected aides to its presidents. The amendment must make clear that it is not about one man's celebrity. Approximately seven hundred foreign-born Americans have won the Medal of Honor and over sixty thousand proudly serve in the United States military today (Siskind 5). The "natural-born" clause must be removed to provide each of these people—over half a million naturalized in 2003 alone—with equal footing to those who were born into citizenship rather than working for it (United States).

Since the passing of the Bill of Rights, only seventeen amendments have been ratified. This process takes time and overwhelming congressional and statewide support. To alter the Constitution, a proposed amendment must pass with a two-thirds "super-majority" in both the House of Representatives and the Senate. In addition, the proposal must find favor in two-thirds (38) of state legislatures. In short, this task will not be easy. In order for this change to occur, a grassroots campaign must work to dispel misinformation regarding naturalized citizens and to force the hands of senators and representatives wishing to retain their congressional

Lee gives examples of people who are qualified to become president yet are ineligible.

Lee explains the process of amending the Constitution and ends with a call for action.

Lee 4

seats. We must take this proposal to ethnicity-specific political groups from both sides of the aisle, business organizations, and community activist groups. We must convince representatives that this issue matters. Only through raising voices and casting votes can the people enact change. Only then can every American child see the possibility for limitless achievement and equality. Only then can everyone find the same sense of pride in the possibility for true American diversity in the highest office in the land.

Lee 5

Works Cited

Ginsberg, Gordon. "Citizenship: Expatriation: Distinction between Naturalized and Natural Born Citizens." *Michigan Law Review* 50 (1952): 926-29. *JSTOR*. Web. 6 Mar. 2009.

Kasindorf, Martin. "Should the Constitution Be Amended for Arnold?" *USA Today* 2 Dec. 2004. *LexisNexis Academic*. Web. 8 Mar. 2009.

Mathews, Joe. "Maybe Anyone Can Be President." *Los Angeles Times* 2 Feb. 2005: A1. *LexisNexis Academic*. Web. 6 Mar. 2009.

Pryor, Jill A. "The Natural Born Citizen Clause and Presidential Eligibility: An Approach for Resolving Two Hundred Years of Uncertainty." *Yale Law Journal* 97.5 (1988): 881-99. Print.

Siskind, Lawrence J. "Why Shouldn't Arnold Run?" *Recorder* 10 Dec. 2004: 5. *LexisNexis Academic*. Web. 10 Mar. 2009.

United States. Dept. of Commerce. Census Bureau. "The Fourth of July 2005." *Facts for Features*. US Dept. of Commerce, 27 June 2005. Web. 17 Mar. 2009.

For additional writing resources that will help you master the objectives of this chapter, go to your **MyLab**.

Designing and Presenting Arguments

PART

4

14 | Designing Multimedia Arguments

QUICK TAKE

In this chapter you will learn to

1. Identify the advantages and disadvantages of different media for reaching your audience (see page 207)

2. Analyze how an image or a graphic communicates to an audience (see page 208)

3. Describe the argument made by an image or a graphic (see page 208)

4. List the elements important to designing a print page (see page 209)

5. Create effective multimedia projects involving images, Web site production, audio, and video (see page 210)

rguments do not communicate with words alone. Even written arguments that do not contain graphics or images have a look and feel that also communicate meaning. Many arguments depend on presenting information visually, in multimedia, or in images, in addition to using written language. Using effective design strategies will make your arguments more engaging and compelling.

Think About Which Media Will Reach Your Audience

Before you graduate from college, likely you will find occasions when you want to persuade an audience beyond your teacher, classmates, and friends—possibly for your work, possibly for an organization you belong to, or possibly because an issue concerns you. You may have a clear sense of your message and the good reasons to support that message. But no matter how good your argument, nothing will happen unless you can command the scarcest commodity in our multitasking world—the attention of your audience.

Most college assignments specify the medium, which is typically a printed paper that you submit to the instructor. In the workplace and in life outside college, the choice of medium often isn't immediately evident. For example, if you want to address a neighborhood issue, would a brochure or a Web site be more effective?

Think about your options.

PRINTED TEXT

- Advantages: Low technological requirements to produce; complex, in-depth arguments are possible.
- Disadvantages: Unless published in an established forum like a newspaper, it can be difficult to get people to read the argument.

WEB SITE

- Advantages: Inexpensive to create and allows images, video, audio, and animations to be embedded.
- Disadvantages: How do people find your Web site among the millions of other sites?

BLOG

- Advantages: Inexpensive to create and many sites host blogs.
- Disadvantages: Requires frequent, interesting content to keep readers coming back.

AUDIO PODCAST

- Advantages: Inexpensive to create and can be downloaded from a Web site.
- Disadvantages: Requires some audio editing skills. Like other Web-based media, you have to have a strategy for getting people to listen.

VIDEO

- Advantages: Can be uploaded to sites like YouTube and Vimeo.
- Disadvantages: Producing quality original video takes time, equipment, and editing skills.

Know When to Use Visual Evidence

Personal computers, digital cameras, scanners, printers, and the Web have made it easy to include images and graphics in writing and link to audio and video. But these technologies don't tell you if, when, or how images and graphics should be used.

Think about what an image or graphic communicates

- **What are your readers' expectations for the medium you are using?** Most essays don't include images; most Web sites and brochures do.

- **What is the purpose for an image or graphic?** Does it illustrate a concept? Does it highlight an important point? Does it show something that is hard to explain with words alone? If you don't know the purpose, you may not need the image.

- **Where should an image or graphic be placed in your text?** Images should be as close as possible to the relevant point in your text.

- **What will readers focus on when they see the image?** Will they focus on the part that matters? If not, you may need to crop the image.

- **What explanation do readers need in order to understand the image?** Provide informative captions for the images and graphics you use, and refer to them in your text.

Think About the Argument an Image Makes

Images don't speak for themselves, but if they are referenced in your text and captioned, they can make supporting arguments. Think strategically when you include arguments.

Say, for example, you are making a proposal argument for more students to become more involved in feeding homeless people in your city. Students are aware that there are homeless people, but many students are not aware of organizations that deliver food to hungry people. You might want to photograph the volunteers instead of homeless people.

Volunteers work to make sandwiches that will be distributed by a food truck to homeless people.

Think about the argument a chart or graph makes

Charts and graphs are useful for visually representing statistical trends and for making comparisons. For example, the rising national debt became a hotly debated issue during the administrations of George W. Bush and Barack Obama. Many graphs were used in the debate to show the dramatic rise of federal debt. But if you want to make a causal argument that lowering the income tax rate for the rich contributed to the rise in the debt, you might use a line graph.

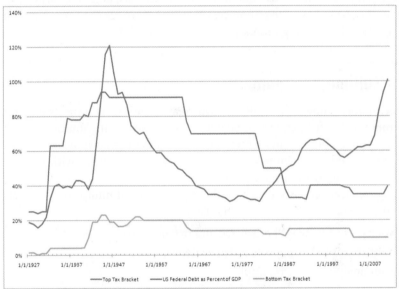

Line graph comparing the national debt with the highest and lowest income tax rates.

Design Arguments for Print

Writing on a computer gives you a range of options for designing a page that is appropriate to your assignment. Thinking about design will lead to a more effective presentation of your argument.

- **Choose the orientation, size of your page, and number of columns.** You can usually use the defaults on your computer for academic essays (remember to select double-spacing for line spacing if the default is single-spaced). For other kinds of texts you may want a horizontal rather than a vertical orientation, a size other than a standard sheet of paper, and two or more columns rather than one.

- **Divide your text into units.** The paragraph is the basic unit of extended writing, but also think about when to use lists. This list is a bulleted list. You can also use a numbered list.

- **Use left-aligned text with a ragged-right margin.** Fully justified text aligns the right margin, which gives a more formal look but can also leave unsightly rivers of extra white space running through the middle of your text. Ragged-right text is easier to read.

■ **Be conscious of white space.** White space can make your text more readable and set off more important elements. Headings stand out more with white space surrounding them. Leave room around graphics. Don't crowd words too close to graphics because both the words and the visuals will become hard to read.

■ **Be aware of MLA and APA design specifications.** MLA and APA styles have specifications for margins, indentions, reference lists, and other aspects of paper formatting. See the sample paper on pages 276–282 for guidelines on designing a paper using MLA style.

Design Multimedia Arguments

Digital technologies now make it possible to create multimedia projects on your home computer that formerly required entire production staffs. You can publish multimedia projects on the Internet (either as Web sites or as downloadable files), as stand-alone media distributed on CDs and DVDs, or in print with posters, brochures, and essays with images.

College viewers and listeners have the expectations of multimedia projects that they do of essays and research papers. They expect

■ your project to be well organized and free of errors,

■ your claims to be supported with evidence,

■ your analysis to be insightful,

■ your sources to be documented, and

■ your work clearly distinguished from the work of others.

Creating multimedia projects

If you decide to create a multimedia project, find out what resources are available for students on your campus. Many colleges and universities have digital media labs, which offer workshops and can provide video and audio studios, technical assistance, equipment, and software. Look for links to digital media services on your college's Web site.

Oral presentation with visuals (see Chapter 15)

Essay with images

■ **Example project**: Evaluation argument concerning the poor condition of parks in your city

■ Plan: Visit several parks, make notes, and take photographs.

■ Produce: Write the project. Edit your images with an image editor and insert them in your project with captions.

■ Edit: Revise with the comments of classmates and your instructor.

Web site production

- **Example project:** Web site making a definition argument that censorship of the Internet is a violation of the right to free speech
- **Plan:** Collect all the materials you will need for your site including text; digital images; graphics; and audio, video, and animation files.
- **Produce:** If you don't have a Web editor on your computer, find a campus lab that has Dreamweaver or similar software. Upload your site to a server. Many colleges offer server space to host student Web sites.
- **Edit:** Test your site to ensure that all links are working and all images and other files are showing up correctly. Edit with a Web editor.

Audio production

- **Example project:** Oral history of neighborhood residents making a causal argument about why a neighborhood declined after a freeway was built through the middle of it
- **Plan:** Arrange and record interviews and write a script.
- **Produce:** Reserve a campus audio production lab or record on your computer. Create an audio file by combining the interviews with your narration.
- **Edit:** Edit with an audio editor. Export the video into a format such as WAV or MP3 that you can put on the Web or share as a downloadable file.

Video production

- **Example project:** Proposal to create bike lanes on a busy street near your campus
- **Plan:** Identify locations, get permission to film if necessary, and write a script.
- **Produce:** Shoot video of the street with cars and bikes competing. Interview cyclists, drivers, and local business owners about their sense of urgency of the problem and the effects of creating bike lanes.
- **Edit:** Edit with a video editor. Export the video into a format such as QuickTime that you can put on the Web or share as a downloadable file.

For additional writing resources that will help you master the objectives of this chapter, go to your **MyLab**.

15 | Presenting Arguments

Plan a Presentation

If you are assigned to give a presentation, look carefully at the assignment for guidance on finding a topic. The process for finding a topic is similar to a written assignment (see Chapter 3). If your assignment requires research, you will need to document the sources of information just as you do for a research paper (see Chapters 16–19).

Start with your goal in mind

What is the real purpose of your presentation? Are you informing, persuading, or motivating? Take the elevator test. Imagine you are in an elevator with the key people who can approve or reject your ideas. Their schedule is very tight. You have only thirty seconds to convince them. Can you make your case?

This scenario is not far-fetched. One executive demanded that every new idea had to be written in one sentence on the back of a business card. What's your sentence?

It's all about your audience

Who is your audience? In college your audience is often your instructor and fellow students—an audience you know well. Many times you will not have this advantage.

Take a few minutes to answer these questions.

- Will my audience be interested in the topic?
- Why does it matter to them?
- What are they likely to know and believe about the topic?
- What are they likely to not know?
- Where are they likely to disagree?
- What do I want them to do?
- How much time do I have?
- If they remember only one thing, what should it be?

Get organized

Start with pen and paper before you begin creating slides. Post-it notes are another useful planning tool.

- **Make a list of key points.** Think about the best order for your major points.
- **Plan your introduction.** Your success depends on your introduction. You must gain the attention of your audience, introduce your topic, indicate why it's important, and give a sense of where you are headed. It's a tall order, but if you don't engage your audience in the first two minutes, you will lose them.
- **Plan your conclusion.** You want to end on a strong note. Stopping abruptly or rambling on only to tail off leaves your audience with a bad impression. Give your audience something to take away, a compelling example or an idea that captures the gist of your presentation.

Build content

Content alone does not make a presentation successful, but you cannot succeed without solid content. Support your major points with relevant evidence.

- **Facts.** Speakers who know their facts build credibility.
- **Statistics.** Effective use of statistics can give the audience the impression that you have done your homework. Statistics can also indicate that a particular example is representative.
- **Statements by authorities.** Quotations from credible experts can support key points.
- **Narratives.** Narratives are brief stories that illustrate key points. Narratives can hold the attention of the audience—but keep them short or they will become a distraction.

Design Visuals for a Presentation

Less is more with slides. One text-filled slide after another is mind-numbingly dull. Presentations using slides don't have to be this bad.

Keep it simple

Imagine you are making an argument that fewer animals would be euthanized at animal shelters if more people in your city knew that they could save a pet's life by adopting it. You could fill your slides with statistics alone. Or you tell your audience the facts while showing them slides that give emotional impact to your numbers.

Simple design rules! Keep in mind these principles:

- One point per slide
- Very few fonts
- Quality photos, not clipart
- Less text, more images
- Easy on the special effects

Compare the following examples.

Pet Overpopulation in the United States

- Estimated number of animals that enter shelters each year: 6-8 million
- Estimated number of animals euthanized at shelters each year: 3-4 million
- Estimated number of animals adopted at shelters each year: 3-4 million

Source: "HSUS Pet Overpopulation Estimates." *Humane Society of the U.S.* Humane Society of the U.S., 9 Nov. 2009. 18 Oct. 2010.

Pet Overpopulation in the United States

- Estimated number of animals entering shelters each year: 6-8 million
- Estimated number of animals euthanized at shelters each year: 3-4 million
- Estimated number of animals adopted at shelters: 3-4 million

Source: "HSUS Pet Overpopulation Estimates." *Humane Society of the U.S.* Humane Society of the U.S., 9 Nov. 2009. Web. 18 Oct. 2010.

Save a pet

Which slide makes the point most effectively?

But what if you have a lot of data to show? Make a handout that the audience can study later. They can make notes on your handout, which gives them a personal investment. Keep your slides simple and emphasize the main points in the presentation.

Use audio and video clips strategically

Short audio and video clips can offer concrete examples and add some variety to your presentation. An audience appreciates hearing and even seeing the people you interview. PowerPoint makes it simple to embed the files within a presentation. Be careful, however, in using the built-in sound effects in PowerPoint such as canned applause. Most sound effects are annoying and make you come off as inexperienced.

Deliver an Effective Presentation

If you are not passionate about your subject, you will never get your audience committed to your subject, no matter how good your slides. Believe in what you say; enthusiasm is contagious.

It's all about you

The audience didn't come to see the back of your head in front of slides. Move away from the podium and connect with them. Make strong eye contact with individuals. You will make everyone feel like you were having a conversation instead of giving a speech.

Prepare in advance

Practice your presentation, even if you have to speak to an empty chair. Check out the room and equipment in advance. If you are using your laptop with a projector installed in the room, make sure it connects. If the room has a computer connected to the projector, bring your presentation on a flash drive and download it to the computer. PowerPoint works much the same on a Mac or Windows platform.

Be professional

Pay attention to the little things.

- **Proofread carefully.** A glaring spelling error can destroy your credibility.
- **Be consistent.** If you randomly capitalize words or insert punctuation, your audience will be distracted.

- **Pay attention to the timing of your slides.** Stay in sync with your slides. Don't leave a slide up when you are talking about something else.

- **Use the "B" key.** If you get sidetracked, press the "B" key, which makes the screen go blank so the audience can focus on you. When you are ready to resume, press the "B" key again and the slide reappears.

- **Involve your audience.** Invite response during your presentation where appropriate, and leave time for questions at the end.

- **Add a bit of humor.** Humor can be tricky, especially if you don't know your audience well. But if you can get your audience to laugh, they will be on your side.

- **Slow down.** When you are nervous, you tend to go too fast. Stop and breathe. Let your audience take in what's on your slides.

- **Finish on time or earlier.** Your audience will be grateful.

- **Be courteous and gracious.** Remember to thank anyone who helped you and the audience for their comments. Eventually you will run into someone who challenges you, sometimes politely, sometimes not. If you remain cool and in control, the audience will remember your behavior long after the words are forgotten.

Convert a Written Text into a Presentation

The temptation when converting a written text into a presentation is to dump sentences and paragraphs onto the slides. Indeed, it's simple enough to cut and paste big chunks of text, but you risk losing your audience.

Make a list of the main points in your written text, and then decide which ones you need to show on slides and which you can tell the audience. Your voice supplies most of the information; your slides help your audience to remember and organize your presentation.

People learn better when your oral presentation is accompanied by engaging images and graphics. Slides can also add emotional involvement.

Unwanted dogs

Carlos

a playful mixed-breed pup who was recently adopted

Arrange your slides so they tell a story. For example, if you are arguing that fewer dogs would be euthanized if your city were more active in promoting adoption, you can show slides that give statistics, or you can report statistics in your presentation while letting your audience identify with individual dogs.

For additional writing resources that will help you master the objectives of this chapter, go to your **MyLab**.

Researching Arguments

PART

5

16 | Planning Research

QUICK TAKE

In this chapter you will learn to

1. Analyze an assignment or research task (see below)
2. Find a subject and develop a research question (see page 221)
3. Gather information through field research, including interviews, surveys, and observations (see page 222)
4. Draft a working thesis to guide you through further research and the development of your argument (see page 225)

Analyze the Research Task

Research is a creative process, which is another way of saying it is a messy process. Even though the process is complex, your results will improve if you keep the big picture in mind while you are immersed in research. If you have an assignment that requires research, look closely at what you are being asked to do.

Look for key words

Often the assignment will tell you what is expected.

- An assignment that asks you, for example, how the usual *definition* of intellectual property applies to YouTube invites you to write a definition argument (see Chapter 8).
- An *analysis of causes* requires you to write a causal argument (see Chapter 9).
- An *evaluation* requires you to make critical judgments based on criteria (see Chapter 10).
- A *proposal* requires you to assemble evidence in support of a solution to a problem or a call for the audience to do something (see Chapter 13).

Identify your potential readers

- How familiar are your readers with your subject?
- What background information will you need to supply?
- If your subject is controversial, what opinions or beliefs are your readers likely to hold?
- If some readers are likely to disagree with you, how can you convince them?

Assess the project's length, scope, and requirements

- What kind of research are you being asked to do?
- What is the length of the project?
- What kinds and number of sources or field research are required?
- Which documentation style is required such as MLA (see Chapter 20) or APA (see Chapter 21)?

Set a schedule

- Note the due dates on the assignment for drafts and final versions.
- Set dates for yourself on finding and evaluating sources, drafting your thesis, creating a working bibliography, and writing a first draft.
- Give yourself enough time to do a thorough job.

Find a Subject

One good way to begin is by browsing, which may also show you the breadth of possibilities included in a topic and possibly lead you to new topics (see Chapter 3).

You might begin browsing by doing one or more of the following.

- **Visit "Research by Subject" on your library's Web site.** Clicking on a subject such as "African and African American Studies" will take you to a list of online resources. Often you can find an e-mail link to a reference librarian who can assist you.
- **Look for topics in your courses.** Browse your course notes and readings. Are there any topics you might want to explore in greater depth?
- **Browse a Web subject directory.** Web subject directories, including *Yahoo Directory* (dir.yahoo.com), are useful when you want to narrow a topic or learn what subcategories a topic might contain. In addition to

the Web subject directories, your library's Web site may have a link to the *Opposing Viewpoints* database.

■ **Look for topics as you read.** When you read actively, you ask questions and respond to ideas in the text. Review what you wrote in the margins or the notes you have made about something you read that interested you. You may find a potential topic.

Ask a Research Question

Often you'll be surprised by the amount of information your initial browsing uncovers. Your next task will be to identify a question for your research project within that mass of information. This **researchable question** will be the focus of the remainder of your research and ultimately of your research project or paper. Browsing on the subject of organic foods, for example, might lead you to one of the following researchable questions.

■ How do farmers benefit from growing organic produce?
■ Why are organic products more expensive than nonorganic products?
■ Are Americans being persuaded to buy more organic products?

Once you have formulated a research question, you should begin thinking about what kind of research you will need to do to address the question.

Gather Information About the Subject

Most researchers rely partly or exclusively on the work of others as sources of information. Research based on the work of others is called **secondary research**. In the past this information was contained almost exclusively in collections of print materials housed in libraries, but today enormous amounts of information are available through library databases and on the Web (see Chapter 17).

Much of the research done at a university creates new information through **primary research**—experiments, examination of historical documents—and **field research**, including data-gathering surveys, interviews, and detailed observations, described below.

Conducting field research

Sometimes you may be researching a question that requires you to gather firsthand information with field research. For example, if you are researching a campus issue such as the impact of a new technology fee on students' budgets, you may need to conduct interviews, make observations, and give a survey.

Interviews

College campuses are a rich source of experts in many areas, including people on the faculty and in the surrounding community. Interviewing experts on your research subject can help build your knowledge base. You can use interviews to discover what the people most affected by a particular issue are thinking, such as why students object to some fees and not others.

Arrange interviews

Before you contact anyone, think carefully about your goals. Knowing what you want to find out through your interviews will help you determine whom you need to interview and what questions you need to ask. Use these guidelines to prepare for an interview.

- Decide what you want or need to know and who best can provide that information for you.
- Schedule each interview in advance, and let the person know why you are conducting the interview. Estimate how long your interview will take, and tell your subject how much of her or his time you will need.
- Choose a location that is convenient for your subject but not too chaotic or loud. An office or study room is better than a noisy cafeteria.
- Plan your questions in advance. Write down a few questions and have a few more in mind. Background reading will avoid unnecessary questions.
- If you want to record the interview, ask for permission in advance. A recording device might intimidate the person you are interviewing.

Conduct interviews

- Come prepared with your questions, a notebook, and a pen or pencil.
- If you plan to record the interview (with your subject's permission), make sure whatever recording device you use has an adequate power supply and will not run out of tape, disk space, or memory.
- Listen carefully so you can follow up on key points. Make notes when important questions are raised or answered, but don't attempt to transcribe every word the person is saying.
- When you are finished, thank your subject, and ask his or her permission to get in touch again if you have additional questions.

Surveys

Extensive surveys that can be projected to large populations, like the ones used in political polls, require the effort of many people. Small surveys, however, often can provide insight on local issues, such as what percentage of students might be affected if library hours were reduced.

Plan surveys

What information do you need for your research question? Decide what exactly you want to know and design a survey that will provide that information. Likely you will want both close-ended questions (multiple choice, yes or no, rating scale) and open-ended questions that allow detailed responses. To create a survey, follow these guidelines.

- Write a few specific, unambiguous questions. People will fill out your survey quickly. If the questions are confusing, the results will be meaningless.
- Include one or two open-ended questions, such as "What do you like about X?" or "What don't you like about X?" Open-ended questions can be difficult to interpret, but sometimes they turn up information you had not anticipated.
- Test the questions on a few people before you conduct the survey.
- Think about how you will interpret your survey. Multiple-choice formats make data easy to tabulate, but often they miss key information. Open-ended questions will require you to figure out a way to sort responses into categories.

Administer surveys

- Decide on who you need to survey and how many respondents your survey will require. For example, if you want to claim that the results of your survey represent the views of residents of your dormitory, your method of selecting respondents should give all residents an equal chance to be selected. Don't select only your friends.
- Decide how you will contact participants in your survey. If you are conducting your survey on private property, you will need permission from the property owner. Likewise, e-mail lists and lists of mailing addresses are usually guarded closely to preserve privacy. You will need to secure permission from the appropriate parties if you want to contact people via an e-mail list.
- If you mail or e-mail your survey, include a statement about what the survey is for.

Observations

Observing can be a valuable source of data. For example, if you are researching why a particular office on your campus does not operate efficiently, observe what happens when students enter and how the staff responds to their presence.

Make observations

- Choose a place where you can observe with the least intrusion. The less people wonder about what you are doing, the better.
- Carry a notebook and write extensive field notes. Record as much information as you can, and worry about analyzing it later.
- Record the date, exactly where you were, exactly when you arrived and left, and important details like the number of people present.
- Write on one side of your notebook so you can use the facing page to note key observations and analyze your data later.

Analyze observations

You must interpret your observations so they make sense in the context of your argument. Ask yourself the following questions.

- What patterns of behavior did you observe?
- How was the situation you observed unique? How might it be similar to other locations?
- What constituted "normal" activity during the time when you were observing? Did anything out of the ordinary happen?
- Why were the people there? What can you determine about the purposes of the activities you observed?

Draft a Working Thesis

Once you have done some preliminary research into your question, you can begin to craft a working thesis. Let's take one topic as an example—the increasing popularity of organic products, including meat, dairy products, and produce. If you research this topic, you will discover that due to this trend, large corporations such as Walmart are beginning to offer organic products in their stores. However, the enormous demand for organic products is actually endangering smaller organic farmers and producers. As you research the question of why small farmers and producers in the United States are endangered and what small farmers and producers in other countries have done to protect themselves, a working thesis begins to emerge.

Write your subject, research question, and working thesis on a note card or sheet of paper. Keep your working thesis handy. You may need to revise it several times until the wording is precise. As you research, ask yourself, does this information tend to support my thesis? Information that does not support your thesis is still important! It may lead you to adjust your thesis or even to abandon it altogether. You may need to find another source or reason that shows your thesis is still valid.

Example

SUBJECT: Increased demand for organic products endangering smaller farmers and producers.

RESEARCH QUESTION: How can successful smaller organic farmers and producers protect themselves from becoming extinct?

WORKING THESIS: In order to meet the increasing demand for organic products that has been created by larger corporations such as Walmart, smaller organic farmers and producers should form regional co-ops. These co-ops will work together to supply regional chains, much as co-ops of small farmers and dairies in Europe work together, thereby cutting transportation and labor costs and ensuring their survival in a much-expanded market.

For additional writing resources that will help you master the objectives of this chapter, go to your **MyLab**.

17 | Finding Sources

Develop Strategies for Finding Sources

The distinction between doing research online and in the library is blurring as more and more libraries make their collections accessible on the Web. Nevertheless, libraries still contain many resources not available on the Web. Even more important, libraries have professional research librarians who can help you locate sources quickly.

Determine where to start looking

Searches using *Google* or *Yahoo!* turn up thousands of items, many of which are often not useful for research. Considering where to start is the first step.

Scholarly books and articles in scholarly journals often are the highest-quality sources, but the lag in publication time makes them less useful for very current topics. Newspapers cover current issues, but often not in the depth of books and scholarly journals. Government Web sites and publications are often the best for finding statistics and are also valuable for researching science and medicine.

Learn the art of effective keyword searches

Keyword searches take you to the sources you need. Start with your working thesis and generate a list of possible keywords for researching your thesis.

First, think of keywords that make your search more specific. For example, a search for sources related to Internet privacy issues might focus more specifically on privacy *and*

Internet
cookies
Web profiling
Flash
spyware

You should also think about more general ways to describe what you are doing—what synonyms can you think of for your existing terms? Other people may have discussed the topic using those terms instead. Instead of relying on "privacy," you can also try keywords like

identity theft
data protection
electronic records

You can even search using terms that refer to related people, events, or movements that you are familiar with.

Facebook
Internet vigilantism
Google+
phishing

Many databases have a thesaurus that can help you find more keywords.

Find Sources in Databases

Sources found through library **databases** have already been filtered for you by professional librarians. They will include some common sources like popular magazines and newspapers, but the greatest value of database sources are the many journals, abstracts, studies, e-books, and other writing produced by specialists whose work has been scrutinized and commented on by other experts. When you read a source from a library database, chances are you are hearing an informed voice in an important debate.

Locate databases

You can find databases on your library's Web site. Sometimes you will find a list of databases. Sometimes you select a subject, and then you are directed to databases. Sometimes you select the name of a database vendor such as *EBSCO* or *ProQuest*. The vendor is the company that provides databases to the library.

Use databases

Your library has a list of databases and indexes by subject. If you can't find this list on your library's Web site, ask a **reference librarian** for help. Follow these steps to find articles.

1. Select a database appropriate to your subject or a comprehensive database like *Academic Search Complete, Academic Search Premier,* or *LexisNexis Academic.*

2. Search the database using your list of keywords.

3. Once you have chosen an article, print or e-mail to yourself the complete citation to the article. Look for the e-mail link after you click on the item you want.

4. Print or e-mail to yourself the full text if it is available. The full text is better than cutting and pasting because you might lose track of which words are yours, leading to unintended plagiarism.

5. If the full text is not available, check the online library catalog to see if your library has the journal.

Your library will probably have printed handouts or online information that tells you which database to use for a particular subject. Ask a librarian who works at the reference or information desk to help you.

If you wish to get only full-text articles, you can filter your search by checking that option. Full-text documents give you the same text you would find in print. Sometimes the images are not reproduced in the HTML versions, but the PDF versions show the actual printed copy. Get the PDF version if it is available. Articles in HTML format usually do not contain the page numbers.

Common Databases

Academic OneFile	Indexes periodicals from the arts, humanities, sciences, social sciences, and general news, with full-text articles and images. (*Formerly Expanded Academic ASAP*)
Academic Search Premier and Complete	Provide full-text articles for thousands of scholarly publications, including social sciences, humanities, education, computer sciences, engineering, language and linguistics, literature, medical sciences, and ethnic-studies journals.

(*Continued*)

Common Databases

ArticleFirst	Indexes journals in business, the humanities, medicine, science, and social sciences.
EBSCOhost Research Databases	Gateway to a large collection of EBSCO databases, including *Academic Search Premier* and *Complete, Business Source Premier* and *Complete, ERIC,* and *Medline.*
Factiva	Provides full-text articles on business topics, including articles from the *Wall Street Journal.*
Google Books	Allows you to search within books and gives you snippets surrounding search terms for copyrighted books. Many books out of copyright have the full text. Available for everyone.
Google Scholar	Searches scholarly literature according to criteria of relevance. Available for everyone.
General OneFile	Contains millions of full-text articles about a wide range of academic and general-interest topics.
LexisNexis Academic	Provides full text of a wide range of newspapers, magazines, government and legal documents, and company profiles from around the world.
Opposing Viewpoints Resource Center	Provides full-text articles representing differing points of view on current issues.
ProQuest Databases	Like EBSCOhost, ProQuest is a gateway to a large collection of databases with over 100 billion pages, including the best archives of doctoral dissertations and historical newspapers.

Find Sources on the Web

Because anyone can publish on the Web, there is no overall quality control and there is no system of organization—two strengths we take for granted in libraries. Nevertheless, the Web offers you some resources for current topics that would be difficult or impossible to find in a library. The key to success is knowing where you are most likely to find current and accurate information about the particular question you are researching, and knowing how to access that information.

Use search engines wisely

Search engines designed for the Web work in ways similar to library databases and your library's online catalog but with one major difference. Databases typically do some screening of the items they list, but search engines potentially take you to everything on the Web—millions of pages in all. Consequently, you have to work harder to limit searches on the Web or you can be deluged with tens of thousands of items.

Kinds of search engines

A search engine is a set of programs that sort through millions of items at incredible speed. There are four basic kinds of search engines.

1. **Keyword search engines** (e.g., *Bing, Google, Yahoo!*). Keyword search engines give different results because they assign different weights to the information they find.

2. **Meta-search engines** (e.g., *Dogpile, MetaCrawler, Surfwax*). Meta-search engines allow you to use several search engines simultaneously. While the concept is sound, metasearch agents are limited because many do not access *Google* or *Yahoo!*

3. **Web directories** (e.g., *Britannica.com, Yahoo! Directory*). Web directories classify Web sites into categories and are the closest equivalent to the cataloging system used by libraries. On most directories professional editors decide how to index a particular Web site. Web directories also allow keyword searches.

4. **Specialized search engines** are designed for specific purposes:

   - regional search engines (e.g., *Baidu* for China)
   - medical search engines (e.g., *WebMD*)
   - legal search engines (e.g., *Lexis*)
   - job search engines (e.g., *Monster.com*)
   - property search engines (e.g., *Zillow*)

Advanced searches

Search engines often produce too many hits and are therefore not always useful. If you look only at the first few items, you may miss what is most valuable. The alternative is to refine your search. Most search engines offer you the option of an advanced search, which gives you the opportunity to limit numbers.

The advanced searches on *Google* and *Yahoo!* give you the options of using a string of words to search for sites that contain (1) all the words, (2) the exact phrase, (3) any of the words, or (4) that do not contain certain words. They also allow you to specify the site, the date range, the file format, and the domain. For example, if you want to limit a search for *identity theft statistics* to reliable government Web sites, you can specify the domain as **.gov**.

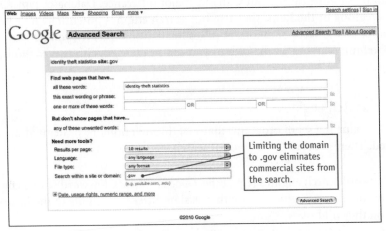

An advanced search on *Google* for government (.gov) sites only.

The **OR** operator is useful if you don't know exactly which term will get the results you want, especially if you are searching within a specific site. For example, you could try this search: "face-to-face OR f2f site:webworkerdaily.com."

You can also exclude terms by putting a minus sign before the term. If you want to search for social network privacy, but not *Facebook*, try "social network privacy–Facebook."

Find online government sources

The federal government has made many of its publications available on the Web. Also, many state governments now publish important documents on the Web. Often the most current and most reliable statistics are government statistics. Among the more important government resources are the following.

- **Bureau of Labor Statistics** (www.bls.gov/). Source for official U.S. government statistics on employment, wages, and consumer prices
- **Census Bureau** (www.census.gov/). Contains a wealth of links to sites for population, social, economic, and political statistics, including the *Statistical Abstract of the United States* (www.census.gov/compendia/statab/)
- **Centers for Disease Control** (www.cdc.gov/). Authoritative and trustworthy source for health statistics
- **CIA World Factbook** (www.cia.gov/library/publications/the-world-factbook/). Resource for geographic, economic, demographic, and political information on the nations of the world
- **Library of Congress** (www.loc.gov/). Many of the resources of the largest library in the world are available on the Web
- **NASA** (www.nasa.gov/). A rich site with much information and images concerning space exploration and scientific discovery
- **National Institutes of Health** (www.nih.gov/). Extensive health information including MedlinePlus searches
- **Thomas** (thomas.loc.gov/). The major source of legislative information, including bills, committee reports, and voting records of individual members of Congress
- **USA.gov** (www.usa.gov/). The place to start when you are not sure where to look for government information

Find online reference sources

Your library's Web site has a link to reference sites, either on the main page or under another heading like "research tools."

Reference sites are usually organized by subject, and you can find resources under the subject heading.

- **Business information** (links to business databases and sites like *Hoover's* that profiles companies)
- **Dictionaries** (including the *Oxford English Dictionary* and various subject dictionaries and language dictionaries)
- **Education** (including *The College Blue Book* and others)
- **Encyclopedias** (including *Britannica Online* and others)
- **Government information** (links to federal, state, and local Web sites)
- **Reference books** (commonly used books like atlases, almanacs, biographies, handbooks, and histories)
- **Statistics and demographics** (links to federal, state, and local government sites; *FedStats* [www.fedstats.gov/] is a good place to start)

Search interactive media

The Internet allows you to access other people's opinions on thousands of topics. Millions of people post messages on discussion lists and groups, *Facebook* groups, blogs, RSS feeds, *Twitter*, and so on. Much of what you read on interactive media sites is undocumented and highly opinionated, but you can still gather important information about people's attitudes and get tips about other sources, which you can verify later.

Several search engines have been developed for interactive media. *Facebook* and *Twitter* also have search engines for their sites.

Discussion list search engines

- **Big Boards** (www.big-boards.com). Tracks over two thousand of the most active discussion forums
- **Google Groups** (groups.google.com). Archives discussion forums dating back to 1981
- **Yahoo! Groups** (groups.yahoo.com). A directory of groups by subject

Blog search engines

- **Bloglines** (www.bloglines.com). Web-based aggregator that delivers RSS feeds
- **Google Blog Search** (blogsearch.google.com). Searches blogs in several languages besides English
- **IceRocket** (blogs.icerocket.com). Searches blogs, *MySpace*, and *Twitter*
- **Technorati** (www.technorati.com). Searches blogs and other user-generated content

Know the limitations of *Wikipedia*

Wikipedia is a valuable resource for current information and for popular culture topics that are not covered in traditional encyclopedias. You can find out, for example, that SpongeBob SquarePants's original name was "SpongeBoy," but the name had already been copyrighted.

Nevertheless, many instructors and the scholarly community in general do not consider *Wikipedia* a reliable source of information for a research paper. The fundamental problem with *Wikipedia* is stability, not whether the information is correct or incorrect. *Wikipedia* and other wikis constantly change. The underlying idea of documenting sources is that readers can consult the same sources that you consulted. Consult other sources to confirm what you find on *Wikipedia* and cite those sources. Often the *Wikipedia* entry includes a list of references that you can use as a starting point for your own research.

Find Multimedia Sources

Massive collections of images; audio files including music, speeches, and podcasts; videos; maps, charts, and graphs; and other resources are now available on the Web.

Find images

The major search engines for images include the following.

- **Bing Images** (www.bing.com/images/)
- **Google Image Search** (images.google.com/)
- **Picsearch** (www.picsearch.com/)
- **Yahoo! Image Search** (images.search.yahoo.com)

Libraries and museums also offer large collections of images that may help you in your research. For example, the American Memory collection in the Library of Congress offers an important visual record of the history of the United States (memory.loc.gov/ammem/).

Find videos

- **Bing Videos** (www.bing.com/videos/)
- **blinkx** (www.blinkx.com/)
- **Google Videos** (video.google.com/)
- **Vimeo** (vimeo.com)
- **Yahoo! Video Search** (video.search.yahoo.com)
- **YouTube** (www.youtube.com)

Find podcasts

- **iTunes Podcast Resources** (www.apple.com/itunes/podcasts/)
- **PodcastDirectory.com** (www.podcastdirectory.com/)

Find charts, graphs, and maps

You can find statistical data represented in charts and graphs on many government Web sites.

- **Statistical Abstract of the United States** (www.census.gov/compendia/statab/)
- **Google Earth** (earth.google.com/)

- **National Geographic Map Machine**
  (mapmachine.nationalgeographic.com/)
- **Perry Casteñada Map Collection, University of Texas**
  (www.lib.utexas.edu/maps/map_sites/map_sites.html)

Respect copyright

Just because images, videos, and other multimedia files are easy to download from the Web does not mean that everything is available for you to use. Look for the creator's copyright notice and suggested credit line. This notice will tell you if you can reproduce the multimedia file. Include properly formatted citations for each electronic resource you include in your paper.

Find Print Sources

Print sources may seem "old fashioned" if you grew up with the Internet. You might even feel a little bit intimidated by them. But they are the starting point for much of the research done by experts. In college and beyond, they are indispensable. No matter how current the topic you are researching, you will likely find information in print sources that is simply not available online.

Print sources have other advantages as well.

- Books are shelved according to subject, allowing easy browsing.
- Books often have bibliographies, directing you to other research on the subject.
- You can search for books in multiple ways: author, title, subject, or call letter.
- The majority of print sources have been evaluated by scholars, editors, and publishers, who decided whether they merited publication.

Find books

Nearly all libraries now shelve books according to the Library of Congress Classification System, which uses a combination of letters and numbers to give you the book's unique location in the library. The Library of Congress call number begins with a letter or letters that represent the broad subject area into which the book is classified.

Locating books in your library

The floors of your library where books are shelved are referred to as the stacks. The call number will enable you to find the item in the stacks. You will need to consult the locations guide for your library, which gives the level and section where an item is shelved.

Locating e-books

Use your library's online catalog to find e-books the same way you find printed books. You'll see on the record "e-book" or "electronic resource." Click on the link and you can read the book and often download a few pages.

Find journal articles

Like books, **scholarly journals** provide in-depth examinations of subjects. The articles in scholarly journals are written by experts, and they usually contain lists of references that can guide you to other research on a subject.

Popular journals are useful for gaining general information. Articles in popular magazines are usually short with few, if any, source references and are typically written by journalists. Some instructors frown on using popular magazines, but these journals can be valuable for researching current opinion on a particular topic.

Many scholarly journals and popular magazines are available on your library's Web site. Find them the same way you look for books, using your library's online catalog. Databases increasingly contain the full text of articles, allowing you to read and copy the contents onto your computer. If the article you are looking for isn't available online, the paper copy will be shelved with the books in your library.

For additional writing resources that will help you master the objectives of this chapter, go to your **MyLab**.

18 | Evaluating and Recording Sources

QUICK TAKE

In this chapter you will learn to

1. Use the working thesis to decide a source's relevance (see below)
2. Distinguish among sources: anonymous versus edited, popular versus scholarly, and primary versus secondary sources (see page 239)
3. Evaluate library database and print sources (see page 241)
4. Evaluate the quality of Web sources (see page 242)
5. Keep track of sources, including recording all the information you need to cite a source (see page 244)

Determine the Relevance of Sources

Whether you use print or online sources, a successful search will turn up many more items than you can expect to use in your final product. You have to make a series of decisions as you evaluate your material. Use your research question and working thesis to create guidelines for yourself about importance and relevance.

If you ask a research question about contemporary events such as the NCAA's policy on compensating student athletes (see pages 108–112), you will need to find both background information and current information. You will need to know, for example, the most recent statistics on how many scholarship athletes actually graduate because the NCAA's main defense of not paying scholarship athletes is that they get a free education.

Use these guidelines to determine the importance and relevance of your sources to your research question.

- Does your research question require you to consult primary or secondary sources?
- Does a source you have found address your question?
- Does a source support or disagree with your working thesis? (You should not throw out work that challenges your views. Representing opposing views accurately enhances your credibility.)
- Does a source add significant information?

■ Is the source current? (For most topics try to find the most up-to-date information.)

■ What indications of possible bias do you note in the source?

Determine the Quality of Sources

In the digital era, we don't lack for information, but we do lack filters for finding quality information. Two criteria will help you to make a beginning assessment of quality: individual vs. edited sources and popular vs. scholarly sources.

Distinguish individual and anonymous sources from edited sources

Anyone with a computer and Internet access can put up a Web site. Furthermore, they can put up sites anonymously or under an assumed name. It's no wonder that so many Web sites contain misinformation or are intentionally deceptive.

In general, sources that have been edited and published in scholarly journals, scholarly books, major newspapers, major online and print magazines, and government Web sites are considered of higher quality than what an individual might put on a personal Web site, a Facebook page, a user review, or in a blog.

Edited sources can have biases, and indeed some are quite open about their perspectives. *National Review* offers a conservative perspective, the *Wall Street Journal* is pro-business, and the *Nation* is a liberal voice. The difference from individual and anonymous sites is that we know the editorial perspectives of these journals, and we expect the editors to check the facts. On self-published Web sites and in self-published books, anything goes.

Distinguish popular sources from scholarly sources

Scholarly books and **scholarly journals** are published by and for experts. Scholarly books and articles published in scholarly journals undergo a **peer review** process in which a group of experts in a field reviews them for their scholarly soundness and academic value. Scholarly books and articles in scholarly journals include

■ author's name and academic credentials and
■ a list of works cited.

Newspapers, popular books, and **popular magazines** vary widely in quality. Newspapers and popular magazines range from highly respected publications such as the *Los Angeles Times, Scientific American,* and the *Atlantic Monthly* to the sensational tabloids at grocery-store checkouts. Popular sources are not peer reviewed and require more work on your part to determine their quality. EBSCO-host databases allow you to limit searches to scholarly journals.

Distinguish primary sources from secondary sources

Another key distinction for researchers is primary versus secondary sources. In the humanities and fine arts, **primary sources** are original, creative works and original accounts of events written close to the time they occurred. **Secondary sources** interpret creative works and primary sources of events.

In the sciences, primary sources are the factual results of experiments, observations, clinical trials, and other factual data. Secondary sources analyze and interpret those results.

Read sources critically

Evaluating sources requires you to read critically, which includes the following.

- Identifying the source, which is not always easy on the Web
- Identifying the author and assessing the author's credentials
- Understanding the content—what the text says
- Recognizing the author's purpose—whether the author is attempting to reflect, inform, or persuade
- Recognizing biases in the choices of words, examples, and structure
- Recognizing what the author does not include or address
- Developing an overall evaluation that takes into account all of the above

Evaluate the quality of visual sources

Evaluating the quality of visual sources involves skills similar to critical reading. Similar to critical reading, you should

- identify and assess the source,
- identify the creator,
- identify the date of creation,
- describe the content,
- assess the purpose, and
- recognize how the purpose influences the image, graphic, or video.

For visuals including charts and graphs, pay attention to the source of any data presented and see that the data are presented fairly.

Evaluate Database and Print Sources

Books are expensive to print and distribute, so book publishers generally protect their investment by providing some level of editorial oversight. Printed and on-line materials in your library undergo another review by professional librarians who select them to include in their collections.

This initial screening doesn't free you, however, from the responsibility of evaluating the quality of the sources. Many printed and database sources contain their share of inaccurate, misleading, and biased information. Also, all sources carry the risk of becoming outdated if you are looking for current information.

Checklist for evaluating database and print sources

Over the years librarians have developed a set of criteria for evaluating sources, and you should apply them in your research.

1. **Source.** Who published the book or article? Enter the publisher's name on *Google* or another search engine to learn about the publisher. Scholarly books and articles in scholarly journals are generally more reliable than popular magazines and books, which tend to emphasize what is sensational or entertaining at the expense of accuracy and comprehensiveness.

2. **Author.** Who wrote the book or article? Enter the author's name on *Google* or another search engine to learn more about him or her. What are the author's qualifications? Does the author represent an organization?

3. **Timeliness.** How current is the source? If you are researching a fast-developing subject such as treating ADHD, then currency is very important, but even historical topics are subject to controversy or revision.

4. **Evidence.** Where does the evidence come from—facts, interviews, observations, surveys, or experiments? Is the evidence adequate to support the author's claims?

5. **Biases.** Can you detect particular biases of the author? How do the author's biases affect the interpretation offered?

6. **Advertising.** For print sources, is advertising a prominent part of the journal or newspaper? How might the ads affect the credibility or the biases of the information that gets printed?

Evaluate Web Sources

Researching on the Web has been compared to drinking from a fire hose. The key to success is not only getting the torrent down to the size of a glass, but also making sure the water in the glass is pure enough to drink.

Pay attention to domain names

Domain names can give you clues about the quality of a Web site.

- **.com** Commercial site. The information on a .com site is generally about a product or company. While the information may be accurate, keep in mind that the purpose of the site may be to sell a product or service.
- **.edu** Educational institution. The suffix tells you the site is on a school server, ranging from kindergarten to higher education. If the information is from a department or research center, it is generally credible, but if the site is an individual's, treat it as you would other kinds of self-published information.
- **.gov** Government. If you see this suffix, you're viewing a federal government site. Most government sites are considered credible sources.
- **.org** Nonprofit organization. Initially, nonpartisan organizations like the Red Cross used this domain, but increasingly partisan political groups and commercial interests have taken the .org suffix. Evaluate these sites carefully.
- **.mil** Military. This domain suffix is owned by the various branches of the armed forces.
- **.net** Network. Anyone can use this domain. Seek out information about the site's origin.

Be alert for biased Web sites

Nearly every large company and political and advocacy organization has a Web site. We expect these sites to represent the company or the point of view of the organization. Many sites on the Web, however, are not so clearly labeled.

For example, if you do a search for "Sudden Infant Death Syndrome (SIDS)" and "vaccines," you'll find near the top of the list an article titled "Vaccines and Sudden Infant Death Syndrome (SIDS): A Link?" (www.thinktwice.com/sids.htm). The article concludes that vaccines cause SIDS. If you look at the home page—www.thinktwice.com—you'll find that the site's sponsor, Global Vaccine Institute, opposes all vaccinations of children.

Always look for other objective sources for verification of your information. The U.S. Centers for Disease Control publishes fact sheets with the latest information about diseases and their prevention (www.cdc.gov/vaccinesafety/Concerns/sids_faq.html). The fact sheet on SIDS and vaccines reports that people associate sudden infant death syndrome with vaccinations because babies are given vaccinations when they are between 2 and 4 months old, the same age babies die of SIDS. There is no scientific evidence that vaccines cause SIDS.

Checklist for evaluating Web sources

Web sources present special challenges for evaluation. When you find a Web page by using a search engine, you will often go deep into a complex site without having any sense of the context for that page. To evaluate the credibility of the site, you would need to examine the home page, not just the specific page you get to first. Use the following criteria for evaluating Web sites.

1. **Source.** What organization sponsors the Web site? Look for the site's owner at the top or bottom of the home page or in the Web address. Enter the owner's name on *Google* or another search engine to learn about the organization. If a Web site doesn't indicate ownership, then you have to make judgments about who put it up and why.

2. **Author.** Is the author identified? Look for an "About Us" link if you see no author listed. Enter the author's name on *Google* or another search engine to learn more about the author. Often Web sites give no information about their authors other than an e-mail address, if that. In such cases, it is difficult or impossible to determine the author's qualifications. Be cautious about information on an anonymous site.

3. **Purpose.** Is the Web site trying to sell you something? Many Web sites are infomercials that might contain useful information, but they are no more trustworthy than other forms of advertising. Is the purpose to entertain? to inform? to persuade?

4. **Timeliness.** When was the Web site last updated? Look for a date on the home page. Many Web pages do not list when they were last updated; thus you cannot determine their currency.

5. **Evidence.** Are sources of information listed? Any factual information should be supported by indicating where the information came from. Reliable Web sites that offer information will list their sources.

6. **Biases.** Does the Web site offer a balanced point of view? Many Web sites conceal their attitude with a reasonable tone and seemingly factual evidence such as statistics. Citations and bibliographies do not ensure that a site is reliable. Look carefully at the links and sources cited, and peruse the "About Us" link if one is available.

Keep Track of Sources

As you begin to collect your sources, make sure you get full bibliographic information for everything you might want to use in your project. Decide which documentation style you will use. (Two major documentation styles—MLA and APA—are explained in detail in Chapters 20 and 21.)

Locate elements of a citation in database sources

For any sources you find on databases, MLA style requires you to provide the full print information, the name of the database in italics, the medium of publication (*Web*), and the date you accessed the database. If page numbers are not included, use *n. page.* Do not include the URL of the database.

See pages 262–263 for detailed coverage.

Author's name	Shaughnessy, Dan
Title of article	"They've Had Some Chief Concerns"
Publication information	
Name of periodical	*Boston Globe*
Date of publication	12 Oct. 2007
Section and page number	C5
Database information	
Name of database	*LexisNexis Academic*
Medium of publication	Web
Date you accessed the site	19 Apr. 2010

Citation in MLA-style list of works cited

Shaughnessy, Dan. "They've Had Some Chief Concerns." *Boston Globe* 12 Oct. 2007: C5. *LexisNexis Academic.* Web. 19 Apr. 2010.

Many databases include a feature that shows you how to cite the source; some have a built-in citation generator. Double-check the format before you include the citation in your paper to ensure accuracy.

Locate elements of a citation in online sources

As you conduct your online research, make sure you collect the necessary biblio-graphic information for everything you might want to use as a source. Because of the potential volatility of online sources (they can and do disappear overnight), their citations require extra information. Depending on the citation format you use, you'll arrange this information in different ways.

See page 263 for detailed coverage.

Author's name	Zaiger, Alan Scher
Title of work	"Study: NCAA Graduation Rate Comparisons Flawed"
Title of the overall Web site	*ABC News*
Publication information	
Publisher or sponsor	ABC News
Date of publication	20 Apr. 2010
Medium of publication	Web
Date you accessed the site	1 Nov. 2010

Citation in MLA-style list of works cited

Zaiger, Alan Scher. "Study: NCAA Graduation Rate Comparisons Flawed." *ABC News*. ABC News, 20 Apr. 2010. Web. 1 Nov. 2010.

Locate elements of a citation in print sources

For books you will need, at minimum, the following information, which can typi-cally be found on the front and back of the title page.

See page 263 for detailed coverage.

Author's name	Fleitz, David L.
Title of the book	Louis Sockalexis: The First Cleveland Indian
Publication information	
Place of publication	Jefferson
Name of publisher	McFarland
Date of publication	2002
Medium of publication	Print

Citation in MLA-style list of works cited

Fleitz, David L. *Louis Sockalexis: The First Cleveland Indian*. Jefferson: McFarland, 2002. Print.

See pages 261–262 for detailed coverage.

For additional writing resources that will help you master the objectives of this chapter, go to your **MyLab**.

19 | Writing the Research Project

QUICK TAKE

In this chapter you will learn to

1. Assess the thesis for your research project and determine your contribution and main points (see below)
2. Define plagiarism and give examples of plagiarism in college writing (see page 248)
3. Avoid plagiarism in quoting sources (see page 250)
4. Avoid plagiarism in summarizing and paraphrasing (see page 253)
5. Decide when to quote and when to paraphrase (see page 255)
6. Integrate quotations into your text, including using signal phrases and block quotations (see page 255)

Review Your Goals and Plan Your Organization

If you have chosen a subject you're interested in, asked questions about it, and researched it thoroughly, you have a wealth of ideas and information to communicate to your audience.

Review your assignment and thesis

Before you begin writing a research project, review the assignment to remind yourself of the purpose of your argument, your potential readers, and the requested length of the finished paper.

By now you should have formulated a **working thesis**, which will be the focus of your project. You also should have located, read, evaluated, and taken notes on enough source material to write your project, and perhaps have conducted field research. At this stage in the writing process, your working thesis may be rough and may change as you write your draft, but having a working thesis will help keep your project focused.

Determine your contribution

A convincing and compelling source-based argument does not make claims based solely on the word of you, the writer. To be persuasive, it must draw on the expertise and reputations of others as well. However, you must also demonstrate that you have thought about and synthesized the evidence you have gathered from your sources, and you must show your readers which elements of your project represent your original thinking.

Determine exactly what you are adding to the larger conversation about your subject by answering these questions.

- Whom do you agree with?
- Whom do you disagree with?
- Which positions do you agree with but can add an additional point or example to?
- What original analysis or theorizing do you have to offer?

See pages 31–34 for examples of how to identify your contribution in relation to your sources.

Determine your main points

Look back over your notes on your sources and determine how to group the ideas you researched. Decide what your major points will be and how those points support your thesis. Group your research findings so that they match up with your major points.

Now it is time to create a working outline. Always include your thesis at the top of your outline as a guiding light. Some writers create formal outlines with roman numerals and the like; others compose the headings for the paragraphs of their project and use them to guide their draft; still others may start writing and then determine how they will organize their draft when they have a few paragraphs written. Experiment and decide which method works best for you.

Avoid Plagiarism

Plagiarism means claiming credit for someone else's intellectual work no matter whether it's to make money or get a better grade. Intentional or not, plagiarism has dire consequences. Reputable authors have gotten into trouble through carelessness by copying passages from published sources without acknowledging those sources. A number of famous people have had their reputations tarnished by accusations of plagiarism, and several prominent journalists have lost their jobs and careers for copying the work of other writers and passing it off as their own.

Deliberate plagiarism

If you buy a paper on the Web, copy someone else's paper word for word, or take an article off the Web and turn it in as yours, it's plain stealing, and people who take that risk should know that the punishment can be severe—usually failure for the course and sometimes expulsion. Deliberate plagiarism is easy for your instructors to spot because they recognize shifts in style, and it is easy for them to use search engines to find the sources of work stolen from the Web.

Patch plagiarism

The use of the Web has increased instances of plagiarism in college. Some students view the Internet as a big free buffet where they can grab anything, paste it in a file, and submit it as their own work. Other students intend to submit work that is their own, but they commit patch plagiarism because they aren't careful in taking notes to distinguish the words of others from their own words.

What you are not required to acknowledge

Fortunately, common sense governs issues of academic plagiarism. The standards of documentation are not so strict that the source of every fact you cite must be acknowledged. You do not have to document the following.

- **Facts available from many sources.** For example, many reference sources report that the death toll of the sinking of the *Titanic* on April 15, 1912, was around 1,500.
- **Results of your own field research.** If you take a survey and report the results, you don't have to cite yourself. You do need to cite individual interviews.

What you are required to acknowledge

The following sources should be acknowledged with an in-text citation and an entry in the list of works cited (MLA style) or the list of references (APA style).

- **Quotations.** Short quotations should be enclosed within quotation marks, and long quotations should be indented as a block. See page 256 for how to integrate quotations with signal phrases.
- **Summaries and paraphrases.** Summaries represent the author's argument in miniature as accurately as possible. Paraphrases restate the author's argument in your own words.
- **Facts that are not common knowledge.** For facts that are not easily found in general reference works, cite the source.
- **Ideas that are not common knowledge.** The sources of theories, analyses, statements of opinion, and arguable claims should be cited.
- **Statistics, research findings, examples, graphs, charts, and illustrations.** As a reader you should be skeptical about statistics and research findings when the source is not mentioned. When a writer does not cite the sources of statistics and research findings, there is no way of knowing how reliable the sources are or whether the writer is making them up.

Plagiarism in college writing

If you find any of the following problems in your academic writing, you may be guilty of plagiarizing someone else's work. Because plagiarism is usually inadvertent, it is especially important that you understand what constitutes using sources responsibly. Avoid these pitfalls.

- **Missing attribution.** Make sure the author of a quotation has been identified. Include a lead-in or signal phrase that provides attribution to the source, and identify the author in the citation.

- **Missing quotation marks.** You must put quotation marks around material quoted directly from a source.

- **Inadequate citation.** Give a page number to show where in the source the quotation appears or where a paraphrase or summary is drawn from.

- **Paraphrase relies too heavily on the source.** Be careful that the wording or sentence structure of a paraphrase does not follow the source too closely.

- **Distortion of meaning.** Don't allow your paraphrase or summary to distort the meaning of the source, and don't take a quotation out of context, resulting in a change of meaning.

- **Missing works-cited entry.** The Works Cited page must include all the works cited in the project.

- **Inadequate citation of images.** A figure or photo must appear with a caption and a citation to indicate the source of the image. If material includes a summary of data from a visual source, an attribution or citation must be given for the graphic being summarized.

Avoid plagiarism when taking notes

The best way to avoid unintentional plagiarism is to take care to distinguish source words from your own words. Don't mix words from the source with your own words.

- ◼ **Create a working bibliography and make separate files for content notes.** Create a file for each source and label it clearly with the author's name. If you work on paper, use a separate page for each source. At the top of each page, write down all the information you need for a list of works cited or a list of references in your working bibliography.

- ◼ **If you copy anything from a source when taking notes, place those words in quotation marks and note the page number(s) where those words appear.** If you copy words from an online source, take special care to note the source. You could easily copy online material and later not be able to find where it came from.

■ **Print out the entire source so you can refer to it later.** Having photocopies or complete printed files allows you to double-check later that you haven't used words from the source by mistake and that any words you quote are accurate.

Avoid Plagiarism When Quoting Sources

Effective research writing builds on the work of others. You can summarize or paraphrase the work of others, but often it is best to let the authors speak in your text by quoting their exact words. Indicate the words of others by placing them inside quotation marks.

Most people who get into plagiarism trouble lift words from a source and use them without quotation marks. Look carefully at this example to see where the line is drawn. In the following passage, Steven Johnson takes sharp issue with the metaphor of surfing applied to the Web:

> The concept of "surfing" does a terrible injustice to what it means to navigate around the Web. . . .What makes the idea of cybersurf so infuriating is the implicit connection drawn to television. Web surfing, after all, is a derivation of channel surfing—the term thrust upon the world by the rise of remote controls and cable panoply in the mid-eighties. . . . Applied to the boob tube, of course, the term was not altogether inappropriate. Surfing at least implied that channel-hopping was more dynamic, more involved, than the old routine of passive consumption. Just as a real-world surfer's enjoyment depended on the waves delivered up by the ocean, the channel surfer was at the mercy of the programmers and network executives. The analogy took off because it worked well in the one-to-many system of cable TV, where your navigational options were limited to the available channels.
>
> But when the term crossed over to the bustling new world of the Web, it lost a great deal of precision. . . . Web surfing and channel surfing are genuinely different pursuits; to imagine them as equivalents is to ignore the defining characteristics of each medium. Or at least that's what happens in theory. In practice, the Web takes on the greater burden. The television imagery casts the online surfer in the random, anesthetic shadow of TV programming, roaming from site to site like a CD player set on shuffle play. But what makes the online world so revolutionary is the fact that there *are* connections between each stop on a Web itinerant's journey. The links that join those various destinations are links of association, not randomness. A channel surfer hops back and forth between different channels because she's bored. A Web surfer clicks on a link because she's interested.

> —Steven Johnson. *Interface Culture: How New Technology Transforms the Way We Create and Communicate.*
> New York: Harper, 1997. 107–09.

If you were writing a paper or creating a Web site that concerns Web surfing, you might want to mention the distinction that Johnson makes between channel surfing and surfing on the Web.

Quoting directly

If you quote directly, you must place quotation marks around all words you take from the original:

> One observer marks this contrast: "A channel surfer hops back and forth between different channels because she's bored. A Web surfer clicks on a link because she's interested" (Johnson 109).

Notice that the quotation is introduced and not just dropped in. This example follows MLA style, where the citation—(Johnson 109)—goes outside the quotation marks but before the final period. In MLA style, source references are made according to the author's last name, which refers you to the full citation in the list of works cited at the end. Following the author's name is the page number where the quotation can be located. (Notice that there is no comma after the name.)

Attributing every quotation

If the author's name appears in the sentence, cite only the page number, in parentheses:

> According to Steven Johnson, "A channel surfer hops back and forth between different channels because she's bored. A Web surfer clicks on a link because she's interested" (109).

Quoting words that are quoted in your source

Use single quotation marks to quote material that is already quoted in your source:

> Steven Johnson uses the metaphor of a Gothic cathedral to describe a computer interface: "'The principle of the Gothic architecture,' Coleridge once said, 'is infinity made imaginable.' The same could be said for the modern interface" (42).

Avoid Plagiarism When Summarizing and Paraphrasing

Summarizing

When you summarize, you state the major ideas of an entire source or part of a source in a paragraph or perhaps even a sentence. The key is to put the summary in your own words. If you use words from the source, you must put those words within quotation marks.

Plagiarized

> Steven Johnson argues in *Interface Culture* that the concept of "surfing" is misapplied to the Internet because channel surfers hop back and forth between different channels because they're bored, but Web surfers click on links because they're interested.

[Most of the words are lifted directly from the original; see page 251.]

Acceptable summary

> Steven Johnson argues in *Interface Culture* that the concept of "surfing" is misapplied to the Internet because users of the Web consciously choose to link to other sites while television viewers mindlessly flip through the channels until something catches their attention.

Paraphrasing

When you paraphrase, you represent the idea of the source in your own words at about the same length as the original. You still need to include the reference to the source of the idea. The following example illustrates an unacceptable paraphrase.

Plagiarized

> Steven Johnson argues that the concept of "surfing" does a terrible injustice to what it means to navigate around the Web. What makes the idea of Web surfing infuriating is the association with television. Surfing is not a bad metaphor for channel hopping, but it doesn't fit what people do on the Web. Web surfing and channel surfing are truly different activities; to imagine them as the same is to ignore their defining characteristics. A channel surfer skips around because she's bored while a Web surfer clicks on a link because she's interested (107-09).

Even though the source is listed, this paraphrase is unacceptable. Too many of the words in the original are used directly here, including much or all of entire sentences. When a string of words is lifted from a source and inserted without quotation marks, the passage is plagiarized. Changing a few words in a sentence is not a paraphrase. Compare these two sentences.

Source

> Web surfing and channel surfing are genuinely different pursuits; to imagine them as equivalents is to ignore the defining characteristics of each medium.

Unacceptable paraphrase

> Web surfing and channel surfing are truly different activities; to imagine them as the same is to ignore their defining characteristics.

The paraphrase takes the structure of the original sentence and substitutes a few words. It is much too similar to the original.

> **A true paraphrase represents an entire rewriting of the idea from the source.**

Acceptable paraphrase

> Steven Johnson argues that "surfing" is a misleading term for describing how people navigate on the Web. He allows that "surfing" is appropriate for clicking across television channels because the viewer has to interact with what the networks and cable companies provide, just as the surfer has to interact with what the ocean provides. Web surfing, according to Johnson, operates at much greater depth and with much more consciousness of purpose. Web surfers actively follow links to make connections (107-09).

Even though this paraphrase contains a few words from the original, such as *navigate* and *connections*, these sentences are original in structure and wording while accurately conveying the meaning of the source.

Decide When to Quote and When to Paraphrase

The general rule in deciding when to include direct quotations and when to paraphrase lies in the importance of the original wording.

- If you want to refer to an idea or fact and the original wording is not critical, make the point in your own words.
- Save direct quotations for language that is memorable or conveys the character of the source.

Use quotations effectively

Quotations are a frequent problem area in research projects. Review every quotation to ensure that each is used effectively and correctly.

- **Limit the use of long quotations.** If you have more than one block quotation on a page, look closely to see if one or more can be paraphrased or summarized. Use direct quotations only if the original wording is important.
- **Check that each quotation is supporting your major points rather than making major points for you.** If the ideas rather than the original wording are what's important, paraphrase the quotation and cite the source.
- **Check that each quotation is introduced and attributed.** Each quotation should be introduced and the author or title named. Check for signal phrases that signal a quotation: Smith *claims*, Jones *argues*, Brown *states*.
- **Check that each quotation is properly formatted and punctuated.** Prose quotations longer than four lines (MLA) or forty words (APA) should be indented 1 inch in MLA style or 1/2 inch in APA style. Shorter quotations should be enclosed within quotation marks.
- **Check that you cite the source for each quotation.** You are required to cite the sources of all direct quotations, paraphrases, and summaries.
- **Check the accuracy of each quotation.** It's easy to leave out words or mistype a quotation. Compare what is in your project to the original source. If you need to add words to make the quotation grammatical, make sure the added words are in brackets. Use ellipses to indicate omitted words.
- **Read your project aloud to a classmate or a friend.** Each quotation should flow smoothly when you read your project aloud. Put a check beside rough spots as you read aloud so you can revise later.

Use signal phrases

Signal verbs often indicate your stance toward a quotation. Introducing a quotation with "X says" or "X believes" tells your readers nothing. Find a livelier verb that suggests how you are using the source. For example, if you write "X contends," your reader is alerted that you likely will disagree with the source. Be as precise as possible.

Signal phrases that report information or a claim

X argues that . . .

X asserts that . . .

X claims that . . .

X observes that . . .

As X puts it, . . .

X reports that . . .

As X sums it up, . . .

Signal phrases when you agree with the source

X affirms that . . .

X has the insight that . . .

X points out insightfully that . . .

X theorizes that . . .

X verifies that . . .

Signal phrases when you disagree with the source

X complains that . . .

X contends that . . .

X denies that . . .

X disputes that . . .

X overlooks that . . .

X rejects that . . .

X repudiates that . . .

Signal phrases in the sciences

Signal phrases in the sciences often use the past tense, especially for interpretations and commentary.

X described . . .

X found . . .

X has suggested . . .

Introduce block quotations

Long direct quotations, called **block quotations**, are indented from the margin instead of being placed in quotation marks. In MLA style, a quotation longer than four lines should be indented 1 inch. A quotation of forty words or longer is indented 1/2 inch in APA style. In both MLA and APA styles, long quotations are double-spaced. You still need to integrate a block quotation into the text of your project by mentioning who wrote or said it.

- No quotation marks appear around the block quotation.
- Words quoted in the original retain the double quotation marks.
- The page number appears in parentheses after the period at the end of the block quotation.

It is a good idea to include at least one or two sentences following the quotation to describe its significance to your thesis.

Double-check quotations

Whether they are long or short, you should double-check all quotations you use to be sure they are accurate and that all words belonging to the original are set off with quotation marks or placed in a block quotation. If you wish to leave out words from a quotation, indicate the omitted words with ellipses (. . .), but make sure you do not alter the meaning of the original quotation. If you need to add words of your own to a quotation to make the meaning clear, place your words in square brackets.

Write a Draft

Some writers begin by writing the title, first paragraph, and concluding paragraph.

Write a specific title

A bland, generic title says to readers that you are likely to be boring.

Generic

> Good and Bad Fats

Specific titles are like tasty appetizers; if you like the appetizer, you'll probably like the main course.

Specific

> The Secret Killer: Hydrogenated Fats

Write an engaging introduction

Get off to a fast start. If, for example, you want to alert readers to the dangers of partially hydrogenated oils in the food we eat, you could begin by explaining the difference in molecular structure between natural unsaturated fatty acids and trans-fatty acids. And you would probably lose your readers by the end of the first paragraph.

Instead, let readers know what is at stake along with giving some background and context; consider dramatizing a problem that your paper will address. State your thesis early on. Then go into the details in the body of your project.

Write a strong conclusion

The challenge in writing ending paragraphs is to leave the reader with something provocative, something beyond pure summary of the previous paragraphs. Connect back to your thesis, and use a strong concluding image, example, question, or call to action to leave your readers with something to remember and think about.

Review and Revise

After you've gone through the peer editing process or assessed your own draft, sit down with your project and consider the changes you need to make. Start from the highest level, reorganizing paragraphs and possibly even cutting large parts of your project and adding new sections. If you make significant revisions, likely you will want to repeat the overall evaluation of your revised draft when you finish (see Chapter 4).

When you feel your draft is complete, begin the editing phase. Use the guidelines on pages 51–52 to revise style and grammatical errors. Finally, proofread your project, word by word, checking for mistakes.

> For additional writing resources that will help you master the objectives of this chapter, go to your **MyLab**.

20 | Documenting Sources in MLA Style

QUICK TAKE

In this chapter you will learn to

1. Describe the elements of MLA documentation, including in-text references and the works-cited list (see below)
2. Identify the basic patterns for MLA in-text citations (see page 264)
3. Identify the basic patterns for MLA works-cited entries, including entries for books, periodicals, databases, online sources, and nonprint sources (see page 267)
4. Format research papers using MLA style (see page 276)

The two styles of documentation used most frequently are APA style and MLA style. APA stands for American Psychological Association, which publishes a style manual used widely in the social sciences and education (see Chapter 21). MLA stands for the Modern Language Association, and its style is the norm for the humanities and fine arts, including English and rhetoric and composition. If you have questions that this chapter does not address, consult the *MLA Handbook for Writers of Research Papers,* Seventh Edition (2009), and the *MLA Style Manual and Guide to Scholarly Publishing,* Third Edition (2008).

Elements of MLA Documentation

Citing a source in your paper

Citing sources is a two-part process. When readers find a reference to a source (called an in-text or parenthetical citation) in the body of your paper, they can turn to the works-cited list at the end and find the full publication information. Place the author's last name and the page number inside parentheses at the end of the sentence.

Anticipating the impact of Google's project of digitally scanning books in major research libraries, one observer predicts that "the real magic will come in the second act, as each word in each book is cross-linked, clustered, cited, extracted, indexed, analyzed, annotated, remixed, reassembled and woven deeper into the culture than ever before" (Kelly 43).

Author not mentioned in text

If you mention the author's name in the sentence, you do not have to put the name in the parenthetical reference at the end. Just cite the page number.

> Anticipating the impact of Google's project of digitally scanning books in major research libraries, Kevin Kelly predicts that "the real magic will come in the second act, as each word in each book is cross-linked, clustered, cited, extracted, indexed, analyzed, annotated, remixed, reassembled and woven deeper into the culture than ever before" (43).

Author mentioned in text

The corresponding entry in the works-cited list at the end of your paper would be as follows.

Works Cited

> Kelly, Kevin. "Scan This Book!" *New York Times* 14 May 2006, late ed., sec 6: 43+. Print.

Entry in the works-cited list

Citing an entire work, a Web site, or another electronic source

If you wish to cite an entire work (a book, a film, a performance, and so on), a Web site, or an electronic source that has no page numbers or paragraph numbers, MLA style instructs that you mention the name of the person (for example, the author or director) in the text with a corresponding entry in the works-cited list. You do not need to include the author's name in parentheses. If you cannot identify the author, mention the title in your text.

> Joel Waldfogel discusses the implications of a study of alumni donations to colleges and universities, observing that parents give generously to top-rated colleges in the hope that their children's chances for admission will improve.

Author mentioned in text

Works Cited

> Waldfogel, Joel. "The Old College Try." *Slate*. Washington Post Newsweek Interactive, 6 July 2007. Web. 27 Jan. 2010.

MLA style requires the medium of publication (print, Web, performance, etc.) to be included in each citation.

Creating an MLA-style works-cited list

To create your works-cited list, go through your paper and find every reference to the sources you consulted during your research. Each in-text reference must have an entry in your works-cited list. Do not include any sources on your works-cited list that you do not refer to in your paper.

Organize your works-cited list alphabetically by authors' last names or, if no author is listed, the first word in the title other than *a*, *an*, or *the*. (See pages 281–282 for a sample works-cited list.) MLA style uses four basic forms for entries in the works-cited list: books, periodicals (scholarly journals, newspapers, magazines), online library database sources, and other online sources (Web sites, discussion forums, blogs, online newspapers, online magazines, online government documents, and e-mail messages). There are also specific formats for citation of interviews, images, music, and film.

Works-cited entries for books

Entries for books have three main elements.

Pollan, Michael. *In Defense of Food: An Eater's Manifesto*. New York: Penguin, 2008. Print.

1. Author's name.
- List the author's name with the last name first, followed by a period.

2. *Title of book*.
- Find the exact title on the title page, not the cover.
- Separate the title and subtitle with a colon.
- Italicize the title and put a period at the end.

3. Publication information.
- Give the city of publication and a colon.
- Give the name of the publisher, using accepted abbreviations, and a comma.
- Give the date of publication, followed by a period.
- Give the medium of publication (Print), followed by a period.

Works-cited entries for periodicals

Entries for periodicals (scholarly journals, newspapers, magazines) have three main elements.

Pilgrim, Sarah, David Smith, and Jules Pretty. "A Cross-Regional Assessment of the Factors Affecting Ecoliteracy: Implications for Policy and Practice." *Ecological Applications* 17.6 (2007): 1742-51. Print.

1. Author's name.
- List the author's name with the last name first, followed by a period.

2. "Title of article."
- Place the title of the article inside quotation marks.
- Insert a period before the closing quotation mark.

3. Publication information.
- Italicize the title of the journal.
- Give the volume number.
- List the date of publication, in parentheses, followed by a colon.
- List the page numbers, followed by a period. (Note: MLA uses hyphens in page spans and does not use full numbers.)
- Give the medium of publication (Print), followed by a period.

Works-cited entries for library database sources

Basic entries for library database sources have four main elements.

Damiano, Jessica. "Growing Vegetables in Small Spaces: Train Them up Trellises and Plant Crops in Succession." *Newsday* 2 May 2010: G107. *LexisNexis Academic.* Web. 8 Apr. 2010.

1. Author's name.
- List the author's name with the last name first, followed by a period.

2. "Title of article."
- Place the title of the article inside quotation marks.
- Insert a period before the closing quotation mark.

3. Print publication information
- Give the print publication information in standard format, in this case for a periodical (see pages 270–272).

4. Database information
- Italicize the name of the database, followed by a period.
- List the medium of publication, followed by a period. For all database sources, the medium of publication is *Web*.
- List the date you accessed the source (day, month, and year), followed by a period.

Works-cited entries for other online sources

Basic entries for online sources (Web sites, discussion forums, blogs, online newspapers, online magazines, online government documents, and e-mail messages) have three main elements. Sometimes information such as the author's name or the date of publication is missing from the online source. Include the information you are able to locate.

There are many formats for the different kinds of electronic publications. Here is the format of an entry for an online article.

Jacobs, Ruth. "Organic Garden Gives Back." *Colby Magazine* 99.1 (2010): n. pag. Web. 2 Apr. 2010.

1. Author's name.
- List the author's name with the last name first, followed by a period.

2. "Title of work"; Title of the overall Web site
- Place the title of the work inside quotation marks if it is part of a larger Web site.
- Italicize the name of the overall site if it is different from the title of the work.
- Some Web sites are updated periodically, so list the version if you find it (e.g., 2010 edition).

3. Publication information.
- List the publisher or sponsor of the site, followed by a comma. If not available, use *N.p.* (for *no publisher*).
- List the date of publication if available; if not, use *n.d.* (for no date)
- List the medium of publication (*Web*).
- List the date you accessed the source (day, month, and year).

MLA In-Text Citations

1. Author named in your text

Put the author's name in a signal phrase in your sentence. Put the page number in parentheses at the end of the sentence.

> Sociologist Daniel Bell called this emerging U.S. economy the "postindustrial society" (3).

2. Author not named in your text

Put the author's last name and the page number inside parentheses at the end of the sentence.

> In 1997, the Gallup poll reported that 55% of adults in the United States think secondhand smoke is "very harmful," compared to only 36% in 1994 (Saad 4).

3. Work by a single author

The author's last name comes first, followed by the page number. There is no comma.

> (Bell 3)

4. Work by two or three authors

The authors' last names follow the order of the title page. If there are two authors, join the names with *and*. If there are three authors, use a comma between the first two names and a comma with *and* before the last name.

> (Francisco, Vaughn, and Lynn 7)

5. Work by four or more authors

You may use the phrase *et al.* (meaning "and others") for all names but the first, or you may write out all the names. Make sure you use the same method for both the in-text citations and the works-cited list.

> (Abrams et al. 1653)

6. Work by an unnamed author

Use a shortened version of the title that includes at least the first important word. Your reader will use the shortened title to find the full title in the works-cited list.

> A review in the *New Yorker* of Ryan Adams's new album focuses on the artist's age ("Pure" 25).

Notice that "Pure" is in quotation marks because it is the shortened title of an article. If it were a book, the short title would be in italics.

7. Work by a group or organization

Treat the group or organization as the author, but try to identify the group author in the text and place only the page number in parentheses. Shorten terms that are commonly abbreviated.

> According to the *Irish Free State Handbook*, published by the Ministry for Industry and Finance, the population of Ireland in 1929 was approximately 4,192,000 (23).

8. Quotations longer than four lines

When using indented (block) quotations of more than four lines, place the period *before* the parentheses enclosing the page number.

> In her article "Art for Everybody," Susan Orlean attempts to explain the popularity of painter Thomas Kinkade:
>> People like to own things they think are valuable. . . .
>> The high price of limited editions is part of their appeal:
>> it implies that they are choice and exclusive, and that
>> only a certain class of people will be able to
>> afford them. (128)
>
> This same statement could possibly also explain the popularity of phenomena like PBS's *Antiques Road Show*.

If the source is longer than one page, provide the page number for each quotation, paraphrase, and summary.

9. Web sources including Web pages, blogs, podcasts, wikis, videos, and other multimedia sources

Give the author's name in the text instead of in parentheses.

> Andrew Keen ironically used his own blog to claim that "blogs are boring to write (yawn), boring to read (yawn) and boring to discuss (yawn)."

If you cannot identify the author, mention the title in your text.

> The podcast "Catalina's Cubs" describes the excitement on Catalina Island when the Chicago Cubs went there for spring training in the 1940s.

10. Work in an anthology

Cite the name of the author of the work within an anthology, not the name of the editor of the collection. Alphabetize the entry in the list of works cited by the author, not the editor.

> In "Beard," Melissa Jane Hardie explores the role assumed by Elizabeth Taylor as the celebrity companion of gay actors including Rock Hudson and Montgomery Clift (278-79).

11. Two or more works by the same author

When an author has two or more items in the works-cited list, distinguish which work you are citing by using the author's last name and then a shortened version of the title of each source.

> The majority of books written about coauthorship focus on partners of the same sex (Laird, *Women* 351).

Note that *Women* is italicized because it is the name of a book; if an article were named, quotation marks would be used.

12. Different authors with the same last name

If your list of works cited contains items by two or more different authors with the same last name, include the initial of the first name in the parenthetical reference.

> Web surfing requires more mental involvement than channel surfing (S. Johnson 107).

Note that a period follows the initial.

13. Two or more sources within the same sentence

Place each citation directly after the statement it supports.

> In the 1990s, many sweeping pronouncements were made that the Internet is the best opportunity to improve education since the printing press (Ellsworth xxii) or even in the history of the world (Dyrli and Kinnaman 79).

14. Two or more sources within the same citation

If two sources support a single point, separate them with a semicolon.

> (McKibbin 39; Gore 92)

15. Work quoted in another source

When you do not have access to the original source of the material you wish to use, put the abbreviation *qtd. in* (quoted in) before the information about the indirect source.

> National governments have become increasingly what Ulrich Beck, in a 1999 interview, calls "zombie institutions"—institutions that are "dead and still alive" (qtd. in Bauman 6).

16. Literary works

To supply a reference to a literary work, you sometimes need more than a page number from a specific edition. Readers should be able to locate a quotation in any edition of the book. Give the page number from the edition that you are using, then a semicolon and other identifying information.

> "Marriage is a house" is one of the most memorable lines in *Don Quixote* (546; pt. 2, bk. 3, ch. 19).

MLA Works-Cited List: Books

One author

17. Book by one author

The author's last name comes first, followed by a comma, the first name, and a period.

> Doctorow, E. L. *The March*. New York: Random, 2005. Print.

18. Two or more books by the same author

In the entry for the first book, include the author's name. In the second entry, substitute three hyphens and a period for the author's name. List the titles of books by the same author in alphabetical order.

> Grimsley, Jim. *Boulevard*. Chapel Hill: Algonquin, 2002. Print.
> ---. *Dream Boy*. New York: Simon, 1995. Print.

Multiple authors

19. Book by two or three authors

Second and subsequent authors' names appear first name first. A comma separates the authors' names.

> Chapkis, Wendy, and Richard J. Webb. *Dying to Get High: Marijuana as Medicine.* New York: New York UP, 2008. Print.

20. Book by four or more authors

You may use the phrase *et al.* (meaning "and others") for all authors but the first, or you may write out all the names. Use the same method in the in-text citation as you do in the works-cited list.

> Zukin, Cliff, et al. *A New Engagement? Political Participation, Civic Life, and the Changing American Citizen.* New York: Oxford UP, 2006. Print.

Anonymous and group authors

21. Book by an unknown author

Begin the entry with the title.

> *Encyclopedia of Americana.* New York: Somerset, 2001. Print.

22. Book by a group or organization

Treat the group as the author of the work.

> United Nations. *The Charter of the United Nations: A Commentary.* New York: Oxford UP, 2000. Print.

23. Religious texts

Do not italicize the title of a sacred text, including the Bible, unless you are citing a specific edition.

> Holy Bible. King James Text: Modern Phrased Version. New York: Oxford UP, 1980. Print.

Imprints, reprints, and undated books

24. Book with no publication date

If no year of publication is given but can be approximated, put a *c.* ("circa") and the approximate date in brackets: [c. 2009]. Otherwise, put *n.d.* ("no date"). For works before 1900, you do not need to list the publisher.

> O'Sullivan, Colin. *Traditions and Novelties of the Irish Country Folk.* Dublin, [c. 1793]. Print.

> James, Franklin. *In the Valley of the King.* Cambridge: Harvard UP, n.d. Print.

25. Reprinted works

For works of fiction that have been printed in many different editions or reprints, give the original publication date after the title.

> Wilde, Oscar. *The Picture of Dorian Gray*. 1890. New York: Norton, 2001. Print.

Parts of books

26. Introduction, foreword, preface, or afterword

Give the author and then the name of the specific part being cited. Next, name the book. Then, if the author for the whole work is different, put that author's name after the word *By*. Place inclusive page numbers at the end.

> Benstock, Sheri. Introduction. *The House of Mirth*. By Edith Wharton. Boston: Bedford-St. Martin's, 2002. 3-24. Print.

27. Single chapter written by same author as the book

> Ardis, Ann L. "Mapping the Middlebrow in Edwardian England." *Modernism and Cultural Conflict: 1880-1922*. Cambridge: Cambridge UP, 2002. 114-42. Print.

28. Selection from an anthology or edited collection

> Sedaris, David. "Full House." *The Best American Nonrequired Reading 2004*. Ed. Dave Eggers. Boston: Houghton, 2004. 350-58. Print.

29. Article in a reference work

You can omit the names of editors and most publishing information for an article from a familiar reference work. Identify the edition by date. There is no need to give the page numbers when a work is arranged alphabetically. Give the author's name, if known.

> "Utilitarianism." *The Columbia Encyclopedia*. 6th ed. 2001. Print.

Editions and translations

30. Book with an editor

List an edited book under the editor's name if your focus is on the editor. Otherwise, cite an edited book under the author's name as shown in the second example below.

> Lewis, Gifford, ed. *The Big House of Inver*. By Edith Somerville and Martin Ross. Dublin: Farmar, 2000. Print.

> Somerville, Edith, and Martin Ross. *The Big House of Inver*. Ed. Gifford Lewis. Dublin: Farmar, 2000. Print.

31. Book with a translator

> Benjamin, Walter. *The Arcades Project*. Trans. Howard Eiland and Kevin McLaughlin. Cambridge: Harvard UP, 1999. Print.

32. Second or subsequent edition of a book

> Hawthorn, Jeremy, ed. *A Concise Glossary of Contemporary Literary Theory*. 3rd ed. London: Arnold, 2001. Print.

Multivolume works

33. Multivolume work
Identify both the volume you have used and the total number of volumes in the set.

> Samuel, Raphael. *Theatres of Memory*. Vol. 1. London: Verso, 1999. 2 vols. Print.

If you refer to more than one volume, identify the specific volume in your in-text citations, and list the total number of volumes in your list of works cited.

> Samuel, Raphael. *Theatres of Memory*. 2 vols. London: Verso, 1999. Print.

MLA Works-Cited List: Periodicals
Journal articles

34. Article by one author

> Mallory, Anne. "Burke, Boredom, and the Theater of Counterrevolution." *PMLA* 118.2 (2003): 329-43. Print.

35. Article by two or three authors

> Miller, Thomas P., and Brian Jackson. "What Are English Majors For?" *College Composition and Communication* 58.4 (2007): 825-31. Print.

36. Article by four or more authors

You may use the phrase *et al.* (meaning "and others") for all authors but the first, or you may write out all the names.

> Breece, Katherine E., et al. "Patterns of mtDNA Diversity in Northwestern North America." *Human Biology* 76.1 (2004): 33-54. Print.

Pagination in journals

37. Article in a scholarly journal

List the volume and issue number after the name of the journal.

> Duncan, Mike. "Whatever Happened to the Paragraph?" *College English* 69.5 (2007): 470-95. Print.

38. Article in a scholarly journal that uses only issue numbers

List the issue number after the name of the journal.

> McCall, Sophie. "Double Vision Reading." *Canadian Literature* 194 (2007): 95-97. Print.

Magazines

39. Monthly or seasonal magazines

Use the month (or season) and year in place of the volume. There is no comma before the date. Abbreviate the names of all months except May, June, and July.

> Barlow, John Perry. "Africa Rising: Everything You Know about Africa Is Wrong." *Wired* Jan. 1998: 142-58. Print.

40. Weekly or biweekly magazines

Give both the day and the month of publication, as listed on the issue.

> Brody, Richard. "A Clash of Symbols." *New Yorker* 25 June 2007: 16. Print.

Newspapers

41. Newspaper article by one author

The author's last name comes first, followed by a comma and the first name.

> Marriott, Michel. "Arts and Crafts for the Digital Age." *New York Times* 8 June 2006, late ed.: C13. Print.

42. Article by two or three authors

The second and subsequent authors' names are printed in regular order, first name first:

> Schwirtz, Michael, and Joshua Yaffa. "A Clash of Cultures at a Square in Moscow." *New York Times* 11 July 2007, late ed.: A9. Print.

43. Newspaper article by an unknown author

Begin the entry with the title.

> "The Dotted Line." *Washington Post* 8 June 2006, final ed.: E2. Print.

Reviews, editorials, letters to the editor

44. Review

If there is no title, just name the work reviewed.

> Mendelsohn, Daniel. "The Two Oscar Wildes." Rev. of *The Importance of Being Earnest*, dir. Oliver Parker. *The New York Review of Books* 10 Oct. 2002: 23-24. Print.

45. Editorial

> "Hush-hush, Sweet Liberty." Editorial. *Los Angeles Times* 7 July 2007: A18. Print.

46. Letter to the editor

> Doyle, Joe. Letter. *Direct* 1 July 2007: 48. Print.

MLA Works-Cited List: Library Database Sources

47. Work from a library database

Begin with the print publication information, then the name of the database (italicized), the medium of publication (*Web*), and the date of access.

> Snider, Michael. "Wired to Another World." *Maclean's* 3 Mar. 2003: 23-24. *Academic Search Premier*. Web. 14 Jan. 2010.

MLA Works-Cited List: Online Sources
Web publications

When do you list a URL? MLA style no longer requires including URLs of Web sources. URLs are of limited value because they change frequently and they can be specific to an individual search. Include the URL as supplementary information only when your readers probably cannot locate the source without the URL.

48. Publication by a known author

> Boerner, Steve. "Leopold Mozart." *The Mozart Project: Biography.* The Mozart Project, 21 Mar. 1998. Web. 30 Oct. 2010.

49. Publication by a group or organization

If a work has no author's or editor's name listed, begin the entry with the title.

> "State of the Birds." *Audubon.* National Audubon Society, 2008. Web. 19 Aug. 2010.

50. Article in a scholarly journal on the Web

Some scholarly journals are published on the Web only. List articles by author, title, name of journal in italics, volume and issue number, and year of publication. If the journal does not have page numbers, use *n. pag.* in place of page numbers. Then list the medium of publication (*Web*) and the date of access (day, month, and year).

> Fleckenstein, Kristie. "Who's Writing? Aristotelian Ethos and the Author Position in Digital Poetics." *Kairos* 11.3 (2007): n. pag. Web. 6 Apr. 2010.

51. Article in a newspaper on the Web

The first date is the date of publication; the second is the date of access.

> Brown, Patricia Leigh. "Australia in Sonoma." *New York Times.* New York Times, 5 July 2008. Web. 3 Aug. 2010.

52. Article in a magazine on the Web

> Brown, Patricia Leigh. "The Wild Horse Is Us." *Newsweek.* Newsweek, 1 July 2008. Web. 12 Dec. 2010.

53. Book on the Web

> Prebish, Charles S., and Kenneth K. Tanaka. *The Faces of Buddhism in America*. Berkeley: U of California P, 2003. *eScholarship Editions*. Web. 2 May 2010.

Other online sources

54. Blog entry

If there is no sponsor or publisher for the blog, use *N.p.*

> Arrington, Michael. "Think Before You Voicemail." *TechCrunch*. N.p., 5 July 2008. Web. 10 Sept. 2010.

55. E-mail

Give the name of the writer, the subject line, a description of the message, the date, and the medium of delivery (*E-mail*).

> Ballmer, Steve. "A New Era of Business Productivity and Innovation." Message to Microsoft Executive E-mail. 30 Nov. 2010. E-mail.

56. Video on the Web

Video on the Web often lacks a creator and a date. Begin the entry with a title if you cannot find a creator. Use *n.d.* if you cannot find a date.

> Wesch, Michael. *A Vision of Students Today*. *YouTube*. YouTube, 2007. Web. 28 May 2010.

57. Personal home page

List *Home page* without quotation marks in place of the title. If no date is listed, use *n.d.*

> Graff, Harvey J. Home page. Dept. of English, Ohio State U, n.d. Web. 15 Nov. 2010.

58. Wiki entry

A wiki is a collaborative writing and editing tool. Although some topic-specific wikis are written and carefully edited by recognized scholars, the more popular wiki sites—such as *Wikipedia*—are often considered unreliable sources for academic papers.

> "Snowboard." *Wikipedia*. Wikimedia Foundation, 2009. Web. 30 Jan. 2010.

59. Podcast

Sussingham, Robin. "All Things Autumn." No. 2. *HighLifeUtah*. N.p.,
20 Nov. 2006. Web. 28 Feb. 2010.

60. PDFs and digital files

PDFs and other digital files can often be downloaded through links. Determine the kind of work you are citing, include the appropriate information for the particular kind of work, and list the type of file.

Glaser, Edward L., and Albert Saiz. "The Rise of the Skilled City." Discussion
Paper No. 2025. Harvard Institute of Economic Research. Cambridge:
Harvard U, 2003. PDF file.

MLA Works-Cited List: Other Sources

61. Sound recording

McCoury, Del, perf. "1952 Vincent Black Lightning." By Richard Thompson.
Del and the Boys. Ceili, 2001. CD.

62. Film

Begin with the title in italics. List the director, the distributor, the date, and the medium. Other data, such as the names of the screenwriters and performers, is optional.

Wanted. Dir. Timur Bekmambetov. Perf. James McAvoy, Angelina Jolie, and
Morgan Freeman. Universal, 2008. Film.

63. DVD

No Country for Old Men. Dir. Joel Coen and Ethan Coen. Perf. Tommy Lee
Jones, Javier Bardem, and Josh Brolin. Paramount, 2007. DVD.

64. Television or radio program

"Kaisha." *The Sopranos*. Perf. James Gandolfini, Lorraine Bracco, and Edie
Falco. HBO. 4 June 2006. Television.

65. Personal interview

Andrews, Michael. Personal interview. 25 Sept. 2010.

Sample MLA paper

Brian Witkowski

Professor Mendelsohn

RHE 309K

3 May 2010

Need a Cure for Tribe Fever?

How About a Dip in the Lake?

Everyone is familiar with the Cleveland Indians' Chief Wahoo logo—and I do mean everyone, not just Clevelanders. Across America people wear the smiling mascot on Cleveland Indians caps and jerseys, and recent trends in sports merchandise have popularized new groovy multicolored Indians sportswear. Because of lucrative contracts between major league baseball and Little League, youth teams all over the country don Cleveland's famous (or infamous) smiling Indian each season as fresh-faced kids scamper onto the diamonds looking like mini major leaguers (Liu). Various incarnations of the famous Chief Wahoo—described by writer Ryan Zimmerman as "a grotesque caricature grinning idiotically through enormous bucked teeth"—have been around since the 1940s. Now redder and even more cartoonish than the original hook-nosed, beige Indian with a devilish grin, Wahoo often passes as a cheerful baseball buddy like the San Diego Chicken or the St. Louis Cardinals' Fredbird.

Though defined by its distinctive logo, Cleveland baseball far preceded its famous mascot. The team changed from the Forest Citys to the Spiders to the Bluebirds/Blues to the Broncos to the Naps and finally to the Indians. Dubbed the Naps in 1903 in honor of its star player and manager Napoleon Lajoie, the team gained their current appellation in 1915. After Lajoie was traded, the team's president challenged sportswriters to devise a suitable "temporary" label for the floundering club. Publicity material claims that the writers decided on the Indians to celebrate Louis Sockalexis, a Penobscot Indian who played for the team from 1897 to 1899. With a high batting average and the notability of being the first Native American in professional baseball, Sockalexis was immortalized by the new Cleveland label (Schneider 10-23). (Contrary to popular lore, some cite alternative—and less reverent—motivations behind the team's

---

Annotations (margin notes):

Include your last name and page number as page header, beginning with the first page, 1/2" from the top.

MLA style does not require a title page. Ask your instructor whether you need one.

Center your title. Do not put the title in quotation marks or type it in all capital letters.

Use 1" margins all around. Double-space everything.

Cite publications by the name of the author (or authors).

Indent each paragraph 1/2" on the ruler in your word processing program.

Witkowski 2

naming and point to a lack of Sockalexis publicity in period newspaper articles discussing the team's naming process [Staurowsky 95-97].) Almost ninety years later, the "temporary" name continues to raise eyebrows, in both its marketability and its ideological questionability.

Today the logo is more than a little embarrassing. Since the high-profile actions of the American Indian Movement (AIM) in the 1970s, sports teams around the country—including the Indians—have been criticized for their racially insensitive mascots. Native American groups question these caricatured icons—not just because of grossly stereotyped mascots, but also because of what visual displays of team support say about Native American culture. Across the country, professional sporting teams, as well as high schools and colleges, perform faux rituals in the name of team spirit. As Tim Giago, publisher of *The Lakota Times*, a weekly South Dakotan Native American newspaper, has noted,

> The sham rituals, such as the wearing of feathers, smoking of so-called peace pipes, beating of tomtoms, fake dances, horrendous attempts at singing Indian songs, the so-called war whoops, and the painted faces, address more than the issues of racism. They are direct attacks upon the spirituality of the Indian people. (qtd. in Wulf)

Controversy over such performances still fuels the fire between activists and alumni at schools such as the University of Illinois at Champaign-Urbana, where during many decades of football halftimes fans cheered the performance of a student (often white) dressed as Chief Illiniwek. In March of 2007, the University of Illinois board of trustees voted in a nearly unanimous decision to retire the mascot's name, regalia and image ("Illinois").

Since 1969, when Oklahoma disavowed its "Little Red" mascot, more than 600 school and minor league teams have followed a more ethnically sensitive trend and ditched their "tribal" mascots (Price). High-profile teams such as Stanford, St. Johns University, and Miami (Ohio) University have changed their team names from the Indians to the Cardinal (1972), the Redmen to the Red Storm (1993), and the Redskins to the Redhawks (1996), respectively. In 2005, the NCAA officially ruled that "colleges whose nicknames or mascots refer to American Indians will not be permitted to hold National Collegiate Athletic Association tournament events" (Wolverton). By September 2005, only seventeen schools remained in violation (Wolverton). While many people see such controversies as mere bowing to the pressures of the late twentieth and early twenty-first centuries, others see the mascot issue as a topic well worthy of debate.

Cleveland's own Chief Wahoo has far from avoided controversy. Multiple conflicts between Wahoo devotees and dissenters occur annually during the baseball season. At the opening game of 1995, fifty Native Americans and supporters took stations around Jacobs Field to demonstrate against the use of the cartoonish smiling crimson mascot (Kropk). Arrests were made in 1998 when demonstrators from the United Church of Christ burned a three-foot Chief Wahoo doll in effigy ("Judge"). Opinions on the mascot remain mixed. Jacoby Ellsbury, outfielder for the Boston Red Sox and a member of the Colorado River Indian Tribes, said in 2007, "I'm not offended [by the mascot]. You can look at it two different ways. You can look at it that it's offensive or you can look at it that they are representing Native Americans. Usually I'll try to take the positive out of it" (Shaughnessy). Nonetheless, Ellsbury still acknowledges that he "can see both sides of [the controversy]" (Shaughnessy). Wedded to their memorabilia, fans proudly stand behind their Indian as others lobby vociferously for its removal, splitting government officials, fans, and social and religious groups.

In 2000, Cleveland mayor Michael White came out publicly against the team mascot, joining an already established group of religious leaders, laypersons, and civil rights activists who had demanded Wahoo's retirement. African American religious and civic leaders such as Rev. Gregory A. Jacobs pointed to the absurdity of minority groups who embrace the Wahoo symbol. "Each of us has had to fight its [sic] own battle, quite frankly," Jacobs stated. "We cannot continue to live in this kind of hypocrisy that says, Yes, we are in solidarity with my [sic] brothers and sisters, yet we continue to exploit them" (qtd. in Briggs).

This controversy also swirls outside of the greater Cleveland area. In 2009, the image of Wahoo was removed from the team's training complex in Goodyear, Arizona ("Cleveland"), while the *Seattle Times* went so far as to digitally remove the Wahoo symbol from images of the Cleveland baseball cap ("Newspaper"). As other teams make ethnically sensitive and image-conscious choices to change their mascots, Cleveland stands firm in its resolve to retain Chief Wahoo. Despite internal division and public ridicule fueled by the team icon, the city refuses to budge.

Cleveland's stubbornness on the issue of Wahoo runs contrary to the city's recently improved image and downtown revitalization. As a native of Cleveland, I understand the power of "Tribe Fever" and the unabashed pride one feels when wearing Wahoo garb during a winning (or losing) season. Often it is not until we leave northeastern Ohio that we realize the negative image that Wahoo projects. What then can Cleveland do to simultaneously save face and bolster its burgeoning positive city image? I propose that the team finally change the "temporary" Indians label. In a city so proud of its diverse ethnic heritage—African American, Italian American, and Eastern European American to name a few examples—why stand as a bearer of retrograde ethnic politics? Cleveland should take this opportunity to link its positive Midwestern image to the team of which it is so proud. I propose changing the team's name to the Cleveland Lakers.

The city's revival in the last twenty years has embraced the geographic and aesthetic grandeur of Lake Erie. Disavowing its "mistake on the lake" moniker of the late 1970s, Cleveland has traded aquatic pollution fires for a booming lakeside business district. Attractions such as the Great Lakes Science Center, the Rock and Roll Hall of Fame, and the new Cleveland Browns Stadium take advantage of the beauty of the landscape and take back the lake. Why not continue this trend through one of the city's biggest and highest-profile moneymakers: professional baseball? By changing the team's name to the Lakers, the city would gain national advertisement for one of its major selling points, while simultaneously announcing a new ethnically inclusive image that is appropriate to our wonderfully diverse city. It would be a public relations triumph for the city.

Of course this call will be met with many objections. Why do we have to buckle to pressure? Do we not live in a free country? What fans and citizens alike need to keep in mind is that ideological pressures would not be the sole motivation for this move. Yes, retiring Chief Wahoo would take Cleveland off AIM's hit list. Yes, such a move would promote a kinder and gentler Cleveland. At the same time, however, such a gesture would work toward uniting the community. So much civic division exists over this issue that a renaming could help start to heal these old wounds.

Additionally, this type of change could bring added economic prosperity to the city. First, a change in name will bring a new wave of team merchandise. Licensed sports apparel generates more than a 10-billion-dollar annual retail business in the United States, and teams have proven repeatedly that new uniforms and logos can provide new capital. After all, a new logo for the Seattle Mariners bolstered severely slumping merchandise sales (Lefton). Wahoo devotees need not panic; the booming vintage uniform business will keep him alive, as is demonstrated by the current ability to purchase replica 1940s jerseys with the old Indians logo. Also, good press created by this change will hopefully help increase tourism in Cleveland. If the goodwill created by the Cleveland Lakers can prove half as profitable as the Rock and Roll Hall of Fame, then local businesses will be humming a happy tune. Finally, if history repeats itself, a change to a more culturally inclusive logo could, in and of itself, prove to be a cash cow. When Miami University changed from the Redskins to the Redhawks, it saw alumni donations skyrocket (Price). A less divisive mascot would prove lucrative to the ball club, the city, and the players themselves. (Sluggers with inoffensive logos make excellent spokesmen.)

Perhaps this proposal sounds far-fetched: Los Angeles may seem to have cornered the market on Lakers. But where is their lake? (The Lakers were formerly the Minneapolis Lakers, where the name makes sense in the "Land of 10,000 Lakes.") Various professional and collegiate sports teams—such as baseball's San Francisco Giants and football's New York Giants—share a team name, so licensing should not be an issue. If Los Angeles has qualms about sharing the name, perhaps Cleveland could persuade Los Angeles to become the Surfers or the Stars; after all, Los Angeles players seem to spend as much time on the big and small screens as on the court.

Witkowski 6

Now is the perfect time for Cleveland to make this jump. Perhaps a new look will help usher in a new era of Cleveland baseball and a World Series ring to boot. Through various dry spells, the Cleveland Indians institution has symbolically turned to the descendants of Sockalexis, asking for goodwill or a latter-generation Penobscot slugger (Fleitz 3). Perhaps the best way to win goodwill, fortunes, and the team's first World Series title since 1948 would be to eschew a grinning life-size Chief Wahoo for the new Cleveland Laker, an oversized furry monster sporting water wings, cleats, and a catcher's mask. His seventh-inning-stretch show could include an air-guitar solo with a baseball bat as he quietly reminds everyone that the Rock Hall is just down the street.

Witkowski 7

Center "Works Cited" on a new page.

Works Cited

Briggs, David. "Churches Go to Bat Against Chief Wahoo." *Cleveland Plain Dealer* 25 Aug. 2000: 1A. *LexisNexis Academic*. Web. 19 Apr. 2010.

Double-space all entries. Indent all but the first line in each entry one-half inch.

"Cleveland Indians' Chief Wahoo Logo Left Off Team's Ballpark, Training Complex in Goodyear, Arizona." *Cleveland.com*. Cleveland Plain Dealer, 12 Apr. 2009. Web. 23 Apr. 2010.

Fleitz, David L. *Louis Sockalexis: The First Cleveland Indian*. Jefferson: McFarland, 2002. Print.

"Illinois Trustees Vote to Retire Chief Illiniwek." *ESPN*. ESPN Internet Ventures, 13 Mar. 2007. Web. 26 Apr. 2010.

Alphabetize entries by the last names of the authors or by the first important word in the title if no author is listed.

"Judge Dismisses Charges Against City in Wahoo Protest." *Associated Press* 6 Aug. 2001. *LexisNexis Academic*. Web. 19 Apr. 2010.

Kropk, M. R. "Chief Wahoo Protestors Largely Ignored by Fans." *Austin American Statesman* 6 May 1995: D4. Print.

Lefton, Terry. "Looks Are Everything: For New Franchises, Licensing Battles Must Be Won Long Before the Team Even Takes the Field." *Sport* 89 (May 1998): 32. Print.

Italicize the titles of books and periodicals.

Liu, Caitlin. "Bawl Game." *Portfolio.com*. Condé Nast, 21 Oct. 2008.
    Web. 28 Apr. 2009.

"Newspaper Edits Cleveland Indian Logo from Cap Photo." *Associated
    Press* 31 Mar. 1997. *LexisNexis Academic*. Web. 27 Apr. 2010.

Price, S. L. "The Indian Wars." *Sports Illustrated* 4 Mar. 2002: 66+.
    Academic OneFile. Web. 20 Apr. 2010.

Schneider, Russell. *The Cleveland Indians Encyclopedia*. Philadelphia:
    Temple UP, 1996. Print.

Shaughnessy, Dan. "They've Had Some Chief Concerns." *Boston Globe* 12
    October 2007: C5. *LexisNexis Academic*. Web. 19 Apr. 2010.

Staurowsky, Ellen J. "Sockalexis and the Making of the Myth at the Core of
    the Cleveland's 'Indian' Image." *Team Spirits: The Native American
    Mascots Controversy*. Eds. C. Richard King and Charles Fruehling
    Springwood. Lincoln: U of Nebraska P, 2001. 82-106. Print.

Wolverton, Brad. "NCAA Restricts Colleges With Indian Nicknames and
    Mascots." *Chronicle of Higher Education* 2 Sept. 2005: A65.
    ProQuest. Web. 25 Apr. 2010.

Wulf, Steve. "A Brave Move." *Sports Illustrated* 24 Feb. 1992: 7. Print.

Zimmerman, Ryan. "The Cleveland Indians' Mascot Must Go." *Christian
    Science Monitor* 15 Oct. 2007: 5. *LexisNexis Academic*. Web. 19
    Apr. 2010.

Check to make sure all the sources you have cited in your text are in the list of works cited.

For additional writing resources that will help you master the objectives of this chapter, go to your **MyLab**.

21 | Documenting Sources in APA Style

QUICK TAKE

In this chapter you will learn to

1. Describe the elements of APA documentation style, including in-text citations and the References list (see below)
2. Identify the basic patterns for APA in-text citations (see page 286)
3. Identify the basic patterns for APA References entries, including entries for books, periodicals, databases, online sources, and nonprint sources (see page 288)

Papers written for the social sciences, including government, linguistics, psychology, sociology, and education, frequently use the APA documentation style. For a detailed treatment of APA style, consult the *Publication Manual of the American Psychological Association*, sixth edition (2010).

Elements of APA Documentation

Citing a source in your paper

APA style emphasizes the date of publication. When you cite an author's name in the body of your paper, always include the date of publication. Notice too that APA style includes the abbreviation for page "(p.)" in front of the page number. A comma separates each element of the citation.

> Zukin (2004) observes that teens today begin to shop for themselves at age 13 or 14, "the same age when lower-class children, in the past, became apprentices or went to work in factories" (p. 50).

If the author's name is not mentioned in the sentence, cite the author, date, and page number inside parentheses.

> One sociologist notes that teens today begin to shop for themselves at age 13 or 14, "the same age when lower-class children, in the past, became apprentices or went to work in factories" (Zukin, 2004, p. 50).

The corresponding entry in the references list would be as follows.

Zukin, S. (2004). *Point of purchase: How shopping changed American culture.* New York, NY: Routledge.

Creating an APA-style references list

To create your references list, go through your paper and find every reference to the sources you consulted during your research. Each in-text citation must have an entry in your references list.

Organize your references list alphabetically by authors' last names or, if no author is listed, the first word in the title other than *a, an,* or *the.* APA style uses three basic forms for entries in the references list: books, periodicals (scholarly journals, newspapers, magazines), and online sources (online library database sources, Web sites, blogs, online newspapers, online magazines, and online government documents).

References entries for books

Orum, A. M., & Chen, X. (2003). *The world of cities: Places in comparative and historical perspective.* Malden, MA: Blackwell.

1. Author's or editor's name.
- List the author's name with the last name first, followed by a comma and the author's initials.
- Join two authors' names with an ampersand.
- If an editor, put "(Ed.)" after the name: Kavanaugh, P. (Ed.).

2. (Year of publication).
- Give the year of publication in parentheses. If no year of publication is given, write *(n.d.)* ("no date") : Smith, S. (n.d.).
- If it is a multivolume edited work, published over a period of more than one year, put the time span in parentheses: Smith, S. (1999–2001).

3. Title of book.
- Italicize the title.
- Capitalize only the first word, proper nouns, and the first word after a colon.
- If the title is in a foreign language, copy it exactly as it appears on the title page.

4. Publication information.

- For all books list the city with a two-letter state abbreviation (or full country name) after the city name. If more than one city is given on the title page, list only the first.
- Do not shorten or abbreviate words like *University* or *Press*. Omit words such as *Co.*, *Inc.*, and *Publishers*.

References entries for periodicals

Lee, E. (2007). Wired for gender: Experientiality and gender-stereotyping in computer-mediated communication. *Media Psychology, 10,* 182–210.

1. Author's name.

- List the author's name, last name first, followed by the author's initials.
- Join two authors' names with a comma and an ampersand.

2. (Year of publication).

- Give the year the work was published in parentheses.

3. Title of article.

- Do not use quotation marks. If there is a book title in the article title, italicize it.
- Capitalize only the first word of the title, the first word of the subtitle, and any proper nouns in the title.

4. Publication information.

- Italicize the journal name.
- Capitalize all nouns, verbs, and pronouns, and the first word of the journal name. Do not capitalize any article, preposition, or coordinating conjunction unless it is the first word of the title or subtitle.
- Put a comma after the journal name.
- Italicize the volume number and follow it with a comma.
- If each issue of the journal begins on page 1, give the issue number in parentheses, followed by comma.
- Give page numbers of the article (see sample references 19 and 20 for more on pagination). Note: APA uses N dashes in page spans and provides the full numbers.

References entries for online sources

> Department of Justice. Federal Bureau of Investigation. (2004). Hate crime statistics 2004: Report summary. Retrieved from http://www.fbi.gov /ucr/hc2004/openpage.htm

1. Author's name, associated institution, or organization.
- List the author's name, if given, with the last name first, followed by the author's initials.
- If the only authority you find is a group or organization (as in this example), list its name as the author.
- If the author or organization is not identified, begin the reference with the title of the document.

2. (Date of publication).
- List the date the site was produced, last revised, or copyrighted.

3. Title of page or article.
- If you are citing a page or article that has a title, treat the title like an article in a periodical. If you are citing an entire Web site, treat the name like a book.
- If the Web site has no title, list it by author or creator.

4. Retrieval information
- If your source has been assigned a DOI (Digital Object Identifier), list it after the title. Do not add a period at the end of a DOI.
- If the source does not have a DOI, list the URL of the journal's home page.

APA In-Text Citations

1. **Author named in your text**

> Influential sociologist Daniel Bell (1973) noted a shift in the United States to the "postindustrial society" (p. 3).

2. **Author not named in your text**

> In 1997, the Gallup poll reported that 55% of adults in the United States think secondhand smoke is "very harmful," compared to only 36% in 1994 (Saad, 1997, p. 4).

3. Work by a single author

(Bell, 1973, p. 3)

4. Work by two authors

Notice that APA uses an ampersand (&) with multiple authors' names rather than *and*.

(Suzuki & Irabu, 2002, p. 404)

5. Work by three to five authors

The authors' last names follow the order of the title page.

(Francisco, Vaughn, & Romano, 2001, p. 7)

Subsequent references can use the first name and *et al.*

(Francisco et al., 2001, p. 17)

6. Work by six or more authors

Use the first author's last name and *et al.* for all in-text references.

(Swallit et al., 2004, p. 49)

7. Work by a group or organization

Identify the group author in the text and place only the page number in parentheses.

The National Organization for Women (2001) observed that this "generational shift in attitudes towards marriage and childrearing" will have profound consequences (p. 325).

8. Work by an unknown author

Use a shortened version of the title (or the full title if it is short) in place of the author's name. Capitalize all key words in the title. If it is an article title, place it in quotation marks.

("Derailing the Peace Process," 2003, p. 44)

9. Quotations of 40 words or longer

Indent long quotations 1/2 inch and omit quotation marks. Note that the period appears before the parentheses in an indented block quote.

> Orlean (2001) has attempted to explain the popularity of the painter Thomas Kinkade:
>> People like to own things they think are valuable. . . . The high price of limited editions is part of their appeal; it implies that they are choice and exclusive, and that only a certain class of people will be able to afford them. (p. 128)

APA References List: Books

10. Book by one author

The author's last name comes first, followed by a comma and the author's initials.

> Ball, E. (2000). *Slaves in the family*. New York, NY: Ballantine Books.

If an editor, put "(Ed.)" in parentheses after the name.

> Kavanagh, P. (Ed.). (1969). *Lapped furrows*. New York, NY: Hand Press.

11. Book by two authors

Join two authors' names with a comma and ampersand.

> Hardt, M., & Negri, A. (2000). *Empire*. Cambridge, MA: Harvard University Press.

If editors, use "(Eds.)" after the names.

> McClelland, D., & Eismann, K. (Eds).

12. Book by three or more authors

List last names and initials for up to seven authors, with an ampersand between the last two names. For works with eight or more authors, list the first six names, then an ellipsis, then the last author's name.

> Anders, K., Child, H., Davis, K., Logan, O., Petersen, J., Tymes, J., . . . Johnson, S.

13. Chapter in an edited collection

Add "In" after the selection title and before the names of the editor(s).

Howard, A. (1997). Labor, history, and sweatshops in the new global economy. In A. Ross (Ed.), *No sweat: Fashion, free trade, and the rights of garment workers* (pp. 151–172). New York, NY: Verso.

14. Published dissertation or thesis

If the dissertation you are citing is published by University Microfilms International (UMI), provide the order number as the last item in the entry.

Price, J. J. (1998). Flight maps: Encounters with nature in modern American culture. *Dissertation Abstracts International, 59*(5), 1635. (UMI No. 9835237)

15. Government document

When the author and publisher are identical, use "Author" as the name of the publisher.

U.S. Environmental Protection Agency. (2002). *Respiratory health effects of passive smoking: Lung cancer and other disorders.* (EPA Publication No. 600/6-90/006 F). Washington, DC: Author.

APA References List: Periodicals

16. Article by one author

Kellogg, R. T. (2001). Competition for working memory among writing processes. *American Journal of Psychology, 114,* 175–192.

17. Article by multiple authors

Write out all of the authors' names, up to seven authors. For works with eight or more authors, list the first six names, then an ellipsis, then the last author's name.

Blades, J., & Rowe-Finkbeiner, K. (2006). The motherhood manifesto. *The Nation, 282*(20), 11–16.

18. Article by a group or organization

National Organization for Women (2002). Where to find feminists in Austin. *The NOW guide for Austin women.* Austin, TX: Chapter Press.

19. Article in a journal with continuous pagination

Include the volume number and the year, but not the issue number.

Engen, R., & Steen, S. (2000). The power to punish: Discretion and sentencing reform in the war on drugs. *American Journal of Sociology, 105,* 1357–1395.

20. Article in a journal paginated by issue

List the issue number in parentheses (not italicized) after the volume number. For a popular magazine that does not commonly use volume numbers, use the season or date of publication.

McGinn, D. (2006, June 5). Marriage by the numbers. *Newsweek, 40*–48.

21. Monthly publication

Barlow, J. P. (1998, January). Africa rising: Everything you know about Africa is wrong. *Wired, 142*–158.

22. Newspaper article

Hagenbaugh, B. (2005, April 25). Grads welcome an uptick in hiring. *USA Today,* p. A1.

APA References List: Library Database Sources

23. Document from a library database

Increasingly, articles are accessed online. Because URLs frequently change, many scholarly publishers have begun to use a Digital Object Identifier (DOI), a unique alphanumeric string that is permanent. If a DOI is available, use the DOI.

APA no longer requires listing the names of well-known databases. The article below was retrieved from the PsychARTICLES database, but there is no need to list the database, the retrieval date, or the URL if the DOI is listed.

Erdfelder, E. (2008). Experimental psychology: Good news. *Experimental Psychology, 55*(1), 1–2. doi:0.1027/1618-3169.55.1.1

APA References List: Online Sources

24. Online publication by a known author

Authorship is sometimes hard to discern for online sources. If you do have an author or creator to cite, follow the rules for periodicals and books.

> Carr, A. (2003, May 22). AAUW applauds senate support of title IX resolution. Retrieved from http://www.aauw.org/about/newsroom/press_releases /030522.cfm

25. Online publication by a group or organization

If the only authority you find is a group or organization, list its name as the author.

> Girls Incorporated. (2003). Girls' bill of rights. Retrieved from http://www.girlsinc.org/gc/page.php?id=9

26. Article in an online scholarly journal

> Brown, B. (2004). The order of service: the practical management of customer interaction. *Sociological Research Online, 9*(4). Retrieved from http://www.socresonline.org.uk/9/4/brown.html

27. Article in an online newspaper

> Slevin, C. (2005, April 25). Lawmakers want to put limits on private toll roads. *Boulder Daily Camera*. Retrieved from http://www.dailycamera.com

28. Article in an online magazine

> Pein, C. (2005, April 20). Is Al-Jazeera ready for prime time? *Salon*. Retrieved from http://www.salon.com

APA References List: Other Sources

29. Television program

> Burgess, M., & Green, M. (Writers). (2004). Irregular around the margins. [Television series episode]. In D. Chase (Producer), *The sopranos*. New York: HBO.

30. Film, Video, or DVD

> Kaurismäki, A. (Director). (1999). *Leningrad cowboys go America* [DVD]. United States: MGM.

31. Musical recording

List both the title of the song and the title of the album or CD. In the in-text citation, include side or track numbers.

> Lowe, N. (2001). Lately I've let things slide. On *The convincer* [CD]. Chapel Hill, NC: Yep Roc Records.

> For additional writing resources that will help you master the objectives of this chapter, go to your **MyLab**.

Contemporary Arguments

PART

6

22 | Negotiating the Environment

American Environmentalism

Most people agree that the modern environmental movement emerged from the work of two people: Aldo Leopold, who outlined a "land ethic" in his 1948 book *A Sand County Almanac*; and Rachel Carson, whose 1962 book *Silent Spring* sounded a national alarm against pesticides commonly used in the agriculture industry, particularly DDT. Together Leopold and Carson argued persuasively for a new sense of our relationship to our environment, for the conviction that we should be living in balance with nature, not in domination over it. Both books ultimately influenced not only agricultural practice but also efforts to protect endangered species, to regulate population growth, and to clean up our air and water resources. When President Richard Nixon created the Environmental Protection Agency in 1973, environmental concern became institutionalized in the United States; most states created their own departments of natural resources or environmental protection soon afterward.

Dams on the Klamath River in Oregon provide water to power plants, which in turn supply clean electricity. But dams also affect fish and other wildlife, farmers, and Native Americans who live along the river. When people decide to build a dam, whose priorities should be considered?

In part, Aldo Leopold and Rachel Carson were successful because their appeals struck a chord deep within many Americans. For in a very real sense environmentalism is anything but modern. Ingrained deep within the American character, it derives from a respect for the land—the American Eden—that is evident in the legend of Rip Van Winkle, in the work of Hudson River painters such as Thomas Cole, in the landscape architecture of Frederick Law Olmsted, in Henry David Thoreau's *Walden* and in Ralph Waldo Emerson's Transcendentalist writings in the 1850s, in John

> We are the most dangerous species of life on the planet, and every other species, even the earth itself, has cause to fear our power to exterminate. But we are also the only species which, when it chooses to do so, will go to great effort to save what it might destroy.
>
> —WALLACE STEGNER

Muir's testimonials about Yosemite, and in Theodore Roosevelt's withdrawals into the Badlands and his campaign to begin a system of national parks. Of course, the exploitation of the American green world for profit is also ingrained in our national character. Even as some Americans were revering the land as a special landscape that sustained them physically and spiritually, pioneers moving westward were subduing it for their own purposes, in the process spoiling rivers and air and virgin forests—and native peoples—in the name of development.

In this photograph of an environmental rally in Washington, D.C., what images evoke environmental themes?

Contemporary Arguments

Today, tensions between preserving nature and using nature are perhaps as high as they have ever been. When the BP spill dumped millions of gallons of crude oil into the Gulf of Mexico in 2010, the debate between exploiters of nature and preservers of nature became particularly fierce. The tensions inherent in the two positions help to explain why environmental issues remain so prevalent in public discourse.

■ What are—and what should be—the proper relationships among science, technology, and the environment?

■ What is the appropriate relationship between people and the natural environment?

■ How can humans balance resource development and resource protection—with "resources" including everything from timber and coal to streams and animals?

■ What are the nature and extent of global warming, and what counter-measures does it require?

■ How can poorer nations develop economically without negative global environmental repercussions?

Such questions are debated each day in all media, especially as organized environmental groups are legion, ranging from the activist Earth First! (whose 10,000 members sometimes advocate direct action in support of environmental aims) to more mainstream groups such as the Sierra Club or the Nature Conservancy. The Nature Conservancy has created a membership of about a million in an explicit effort to create partnerships between scientists and businesspeople in the interests of environmental reform. On the other hand, conservatives such as Rush Limbaugh

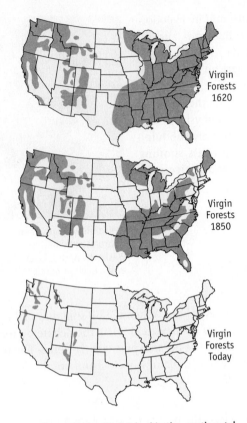

Virgin
Forests
1620

Virgin
Forests
1850

Virgin
Forests
Today

How virgin forests have diminished in the continental United States.

Source: *Atlas of the Historical Georgraphy of the United States*, ed. C. O. Paullin.

and Sarah Palin have often ridiculed the efforts of environmentalists in the interest of a relatively unbridled developmentalism that is in the optimistic tradition of nineteenth-century free enterprise.

Debates about environmental issues are part and parcel of American culture. In the following pages you will find a sampling of the arguments concerning our relationship to the natural world. Three selections (by Rachel Carson, Edward O. Wilson, and Wallace Stegner) offer philosophical perspectives and relate environmental ethics to human societies and practices—thereby providing context for a host of other, specific arguments, such as those about global warming and sustainability. We also present an argument and counterargument (by Chris Peckham and Mark Wright) on a particular issue of expediency: Do we have the financial resources to spend on saving exotic animal species (like pandas) when there are so many other pressing environmental issues before us?

Then this chapter turns to an important Issue in Focus, environmental sustainability: the question of whether the human race needs to change many of its most deeply held habits and practices in order to ward off ecological and human catastrophe. We include a range of perspectives on the matter, everything from Wendell Berry's eloquent and passionate advocacy for sustainable practices—environmental and economic practices, but also moral and cultural ones—to a statement by the National Association of Scholars that critiques nine shortcomings that the NAS sees within the sustainability movement. This Issue in Focus includes attacks on large corporations as greedy destroyers—and a defense of large corporations (by Jared Diamond) as the key agent toward meeting sustainability challenges. You will encounter a defense of the beef industry from a sustainability perspective and a critique of the "sustainable" organic food ideal. In addition, you'll read a journal article on land-use issues relative to urban sprawl and ways that citizens can negotiate viable solutions to them.

How serious is our current environmental predicament? Are some of our cultural practices truly unsustainable and destructive? What are the best ways to ensure that future generations will inherit a planet able to sustain happiness and prosperity? Must we give up many creature comforts in order to survive in a healthy environment? Must population controls be instituted in order to stave off mass starvation? What compromises must we make to balance economic growth, technological advancement and innovation, the preservation of green spaces, environmental quality, and biodiversity—and what should be our priorities?

Brown pelicans are common along the coasts of the South and California, but they were headed toward extinction by 1970 because the pesticide DDT caused their eggs to be too thin to support developing chicks to maturity. Although DDT was banned in the United States, many countries continue to use it for agricultural spraying and malaria control even though insects and mosquitoes have developed resistance to it.

Rachel Carson

The Obligation to Endure

Rachel Carson (1907–1964) was raised in Springdale, Pennsylvania, 18 miles up the Allegheny River from Pittsburgh, where she developed the love of nature that she maintained throughout her life. At age 22, she began her career as a marine biologist at Woods Hole, Massachusetts, and she later went to graduate school at Johns Hopkins University in Baltimore. In 1936, she began working in the agency that later became the U.S. Fish and Wildlife Service. A meticulous scientist, Carson wrote three highly praised books about the sea and wetlands: *Under the Sea Wind* (1941), *The Sea Around Us* (1951), and *The Edge of the Sea* (1954).

When Carson decided to write *Silent Spring* (published in 1962), it marked a great change in her life. For the first time, she became an environmental activist in addition to being an enthusiastic writer about nature. During the 1950s she had grown progressively alarmed at the effects of the chemical DDT on fish, waterfowl, and birds. When her initial alarms went unheard, because DDT was contributing to substantial increases in agricultural production and controlling disease-spreading insects, she decided to write a short book to raise public consciousness. That book was *Silent Spring*, one of the most important books of the past century.

What follows are the famous first chapter and beginning sections of the second chapter of *Silent Spring*. Notice how the two chapters use very different rhetorical tactics in order to persuade readers and move them to act.

I.

There was once a town in the heart of America where all life seemed to live in harmony with its surroundings. The town lay in the midst of a checkerboard of prosperous farms, with fields of grain and hillsides of orchards where, in spring, white clouds of bloom drifted above the green fields. In autumn, oak and maple and birch set up a blaze of color that flamed and flickered across a backdrop of pines. Then foxes barked in the hills and deer silently crossed the fields, half hidden in the mists of the fall mornings.

2   Along the roads, laurel, viburnum and alder, great ferns and wildflowers delighted the traveler's eye through much of the year. Even in winter the roadsides were places of beauty, where countless birds came to feed on the berries and on the seed heads of the dried weeds rising above the snow. The countryside was, in fact, famous for the abundance and the variety of its bird life, and when the flood of migrants was pouring through in spring and fall people traveled from great distances to observe them. Others came to fish the streams, which flowed clear and cold out of the hills and contained shady pools where trout lay. So it had been from the days many years ago when the first settlers raised their houses, sank their wells, and built their barns.

3   Then a strange blight crept over the area and everything began to change. Some evil spell had settled on the community: mysterious maladies swept the flocks of chickens; the cattle and sheep sickened and died. Everywhere was a shadow of death. The farmers spoke of much illness among their families. In the town the doctors had become more and more puzzled by new kinds of sickness appearing among their patients. There had been several sudden and unexpected deaths not only among adults but even among children, who would be stricken suddenly while at play and die within a few hours.

4   There was a strange stillness. The birds, for example—where had they gone? Many people spoke of them, puzzled and disturbed. The feeding stations in the backyards were deserted. The few birds seen anywhere were moribund; they trembled violently and could not fly. It was a spring without voices. On the mornings that had once throbbed with the dawn chorus of robins, catbirds, doves, jays, wrens, and scores of other bird voices there was now no sound; only silence lay over the fields and woods and marsh.

5   On the farms the hens brooded, but no chicks hatched. The farmers complained that they were unable to raise any pigs—the litters were small and the young survived only a few days. The apple trees were coming into bloom but no bees droned among the blossoms, so there was no pollination and there would be no fruit.

6   The roadsides, once so attractive, were now lined with browned and withered vegetation as though swept by fire. These, too, were silent, deserted by all living things. Even the streams were now lifeless. Anglers no longer visited them, for all the fish had died.

7   In the gutters under the eaves and between the shingles of roofs, a white granular powder still showed a few patches; some weeks before it had fallen like snow upon the roofs and the lawns, the fields and the streams.

8   No witchcraft, no enemy action had silenced the rebirth of new life in this stricken world. The people had done it themselves.

9   This town does not actually exist, but it might easily have a thousand counterparts in America or elsewhere in the world. I know of no community that has experienced all the misfortunes I describe. Yet every one of these disasters has actually happened somewhere, and many real communities have already suffered a substantial number of them. A grim specter has crept upon us almost unnoticed, and this imagined tragedy may easily become a stark reality we all shall know

     What has already silenced the voices of spring in countless towns in America? This book is an attempt to explain.

II.

The history of life on earth has been a history of interaction between living things and their surroundings. To a large extent, the physical form and the habits of the earth's vegetation and its animal life have been molded by the environment. Considering the whole span of earthly time, the opposite effect, in which life actually modifies its surroundings, has been relatively slight. Only within the moment of time represented by the present century has one species—man—acquired significant power to alter the nature of his world.

2   During the past quarter century this power has not only increased to one of disturbing magnitude but it has changed in character. The most alarming of all man's assaults upon the environment is the contamination of air, earth, rivers, and sea with dangerous and even lethal materials. This pollution is for the most part irrecoverable; the chain of evil it initiates not only in the world that must support life but in living tissues is for the most part irreversible. In this now universal contamination of the environment, chemicals are the sinister and little-recognized partners of radiation in changing the very nature of the world—the very nature of its life. Strontium 90, released through nuclear explosions into the air, comes to earth in rain or drifts down as fallout, lodges in soil, enters into the grass or corn or wheat grown there, and in time takes up its abode in the bones of a human being, there to remain until his death. Similarly, chemicals sprayed on croplands or forests or gardens lie long in soil, entering into living organisms, passing from one to another in a chain of poisoning and death. Or they pass mysteriously by underground streams until they emerge and, through the alchemy of air and sunlight, combine into new forms that kill vegetation, sicken cattle, and work unknown harm on those who drink from once pure wells. As Albert Schweitzer has said, "Man can hardly even recognize the devils of his own creation."

     It took hundreds of millions of years to produce the life that now inhabits the earth—eons of time in which that developing and evolving and diversifying life reached a state of adjustment and balance with its surroundings. The environment, rigorously shaping and directing the life it supported, contained elements that were hostile as well as supporting. Certain rocks gave out dangerous radiation; even within the light of the sun, from which all life draws its energy, there were short-wave radiations with power to injure.

Given time—time not in years but in millennia—life adjusts, and a balance has been reached. For time is the essential ingredient; but in the modern world there is no time.

4   The rapidity of change and the speed with which new situations are created follow the impetuous and heedless pace of man rather than the deliberate pace of nature. Radiation is no longer merely the background radiation of rocks, the bombardment of cosmic rays, the ultraviolet of the sun that have existed before there was any life on earth; radiation is now the unnatural creation of man's tampering with the atom. The chemicals to which life is asked to make its adjustment are no longer merely the calcium and silica and copper and all the rest of the minerals washed out of the rocks and carried in rivers to the sea; they are the synthetic creations of man's inventive mind, brewed in his laboratories, and having no counterparts in nature.

5   To adjust to these chemicals would require time on the scale that is nature's; it would require not merely the years of a man's life but the life of generations. And even this, were it by some miracle possible, would be futile, for the new chemicals come from our laboratories in an endless stream; almost five hundred annually find their way into actual use in the United States alone. The figure is staggering and its implications are not easily grasped—500 new chemicals to which the bodies of men and animals are required somehow to adapt each year, chemicals totally outside the limits of biologic experience.

6   Among them are many that are used in man's war against nature. Since the mid-1940's over 200 basic chemicals have been created for use in killing insects, weeds, rodents, and other organisms described in the modern vernacular as "pests"; and they are sold under several thousand different brand names.

7   These sprays, dusts, and aerosols are now applied almost universally to farms, gardens, forests, and homes—nonselective chemicals that have the power to kill every insect, the "good" and the "bad," to still the song of birds and the leaping of fish in the streams, to coat the leaves with a deadly film, and to linger on in soil—all this though the intended target may be only a few weeds or insects. Can anyone believe it is possible to lay down such a barrage of poisons on the surface of the earth without making it unfit for all life? They should not be called "insecticides," but "biocides."

8   The whole process of spraying seems caught up in an endless spiral. Since DDT was released for civilian use, a process of escalation has been going on in which ever more toxic materials must be found. This has happened because insects, in a triumphant vindication of Darwin's principle of the survival of the fittest, have evolved super races immune to the particular insecticide used, hence a deadlier one has always to be developed—and then a deadlier one than that. It has happened also because, for reasons to be described later, destructive insects often undergo a "flareback," or resurgence, after spraying, in numbers greater than before. Thus the chemical war is never won, and all life is caught in its violent crossfire.

9   Along with the possibility of the extinction of mankind by nuclear war, the central problem of our age has therefore become the contamination of man's total environment with such substances of incredible potential for harm—substances that accumulate in the tissues of plants and animals and even penetrate the germ cells to shatter or alter the very material of heredity upon which the shape of the future depends.

10   Some would-be architects of our future look toward a time when it will be possible to alter the human germ plasm by design. But we may easily be doing so now by

inadvertence, for many chemicals, like radiation, bring about gene mutations. It is ironic to think that man might determine his own future by something so seemingly trivial as the choice of an insect spray.

11   All this has been risked—for what? Future historians may well be amazed by our distorted sense of proportion. How could intelligent beings seek to control a few unwanted species by a method that contaminated the entire environment and brought the threat of disease and death even to their own kind? Yet this is precisely what we have done. We have done it, moreover, for reasons that collapse the moment we examine them. We are told that the enormous and expanding use of pesticides is necessary to maintain farm production. Yet is our real problem not one of *overproduction*? Our farms, despite measures to remove acreages from production and to pay farmers *not* to produce, have yielded such a staggering excess of crops that the American taxpayer in 1962 is paying out more than one billion dollars a year as the total carrying cost of the surplus-food storage program. And is the situation helped when one branch of the Agriculture Department tries to reduce production while another states, as it did in 1958, "It is believed generally that reduction of crop acreages under provisions of the Soil Bank will stimulate interest in use of chemicals to obtain maximum production on the land retained in crops."

12   All this is not to say there is no insect problem and no need of control. I am saying, rather, that control must be geared to realities, not to mythical situations, and that the methods employed must be such that they do not destroy us along with the insects. . . . ■

Edward O. Wilson

The Conservation Ethic

Edward O. Wilson, a long-time Harvard professor and an entomologist with a special interest in ants, is one of the world's leading naturalists. He has won the Pulitzer Prize (twice) and the National Medal of Science, among other awards. Many of his books, including *The Diversity of Life, Naturalist,* and *Biophilia*, emphasize the vitality of species diversity and decry activities that cause the extinction of particular species. Wilson points out the value of even the smallest bugs and plants as integral parts of life systems. The following text, from *Biophilia* (1984), outlines important connections between ecology and ethics.

When very little is known about an important subject, the questions people raise are almost invariably ethical. Then as knowledge grows, they become more concerned with information and amoral, in other words more narrowly intellectual. Finally, as understanding becomes sufficiently complete, the questions turn ethical again. Environmentalism is now passing from the first to the second phase, and there is reason to hope that it will proceed directly on to the third.

2   The future of the conservation movement depends on such an advance in moral reasoning. Its maturation is linked to that of biology and a new hybrid field, bioethics, that deals with the many technological advances recently made possible by biology. Philosophers and scientists are applying a more formal analysis to such complex problems as the allocations of scarce organ transplants, heroic but extremely expensive efforts to prolong life, and the possible use of genetic engineering to alter human heredity. They have only begun to consider the relationships between human beings and organisms with the same rigor. It is clear that the key to precision lies in the understanding of motivation, the ultimate reasons why people care about one thing but not another—why, say, they prefer a city with a park to a city alone. The goal is to join emotion with the rational analysis of emotion in order to create a deeper and more enduring conservation ethic.

3   Aldo Leopold, the pioneer ecologist and author of *A Sand County Almanac*, defined an ethic as a set of rules invented to meet circumstances so new or intricate, or else encompassing responses so far in the future, that the average person cannot foresee the final outcome. What is good for you and me at this moment might easily sour within ten years, and what seems ideal for the next few decades could ruin future generations. That is why any ethic worthy of the name has to encompass the distant future. The relationships of ecology and the human mind are too intricate to be understood entirely by unaided intuition, by common sense—that overrated capacity composed of the set of prejudices we acquire by the age of eighteen.

4   Values are time-dependent, making them all the more difficult to carve in stone. We want health, security, freedom, and pleasure for ourselves and our families. For distant generations we wish the same but not at any great personal cost. The difficulty created for the conservation ethic is that natural selection has programmed people to think mostly in physiological time. Their minds travel back and forth across hours, days, or at most a hundred years. The forests may all be cut, radiation slowly rise, and the winters grow steadily colder, but if the effects are unlikely to become decisive for a few generations, very few people will be stirred to revolt. Ecological and evolutionary time, spanning centuries and millennia, can be conceived in an intellectual mode but has no immediate emotional impact. Only through an unusual amount of education and reflective thought do people come to respond emotionally to far-off events and hence place a high premium on posterity.

5   The deepening of the conservation ethic requires a greater measure of evolutionary realism, including a valuation of ourselves as opposed to other people. What do we really owe our remote descendants? At the risk of offending some readers I will suggest: Nothing. Obligations simply lose their meaning across centuries. But what do we owe ourselves in planning for them? Everything. If human existence has any verifiable meaning, it is that our passions and toil are enabling mechanisms to continue that existence unbroken, unsullied, and progressively secure. It is for ourselves, and not for them or any abstract morality, that we think into the distant future. The precise manner in which we take this measure, how we put it into words, is crucially important. For if the whole process of our life is directed toward preserving our species and personal genes, preparing for future generations is an expression of the highest morality of which human beings are capable. It follows that the destruction of

the natural world in which the brain was assembled over millions of years is a risky step. And the worst gamble of all is to let species slip into extinction wholesale, for even if the natural environment is conceded more ground later, it can never be reconstituted in its original diversity. The first rule of the tinkerer, Aldo Leopold reminds us, is to keep all the pieces.

6   This proposition can be expressed another way. What event likely to happen during the next few years will our descendants most regret? Everyone agrees, defense ministers and environmentalists alike, that the worst thing possible is global nuclear war. If it occurs the entire human species is endangered; life as normal human beings wish to live it would come to an end. With that terrible truism acknowledged, it must be added that if no country pulls the trigger the worst thing that will *probably* happen—in fact is already well underway—is not energy depletion, economic collapse, conventional war, or even the expansion of totalitarian governments. As tragic as these catastrophes would be for us, they can be repaired within a few generations. The one process now going on that will take millions of years to correct is the loss of genetic and species diversity by the destruction of natural habitats. This is the folly our descendants are least likely to forgive us.

7   Extinction is accelerating and could reach ruinous proportions during the next twenty years. Not only are birds and mammals vanishing but such smaller forms as mosses, insects, and minnows. A conservative estimate of the current extinction rate is one thousand species a year, mostly from the destruction of forests and other key habitats in the tropics. By the 1990s the figure is expected to rise past ten thousand species a year (one species per hour). During the next thirty years fully one million species could be erased.

8   Whatever the exact figure—and the primitive state of evolutionary biology permits us only to set broad limits—the current rate is still the greatest in recent geological history. It is also much higher than the rate of production of new species by ongoing evolution, so that the net result is a steep decline in the world's standing diversity. Whole categories of organisms that emerged over the past ten million years, among them the familiar condors, rhinoceros, manatees, and gorillas, are close to the end. For most of their species, the last individuals to exist in the wild state could well be those living there today. It is a grave error to dismiss the hemorrhaging as a "Darwinian" process, in which species autonomously come and go and man is just the latest burden on the environment. Human destructiveness is something new under the sun. Perhaps it is matched by the giant meteorites thought to smash into the Earth and darken the atmosphere every hundred million years or so (the last one apparently arrived 65 million years ago and contributed to the extinction of the dinosaurs). But even that interval is ten thousand times longer than the entire history of civilization. In our own brief lifetime humanity will suffer an incomparable loss in aesthetic value, practical benefits from biological research, and worldwide biological stability. Deep mines of biological diversity will have been dug out and carelessly discarded in the course of environmental exploitation, without our even knowing fully what they contained.

9   The time is late for simple answers and divine guidance, and ideological confrontation has just about run its course. Little can be gained by throwing sand in the gears of industrialized society, even less by perpetuating the belief that we can solve

Aldo Leopold

Excerpts from "The Land Ethic"

Aldo Leopold (1887–1948) was one of the most influential nature writers of the twentieth century and one of the founders of modern ecology. He was completing his essay "The Land Ethic" when he died while fighting a brushfire in a neighbor's field. It appeared in Leopold's posthumously published A Sand County Almanac *(1949). As the following excerpts illustrate, the essay offers a new way of understanding our relationship with the environment—an understanding that has powerfully influenced environmental policy debates in the United States.*

The Ethical Sequence

The first ethics dealt with the relation between individuals; the Mosaic Decalogue is an example. Later accretions dealt with the relation between the individual and society. The Golden Rule tries to integrate the individual to society; democracy to integrate social organization to the individual.

There is as yet no ethic dealing with man's relation to land and to the animals and plants which grow upon it.

The Community Concept

All ethics so far evolved rest upon a single premise: that the individual is a member of a community of interdependent parts. His instincts prompt him to compete for his place in that community, but his ethics prompt him also to cooperate (perhaps in order that there may be a place to compete for).

The land ethic simply enlarges the boundaries of the community to include soils, waters, plants, and animals, or collectively: the land.

any problem created by earlier spasms of human ingenuity. The need now is for a great deal more knowledge of the true biological dimensions of our problem, civility in the face of common need, and the style of leadership once characterized by Walter Bagehot as agitated moderation.

10   Ethical philosophy is a much more important subject than ordinarily conceded in societies dominated by religious and ideological orthodoxy. It faces an especially severe test in the complexities of the conservation problem. When the time scale is expanded to encompass ecological events, it becomes far more difficult to be certain about the wisdom of any particular decision. Everything is riddled with ambiguity; the middle way turns hard and general formulas fail with dispiriting consistency. Consider that a man who is a villain to his contemporaries can become a hero to his descendants. If a tyrant were to carefully preserve his nation's land and natural resources for his personal needs while keeping his people in poverty, he might unintentionally be-

The Ecological Conscience

Obligations have no meaning without conscience, and the problem we face is the extension of the social conscience from people to land.

Substitutes for a Land Ethic

A system of conservation based solely on economic self-interest is hopelessly lopsided. It tends to ignore, and thus eventually to eliminate, many elements in the land community that lack commercial value, but that are (as far as we know) essential to its healthy functioning.

The Land Pyramid

Land, then, is not merely soil; it is a fountain of energy flowing through a circuit of soils, plants, and animals. Food chains are the living channels which conduct energy upward; death and decay return it to the soil.

Land Health and the A–B Cleavage

We see repeated the same basic paradoxes: man the conqueror *versus* man the biotic citizen; science the sharpener of his sword *versus* science the searchlight on his universe; land the slave and servant *versus* land the collective organism.

The Outlook

Examine each question in terms of what is ethically and esthetically right, as well as what is economically expedient. A thing is right when it tends to preserve the integrity, stability, and beauty of the biotic community. It is wrong when it tends otherwise.

queath a rich, healthful environment to a reduced population for enjoyment in later, democratic generations. This caudillo will have improved the long-term welfare of his people by giving them greater resources and more freedom of action. The exact reverse can occur as well: today's hero can be tomorrow's destroyer. A popular political leader who unleashes the energies of his people and raises their standard of living might simultaneously promote a population explosion, overuse of resources, flight to the cities, and poverty for later generations. Of course these two extreme examples are caricatures and unlikely to occur just so, but they suffice to illustrate that, in ecological and evolutionary time, good does not automatically flow from good or evil from evil. To choose what is best for the near future is easy. To choose what is best for the distant future is also easy. But to choose what is best for both the near and distant futures is a hard task, often internally contradictory, and requiring ethical codes yet to be formulated. ■

Many species of frogs and toads are disappearing throughout the world at a rapid rate. The causes of this decline appear to be numerous, but in the Amazon basin, the primary cause is loss of habitat from deforestation. Frogs and toads occupy an important niche on the food chain, and their loss negatively affects all other species.

Chris Packham and Mark Wright

Should Pandas Be Left to Face Extinction?

In September 2009, the well-known British naturalist, photographer, and writer Chris Packham (born 1961) created an international furor when during a radio interview he proposed that giant pandas ought to be allowed to go extinct. A fierce advocate for nature and wildlife, he nevertheless contends that so-called "T-shirt animals" (like pandas) get far too much attention and draw resources from far more critical environmental concerns. On September 23, 2009, the British newspaper *The Guardian* carried a debate between Packham and Mark Wright that we reprint below. Wright, a leading scientist at the

World Wide Fund for Nature, was one of a great many who disagreed with Packham. Scientists are estimating that half the species on earth may become extinct in the next century. After the debate, we reprint several blog postings from around the world that commented on Packham's position. The blogs appeared on the *RadioTimes* Web site in the final days of September.

Yes, says Chris Packham

I don't want the panda to die out. I want species to stay alive—that's why I get up in the morning. I don't even kill mosquitoes or flies. So if pandas can survive, that would be great. But let's face it: conservation, both nationally and globally, has a limited amount of resources, and I think we're going to have to make some hard, pragmatic choices.

2   The truth is, pandas are extraordinarily expensive to keep going. We spend millions and millions of pounds on pretty much this one species, and a few others, when we know that the best thing we could do would be to look after the world's biodiversity hotspots with greater care. Without habitat, you've got nothing. So maybe if we took all the cash we spend on pandas and just bought rainforest with it, we might be doing a better job.

3   Of course, it's easier to raise money for something fluffy. Charismatic megafauna like the panda do appeal to people's emotional side, and attract a lot of public attention. They are emblematic of what I would call single-species conservation: i.e., a focus on one animal. This approach began in the 1970s with Save the Tiger, Save the Panda, Save the Whale, and so on, and it is now out of date. I think pandas have had a valuable role in raising the profile of conservation, but perhaps "had" is the right word.

4   Panda conservationists may stand up and say, "It's a flagship species. We're also conserving Chinese forest, where there is a whole plethora of other things." And when that works, I'm not against it. But we have to accept that some species are stronger than others. The panda is a species of bear that has gone herbivorous, and that eats a type of food that isn't all that nutritious, and that dies out sporadically. It is susceptible to various diseases, and, up until recently, it has been almost impossible to breed in captivity. They've also got a very restricted range, which is ever decreasing, due to encroachment on their habitat by the Chinese population. Perhaps the panda was already destined to run out of time.

5   Extinction is very much a part of life on earth. And we are going to have to get used to it in the next few years because climate change is going to result in all sorts of disappearances. The last large mammal extinction was another animal in China—the Yangtze river dolphin, which looked like a worn-out piece of pink

soap with piggy eyes and was never going to make it on to anyone's T-shirt. If that had appeared beautiful to us, then I doubt very much that it would be extinct. But it vanished, because it was pig-ugly and swam around in a river where no one saw it. And now, sadly, it has gone for ever.

6   I'm not trying to play God; I'm playing God's accountant. I'm saying we won't be able to save it all, so let's do the best we can. And at the moment I don't think our strategies are best placed to do that. We should be focusing our conservation endeavours on biodiversity hotspots, spreading our net more widely and looking at good-quality habitat maintenance in order to preserve as much of the life as we possibly can, using hard science to make educated decisions as to which species are essential to a community's maintenance. It may well be that we can lose the cherries from the cake. But you don't want to lose the substance. Save the Rainforest, or Save the Kalahari: that would be better.

No, says Mark Wright

7   You are reading this because it is about giant pandas. We could have this argument about the frogs of the rainforest and the issues would be identical, but the ability to get people's attention would be far lower. So in that sense, yes, you could argue that conservationists capitalize on the panda's appeal.

8   And, to be fair, I can understand where Chris Packham is coming from. Everywhere you look on this planet there are issues to be addressed, and we have finite resources. So we do make really horrible choices. But nowadays, almost exclusively, when people work in conservation they focus on saving habitats.

9   Chris has talked about pandas being an evolutionary cul-de-sac, and it's certainly unusual for a carnivore to take up herbivory. But there are many, many other species that live in a narrowly defined habitat. When he says that if you leave them be, they will die out, that's simply not true. If we don't destroy their habitat they will just chunter along in the same way that they have for the thousands of years.

10   And besides, in terms of its biodiversity and the threats it faces, I think that the part of China where pandas live should be on the preservation list anyway. The giant panda shares its habitat with the red panda, golden monkeys, and various birds that are found nowhere else in the world. The giant panda's numbers are increasing in the wild, so I don't see them dying out, and I haven't heard anything to suggest that other biodiversity isn't thriving equally.

11   It is true, though, that there some cases where preserving an animal is not the best use of resources. If you asked 100 conservationists—even at the World Wide Fund—you would proba-

bly get 90 different answers, but look at what happened with the northern white rhino in Africa, which we're pretty sure has died out. We lament its loss. But at the same time it had gotten to the stage where the likelihood of success was at a critically low level. If you were doing a battlefield triage system, the rhino would probably have had to be a casualty.

12   Otherwise, charismatic megafauna can be extremely useful. Smaller creatures often don't need a big habitat to live in, so in conservation terms it's better to go for something further up the food chain, because then by definition you are protecting a much larger area, which in turn encompasses the smaller animals.

13   And of course they are an extraordinarily good vehicle for the messages we want to put out on habitat conservation. Look at Borneo, where you instantly think of the orangutans. In the southern oceans, you think of the blue whale. Then there are polar bears in the north. There are things you pull out from the picture because people can relate to them. And it does make a difference.

A giant panda, an example of what Chris Packham calls "T-shirt animals."

Web postings

14   Lay off them! They haven't done anything to you! They are already nearly extinct [so] let them die naturally. How would you like it if they told you to go die? You wouldn't like it, would you? (**Nicola-Lucy**)

15   Nice to hear someone with such a public profile expressing the honest view of the majority within conservation circles. It's long been widely agreed that the long-term success of [conservation] efforts depends on promoting sustainable environments, where the natural world (including all the animals, plants, etc.) will find its own balance without us—as opposed to the reactive preservation on total global numbers of individual species, without regards to impact on local environments.

16   Nicola-Lucy: breathe and relax. I think you may have misread Chris's views on pandas. I think he meant we should 'pull the plug' on plowing so much money into a campaign that has seen no marked improvement for decades now, not go round culling the remaining population. (**Sam**)

17   [Packham's] comments have clearly been made through a lack of understanding of wider conservation projects. By protecting the

panda you are protecting its habitat and environment and therefore protecting the entire ecosystem that it lives within, including the people that need sustainable livelihoods. He's clearly missed the bigger picture that species and humans are intrinsically linked and by saving one you are protecting the longevity of the other. (**Becki**)

18   We pour millions into cats and dogs. Why not get rid of cats and dogs and save the panda! (**Sally**)

19   Becki misses the point spectacularly. Protecting ecosystems is certainly an excellent cause, but there is no need to link that to pandas who seem to have a darwinian instinct for self-elimination. It isn't about money plowed into conservation of habitats. . . . It is more about the ridiculous lengths we humans are going to get them to mate. (**Peter**)

20   This man is an evil, disgusting specimen of humanity. Is this what it's come down to? We can ignore the fact that the economy spends millions on cigarettes every year and this is causing more damage to the universal economy than the pandas are! We were put on this earth to do whatever we can to preserve the earth that we were put on and the animals that we share it with. (**Amy**)

21   I suppose I sit on the fence. I can see both points of view. If it is us humans causing the extinction, then we have a responsibility to do all we can reasonably do to prevent this. . . . However, it does seem to me that the panda has itself chosen to take a path which because of its diet would in any event lead to extinction. So should we step in and do something or allow nature to take its course? (**John**)

22   I think it is terrible that anyone can say that pandas should be left to die. The human race really is arrogant, greedy, etc. Glad I do not eat meat. (**Sue**)

23   I have to admit I've had an unreasonable hatred of pandas ever since I failed to see one in the Quinling Mountains in central China, but even I wouldn't agree that we should let it go extinct. It is certainly an environmental oddity, but before humans impacted on its life it would have been quite a widespread and successful species with a good chance of carrying on for the 3 million years or so that is the average life expectancy of a vertebrate species. To call it an evolutionary failure because human-induced habitat destruction had vastly reduced its range seems a little unfair. Like gorillas and tigers it is a flagship species and as we approach the point of total destruction of most of the world's ecosystems it would seem the best chance for any of them to survive is if they are home to some big charismatic animal. Conserve the panda and you conserve the Golden Takin, the Golden Pheasant, the Golden Snub-Nosed Monkey, not to mention all the other thousands of species that live in the area. (**Julian**)

Wallace Stegner

A Wilderness Letter

Wallace Stegner (1909–1993) was a successful novelist in the United States after World War II. He wrote more than thirty books, including *Angle of Repose*, which won the Pulitzer Prize, and *The Spectator Bird*, which won the National Book Award in 1976. Stegner was also an outspoken conservationist, and his books often feature natural settings and environmental themes. In 1960 he wrote the following letter, a famous argument for the spiritual values found in the wild, to David Pesonen of the Wildland Research Center at the University of California, Berkeley: it helped to persuade Congress to create the National Wilderness Preservation System in 1964.

Los Altos, California
December 3, 1960

David E. Pesonen
Wildland Research Center
Agricultural Experiment Station
243 Mulford Hall
University of California
Berkeley 4, Calif.

Dear Mr. Pesonen:

I believe that you are working on the wilderness portion of the Outdoor Recreation Resources Review Commission's report. If I may, I should like to urge some arguments for wilderness preservation that involve recreation, as it is ordinarily conceived, hardly at all. Hunting, fishing, hiking, mountain-climbing, camping, photography, and the enjoyment of natural scenery will all, surely, figure in your report. So will the wilderness as a genetic reserve, a scientific yardstick by which we may measure the world in its natural balance against the world in its man-made imbalance. What I want to speak for is not so much the wilderness uses, valuable as those are, but the wilderness idea, which is a resource in itself. Being an intangible and spiritual resource, it will seem mystical to the practical minded—but then anything that cannot be moved by a bulldozer is likely to seem mystical to them.

I want to speak for the wilderness idea as something that has helped form our character and that has certainly shaped our history as a people. It has no more to do with recreation than churches have to do with recreation, or than the strenuousness and optimism and expansiveness of what the historians call the "American Dream" have to do with recreation. Nevertheless, since it is only in this recreation survey that the values of wilderness are being compiled, I hope you will permit me to insert this idea between the leaves, as it were, of the recreation report.

Something will have gone out of us as a people if we ever let the remaining wilderness be destroyed; if we permit the last virgin forests to be turned into comic books and plastic cigarette cases; if we drive the few remaining members of the wild species into zoos or to extinction; if we pollute the last clear air and dirty the last clean streams and push our paved roads through the last of the silence, so that never again will Americans be free in their own country from the noise, the exhausts, the stinks of human and automotive waste. And so that never again can we have the chance to see ourselves single, separate, vertical and individual in the world, part of the environment of trees and rocks and soil, brother to the other animals, part of the natural world and competent to belong in it. Without any remaining wilderness we are committed wholly, without chance for even momentary reflection and rest, to a headlong drive into our technological termite-life, the Brave New World of a completely man-controlled environment. We need wilderness preserved—as much of it as is still left, and as many kinds—because it was the challenge against which our character as a people was formed. The reminder and the reassurance that it is still there is good for our spiritual health even if we never once in ten years set foot in it. It is good for us when we are young, because of the incomparable sanity it can bring briefly, as vacation and rest, into our insane lives. It is important to us when we are old simply because it is there—important, that is, simply as an idea.

5   We are a wild species, as Darwin pointed out. Nobody ever tamed or domesticated or scientifically bred us. But for at least three millennia we have been engaged in a cumulative and ambitious race to modify and gain control of our environment, and in the process we have come close to domesticating ourselves. Not many people are likely, any more, to look upon what we call "progress" as an unmixed blessing. Just as surely as it has brought us increased comfort and more material goods, it has brought us spiritual losses, and it threatens now to become the Frankenstein that will destroy us. One means of sanity is to retain a hold on the natural world, to remain, insofar as we can, good animals. Americans still have that chance, more than many peoples; for while we were demonstrating ourselves the most efficient and ruthless environment-busters in history, and slashing and burning and cutting our way through a wilderness continent, the wilderness was working on us. It remains in us as surely as Indian names remain on the land. If the abstract dream of human liberty and human dignity became, in America, something more than an abstract dream, mark it down at least partially to the fact that we were in subdued ways subdued by what we conquered.

6   The Connecticut Yankee, sending likely candidates from King Arthur's unjust kingdom to his Man Factory for rehabilitation, was over-optimistic, as he later admitted. These things cannot be forced, they have to grow. To make such a man, such a democrat, such a believer in human individual dignity, as Mark Twain himself, the frontier was necessary, Hannibal and the Mississippi and Virginia City, and reaching out from those the wilderness; the wilderness as opportunity and idea, the thing that has helped to make an American different from and, until we forget it in the roar of our industrial cities, more fortunate than other men. For an American, insofar as he is new and different at all, is a civilized man who has renewed himself in the wild. The American experience has been the confrontation by old peoples and cultures of a world as new as if it had just risen from the sea. That gave us our hope and our excitement, and the hope and excitement can be passed on to newer Americans,

One of the first conservation districts was formed after the founding of to the Soil Conservation Service, now known as the USDA's Natural Resources Conservation Service, in 1935.

Americans who never saw any phase of the frontier. But only so long as we keep the remainder of our wild as a reserve and a promise—a sort of wilderness bank.

As a novelist, I may perhaps be forgiven for taking literature as a reflection, indirect but profoundly true, of our national consciousness. And our literature, as perhaps you are aware, is sick, embittered, losing its mind, losing its faith. Our novelists are the declared enemies of their society. There has hardly been a serious or important novel in this century that did not repudiate in part or in whole American technological culture for its commercialism, its vulgarity, and the way in which it has dirtied a clean continent and a clean dream. I do not expect that the preservation of our remaining wilderness is going to cure this condition. But the mere example that we can as a nation apply some other criteria than commercial and exploitative considerations would be heartening to many Americans, novelists or otherwise. We need to demonstrate our acceptance of the natural world, including ourselves; we need the spiritual refreshment that being natural can produce. And one of the best places for us to get that is in the wilderness where the fun houses, the bulldozers, and the pavement of our civilization are shut out.

Sherwood Anderson, in a letter to Waldo Frank in the 1920s, said it better than I can. "Is it not likely that when the country was new and men were often alone in the fields and the forest they got a sense of bigness outside themselves that has now in some way been lost. . . . Mystery whispered in the grass, played in the branches of trees overhead, was caught up and blown across the American line in clouds of dust at evening on the prairies. . . . I am old enough to remember tales that strengthen my belief in a deep semi-religious influence that was formerly at work among our people. The flavor of it hangs over the best work of Mark Twain. . . . I can remember old fellows in my home town speaking feelingly of an evening spent on the big empty plains. It had taken the shrillness out of them. They had learned the trick of quiet. . . . "

9   We could learn it too, even yet; even our children and grandchildren could learn it. But only if we save, for just such absolutely non-recreational, impractical, and mystical uses as this, all the wild that still remains to us.

10   It seems to me significant that the distinct downturn in our literature from hope to bitterness took place almost at the precise time when the frontier officially came to an end, in 1890, and when the American way of life had begun to turn strongly urban and industrial. The more urban it has become, and the more frantic with technological change, the sicker and more embittered our literature, and I believe our people, have become. For myself, I grew up on the empty plains of Saskatchewan and Montana and in the mountains of Utah, and I put a very high valuation on what those places gave me. And if I had not been able periodically to renew myself in the mountains and deserts of western America I would be very nearly bughouse. Even when I can't get to the back country, the thought of the colored deserts of southern Utah, or the reassurance that there are still stretches of prairies where the world can be instantaneously perceived as disk and bowl, and where the little but intensely important human being is exposed to the five directions of the thirty-six winds, is a positive consolation. The idea alone can sustain me. But as the wilderness areas are progressively exploited or "improve," as the jeeps and bulldozers of uranium prospectors scar up the deserts and the roads are cut into the alpine timberlands, and as the remnants of the unspoiled and natural world are progressively eroded, every such loss is a little death in me. In us.

11   I am not moved by the argument that those wilderness areas which have already been exposed to grazing or mining are already deflowered, and so might as well be "harvested." For mining I cannot say much good except that its operations are generally short-lived. The extractable wealth is taken and the shafts, the tailings, and the ruins left, and in a dry country such as the American West the wounds men make in the earth do not quickly heal. Still, they are only wounds; they aren't absolutely mortal. Better a wounded wilderness than none at all. And as for grazing, if it is strictly controlled so that it does not destroy the ground cover, damage the ecology, or compete with the wildlife it is in itself nothing that need conflict with the wilderness feeling or the validity of the wilderness experience. I have known enough range cattle to recognize them as wild animals; and the people who herd them have, in the wilderness context, the dignity of rareness; they belong on the frontier, moreover, and have a look of rightness. The invasion they make on the virgin country is a sort of invasion that is as old as Neolithic man, and they can, in moderation, even emphasize a man's feeling of belonging

to the natural world. Under surveillance, they can belong; under control, they need not deface or mar. I do not believe that in wilderness areas where grazing has never been permitted, it should be permitted; but I do not believe either that an otherwise untouched wilderness should be eliminated from the preservation plan because of limited existing uses such as grazing which are in consonance with the frontier condition and image.

12   Let me say something on the subject of the kinds of wilderness worth preserving. Most of those areas contemplated are in the national forests and in high mountain country. For all the usual recreational purposes, the alpine and the forest wildernesses are obviously the most important, both as genetic banks and as beauty spots. But for the spiritual renewal, the recognition of identity, the birth of awe, other kinds will serve every bit as well. Perhaps, because they are less friendly to life, more abstractly nonhuman, they will serve even better. On our Saskatchewan prairie, the nearest neighbor was four miles away, and at night we saw only two lights on all the dark rounding earth. The earth was full of animals—field mice, ground squirrels, weasels, ferrets, badgers, coyotes, burrowing owls, snakes. I knew them as my little brothers, as fellow creatures, and I have never been able to look upon animals in any other way since. The sky in that country came clear down to the ground on every side, and it was full of great weathers, and clouds, and winds, and hawks. I hope I learned something from looking a long way, from looking up, from being much alone. A prairie like that, one big enough to carry the eye clear to the sinking, rounding horizon, can be as lonely and grand and simple in its forms as the sea. It is as good a place as any for the wilderness experience to happen; the vanishing prairie is as worth preserving for the wilderness idea as the alpine forest.

13   So are great reaches of our western deserts, scarred somewhat by prospectors but otherwise open, beautiful, waiting, close to whatever God you want to see in them. Just as a sample, let me suggest the Robbers' Roost country in Wayne County, Utah, near the Capitol Reef National Monument. In that desert climate the dozer and jeep tracks will not soon melt back into the earth, but the country has a way of making the scars insignificant. It is a lovely and terrible wilderness, such as wilderness as Christ and the prophets went out into; harshly and beautifully colored, broken and worn until its bones are exposed, its great sky without a smudge of taint from Technocracy, and in hidden corners and pockets under its cliffs the sudden poetry of springs. Save a piece of country like that intact, and it does not matter in the slightest that only a few people every year will go into it. That is precisely its value. Roads would be a desecration, crowds would ruin it. But those who haven't the strength or youth to go into it and live can simply sit and look. They can look two hundred miles, clear into Colorado: and looking down over the cliffs and canyons of the San Rafael Swell and the Robbers' Roost they can also look as deeply into themselves as anywhere I know. And if they can't even get to the places on the Aquarius Plateau where the present roads will carry them, they can simply contemplate the idea, take pleasure in the fact that such a timeless and uncontrolled part of earth is still there.

14   These are some of the things wilderness can do for us. That is the reason we need to put into effect, for its preservation, some other principle than the principles of exploitation or "usefulness" or even recreation. We simply need that wild country available to us, even if we never do more than drive to its edge and look in. For it can be a means of reassuring ourselves of our sanity as creatures, a part of the geography of hope.

Very sincerely yours,

Wallace Stegner ■

ISSUE IN **FOCUS**

Sustainability

According to the U.S. Census Bureau, the human population reached seven billion in 2012 and is expected to reach nine billion by 2050. Most of the population increase will be in economically "developing" nations like India and China or in Africa and South America, in nations where citizens are aspiring to the living standards common in the Western democracies. Those living standards have traditionally required the consumption (and waste) of increasing amounts of water, energy, breathable air, and other resources. The combination of rapid population increase in the developing world and unsustainable consumption levels in the developed world poses a stark challenge, a challenge that many are taking up through what has become known as the sustainability movement.

Many scientists are claiming that humans are already living beyond the carrying capacity of the Earth. If the "ecological footprint" of humans—that is, the amount that each human being consumes—exceeds the carrying capacity of the earth, then humanity is on a disastrous course that cannot be sustained without dire consequences to the quality of life. In the short run, deficits can temporarily be made up by mining the reserves built up in the past (for example, by drilling for fossil fuels that are destined to run out) or by borrowing from the future (for example, by overfishing the seas until fish supplies run dry or by running up debt). But in the long run such practices obviously cannot succeed.

What is the responsibility of every human being for the happiness and prosperity of future generations? That question now animates citizens involved in the growing sustainability movement, which takes as its goal the promotion of environmental, social, and economic practices that will assure the long-term viability of human life on earth.

A key concept in the sustainability community is stewardship: How can people make use of the Earth's bounty without destroying the planet? How can citizens be good stewards of the advantages they have inherited? Those committed to sustainability are currently intent on ameliorating all kinds of destructive habits—debilitating farming practices, damaging or ineffectual methods of energy production and conservation, even human overpopulation. Deeply involved in arguments about ethics, sustainability advocates are promoting diverse and healthy ecosystems, the renewal of forests and wetlands, a resistance to the use of fossil fuels, concern for climate change, and the redesign of urban and suburban living spaces. On the one hand, sustainability advocates seek to reduce the human impact on ecosystems; they draw from experts in conservation biology, environmental science, agricultural science, even philosophy and religion. On the other hand, sustainability advocates seek to manage and limit the consumption of resources; they draw from experts in economics, law, public policy, energy production, sanitation engineering, urban planning, and transportation engineering, among other fields.

As these lists imply, those attracted to the sustainability ideal come from across the political spectrum. Both radical and reformist principles are present in the movement; deeply conservative, libertarian, even reactionary impulses can be found within the sustainability movement; some contend that capitalism itself is unsustainable, while others believe that free enterprise and competition hold the key to the creating of a more sustainable world. Arguments within the movement are often as fierce, therefore, as arguments directed against people who resist or even ridicule the entire sustainability movement.

A United Nations commission, on March 20, 1987, declared that "sustainable development is development that meets the needs of the present without compromising the ability of future generations to meet their own needs." Since then, the "three pillars" of the sustainability movement have been environmental quality, social equality, and economic reform. But exactly what kinds of reform? The sustainability movement offers an expansive but conflicted social agenda that challenges nearly every human practice. True, some standards have been drafted—the Rainforest Alliance and Fair Trade certification programs and the Common Code for the Coffee Community are well-known examples—but the three pillars have been incompletely accepted and variously interpreted. What exactly is meant by "sustainability"? What should be the specific goals and methods of the movement? Does sustainability require a radical restructuring of political systems and the destruction of multinational corporations? Or does it call for more gradual reforms or for personal changes in individual human desires and appetites?

Here we include an argument by one of the esteemed high priests of the sustainability movement, Wendell Berry. A writer and teacher who grew up on a farm in Kentucky, Berry has been living out sustainability principles since his birth in 1934 and promoting them in a series of widely read and admired essays

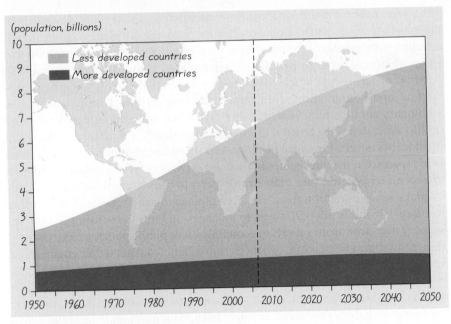

(population, billions)

- Less developed countries
- More developed countries

Projected Worldwide Population Growth.
The world's population is expected to reach 9.1 billion by 2050, with virtually all population growth occurring in less-developed countries.
Source: Finance and Development (Sept 2006, vol 43, no. 3) published by the International Monetary Fund. http://www.imf.org/external/pubs/ft/fandd/2006/09/picture.htm

and poems. In articles such as "What Are People For?" and "Why I Am Not Going to Buy a Computer" and in the poems collected in *Sabbaths* and *The Country of Marriage*, Berry has long explored the ties that connect people and has advocated a simple lifestyle, at odds with new technologies that threaten agrarian ways. In 2012, Berry was invited by the National Endowment for the Humanities to give the prestigious annual Jefferson Lecture, published in a book of his essays and excerpted here, and he used the occasion to argue eloquently for sustainability principles and practices.

But Berry's positions and his withering criticisms of capitalism do not stand unchallenged. As a partial response to the sustainability movement's distrust of large corporations, we offer the decorated scientist Jared Diamond's 2009 essay "Will Big Business Save the Earth?" As a further rejoinder to sustainability enthusiasms, one with direct implications for colleges and college students, we then provide the conservative National Association of Scholars statement "Fixing Sustainability," issued in 2011. Then Nicolette Niman and

Mark Bittman offer arguments that first appeared in 2009 in the *New York Times*. Niman counters those who easily identify sustainability with vegetarianism, while Bittman urges his readers to complicate their attitudes toward what counts as "organic" food and farming. Finally, in an article published in the *American Journal of Public Health*, David Resnick explores the ways smart growth policies can address the problems of urban sprawl, why some oppose such policies, and how using deliberative democracy can help bring communities to consensus.

Together the selections should enlighten you about what sustainability advocates promise—and should stimulate you to take up your own arguments about the matter.

Wendell E. Berry

"It All Turns on Affection": 2012 Jefferson Lecture

"Because a thing is going strong now, it need not go strong for ever," [Margaret] said. "This craze for motion has only set in during the last hundred years. It may be followed by a civilization that won't be a movement, because it will rest upon the earth."

—E. M. Forster, *Howards End* (1910)[1]

One night in the winter of 1907, at what we have always called "the home place" in Henry County, Kentucky, my father, then six years old, sat with his older brother and listened as their parents spoke of the uses they would have for the money from their 1906 tobacco crop. The crop was to be sold at auction in Louisville on the next day. They would have been sitting in the light of a kerosene lamp, close to the stove, warming themselves before bedtime. They were not wealthy people. I believe that the debt on their farm was not fully paid, there would have been interest to pay, there would have been other debts. The depression of the 1890s would have left them burdened. Perhaps, after the income from the crop had paid their obligations, there would be some money that they could spend as they chose. At around two o'clock the next morning, my father was wakened by a horse's shod hooves on the stones of the driveway. His father was leaving to catch the train to see the crop sold.

2   He came home that evening, as my father later would put it, "without a dime." After the crop had paid its transportation to market and the commission on its sale, there was nothing left. Thus began my father's lifelong advocacy, later my brother's and my own, and now my daughter's and my son's, for small farmers and for land-conserving economies.

3   The economic hardship of my family and of many others, a century ago, was caused by a monopoly, the American Tobacco Company, which had eliminated all competitors and thus was able to reduce as it pleased the prices it paid to farmers. The American Tobacco Company was the work of James B. Duke of Durham, North Carolina, and New York City, who, disregarding any other consideration, followed a capitalist logic to absolute control of his industry and, incidentally, of the economic fate of thousands of families such as my own.

4   My effort to make sense of this memory and its encompassing history has depended on a pair of terms used by my teacher, Wallace Stegner. He thought rightly that we Americans, by inclination at least, have been divided into two kinds: "boomers" and "stickers." Boomers, he said, are "those who pillage and run," who want "to make a killing and end up on Easy Street," whereas stickers are "those who settle, and love the life they have made and the place they have made it in."[2] "Boomer" names a kind of person and a kind of ambition that is the major theme, so far, of the history of the European races in our country. "Sticker" names a kind of person and also a desire that is,

so far, a minor theme of that history, but a theme persistent enough to remain significant and to offer, still, a significant hope.

5 The boomer is motivated by greed, the desire for money, property, and therefore power. James B. Duke was a boomer, if we can extend the definition to include pillage *in absentia*. He went, or sent, wherever the getting was good, and he got as much as he could take.

6 Stickers on the contrary are motivated by affection, by such love for a place and its life that they want to preserve it and remain in it. Of my grandfather I need to say only that he shared in the virtues and the faults of his kind and time, one of his virtues being that he was a sticker. He belonged to a family who had come to Kentucky from Virginia, and who intended to go no farther. He was the third in his paternal line to live in the neighborhood of our little town of Port Royal, and he was the second to own the farm where he was born in 1864 and where he died in 1946.

7 We have one memory of him that seems, more than any other, to identify him as a sticker. He owned his farm, having bought out the other heirs, for more than fifty years. About forty of those years were in hard times, and he lived almost continuously in the distress of debt. Whatever has happened in what economists call "the economy," it is generally true that the land economy has been discounted or ignored. My grandfather lived his life in an economic shadow. In an urbanizing and industrializing age, he was the wrong kind of man. In one of his difficult years he plowed a field on the lower part of a long slope and planted it in corn. While the soil was exposed, a heavy rain fell and the field was seriously eroded. This was heartbreak for my grandfather, and he devoted the rest of his life, first to healing the scars and then to his obligation of care. In keeping with the sticker's commitment, he neither left behind the damage he had done nor forgot about it, but stayed to repair it, insofar as soil loss can be repaired. My father, I think, had his father's error in mind when he would speak of farmers attempting, always uselessly if not tragically, "to plow their way out of debt." From that time, my grandfather and my father were soil conservationists, a commitment that they handed on to my brother and to me.

8 It is not beside the point, or off my subject, to notice that these stories and their meanings have survived because of my family's continuing connection to its home place. Like my grandfather, my father grew up on that place and served as its caretaker. It has now belonged to my brother for many years, and he in turn has been its caretaker. He and I have lived as neighbors, allies, and friends. Our long conversation has often taken its themes from the two stories I have told, because we have been continually reminded of them by our home neighborhood and topography. If we had not lived there to be reminded and to remember, nobody would have remembered. If either of us had lived elsewhere, both of us would have known less. If both of us, like most of our generation, had moved away, the place with its memories would have been lost to us and we to it—and certainly my thoughts about agriculture, if I had thought of it at all, would have been much more approximate than they have been.

9 Because I have never separated myself from my home neighborhood, I cannot identify myself to myself apart from it. I am fairly literally flesh of its flesh. It is present in me, and to me, wherever I go. This undoubtedly accounts for my sense of shock when, on my first visit to Duke University, and by surprise, I came face-to-face with James B. Duke in his dignity, his glory perhaps, as the founder of that university. He stands

imperially in bronze in front of a Methodist chapel aspiring to be a cathedral. He holds between two fingers of his left hand a bronze cigar. On one side of his pedestal is the legend: INDUSTRIALIST. On the other side is another single word: PHILANTHROPIST. The man thus commemorated seemed to me terrifyingly ignorant, even terrifyingly innocent, of the connection between his industry and his philanthropy. But I did know the connection. I felt it instantly and physically. The connection was my grandparents and thousands of others more or less like them. If you can appropriate for little or nothing the work and hope of enough such farmers, then you may dispense the grand charity of "philanthropy."

10   After my encounter with the statue, the story of my grandfather's 1906 tobacco crop slowly took on a new dimension and clarity in my mind. I still remembered my grandfather as himself, of course, but I began to think of him also as a kind of man standing in thematic opposition to a man of an entirely different kind. And I could see finally that between these two kinds there was a failure of imagination that was ruinous, that belongs indelibly to our history, and that has continued, growing worse, into our own time.

11   The term "imagination" in what I take to be its truest sense refers to a mental faculty that some people have used and thought about with the utmost seriousness. The sense of the verb "to imagine" contains the full richness of the verb "to see." To imagine is to see most clearly, familiarly, and understandingly with the eyes, but also to see inwardly, with "the mind's eye." It is to see, not passively, but with a force of vision and even with visionary force. To take it seriously we must give up at once any notion that imagination is disconnected from reality or truth or knowledge. It has nothing to do either with clever imitation of appearances or with "dreaming up." It does not depend upon one's attitude or point of view, but grasps securely the qualities of things seen or envisioned.

12   I will say, from my own belief and experience, that imagination thrives on contact, on tangible connection. For humans to have a responsible relationship to the world, they must imagine their places in it. To have a place, to live and belong in a place, to live from a place without destroying it, we must imagine it. By imagination we see it illuminated by its own unique character and by our love for it. By imagination we recognize with sympathy the fellow members, human and nonhuman, with whom we share our place. By that local experience we see the need to grant a sort of preemptive sympathy to all the fellow members, the neighbors, with whom we share the world. As imagination enables sympathy, sympathy enables affection. And it is in affection that we find the possibility of a neighborly, kind, and conserving economy.

13   Obviously there is some risk in making affection the pivot of an argument about economy. The charge will be made that affection is an emotion, merely "subjective," and therefore that all affections are more or less equal: people may have affection for their children and their automobiles, their neighbors and their weapons. But the risk, I think, is only that affection is personal. If it is not personal, it is nothing; we don't, at least, have to worry about governmental or corporate affection. And one of the endeavors of human cultures, from the beginning, has been to qualify and direct the influence of emotion. The word "affection" and the terms of value that cluster around it—love, care,

sympathy, mercy, forbearance, respect, reverence—have histories and meanings that raise the issue of worth. We should, as our culture has warned us over and over again, give our affection to things that are true, just, and beautiful. When we give affection to things that are destructive, we are wrong. A large machine in a large, toxic, eroded cornfield is not, properly speaking, an object or a sign of affection.

14 My grandfather knew, urgently, the value of money, but only of such comparatively small sums as would have paid his debts and allowed to his farm and his family a decent prosperity. He certainly knew of the American Tobacco Company. He no doubt had read and heard of James B. Duke, and could identify him as the cause of a hard time, but nothing in his experience could have enabled him to imagine the life of the man himself.

15 James B. Duke came from a rural family in the tobacco country of North Carolina. In his early life he would have known men such as my grandfather. But after he began his rise as an industrialist, the life of a small tobacco grower would have been to him a negligible detail incidental to an opportunity for large profits. In the minds of the "captains of industry," then and now, the people of the land economies have been reduced to statistical numerals. Power deals "efficiently" with quantities that affection cannot recognize.

16 It may seem plausible to suppose that the head of the American Tobacco Company would have imagined at least that a dependable supply of raw material to his industry would depend upon a stable, reasonably thriving population of farmers and upon the continuing fertility of their farms. But he imagined no such thing. In this he was like apparently all agribusiness executives. They don't imagine farms or farmers. They imagine perhaps nothing at all, their minds being filled to capacity by numbers leading to the bottom line. Though the corporations, by law, are counted as persons, they do not have personal minds, if they can be said to have minds. It is a great oddity that a corporation, which properly speaking has no self, is by definition selfish, responsible only to itself. This is an impersonal, abstract selfishness, limitlessly acquisitive, but unable to look so far ahead as to preserve its own sources and supplies. The selfishness of the fossil fuel industries by nature is self-annihilating; but so, always, has been the selfishness of the agribusiness corporations. Land, as Wes Jackson has said, has thus been made as exhaustible as oil or coal.

17 . . . Corporate industrialism has tended to be, and as its technological and financial power has grown it has tended increasingly to be, indifferent to its sources in what Aldo Leopold called "the land-community": the land, all its features and "resources," and all its members, human and nonhuman, including of course the humans who do, for better or worse, the work of land use.[3] Industrialists and industrial economists have assumed, with permission from the rest of us, that land and people can be divorced without harm. If farmers come under adversity from high costs and low prices, then they must either increase their demands upon the land and decrease their care for it, or they must sell out and move to town, and this is supposed to involve no ecological or economic or social cost. Or if there are such costs, then they are rated as "the price of progress" or "creative destruction."

18   But land abuse *cannot* brighten the human prospect. There is in fact no distinction between the fate of the land and the fate of the people. When one is abused, the other
suffers. The penalties may come quickly to a farmer who destroys perennial cover on a
sloping field. They *will* come sooner or later to a land-destroying civilization such
as ours.

19   And so it has seemed to me less a choice than a necessity to oppose the
boomer enterprise with its false standards and its incomplete accounting, and to es-
pouse the cause of stable, restorative, locally adapted economies of mostly family-
sized farms, ranches, shops, and trades. Naïve as it may sound now, within the
context of our present faith in science, finance, and technology—the faith equally of

Locally Grown...
                Heaven Sent

Shopping farmers' markets as well as grocery stores and
restaurants featuring local produce helps support sustainable
agriculture and family farms.
Every purchase you make is an act of stewardship.

Supporting Family Farms • Kentucky Appalachian Ministry
A Mission Center of the Christian Church (Disciples of Christ)
206 Chestnut Street / Berea, KY 40403

What views on sustainability does this poster from the Kentucky Appalachian Ministry articulate?

"conservatives" and "liberals"—this cause nevertheless has an authentic source in the sticker's hope to abide in and to live from some chosen and cherished small place—which, of course, is the agrarian vision that Thomas Jefferson spoke for, a sometimes honored human theme, minor and even fugitive, but continuous from ancient times until now. Allegiance to it, however, is not a conclusion but the beginning of thought.

20   . . . Economy in its original—and, I think, its proper—sense refers to household management. By extension, it refers to the husbanding of all the goods by which we live. An authentic economy, if we had one, would define and make, on the terms of thrift and affection, our connections to nature and to one another. Our present industrial system also makes those connections, but by pillage and indifference. Most economists think of this arrangement as "the economy." Their columns and articles rarely if ever mention the land-communities and land-use economies. They never ask, in their professional oblivion, why we are willing to do permanent ecological and cultural damage "to strengthen the economy."

21   In his essay, "Notes on Liberty and Property," Allen Tate gave us an indispensable anatomy of our problem. His essay begins by equating, not liberty and property, but liberty and *control* of one's property. He then makes the crucial distinction between ownership that is merely legal and what he calls "effective ownership." If a property, say a small farm, has one owner, then the one owner has an effective and assured, if limited, control over it as long as he or she can afford to own it, and is free to sell it or use it, and (I will add) free to use it poorly or well. It is clear also that effective ownership of a small property is personal and therefore can, at least possibly, be intimate, familial, and affectionate. If, on the contrary, a person owns a small property of stock in a large corporation, then that person has surrendered control of the property to larger shareholders. The drastic mistake our people made, as Tate believed and I agree, was to be convinced "that there is *one* kind of property—just *property*, whether it be a thirty-acre farm in Kentucky or a stock certificate in the United States Steel Corporation." By means of this confusion, Tate said, "Small ownership . . . [Berry's ellipsis] has been worsted by big, dispersed ownership—the giant corporation."[4] (It is necessary to append to this argument the further fact that by now, owing largely to corporate influence, land ownership implies the right to destroy the land-community entirely, as in surface mining, and to impose, as a consequence, the dangers of flooding, water pollution, and disease upon communities downstream.)

22   Tate's essay was written for the anthology, *Who Owns America?*, the publication of which was utterly without effect. With other agrarian writings before and since, it took its place on the far margin of the national dialogue, dismissed as anachronistic, retrogressive, nostalgic, or (to use Tate's own term of defiance) reactionary in the face of the supposedly "inevitable" dominance of corporate industrialism. *Who Owns America?* was published in the Depression year of 1936. It is at least ironic that talk of "effective property" could have been lightly dismissed at a time when many rural people who had migrated to industrial cities were returning to their home farms to survive.

23   In 1936, when to the dominant minds a thirty-acre farm in Kentucky was becoming laughable, Tate's essay would have seemed irrelevant as a matter of course. At that time, despite the Depression, faith in the standards and devices of industrial progress was nearly universal and could not be shaken.

24 But now, three-quarters of a century later, we are no longer talking about theoretical alternatives to corporate rule. We are talking with practical urgency about an obvious need. Now the two great aims of industrialism—replacement of people by technology and concentration of wealth into the hands of a small plutocracy—seem close to fulfillment. At the same time the *failures* of industrialism have become too great and too dangerous to deny. Corporate industrialism itself has exposed the falsehood that it ever was inevitable or that it ever has given precedence to the common good. It has failed to sustain the health and stability of human society. Among its characteristic signs are destroyed communities, neighborhoods, families, small businesses, and small farms. It has failed just as conspicuously and more dangerously to conserve the wealth and health of nature. No amount of fiddling with capitalism to regulate and humanize it, no pointless rhetoric on the virtues of capitalism or socialism, no billions or trillions spent on "defense" of the "American dream," can for long disguise this failure. The evidences of it are everywhere: eroded, wasted, or degraded soils; damaged or destroyed ecosystems; extinction of species; whole landscapes defaced, gouged, flooded, or blown up; pollution of the whole atmosphere and of the water cycle; "dead zones" in the coastal waters; thoughtless squandering of fossil fuels and fossil waters, of mineable minerals and ores; natural health and beauty replaced by a heartless and sickening ugliness. Perhaps its greatest success is an astounding increase in the destructiveness, and therefore the profitability, of war.

25 In 1936, moreover, only a handful of people were thinking about sustainability. Now, reasonably, many of us are thinking about it. The problem of sustainability is simple enough to state. It requires that the fertility cycle of birth, growth, maturity, death, and decay—what Albert Howard called "the Wheel of Life"—should turn continuously in place, so that the law of return is kept and nothing is wasted. For this to happen in the stewardship of humans, there must be a cultural cycle, in harmony with the fertility cycle, also continuously turning in place. The cultural cycle is an unending conversation between old people and young people, assuring the survival of local memory, which has, as long as it remains local, the greatest practical urgency and value. This is what is meant, and is all that is meant, by "sustainability." The fertility cycle turns by the law of nature. The cultural cycle turns on affection. . . .

26 In my reading of the historian John Lukacs, I have been most instructed by his understanding that there is no knowledge but human knowledge, that we are therefore inescapably central to our own consciousness, and that this is "a statement not of arrogance but of humility. It is yet another recognition of the inevitable limitations of mankind."[5] We are thus isolated within our uniquely human boundaries, which we certainly cannot transcend or escape by means of technological devices.

27 But as I understand this dilemma, we are not *completely* isolated. Though we cannot by our own powers escape our limits, we are subject to correction from, so to speak, the outside. I can hardly expect everybody to believe, as I do (with due caution), that inspiration can come from the outside. But inspiration is not the only way the human enclosure can be penetrated. Nature too may break in upon us, sometimes to our delight, sometimes to our dismay.

28 As many hunters, farmers, ecologists, and poets have understood, Nature (and here we capitalize her name) is the impartial mother of all creatures, unpredictable,

never entirely revealed, not my mother or your mother, but nonetheless our mother. If we are observant and respectful of her, she gives good instruction. As Albert Howard, Wes Jackson, and others have carefully understood, she can give us the right patterns and standards for agriculture. If we ignore or offend her, she enforces her will with punishment. She is always trying to tell us that we are not so superior or independent or alone or autonomous as we may think. She tells us in the voice of Edmund Spenser that she is of *all* creatures "the equall mother, / And knittest each to each, as brother unto brother."[6] Nearly three and a half centuries later, we hear her saying about the same thing in the voice of Aldo Leopold: "In short, a land ethic changes the role of *Homo sapiens* from conqueror of the land-community to plain member and citizen of it."[7]

We cannot know the whole truth, which belongs to God alone, but our task nevertheless is to seek to know what is true. And if we offend gravely enough against what we know to be true, as by failing badly enough to deal affectionately and responsibly with our land and our neighbors, truth will retaliate with ugliness, poverty, and disease. The crisis of this line of thought is the realization that we are at once limited and unendingly responsible for what we know and do.

The discrepancy between what modern humans presume to know and what they can imagine—given the background of pride and self-congratulation—is amusing and even funny. It becomes more serious as it raises issues of responsibility. It becomes fearfully serious when we start dealing with statistical measures of industrial destruction.

To hear of a thousand deaths in war is terrible, and we "know" that it is. But as it registers on our hearts, it is not more terrible than one death fully imagined. The economic hardship of one farm family, if they are our neighbors, affects us more painfully than pages of statistics on the decline of the farm population. I can be heartstruck by grief and a kind of compassion at the sight of one gulley (and by shame if I caused it myself), but, conservationist though I am, I am not nearly so upset by an accounting of the tons of plowland sediment borne by the Mississippi River. Wallace Stevens wrote that "Imagination applied to the whole world is vapid in comparison to imagination applied to a detail"[8]—and that appears to have the force of truth . . .

. . . The losses and damages characteristic of our present economy cannot be stopped, let alone restored, by "liberal" or "conservative" tweakings of corporate industrialism, against which the ancient imperatives of good care, homemaking, and frugality can have no standing. The possibility of authentic correction comes, I think, from two already-evident causes. The first is scarcity and other serious problems arising from industrial abuses of the land-community. The goods of nature so far have been taken for granted and, especially in America, assumed to be limitless, but their diminishment, sooner or later unignorable, will enforce change.

A positive cause, still little noticed by high officials and the media, is the by now well-established effort to build or rebuild local economies, starting with economies of food. This effort to connect cities with their surrounding rural landscapes has the advantage of being both attractive and necessary. It rests exactly upon the recognition of human limits and the necessity of human scale. Its purpose, to the extent possible, is to bring producers and consumers, causes and effects, back within the bounds of neighborhood, which is to say the effective reach of imagination, sympathy, affection, and all else that neighborhood implies. An economy genuinely local and neighborly offers to localities a measure of security that they cannot derive from a national or a global economy controlled by people who, by principle, have no local commitment.

34   . . . By now all thoughtful people have begun to feel our eligibility to be instructed by ecological disaster and mortal need. But we endangered ourselves first of all by dismissing affection as an honorable and necessary motive. Our decision in the middle of the last century to reduce the farm population, eliminating the allegedly "inefficient" small farmers, was enabled by the discounting of affection. As a result, we now have barely enough farmers to keep the land in production, with the help of increasingly expensive industrial technology and at an increasing ecological and social cost. Far from the plain citizens and members of the land-community, as Aldo Leopold wished them to be, farmers are now too likely to be merely the land's exploiters.

35   I don't hesitate to say that damage or destruction of the land-community is morally wrong, just as Leopold did not hesitate to say so when he was composing his essay, "The Land Ethic," in 1947. But I do not believe, as I think Leopold did not, that morality, even religious morality, is an adequate motive for good care of the land-community. The *primary* motive for good care and good use is always going to be affection, because affection involves us entirely. And here Leopold himself set the example. In 1935 he bought an exhausted Wisconsin farm and, with his family, began its restoration. To do this was morally right, of course, but the motive was affection. Leopold was an ecologist. He felt, we may be sure, an informed sorrow for the place in its ruin. He imagined it as it had been, as it was, and as it might be. And a profound, delighted affection radiates from every sentence he wrote about it.

36   Without this informed, practical, and *practiced* affection, the nation and its economy will conquer and destroy the country . . .

NOTES

1. *Everyman's Library*, Alfred A. Knopf, New York, 1991, page 355.
2. *Where the Bluebird Sings to the Lemonade Springs*, Random House, New York, 1992, pages xxii & 4.
3. *A Sand County Almanac*, Oxford University Press, New York, 1966, pages 219–220.
4. *Who Owns America?* edited by Herbert Agar and Allen Tate, ISI Books, Wilmington, DE, 1999, † pages 109–114. (First published by Houghton Mifflin Company, Boston, 1936.)
5. *Last Rites*, Yale University Press, New Haven and London, 2009, pages 31 and 35.
6. *The Faerie Queene*, VII, vii, stanza XIV.
7. *A Sand County Almanac*, pages 219–220.
8. *Opus Posthumous*, edited, with an Introduction by Samuel French Morse, Alfred A. Knopf, New York, 1957, page 176.

Jared Diamond

Will Big Business Save the Earth?

There is a widespread view, particularly among environmentalists and liberals, that big businesses are environmentally destructive, greedy, evil and driven by short-term profits. I know—because I used to share that view.

But today I have more nuanced feelings. Over the years I've joined the boards of two environmental groups, the World Wildlife Fund and Conservation International, serving alongside many business executives.

As part of my board work, I have been asked to assess the environments in oil fields, and have had frank discussions with oil company employees at all levels. I've also worked with executives of mining, retail, logging and financial services companies. I've discovered that while some businesses are indeed as destructive as many suspect, others are among the world's strongest positive forces for environmental sustainability.

The embrace of environmental concerns by chief executives has accelerated recently for several reasons. Lower consumption of environmental resources saves money in the short run. Maintaining sustainable resource levels and not polluting saves money in the long run. And a clean image—one attained by, say, avoiding oil spills and other environmental disasters—reduces criticism from employees, consumers and government.

What's my evidence for this? Here are a few examples involving three corporations—Walmart, Coca-Cola and Chevron—that many critics of business love to hate, in my opinion, unjustly.

Let's start with Walmart. Obviously, a business can save money by finding ways to spend less while maintaining sales. This is what Walmart did with fuel costs, which the company reduced by $26 million per year simply by changing the way it managed its enormous truck fleet. Instead of running a truck's engine all night to heat or cool the cab during mandatory 10-hour rest stops, the company installed small auxiliary power units to do the job. In addition to lowering fuel costs, the move eliminated the carbon dioxide emissions equivalent to taking 18,300 passenger vehicles off the road.

Walmart is also working to double the fuel efficiency of its truck fleet by 2015, thereby saving more than $200 million a year at the pump. Among the efficient prototypes now being tested are trucks that burn biofuels generated from waste grease at Walmart's delis. Similarly, as the country's biggest private user of electricity, Walmart is saving money by decreasing store energy use.

Another Walmart example involves lowering costs associated with packaging materials. Walmart now sells only concentrated liquid laundry detergents in North America, which has reduced the size of packaging by up to 50 percent. Walmart stores also have machines called bailers that recycle plastics that once would have been discarded. Walmart's eventual goal is to end up with no packaging waste.

9   One last Walmart example shows how a company can save money in the long run by buying from sustainably managed sources. Because most wild fisheries are managed unsustainably, prices for Chilean sea bass and Atlantic tuna have been soaring. To my pleasant astonishment, in 2006 Walmart decided to switch, within five years, all its purchases of wild-caught seafood to fisheries certified as sustainable.

10   Coca-Cola's problems are different from Walmart's in that they are largely long-term. The key ingredient in Coke products is water. The company produces its beverages in about 200 countries through local franchises, all of which require a reliable local supply of clean fresh water.

11   But water supplies are under severe pressure around the world, with most already allocated for human use. The little remaining unallocated fresh water is in remote areas unsuitable for beverage factories, like Arctic Russia and northwestern Australia.

12   Coca-Cola can't meet its water needs just by desalinizing seawater, because that requires energy, which is also increasingly expensive. Global climate change is making water scarcer, especially in the densely populated temperate-zone countries, like the United States, that are Coca-Cola's main customers. Most competing water use around the world is for agriculture, which presents sustainability problems of its own.

13   Hence Coca-Cola's survival compels it to be deeply concerned with problems of water scarcity, energy, climate change and agriculture. One company goal is to make its plants water-neutral, returning to the environment water in quantities equal to the amount used in beverages and their production. Another goal is to work on the conservation of seven of the world's river basins, including the Rio Grande, Yangtze, Mekong and Danube—all of them sites of major environmental concerns besides supplying water for Coca-Cola.

14   These long-term goals are in addition to Coca-Cola's short-term cost-saving environmental practices, like recycling plastic bottles, replacing petroleum-based plastic in bottles with organic material, reducing energy consumption and increasing sales volume while decreasing water use.

15   The third company is Chevron. Not even in any national park have I seen such rigorous environmental protection as I encountered in five visits to new Chevron-managed oil fields in Papua New Guinea. (Chevron has since sold its stake in these properties to a New Guinea-based oil company.) When I asked how a publicly traded company could justify to its shareholders its expenditures on the environment, Chevron employees and executives gave me at least five reasons.

16   First, oil spills can be horribly expensive: it is far cheaper to prevent them than to clean them up. Second, clean practices reduce the risk that New Guinean landowners become angry, sue for damages and close the fields. (The company has been sued for problems in Ecuador that Chevron inherited when it merged with Texaco in 2001.) Next, environmental standards are becoming stricter around the world, so building clean facilities now minimizes having to do expensive retrofitting later.

17   Also, clean operations in one country give a company an advantage in bidding on leases in other countries. Finally, environmental practices of which employees are proud improve morale, help with recruitment and increase the length of time employees are likely to remain at the company.

In view of all those advantages that businesses gain from environmentally sustainable policies, why do such policies face resistance from some businesses and many politicians? The objections often take the form of one-liners.

- We have to balance the environment against the economy. The assumption underlying this statement is that measures promoting environmental sustainability inevitably yield a net economic cost rather than a profit. This line of thinking turns the truth upside down. Economic reasons furnish the strongest motives for sustainability, because in the long run (and often in the short run as well) it is much more expensive and difficult to try to fix problems, environmental or otherwise, than to avoid them at the outset.

Americans learned that lesson from Hurricane Katrina in August 2005, when, as a result of government agencies balking for a decade at spending several hundred million dollars to fix New Orleans's defenses, we suffered hundreds of billions of dollars in damage—not to mention thousands of dead Americans. Likewise, John Holdren, the top White House science adviser, estimates that solving problems of climate change would cost the United States 2 percent of our gross domestic product by the year 2050, but that not solving those problems would damage the economy by 20 percent to 30 percent of G.D.P.

- Technology will solve our problems. Yes, technology can contribute to solving problems. But major technological advances require years to develop and put in place, and regularly turn out to have unanticipated side effects—consider the destruction of the atmosphere's ozone layer by the nontoxic, nonflammable chlorofluorocarbons initially hailed for replacing poisonous refrigerant gases.
- World population growth is leveling off and won't be the problem that we used to fear. It's true that the rate of world population growth has been decreasing. However, the real problem isn't people themselves, but the resources that people consume and the waste that they produce. Per-person average consumption rates and waste production rates, now 32 times higher in rich countries than in poor ones, are rising steeply around the world, as developing countries emulate industrialized nations' lifestyles.
- It's futile to preach to us Americans about lowering our standard of living: we will never sacrifice just so other people can raise their standard of living. This conflates consumption rates with standards of living: they are only loosely correlated, because so much of our consumption is wasteful and doesn't contribute to our quality of life. Once basic needs are met, increasing consumption often doesn't increase happiness.
- Replacing a car that gets 15 miles per gallon with a more efficient model wouldn't lower one's standard of living, but would help improve all of our lives by reducing the political and military consequences of our dependence on imported oil. Western Europeans have lower per-capita consumption rates than Americans, but enjoy a higher standard of living as measured by access to medical care, financial security after retirement, infant mortality, life expectancy, literacy and public transport.

20   Not surprisingly, the problem of climate change has attracted its own particular crop of objections.

- Even experts disagree about the reality of climate change. That was true 30 years ago, and some experts still disagreed a decade ago. Today, virtually every climatologist agrees that average global temperatures, warming rates and atmospheric carbon dioxide levels are higher than at any time in the earth's recent past, and that the main cause is greenhouse gas emissions by humans. Instead, the questions still being debated concern whether average global temperatures will increase by 13 degrees or "only" by 4 degrees Fahrenheit by 2050, and whether humans account for 90 percent or "only" 85 percent of the global warming trend.

- The magnitude and cause of global climate change are uncertain. We shouldn't adopt expensive countermeasures until we have certainty. In other spheres of life — picking a spouse, educating our children, buying life insurance and stocks, avoiding cancer and so on — we admit that certainty is unattainable, and that we must decide as best we can on the basis of available evidence. Why should the impossible quest for certainty paralyze us solely about acting on climate change? As Mr. Holdren, the White House adviser, expressed it, not acting on climate change would be like being "in a car with bad brakes driving toward a cliff in the fog."

- Global warming will be good for us, by letting us grow crops in places formerly too cold for agriculture. The term "global warming" is a misnomer; we should instead talk about global climate change, which isn't uniform. The global average temperature is indeed rising, but many areas are becoming drier, and frequencies of droughts, floods and other extreme weather events are increasing. Some areas will be winners, while others will be losers. Most of us will be losers, because the temperate zones where most people live are becoming drier.

- It's useless for the United States to act on climate change, when we don't know what China will do. Actually, China will arrive at this week's Copenhagen climate change negotiations with a whole package of measures to reduce its "carbon intensity."

21   While the United States is dithering about long-distance energy transmission from our rural areas with the highest potential for wind energy generation to our urban areas with the highest need for energy, China is far ahead of us. It is developing ultra-high-voltage transmission lines from wind and solar generation sites in rural western China to cities in eastern China. If America doesn't act to develop innovative energy technology, we will lose the green jobs competition not only to Finland and Germany (as we are now) but also to China.

22   On each of these issues, American businesses are going to play as much or more of a role in our progress as the government. And this isn't a bad thing, as corporations know they have a lot to gain by establishing environmentally friendly business practices.

23   My friends in the business world keep telling me that Washington can help on two fronts: by investing in green research, offering tax incentives and passing cap-and-trade legislation; and by setting and enforcing tough standards to ensure that companies with cheap, dirty standards don't have a competitive advantage over those businesses protecting the environment. As for the rest of us, we should get over the misimpression that American business cares only about immediate profits, and we should reward companies that work to keep the planet healthy. ■

Fixing Sustainability and Sustaining Liberal Education

❝Sustainability" is one of the key words of our time. We are six years along in the United Nations' "Decade of Education for Sustainable Development." In the United States, 677 colleges and universities presidents have committed themselves to a sustainability-themed "Climate Commitment." Sustainability is, by a large measure, the most popular social movement today in American higher education. It is, of course, not just a campus movement, but also a ubiquitous presence in the K-12 curriculum, and a staple of community groups, political platforms, appeals to consumers, and corporate policy.

2   In view of the broad popularity of the idea, we realize that a dissenting opinion may be dismissed out of hand. Yet sustainability ought not to be held exempt from critical scrutiny. And the campus movement built around the word "sustainability," is, in our view, very much in need of such scrutiny. This statement presents the National Association of Scholars' considered view of nine ways that the campus sustainability movement has gone wrong. And we offer a proposal for how it can be set right.

3   We came to compose this statement after three years of studying the campus sustainability movement. We have at this point published over one hundred online articles, reports, and interviews on the topic; attended sustainability events; presented findings at academic meetings; and devoted a special issue of our quarterly journal *Academic Questions* to scholarly analyses of the movement's origins and claims. Our policy statement distills what we have learned from this investigation.

1. A MISAPPROPRIATED WORD

4   Our dissent does not aim at the whole of "sustainability." We regard good stewardship of natural and institutional resources and respect for the environment as excellent principles. We have nothing against colleges and universities attempting to trim their budgets by saving energy. But wholesome words standing for wholesome principles do not always stay put. They can be appropriated by political movements seeking to mask unattractive or unworthy ideas.

5   Words can be twisted, and on our campuses this is what has happened to "sustainability." We've seen this before. "Diversity," for example, appealed to tolerance, but was twisted into a rationalization for special privilege and coercive policy. "Multiculturalism" initially seemed a call to appreciate other cultures, but turned out to be primarily an attack on our own. "Sustainability" has followed this crooked path, appealing initially to our obligation to give future generations a clean and healthy planet, but quickly turning into a thicket of ideological prescriptions.

6   In its career as a politically correct euphemism, sustainability has begun to cause some serious mischief.

2. MISTAKING SCARCITY

7 The sustainability movement by and large mistakes the fundamental problem dealt with by the discipline of economics: scarcity. Economics has shown us that scarcity of material goods is basic. Humans can respond to scarcity in many ways, including hoarding, theft, war, and oligarchy. But among the most constructive responses are trade, substitution, the development of markets, and technological innovation.

8 The sustainability movement, however, embraces the notion that the best approach to the problem of scarcity is generally the maximal conservation of existing resources. That can be accomplished only by curtailing use, and in the effort to achieve sharp reductions in the use of resources, the sustainability movement favors government regulation as key. The sustainability movement is, in its essence, neo-Malthusian. (It supposes that, short of intervention, population growth will outstrip resources.)

9 There are, to be sure, advocates of sustainability who are friendlier towards the roles of innovation and markets in addressing future needs, but they do not represent the mainstream of the movement.

3. MALIGNING PROGRESS

10 Historically, progress has depended on finding means to do more with less, or do more by converting the previously unusable into a source of value. Because the sustainability movement has so little confidence in the power of technological innovation, it is essentially anti-progress. Indeed some sustainability advocates openly declare their hostility to the industrialization of the West and the spread of advanced economic structures to the rest of the world. Instead of progress, the sustainability movement prefers control. Progress proceeds through innovation; sustainability through regulation.

11 While not inherently at cross-purposes with progress, regulation can thwart it by replacing market mechanisms with planned allocation, thereby diminishing the incentives for invention. The trade-offs between regulation and innovation will vary from case to case and need to be specifically analyzed. But turning sustainability, as often happens, into a moral imperative, a public icon, a matter of unquestioned doctrine, frustrates rational canvass.

4. MISLEADING ASSUMPTIONS

12 The sustainability movement often simply assumes what it cannot show. Is the world running out of key resources? Has consumption in developed countries reached "unsustainable" levels? In view of global warming or climate change, do we need to institute dramatic changes in the world economy? Such questions, if asked at all, tend to be asked rhetorically, as if the answers were self-evident. Or if the situation requires an answer, we are met with spurious declarations of authority: the Intergovernmental Panel on Climate Change says this; the "consensus" of scientists says that.

13 Sustainability in this sense is becoming a means of question-begging, of preempting discussion about the best ways of dealing with the problem of scarcity.

14 To be sure, the National Association of Scholars does not have its own answers to these important questions. To the extent that the questions are really questions and not just rhetorical devices, they are beyond our scope as an organization to answer.

But it is not beyond our scope to insist on respect for the scientific method and conclusions based on the best available evidence, not mere assumptions packaged to look like science.

5. STIFLING INQUIRY

15 The sustainability movement's aversion to progress and its tendency to assume rather than argue its basic propositions runs against the spirit of higher education. Our institutions of higher learning have long been great centers of inquiry. They have helped to drive technological progress for more than four centuries, and have been instrumental as well in driving economic development. To transform sustainability into mindless mantra—absorbed by students, faculty, and staff through catchword repetition—risks replacing the West's traditional optimism with a reflexive self-denial. That shouldn't be the vocation of America's higher educators.

6. MISUSING AUTHORITY

16 The sustainability movement arrived on campuses mainly at the invitation of college presidents and administrative staff in areas such as student activities and residence life. That means that it largely escaped the scrutiny of faculty members and that it continues to enjoy a position of unearned authority. In many instances, the movement advances by administrative fiat, backed up by outside advocacy groups and students recruited for their zeal in promoting the cause. Agenda-driven organizations—such as the Association for the Advancement of Sustainability in Higher Education (AASHE) and the American College and University Presidents' Climate Commitment (ACUPCC)—have taken advantage of academic sensibilities to turn sustainability into what is in many cases, a campus fetish. Sustainability also gets promoted by resort to pledges, games, competitions, and a whole variety of psychological gimmicks that bypass serious intellectual inquiry.

17 Some results are relatively trivial. For example, at certain institutions, cafeteria trays have been banned to save food, water, and energy, leaving students and staff to juggle dishes, cups, and utensils as they move between counters and tables. Many campuses have also banned the sale of disposable water bottles to reduce plastic waste. Yet however laughable, such petty annoyances have a sinister penumbra. They advertise a willingness to bully that creates a more generalized climate of intimidation, spilling over into other domains.

7. ABUSING FREEDOM

18 One of these is academic freedom, and here the news is worse. As with diversity, some institutions have been pressuring faculties to incorporate "sustainability" across-the-curriculum, requiring reports about the ways in which individual instructors have redesigned their teaching. Quite apart from the practical difficulties this creates in fields like music or philology, it invades the pivotal right of faculty members to interpret their subject matter freely. Belief in the imminence of environmental crisis, or the imperative of laying aside other intellectual priorities to address it, should not be a requirement for

teaching or scholarship, or a standard of good academic citizenship. That it threatens to become so reflects a serious disturbance in the academic climate, to say nothing of being a tell-tale sign of the kind of hubris that infects ideologically empowered administrators.

8. IDEOLOGICAL AGGREGATION

19 When we hear the word "sustainability," most of us think of the environment, but for a long time many sustainability advocates have been staking claims to larger territory. They see sustainability as not just about the environment but also about economics and social justice. The movement takes as its unofficial logo a Venn diagram of three overlapping circles labeled accordingly. And many in the movement believe that to achieve a sustainable society, we must make coordinated radical changes in all three areas. In practice, this means that sustainability is used as a means of promoting to students a view that capitalism and individualism are "unsustainable," morally unworthy, and a present danger to the future of the planet.

20 Many sustainability advocates, particularly those situated in, or allied to, offices of student life, now contend that since moral choices inevitably produce a cascade of environmental consequences, moral reeducation is needed to ensure sustainability. Much of this is directed, at least implicitly, against traditional moral values. Having an affirmative attitude toward homosexuality, for instance, is reinterpreted so as to bear a positive environmental significance. Obviously, moral principles are an entirely valid topic for debate, on campus or off. In a university setting we would prefer this debate—to the degree it is under official auspices—to occur in those courses where it's materially

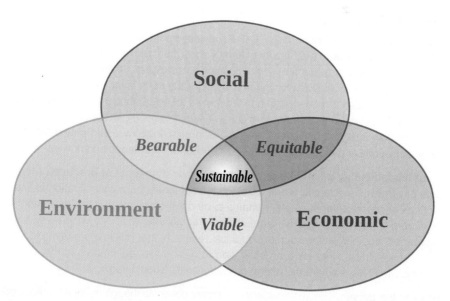

The Venn diagram demonstrates what sustainability advocates see as the relationships between the environmental, economic, and social spheres.

relevant. Needless to say, students should also be completely free to discuss these questions outside the classroom. What should not happen, but nonetheless does, is for the debate to be stage-managed by dormitory-based bureaucrats, under the pretext of furthering the university's educational responsibilities.

9. MYSTIC DOOM

21 Fascination with decline and ruin are nothing new in Western thought. The sustainability movement combines a bureaucratic and regulatory impulse with an updated version of the Romantics' preoccupation with the end of civilization, and with hints of the Christian apocalyptic tradition. These are the "end times" in the view of some sustainability advocates—or potentially so in the eyes of many others. The movement has its own versions of sin and redemption, and in many other respects has a quasi-religious character. For some of the adherents, the earth itself is treated as a sentient deity; others content themselves with the search for the transcendent in Nature.

22 As a creed among creeds, sustainability constitutes an upping of the ideological ante. Feminism, Afro-centrism, gay-liberation, and various other recent fads and doctrines, whatever else they were, were secular, speaking merely to politics and culture. The sustainability movement reaches beyond that, having nothing less than the preservation of life on earth at its heart.

23 The religious creeds of faculty members and students are their own business, but we have reason for concern when dogmatic beliefs are smuggled into the curriculum and made a basis for campus programs as though they were mere extensions of scientific facts.

RECOMMENDATIONS

24 Our list of nine ways in which the sustainability movement has gone wrong, of course, reflects our view of what the university ideally should be. Universities at their best adhere to reasoned discourse and scientific method: reasoned discourse in welcoming all serious perspectives, scientific method in subjecting them to the canons of logic and evidence. Universities are founded on the premise that clear thought must precede action. The sustainability movement as it is now assaults all of these ideals.

25 We can imagine, however, ways in which sustainability could play a far more constructive role in the university. To that end, NAS urges colleges and universities to:

Treat sustainability as an object of inquiry rather than a set of precepts. A great deal of worthwhile scientific work, research in engineering, and investigation in fields such as economics, for example, remains to be done on points that the movement in its current form tends to take for granted. Some of this work is already underway, but it is crowded together with much more dubious "research" that is little more than ideological touting. Universities have an obligation to distinguish legitimate inquiry from its counterfeits. This is where the reform of sustainability should begin.

Restore the debate. The sustainability movement poses as though many long-disputed matters are now settled. This isn't true. For sustainability to play a genuinely constructive part in the intellectual life of the nation's universities, it must submit to both cross-examination and to open dialog. The neo-Malthusian component of the movement (the idea that the world's population is outstripping its resources) is especially in need of the questioning that open debate can provide.

Level the playing field. It won't be much of a debate if sustainability advocates enjoy all the advantages of administrative favor. Advocates of alternative "narratives," such as those who emphasize progress through technological innovation, need comparable levels of support.

Get off the bandwagon. Signing statements like the "American College and University Presidents' Climate Commitment" preempts discussion of matters that should rightly be open for debate and for robust expression of different opinions. Efforts to collectivize opinion and to settle open questions by appealing to the prestige of signatories are, at bottom, anti-intellectual as well as a threat to academic freedom.

Quit bullying the skeptics. Even tenured faculty members complain of the heavy-handed tactics of sustainability advocates in their attempts to silence dissent. Matters are much worse for undergraduate students who often come under the gaze of "sustainabullies"—those students who, often with the encouragement of their colleges, take it upon themselves to enforce the ideology.

Promote intellectual freedom. Sustainability would be a much more attractive idea shorn of its coercive aspect. College and university officials should take care not to turn optional campus activities themed on sustainability into de facto requirements. Making sustainability part of freshman orientation, for example, preempts most students from ever risking the expression of an independent opinion. Advocacy of causes about which individuals can reasonably disagree should always take place in a manner in which disagreement can be voiced without fear of official sanction.

Respect pedagogical freedom. Recent efforts at some colleges and universities to quiz faculty members in every department about their contributions to sustainability in all their classes are another instance of administrative overreach. If sustainability is to thrive as one perspective among many it must be set free from such meddling. Faculty members must be free to interpret course content, and to exclude content they don't believe falls within the purview of their fields. Sustainability is not a subject that should be imposed across the curriculum.

Remember the mission. Make sound education rather than enthusiasm for social causes the essence of the academic mission. Good causes beckon every day. But even the best of social causes is, in the end, a diversion from the real purpose of the university.

26   We encourage college and university presidents, who have so often taken the lead in bringing the sustainability movement to campus, to take the lead again in correcting the excesses of the movement. We also encourage trustees, alumni, faculty members, administrators, and students to raise the pertinent questions and stand fast in their expectations of fair-minded debate.

WHAT'S NEXT

27 At the beginning of this statement we acknowledged that we are critiquing a movement that enjoys widespread popularity. We have no illusions that in setting out a brief summary of that movement's flaws we will prompt an equally widespread reassessment. It is human nature that once people invest themselves in a system of belief, they defend it with vigor and turn away from it only reluctantly and after numerous disappointments. The academy is no exception. Though it espouses in principle the rules of rational inquiry and reliance on unbiased evidence, academics too are prey to the dynamics of ideological conviction.

28 In that light, what purpose does our critique serve? We offer it in the spirit of a constructive alternative. We are far from dismissing the importance of environmental issues or the complicated connections between the environment, economic structures, and social conditions. Our overriding concern is that a movement that is in haste to promote its preferred solutions to what it sees as urgent problems has deflected higher education from its proper role. We seek to remind all those concerned with the future of American higher education what that role is, and to summon the responsible authorities back to their primary work.

29 We do this knowing that a large number of faculty members as well as members of the general public harbor misgivings about the sustainability movement but have all too often found themselves shut out of debate and unable even to find a forum in which to express their doubts. This statement offers those who are already skeptical encouragement. It offers those who have reserved judgment an invitation to embark on their own critical examination of the topic. And it offers those who are currently committed to the sustainability movement a challenge to their settled assumptions and a path to the exit when they are ready to rethink.

30 That rethinking is inevitable. The sustainability movement is, in a word, unsustainable. It runs too contrary to the abiding purposes of higher education; it is too rife with internal contradictions; and it is too contrary to the environmental, economic, and social facts to endure indefinitely. When it begins to sink, we trust that this document will be remembered as offering a useful map for finding higher—and firmer—ground ■

Nicolette Hahn Niman

The Carnivore's Dilemma

I s eating a hamburger the global warming equivalent of driving a Hummer? This week an article in *The Times* of London carried a headline that blared: "Give Up Meat to Save the Planet." Former Vice President Al Gore, who has made climate change his signature issue, has even been assailed for omnivorous eating by animal rights activists.

2 It's true that food production is an important contributor to climate change. And the claim that meat (especially beef) is closely linked to global warming has received

some credible backing, including by the United Nations and University of Chicago. Both institutions have issued reports that have been widely summarized as condemning meat-eating.

3   But that's an overly simplistic conclusion to draw from the research. To a rancher like me, who raises cattle, goats and turkeys the traditional way (on grass), the studies show only that the prevailing methods of producing meat—that is, crowding animals together in factory farms, storing their waste in giant lagoons and cutting down forests to grow crops to feed them—cause substantial greenhouse gases. It could be, in fact, that a conscientious meat eater may have a more environmentally friendly diet than your average vegetarian.

4   So what is the real story of meat's connection to global warming? Answering the question requires examining the individual greenhouse gases involved: carbon dioxide, methane and nitrous oxides.

5   Carbon dioxide makes up the majority of agriculture-related greenhouse emissions. In American farming, most carbon dioxide emissions come from fuel burned to operate vehicles and equipment. World agricultural carbon emissions, on the other hand, result primarily from the clearing of woods for crop growing and livestock grazing. During the 1990s, tropical deforestation in Brazil, India, Indonesia, Sudan and other developing countries caused 15 percent to 35 percent of annual global fossil fuel emissions.

6   Much Brazilian deforestation is connected to soybean cultivation. As much as 70 percent of areas newly cleared for agriculture in Mato Grosso State in Brazil is being used to grow soybeans. Over half of Brazil's soy harvest is controlled by a handful of international agribusiness companies, which ship it all over the world for animal feed and food products, causing emissions in the process.

7   Meat and dairy eaters need not be part of this. Many smaller, traditional farms and ranches in the United States have scant connection to carbon dioxide emissions because they keep their animals outdoors on pasture and make little use of machinery. Moreover, those farmers generally use less soy than industrial operations do, and those who do often grow their own, so there are no emissions from long-distance transport and zero chance their farms contributed to deforestation in the developing world.

8   In contrast to traditional farms, industrial livestock and poultry facilities keep animals in buildings with mechanized systems for feeding, lighting, sewage flushing, ventilation, heating and cooling, all of which generate emissions. These factory farms are also soy guzzlers and acquire much of their feed overseas. You can reduce your contribution to carbon dioxide emissions by avoiding industrially produced meat and dairy products.

9   Unfortunately for vegetarians who rely on it for protein, avoiding soy from deforested croplands may be more difficult: as the Organic Consumers Association notes, Brazilian soy is common (and unlabeled) in tofu and soymilk sold in American supermarkets.

10   Methane is agriculture's second-largest greenhouse gas. Wetland rice fields alone account for as much 29 percent of the world's human-generated methane. In animal farming, much of the methane comes from lagoons of liquefied manure at industrial facilities, which are as nauseating as they sound.

11   This isn't a problem at traditional farms. "Before the 1970s, methane emissions from manure were minimal because the majority of livestock farms in the U.S. were small operations where animals deposited manure in pastures and corrals," the Environmental Protection Agency says. The E.P.A. found that with the rapid rise of factory farms, liquefied manure systems became the norm and methane emissions skyrocketed. You can reduce your methane emissions by seeking out meat from animals raised outdoors on traditional farms.

12   Critics of meat-eating often point out that cattle are prime culprits in methane production. Fortunately, the cause of these methane emissions is understood, and their production can be reduced.

13   Much of the problem arises when livestock eat poor quality forages, throwing their digestive systems out of balance. Livestock nutrition experts have demonstrated that by making minor improvements in animal diets (like providing nutrient-laden salt licks) they can cut enteric methane by half. Other practices, like adding certain proteins to ruminant diets, can reduce methane production per unit of milk or meat by a factor of six, according to research at Australia's University of New England. Enteric methane emissions can also be substantially reduced when cattle are regularly rotated onto fresh pastures, researchers at University of Louisiana have confirmed.

14   Finally, livestock farming plays a role in nitrous oxide emissions, which make up around 5 percent of this country's total greenhouse gases. More than three-quarters of farming's nitrous oxide emissions result from manmade fertilizers. Thus, you can reduce nitrous oxide emissions by buying meat and dairy products from animals that

The E.P.A defines animal feeding operations (AFOs) as operations in which the animals are confined for at least 45 days in a 12-month period and there is no grass or other vegetation in the confinement area during the normal growing season.

were not fed fertilized crops—in other words, from animals raised on grass or raised organically.

15   In contrast to factory farming, well-managed, non-industrialized animal farming minimizes greenhouse gases and can even benefit the environment. For example, properly timed cattle grazing can increase vegetation by as much as 45 percent, North Dakota State University researchers have found. And grazing by large herbivores (including cattle) is essential for well-functioning prairie ecosystems, research at Kansas State University has determined.

16   Additionally, several recent studies show that pasture and grassland areas used for livestock reduce global warming by acting as carbon sinks. Converting croplands to pasture, which reduces erosion, effectively sequesters significant amounts of carbon. One analysis published in the journal Global Change Biology showed a 19 percent increase in soil carbon after land changed from cropland to pasture. What's more, animal grazing reduces the need for the fertilizers and fuel used by farm machinery in crop cultivation, things that aggravate climate change.

17   Livestock grazing has other noteworthy environmental benefits as well. Compared to cropland, perennial pastures used for grazing can decrease soil erosion by 80 percent and markedly improve water quality, Minnesota's Land Stewardship Project research has found. Even the United Nations report acknowledges, "There is growing evidence that both cattle ranching and pastoralism can have positive impacts on biodiversity."

18   As the contrast between the environmental impact of traditional farming and industrial farming shows, efforts to minimize greenhouse gases need to be much more sophisticated than just making blanket condemnations of certain foods. Farming methods vary tremendously, leading to widely variable global warming contributions for every food we eat. Recent research in Sweden shows that, depending on how and where a food is produced, its carbon dioxide emissions vary by a factor of 10.

19   And it should also be noted that farmers bear only a portion of the blame for greenhouse gas emissions in the food system. Only about one-fifth of the food system's energy use is farm-related, according to University of Wisconsin research. And the Soil Association in Britain estimates that only half of food's total greenhouse impact has any connection to farms. The rest comes from processing, transportation, storage, retailing and food preparation. The seemingly innocent potato chip, for instance, turns out to be a dreadfully climate-hostile food. Foods that are minimally processed, in season and locally grown, like those available at farmers' markets and backyard gardens, are generally the most climate-friendly.

20   Rampant waste at the processing, retail and household stages compounds the problem. About half of the food produced in the United States is thrown away, according to University of Arizona research. Thus, a consumer could measurably reduce personal global warming impact simply by more judicious grocery purchasing and use.

21   None of us, whether we are vegan or omnivore, can entirely avoid foods that play a role in global warming. Singling out meat is misleading and unhelpful, especially since few people are likely to entirely abandon animal-based foods. Mr. Gore, for one, apparently has no intention of going vegan. The 90 percent of Americans who eat meat and dairy are likely to respond the same way.

22   Still, there are numerous reasonable ways to reduce our individual contributions to climate change through our food choices. Because it takes more resources to produce meat and dairy than, say, fresh locally grown carrots, it's sensible to cut back on consumption of animal-based foods. More important, all eaters can lower their global warming contribution by following these simple rules: avoid processed foods and those from industrialized farms; reduce food waste; and buy local and in season ∎

Mark Bittman

Eating Food That's Better for You, Organic or Not

I n the six-and-one-half years since the federal government began certifying food as "organic," Americans have taken to the idea with considerable enthusiasm. Sales have at least doubled, and three-quarters of the nation's grocery stores now carry at least some organic food. A Harris poll in October 2007 found that about 30 percent of Americans buy organic food at least on occasion, and most think it is safer, better for the environment and healthier.

2   "People believe it must be better for you if it's organic," says Phil Howard, an assistant professor of community, food and agriculture at Michigan State University.

3   So I discovered on a recent book tour around the United States and Canada.

4   No matter how carefully I avoided using the word "organic" when I spoke to groups of food enthusiasts about how to eat better, someone in the audience would inevitably ask, "What if I can't afford to buy organic food?" It seems to have become the magic cure-all, synonymous with eating well, healthfully, sanely, even ethically.

5   But eating "organic" offers no guarantee of any of that. And the truth is that most Americans eat so badly—we get 7 percent of our calories from soft drinks, more than we do from vegetables; the top food group by caloric intake is "sweets"; and one-third of nation's adults are now obese—that the organic question is a secondary one. It's not unimportant, but it's not the primary issue in the way Americans eat.

6   To eat well, says Michael Pollan, the author of "In Defense of Food," means avoiding "edible food-like substances" and sticking to real ingredients, increasingly from the plant kingdom. (Americans each consume an average of nearly two pounds a day of animal products.) There's plenty of evidence that both a person's health—as well as the environment's—will improve with a simple shift in eating habits away from animal products and highly processed foods to plant products and what might be called "real food." (With all due respect to people in the "food movement," the food need not be "slow," either.)

7   From these changes, Americans would reduce the amount of land, water and chemicals used to produce the food we eat, as well as the incidence of lifestyle diseases linked to unhealthy diets, and greenhouse gases from industrial meat production. All without legislation.

3   And the food would not necessarily have to be organic, which, under the United States Department of Agriculture's definition, means it is generally free of synthetic substances; contains no antibiotics and hormones; has not been irradiated or fertilized with sewage sludge; was raised without the use of most conventional pesticides; and contains no genetically modified ingredients.

9   Those requirements, which must be met in order for food to be labeled "U.S.D.A. Organic," are fine, of course. But they still fall short of the lofty dreams of early organic farmers and consumers who gave the word "organic" its allure—of returning natural nutrients and substance to the soil in the same proportion used by the growing process (there is no requirement that this be done); of raising animals humanely in accordance with nature (animals must be given access to the outdoors, but for how long and under what conditions is not spelled out); and of producing the most nutritious food possible (the evidence is mixed on whether organic food is more nutritious) in the most ecologically conscious way.

10   The government's organic program, says Joan Shaffer, a spokeswoman for the Agriculture Department, "is a marketing program that sets standards for what can be certified as organic. Neither the enabling legislation nor the regulations address food safety or nutrition."

11   People don't understand that, nor do they realize "organic" doesn't mean "local." "It doesn't matter if it's from the farm down the road or from Chile," Ms. Shaffer said. "As long as it meets the standards it's organic."

12   Hence, the organic status of salmon flown in from Chile, or of frozen vegetables grown in China and sold in the United States—no matter the size of the carbon footprint left behind by getting from there to here.

13   Today, most farmers who practice truly sustainable farming, or what you might call "organic in spirit," operate on small scale, some so small they can't afford the requirements to be certified organic by the government. Others say that certification isn't meaningful enough to bother. These farmers argue that, "When you buy organic you don't just buy a product, you buy a way of life that is committed to not exploiting the planet," says Ed Maltby, executive director of the Northeast Organic Dairy Producers Alliance.

3   But the organic food business is now big business, and getting bigger. Professor Howard estimates that major corporations now are responsible for at least 25 percent of all organic manufacturing and marketing (40 percent if you count only processed organic foods). Much of the nation's organic food is as much a part of industrial food production as midwinter grapes, and becoming more so. In 2006, sales of organic foods and beverages totaled about $16.7 billion, according to the most recent figures from Organic Trade Association.

14   Still, those sales amounted to slightly less than 3 percent of overall food and beverage sales. For all the hoo-ha, organic food is not making much of an impact on the way Americans eat, though, as Mark Kastel, co-founder of The Cornucopia Institute, puts it: "There are generic benefits from doing organics. It protects the land from the ravages of conventional agriculture," and safeguards farm workers from being exposed to pesticides.

15   But the questions remain over how we eat in general. It may feel better to eat an organic Oreo than a conventional Oreo, but, says Marion Nestle, a professor at

New York University's department of nutrition, food studies and public health, "Organic junk food is still junk food."

16   Last week, Michelle Obama began digging up a patch of the South Lawn of the White House to plant an organic vegetable garden to provide food for the first family and, more important, to educate children about healthy, locally grown fruits and vegetables at a time when obesity and diabetes have become national concerns.

17   But Mrs. Obama also emphasized that there were many changes Americans can make if they don't have the time or space for an organic garden.

18   "You can begin in your own cupboard," she said, "by eliminating processed food, trying to cook a meal a little more often, trying to incorporate more fruits and vegetables."

19   Popularizing such choices may not be as marketable as creating a logo that says "organic." But when Americans have had their fill of "value-added" and overprocessed food, perhaps they can begin producing and consuming more food that treats animals and the land as if they mattered. Some of that food will be organic, and hooray for that. Meanwhile, they should remember that the word itself is not synonymous with "safe," "healthy," "fair" or even necessarily "good." ∎

David B. Resnik

Urban Sprawl, Smart Growth, and Deliberative Democracy

In the last two decades, public health researchers have demonstrated how the built environment—homes, roads, neighborhoods, workplaces, and other structures and spaces created or modified by people—can affect human health adversely.[1–7] Urban sprawl, a pattern of uncontrolled development around the periphery of a city, is an increasingly common feature of the built environment in the United States and other industrialized nations.[8] Although there is considerable evidence that urban sprawl has adverse environmental impacts and contributes to a variety of health problems—including obesity, diabetes, cardiovascular disease, and respiratory disease[9]—implementation of policies designed to combat sprawl, such as smart growth, has proven to be difficult.[10–17] One of the main difficulties obstructing the implementation of smart-growth policies is the considerable controversy these policies generate. Such controversy is understandable, given the fact that the stakeholders affected by urban-planning policies have conflicting interests and divergent moral and political viewpoints.[4] In some of these situations, deliberative democracy—an approach to resolving controversial public-policy questions that emphasizes open, deliberative debate among the affected parties as an alternative to voting—would be a fair and effective way to resolve urban-planning issues.

URBAN SPRAWL

Urban sprawl in the United States has its origins in the flight to the suburbs that began in the 1950s. People wanted to live outside of city centers to avoid traffic, noise, crime, and other problems, and to have homes with more square footage and yard space.[8,9] As suburban areas developed, cities expanded in geographic size faster than they grew in population. This trend has produced large metropolitan areas with low population densities, interconnected by roads.

Residents of sprawling cities tend to live in single-family homes and commute to work, school, or other activities by automobile.[8,9] People who live in large metropolitan areas often find it difficult to travel even short distances without using an automobile, because of the remoteness of residential areas and inadequate availability of mass transit, walkways, or bike paths. In 2002, the 10 worst US metropolitan areas for sprawl were Riverside–San Bernardino, CA; Greensboro–Winston-Salem–High Point, NC; Raleigh–Durham, NC; Atlanta, GA; Greenville–Spartanburg, SC; West Palm Beach–Boca Raton–Delray Beach, FL; Bridgeport–Stamford–Norwalk–Danbury, CT; Knoxville, TN; Oxnard–Ventura, CA; and Fort Worth–Arlington, TX.[8]

There is substantial evidence that urban sprawl has negative effects on human health and the environment.[4,7,9,19] An urban development pattern that necessitates automobile use will produce more air pollutants, such as ozone and airborne particulates, than a pattern that includes alternatives to automotive transportation. The relationship between air pollution and respiratory problems, such as asthma and lung cancer, is well documented.[4] Cities built around automobile use also provide fewer opportunities to exercise than cities that make it easy for people to walk or bike to school, work, or other activities.[4] Exercise has been shown to be crucial to many different aspects of health, such as weight control, cardiovascular function, stress management, and so on.[20,21]

Because socioeconomically disadvantaged people in sprawling cities may have less access to exercise opportunities and healthy food than do wealthier people, sprawl may also contribute to health inequalities.[22] Urban sprawl can reduce water quality by increasing the amount of surface runoff, which channels oil and other pollutants into streams and rivers.[4] Poor water quality is associated with a variety of negative health outcomes, including diseases of the gastrointestinal tract, kidney disease, and cancer.[23] In addition to air and water pollution, adverse environmental impacts of sprawl include deforestation and disruption of wildlife habitat.[4]

SMART GROWTH

Many public health advocates have recommended smart growth as a potential solution to the problem of urban sprawl.[4,7,9,20] Smart growth can be defined as a policy framework that promotes an urban development pattern characterized by high population density, walkable and bikeable neighborhoods, preserved green spaces, mixed-use development (i.e., development projects that include both residential and commercial uses), available mass transit, and limited road construction.[4,7,11] Smart growth was originally conceptualized as an aesthetically pleasing alternative to urban sprawl that would offer residents a high quality of life and the convenience of local amenities,[24] but it also has many potential health benefits, such as diminished air pollution, fewer

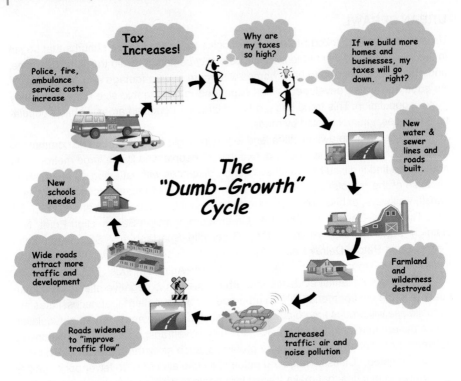

The "Dumb-Growth" Cycle

- Tax Increases!
- Why are my taxes so high?
- If we build more homes and businesses, my taxes will go down. right?
- Police, fire, ambulance service costs increase
- New water & sewer lines and roads built.
- New schools needed
- Farmland and wilderness destroyed
- Wide roads attract more traffic and development
- Increased traffic: air and noise pollution
- Roads widened to "improve traffic flow"

RochesterEnvironment.com aims to encourage dialogue on environmental issues in the area of Rochester, New York. What is the aim of these diagrams? How effective are they?

motor vehicle accidents, lower pedestrian mortality, and increased physical exercise.[4,7] Smart growth is different from the concept of "garden suburbs" because it addresses issues of population density and transportation, not just availability of green space and preservation of agricultural land.[4]

In the 1970s, Portland, Oregon, was the first major city in the United States to establish smart growth urban planning by limiting urban growth to an area around the inner city.[11] Since the 1990s, many other urban areas have encouraged the development of planned communities in which people can live, shop, work, go to school, worship, and recreate without having to travel great distances by automobile. An example of one of these planned communities is Southern Village, situated on 300 acres south of Chapel Hill, North Carolina. Launched in 1996, Southern Village features apartments, townhouses, single-family homes, and a conveniently located town center with a grocery store, restaurants, shops, a movie theater, a dry cleaner, common areas, offices, health care services, a farmer's market, a day-care center, an elementary school, and a church. Southern Village is a walkable community with sidewalks on both sides of the streets and a 1.3-milegreenway running through the middle of town. Southern Village residents have access to mass transit via Chapel Hill's bus system and can enjoy free outdoor concerts in the common areas. More than 3,000 people live in Southern Village.[25]

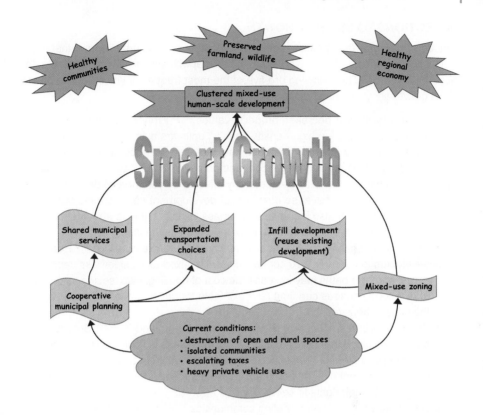

Urban sprawl has occurred largely because land owners and developers have made choices that promote their own economic and personal interests, which do not necessarily coincide with the public good.[18,25] Many community leaders have found it necessary to engage in centralized urban planning to promote smartgrowth.[11] Various laws and regulations can help to control land use and development. One of the most useful land-use policy tools is to change zoning laws to promote mixed-use development.[18] Zoning laws that forbid commercial development in residential areas promote sprawl because they require residents to travel greater distances to buy groceries, shop for clothes, and so on. Zoning laws can also be written to encourage high-density development and to require sidewalks and bike lanes.

Another important policy tool for promoting smart growth is to take steps to prevent development outside of a defined urban area, such as forbidding new housing construction on rural land, or setting administrative boundaries for city services, such as water and sewer connections.[18] The government can also use economic incentives to promote smart growth. Developers that follow smart-growth principles can be deemed eligible for reduced fees that help offset the costs of smart growth development, such as environmental impact fees. Conversely, developers that do not follow smart-growth principles can be subjected to higher fees.[18] Finally, governments can also invest public funds in projects and land uses that facilitate smart growth, such as mass-transit systems, recreation areas, and schools conveniently situated in neighborhoods.[2]

OBJECTIONS TO SMART GROWTH

Although smart growth appears to be a promising alternative to urban sprawl that could benefit public health and the environment, it has met with stiff resistance in some communities.[11,13,15,18,26] The following are five of the most frequently voiced objections to smart growth philosophies and policies:

1. Smart growth can decrease property values.[11–13] Property values may be adversely affected when high-density housing units are built in an area where low-density housing prevails because the increase in population density may exacerbate local traffic, congestion, and crime, which reduces property values. Property values may also be negatively affected by commercial development in a residential area, because commercial development can increase traffic and crime. Crime may also increase when mass transit connects a residential area to a location where crime is more prevalent, such as the inner city.

2. Smart growth can decrease the availability of affordable housing.[14,15] Requiring developers to build planned communities with mixed uses, sidewalks, recreation areas, and bike paths may increase the cost of housing. Also, setting aside large undeveloped spaces can limit land available for development, which drives up the price of housing.

3. Smart growth restricts property owners' use of their land.[10,17,27,28] Suburbanites have complained that laws requiring residential areas to have sidewalks and bike paths deprive them of lawn space. Farmers have protested against laws that prevent development of large portions of agricultural and forestland because this interferes with their rights to sell the land.

4. Smart growth can disrupt existing communities.[11,12,29,30] Low-density, quiet, non-commercial living areas may become high-density, noisy, and commercial. Historically low-income minority communities may be displaced to make room for high-rise, smart-growth housing complexes and upscale commercial development.

5. Smart growth may increase sprawl instead of decreasing it.[11,14] Some opponents of smart growth have argued that it often fails to achieve its intended effect and can actually exacerbate sprawl, traffic, congestion, pollution, and other urban problems.

11   Proponents of smart growth have responded to these and other objections at meetings of county planning boards and city councils, but opposition remains strong. Though smart growth has been a popular buzzword in real estate and urban development since the1990s, some leaders of the movement worry that it has lost momentum.[13,16] One reason why smart growth has stalled is that key stakeholders involved in the debate—real estate developers, land owners, environmentalists, public health advocates, and people living in metropolitan areas affected by smart-growth projects—have divergent interests, and the political process has often been unable to resolve these conflicts.[18]

DELIBERATIVE DEMOCRACY

12   One approach to resolving controversial public-policy questions that may be able to help loosen the smart-growth gridlock is a procedure known as deliberative democracy. Democracy is a form of government in which citizens wield political power by

directly voting on issues, as in referendums, or by electing representatives to make decisions on their behalf.[31] Deliberative democracy emphasizes public deliberation on controversial issues as an alternative to voting.[31-34] In deliberative democracy, public deliberation should meet five conditions[31-34]:

1. Political legitimacy. The parties to the deliberation view the democratic process as a source of political legitimacy and are willing to abide by the decision that is reached.
2. Mutual respect. The parties are committed to respecting each other's diverging interests, goals, and moral, political, or religious viewpoints.
3. Inclusiveness. All parties with an interest in the issue can participate in the deliberative process, and a special effort is made to include those parties who often lack political influence because of socioeconomic status, lack of education, or other factors.
4. Public reason. Parties involved in the deliberation are committed to giving publicly acceptable arguments for their positions, drawing on publicly available evidence and information.
5. Equality. All parties to the deliberation have equal standing to defend and criticize arguments; there is no hierarchy or presumed line of authority.

Deliberative democracy was originally proposed as a method for resolving disagreements on controversial topics for which interested parties have conflicting interests and incompatible moral or political viewpoints, such as abortion, euthanasia, and capital punishment. Proponents of deliberative democracy have argued that public deliberation about controversial topics can be more fair and effective than can traditional democratic procedures, which can be manipulated by powerful interest groups.[31-34] Critics of deliberative democracy have argued that it is an idealized theory of political decision-making whose conditions are often not met in the real world.[35] However, deliberative democracy may be worth trying when other approaches have failed to resolve controversial issues.

The debate about smart growth appears to be a good candidate for application of a deliberative approach because the parties have conflicting interests and divergent moral and political viewpoints.[10,11,18,28] Proponents of smart growth typically argue that collective action must be taken to promote common goods, such as public health, environmental integrity, or overall quality of life.[4,5,7] This type of argument is utilitarian in form because it asserts that public policies should promote the overall good of society.[36,37] Many of the property owners who oppose smart growth assume a libertarian perspective and argue that individual rights may be restricted only to prevent harm to others, not to promote the good of society.[18] According to libertarianism, the role of the state is to protect individual rights to life, liberty, or property; thus, government authority should not be used to redistribute wealth or advance social causes.[38,39] Critics who are concerned that smart growth may reduce the availability of affordable housing or adversely affect minority neighborhoods may subscribe to an egalitarian philosophy, such as Rawls's theory of justice, which holds that public policies should promote the interests of the least advantaged people in society and should not undermine equality of opportunity.[40,41] If smart growth benefits society as a whole at the expense of harming its least advantaged members by reducing the availability of affordable housing or disrupting minority neighborhoods, then it would violate Rawls's egalitarian principles of justice. Thus, the debate about smart growth can be viewed as a conflict among three competing visions of social justice: utilitarianism, libertarianism, and egalitarianism.

DELIBERATING ABOUT SMART GROWTH

15   Smart growth is an important strategy for combating the adverse public health, environmental, and aesthetic effects of urban sprawl. Because proponents and opponents of smart growth have conflicting interests and divergent moral and political viewpoints, deliberative democracy may be a fair and effective procedure for addressing some of the controversies surrounding policy proposals designed to counteract urban sprawl. To implement a deliberative approach, governments should sponsor open community forums on issues related to sprawl and smart growth, such as focus groups, public debates, and town-hall meetings. The deliberations that occur at these public forums should supplement the discussions that take place on county planning board or city council meetings. The goal of these public forums should be to foster open debate, information sharing, constructive criticism, and mutual understanding. Forums should be well-publicized and open to all parties with an interest in the proceedings. A special effort should be made to invite participants from groups that lack political influence.[42] Many communities have already held open forums on smart growth that embody some of the principles of deliberative democracy, but many others have not.[11,18,26] Communities that have not tried the deliberative approach should attempt it; those that have already held open forums should continue deliberating.

REFERENCES

1. Fitzpatrick K. *Unhealthy Places*. New York, NY: Routledge; 2000.
2. Frank L, Engelke P, Schmid T. *Health and Community Design: The Impact of the Built Environment on Physical Activity*. Washington, DC: Island Press; 2003.
3. Jackson RJ. The impact of the built environment on health: an emerging field. *Am J Public Health*. 2003; 93(9): 1382–1384.
4. Frumkin H, Frank L, Jackson R. *Urban Sprawl and Public Health*. Washington, DC: Island Press; 2004.
5. Corburn J. Confronting the challenges in reconnecting urban planning and public health. *Am J Public Health*. 2004; 94(4): 541–546.
6. Rao M, Prasad S, Adshead F, Tissera H. The built environment and health. *Lancet*. 2007; 370(9593): 1111–1113.
7. Jackson R, Kochtitzky C. Creating a healthy environment: the impact of the built environment on public health. Atlanta, GA: Centers for Disease Control and Prevention; 2009. Available at: http://www.cdc.gov/healthyplaces/articles/Creating%20A%20Healthy%20Environment.pdf. Accessed July 12, 2009.
8. Ewing R, Pendall R, Chen D. Sprawl scores for 83 metropolitan regions. Washington, DC: Smart Growth America; 2002. Available at: http://www.smartgrowthamerica.org/sprawlindex/chart.pdf. Accessed July 24, 2009.

9. Frumkin H. Urban sprawl and public health. *Public Health Rep.* 2002; 117(3): 201–217.

10. Whoriskey P. Planners' brains vs. public's brawn: neighbors' hostility to dense projects impairs Md. land preservation. *Washington Post.* August 10, 2004:A1. Available at: http://www.washingtonpost.com/wp-dyn/articles/A52900-2004Aug9 .html. Accessed December 10, 2009.

11. Harris J, Evans J. Sprawl brawl: battle lines drawn in smart growth debate. *Real Estate Issues*, April 2000. Available at: http://recenter.tamu.edu/pdf/1371.pdf. Accessed July 26, 2009.

12. Waite D. It's not smart growth. *Gainesville Sun.* May 22, 2009. Available at: http://www.gainesville.com/article/20090522/NEWS/905229984. Accessed July 25, 2009.

13. Ward B. Report: smart growth failing. *Carroll County Times.* March 11, 2009. Available at: http://www.carrollcountytimes.com/article_4e9dc828-6126-5ffb-9fbf -33a673b3a924.html. Accessed July 26, 2009.

14. Staley S. The peril and promise of smart growth: is Ohio ready for regional planning? Columbus, OH: Buckeye Institute; July 2004. Available at: http:// www.buckeyeinstitute.org/docs/smartgrowth72304.pdf. Accessed December 10, 2009.

15. Orski C, Shaw J. Smart growth? Sprawl-reducing policies suffer setback. *Rocky Mountain News.* July 9, 2005. Available at: http://www.perc.org/articles /article575.php. Accessed December 10, 2009.

16. Hirschhorn J. Why the smart growth movement will fail. Planetizen Web site. Available at: http://www.planetizen.com/node/55. Published June 17, 2002. Accessed December 10, 2009.

17. Berg N. Suburban officials try to build sidewalks amid local opposition. Planetizen Web site. Available at: http://www.planetizen.com/node/26436. Published August 21, 2007. Accessed December 10, 2009.

18. Ramirez de la Cruz E. Local political institutions and smart growth: an empirical study of the politics of compact development. *Urban Aff Rev.* 2009; 45(2): 218–246.

19. Frumkin H. Health, equity, and the built environment. *Environ Health Perspect.* 2005; 113(5): A290–A291.

20. Committee on Environmental Health, Tester JM. The built environment: designing communities to promote physical activity in children. *Pediatrics.* 2009; 123(6): 1591–1598.

21. Sallis JF, Glanz K. Physical activity and food environments: solutions to the obesity epidemic. *Milbank Q.* 2009; 87(1): 123–154.

22. Gordon-Larsen P, Nelson M, Page P, Popkin B. Inequality in the built environment underlies key health disparities in physical activity and obesity. Pediatrics. 2006; 117(2): 417–424.

23. Barzilay J, Weinberg W, Eley J. *The Water We Drink: Water Quality and Its Effects on Health.* Piscataway, NJ: Rutgers University Press; 1999.

24. Fox W, ed. *Ethics and the Built Environment.* New York, NY: Routledge; 2000.

25. Southern Village Web site. Southern Village: a new old neighborhood. Available at: http://www.southernvillage.com/images/sv_history.pdf. Published November 12, 2006. Accessed July 24, 2009.

26. Downs A. Smart growth: why we discuss it more than we do it. *J Am Plann Assoc.* 2005;71(4):367–378.

27. Gilroy L. The human face of smart growth opposition. Reason Foundation Web site. Available at: http://reason.org/news/show/the-human-face-of-smartgrowth. Published September 13, 2002. Accessed December 11, 2009.

28. Utt R. Can both sides of the sprawl debate find common ground on property rights? Heritage Foundation Web site. Available at: http://www.heritage.org/research/smartgrowth/wm730.cfm. Published April 25, 2005. Accessed July 26, 2009.

29. Campbell C. Faulty towers? Construction revives gentrification fears. *Chapel Hill News.* March 4, 2009:A1.

30. Campbell C. Vandals try to fight Greenbridge condos. *News and Observer.* April 28, 2009:B1.

31. Gutmann A, Thompson D, eds. *Why Deliberative Democracy?* Princeton, NJ: Princeton University Press; 2004.

32. Gutmann A, Thompson D. *Democracy and Disagreement.* Cambridge, MA: Harvard University Press; 1998.

33. Cohen J. *Philosophy, Politics, Democracy.* Cambridge, MA: Harvard University Press; 2009.

34. Rawls J. *Political Liberalism.* New York, NY: Columbia University Press; 1993.

35. Fishkin J, Laslett P. *Debating Deliberative Democracy.* Somerset, NJ: Wiley-Blackwell; 2003.

36. Mill J. *Utilitarianism.* 2nd ed. Indianapolis, IN: Hackett; 2002.

37. Singer P. *Practical Ethics.* 2nd ed. Cambridge, UK: Cambridge University Press; 1999.

38. Nozick R. *Anarchy, State, and Utopia.* New York, NY: Basic Books; 1974.

39. Boaz D. *Libertarianism: A Primer.* New York, NY: Free Press; 1998.

40. Rawls J. *A Theory of Justice.* Cambridge, MA: Harvard University Press; 1971.

41. Daniels N. *Just Health.* Cambridge, UK: Cambridge University Press; 2007.

42. Shrader-Frechette K. *Environmental Justice.* New York, NY: Oxford University Press; 2002. ∎

FROM READING TO WRITING

1. Analyze the paired arguments by either Wendell Berry and the National Association of Scholars, or by Berry and Jared Diamond, or by Chris Packham and Mark Wright: How is each argument the product of its audience and purpose? What sources of argument (ethical appeals, emotional appeals, and logical appeals) does each author choose and why? (See Chapter 5 for more on rhetorical analysis.)

2. Compare the various photos and charts that appear on the preceding pages in this chapter. What visual argument does each photo seem to make? (See Chapter 6 for guidance on analyzing visuals.)

3. Write an argument that makes its point by defining a key term related to environmental concerns. You might choose to change someone's attitude toward a particular practice or concept in order to defend or challenge it, for instance, by defining it in a certain way. For example, you might start with the claim that "Green clothes are just a marketing ploy for the fashion industry to cash in on consumers' increased environmental awareness" or "Global warming is actually a blessing in disguise for some of the world." (See Chapter 8 for strategies for writing definition arguments.)

4. Propose a change in policy related to an environmental issue in your community. (See Chapter 13 for help with writing a proposal argument.)

5. Write a rebuttal of an article related to the environment in your local or school newspaper. Imitate, as appropriate, the moves you see in essays by the National Association for Scholars and Nicolette Niman; see Chapter 12 for advice on rebuttals. Consider whether you wish to show the weaknesses in the article, whether you wish to counterargue, or both.

6. Write an essay that recounts a personal experience of yours to make an argumentative point related to the environment. It could be a story about camping or hiking, for example, or a tale of your encounter with some environmental problem or challenge. (See Chapter 11 for advice on writing narrative arguments.)

23 | Education

Joe Heller/PoliticalCartoons.com

Education in American Society

Why have Americans always been so passionate about issues related to education? For one thing, education issues affect every American in a personal way because no other people strive for universal education with the zeal that American do. True, there is a strong anti-intellectual strain in American life, and true, not everyone appreciates the mandate for universal education; but it is also true that Americans do pursue with a passion the ideal of "education for all" both as a means of self-improvement and as the source of the enlightened citizenry required by democratic institutions. For another thing, education issues in America are decided locally and immediately. The relatively decentralized nature of our educational "system" (not that American education is as monolithic as the term *system* implies) encourages continuing and passionate public discussion among citizens interested in shaping the policies and practices of local schools.

What principles should guide educational policy in the United States? That fundamental question, which lies behind most of the debates about education, has been restated in a compelling way by the American philosopher and educational reformer John Dewey: *Should society be a function of education,* or *should education be a function of society?* In other words, should educational institutions be developed to perpetuate American institutions and values and to develop a skilled workforce for the American economy ("education as a function of society")? Or should educational institutions be developed chiefly in order to critique and reform American institutions in the interest of creating a more just and equitable society ("society as a function of education")? To put it yet another way: Should schools emphasize mastery of bodies of knowledge, "what every educated citizen needs to know"? Or instead should they emphasize practical learning skills—problem-solving ability, flexibility, independent thinking, and resourcefulness? Most people would answer "Both": Education should equip people both with practical, vocational abilities and with the critical and communication skills necessary to make for a vibrant, resourceful, just society. Yet that answer only complicates the issue, for in what proportion should schools develop creative criticizers and questioners versus efficient and adjusted workers?

Contemporary Arguments

The arguments included in this chapter bear directly on the issue of "education as a function of society" versus "society as a function of education." Ralph Waldo Emerson's famous "The American Scholar" offers a definition of what a college student should be and do and how a college student should learn—one that continues to shape institutions and individuals. W. E. B. DuBois next offers (in "The Talented Tenth") an argument about the nature of higher education for African Americans that counters the more strictly vocational goals that were emphasized by Booker T. Washington. Later a cartoon strip by Garry B. Trudeau challenges Americans to make higher education a means of enhancing critical thinking and intellectual development.

Another group of arguments addresses the function of primary and secondary education. Margaret Spellings and Gerald Bracey face off over the controversial No Child Left Behind educational reform passed into law in 2001. The act is based on the principle that setting high standards and goals can improve educational outcomes, but critics have been suspicious of the testing required and the mechanisms used to evaluate schools and teachers. Among the critics are John Gatto, who argues against compulsory high school education, and David Brooks, a respected newspaper columnist who has advice for how college students might learn how to improve social cohesion and interpersonal cooperation.

The chapter concludes with an Issue in Focus: Is College Worth the Price? With college tuition rates spiking and the U.S. economy struggling to recover, critics are questioning the wisdom of encouraging so many people to attend college. The

Issue in Focus not only addresses the controversy directly, but it also suggests practical alternatives to college that most high school graduates have not considered.

The readings you encounter should give you a better understanding of the issues that you and your classmates are grappling with right now. As you read, remember that the perennial nature of debates about education can be frustrating, especially to educational leaders. But the very relentlessness of the debates probably brings out the best feature of a democratic society: the freedom of citizens to shape policy through open and public exchange.

Ralph Waldo Emerson

The American Scholar

Ralph Waldo Emerson (1803–1882) originally trained to become a Unitarian minister but instead left that profession to take up what would be a long and celebrated career in writing and public speaking. Emerson was a prolific and original thinker. Many of his ideas formed the basis of the American Transcendentalist movement, which valued spirituality, the natural world, human optimism, and a healthy skepticism toward reason and logic. In "The American Scholar," originally delivered before the Phi Beta Kappa Society in 1837 and excerpted here, Emerson argues for a new and distinctly "American" brand of educational philosophy.

M r. President and Gentlemen,

2   I greet you on the re-commencement of our literary year. Our anniversary is one of hope, and, perhaps, not enough of labor. We do not meet for games of strength or skill, for the recitation of histories, tragedies, and odes, like the ancient Greeks; for parliaments of love and poesy, like the Troubadours; nor for the advancement of science, like our contemporaries in the British and European capitals. Thus far, our holiday has been simply a friendly sign of the survival of the love of letters amongst a people too busy to give to letters any more. As such, it is precious as the sign of an indestructible instinct. Perhaps the time is already come, when it ought to be, and will be, something else; when the sluggard intellect of this continent will look from under its iron lids, and fill the postponed expectation of the world with something better than the exertions of mechanical skill. Our day of dependence, our long apprenticeship to the learning of other lands, draws to a close. The millions, that around us are rushing into life, cannot always be fed on the sere remains of foreign harvests. Events, actions arise, that must be sung, that will sing themselves. Who can doubt, that poetry will revive and lead in a new age, as the star in the constellation Harp, which now flames in our zenith, astronomers announce, shall one day be the pole-star for a thousand years?

3   In this hope, I accept the topic which not only usage, but the nature of our association, seem to prescribe to this day,—the AMERICAN SCHOLAR. Year by year, we

come up hither to read one more chapter of his biography. Let us inquire what light new days and events have thrown on his character, and his hopes.

It is one of those fables, which, out of an unknown antiquity, convey an unlooked-for wisdom, that the gods, in the beginning, divided Man into men, that he might be more helpful to himself; just as the hand was divided into fingers, the better to answer its end.

The old fable covers a doctrine ever new and sublime; that there is One Man,—present to all particular men only partially, or through one faculty; and that you must take the whole society to find the whole man. Man is not a farmer, or a professor, or an engineer, but he is all. Man is priest, and scholar, and statesman, and producer, and soldier. In the *divided* or social state, these functions are parcelled out to individuals, each of whom aims to do his stint of the joint work, whilst each other performs his. The fable implies, that the individual, to possess himself, must sometimes return from his own labor to embrace all the other laborers. But unfortunately, this original unit, this fountain of power, has been so distributed to multitudes, has been so minutely subdivided and peddled out, that it is spilled into drops, and cannot be gathered. The state of society is one in which the members have suffered amputation from the trunk, and strut about so many walking monsters,—a good finger, a neck, a stomach, an elbow, but never a man.

Man is thus metamorphosed into a thing, into many things. The planter, who is Man sent out into the field to gather food, is seldom cheered by any idea of the true dignity of his ministry. He sees his bushel and his cart, and nothing beyond, and sinks into the farmer, instead of Man on the farm. The tradesman scarcely ever gives an ideal worth to his work, but is ridden by the routine of his craft, and the soul is subject to dollars. The priest becomes a form; the attorney, a statute-book; the mechanic, a machine; the sailor, a rope of a ship.

In this distribution of functions, the scholar is the delegated intellect. In the right state, he is, *Man Thinking.* In the degenerate state, when the victim of society, he tends to become a mere thinker, or, still worse, the parrot of other men's thinking.

In this view of him, as Man Thinking, the theory of his office is contained. Him nature solicits with all her placid, all her monitory pictures; him the past instructs; him the future invites. Is not, indeed, every man a student, and do not all things exist for the student's behoof? And, finally, is not the true scholar the only true master? But the old oracle said, 'All things have two handles: beware of the wrong one.' In life, too often, the scholar errs with mankind and forfeits his privilege. Let us see him in his school, and consider him in reference to the main influences he receives.

9   I. The first in time and the first in importance of the influences upon the mind is that of nature. Every day, the sun; and, after sunset, night and her stars. Ever the winds blow; ever the grass grows. Every day, men and women, conversing, beholding and beholden. The scholar is he of all men whom this spectacle most engages. He must settle its value in his mind. What is nature to him? There is never a beginning, there is never an end, to the inexplicable continuity of this web of God, but always circular power returning into itself. Therein it resembles his own spirit, whose beginning, whose ending, he never can find,—so entire, so boundless. Far, too, as her splendors shine, system on system shooting like rays, upward, downward, without centre, without circumference,—in the mass and in the particle, nature hastens to render account of herself to the mind. Classification begins. To the young mind, every thing is individual, stands by itself. By and by, it finds how to join two things, and see in them one nature; then three, then three thousand; and so, tyrannized over by its own unifying instinct, it goes on tying things together, diminishing anomalies, discovering roots running under ground, whereby contrary and remote things cohere, and flower out from one stem. It presently learns, that, since the dawn of history, there has been a constant accumulation and classifying of facts. But what is classification but the perceiving that these objects are not chaotic, and are not foreign, but have a law which is also a law of the human mind? . . .

10   Thus to him, to this school-boy under the bending dome of day, is suggested, that he and it proceed from one root; one is leaf and one is flower; relation, sympathy, stirring in every vein. And what is that Root? Is not that the soul of his soul?—A thought too bold,—a dream too wild. Yet when this spiritual light shall have revealed the law of more earthly natures,—when he has learned to worship the soul, and to see that the natural philosophy that now is, is only the first gropings of its gigantic hand, he shall look forward to an ever expanding knowledge as to a becoming creator. He shall see, that nature is the opposite of the soul, answering to it part for part. One is seal, and one is print. Its beauty is the beauty of his own mind. Its laws are the laws of his own mind. Nature then becomes to him the measure of his attainments. So much of nature as he is ignorant of, so much of his own mind does he not yet possess. And, in fine, the ancient precept, "Know thyself," and the modern precept, "Study nature," become at last one maxim.

11   II. The next great influence into the spirit of the scholar, is, the mind of the Past,—in whatever form, whether of literature, of art, of institutions, that mind is inscribed. Books are the best type of the influence of the past, and perhaps we shall get at the truth,— learn the amount of this influence more conveniently,—by considering their value alone.

12   The theory of books is noble. The scholar of the first age received into him the world around; brooded thereon; gave it the new arrangement of his own mind, and uttered it again. It came into him, life; it went out from him, truth. It came to him, short-lived actions; it went out from him, immortal thoughts. It came to him, business; it went from him, poetry. It was dead fact; now, it is quick thought. It can stand, and it can go. It now endures, it now flies, it now inspires. Precisely in proportion to the depth of mind from which it issued, so high does it soar, so long does it sing.

13   Or, I might say, it depends on how far the process had gone, of transmuting life into truth. In proportion to the completeness of the distillation, so will the purity and imperishableness of the product be. But none is quite perfect. As no air-pump can by any means make a perfect vacuum, so neither can any artist entirely exclude the conventional, the local, the perishable from his book, or write a book of pure thought, that shall

be as efficient, in all respects, to a remote posterity, as to contemporaries, or rather to the second age. Each age, it is found, must write its own books; or rather, each generation for the next succeeding. The books of an older period will not fit this.

Yet hence arises a grave mischief. The sacredness which attaches to the act of creation,—the act of thought,—is transferred to the record. The poet chanting, was felt to be a divine man: henceforth the chant is divine also. . . . [I]nstead of Man Thinking, we have the bookworm. Hence, the book-learned class, who value books, as such; not as related to nature and the human constitution, but as making a sort of Third Estate with the world and the soul. Hence, the restorers of readings, the emendators, the bibliomaniacs of all degrees.

Books are the best of things, well used; abused, among the worst. What is the right use? What is the one end, which all means go to effect? They are for nothing but to inspire. I had better never see a book, than to be warped by its attraction clean out of my own orbit, and made a satellite instead of a system. The one thing in the world, of value, is the active soul. This every man is entitled to; this every man contains within him, although, in almost all men, obstructed, and as yet unborn. The soul active sees absolute truth; and utters truth, or creates. In this action, it is genius; not the privilege of here and there a favorite, but the sound estate of every man. In its essence, it is progressive. The book, the college, the school of art, the institution of any kind, stop with some past utterance of genius. This is good, say they,—let us hold by this. They pin me down. They look backward and not forward. But genius looks forward: the eyes of man are set in his forehead, not in his hindhead: man hopes: genius creates. Whatever talents may be, if the man create not, the pure efflux of the Deity is not his;—cinders and smoke there may be, but not yet flame. There are creative manners, there are creative actions, and creative words; manners, actions, words, that is, indicative of no custom or authority, but springing spontaneous from the mind's own sense of good and fair. . . .

Undoubtedly there is a right way of reading, so it be sternly subordinated. Man Thinking must not be subdued by his instruments. Books are for the scholar's idle times. When he can read God directly, the hour is too precious to be wasted in other men's transcripts of their readings. But when the intervals of darkness come, as come they must,—when the sun is hid, and the stars withdraw their shining,—we repair to the lamps which were kindled by their ray, to guide our steps to the East again, where the dawn is. . . .

It is remarkable, the character of the pleasure we derive from the best books. They impress us with the conviction, that one nature wrote and the same reads. We read the verses of one of the great English poets, of Chaucer, of Marvell, of Dryden, with the most modern joy,—with a pleasure, I mean, which is in great part caused by the abstraction of all *time* from their verses. There is some awe mixed with the joy of our surprise, when this poet, who lived in some past world, two or three hundred years ago, says that which lies close to my own soul, that which I also had wellnigh thought and said. But for the evidence thence afforded to the philosophical doctrine of the identity of all minds, we should suppose some preestablished harmony, some foresight of souls that were to be, and some preparation of stores for their future wants, like the fact observed in insects, who lay up food before death for the young grub they shall never see.

I would not be hurried by any love of system, by any exaggeration of instincts, to underrate the Book. . . . When the mind is braced by labor and invention, the page of whatever book we read becomes luminous with manifold allusion. Every sentence is doubly significant, and the sense of our author is as broad as the world. We then see, what is always true, that, as the seer's hour of vision is short and rare among heavy days and months, so is its record, perchance, the least part of his volume. The discerning will read, in his Plato or Shakespeare, only that least part,—only the authentic utterances of the oracle;—all the rest he rejects, were it never so many times Plato's and Shakespeare's.

19   Of course, there is a portion of reading quite indispensable to a wise man. History and exact science he must learn by laborious reading. Colleges, in like manner, have their indispensable office,—to teach elements. But they can only highly serve us, when they aim not to drill, but to create; when they gather from far every ray of various genius to their hospitable halls, and, by the concentrated fires, set the hearts of their youth on flame. Thought and knowledge are natures in which apparatus and pretension avail nothing. Gowns, and pecuniary foundations, though of towns of gold, can never countervail the least sentence or syllable of wit. Forget this, and our American colleges will recede in their public importance, whilst they grow richer every year.

20   III. There goes in the world a notion, that the scholar should be a recluse, a valetudinarian,—as unfit for any handiwork or public labor, as a penknife for an axe. The so-called 'practical men' sneer at speculative men, as if, because they speculate or *see*, they could do nothing. I have heard it said that the clergy,—who are always, more universally than any other class, the scholars of their day,—are addressed as women; that the rough, spontaneous conversation of men they do not hear, but only a mincing and diluted speech. They are often virtually disfranchised; and, indeed, there are advocates for their celibacy. As far as this is true of the studious classes, it is not just and wise. Action is with the scholar subordinate, but it is essential. Without it, he is not yet man. Without it, thought can never ripen into truth. Whilst the world hangs before the eye as a cloud of beauty, we cannot even see its beauty. Inaction is cowardice, but there can be no scholar without the heroic mind. The preamble of thought, the transition through which it passes from the unconscious to the conscious, is action. Only so much do I know, as I have lived. Instantly we know whose words are loaded with life, and whose not.

21   The world,—this shadow of the soul, or *other me*, lies wide around. Its attractions are the keys which unlock my thoughts and make me acquainted with myself. I run eagerly into this resounding tumult. I grasp the hands of those next me, and take my place in the ring to suffer and to work, taught by an instinct, that so shall the dumb abyss be vocal with speech. I pierce its order; I dissipate its fear; I dispose of it within the circuit of my expanding life. So much only of life as I know by experience, so much of the wilderness have I vanquished and planted, or so far have I extended my being, my dominion. I do not see how any man can afford, for the sake of his nerves and his nap, to spare any action in which he can partake. It is pearls and rubies to his discourse. Drudgery, calamity, exasperation, want, are instructors in eloquence and wisdom. The true scholar grudges every opportunity of action past by, as a loss of power.

22   It is the raw material out of which the intellect moulds her splendid products. A strange process too, this, by which experience is converted into thought, as a mulberry leaf is converted into satin. The manufacture goes forward at all hours. . . .

23   Of course, he who has put forth his total strength in fit actions, has the richest return of wisdom. I will not shut myself out of this globe of action, and transplant an oak into a flower-pot, there to hunger and pine; nor trust the revenue of some single faculty, and exhaust one vein of thought, much like those Savoyards, who, getting their livelihood by carving shepherds, shepherdesses, and smoking Dutchmen, for all Europe,

went out one day to the mountain to find stock, and discovered that they had whittled up the last of their pine-trees. Authors we have, in numbers, who have written out their vein, and who, moved by a commendable prudence, sail for Greece or Palestine, follow the trapper into the prairie, or ramble round Algiers, to replenish their merchantable stock.

If it were only for a vocabulary, the scholar would be covetous of action. Life is our dictionary. Years are well spent in country labors; in town,—in the insight into trades and manufactures; in frank intercourse with many men and women; in science; in art; to the one end of mastering in all their facts a language by which to illustrate and embody our perceptions. I learn immediately from any speaker how much he has already lived, through the poverty or the splendor of his speech. Life lies behind us as the quarry from whence we get tiles and copestones for the masonry of today. This is the way to learn grammar. Colleges and books only copy the language which the field and the work-yard made.

But the final value of action, like that of books, and better than books, is, that it is a resource. That great principle of Undulation in nature, that shows itself in the inspiring and expiring of the breath; in desire and satiety; in the ebb and flow of the sea; in day and night; in heat and cold; and as yet more deeply ingrained in every atom and every fluid, is known to us under the name of Polarity,—these "fits of easy transmission and reflection," as Newton called them, are the law of nature because they are the law of spirit. The mind now thinks; now acts; and each fit reproduces the other. When the artist has exhausted his materials, when the fancy no longer paints, when thoughts are no longer apprehended, and books are a weariness,—he has always the resource *to live.* Character is higher than intellect. Thinking is the function. Living is the functionary. The stream retreats to its source. A great soul will be strong to live, as well as strong to think. . . .

I hear therefore with joy whatever is beginning to be said of the dignity and necessity of labor to every citizen. There is virtue yet in the hoe and the spade, for learned as well as for unlearned hands. And labor is everywhere welcome; always we are invited to work; only be this limitation observed, that a man shall not for the sake of wider activity sacrifice any opinion to the popular judgments and modes of action.

I have now spoken of the education of the scholar by nature, by books, and by action. It remains to say somewhat of his duties.

They are such as become Man Thinking. They may all be comprised in self-trust. The office of the scholar is to cheer, to raise, and to guide men by showing them facts amidst appearances. He plies the slow, unhonored, and unpaid task of observation. . . . He is one, who raises himself from private considerations, and breathes and lives on public and illustrious thoughts. He is the world's eye. He is the world's heart. He is to resist the vulgar prosperity that retrogrades ever to barbarism, by preserving and communicating heroic sentiments, noble biographies, melodious verse, and the conclusions of history. Whatsoever oracles the human heart, in all emergencies, in all solemn hours, has uttered as its commentary on the world of actions,—these he shall receive and impart. And whatsoever new verdict Reason from her inviolable seat pronounces on the passing men and events of today,—this he shall hear and promulgate.

These being his functions, it becomes him to feel all confidence in himself, and to defer never to the popular cry. He and he only knows the world. The world of any moment is the merest appearance. Some great decorum, some fetish of a government, some ephemeral trade, or war, or man, is cried up by half mankind and cried down by the other half, as if all depended on this particular up or down. The odds are that the whole question is not worth the poorest thought which the scholar has lost in listening to the controversy. Let him not quit his belief that a popgun is a popgun, though the ancient and honorable of the earth affirm it to be the crack of doom. In silence, in steadiness, in severe abstraction, let him hold by himself; add observation to observation, patient of neglect, patient of reproach; and bide his own time,—happy enough, if he can satisfy himself alone, that this day he has seen something truly. Success treads on every right step. For the instinct is sure, that prompts him to tell his brother what he thinks. He then learns, that in going down into the secrets of his own mind, he has descended into the secrets of all minds. He learns that he who has mastered any law in his private thoughts, is master to that extent of all men whose language he speaks, and of all into whose language his own can be translated. The poet, in utter solitude remembering his spontaneous thoughts and recording them, is found to have recorded that, which men in crowded cities find true for them also. The orator distrusts at first the fitness of his frank confessions,—his want of knowledge of the persons he addresses,—until he finds that he is the complement of his hearers;—that they drink his words because he fulfils for them their own nature; the deeper he dives into his privatest, secretest presentiment, to his wonder he finds, this is the most acceptable, most public, and universally true. The people delight in it; the better part of every man feels, This is my music; this is myself.

30   In self-trust, all the virtues are comprehended. Free should the scholar be,—free and brave. Free even to the definition of freedom, "without any hindrance that does not arise out of his own constitution." Brave; for fear is a thing, which a scholar by his very function puts behind him. Fear always springs from ignorance. It is a shame to him if his tranquility, amid dangerous times, arise from the presumption, that, like children and women, his is a protected class; or if he seek a temporary peace by the diversion of his thoughts from politics or vexed questions, hiding his head like an ostrich in the flowering bushes, peeping into microscopes, and turning rhymes, as a boy whistles to keep his courage up. So is the danger a danger still; so is the fear worse. Manlike let him turn and face it. Let him look into its eye and search its nature, inspect its origin,—see the whelping of this lion,—which lies no great way back; he will then find in himself a perfect comprehension of its nature and extent; he will have made his hands meet on the other side, and can henceforth defy it, and pass on superior. The world is his, who can see through its pretension. What deafness, what stone-blind custom, what overgrown error you behold, is there only by sufferance,—by your sufferance. See it to be a lie, and you have already dealt it its mortal blow.

31   Yes, we are the cowed,—we the trustless. It is a mischievous notion that we are come late into nature; that the world was finished a long time ago. As the world was plastic and fluid in the hands of God, so it is ever to so much of his attributes as we bring to it. To ignorance and sin, it is flint. They adapt themselves to it as they may; but in proportion as a man has any thing in him divine, the firmament flows before him and takes his signet and form. Not he is great who can alter matter, but he who can alter my state of mind. They are the kings of the world who give the color of their present thought to all nature and all art, and persuade men by the cheerful serenity of their carrying the matter, that this thing which they do, is the apple which the ages have desired to pluck, now at last ripe, and inviting nations to the harvest. The great man makes the

great thing. Wherever Macdonald sits, there is the head of the table. Linnaeus makes botany the most alluring of studies, and wins it from the farmer and the herb-woman; Davy, chemistry; and Cuvier, fossils. The day is always his, who works in it with serenity and great aims. The unstable estimates of men crowd to him whose mind is filled with a truth, as the heaped waves of the Atlantic follow the moon.

For this self-trust, the reason is deeper than can be fathomed,—darker than can be enlightened. I might not carry with me the feeling of my audience in stating my own belief. But I have already shown the ground of my hope, in adverting to the doctrine that man is one. I believe man has been wronged; he has wronged himself. He has almost lost the light, that can lead him back to his prerogatives. Men are become of no account. Men in history, men in the world of today are bugs, are spawn, and are called 'the mass' and `the herd.' In a century, in a millennium, one or two men; that is to say,— one or two approximations to the right state of every man. All the rest behold in the hero or the poet their own green and crude being,—ripened; yes, and are content to be less, so *that* may attain to its full stature. What a testimony,—full of grandeur, full of pity, is borne to the demands of his own nature, by the poor clansman, the poor partisan, who rejoices in the glory of his chief. The poor and the low find some amends to their immense moral capacity, for their acquiescence in a political and social inferiority. They are content to be brushed like flies from the path of a great person, so that justice shall be done by him to that common nature which it is the dearest desire of all to see enlarged and glorified. They sun themselves in the great man's light, and feel it to be their own element. They cast the dignity of man from their downtrod selves upon the shoulders of a hero, and will perish to add one drop of blood to make that great heart beat, those giant sinews combat and conquer. He lives for us, and we live in him.

Men such as they are, very naturally seek money or power; and power because it is as good as money,—the "spoils," so called, "of office." And why not? for they aspire to the highest, and this, in their sleep-walking, they dream is highest. Wake them, and they shall quit the false good, and leap to the true, and leave governments to clerks and desks. This revolution is to be wrought by the gradual domestication of the idea of Culture. The main enterprise of the world for splendor, for extent, is the upbuilding of a man. Here are the materials strown along the ground. The private life of one man shall be a more illustrious monarchy,—more formidable to its enemy, more sweet and serene in its influence to its friend, than any kingdom in history. For a man, rightly viewed, comprehendeth the particular natures of all men. Each philosopher, each bard, each actor, has only done for me, as by a delegate, what one day I can do for myself. The books which once we valued more than the apple of the eye, we have quite exhausted. What is that but saying, that we have come up with the point of view which the universal mind took through the eyes of one scribe; we have been that man, and have passed on. First, one; then, another; we drain all cisterns, and, waxing greater by all these supplies, we crave a better and more abundant food. The man has never lived that can feed us ever. The human mind cannot be enshrined in a person, who shall set a barrier on any one side to this unbounded, unboundable empire. It is one central fire, which, flaming now out of the lips of Etna, lightens the capes of Sicily; and, now out of the throat of Vesuvius, illuminates the towers and vineyards of Naples. It is one light which beams out of a thousand stars. It is one soul which animates all men. . . .■

W. E. B. DuBois

The Talented Tenth

William Edward Burghardt DuBois (1868–1963) was determined to expedite the emancipation of African Americans. Having received his education from Fisk (1885–1888) and from Harvard (where he received his PhD in 1895), he launched a distinguished career as a social scientist, social critic, social reformer, and civil rights leader. He wrote many books, played a prominent role in the founding of the NAACP (in 1909), and for many years edited its magazine, *Crisis*.

DuBois's theories brought him into conflict with the most influential African American working at the turn of the century, Booker T. Washington. Washington preached a policy of accommodation. He felt that African Americans could best achieve social and legal progress by gradually winning the respect of whites through hard work and personal virtue, and he founded Tuskegee Institute as a means of improving and extending vocational education. DuBois, by contrast, in his famous 1903 book *The Souls of Black Folk*, charged that Washington's approach would only perpetuate injustice. Later that year, in "The Talented Tenth," DuBois elaborated his position on higher education for African Americans. DuBois revisited the subject of "The Talented Tenth" throughout his career.

The Negro race, like all races, is going to be saved by its exceptional men. The problem of education, then, among Negroes must first of all deal with the Talented Tenth: it is the problem of developing the Best of this race that they may guide the Mass away from the contamination and death of the Worst, in their own and other races. Now the training of men is a difficult and intricate task. Its technique is a matter for educational experts, but its object is for the vision of seers. If we make money the object of man-training, we shall develop money-makers but not necessarily men; if we make technical skill the object of education, we may possess artisans but not, in nature, men. Men we shall have only as we make manhood the object of the work of the schools—intelligence, broad sympathy, knowledge of the world that was and is, and of the relation of men to it—this is the curriculum of that Higher Education which must underlie true life. On this foundation we may build bread winning, skill of hand and quickness of brain, with never a fear lest the child and man mistake the means of living for the object of life.

2   If this be true—and who can deny it—three tasks lay before me: first to show from the past that the Talented Tenth as they have risen among American Negroes have been worthy of leadership; secondly to show how these men may be educated and developed; and thirdly to show their relation to the Negro problem.

3   You misjudge us because you do not know us. From the very first it has been the educated and intelligent of the Negro people that have led and elevated the mass, and the sole obstacles that nullified and retarded their efforts were slavery and race prejudice: for what is slavery but the legalized survival of the unfit and the nullification of the work of natural internal leadership? Negro leadership therefore sought from the first to rid the race of this awful incubus that it might make way for natural selection and the survival of the

fittest. In colonial days came Phillis Wheatley and Paul Cuffe striving against the bars of prejudice; and Benjamin Banneker, the almanac maker, voiced their longings when he said to Thomas Jefferson, "I freely and cheerfully acknowledge that I am of the African race and in colour which is natural to them, of the deepest dye; and it is under a sense of the most profound gratitude to the Supreme Ruler of the Universe, that I now confess to you that I am not under that state of tyrannical thraldom and inhuman captivity to which too many of my brethren are doomed, but that I have abundantly tasted of the fruition of those blessings which proceed from that free and unequalled liberty with which you are favored."

4 Then came Dr. James Derham, who could tell even the learned Dr. Rush something of medicine, and Lemuel Haynes, to whom Middlebury College gave an honorary A. M. in 1804. These and others we may call the Revolutionary group of distinguished Negroes—they were persons of marked ability, leaders of a Talented Tenth, standing conspicuously among the best of their time. They strove by word and deed to save the color line from becoming the line between the bond and free, but all they could do was nullified by Eli Whitney and the Curse of Gold. So they passed into forgetfulness.

5 But their spirit did not wholly die; here and there in the early part of the century came other exceptional men. Some were natural sons of unnatural fathers and were given often a liberal training and thus a race of educated mulattoes sprang up to plead for black men's rights. There was Ira Aldridge, whom all Europe loved to honor; there was that Voice crying in the Wilderness, David Walker.

6 In 1831 there met that first Negro convention in Philadelphia, at which the world gaped curiously but which bravely attacked the problems of race and slavery, crying out against persecution and declaring that "Laws as cruel in themselves as they were unconstitutional and unjust, have in many places been enacted against our poor, unfriended and unoffending brethren (without a shadow of provocation on our part), at whose bare recital the very savage draws himself up for fear of contagion—looks noble and prides himself because he bears not the name of Christian." Side by side this free Negro movement, and the movement for abolition, strove until they merged in to one strong stream. Too little notice has been taken of the work which the Talented Tenth among Negroes took in the great abolition crusade. From the very day that a Philadelphia colored man became the first subscriber to Garrison's "Liberator," to the day when Negro soldiers made the Emancipation Proclamation possible, black leaders worked shoulder to shoulder with white men in a movement, the success of which would have been impossible without them. There was Purvis and Remond, Pennington and Highland Garnett, Sojourner Truth and Alexander Crummel, and above all, Frederick Douglass—what would the abolition movement have been without them? They stood as living examples of the possibilities of the Negro race, their own hard

experiences and well wrought culture said silently more than all the drawn periods of orators—they were the men who made American slavery impossible.

7   And so we come to the present—a day of cowardice and vacillation, of strident wide-voiced wrong and faint hearted compromise; of double-faced dallying with Truth and Right. Who are today guiding the work of the Negro people? The "exceptions" of course. And yet so sure as this Talented Tenth is pointed out, the blind worshippers of the Average cry out in alarm: "These are exceptions, look here at death, disease and crime—these are the happy rule." Of course they are the rule, because a silly nation made them the rule: Because for three long centuries this people lynched Negroes who dared to be brave, raped black women who dared to be virtuous, crushed dark-hued youth who dared to be ambitious, and encouraged and made to flourish servility and lewdness and apathy. But not even this was able to crush all manhood and chastity and aspiration from black folk. A saving remnant continually survives and persists, continually aspires, continually shows itself in thrift and ability and character. Exceptional it is to be sure, but this is its chiefest promise; it shows the capability of Negro blood, the promise of black men. Do Americans ever stop to reflect that there are in this land a million men of Negro blood, well-educated, owners of homes, against the honor of whose womanhood no breath was ever raised, whose men occupy positions of trust and usefulness, and who, judged by any standard, have reached the full measure of the best type of modern European culture? Is it fair, is it decent, is it Christian to ignore these facts of the Negro problem, to be-little such aspiration, to nullify such leadership and seek to crush these people back into the mass out of which by toil and travail, they and their fathers have raised themselves?

8   Can the masses of the Negro people be in any possible way more quickly raised than by the effort and example of this aristocracy of talent and character? Was there ever a nation on God's fair earth civilized from the bottom upward? Never; it is, ever was and ever will be from the top downward that culture filters. The Talented Tenth rises and pulls all that are worth the saving up to their vantage ground. This is the history of human progress; and the two historic mistakes which have hindered that progress were the thinking first that no more could ever rise save the few already risen: or second, that it would better the unrisen to pull the risen down.

9   How then shall the leaders of a struggling people be trained and the hands of the risen few strengthened? There can be but one answer: The best and most capable of their youth must be schooled in the colleges and universities of the land. We will not quarrel as to just what the university of the Negro should teach or how it should teach it—I willingly admit that each soul and each race-soul needs its own peculiar curriculum. But this is true: A university is a human invention for the transmission of knowledge and culture from generation to generation, through the training of quick minds and pure hearts, and for this work no other human invention will suffice, not even trade and industrial schools.

10   All men cannot go to college but some men must; every isolated group or nation must have its yeast, must have for the talented few centers of training where men are not so mystified and befuddled by the hard and necessary toil of earning a living, as to have no aims higher than their bellies, and no God greater than Gold. This is true training, and thus in the beginning were the favored sons of the freedmen trained. Out of the colleges of the North came, after the blood of war, Ware, Cravath,

Chase, Andrews, Bumstead and Spence to build the foundations of knowledge and civilization in the black South. Where ought they to have begun to build? At the bottom, of course, quibbles the mole with his eyes in the earth. Aye! truly at the bottom, at the very bottom; at the bottom of knowledge, down in the very depths of knowledge there where the roots of justice strike into the lowest soil of Truth. And so they did begin; they founded colleges, and up from the colleges shot normal schools, and out from the normal schools went teachers, and around the normal teachers clustered other teachers to teach the public schools; the college trained in Greek and Latin and mathematics, 2,000 men; and these men trained full 50,000 others in morals and manners, and they in turn taught thrift and the alphabet to nine millions of men, who today hold $300,000,000 of property. It was a miracle—the most wonderful peace-battle of the 19th century, and yet today men smile at it, and in fine superiority tell us that it was all a strange mistake; that a proper way to found a system of education is first to gather the children and buy them spelling books and hoes; afterward men may look about for teachers, if haply they may find them; or again they would teach men Work, but as for Life—why, what has Work to do with Life, they ask vacantly.

1   Was the work of these college founders successful; did it stand the test of time? Did the college graduates, with all their fine theories of life, really live? Are they useful men helping to civilize and elevate their less fortunate fellows? Let us see. Omitting all institutions which have not actually graduated students from a college course, there are today in the United States thirty-four institutions giving something above high school training to Negroes and designed especially for this race.

2   Three of these were established in border States before the War; thirteen were planted by the Freedmen's Bureau in the years 1864–1869; nine were established between 1870 and 1880 by various church bodies: five were established after 1881 by Negro churches; and four are state institutions supported by United States' agricultural funds. In most cases the college departments are small adjuncts to high and common schoolwork. As a matter of fact six institutions—Atlanta, Fisk, Howard, Shaw, Wilberforce and Leland—are the important Negro colleges so far as actual work and number of students are concerned. In all these institutions, seven hundred and fifty Negro college students are enrolled. In grade the best of these colleges are about a year behind the smaller New England colleges and a typical curriculum is that of Atlanta University. Here students from the grammar grades, after a three years' high school course, take a college course of 136 weeks. One-fourth of this time is given to Latin and Greek; one-fifth, to English and modern languages; one-sixth, to history and social science; one-seventh, to natural science; one-eighth to mathematics; and one-eighth to philosophy and pedagogy.

3   In addition to these students in the South, Negroes have attended Northern colleges for many years. As early as 1826 one was graduated from Bowdoin College, and from that time till today nearly every year has seen elsewhere, other such-graduates. They have, of course, met much color prejudice. Fifty years ago very few colleges would admit them at all. Even today no Negro has ever been admitted to Princeton, and at some other leading institutions they are rather endured than encouraged. Oberlin was the great pioneer in the work of blotting out the color line in colleges, and has more Negro graduates by far than any other Northern college.

14   The total number of Negro college graduates up to 1899 (several of the graduates of that year not being reported), was as follows:

	Negro Colleges	White Colleges
Before '76	137	75
'75–80	143	22
'80–85	250	31
'85–90	413	43
'90–95	465	66
'95–99	475	88
Class Unknown	57	64
Total	1,914	390

15   Of these graduates 2,079 were men and 252 were women; 50 per cent of Northern-born college men come South to work among the masses of their people, at a sacrifice which few people realize; nearly 90 per cent of the Southern-born graduates instead of seeking that personal freedom and broader intellectual atmosphere which their training has led them, in some degree, to conceive, stay and labor and wait in the midst of their black neighbors and relatives.

16   The most interesting question, and in many respects the crucial question, to be asked concerning college-bred-Negroes, is: Do they earn a living? It has been intimated more than once that the higher training of Negroes has resulted in sending into the world of work, men who could find nothing to do suitable to their talents. Now and then there comes a rumor of a colored college man working at menial service, etc. Fortunately, returns as to occupations of college-bred Negroes, gathered by the Atlanta conference, are quite full—nearly sixty per cent of the total number of graduates.

17   This enables us to reach fairly certain conclusions as to the occupations of all college-bred Negroes. Of 1,312 persons reported, there were:

    701 Teachers:
        Presidents and Deans, 19
        Teacher of Music, 7
        Professors, Principals and Teachers, 675
    221 Clergymen:
        Bishop, 1
        Chaplains U.S. Army, 2
        Missionaries, 9
        Presiding Elders, 12
        Preachers, 197
    83 Physicians:
        Doctors of Medicine, 76
        Druggists, 4
        Dentists, 3
    74 Students
    62 Lawyers

53 in Civil Service:
U.S. Minister Plenipotentiary, 1
U.S. Consul, 1
U.S. Deputy Collector, 1
U.S. Gauger, 1
U.S. Postmasters, 2
U.S. Clerks, 44
State Civil Service, 2
City Civil Service, 1
47 Business Men:
Merchants, etc., 30
Managers, 13
Real Estate Dealers, 4
26 Farmers
22 Clerks and Secretaries:
Secretary of National Societies, 7
Clerks, etc., 15
9 Artisans
9 Editors
5 Miscellaneous

18 These figures illustrate vividly the function of the college-bred Negro. He is, as he ought to be, the group leader, the man who sets the ideals of the community where he lives, directs its thoughts and heads its social movements. It need hardly be argued that the Negro people need social leadership more than most groups; that they have no traditions to fall back upon, no long established customs, no strong family ties, no well defined social classes. All these things must be slowly and painfully evolved. The preacher was, even before the war, the group leader of the Negroes, and the church their greatest social institution. Naturally this preacher was ignorant and often immoral, and the problem of replacing the older type by better educated men has been a difficult one. Both by direct work and by direct influence on other preachers, and on congregations, the college-bred preacher has an opportunity for reformatory work and moral inspiration, the value of which cannot be overestimated.

19 It has, however, been in the furnishing of teachers that the Negro college has found its peculiar function. Few persons realize how vast a work, how mighty a revolution has been thus accomplished. To furnish five millions and more of ignorant people with teachers of their own race and blood, in one generation, was not only a very difficult undertaking, but a very important one, in that it placed before the eyes of almost every Negro child an attainable ideal. It brought the masses of the blacks in contact with modern civilization, made black men the leaders of their communities and trainers of the new generation. In this work college-bred Negroes were first teachers, and then teachers of teachers. And here it is that the broad culture of college work has been of peculiar value. Knowledge of life and its wider meaning, has been the point of the Negro's deepest ignorance, and the sending out of teachers whose training has not been simply for bread winning, but also for human culture, has been of inestimable value in the training of these men.

20 In earlier years the two occupations of preacher and teacher were practically the only ones open to the black college graduate. Of later years a larger diversity of life among his people, has opened new avenues of employment. Nor have these college

men been paupers and spendthrifts: 557 college-bred Negroes owned in 1899, $1,342,862.50 worth of real estate (assessed value), or $2,411 per family. The real value of the total accumulations of the whole group is perhaps about $10,000,000, or $5,000 a piece. Pitiful is it not beside the fortunes of oil kings and steel trusts, but after all is the fortune of the millionaire the only stamp of true and successful living? Alas! it is, with many and there's the rub.

21   The problem of training the Negro is today immensely complicated by the fact that the whole question of the efficiency and appropriateness of our present systems of education, for any kind of child, is a matter of active debate, in which final settlement seems still afar off. Consequently it often happens that persons arguing for or against certain systems of education for Negroes, have these controversies in mind and miss the real question at issue. The main question, so far as the Southern Negro is concerned, is: What under the present circumstance, must a system of education do in order to raise the Negro as quickly as possible in the scale of civilization? The answer to this question seems to me clear: It must strengthen the Negro's character, increase his knowledge and teach him to earn a living. Now it goes without saying that it is hard to do all these things simultaneously or suddenly and that at the same time it will not do to give all the attention to one and neglect the others: we could give black boys trades, but that alone will not civilize a race of ex-slaves; we might simply increase their knowledge of the world, but this would not necessarily make them wish to use this knowledge honestly; we might seek to strengthen character and purpose, but to what end if this people have nothing to eat or to wear? A system of education is not one thing, nor does it have a single definite object, nor is it a mere matter of schools. Education is that whole system of human training within and without the school house walls, which molds and develops men. If then we start out to train an ignorant and unskilled people with a heritage of bad habits, our system of training must set before itself two great aims—the one dealing with knowledge and character, the other part seeking to give the child the technical knowledge necessary for him to earn a living under the present circumstances. These objects are accomplished in part by the opening of the common schools on the one hand, and of the industrial schools on the other. But only in part, for there must also be trained those who are to teach these schools—men and women of knowledge and culture and technical skill who understand modern civilization, and have the training and aptitude to impart it to the children under them. There must be teachers, and teachers of teachers, and to attempt to establish any sort of a system of common and industrial school training, without *first* (and I say *first* advisedly) without *first* providing for the higher training of the very best teachers, is simply throwing your money to the winds. School houses do not teach themselves—piles of brick and mortar and machinery do not send out *men*. It is the trained, living human soul, cultivated and strengthened by long study and thought, that breathes the real breath of life into boys and girls and makes them human, whether they be black or white, Greek, Russian or American. Nothing, in these latter days, has so dampened the faith of thinking Negroes in recent educational movements, as the fact that such movements have been accompanied by ridicule and denouncement and decrying of those very institutions of higher training which made the Negro public school possible, and make Negro industrial schools thinkable. It was Fisk, Atlanta, Howard and Straight, those colleges born of the

faith and sacrifice of the abolitionist, that placed in the black schools of the South the 30,000 teachers and more, which some, who depreciate the work of these higher schools, are using to teach their own new experiments. If Hampton, Tuskegee and the hundred other industrial schools prove in the future to be as successful as they deserve to be, then their success in training black artisans for the South will be due primarily to the white colleges of the North and the black colleges of the South, which trained the teachers who today conduct these institutions. There was a time when the American people believed pretty devoutly that a log of wood with a boy at one end and Mark Hopkins at the other represented the highest ideal of human training. But in these eager days it would seem that we have changed all that and think it necessary to add a couple of saw-mills and a hammer to this outfit, and, at a pinch, to dispense with the services of Mark Hopkins.

22   I would not deny, or for a moment seem to deny, the paramount necessity of teaching the Negro to work, and to work steadily and skillfully; or seem to depreciate in the slightest degree the important part industrial schools must play in the accomplishment of these ends, but I *do* say, and insist upon it, that it is industrialism drunk with its vision of success, to imagine that its own work can be accomplished without providing for the training of broadly cultured men and women to teach its own teachers, and to teach the teachers of the public schools.

23   But I have already said that human education is not simply a matter of schools; it is much more a matter of family and group life—the training of one's home, of one's daily companions, of one's social class. Now the black boy of the South moves in a black world—a world with its own leaders, its own thoughts, its own ideals. In this world he gets by far the larger part of his life training, and through the eyes of this dark world he peers into the veiled world beyond. Who guides and determines the education which he receives in his world? His teachers here are the group-leaders of the Negro people—the physicians and clergymen, the trained fathers and mothers, the influential and forceful men about him of all kinds; here it is, if at all, that the culture of the surrounding world trickles through and is handed on by the graduates of the higher schools. Can such culture training of group leaders be neglected? Can we afford to ignore it? Do you think that if the leaders of thought among Negroes are not trained and educated thinkers, that they will have no leaders? On the contrary a hundred half-trained demagogues will still hold the places they so largely occupy now, and hundreds of vociferous busy-bodies will multiply. You have no choice; either you must help furnish this race from within its own ranks with thoughtful men of trained leadership, or you must suffer the evil consequences of a headless misguided rabble.

24   I am an earnest advocate of manual training and trade teaching for black boys, and for white boys, too. I believe that next to the founding of Negro colleges the most valuable addition to Negro education since the war, has been industrial training for black boys. Nevertheless, I insist that the object of all true education is not to make men carpenters, it is to make carpenters men; there are two means of making the carpenter a man, each equally important: the first is to give the group and community in which he works, liberally trained teachers and leaders to teach him and his family what life means; the second is to give him sufficient intelligence and technical skill to make

him an efficient workman. The first object demands the Negro college and college-bred men—not a quantity of such colleges, but a few of excellent quality; not too many college-bred men, but enough to leaven the lump, to inspire the masses, to raise the Talented Tenth to leadership. The second object demands a good system of common schools, well-taught, conveniently located and properly equipped.

25   What is the chief need for the building up of the Negro public school in the South? The Negro race in the South needs teachers today above all else. This is the concurrent testimony of all who know the situation. For the supply of this great demand two things are needed—institutions of higher education and money for school houses and salaries. It is usually assumed that a hundred or more institutions for Negro training are today turning out so many teachers and college-bred men that the race is threatened with an over-supply. This is sheer nonsense. There are today less than 3,000 living Negro college graduates in the United States, and less than 1,000 Negroes in college. Moreover, in the 164 schools for Negroes, 95 per cent of their students are doing elementary and secondary work, work which should be done in the public schools. Over half the remaining 2,157 students are taking high school studies. The mass of so-called "normal" schools for the Negro are simply doing elementary common school work, or, at most, high school work, with a little instruction in methods. The Negro colleges and the post-graduate courses at other institutions are the only agencies for the broader and more careful training of teachers. The work of these institutions is hampered for lack of funds. It is getting increasingly difficult to get funds for training teachers in the best modern methods, and yet all over the South, from State Superintendents, county officials, city boards and school principals comes the wail, "We need TEACHERS!" and teachers must be trained. As the fairest minded of all white Southerners, Atticus G. Haygood, once said: "The defects of colored teachers are so great as to create an urgent necessity for training better ones. Their excellencies and their successes are sufficient to justify the best hopes of success in the effort, and to vindicate the judgment of those who make large investments of money and service to give to colored students opportunity for thoroughly preparing themselves for the work of teaching children of their people."

26   The truth of this has been strikingly shown in the marked improvement of white teachers in the South. Twenty years ago the rank and file of white public school teachers were not as good as the Negro teachers. But they, by scholarships and good salaries, have been encouraged to thorough normal and collegiate preparation, while the Negro teachers have been discouraged by starvation wages and the idea that any training will do for a black teacher. If carpenters are needed it is well and good to train men as carpenters. But to train men as carpenters, and then set them to teaching is wasteful and criminal; and to train men as teachers and then refuse them living wages, unless they become carpenters, is rank nonsense.

27   The United States Commissioner of Education says in his report for 1900: "For comparison between the white and colored enrollment in secondary and higher education, I have added together the enrollment in high schools and secondary schools, with the attendance on colleges and universities, not being sure of the actual grade of work done in the colleges and universities. The work done in the secondary schools is reported in such detail in this office, that there can be no doubt of its grade."

28   He then makes the following comparisons of persons in every million enrolled in secondary and higher education:

	Whole Country	Negroes
1880	4,362	1,289
1900	10,743	2,061

And he concludes: "While the number in colored high schools and colleges had increased somewhat faster than the population, it had not kept pace with the average of the whole country, for it had fallen from 30 per cent to 24 per cent of the average quota. Of all colored pupils, one (1) in one hundred was engaged in secondary and higher work, and that ratio has continued substantially for the past twenty years. If the ratio of colored population in secondary and higher education is to be equal to the average for the whole country, it must be increased to five times its present average." And if this be true of the secondary and higher education, it is safe to say that the Negro has not one-tenth his quota in college studies. How baseless, therefore, is the charge of too much training! We need Negro teachers for the Negro common schools, and we need first-class normal schools and colleges to train them. This is the work of higher Negro education and it must be done.

29   Further than this, after being provided with group leaders of civilization, and a foundation of intelligence in the public schools, the carpenter, in order to be a man, needs technical skill. This calls for trade schools. Now trade schools are not nearly such simple things as people once thought. The original idea was that the "Industrial" school was to furnish education, practically free, to those willing to work for it: it was to "do" things—i.e.: become a center of productive industry, it was to be partially, if not wholly, self-supporting, and it was to teach trades. Admirable as were some of the ideas underlying this scheme, the whole thing simply would not work in practice; it was found that if you were to use time and material to teach trades thoroughly, you could not at the same time keep the industries on a commercial basis and make them pay. Many schools started out to do this on a large scale and went into virtual bankruptcy. Moreover, it was found also that it was possible to teach a boy a trade mechanically, without giving him the full educative benefit of the process, and, vice versa, that there was a distinctive educative value in teaching a boy to use his hands and eyes in carrying out certain physical processes, even though he did not actually learn a trade. It has happened, therefore, in the last decade, that a noticeable change has come over the industrial schools. In the first place the idea of commercially remunerative industry in a school is being pushed rapidly to the background. There are still schools with shops and farms that bring an income, and schools that use student labor partially for the erection of their buildings and the furnishing of equipment. It is coming to be seen, however, in the education of the Negro, as clearly as it has been seen in the education of the youths the world over, that it is the *boy* and not the material product, that is the true object of education. Consequently the object of the industrial school came to be the thorough training of boys regardless of the cost of the training, so long as it was thoroughly well done.

30   Even at this point, however, the difficulties were not surmounted. In the first place modern industry has taken great strides since the war, and the teaching of trades is no longer a simple matter. Machinery and long processes of work have greatly changed the work of the carpenter, the ironworker and the shoemaker. A really efficient workman must be today an intelligent man who has had good technical training in addition to thorough common school, and perhaps even higher training. To meet this situation the industrial schools began a further development; they established distinct Trade Schools for the thorough training of better class artisans, and at the same time they sought to preserve for the purposes of general education, such of the simpler processes of elementary trade learning as were best suited therefor. In this differentiation of the Trade School and manual training, the best of the industrial schools simply followed the plain trend of the present educational epoch. A prominent educator tells us that, in Sweden, "In the beginning the economic conception was generally adopted, and everywhere manual training was looked upon as a means of preparing the children of the common people to earn their living. But gradually it came to be recognized that manual training has a more elevated purpose, and one, indeed, more useful in the deeper meaning of the term. It came to be considered as an educative process for the complete moral, physical and intellectual development of the child."

31   Thus, again, in the manning of trade schools and manual training schools we are thrown back upon the higher training as its source and chief support. There was a time when any aged and wornout carpenter could teach in a trade school. But not so today. Indeed the demand for college-bred men by a school like Tuskegee, ought to make Mr. Booker T. Washington the firmest friend of higher training. Here he has as helpers the son of a Negro senator, trained in Greek and the humanities and graduated at Harvard; the son of a Negro congressman and lawyer, trained in Latin and mathematics, and graduated at Oberlin; he has as his wife, a woman who read Virgil and Homer in the same class room with me; he has as college chaplain, a classical graduate of Atlanta University; as teacher of science, a graduate of Fisk; as teacher of history, a graduate of Smith,—indeed some thirty of his chief teachers are college graduates, and instead of studying French grammars in the midst of weeds, or buying pianos for dirty cabins, they are at Mr. Washington's right hand helping him in a noble work. And yet one of the effects of Mr. Washington's propaganda has been to throw doubt upon the expediency of such training for Negroes, as these persons have had.

32   Men of America, the problem is plain before you. Here is a race transplanted through the criminal foolishness of your fathers. Whether you like it or not the millions are here, and here they will remain. If you do not lift them up, they will pull you down. Education and work are the levers to uplift a people. Work alone will not do it unless inspired by the right ideals and guided by intelligence. Education must not simply teach work—it must teach Life. The Talented Tenth of the Negro race must be made leaders of thought and missionaries of culture among their people. No others can do this work and Negro colleges must train men for it. The Negro race, like all other races, is going to be saved by its exceptional men. ∎

Garry B. Trudeau

Teaching Is Dead

Garry B. Trudeau (born 1948) is one of America's most influential (and controversial) political and social commentators. His vehicle is the comic strip "Doonesbury," which appears in more than 850 newspapers and whose audience may top 100 million readers. What exactly does this cartoon argue about the nature of current higher education?

Margaret Spellings

Remarks at the 2006 No Child Left Behind Summit

Born in 1957, Margaret Spellings became Secretary of Education in 2005. In that role, she stressed accountability and assessment of education in secondary schools. In the following speech, delivered to the No Child Left Behind Summit held in Philadelphia in 2006, Spellings recounts what she takes to be the positive results of this educational reform movement. Compare her use of statistics and her sense of the goals of education with those provided by Gerald Bracey in the essay that follows this one.

Thank you, Paul Vallas, for introducing me. You're a terrific leader and manager, and you've achieved great results. Since you came here, student achievement has risen by 11 points in reading and 17 points in math. Fifth grade math scores alone increased by 26 points. All this, and you've balanced your budget, too. Clearly, your background in economics has been a tremendous asset to your school districts . . . and to the students and parents they serve.

2 As Paul or any successful business leader will tell you, high standards and accountability are the foundation for success. That's Business 101. It's the same in education, and a few years ago with No Child Left Behind, we made that foundation permanent.

3 With this law, we set a historic goal for our country: every child learning on grade level by 2014. This is the first in a series of departmental summits—public discussions to help educators and administrators ensure our students reach that goal. I'm looking forward to future events on other topics . . . including how to serve more students more effectively . . . and how to close the achievement gap between children from different races, backgrounds, and ZIP codes.

4 All of us know that the hard work of educating our students happens in classrooms, not in the superintendent's office, the state legislature, the U.S. Capitol—or for that matter, the Education Secretary's office. So I'd like to take a moment to say thank you to all of the teachers who are here.

5 I would like to thank the American Federation of Teachers for joining us. I've appreciated AFT's input on many key policy issues, especially their great work on reading, and we have a great working relationship. Just last night, I was with Nat LaCour at the teacher of the year celebration. I also want to thank the NEA for being here; one of their own, Kim Oliver, was honored yesterday as the new Teacher of the Year for 2006.

6 Yesterday I stood on the White House lawn and watched President Bush proclaim Kim National Teacher of the Year. She said she chose to be a teacher because like all of us, she was lucky enough to have a teacher who challenged her.

7 Everywhere I go, I am inspired by hard-working teachers who believe that every child deserves a quality education. And like Kim, when they look at a struggling student, they see nothing but potential. You can feel it when you walk into their classrooms—their confidence and great expectations are palpable.

8   I recently met a local teacher of the year in Spokane, Washington. She had earned that honor after 17 years of teaching elementary school—but the most recent ones were different. She told me she was a better teacher today than she was five years ago because of No Child Left Behind.

9   That's probably the best compliment this law could get. Because at its heart, it was intended to help teachers help students reach their potential. And all of us must do everything we can to support educators in this most important task.

10   We at the Department of Education are offering free workshops on effective strategies for teachers. Our training is certified in all 50 states and the District of Columbia. Through our online courses at Ed.gov, teachers may even obtain Highly Qualified Teacher status without ever leaving their homes.

11   Before No Child Left Behind, if a parent asked how a school was doing, we couldn't really answer the question. We had very little data about how to track year-to-year progress . . . and often no benchmarks for success.

12   This law is helping us learn about what works in our schools. And clearly, high standards and accountability are working. Over the last 5 years, our 9-year-olds have made more progress in reading than in the previous 28 combined. Scores are at all-time highs for African-American and Hispanic students.

13   We're also learning about what we need to improve. And we've reached a point where we must make some tough decisions and confront some sacred cows.

14   If we're going to have all students learning on grade level by 2014, we've got to start running faster and doing more. We're seeing it's possible. Delaware, Kansas, North Carolina, and Oklahoma are on track to reaching our goal in elementary school reading. But many others are not yet.

15   As leaders, as policymakers, and as parents, it's our job to help those schools reach their full potential. And it's our job to make sure every child has the knowledge and skills to succeed.

16   We have a saying in Texas, "if all you ever do is all you've ever done, then all you'll ever get is all you've ever got." And in my experience, if you just put more money for the same old things in the same old system, it usually means you'll get the same old results. Until every child can read and do math on grade level, the same old thing won't be enough. Not by a long shot. If we're serious about our 2014 goal—and I know we are—then we've got to change some things.

17   Business as usual doesn't always serve the needs of teachers or students. For example, today, you're most likely to find the most experienced and qualified teachers in our wealthiest communities. But in high-poverty middle and high schools, only half of math teachers majored or minored in the field they're teaching.

18   We don't serve teachers or students well by placing our least experienced teachers in our most challenging environments. Nor do we serve teachers well by asking them to teach subjects they don't know much about. It's not right, it's not fair, and it sets teachers—and students—up for failure.

19   A lot of you are superintendents and administrators who, like me, are responsible for addressing problems like these. And having worked in education at the state and local levels, I understand the challenges you face. When you're hearing from school boards, parents, your state officials, and the Secretary of Education . . . it can be hard to reconcile the different interests and different expectations. But students are counting on us to make sure the system serves their needs and priorities—and not just the grown-ups.

20   So I'm calling on each and every one of you to apply strategies like the ones you'll hear about today. This is not a show-and-tell. I want this event to kick off some serious debates about how to solve the issues we're facing.

21   For example, how can we reform our personnel system to make sure our most challenging schools are served by our most effective teachers? Shouldn't we track the results they're getting with students and learn from that data? Since we know that teachers with strong content knowledge get better results, shouldn't we reach out to professionals from other fields to bring them into our classrooms, especially when our shortages in these critical areas are so great?

22   The President and the Congress recently created a $100 million Teacher Incentive Fund to encourage more experienced teachers to go to high-poverty schools, and reward them for results—an approach that has been shown to positively impact student performance.

23   The fund also supports state and local administrators who develop proven models that others could replicate—and I encourage all of you who are here to take advantage of that opportunity. We'll start accepting applications for the new Teacher Incentive Fund on Monday, just in time to kick off the Department's Celebrating Teachers Week.

24   In addition, my department will continue to support teachers with significant resources, including more than 3 billion dollars this year. Today you'll hear from some people who are using those resources in innovative and effective ways.

25   We're also faced with a shortage of qualified teachers in math, science, and critical foreign languages—and to overcome it, we must make some changes. That's why the President has also called for $122 million to help prepare 70,000 teachers to lead AP and International Baccalaureate classes . . . and $25 million to help recruit 30,000 math and science professionals to be adjunct teachers in these essential subject areas.

26   This is urgent work . . . and to have all kids on grade level by 2014, we only have time to do what works. As all of you know, our children aren't growing up in the same world we did. You can't pick up a newspaper or magazine these days without reading about global competitiveness. But after traveling around the country and meeting so many great educators, and after meeting the awesome teachers of the year yesterday at the White House—including Pennsylvania's own Barbara Benglian—I know we have nothing to fear.

27   Last week I visited a middle school in Maryland with President Bush and saw sixth graders learning about astronomy, robotic engineering, and aerospace technology—and loving it. We went into a class called Introduction to Robotic Systems, and the teacher walked up to the President and said, "Welcome to the future!" And he was right.

28   The class was full of students asking "what if" questions. They had high expectations and a lot of confidence, and they knew they could make a difference.

29   There are certain things you can't teach in a classroom that our students already have—qualities like creativity, diversity, and entrepreneurship. Our job is to give them the knowledge and skills to compete. Fortunately, we have plenty of great teachers who are up to the task.

30   That's why, like the President, I don't fear foreign competition. Students and teachers like this remind us that America has always been the most innovative society in the world. And together, we will make sure we always are. We know our goal of getting all students to grade level by 2014 is attainable, and as the title of this summit says, teachers will make it happen. ■

David Horsey/Seattlepi/Hearst Corporation

Gerald W. Bracey

The Condition of Public Education

Gerald W. Bracey, who holds a PhD in psychology, has regularly used his writing to comment on the state of education in America, and especially to critique what he considers to be serious flaws in our educational policies. He is an associate of the High/Scope Educational Research Foundation, a fellow at the Educational Policy Studies Laboratory at Arizona State University, and a fellow at the Education and the Public Interest Center at the University of Colorado at Boulder. He has also been one of the most outspoken critics of the policies of No Child Left Behind, even calling for the abolition of the Department of Education. In the essay below from the October 2006 *Phi Beta Kappan*, an excerpt of a longer study, Bracey examines the ways that statistics can be, and have been, used to suggest that No Child Left Behind is working.

N ewt Gingrich has suggested that Democrats run their election campaigns on a simple slogan: "Had enough?"[1] Bush Administration shenanigans and Congressional political ploys so brazen as to be unbelievable—for instance, tying a rise in the minimum wage that would benefit millions to a reduction in the estate tax that would benefit the nation's 7,500 wealthiest families—had me nodding in agreement. Herewith, the year in review.

DESPERATELY SEEKING STRAWS TO GRASP

2   "This law is helping us learn about what works in our schools. And clearly, high standards and accountability are working. Over the last five years, our 9-year-olds have made more progress in reading than in the previous 28 combined." So said Margaret Spellings at the No Child Left Behind Summit in April 2006, referring to gains on the National Assessment of Educational Progress (NAEP).[2] In statistical circles, what the secretary is doing is called "cherry picking." And in this instance, careless and self-serving cherry picking, too. Those last five years Spellings spoke of span 1999 to 2004. For two of those years Bill Clinton was President, and it is possible that all that gain—all 7 points—occurred on his watch. In two of those five years, NCLB did not exist. In 2001–02, NCLB (signed into law in January 2002) would have been in existence only three months before a NAEP assessment—had there been one. And given the confusion that reigned from 2002 to 2004 and the hostility between the states and the U.S. Department of Education, it is not likely that much gain occurred then. (Remember that in 2002, then-Secretary Rod Paige accused some states of trying to "ratchet down their standards" and thus of being "enemies of equal justice and equal opportunity and . . . apologists for failure."[3] It's surprising he didn't go on to call them terrorist organizations.)

3   Spellings' statement is true only if you start in NAEP's first trend year, 1971. Begin in the year of NAEP's previous trend high point, 1980, and the gain would be only 4 points. Then, too, there was no gain from 1999 to 2004 for 13-year-olds and a decline of 3 points for 17-year-olds. And why didn't she mention math trends, since 9-year-olds showed a 9-point gain and 13-year-olds a 5-point gain? Seventeen-year-olds, though, showed a 1-point decline.

4   Spellings also said, "Scores are at all-time highs for African American and Hispanic students."[4] Well, if she meant reading scores for 9-year-olds, that was true. But it wasn't true for 17-year-old blacks or 13- and 17-year-old Hispanics (13-year-old blacks were at an all-time high by a single point). The statement would have been true, too, in mathematics, except for black and Hispanic 17-year-olds.

5   The regular NAEP assessment of 2005, though, proved less upbeat. The "regular" NAEP assessments, the ones billed as "the nation's report card," change items over time in conjunction with curricular shifts; the NAEP that yields trends administers the same items at each assessment. In the regular assessment for 2005, fourth-grade reading reached the same level as it had at the onset of NCLB in 2002, and eighth-grade reading declined 2 points. In math, scores rose 3 points for fourth-graders from 2003 and 1 point for eighth-graders.

6   In reading, the proportion of students at or above the proficient level was static for fourth-graders at 31% and fell for eighth-graders from 33% to 31%. In mathematics, the proportion of fourth-graders at or above proficient rose from 32% to 36%, while for eighth-graders it rose from 29% to 30%. While "the Administration scrambled to put the best face on the numbers and to defend the law that some complain forces a test-driven curriculum on the classroom," Lois Romano reported in the *Washington Post*, Ross Wiener of the Education Trust had a more common reaction: "No one can be satisfied with these results. There's been a discernible slowdown in progress since `03, at a time when we desperately need to accelerate gains. The absence of particularly bad news isn't the same as good news."[5] As for President Bush's comment that the

achievement gaps were narrowing and "that's positive and that's important," Wiener countered, "It is meager progress. Students of color and low-income students continue to be educated at levels far below their affluent peers."[6]

7   For many people, Wiener's views raised the question, "Is NCLB working?" Two reports that appeared within two weeks of each other said "No."[7] Both studies analyzed the regular NAEP assessments, not the trend data.

8   In the first of these reports, researchers at Policy Analysis for California Education (PACE) at the University of California, Berkeley, examined reading trends for 12 states on both the state tests and NAEP. (The states were Arizona, California, Illinois, Iowa, Kentucky, Massachusetts, Nebraska, New Jersey, North Carolina, Oklahoma, Texas, and Washington.) The states began with much higher proportions of "state-proficient" students; the average gap between state-defined proficiency and NAEP-defined proficiency was 38%; the smallest gap was in Massachusetts at 10%; the largest, in Texas at 55%.

9   The gap in itself is of no great import. Both state standards and NAEP achievement levels for determining proficiency are wholly arbitrary—both lack any connection to external criteria for validation—and the NAEP levels are far too high. For instance, U.S. fourth-graders were 11th in math and third in science among the 26 nations that participated in the 1995 Third International Mathematics and Science Study (TIMSS). But NAEP found only 18% of fourth-graders to be proficient or better in math and 26% to be proficient or better in science. Still, for analyzing changes over time, rather than for absolute differences, the NAEP levels can be useful. The following table shows the annual gains in fourth-grade reading and math in pre- and post-NCLB years.

	Reading		Math	
	STATE	NAEP	STATE	NAEP
Pre-NCLB Gains	2.6	0.4	2.7	1.5
Post-NCLB Gains	1.9	−0.2	2.9	2.4

10   As we can readily see, the post-NCLB gains in reading are smaller on both state tests and NAEP. There is actually a loss on NAEP. In math, the state test gains post-NCLB are about the same as prior to the law, while the gains in NAEP mathematics have picked up. Among the states, only Arkansas managed a reading gain of more than 1% per year on NAEP. In math, the annual gains on NAEP ranged from 1.3% in Illinois to 4.0% in Arkansas. Now, if Arkansas can sustain these gains, it can reach 100% proficiency in math by 2024—only a decade late. In Illinois, 100% proficiency in math could be attained by 2057. Both projections are hopelessly optimistic, though, because they are based on the unrealistic assumption that equally large increases in gains will occur each year.

11   The U.S. Department of Education (ED) took its usual approach to such information: it attempted to defame the messenger. Kevin Sullivan, identified by the *Los Angeles Times* as a spokesman for ED, said that PACE "has a track record of putting out flawed and misleading information about No Child Left Behind."[8]

12   As this issue went to press around Labor Day, I had no comments from Mr. Sullivan or any ED official on the new PACE study. Nor has anyone at ED addressed the similar study conducted by Jaekyung Lee of SUNY, Buffalo, for the Harvard Civil Rights

Project. Given that Douglas Harris, Gene Glass, and Robert Linn reviewed Lee's study, it is not likely to fall victim to ED's derogation. At least, not for its methodology. Although Lee uses quite different methods from those used by the PACE researchers, his study produced results similar to PACE's:

> NCLB did not have a significant impact on improving reading and math achievement across the nation and states. Based on the NAEP results, the national average achievement remains flat in reading and grows at the same pace in math after NCLB than before. In grade 4 math, there was a temporary improvement right after NCLB, but it was followed by a return to the pre-reform growth rate. . . .
>
> NCLB has not helped the nation and states significantly narrow the achievement gap. . . .
>
> NCLB's attempt to scale up the alleged success of states that adopted test-driven accountability policy prior to NCLB (e.g., Florida, North Carolina, Texas) did not work. It neither enhanced [these] states' earlier academic improvement nor transferred the effects of a test-driven accountability system to states that adopted test-based accountability under NCLB. . . .
>
> The higher the stakes of state assessments, the greater the discrepancies between NAEP and state assessment results. These discrepancies were particularly large for poor, black, and Hispanic students.

13   That last finding—the higher the stakes, the higher the state/NAEP discrepancy—does not describe a perfect relationship, but it also comes as no surprise. Lee and colleague Kenneth Wong of Brown University had earlier constructed an index to measure state accountability levels.[9] Using this index, Lee found that the correlation between the height of the stakes and the size of the NAEP/state discrepancy was +.36. Not huge, but statistically significant.

14   At the state level, few states showed increases in NAEP reading, and none showed accelerated growth after the law was passed. Lee states that eighth-graders maintained growth similar to that seen pre-NCLB but that fourth-graders showed accelerated growth in math in the post-NCLB years. Lee notes, though, that most of the improved growth occurred between 2000 and 2003 and that growth returned to its pre-NCLB rate afterward. But, as mentioned earlier, NCLB came into existence only in January 2002, and it probably had no influence on what was happening in the last half of the 2001–02 school year. Thus, if NCLB affected math growth in the period from 2000 to 2003, it would have had to work its wonders in a single school year, 2002–03. (There were no NAEP data to examine for 2001–02.) As also mentioned, given the haphazard implementation of NCLB, this seems most unlikely. It is at least possible that the rate increases took place prior to NCLB.

15   Commenting on the NAEP trend results of 2004, Secretary Spellings declared, "Changing the direction of America's schools is like turning the Queen Mary, a large ship whose captain can't change course on a dime. The goal requires a lot of time and effort, but we are beginning to turn our own Queen Mary around."[10] That might or might not be true of the trend analysis. The analyses of regular NAEP data by PACE and by Lee make it clear that, as far as regular NAEP assessments go, the liner is dead in the water.

NCLB: A THREAT TO THE NATION'S GLOBAL COMPETITIVENESS?

16　　　At that NCLB Summit in April, Spellings also said, "There are certain things you can't teach in a classroom that our students *already have—qualities like creativity, diversity, and entrepreneurship.* Our job is to give them the knowledge and skills to compete. . . . America has always been the most innovative society in the world. And together, we will make sure we always are"[11] (emphasis added).

17　　　This might be the first time diversity has been listed with creativity and entrepreneurship as a personal quality, but many people believe that those qualities of creativity and entrepreneurship are what keep the nation competitive in the first place. The minister of education of Singapore certainly thinks so. Tharman Shanmugaratnam told *Newsweek* pundit Fareed Zakaria that Singapore had a test meritocracy while America had a talent meritocracy. "We cannot use tests to measure creativity, ambition, or the willingness of students to question conventional wisdom. These are areas where Singapore must learn from America."[12] Even allowing that the minister is being a bit disingenuous—the last thing a totalitarian society like Singapore wants is a cadre of young people who question conventional wisdom—his comment on tests rings true.

18　　　Zakaria had approached the minister because he was intrigued that kids from Singapore aced tests but that, "ten or twenty years later, it is the American kids who are ahead. Singapore has few truly top-ranked scientists, entrepreneurs, inventors, business executives, or academics. American kids test much worse, but seem to do better later in life and in the real world." A Singaporean father who had lived in the U.S. for a period before returning to his island nation confirmed the minister's assertions, telling Zakaria, "In the American school, when my son would speak up, he was applauded and encouraged. In Singapore, he's seen as pushy and weird." Schooling in Singapore "is a chore. Work hard, memorize, test well." The father placed his son in an American-style private school.

19　　　Similarly, Joseph Renzulli, who directs the National Research Center on the Gifted and Talented, housed at the University of Connecticut, had Japanese visitors tell him, "Your schools have produced a continuous flow of inventors, designers, entrepreneurs, and innovative leaders,"[13] They noticed American creativity and thought the schools had something to do with it.

20　　　It is not only between Asian and American schools that one sees the contrast between passive memorization and active participation in the learning process. A *Washington Post* op-ed from a few years ago described the writer's frustrations trying to get Scottish high-schoolers to discuss Shakespeare. "It took months of badgering before I was able to get my Scottish students to speak up in class. They simply weren't accustomed to asking questions or tossing around their own observations. American schools teach American kids to ask questions. They teach students to be curious, skeptical, even contrary. . . . At their best, they teach kids to challenge the teachers."[14]

21　　　But Spellings doesn't get it. She visited a school in 2006 and reported that "the class was full of students asking 'what if' questions."[15] But she doesn't see the connection between questions, creativity, and competitiveness. How does she think American kids got those qualities that "they already have" in the first place? Is it something in the water? She needs a long chat with Robert Sternberg, dean of the College of Arts and Sciences at Tufts University. Sternberg calls creativity a habit. If you don't arrange conditions for people to practice the habit, it won't develop. And, he contends, "the increasingly massive and far-reaching use of conventional standardized tests is one of the most effective, if unintentional, vehicles this country has created for suppressing creativity."[16] There is nothing creative about taking a test. Aside from a few rare exceptions, taking a test is the opposite of asking a question.

22   As I have said before, we'd better think more than twice about replacing a culture that cultivates asking questions with one that worships high test scores. Somebody needs to give Secretary Spellings a wake-up call.

Notes

1. Quoted in Karen Tumulty and Mike Allen, "Republicans on the Run," *Time*, 3 April 2006.
2. "Remarks by Secretary Spellings at No Child Left Behind Summit," U.S. Department of Education, 27 April 2006, www.ed.gov/news. Search on "Press Releases."
3. "Letter Released from U.S. Education Secretary Paige to State School Chiefs on Implementing No Child Left Behind Act," U.S. Department of Education, 23 October 2002.
4. "Remarks by Secretary Spellings."
5. Lois Romano, "Test Scores Move Little in Math, Reading," *Washington Post*, 20 October 2005, p. A-3.
6. Ibid.
7. Bruce Fuller et al., *Is the No Child Left Behind Act Working?* (Berkeley: Policy Analysis for California Education, 2006); and Jaekyung Lee, *Tracking Achievement Gaps and Assessing the Impact of NCLB on the Gaps* (Cambridge, Mass.: Civil Rights Project, Harvard University, June 2006).
8. Mitchell Landsberg, "Reading Gains Slowing, Study Says," *Los Angeles Times*, 20 June 2006.
9. Jaekyung Lee and Kenneth Wong, "The Impact of Accountability on Racial and Socioeconomic Equity: Considering Both School Resources and Achievement Outcomes," *American Educational Research Journal*, Winter 2004, pp. 797–832.
10. "Spellings Hails New National Report Card Results," U.S. Department of Education, 14 July 2005, www.ed.gov/news. Search on "Press Releases."
11. "Remarks by Secretary Spellings."
12. Fareed Zakaria, "We All Have a Lot to Learn," *Newsweek*, 9 January 2006, www.msnbc.msn.com/id/10663340/site/newsweek.
13. Joseph Renzulli, "A Quiet Crisis Is Clouding the Future of R & D," *Education Week*, 25 May 2005, pp. 32–33.
14. Amy Biancolli, "At Least Our Kids Ask Questions," *Washington Post*, 27 April 2001, p. A-23.
15. "Remarks by Secretary Spellings."
16. Robert J. Sternberg, "Creativity Is a Habit," *Education Week*, 22 February 2006, p. 47. ■

David Brooks

Sam Spade at Starbucks

David Brooks, born in 1961, raised in New York City, and educated at the University of Chicago, is a popular social columnist whose work appears regularly in the *New York Times* and on PBS. He has also written for the *Wall Street Journal, Newsweek,* and other magazines, and his books include *Bobos in Paradise: The New Upper Class and How They Got There* (2000), *On Paradise Drive* (2004), and *The Social Animal: The Hidden Sources of Love, Character, and Achievement* (2011). The following essay appeared in the *New York Times* and many other newspapers on April 12, 2012.

If you attend a certain sort of conference, hang out at a certain sort of coffee shop or visit a certain sort of university, you've probably run into some of these wonderful young people who are doing good. Typically, they've spent a year studying abroad. They've traveled in the poorer regions of the world. Now they have devoted themselves to a purpose larger than self.

2 Often they are bursting with enthusiasm for some social entrepreneurship project: making a cheap water-purification system, starting a company that will empower Rwandan women by selling their crafts in boutiques around the world.

3 These people are refreshingly uncynical. Their hip service ethos is setting the moral tone for the age. Idealistic and uplifting, their worldview is spread by enlightened advertising campaigns, from Benetton years ago to everything Apple has ever done.

4 It's hard not to feel inspired by all these idealists, but their service religion does have some shortcomings. In the first place, many of these social entrepreneurs think they can evade politics. They have little faith in the political process and believe that real change happens on the ground beneath it.

5 That's a delusion. You can cram all the nongovernmental organizations you want into a country, but if there is no rule of law and if the ruling class is predatory then your achievements won't add up to much.

6 Furthermore, important issues always spark disagreement. Unless there is a healthy political process to resolve disputes, the ensuing hatred and conflict will destroy everything the altruists are trying to build.

7 There's little social progress without political progress. Unfortunately, many of today's young activists are really good at thinking locally and globally, but not as good at thinking nationally and regionally.

Second, the prevailing service religion underestimates the problem of disorder. Many of the activists talk as if the world can be healed if we could only insert more care, compassion and resources into it.

History is not kind to this assumption. Most poverty and suffering—whether in a country, a family or a person—flows from disorganization. A stable social order is an artificial accomplishment, the result of an accumulation of habits, hectoring, moral stricture and physical coercion. Once order is dissolved, it takes hard measures to restore it.

10   Yet one rarely hears social entrepreneurs talk about professional policing, honest courts or strict standards of behavior; it's more uplifting to talk about microloans and sustainable agriculture.

11   In short, there's only so much good you can do unless you are willing to confront corruption, venality and disorder head-on. So if I could, presumptuously, recommend a reading list to help these activists fill in the gaps in the prevailing service ethos, I'd start with the novels of Dashiell Hammett or Raymond Chandler, or at least the movies based on them.

12   The noir heroes like Sam Spade in "The Maltese Falcon" served as models for a generation of Americans, and they put the focus squarely on venality, corruption and disorder and how you should behave in the face of it.

13   A noir hero is a moral realist. He assumes that everybody is dappled with virtue and vice, especially himself. He makes no social-class distinction and only provisional moral distinctions between the private eyes like himself and the criminals he pursues. The assumption in a Hammett book is that the good guy has a spotty past, does spotty things and that the private eye and the criminal are two sides to the same personality.

14   He (or she—the women in these stories follow the same code) adopts a layered personality. He hardens himself on the outside in order to protect whatever is left of the finer self within.

15   He is reticent, allergic to self-righteousness and appears unfeeling, but he is motivated by a disillusioned sense of honor. The world often rewards the wrong things, but each job comes with obligations and even if everything is decaying you should still take pride in your work. Under the cynical mask, there is still a basic sense of good order, that crime should be punished and bad behavior shouldn't go uncorrected. He knows he's not going to be uplifted by his work; that to tackle the hard jobs he'll have to risk coarsening himself, but he doggedly plows ahead.

16   This worldview had a huge influence as a generation confronted crime, corruption, fascism and communism. I'm not sure I can see today's social entrepreneurs wearing fedoras and trench coats. But noir's moral realism would be a nice supplement to today's prevailing ethos. It would fold some hardheadedness in with today's service mentality. It would focus attention on the core issues: order and rule of law. And it would be necessary. Contemporary Washington, not to mention parts of the developing world, may be less seedy than the cities in the noir stories, but they are equally laced with self-deception and self-dealing. ∎

John Gatto

Against Education: How Public Education Cripples Our Kids, and Why

John Gatto (born 1935) became an award-winning teacher in the New York City school system after trials in other professions, including that of hot dog salesman, songwriter, jewelry designer, and scriptwriter. After he retired from teaching in 1991 (when he had just been named New York State Teacher of the Year), he became active and visible in the education reform movement. Critical of compulsory education, he announced his retirement in a *Wall Street Journal* op-ed piece in 1991 and has continued to write since then. His *Underground History of American Education* appeared in 2001; *Weapons of Mass Instruction* was published in 2008; and the following essay was published in *Harper's* magazine in September 2003.

Do we really need school? I don't mean education, just forced schooling: six classes a day, five days a week, nine months a year, for twelve years. Is this deadly routine really necessary? And if so, for what? Don't hide behind reading, writing, and arithmetic as a rationale, because 2 million happy homeschoolers have surely put that banal justification to rest. Even if they hadn't, a considerable number of well-known Americans never went through the twelve-year wringer our kids currently go through, and they turned out all right. George Washington, Benjamin Franklin, Thomas Jefferson, Abraham Lincoln? Someone taught them, to be sure, but they were not products of a school system, and not one of them was ever "graduated" from a secondary school. Throughout most of American history, kids generally didn't go to high school, yet the unschooled rose to be admirals, like Farragut; inventors, like Edison; captains of industry, like Carnegie and Rockefeller; writers, like Melville and Twain and Conrad; and even scholars, like Margaret Mead. In fact, until pretty recently people who reached the age of thirteen weren't looked upon as children at all. Ariel Durant, who co-wrote an enormous, and very good, multivolume history of the world with her husband, Will, was happily married at fifteen, and who could reasonably claim that Ariel Durant was an uneducated person? Unschooled, perhaps, but not uneducated.

We have been taught (that is, schooled) in this country to think of "success" as synonymous with, or at least dependent upon, "schooling," but historically that isn't true in either an intellectual or a financial sense. And plenty of people throughout the world today find a way to educate themselves without resorting to a system of compulsory secondary schools that all too often resemble prisons. Why, then, do Americans confuse education with just such a system? What exactly is the purpose of our public schools?

Mass schooling of a compulsory nature really got its teeth into the United States between 1905 and 1915, though it was conceived of much earlier and pushed for throughout most of the nineteenth century. The reason given for this enormous up-heaval of family life and cultural traditions was, roughly speaking, threefold:

1. To make good people.
2. To make good citizens.
3. To make each person his or her personal best.

These goals are still trotted out today on a regular basis, and most of us accept them in one form or another as a decent definition of public education's mission, however short schools actually fall in achieving them. But we are dead wrong. Compounding our error is the fact that the national literature holds numerous and surprisingly consistent statements of compulsory schooling's true purpose. We have, for example, the great H. L. Mencken, who wrote in *The American Mercury* for April 1924 that the aim of public education is not

> to fill the young of the species with knowledge and awaken their intelligence. . . . Nothing could be further from the truth. The aim . . . is simply to reduce as many individuals as possible to the same safe level, to breed and train a standardized citizenry, to put down dissent and originality. That is its aim in the United States . . . and that is its aim everywhere else.

5 Because of Mencken's reputation as a satirist, we might be tempted to dismiss this passage as a bit of hyperbolic sarcasm. His article, however, goes on to trace the template for our own educational system back to the now vanished, though never to be forgotten, military state of Prussia. And although he was certainly aware of the irony that we had recently been at war with Germany, the heir to Prussian thought and culture, Mencken was being perfectly serious here. Our educational system really is Prussian in origin, and that really is cause for concern.

6 The odd fact of a Prussian provenance for our schools pops up again and again once you know to look for it. William James alluded to it many times at the turn of the century. Orestes Brownson, the hero of Christopher Lasch's 1991 book, *The True and Only Heaven*, was publicly denouncing the Prussianization of American schools back in the 1840s. Horace Mann's "Seventh Annual Report" to the Massachusetts State Board of Education in 1843 is essentially a paean to the land of Frederick the Great and a call for its schooling to be brought here. That Prussian culture loomed large in America is hardly surprising, given our early association with that utopian state. A Prussian served as Washington's aide during the Revolutionary War, and so many German-speaking people had settled here by 1795 that Congress considered publishing a German-language edition of the federal laws. But what shocks is that we should so eagerly have adopted one of the very worst aspects of Prussian culture: an educational system deliberately designed to produce mediocre intellects, to hamstring the inner life, to deny students appreciable leadership skills, and to ensure docile and incomplete citizens—all in order to render the populace "manageable."

7 It was from James Bryant Conant—president of Harvard for twenty years, WWI poison-gas specialist, WWII executive on the atomic-bomb project, high commissioner of the American zone in Germany after WWII, and truly one of the most influential figures of the twentieth century—that I first got wind of the real purposes of American schooling. Without Conant, we would probably not have the same style and degree of

standardized testing that we enjoy today, nor would we be blessed with gargantuan high schools that warehouse 2,000 to 4,000 students at a time, like the famous Columbine High in Littleton, Colorado. Shortly after I retired from teaching I picked up Conant's 1959 book-length essay, *The Child the Parent and the State*, and was more than a little intrigued to see him mention in passing that the modern schools we attend were the result of a "revolution" engineered between 1905 and 1930. A revolution? He declines to elaborate, but he does direct the curious and the uninformed to Alexander Inglis's 1918 book, *Principles of Secondary Education*, in which "one saw this revolution through the eyes of a revolutionary."

8   Inglis, for whom a lecture in education at Harvard is named, makes it perfectly clear that compulsory schooling on this continent was intended to be just what it had been for Prussia in the 1820s: a fifth column into the burgeoning democratic movement that threatened to give the peasants and the proletarians a voice at the bargaining table. Modern, industrialized, compulsory schooling was to make a sort of surgical incision into the prospective unity of these underclasses. Divide children by subject, by age-grading, by constant rankings on tests, and by many other more subtle means, and it was unlikely that the ignorant mass of mankind, separated in childhood, would ever reintegrate into a dangerous whole.

9   Inglis breaks down the purpose—the actual purpose—of modern schooling into six basic functions, any one of which is enough to curl the hair of those innocent enough to believe the three traditional goals listed earlier:

1. The *adjustive* or *adaptive* function. Schools are to establish fixed habits of reaction to authority. This, of course, precludes critical judgment completely. It also pretty much destroys the idea that useful or interesting material should be taught, because you can't test for reflexive obedience until you know whether you can make kids learn, and do, foolish and boring things.

2. The *integrating* function. This might well be called "the conformity function," because its intention is to make children as alike as possible. People who conform are predictable, and this is of great use to those who wish to harness and manipulate a large labor force.

3. The *diagnostic and directive* function. School is meant to determine each student's proper social role. This is done by logging evidence mathematically and anecdotally on cumulative records. As in "your permanent record." Yes, you do have one.

4. The *differentiating* function. Once their social role has been "diagnosed," children are to be sorted by role and trained only so far as their destination in the social machine merits—and not one step further. So much for making kids their personal best.

5. The *selective* function. This refers not to human choice at all but to Darwin's theory of natural selection as applied to what he called "the favored races." In short, the idea is to help things along by consciously attempting to improve the breeding stock. Schools are meant to tag the unfit—with poor grades, remedial placement, and other punishments—clearly enough that their peers will accept them as inferior and effectively bar them from the reproductive sweepstakes. That's what all those little humiliations from first grade onward were intended to do: wash the dirt down the drain.

6. The *propaedeutic* function. The societal system implied by these rules will require an elite group of caretakers. To that end, a small fraction of the kids will

quietly be taught how to manage this continuing project, how to watch over and control a population deliberately dumbed down and declawed in order that government might proceed unchallenged and corporations might never want for obedient labor.

10   That, unfortunately, is the purpose of mandatory public education in this country. And lest you take Inglis for an isolated crank with a rather too cynical take on the educational enterprise, you should know that he was hardly alone in championing these ideas. Conant himself, building on the ideas of Horace Mann and others, campaigned tirelessly for an American school system designed along the same lines. Men like George Peabody, who funded the cause of mandatory schooling throughout the South, surely understood that the Prussian system was useful in creating not only a harmless electorate and a servile labor force but also a virtual herd of mindless consumers. In time a great number of industrial titans came to recognize the enormous profits to be had by cultivating and tending just such a herd via public education, among them Andrew Carnegie and John D. Rockefeller.

11   There you have it. Now you know. We don't need Karl Marx's conception of a grand warfare between the classes to see that it is in the interest of complex management, economic or political, to dumb people down, to demoralize them, to divide them from one another, and to discard them if they don't conform. Class may frame the proposition, as when Woodrow Wilson, then president of Princeton University, said the following to the New York City School Teachers Association in 1909: "We want one class of persons to have a liberal education, and we want another class of persons, a very much larger class, of necessity, in every society, to forgo the privileges of a liberal education and fit themselves to perform specific difficult manual tasks." But the motives behind the disgusting decisions that bring about these ends need not be class-based at all. They can stem purely from fear, or from the by now familiar belief that "efficiency" is the paramount virtue, rather than love, liberty, laughter, or hope. Above all, they can stem from simple greed.

12   There were vast fortunes to be made, after all, in an economy based on mass production and organized to favor the large corporation rather than the small business or the family farm. But mass production required mass consumption, and at the turn of the twentieth century most Americans considered it both unnatural and unwise to buy things they didn't actually need. Mandatory schooling was a godsend on that count. School didn't have to train kids in any direct sense to think they should consume nonstop, because it did something even better: it encouraged them not to think at all. And that left them sitting ducks for another great invention of the modern era—marketing.

13   Now, you needn't have studied marketing to know that there are two groups of people who can always be convinced to consume more than they need to: addicts and children. School has done a pretty good job of turning our children into addicts, but it has done a spectacular job of turning our children into children. Again, this is no accident. Theorists from Plato to Rousseau to our own Dr. Inglis knew that if children could be cloistered with other children, stripped of responsibility and independence, encouraged to develop only the trivializing emotions of greed, envy, jealousy, and fear, they would grow older but never truly grow up. In the 1934 edition of his once well-known book *Public Education in the United States*, Ellwood P. Cubberley detailed and praised the

way the strategy of successive school enlargements had extended childhood by two to six years, and forced schooling was at that point still quite new. This same Cubberley— who was dean of Stanford's School of Education, a textbook editor at Houghton Mifflin, and Conant's friend and correspondent at Harvard—had written the following in the 1922 edition of his book *Public School Administration*: "Our schools are . . . factories in which the raw products (children) are to be shaped and fashioned. . . . And it is the business of the school to build its pupils according to the specifications laid down."

It's perfectly obvious from our society today what those specifications were. Maturity has by now been banished from nearly every aspect of our lives. Easy divorce laws have removed the need to work at relationships; easy credit has removed the need for fiscal self-control; easy entertainment has removed the need to learn to entertain oneself; easy answers have removed the need to ask questions. We have become a nation of children, happy to surrender our judgments and our wills to political exhortations and commercial blandishments that would insult actual adults. We buy televisions, and then we buy the things we see on the television. We buy computers, and then we buy the things we see on the computer. We buy $150 sneakers whether we need them or not, and when they fall apart too soon we buy another pair. We drive SUVs and believe the lie that they constitute a kind of life insurance, even when we're upside-down in them. And, worst of all, we don't bat an eye when Ari Fleischer tells us to "be careful what you say," even if we remember having been told somewhere back in school that America is the land of the free. We simply buy that one too. Our schooling, as intended, has seen to it.

Now for the good news. Once you understand the logic behind modern schooling, its tricks and traps are fairly easy to avoid. School trains children to be employees and consumers; teach your own to be leaders and adventurers. School trains children to obey reflexively; teach your own to think critically and independently. Well-schooled kids have a low threshold for boredom; help your own to develop an inner life so that they'll never be bored. Urge them to take on the serious material, the *grown-up* material, in history, literature, philosophy, music, art, economics, theology—all the stuff schoolteachers know well enough to avoid. Challenge your kids with plenty of solitude so that they can learn to enjoy their own company, to conduct inner dialogues. Well-schooled people are conditioned to dread being alone, and they seek constant companionship through the TV, the computer, the cell phone, and through shallow friendships quickly acquired and quickly abandoned. Your children should have a more meaningful life, and they can.

First, though, we must wake up to what our schools really are: laboratories of experimentation on young minds, drill centers for the habits and attitudes that corporate society demands. Mandatory education serves children only incidentally; its real purpose is to turn them into servants. Don't let your own have their childhoods extended, not even for a day. If David Farragut could take command of a captured British warship as a preteen, if Thomas Edison could publish a broadsheet at the age of twelve, if Ben Franklin could apprentice himself to a printer at the same age (then put himself through a course of study that would choke a Yale senior today), there's no telling what your own kids could do. After a long life, and thirty years in the public school trenches, I've concluded that genius is as common as dirt. We suppress our genius only because we haven't yet figured out how to manage a population of educated men and women. The solution, I think, is simple and glorious. Let them manage themselves. ■

Is College Worth the Price?

It's an old story," says Anthony P. Carnevale, director of Georgetown University's Center on Education and the Workforce and one of the authors featured in this section: "When economic downturns hit, unemployment rates spiral and tales of college graduates forced to tend bar or mop floors proliferate."

THE NON-TUITION COSTS OF EDUCATION

High school grads often look at the bill for their upcoming 4 years of college in disbelief. Thankfully, student loans often cover the cost of actually getting them into the classroom, but what about all the additional expenses that come along with their four years away from home? Living on their own for the first time is costly, especially in the fast-paced world of the college social scene.

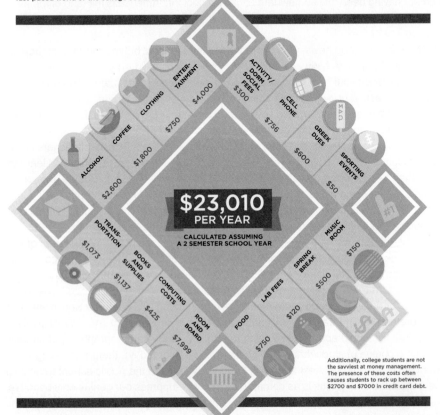

ENTERTAINMENT $4,000
CLOTHING $750
ACTIVITY/DORM SOCIAL FEES $300
CELL PHONE $756
COFFEE $1,800
GREEK DUES $600
ALCOHOL $2,600
SPORTING EVENTS $50
TRANSPORTATION $1,073

$23,010 PER YEAR
CALCULATED ASSUMING A 2 SEMESTER SCHOOL YEAR

MUSIC ROOM $150
BOOKS AND SUPPLIES $1,137
COMPUTING COSTS $425
ROOM AND BOARD $7,999
FOOD $750
LAB FEES $120
SPRING BREAK $500

Additionally, college students are not the savviest at money management. The presence of these costs often causes students to rack up between $2700 and $7000 in credit card debt.

But is the story really so old? Fifty years ago, according to the National Center for Education Statistics, about 45 percent of 1.7 million high school graduates went to college. By 2010, that number had nearly doubled, with 68 percent of 3.2 million high school graduates pursuing a college education. In short, more people—many more—than ever before are attending college before entering the workforce.

According to the *Concise Encyclopedia of Economics*, opinions about the "necessity" of a college degree have fluctuated for decades, often in correspondence with the rising and falling increase in salary for college graduates. But regardless of arguments made in decades past, one thing is clear: Today, college is on more people's minds than ever before. What should we make of its worth? And what parameters we should use to *define* its worth in the first place?

Many think that college's Golden Age has come and gone. College, they say, has become "the new high school"—and, as it grows more and more common for people to attend college, the degree means less and less. Not only that, tuition

ALCOHOL
Don't let their schedules fool you, college kids always find time to party. In fact, partying is such a staple of the college like that the average student spends $2,600/year on beer.

ACTIVITY/DORM SOCIAL FEES
Many students decide to join a fraternity or sorority to take advantage of the social life. Greek life isn't free however – dues can cost about $600/year.

COFFEE
Between exciting social life, class projects, studying, and part time work, a daily dose of caffeine is nearly required to function. All those morning Starbucks lattés can add up to $1,800/year.

CELL PHONE
A cell phone is a survival tool in college. The average cell phone bill is around $63/month.

CLOTHING
College is a chance to redefine oneself, to transform one's image, and of course, to get dates with style. To that end, college students spend around $750/year on new clothes.

GREEK DUES
Many students decide to join a fraternity or sorority to take advantage of the social life. Greek life isn't free however – dues can cost about $600/year.

ENTERTAINMENT
And where do they take all the new dates you meet at college? To the movies, concerts, plays, resturants, and on and on. In fact, the average college student spends around $4,000 per year on entertainment.

SPORTING EVENTS
Each year, college students throw on their face paint, don big foam fingers, and support their school at at least one sports game. The average cost of a college football game is around $50.

BOOKS AND SUPPLIES
The national average cost of books and class supplies for the 2010 – 2011 school year was $1,137.

FOOD
Of course, not every meal can be eaten on campus, especially with all those late nights exploring the new city. Assuming the student eats the majority of their meals on campus, extra food costs typically run around $750 per year.

COMPUTING COSTS
The average retail price of a new laptop for college is around $1700. This works out to about $425/year in computing costs.

LAB FEES
Most degrees require students to take at least one science class and/or art class. Lab fees for such classes typically run around $60/semester per class.

ROOM AND BOARD
Room and board fees cover the cost of on-campus housing and a meal plan for food served in the school cafeteria. In 2008 these costs stood around $7999/year average.

SPRING BREAK
If ever there was a reason to crack open beers at 9 AM on a beach, spring break at college is it. The average cost of a trip to any of the popular spring break destinations is $500.

TRANSPORATION
Between exploring their new city and traveling home on the holidays, students living on-campus from the 2010 - 2011 school year spent an average of $1,073 on transportation.

MUSIC ROOM
Students who take music classes need to rent practice rooms to rehearse. This generally costs about $75 per semester, depending on the school.

Sources: www.collegeboard.com | abcnews.go.com | walletpop.com | college.lovetoknow.com | collegeboard.com | youngadults.about.com | mainstreet.com | degreecentral.com | icsellinghope.com | campuscalm.com | blog.oregonlive.com

prices are sky-rocketing, leaving increasing numbers of college graduates in large amounts of debt—and without the employment opportunities to pay it back. Opponents of a "college education for all!" approach often cite statistics indicating that the gap in salaries between college and high school graduates is shrinking, while additional statistics suggest there are more college graduates than there are jobs requiring a college degree. Furthermore, say some critics, the myth that a diploma is necessary for successful entry into the job market diminishes opportunities for those equally capable but less officially "qualified" candidates. While few if any opponents would advocate for the complete abolition of the university system, they do argue that college degrees are appropriate mostly for the few, and not the many—and that a system that purports college to be the "be all and end all" of personal advancement is damaging to both individuals and society as a whole.

Not so fast, say others. Proponents of the college experience often discredit the statistics cited by naysayers. They argue that college graduates still consistently earn more than those who entered the work force immediately after high school, and that the employment sector maintains continual demand for those bearing a college degree. In fact, they say, more employers than ever require post-secondary degrees (whether two- or four-year) as a condition for consideration—a trend often attributed to technological advances and the concomitant need for employees to be educated in the use of those technologies. Then there are the social benefits derived from a college-educated population. "Individuals who have had the opportunity to go to college have a greater probability of having the resources to develop into productive and engaged citizens," says the Solutions for Our Future Project (an organization dedicated to educating the public about the social benefits of higher education). Meanwhile, the Policy Institute cautions that "while the costs incurred educating our society are enormous, and growing, we must be aware that the costs of failing to do so might be even greater."

Advocates for some form of middle ground assert that "degrees" and "education" are not necessarily the same thing. While *degrees* may not be worth the cost, the principle of *education* is—but in order to honor it, we need to change the system so that it focuses more on nurturing well-rounded individuals and less on churning out diplomas. Furthermore, say some, society should do away with funneling high school graduates directly into college regardless of interests or career aspirations. Instead, college should be approached on a case-by-case basis, pursued only if it enhances an individual's goals or is the necessary means to working in a particular career.

In this Issue in Focus, we present arguments that represent many of these divergent viewpoints. First, Anthony Carnevale argues in a January 2011 essay in *Inside Higher Ed* that college is still very much worth it, primarily from an economic perspective. Richard Vedder, an economist, counters Carnevale's arguments directly, asserting that college is not a wise investment for the majority of high school graduates. Clive Crook argues (in an essay first published in 2006 in the *Atlantic*) that education is important, but not a "cure-all" for the nation's various social and economic challenges. Finally, Gregory Kristof recommends another middle ground: taking a "gap year" off between high school and college.

Will a college degree be "worth it" in your life? As you read, pay attention not only to the claims that are made but also to *how* they are made: Do the articles cite statistics, and if so, how might this data be skewed or interpreted in ways that can support seemingly divergent arguments? Do you find statistical evidence to be more compelling than personal anecdotes, interviews with experts, or rhetorical reasoning? Should college's "worth" be based purely on the numbers, or does education offer more intangible (and perhaps even more important) benefits than can be captured by career statistics? Should everybody go to college, or should college be reserved for the few? Are there alternative paths to education that are just as viable and valid as college, or is a college degree, these days, a necessity? These are issues to confront as you contemplate the beginning of your college experience.

Anthony P. Carvenale

College Is Still Worth It

It's an old story: when economic downturns hit, unemployment rates spiral and tales of college graduates forced to tend bar or mop floors proliferate. So, too, do the assertions of experts and budget-constrained political leaders that young people don't need costly postsecondary education in a job market that has little use for college degrees.

Those who make the "skip college" argument [1] often bolster their arguments with official state and national Bureau of Labor Statistics (BLS) data suggesting that the U.S. higher education system has been turning out far more college grads than current or future job openings require.

To a public wary of paying steep tuition bills in a depressed economy, it all sounds alarming and—with the backing of national and state government BLS data—authoritative.

There's just one problem with the official BLS statistics: they're wrong.

BLS data assigns occupations a "required" education level. Their numbers assert that 16.6 percent of jobs, or nearly 25 million jobs, require a bachelor's; in reality, over 30.7 million jobs, or 20.4 percent are filled with workers who have a bachelor's.

The BLS also holds that 6.1 million jobs (4.1 percent) require an associate degree, when 14 million jobs across the economy are actually filled by those with associate-degree holders. The BLS data, therefore, imply that Americans are overeducated.

The most persuasive evidence that the BLS numbers are wrong are earnings data, which show that employers across the country pay a "wage premium" to college graduates, even in occupations that BLS does not consider "college" jobs. This simply means that businesses pay more money to workers with degrees than to those without because employers believe that postsecondary educated workers are more valuable.

And employers aren't just hiring degrees. Over the decades, this premium has ebbed and flowed, but the longer-term trend in demand for college graduates has risen

9   consistently. The college wage premium over high school graduates dropped significantly in the 1970s when vast numbers of college-educated Baby Boomers and males who went to college instead of Vietnam flooded the job market.

      When the baby boomers aged beyond their prime college age years and the Vietnam draft ended, most expected a plunge in college-going. The rate of college-going did fall off, but not nearly as much as most experts predicted. Instead, a sharp upswing in the demand for college-educated workers kept college enrollments growing. Moreover, since the early 1980s, college completion has been unable to keep pace with employer demand. As a result, the college wage premium over high school degrees skyrocketed from roughly 30 percent to 74 percent at present. Hardly a sign of an oversupply of college talent.

10   To dismiss the significance of wage data requires a belief that employers across the country have systematically hired overqualified workers for their job openings and then grossly overpaid them for the past three decades. Consider the implications: It would mean that employers followed the law of supply and demand in the 1970s by cutting back the wage premium, but completely cast it aside in subsequent years by inexplicably throwing extra money at college-educated workers.

11   It would mean that, by 2008, more than a *third* of all workers with postsecondary education were receiving an appreciable economic benefit from their degrees that reasonable employers should never have paid. In short, if all of this is true, then chaos reigns: economic markets don't work, employers are irrational, and preparing children for college is naive for all but a select few.

12   There is a better explanation for the puzzling official data that suggest we are producing too many college graduates.

OFFICIAL EDUCATION DEMAND NUMBERS HAVE SERIOUS FLAWS

13   Bureau of Labor Statistics data, as mentioned, underpin the argument that America overproduces college graduates by the millions. Among the chronically overqualified and overpaid are 43 percent of nuclear technicians who have attained more than the "required" associate degree, and the 80 percent of commercial pilots who hold more than their "required" certificate.

14   While we have high regard for the BLS, and believe that its national and state-level occupational and employment data are unimpeachable, we cannot say the same for its education numbers. They are an offhand byproduct of its other data—and of substantially lower quality.

15   One significant flaw in the BLS method is that it categorizes occupations as either "college" or "non-college," a methodology that is both subjective and static. A better approach, typical of mainstream economic analysis, is to track actual earnings of college graduates to determine the demand for postsecondary education. We reason that if the wages of college-educated workers within an occupation are high and/or rising relative to people with high school diplomas or less, that reflects a tangible advantage conferred by postsecondary education. People with college degrees in these occupations, therefore, are not overeducated because they are actually gaining value in return for their educational investment. While all degrees may not produce equal

returns, in virtually every case, the return is far greater than the cost of obtaining the diploma.

16   In contrast, we do not define the "college labor market" as the BLS does, with its set of "college" occupations that cover the traditional white-collar and professional jobs. The official BLS data assign an education level to an occupation based on the lowest level of education attainment necessary to access the occupation. This approach is remarkably static and fails to adjust to changing economic realities.

17   For one, it misses the shift toward increased postsecondary requirements within occupations that are not traditionally deemed "college jobs." Labor economists agree that there has been a consistent shift toward increased postsecondary requirements across a growing share of occupations that previously did not require two- or four-year college degrees. Examples in the white-collar world include increasing demand for college degrees among managers, health care workers, and a wide variety of office workers, from insurance agents to building inspectors. Examples in the blue- and pink-collar world include increasing degree requirements among production workers, health care technicians, and utility and transportation workers.

TECHNOLOGY DRIVES ONGOING DEMAND FOR BETTER-EDUCATED WORKERS

18   The standard explanation in the economic literature for such shifts is "skill-biased technology change." The core mechanism behind this concept in our current economy is the computer, which automates repetitive tasks and increases the relative value of non-repetitive tasks in individual occupations. Performing these more sophisticated tasks successfully typically requires more skill, training and education.

19   Wage data show that employers have tended to hire workers with postsecondary credentials for these more complex positions—and pay a wage premium to get them. As a result, we view a "college job" as any position that gives substantial earnings returns to a college degree, irrespective of occupation, whether an individual is an insurance agent or a rocket scientist.

20   Our method for tracking education demand is also careful to minimize counting statistical outliers such as bartenders, cab drivers and janitors with BAs and graduate degrees. These kinds of mismatches between degrees and low-skilled jobs—a phenomenon sometimes called "over-education"—are relatively small in number and don't matter much in an economy of nearly 150 million jobs. In addition, most such workers won't stay in those positions long-term. They eventually move on to better-paying jobs. Over a 10-year period, each cashier job has 13 incumbents who permanently leave the occupation; among medical doctors, that replacement rate is only one.

21   People rarely leave jobs that require a college education because they have the best earnings, benefits and working conditions. There are many more brain surgeons who used to be cashiers than there are cashiers who used to be brain surgeons. A brain surgeon never starts as a brain surgeon, but would have likely had all types of jobs before entering college and medical school. Most jobs people hold in high school are in retail, food services, and other low-skill, low-wage jobs, and future brain surgeons are no exception.

22   In addition, low-skill, non-college positions tend to be greatly overrepresented in the official jobs data because so many of them are part-time. Although low-wage, low-skill jobs make up 20 percent of all jobs in a single year, they only make up 14 percent of the hours worked. Jobs that require a BA or better make up 30 percent of all jobs, but 75 percent of those are full-time, full-year jobs, compared with 64 percent of jobs that require a high school diploma or less.

23   There are, then, a number of serious flaws with the BLS education demand numbers, ranging from the designation of college and non-college occupations to their failure to reflect rising education requirements across virtually every occupational category. Still, because the BLS has a stellar—and deserved—reputation for its employment data, its static and misleading metrics on education requirements are treated with undue credibility. BLS numbers are widely used by social scientists to gauge education demand, and yet their accuracy receives little serious scrutiny.

CENSUS NUMBERS OFFER VALUABLE TEST OF BLS EDUCATION DEMAND PROJECTIONS

24   As it turns out, though, there is an effective test to gauge the validity of education demand projections based on BLS data. The Census Bureau actually counts the number of workers with college degrees in the workforce and tracks their earnings on the job. As time passes and the Census data catch up with the BLS projections, we can determine if those projections were accurate. To get to the punch line: BLS projections always under-predict demand for college educations.

25   For instance, when we compare the BLS projections for 2006 and the actual count of people in the labor force with degrees during that year, we see that the Bureau undercounted the true number of postsecondary-educated workers by 17 million in 2006, or roughly 30 percent, and by 22 million, or 40 percent in 2008. The alternative method we introduced in Help Wanted [2] missed by just 4 percent.

26   The bottom line is that the BLS predictions didn't even come close to what actually happened in the economy. The only way to reconcile those projections with real life is to assert that the Bureau's projections reflect the number of college degrees employers actually *require,* not the actual numbers of college-educated workers they decide to hire. If this is the case, then employers not only hired millions of overqualified workers in 2006 and 2008, but paid wage premiums of more than 70 percent for the privilege—a notion, as we said earlier, that requires a belief that business owners across the nation and economic markets as a whole have taken leave of their senses.

SPATE OF MEDIA STORIES ON VALUE OF COLLEGE FUELS NEEDLESS FEARS

27   And yet, much of the media coverage of the issue would have us believe college isn't worth it.

28   Stories on the value of college tend to follow the business cycle, and when the cycle is down, journalists often find it easy to write a story that bucks the conventional wisdom. Headlines that suggest postsecondary education no longer pays off in the

labor market are news because they play into middle-class parents' fears that they will not be able to give their children the advantages they had. The bad advice gets more and more pointed as the recession deepens.

29   This year, the *New York Times* offered "Plan B: Skip College," while the *Washington Post* ran "Parents Crunch the Numbers and Wonder, Is College Still Worth It?" Even the *Chronicle of Higher Education* has succumbed, [3] recently running "Here's Your Diploma. Now Here's Your Mop."—a story about a college graduate working as a janitor that implies a college degree may not be worthwhile in today's economic climate.

30   And if college educated workers were overpaid by 75 percent and oversupplied by 40 percent, why wouldn't they be the first fired and last hired in these tough times? It is true that unemployment rates are relatively high among college grads. When it rains long enough and hard enough, everyone gets wet. But the unemployment rate for all workers with college degrees is a quarter the rate for high school graduates.

31   And it's true, as the *New York Times* pointed out in an editorial [4] on December 13, that the unemployment rate for freshly minted college grads was 9.2 percent, not much different from the 9.8 percent unemployment rate for all workers. But the *Times* didn't bother to mention that the unemployment rate for freshly minted high school graduates was 35 percent.

32   The current recession isn't the first to produce such gloom. The *New York Times* and other prominent newspapers were printing similar stories in the early 1980s, during the last severe recession. At that time, the *Times* ran headlines like "The Underemployed: Working for Survival Instead of Careers."

33   And it's not just the journalists who get gloomy. The *New York Times* quoted Ronald Kutscher, associate commissioner at the Bureau of Labor Statistics in 1984, as saying, "We are going to be turning out about 200,000 to 300,000 too many college graduates a year in the '80s." Yet the 1980s was a decade that saw an unprecedented rise in the wage premium for college-educated workers over high school-educated workers. The wage premium for college degrees over high school degrees increased from 30 percent to more than 80 percent—evidence that the postsecondary system was under-producing college graduates, not that, as Kutscher went on to say, "the supply far exceeds the demand."

34   The gloomy stories, the high unemployment among college graduates and the misleading official data are unlikely to keep many middle- and upper-class youth from going to college. Higher education is a value that such families are unlikely to abandon, regardless of economic pressures. Instead, the real tragedy of these headlines is the message they send to less privileged youth for whom college is not an assumed path. The negative press on college fuels pre-existing biases among working families that college is neither accessible nor worth the cost and effort. Moreover, the bad press and worse data strengthen the hand of elitists [5] who argue that college should be the exclusive preserve of those born into the right race, ethnicity and bank account.

35   It is important to note that current evidence demonstrates increasing demand for college graduates, and the future promises more of the same. By 2018, our own projections from the "Help Wanted" study show that 63 percent of jobs nationwide will

require some form of postsecondary degree. Moreover, postsecondary education has become the only way to secure middle-class earnings in America and, for the least advantaged among us, is now the only way to escape poverty. In 1970, about 60 percent of Americans who attained middle-class status were high school graduates or dropouts. Today, only 46 percent can be found there. In contrast, 44 percent of the top three income deciles had postsecondary education in 1970; today, 81 percent do.

36   The press coverage and expert stumbles don't reflect the empirical reality, but they are symptomatic of a mundane human instinct. People tend to project what's happening in the present into the distant future. If housing prices are great, they'll be that way forever! If job creation is slow, it will be that way forever! If college graduates have to work as bartenders in the depth of a recession, their degrees will never get them ahead! The reality is that jobs come and go with economic cycles. But what lies beneath the economic cycles, and what has remained constant, is the relentless engine of technological change that demands more skilled workers. There is no indication that the trend has suddenly reversed itself.

COLLEGE IS STILL THE BEST SAFE HARBOR IN BAD ECONOMIC TIMES

37 Meanwhile, when jobs disappear, college is the best safe harbor for waiting out the recession and improving your hiring prospects in anticipation of the recovery. Indeed, college-educated workers are much more likely to be employed than their high school-educated counterparts, even during a recession.

38   Irrespective of the current economic conditions, individuals need to consider college as a lifelong investment decision. Likewise, the investment horizon for economic development needs to be measured in decades, not annual budget cycles. Skipping or shortening college on the basis of a headline or even a few years of bad economic news is foolish for individuals whose careers will span 40 or more years of working life. On average, skipping an associate degree will cost a high school graduate half a million dollars in earnings, and skipping a bachelor's degree will cost $1 million in potential earnings over a lifetime.

39   Many argue that the value of college is declining as tuition rises. [6] However, while it is true that the sticker price cost of going to college has risen faster than the inflation rate, the college wage premium has risen even faster, both in terms of the cost of going to college and the inflation rate. The best measure of the value of college is the net present value of going to college. Here we discount the lifetime earnings by the real interest rate, and discount the principal and interest payments from taking out a college loan (a $60,000 loan). Once we've done that, the most accurate estimation of the average value of a college education over a high school education is still $1 million dollars (net present value).

40   Our own forthcoming research shows that we have under-produced college graduates by almost 10 million since 1983. We also find in Help Wanted that through 2018, at least three million jobs that require postsecondary education and training will be unfilled due to lack of supply. The share of jobs for those with a high school education or

less is shrinking. In 1973, high school graduates and dropouts accounted for 72 percent of jobs, while by 2007 it was 41 percent. The opposite has happened for those with at least some college: the share of jobs has increased from 28 percent in 1973 to 59 percent in 2007, and is projected to be 63 percent by 2018. Likewise, the share of national wage income from college-educated workers has increased from 38 percent to 73 percent since 1970, and there is every reason to believe that this trend will continue.

1   We believe there is no doubt about the requirements of our fast-approaching economic future: we need more college graduates, not fewer. But at the very time we need our higher-education system to kick into high gear, it is under pressure to apply the brakes instead.

2   While the economics of higher education are clear, the politics are not. The economy's lackluster demand in recession, coupled with media stories questioning the value of college, makes it easier to excuse cuts in public funding for postsecondary education. In the short term, federal stimulus funds have helped fill the gaps for postsecondary cuts driven by declining state revenues. But the stimulus funds will be unavailable after 2011, and federal money can't make up the difference indefinitely. In fact, it's an easy target for the chopping block. Higher education is especially vulnerable in the debate about public priorities because it lacks the core constituency and the immediacy of such issues as Social Security or homeland security.

3   Still, it's clear that reducing funding for postsecondary education is both bad economic and social policy. The consequences of slashing higher education budgets is a decision that will effect inequality for the next several decades by determining who gets access to middle-class careers. And, slowing the stream of college graduates into the economy threatens to leave employers without the skilled workers they need to thrive in a fiercely competitive economy.

4   While doubts about spending on higher education are understandable in the depths of a catastrophic recession, the potential consequences of succumbing to gloom and relying on flawed data to inform decisions about the value of postsecondary education are ruinous.

5   Bad numbers on the economic value of college encourage disinvestment in college both by individuals and government. And disinvestment in higher education is bad news not only for our higher education system, but for our economy—and for the lives and futures of millions of Americans.

LINKS

1. http://www.nebhe.org/2010/11/30/the-real-education-crisis-are-35-of-all-college-degrees-in-new-england-unnecessary/
2. http://cew.georgetown.edu/jobs2018/
3. http://chronicle.com/article/Heres-Your-Diploma-Now/124982/
4. http://www.nytimes.com/2010/12/14/opinion/14tue1.html
5. http://www.aei.org/article/101207
6. http://www.insidehighered.com/news/2008/04/07/miller ∎

Richard Vedder

For Many, College Isn't Worth It

I n this space last Friday, Anthony Carnevale strongly and lengthily argued [1] that "college is still worth it." He implicitly criticized those, including me [2], who rely on U.S. Bureau of Labor Statistics (BLS) data showing that the number of college graduates exceeds the number of available jobs that require a college degree. While he says many things, he has two main points. First, "There's just one problem with the official BLS statistics: they're wrong." Second, he notes that "the most persuasive evidence that the BLS numbers are wrong are earnings data which show employers across the country pay a 'wage premium' for college graduates. . . ."

2   I will argue that the BLS data are, in fact, pretty good, and that while Carnevale is factually correct about the earnings data, his interpretation of it is, at the minimum, misleading. Moreover, I will further argue that what is involved here is a classic application of what economists over the age of 50 call "Say's Law" (i.e., the theory suggesting that supply creates its own demand; economists under 50 are largely ignorant of it because they have no knowledge of the evolution of their own discipline, reflecting the general abandonment of thorough teaching of the history of economic thought).

3   Furthermore, I will argue that diplomas are a highly expensive and inefficient screening device used by employers who are afraid to test potential employee skills owing to a most unfortunate Supreme Court decision and related legislation. Finally, I will assert that Carnevale and others who argue "college has a high payoff" are comparing apples with oranges—i.e., they are making totally inappropriate comparisons that lead to skewed conclusions.

4   An even-handed interpretation of the data is that college *is* "worth it" for some significant number of young people, but is a far more problematic investment for others. The call by President Obama, the Lumina and Gates Foundations, and many higher education advocates to rapidly and radically increase the number of college graduates is fundamentally off-base.

THE BLS DATA

5   Carnevale essentially argues that the BLS data are pretty bad, mainly because earnings data show that employers pay workers with college degrees a wage premium, which would be irrational if the education associated with a college degree were not valuable for the job in question. Indeed, "a better approach" to this question, according to Carnevale, would be "to track actual earnings of college graduates to determine the demand for postsecondary education." Additionally, Carnevale accurately notes that there are some variations within skills required within some of the BLS occupational categories, and it is possible that for some jobs a college degree would be necessary or highly desirable, while for others it would not be.

6   However, Carnevale's overall description of the BLS data and its system for categorizing education requirements is far from accurate. For instance, Carnevale blandly

declares that "[t]he official BLS data assign an education level to an occupation based on the lowest level of education attainment necessary to access the occupation." Actually, as the BLS makes quite clear on its website [3], it "assign[s] what [its] research suggests was the most significant source of education or training" for each occupation. (Apparently Carnevale confuses a proposed change to the BLS category system—and one which isn't going to be implemented [4] at that—with the system currently in place.) Furthermore, the BLS also noted that its data do in some cases understate educational requirements, but in others they overstate it, suggesting that, in the aggregate, the BLS data can be viewed as reasonably sound.

Another problem with Carnevale's critique of the BLS data is that, in reality, the BLS dataset is arguably superior to that developed by Carnevale and his colleagues. This point was made a couple of months ago by Paul E. Harrington and Andrew M. Sum [5] when they observed that taking Carnevale's approach "assumes a world where no under-employment or mal-employment of college graduates exists." On the other hand, the BLS dataset is robust enough to account for underemployment, albeit perhaps imperfectly.

Carnevale's criticism of the BLS data is nothing, however, compared to that of Cliff Adelman of the Institute for Higher Education policy, who, in commenting on Carnevale's article, said "the base data are bizarre," claiming the statistics misrepresented the numbers in some occupations (he focused on solar panel installers and like occupations) by a huge magnitude. Adelman simply misread the data—badly—as Carnevale himself has indicated in a response.

Before turning to Carnevale's earnings-based argument, I want to comment on his remark about "statistical outliers such as bartenders, cab drivers and janitors with B.A.s and graduate degrees. . . . These kinds of mismatches between degrees and low-skilled jobs . . . are relatively small in number and don't matter much. . . . "

Hogwash. The BLS tells us that for waiters and waitresses alone, there are more than one-third of a million who hold B.A. degrees or more—not an inconsequential number. And the BLS data would indicate that, *in total*, about 17 million college graduates have jobs that do not require a college degree. Not only is that 11 percent or so of the total labor force, hardly a "relatively small" number, but, more relevantly, it constitutes well over 30 percent of the working college graduates in the U.S. —a number of mammoth proportions.

Carnevale argues that a large portion of these persons are short-term in these jobs, and that they typically move on into more appropriate jobs later on. I am the first to admit the turnover rate of waiters is greater than that of physicians, but so what? If roughly one-third of college graduates in general are in jobs not requiring college-level training, that is far more than frictional unemployment—workers temporarily taking a low paying job while awaiting more permanent employment. And that certainly is not simply a function of the recession, although that phenomenon no doubt has aggravated the problem.

THE EARNINGS DATA

Carnevale is absolutely correct that college graduates on average earn more than those with lesser formal educational certifications. And I would agree that on average college graduates have a higher productivity per worker (justifying the higher pay) than those merely possessing high school diplomas. Therefore, for many, going to college is a good personal investment decision.

13   But to a considerable extent, the reason college graduates have higher pay has little to do with what they learned in college *per se*. Suppose an employer has two applicants, who in personal interviews seemed similar in quality. The employer likely will choose the college graduate over the high school graduate because, on average, college graduates have higher levels of cognitive skills (as measured by IQ tests or similar instruments), are more likely to have relatively high levels of motivation and discipline developed before attending college, have more general knowledge about the world in which we live, etc. Hence such employees are often offered a wage premium, since the anticipated level of performance of the college graduate is perceived to be higher. The diploma serves as a screening device that allows businesses to narrow down the applicant pool quickly and almost without cost to the employer, but with a huge financial cost to the individual earning the diploma (often at least $100,000), and to society at large in the form of public subsidies.

14   For the past several decades, moreover, the ability of employers to find other means of certifying competence and skills has been severely circumscribed by judicial decisions and laws. In *Griggs v. Duke Power* (1971), the U.S. Supreme Court essentially outlawed employer testing of prospective workers where the test imparted a "disparate impact" on members of minority groups. Cautious employers have sharply reduced such testing, and are now forced to rely on other measures of competence, namely the possession of a college diploma.

15   This perception that college is primarily a screening device rather than the source of a true vocationally relevant curriculum is supported by a good deal of data that show college students spend relatively little time in academic studies (e.g., the Time Use Survey [6] data of the BLS). The most notable recent effort, utilizing detailed data from the National Survey of Student Engagement, is examined in Richard Arum and Josipa Roksa's new book *Academically Adrift: Limited Learning on College Campuses* [7], just released by the University of Chicago Press. "How much are students actually learning in contemporary higher education? The answer for many undergraduates, we have concluded, is not much," write Arum and Roksa.

SAY'S LAW AND CREDENTIAL INFLATION

16   The economist Jean Baptiste Say, writing in 1803, formulated his "law of markets," which can be roughly summarized as: "supply creates its own demand." In the context of American higher education, colleges have supplied millions of graduates over recent decades—more than needed to fill jobs that historically have been considered ones requiring the skills associated with a college education. Therefore, employers are flooded with applicants who possess college degrees, and given the inherently better character and intellectual traits that college graduates on average have, the employers demand a diploma for a job. The rise in the supply of diplomas created the demand for them, not the other way around.

17   Jobs that have not changed much over time, such as serving as a mail carrier or restaurant manager, now have large numbers of college graduates filling them, relative to the past. This is almost certainly mainly a manifestation of what might be termed

"credential inflation." To be sure, the quality of high school graduates may have declined over time somewhat owing to the mediocre state of our public schools, but it is hard to believe this is important in explaining the rise in, say, college-educated mail carriers.

APPLES AND ORANGES: RISK-TAKING IN ATTENDING COLLEGE

18 A huge problem in any analysis such as that performed by Carnevale is that it ignores the vast number of students who enter college and do not complete a degree. While I am the first to admit there are some problems with the underlying IPEDS data used to measure dropout rates, it is probably nonetheless true that at least two out of every five persons entering college full-time fail to graduate within *six* years. There is a huge risk associated with enrolling in college: you might not graduate. A person considering a $100,000 investment in 1,000 shares of XYZ Corporation common stock at $100 a share is assured that he or she will have those 1,000 shares, although there are some risks associated with the shares declining in value over time. A person making a $100,000 investment in a B.A. degree is *not* assured that he or she will obtain the investment—i.e., actually graduate in a timely fashion.

19 For years, economists have written that the rate of return on college investments tends to be high—10 percent is an oft-cited estimate, greater than the average investor is likely to earn in alternatives such as stocks, bonds or real estate. Thus the studies have concluded that going to college typically makes sense, independent of any non-pecuniary advantages college offers. Yet these studies have failed to account for the added risk associated with it—the probability of dropping out.

20 Two new studies have attempted to correct for this problem, one by Gonzalo Castex and the other by Kartik Athreya and Janice Eberly [8]. They suggest that the reported superior rate of return on investing in college disappears when investments are adjusted for risk.

21 At the individual student level, it is possible to reasonably estimate the risk. A student who was at the top of her class at a top-flight suburban high school, had a composite SAT score of 1500, and plans to attend a private college with relatively low dropout rates is probably going to get a reasonable return on her investment, although even that is no certainty. By contrast, a student who is below average in his graduating class from a mediocre high school, has a combined SAT score of 850, and is considering a college with high dropout rates is very likely not to graduate even in six years, and probably will get a very low return on his college investment. That student might well do much better by going to a certificate program at a career college, learning to be a truck driver, or becoming a barber, for example.

22 In short, a good maxim is "different strokes for different folks." A one-size-fits-all solution does not work as long as human beings have vastly different aptitudes, skills, motivations, etc. On balance, we are probably over-invested in higher education, not under-invested. The earnings data reflect less about human capital accumulation imparted to college graduates by their collegiate experiences than the realities of information costs associated with job searches.

23 With fewer public subsidies of higher education, I suspect much or all of the problem would disappear: College enrollments would reach levels consistent with the needs of our economy and the personal economic welfare of those attending.

LINKS

1. http://www.insidehighered.com/views/2011/01/14/
   carnevale_college_is_still_worth_it_for_americans
2. http://collegeaffordability.blogspot.com/search/label/underemployment
3. http://www.bls.gov/emp/ep_education_tech.htm
4. http://www.bls.gov/emp/ep_propedtrain.htm
5. http://www.nebhe.org/2010/11/08/college-labor-shortages-in-2018/
6. http://www.bls.gov/tus/charts/students.htm
7. http://www.insidehighered.com/news/2011/01/18/
   study_finds_large_numbers_of_college_students_don_t_learn_much
8. http://www.aeaweb.org/aea/2011conference/program/preliminary.php?search_
   string=eberly&search_type=last_name&search=Search ■

...FOR THE NEXT THIRTY YEARS

Clive Crook

A Matter of Degrees: Why College Is Not an Economic Cure-All

It is unusual nowadays to venture more than five minutes into any debate about the American economy—about widening income inequality, say, or threats to the country's global competitiveness, or the squeeze on the middle class—without somebody invoking the great economic cure-all: education. We must improve it. For a moment, partisan passions subside and everybody nods.

2   But only for a moment. How, exactly, do we improve education? Where does the problem reside—in elementary schools, high schools, or colleges? Is the answer to recruit better teachers, or to get more students moving from high school to university? Should we spend more public money? Change the way schools are organized and paid for (supporting charter schools and vouchers, perhaps)? In no time, correctly orthogonal positions are laid down, and the quarreling resumes. But nobody challenges the importance of the issue. The centrality of education as a driver of the nation's economic prospects appears beyond dispute.

3   Yet the connections between education and economics are not as they seem. To rest the case for improving schools and colleges largely on economic grounds is a mistake. It distorts education policy in unproductive ways. And though getting education right surely matters, more is at stake than a slight increase in economic growth.

4   Everybody understands that, as a rule of thumb, more school means a bigger paycheck. On average, having a college degree, rather than just a high-school degree, increases your earnings by about two-thirds. A problem arises, however, if you try to gross up these gains across the whole population. If an extra year of education equipped students with skills that increased their productivity, then giving everybody another year of school or college would indeed raise everybody's income. But take the extreme case, and suppose that the extra year brought no gain in productive skills. Suppose it merely sorted people, signaling "higher ability" to a would-be employer. Then giving an extra year of school to everybody would raise nobody's income, because nobody's position in the ordering would change. The private benefit of more education would remain, but the social benefit would be zero.

5   Would sending everybody to Harvard raise everybody's future income by the full amount of the "Harvard premium"? Yes, if the value of a degree from Harvard resided in the premium skills you acquired there (and if the college's classrooms could be scaled up a little). Well, ask any Harvard graduate about the teaching. The value of a degree from Harvard lies mainly in the sorting that happens during the application process. So the answer is no: if everybody went to Harvard, the Harvard premium would collapse.

6   In the case of an extra year of education, it need not be all or nothing; another year of study usually does impart *some* productivity-enhancing skill. But how much? A year of extra training in computer programming presumably has a direct material value. An extra year spent learning medieval history might improve a student's intellectual self-discipline and ability to think analytically, but has lower material utility: nobody studies feudal land grants for the boost to lifetime earnings. So aggregated figures such as the proportion of high-school graduates going on to college—a number that is constantly cited and compared internationally—tell you very little.

7   Totting up college matriculations as a way of measuring national success is doubly ill-conceived if the signaling function flips over, so that a college education becomes the norm, and college nonattendance is taken to mean "unfit for most jobs."

8   In 2004, 67 percent of American high-school graduates went straight on to college, compared with just under half in 1972. This is widely applauded. It looks like progress—but is it really? Failing to go to college did not always mark people out as rejects, unfit for any kind of well-paid employment. But now, increasingly, it does. In a

cruel paradox, this may be one reason why parental incomes better predict children's incomes in the United States than they used to—in other words, one reason why America is becoming less meritocratic. A college degree has become an expensive passport to good employment, one for which drive and ability less often can substitute, yet one that looks unaffordable to many poor families.

9   Many occupations are suffering from chronic entry-requirement inflation. Hotels, for instance, used to appoint junior managers from among the more able, energetic, and presentable people on their support or service staff, and give them on-the-job training. Today, according to the Bureau of Labor Statistics, around 800 community and junior colleges offer two-year associate degrees in hotel management. In hotel chains, the norm now is to require a four-year bachelor's or master's degree in the discipline.

10   For countless other jobs that once required little or no formal academic training—preschool teacher, medical technician, dental hygienist, physical-therapy assistant, police officer, paralegal, librarian, auditor, surveyor, software engineer, financial manager, sales manager, and on and on—employers now look for a degree. In some of these instances, in some jurisdictions, the law requires one. All of these occupations are, or soon will be, closed to nongraduates. At the very least, some of the public and private investment in additional education needs to be questioned.

11   To be sure, today's IT-driven world is creating a genuine need for some kinds of better-educated workers. It is the shortage of such people, according to most politicians and many economists, that is causing the well-documented rise in income inequality. Both to spur the economy and to lessen inequality, they argue, the supply of college graduates needs to keep rising.

12   It seems plausible, but this theory too is often overstated, and does not fit the facts particularly well. The college wage premium rose rapidly for many years, up to the late 1990s. Since then it has flattened off, just when the pace of innovation would have led you to expect a further acceleration. An even more awkward fact is that especially in the past decade or so, rising inequality has been driven by huge income increases at the very top of the distribution. In the wide middle, where differences in educational attainment ought to count, changes in relative earnings have been far more subdued. During the 1990s, CEO salaries roughly doubled in inflation-adjusted terms. But median pay actually went up more slowly than pay at the bottom of the earnings distribution, and even pay at the 90th percentile (highly educated workers, mostly, but not CEOs) increased only a little faster than median wages. Today, shortages of narrowly defined skills *are* apparent in specific industries or parts of industries—but simply pushing more students through any kind of college seems a poorly judged response.

13   The country will continue to need cadres of highly trained specialists in an array of technical fields. In many cases, of course, the best place to learn the necessary skills will be a university. For many and perhaps most of us, however, university education is not mainly for acquiring directly marketable skills that raise the nation's productivity. It is for securing a higher ranking in the labor market, and for cultural and intellectual enrichment. Summed across society, the first of those purposes cancels out. The second does not. That is why enlightenment, not productivity, is the chief social justification for four years at college.

14   Shoving ever more people from high school to college is not only of dubious economic value, it is unlikely to serve the cause of intellectual enrichment if the new students are reluctant or disinclined. Yet there are still large prizes to be had through educational reform—certainly in enlightenment and perhaps in productivity. They simply lurk farther down the educational ladder.

15   The most valuable attribute for young people now entering the workforce is adaptability. This generation must equip itself to change jobs readily, and the ability to retrain, whether on the job or away from the job, will be crucial. The necessary intellectual assets are acquired long before college, or not at all. Aside from self-discipline and the capacity to concentrate, they are preeminently the core-curriculum skills of literacy and numeracy.

16   Illiteracy has always cut people off from the possibility of a prosperous life, from the consolations of culture, and from full civic engagement. In the future, as horizons broaden for everybody else, people lacking these most basic skills will seem even more imprisoned. The most recent National Assessment of Adult Literacy found that 30 million adult Americans have less than basic literacy (meaning, for instance, that they find it difficult to read mail, or address an envelope). Three out of ten seniors in public high schools still fail to reach the basic-literacy standard. Progress on literacy would bring great material benefits, of course, for the people concerned and some benefits for the wider economy—but those benefits are not the main reason to make confronting illiteracy the country's highest educational priority.

17   In addressing the nation's assorted economic anxieties—over rising inequality, the stagnation of middle-class incomes, and the fading American dream of economic opportunity—education is not the longed-for cure-all. Nor is anything else. The debate about these issues will have to range all across the more bitterly disputed terrains of public policy—taxes, public spending, health care, and more. It is a pity, but in the end a consensus that blinds itself to the complexity of the issues is no use to anyone. ∎

Gregory Kristof

On the Ground with a "Gap Year"

I t took place on a frosty peak tucked away in the Tibetan highlands: my friend Rick and I walked in on a group of monks as they were on their knees, groaning.

2   They were performing secret rituals involving yak butter.

3   Peeking out from behind animal fur curtains, Rick and I hoped that they hadn't noticed us yet. They hummed and sat in rows facing a stage of yak butter candles that threw images against the walls like kicked hacky sacks. Back in the shadows, I worried: What would happen if they saw two white dudes chillin' behind the furs?

4   "Pssst," Rick said. "I think we should leave."

5   "Let's make for the door." I said.

6   I flattened myself against the back of the room, inching toward the door. Take it slow, I told myself. Don't drag your feet. Hurry up! I just had a few more feet to go. Two steps to go. Wow, I would make a great spy.

7   One step. And then—right as I was considering tacking on two zeros to the front of my name—ZINGZAMEMEM-BzerrBzerrBzerr . . .

8   I know, my ringtone sucks. Eyes caved in on me. I sort of just lay there on the dirt floor, not moving much, just looking up sporadically at the curious faces, and feeling sorry that I had disrupted their ritual. And yet I felt warm inside because I was here, getting caught in a mountain temple by Buddhist monks, and not where I shoulda-coulda-woulda been: listening to a PowerPoint lecture in a Boston classroom.

9   My decision to defer college for a year wasn't easy. In my New York high-school, nearly every kid treads the usual path from graduation to college. Upon hearing that I would hop off the traditional academic bandwagon, some teachers, friends, and other parents would respond with "That sounds great!" while murmuring comforting remarks that I would probably turn out ok.

10   I was extremely excited about college, so it was tough to say "Not this time" to the bounty of friends and general awesomeness that my Freshman year would most assuredly bring me.

11   But I remember thinking how most of my great high school memories were localized capsules, like dots on paper waiting to be connected. A great weekend here, a good report card there. It was only when I extracted myself from each individual moment that I would realize that the damn picture still wouldn't come into focus. Where was I going? Where did I want to go?

12   I wanted more. I wanted to see how the other half lived, to learn the things that weren't found in books, to live a phantasmagoria of unforgettable experiences. I wanted to experience a life in which images glided by like kangaroos on rollerblades.

13   So I went to China. So far, I've rock-climbed above Buddhist grottos, showered in underground waterfalls, squeaked my way across 13th century temples hanging halfway up cliffs, and stayed in earthquake-ravaged villages where everyone still dwells in tents. In a one-street town whose sole cab driver appeared to be blind, Rick and I went deep inside one of the world's most dazzling monasteries to party with monks (the scene was about as bangin' as what you'd expect from a group of pacifists). I've motorcycled across a frozen holy lake in the Himalayas, and I've stared into giant volcano pits on the North Korean border.

14   Not all of this was safe and rosy. Rick and I spent one night fending off wild dogs with a metal bar and headlamp, after escaping from the clutches of a hawk-nosed Tibetan with a few loose screws. We finally found a place to stay (by barging into a man's tent at 5 a.m. and striking a deal with him to spend the night), but still, the Himalayan winter nearly turned us into popsicles.

15   I even learned the in's and out's of the squat toilet. Do not sink too low when you squat. Trust me.

16   And while we are on the subject of appropriate dinner table conversation, let me warn you never to pee into a strong oncoming Tibetan wind. Unless you are seeking a novel and roundabout face-washing technique. Believe me, it happened.

So if you are willing to unrut your wheels, if you enjoy hopscotching through the world of motorcycles and open prairie, or if you're just searching for that extra boost to send yourself hurtling down a road less traveled, then perhaps a year abroad is right for you. Think about it in particular if you're going to study a language in college: why pay expensive tuition to learn Spanish in the States when you can learn it more thoroughly and cheaply in Bolivia?

Even a gap year's undesired moments can have a palliative benefit. Setting off for remote mountain villages, only to discover that they have been utterly abandoned; triumphantly finding a town's only bathroom, only to discover that the mud you are now standing in is not actually mud; these are the curve balls that keep you on your toes, that preserve in your life what remains of childhood spontaneity.

A gap year is a larky way to mature out of youth. But if you do it right, it's also a way to keep it.

I nearly forgot to mention that the original purpose of traveling to China was to bolster my Chinese at Tsinghua University in Beijing. Thanks to its great program, as well as the superb Ruiwen school in Dalian, I'm now fluent. But talent in Chinese doesn't compare with talent in analyzing terrain for wild dog hangouts, or with kaleidoscopic memories that will refract experiences for a lifetime.

So, graduating seniors, now's the time to search the Web for travel abroad programs. Check out Global Citizen Year for a mini peace corps experience. If you're less interested in a formal program, just do what I did: sign up for a foreign language school and book a flight. Because of the dollar's purchasing power, travel in China is very cheap—a rebuttal to those who think gap years are only for rich kids. I hope you choose to defer enrollment for one year, and I hope that your gap year, like mine, goes wrong in all the right ways.

When college does roll around, you'll already have gone through your own freshman orientation. After getting lost in a remote village because I was seeking a familiar temple but was approaching it from a completely different direction, I learned that where you are going is not all that matters. Where you are coming from matters, too.

It's like this: Spend time huddling for candle warmth on the Tibetan Plateau, and the C in physics ain't gonna seem so harsh.

Eventually the dots begin to connect themselves. That's when I discovered that I got more than what I'd bargained for. I initially wanted simply to get a sense of where I was headed for the next few years. But the poverty I encountered in western China irrevocably challenged me. I felt, on the most profound of levels, the realness of others. I became just one person among very, very many. Especially since I was in China.

Speaking of melting into the background, that was exactly my wish that evening when my friend and I got caught in the temple.

"I'm just a traveler," I said. After an ungolden silence, a monk stepped forward: "Come eat with us."

Rick and I spent the rest of that evening under a temple rooftop somewhere among the Himalayan foothills—I couldn't find the place now. We and the incredibly hospitable monks traded stories and cheers over yak meat, yak cheese, and yak butter tea well past my bedtime.

Who says you need a classroom for an education? ■

FROM READING TO WRITING

1. There are two explicit rebuttals in this chapter: Gerald Bracey refutes Margaret Spellings, and Richard Vedder answers the argument of Anthony Carnevale. Find an essay in a local publication that is related to education issues and that you disagree with, and then compose a rebuttal. (Consult Chapter 12 on writing a rebuttal.)

2. Gregory Kristof concludes this chapter with an argument that depends on personal experience. Write a narrative of your own experiences that supports your point of view about a specific educational practice or policy. (For more on narrative arguments, see Chapter 11.)

3. Evaluate some policy or practice related to education in your community; it could concern a teacher, an academic department, the food, Greek life, admissions practices, tuition rates, or anything else. Be sure to base your evaluation on specific criteria, such as those described in Chapter 10.

4. This book reproduces an ad from Hofstra University related to education (see Chapter 6). Locate other ads for colleges (in magazines, newspapers, or college Web sites), and analyze the nature of the arguments presented. How do those ads present and support their arguments? Look carefully as well at the cartoons in this chapter: what specific arguments are offered in those cartoons, and what good reasons are offered in support?

5. Education arguments frequently depend on definitions. "Higher education is nothing but a big business," someone might say, for example. Or "Liberal arts education is turning into vocational education." Compose your own argument that redefines some concept or topic related to education—high school or college sports, for example; or Greek life; or charter schools, or whatever. (For advice on definition arguments, see Chapter 8.)

6. Imagine that Ralph Waldo Emerson and W. E. B. Dubois were involved in a conversation about the nature and goals of education. Judging from the essays by those two thinkers that are reproduced in this chapter, do you think they would have any areas of agreement, any common ground? And what issues would separate them?

7. Would you say that a particular school or university that you are familiar with has markedly improved or deteriorated over the years? If so, what caused that advance or decline? (For advice on causal arguments, see Chapter 9.)

24 | Globalization: Importing and Exporting America

America meets the world as the iconic golden arches mix with Japanese characters at the world's busiest McDonald's restaurant in Tokyo. Is the world becoming more like America, or is America becoming more global?

America's Place in the World—and the World's Place in America

The place of America and Americans in relation to the rest of the world has always been an important topic in the national conversation. A product itself of globalization (embodied in the figure of Christopher Columbus) and created through the force of European colonialism, the United States has taken an increasing role in international affairs since its founding. But globalization has only grown more important, it seems, since the end of the Cold War (which seemed to leave the United States as the world's only superpower); since the development of economic reforms in China, in the European Union, and in other parts of the world (which are challenging the primacy of American economic power); and especially since the events of September 11, 2001, and the subsequent war in Iraq (which have compromised our will to work cooperatively with traditional allies). Indeed, according to a survey released on August 18, 2004, by the Pew Research Center for the People and the Press, the American public has a divided, even paradoxical opinion about the place of the United States in the world. On the one hand, Americans agree that the United States has assumed a more powerful role as a world leader, but, on the other hand, they concede that America also seems less respected around the world. Americans reject the role of the United States as a single world leader, but they also reject the pull toward isolation. More generally, then, Americans are confronting the issue of what has come to be known as globalization—that is, the general impact of various nations on each other and more particularly the impact of American culture on other nations and cultures, and their impact on the United States.

Some of that impact is economic, as the United States outsources manufacturing jobs to other nations, shifts in the direction of a service economy, and exports its ideologies (e.g., representative democracy, women's rights, resistance to sweatshop labor, pluralistic religious tolerance). Other effects are military and political, as leaders and citizens debate the wisdom of various options. (For example, should our nation behave as a kind of American empire, free to impose its wishes and will on others? Should our foreign policy be an effort to export democracy, even at the point of a gun? Or should we cooperate more broadly with allies, cultivate new friends, and respect the right of each nation to self-determination? Should the United States close off its borders, literally and figuratively, to follow a kind of neo-isolationism?) Yet other effects are broadly cultural, as Americans import some of the cultural practices and values of others (as in popular songs, films, restaurants, fashions, and so forth) and export our own cultural values and traditions to others. This chapter offers arguments about one or another aspect of these questions related to globalization.

Workers at a call center in New Delhi, India, take a break between calls.

Contemporary Arguments

The arguments in this chapter focus on the exchange of capital and cultural goods between the United States and other nations. Todd Gitlin's essay uses iconic American cultural signs to argue that the global village today has a distinctly American flavor—though that flavor blends and changes in its new environments. In an essay about Walmart and Mexico, Laura Carlsen (a long-time student of the economic effects of American business on Mexican life) discusses her concern about the broader impact of American economic power on the cultures of other nations. Thomas Friedman explains approvingly the new "flat world" that globalization is creating. Richard Florida counters Friedman by arguing that the world is actually not "flat" but "spiky." Robyn Meredith and Suzanne Hoppough tout the economic benefits of globalization in a way that counters Carlsen. And Sadanand Dhume interprets the Best Picture of 2008, *Slumdog Millionaire*, as the product of a thoroughly globalized mentality and "a metaphor for India in the age of globalization."

While the topics discussed in this chapter are varied, all of the readings bring up similar questions about the movement between cultures—of people, goods, values, images, and communication. Those questions come together in the Issue in Focus, on the topic of immigration. What are the effects of globalization? What do you think about American importation of cultural forms from other nations? What about exportation of American culture that is welcomed—even sought out—by people in other nations? Is this importation and exportation dangerous, enriching, or some complicated mixture of the two?

Todd Gitlin

Under the Sign of Mickey Mouse & Co.

Todd Gitlin is a professor of journalism and sociology at Columbia University. A leading and longtime culture critic who writes for a variety of publications (including *Mother Jones*, a popular magazine with a left-of-center appeal, especially to younger readers), he has received several prestigious grants and fellowships, including one from the MacArthur Foundation. His books include *Media Unlimited: How the Torrent of Images and Sounds Overwhelms Our Lives* (2002), *Letters to a Young Activist* (2003), and *The Bulldozer and the Big Tent: Blind Republicans, Lame Democrats, and the Recovery of American Ideals* (2007). The selection below comes from the last chapter of *Media Unlimited*.

Everywhere, the media flow defies national boundaries. This is one of its obvious, but at the same time amazing, features. A global torrent is not, of course, the master metaphor to which we have grown accustomed. We're more accustomed to Marshall McLuhan's *global village*. Those who resort to this metaphor casually often forget that if the world is a global village, some live in mansions on the hill, others in huts. Some dispatch images and sounds around town at the touch of a button; others collect them at the touch of *their* buttons. Yet McLuhan's image reveals an indispensable half-truth. If there is a village, it speaks American. It wears jeans, drinks Coke, eats at the golden arches, walks on swooshed shoes, plays electric guitars, recognizes Mickey Mouse, James Dean, E.T., Bart Simpson, R2-D2, and Pamela Anderson.

2   At the entrance to the champagne cellar of Piper-Heidsieck in Reims, in eastern France, a plaque declares that the cellar was dedicated by Marie Antoinette. The tour is narrated in six languages, and at the end you walk back upstairs into a museum featuring photographs of famous people drinking champagne. And who are they?

AISLIN
THE GAZETTE
Montreal
CANADA

Aislin/Cartoonists & Writers Syndicate

Perhaps members of today's royal houses, presidents or prime ministers, economic titans or Nobel Prize winners? Of course not. They are movie stars, almost all of them American—Marilyn Monroe to Clint Eastwood. The symmetry of the exhibition is obvious, the premise unmistakable: Hollywood stars, champions of consumption, are the royalty of this century, more popular by far than poor doomed Marie.

3   Hollywood is the global cultural capital—capital in both senses. The United States presides over a sort of World Bank of styles and symbols, an International Cultural Fund of images, sounds, and celebrities. The goods may be distributed by American-, Canadian-, European-, Japanese-, or Australian-owned multinational corporations, but their styles, themes, and images do not detectably change when a new board of directors takes over. Entertainment is one of America's top exports. In 1999, in fact, film, television, music, radio, advertising, print publishing, and computer software together *were* the top export, almost $80 billion worth, and while software alone accounted for $50 billion of the total, some of that category also qualifies as entertainment—video games and pornography, for example. Hardly anyone is exempt from the force of American images and sounds. French resentment of Mickey Mouse, Bruce Willis, and the rest of American civilization is well known. Less well known, and rarely acknowledged by the French, is the fact that *Terminator 2* sold 5 million tickets in France during the month it opened—with no submachine guns at the heads of the customers. The same culture minister, Jack Lang, who in 1982 achieved a moment of predictable notoriety in the United States for declaring that *Dallas* amounted to cultural imperialism, also conferred France's highest honor in the arts on Elizabeth Taylor and Sylvester Stallone. The point is not hypocrisy pure and simple but something deeper, something obscured by a single-minded emphasis on American power: dependency. American popular culture is the nemesis that hundreds of millions—perhaps billions—of people love, and love to hate. The antagonism and the dependency are inseparable, for the media flood—essentially American in its origin, but virtually unlimited in its reach—represents, like it or not, a common imagination.

4   How shall we understand the Hong Kong T-shirt that says "I Feel Coke"? Or the little Japanese girl who asks an American visitor in all innocence, "Is there really a Disneyland in America?" (She knows the one in Tokyo.) Or the experience of a German television reporter sent to Siberia to film indigenous life, who after flying out of Moscow and then traveling for days by boat, bus, and jeep, arrives near the Arctic Sea where live a tribe of Tungusians known to ethnologists for their bearskin rituals. In the community store sits a grandfather with his grandchild on his knee. Grandfather is dressed in traditional Tungusian clothing. Grandson has on his head a reversed baseball cap.

5   American popular culture is the closest approximation today to a global lingua franca, drawing the urban and young in particular into a common cultural zone where they share some dreams of freedom, wealth, comfort, innocence, and power—and perhaps most of all, youth as a state of mind. In general, despite the rhetoric of "identity," young people do not live in monocultures. They are not monocular. They are both local and cosmopolitan. Cultural bilingualism is routine. Just as their "cultures" are

neither hard-wired nor uniform, so there is no simple way in which they are "American-ized," though there are American tags on their experience—low-cost links to status and fun. Everywhere, fun lovers, efficiency seekers, Americaphiles, and Americaphobes alike pass through the portals of Disney and the arches of McDonald's wearing Levi's jeans and Gap jackets. Mickey Mouse and Donald Duck, John Wayne, Marilyn Monroe, James Dean, Bob Dylan, Michael Jackson, Madonna, Clint Eastwood, Bruce Willis, the multicolor chorus of Coca-Cola, and the next flavor of the month or the universe are the icons of a curious sort of one-world sensibility, a global semiculture. America's bid for global unification surpasses in reach that of the Romans, the British, the Catholic Church, or Islam; though without either an army or a God, it requires less. The Tungusian boy with the reversed cap on his head does not automatically think of it as "American," let alone side with the U.S. Army.

6   The misleadingly easy answer to the question of how American images and sounds became omnipresent is: American imperialism. But the images are not even faintly force-fed by American corporate, political, or military power. The empire strikes from inside the spectator as well as from outside. This is a conundrum that deserves to be approached with respect if we are to grasp the fact that Mickey Mouse and Coke are everywhere recognized and often enough *enjoyed*. In the peculiar unification at work throughout the world, there is surely a supply side, but there is not only a supply side. Some things are true even if multinational corporations claim so: there is demand.

7   What do American icons and styles mean to those who are not American? We can only imagine—but let us try. What young people graced with disposable income encounter in American television shows, movies, soft drinks, theme parks, and American-labeled (though not American-manufactured) running shoes, T-shirts, baggy pants, ragged jeans, and so on, is a way of being in the world, the experience of a flow of ready feelings and sensations bobbing up, disposable, dissolving, segueing to the next and the next after that. It is a quality of immediacy and casualness not so different from what Americans desire. But what the young experience in the video game arcade or the music megastore is more than the flux of sensation. They flirt with a loose sort of social membership that requires little but a momentary (and monetary) surrender. Sampling American goods, images, and sounds, they affiliate with an empire of informality. Consuming a commodity, wearing a slogan or a logo, you affiliate with disaffiliation. You make a limited-liability connection, a virtual one. You borrow some of the effervescence that is supposed to emanate from this American staple, and hope to be recognized as one of the elect. When you wear the Israeli version that spells *Coca-Cola* in Hebrew, you express some worldwide connection with unknown peers, or a sense of irony, or both—in any event, a marker of membership. In a world of ubiquitous images, of easy mobility and casual tourism, you get to feel not only local or national but global—without locking yourself in a box so confining as to deserve the name "identity."

8   We are seeing on a world scale the familiar infectious rhythm of modernity. The money economy extends its reach, bringing with it a calculating mentality. Even in the poor countries it stirs the same hunger for private feeling, the same taste for disposable

labels and sensations on demand, the same attention to fashion, the new and the now, that cropped up earlier in the West. Income beckons; income rewards. The taste for the marketed spectacle and the media-soaked way of life spreads. The culture consumer may not like the American goods in particular but still acquires a taste for the media's speed, formulas, and frivolity. Indeed, the lightness of American-sponsored "identity" is central to its appeal. It imposes few burdens. Attachments and affiliations coexist, overlap, melt together, form, and re-form.

9   Marketers, like nationalists and fundamentalists, promote "identities," but for most people, the melange is the message. Traditional bonds bend under pressure from imports. Media from beyond help you have your "roots" and eat them, too. You can watch Mexican television in the morning and American in the afternoon, or graze between Kurdish and English. You can consolidate family ties with joint visits to Disney World—making Orlando, Florida, the major tourist destination in the United States, and the Tokyo and Marne-la-Vallée spin-offs massive attractions in Japan and France. You can attach to your parents, or children, by playing oldie music and exchanging sports statistics. You plunge back into the media flux, looking for—what? Excitement? Some low-cost variation on known themes? Some next new thing? You don't know just what, but you will when you see it—or if not, you'll change channels.

10   As devotees of Japanese video games, Hong Kong movies, and Mexican *telenovelas* would quickly remind us, the blends, juxtapositions, and recombinations of popular culture are not just American. American and American-based models, styles, and symbols are simply the most far-flung, successful, and consequential. In the course of a century, America's entertainment corporations succeeded brilliantly in cultivating popular expectations for entertainment—indeed, the sense of a *right* to be entertained, a right that belongs to the history of modernity, the rise of market economies and individualism. The United States, which began as Europe's collective fantasy, built a civilization to deliver the goods for playing, feeling, and meaning. Competitors ignore its success at their own peril, financial and otherwise. ∎

Laura Carlsen

Walmart vs. Pyramids

Laura Carlsen is the director of the Americas Program for the International Relations Center (formerly the Interhemispheric Resource Center), which provides policy analysis and options for economic policy involving North, Central, and South America. A graduate of Stanford University, in 1986 she received a Fulbright Scholarship to study the impact on women of the Mexican economic crisis.

She continues to reside in Mexico City. Carlsen has also written about trade agreements and other economic issues impacting Mexico. The article reprinted below appeared in several places in October and November of 2004, including New York University's Global Beat Syndicate, the *Common Dreams* Web site (www. commondreams.org), and *Human Quest*, an academic journal of religion and philosophy.

The showdown is rife with symbolism. Walmart's expansion plans in Mexico have brought about a modern-day clash of passions and principles at the site of one of the earth's first great civilizations.

2   Several months ago Walmart, the world's largest retail chain, quietly began constructing a new store in Mexico—the latest step in a phenomenal takeover of Mexico's supermarket sector. But the expansion north of Mexico City is not just part of Walmart's commercial conquest of Mexico. It is infringing on the cultural foundations of the country. The new store is just 3,000 meters from the Pyramid of the Sun, the tallest structure in the ancient city of Teotihuacan.

3   The Teotihuacan Empire is believed to have begun as early as 200 B.C. Its dominion stretched deep into the heart of Mayan country in Guatemala and throughout present-day Mexico. At its peak, Teotihuacan was a thriving city of about 200,000 inhabitants, but the civilization declined in 700 A.D. under circumstances still shrouded in mystery.

4   Since then, other tribes and civilizations, including the Aztecs and contemporary Mexican society, have claimed the "City of the Gods" as their heritage. The grand human accomplishment it represents and the power of its architectural, historical and, for many, spiritual legacy is central to Mexico's history and culture.

5   While little is known for certain about the rise and fall of Teotihuacan, much is known about the rise of the Walmart empire. From a store in Rogers, Arkansas founded by the Walton brothers in 1962, the enterprise grew in the breathtakingly short period of 42 years into the world's largest company.

6   In Mexico, its conquest of the supermarket sector began by buying up the nation's extensive chain, Aurrerá, beginning in 1992. Today, with 657 stores, Mexico is home to more Walmarts and their affiliates than any other country outside the United States. Walmart is now Mexico's largest private employer, with

over 100,000 employees. But recent studies in the United States, where resistance to the megastores has been growing, show that job creation is often job displacement, because Walmarts put local stores out of business, leading to net job losses.

7   Walmart has revolutionized the labor and business world by working cheap and growing big. Labor costs are held down through anti-union policies, the hiring of undocumented workers in the United States, alleged discrimination against women and persons with disabilities, and cutbacks in benefits. Prices paid suppliers are driven down by outsourcing competition. Buoyed by $244.5 billion dollars in annual net sales, the chain can afford to make ever deeper incursions into Mexico's retail sector.

8   A diverse group of local merchants, artists, actors, academics and indigenous organizations are leading the opposition, protesting that the store damages Mexico's rich cultural heritage. Through ceremonies, hunger strikes, demonstrations and press coverage, the movement to defend the site has kept the conflict in the public eye and heightened the public-opinion costs to Walmart. Now opponents have taken their concerns to the Mexican Congress and UNESCO.

9   Some ancient ruins have already been found on the store's new site, and Walmart construction workers told the national daily, *La Jornada,* that they had orders to hide any archaeological relics they found. Normally, the presence of relics requires that further excavation be carried out painstakingly or halted altogether. But the booming Walmart corporation clearly has no time for such delays.

10   The dispute in Teotihuacan today is not a battle between the past and the future. It is a struggle over a country's right to define itself. For defenders of the ancient site, the foremost symbol of the nation's cultural heritage also constitutes part of its contemporary integrity. Modern Mexico is still a country that defines itself by legends, and whose collective identity—unlike its neophyte northern neighbor—reaches back thousands of years.

11   In this context, Walmart is a symbol of the cultural insensitivity of rampant economic integration. While its actions may be technically legal, in the end Walmart could pay a high price for this insensitivity . . . and if there is anything Walmart hates, it is high prices.

Thomas Friedman

Why the World Is Flat

The online magazine *Wired* published the following interview in May 2005. Daniel Pink, the author of several books himself on globalization, as well as numerous articles in the *New York Times*, conducted the interview since he is a contributing editor for *Wired*. Friedman, author and syndicated columnist, is described fully in the introduction.

Thirty-five years ago this summer, the golfer Chi Chi Rodriguez was competing in his seventh U.S. Open, played that year at Hazeltine Country Club outside Minneapolis. Tied for second place after the opening round, Rodriguez eventually finished 27th, a few strokes ahead of such golf legends as Jack Nicklaus, Arnold Palmer, and Gary Player. His caddy for the tournament was a 17-year-old local named Tommy Friedman.

2   Rodriguez retired from golf several years later. But his caddy—now known as Thomas L. Friedman, foreign affairs columnist for the *New York Times* and author of the new book *The World Is Flat: A Brief History of the Twenty-First Century*—has spent his career deploying the skills he used on the golf course: describing the terrain, shouting warnings and encouragement, and whispering in the ears of big players. After ten years of writing his twice-weekly foreign affairs column, Friedman has become the most influential American newspaper columnist since Walter Lippmann.

3   One reason for Friedman's influence is that, in the mid-'90s, he staked out the territory at the intersection of technology, financial markets, and world trade, which the foreign policy establishment, still focused on cruise missiles and throw weights, had largely ignored. "This thing called globalization," he says, "can explain more things in more ways than anything else."

4   Friedman's 1999 book, *The Lexus and the Olive Tree: Understanding Globalization*, provided much of the intellectual framework for the debate. "The first big book on globalization that anybody actually read," as Friedman describes it, helped make him a fixture on the Davos-Allen Conference-Renaissance Weekend circuit. But it also made him a lightning rod. He's been accused of "rhetorical hyperventilation" and dismissed as an "apologist" for global capital. The columnist Molly Ivins even dubbed top-tier society's lack of concern for the downsides of globalization "the Tom Friedman Problem."

5   After 9/11, Friedman says, he paid less attention to globalization. He spent the next three years traveling to the Arab and Muslim world trying to get at the roots of the attack on the U.S. His columns on the subject earned him his third Pulitzer Prize. But Friedman realized that while he was writing about terrorism, he missed an even bigger story: Globalization had gone into overdrive. So in a three-month burst last year, he wrote *The World Is Flat* to explain his updated thinking on the subject.

6   Friedman enlisted some impressive editorial assistance. Bill Gates spent a day with him to critique the theory. Friedman presented sections of the book to the strategic

planning unit at IBM and to Michael Dell. But his most important tutors were two Indians: Nandan Nilekani, CEO of Infosys, and Vivek Paul, a top executive at Wipro. "They were the guys who really cracked the code for me."

Wired sat down with Friedman in his office at the Times' Washington bureau to discuss the flattening of the world.

WIRED: What do you mean the world is flat?
FRIEDMAN: I was in India interviewing Nandan Nilekani at Infosys. And he said to me, "Tom, the playing field is being leveled." Indians and Chinese were going to compete for work like never before, and Americans weren't ready. I kept chewing over that phrase—"the playing field is being leveled"—and then it hit me: Holy mackerel, the world is becoming flat. Several technological and political forces have converged, and that has produced a global, Web-enabled playing field that allows for multiple forms of collaboration without regard to geography or distance—or soon, even language.

So, we're talking about globalization enhanced by things like the rise of open source?
This is Globalization 3.0. In Globalization 1.0, which began around 1492, the world went from size large to size medium. In Globalization 2.0, the era that introduced us to multinational companies, it went from size medium to size small. And then around 2000 came Globalization 3.0, in which the world went from being small to tiny. There's a difference between being able to make long distance phone calls cheaper on the Internet and walking around Riyadh with a PDA where you can have all of Google in your pocket. It's a difference in degree that's so enormous it becomes a difference in kind.

Is that why the Netscape IPO is one of your "10 flatteners"? Explain.
Three reasons. Netscape brought the Internet alive with the browser. They made the Internet so that Grandma could use it and her grandchildren could use it. The second thing that Netscape did was commercialize a set of open transmission protocols so that no company could own the Net. And the third is that Netscape triggered the dotcom boom, which triggered the dotcom bubble, which triggered the overinvestment of a trillion dollars in fiber-optic cables.

Are you saying telecommunications trumps terrorism? What about September 11? Isn't that as important?
There's no question flattening is more important. I don't think you can understand 9/11 without understanding flattening.

This is probably the first book by a major foreign affairs thinker that talks about the world-changing effects of . . . supply chains.
[Friedman laughs.]

Why are supply chains so important?
They're incredible flatteners. For UPS to work, they've got to create systems with customs offices around the world. They've got to design supply chain algorithms so when you take that box to the UPS Store, it gets from that store to its hub and then out. Everything they are doing is taking fat out of the system at every joint. I was in India after the nuclear alert of 2002. I was interviewing Vivek Paul at Wipro shortly after he'd gotten an email from one of their big American clients saying, "We're now looking for an alternative to you. We don't want to be looking for an alternative to

you. You don't *want* us to be looking for an alternative to you. Do something about this!" So I saw the effect that India's being part of this global supply chain had on the behavior of the Indian business community, which eventually filtered up to New Delhi.

14 **And that's how you went from your McDonald's Theory of Conflict Prevention—two countries that have a McDonald's will never go to war with each other—to the Dell Theory of Conflict Prevention.**
Yes. No two countries that are both part of a major global supply chain like Dell's will fight against each other as long as they are both part of that supply chain. When I'm managing your back room, when I'm managing your HR, when I'm doing your accounting—that's way beyond selling you burgers. We are intimately in bed with each other. And that has got to affect my behavior.

15 **In some sense, then, the world is a gigantic supply chain. And you don't want to be the one who brings the whole thing down.**
Absolutely.

16 **Unless your goal is to bring the whole thing down. Supply chains work for al Qaeda, too, don't they?**
Al Qaeda is nothing more than a mutant supply chain. They're playing off the same platform as Walmart and Dell. They're just not restrained by it. What is al Qaeda? It's an open source religious political movement that works off the global supply chain. That's what we're up against in Iraq. We're up against a suicide supply chain. You take one bomber and deploy him in Baghdad, and another is manufactured in Riyadh the next day. It's exactly like when you take the toy off the shelf at Walmart and another is made in Shen Zhen the next day.

The 10 Great Levelers

1. **Fall of the Berlin Wall**
   The events of November 9, 1989, tilted the worldwide balance of power toward democracies and free markets.

2. **Netscape IPO**
   The August 9, 1995, offering sparked massive investment in fiber-optic cables.

3. **Work flow software**
   The rise of apps from PayPal to VPNs enabled faster, closer coordination among far-flung employees.

4. **Open-sourcing**
   Self-organizing communities, à la Linux, launched a collaborative revolution.

5. **Outsourcing**
   Migrating business functions to India saved money *and* a third world economy.

The book is almost dizzily optimistic about India and China, about what flattening will bring to these parts of the world.

I firmly believe that the next great breakthrough in bioscience could come from a 15-year-old who downloads the human genome in Egypt. Bill Gates has a nice line: He says, 20 years ago, would you rather have been a B-student in Poughkeepsie or a genius in Shanghai? Twenty years ago you'd rather be a B-student in Poughkeepsie. Today?

Not even close.

Not even close. You'd much prefer to be the genius in Shanghai because you can now export your talents anywhere in the world.

As optimistic as you are about that kid in Shanghai, you're not particularly optimistic about the US.

I'm worried about my country. I love America. I think it's the best country in the world. But I also think we're not tending to our sauce. I believe that we are in what Shirley Ann Jackson [president of Rensselaer Polytechnic Institute] calls a "quiet crisis." If we don't change course now and buckle down in a flat world, the kind of competition our kids will face will be intense and the social implications of not repairing things will be enormous.

You quote a CEO who says that Americans have grown addicted to their high salaries, and now they're going to have to earn them. Are Americans suffering from an undue sense of entitlement?

Somebody said to me the other day that—I wish I had this for the book, but it's going to be in the paperback—the entitlement we need to get rid of is our sense of entitlement.

6. **Offshoring**

Contract manufacturing elevated China to economic prominence.

7. **Supply-chaining**

Robust networks of suppliers, retailers, and customers increased business efficiency. See Walmart.

8. **Insourcing**

Logistics giants took control of customer supply chains, helping mom-and-pop shops go global. See UPS and FedEx.

9. **In-forming**

Power searching allowed everyone to use the Internet as a "personal supply chain of knowledge." See Google.

10. **Wireless**

Like "steroids," wireless technologies pumped up collaboration, making it mobile and personal.

21 **Let's talk about the critics of globalization. You say that you don't want the antiglobalization movement to go away. Why?**

I've been a critic of the antiglobalization movement, and they've been a critic of me, but the one thing I respect about the movement is their authentic energy. These are not people who don't care about the world. But if you want to direct your energy toward helping the poor, I believe the best way is not throwing a stone through a McDonald's window or protesting World Bank meetings. It's through local governance. When you start to improve local governance, you improve education, women's rights, transportation.

22 **It's possible to go through your book and conclude it was written by a US senator who wants to run for president. There's a political agenda in this book.**

Yes, absolutely.

23 **You call for portable benefits, lifelong learning, free trade, greater investment in science, government funding for tertiary education, a system of wage insurance. Uh, Mr. Friedman, are you running for president?**

[*Laughs loudly.*] No, I am not running for president!

24 **Would you accept the vice presidential nomination?**

I just want to get my Thursday column done!

25 **But you are outlining an explicit agenda.**

You can't be a citizen of this country and not be in a hair-pulling rage at the fact that we're at this inflection moment and nobody seems to be talking about the kind of policies we need to get through this flattening of the world, to get the most out of it and cushion the worst. We need to have as focused, as serious, as energetic, as sacrificing a strategy for dealing with flatism as we did for communism. This is the challenge of our day.

26 **Short of Washington fully embracing the Friedman doctrine, what should we be doing? For instance, what advice should we give to our kids?**

When I was growing up, my parents told me, "Finish your dinner. People in China and India are starving." I tell my daughters, "Finish your homework. People in India and China are starving for your job."

27 **Think about your own childhood for a moment. If a teenage Tommy Friedman could somehow have been transported to 2005, what do you think he would have found most surprising?**

That you could go to PGA.com and get the scores of your favorite golfer in real time. That would have been amazing.

Richard Florida

The World in Numbers: The World Is Spiky

Richard Florida (born 1957) is a professor at the University of Toronto, but he is also a prominent and respected public intellectual who writes for a broad readership. In addition to several books, he has written many articles about global trends and economic development strategies for the *New York Times*, the *Wall Street Journal*, and other newspapers and magazines, and he appears frequently as a commentator on CNN, PBS, and CBS. Since 2011 he has been a senior editor for the *Atlantic* (a leading magazine on culture and literature since its founding before the Civil War), where the following article appeared in 2005. Among other things, it is a response to Thomas Friedman's argument that "the world is flat."

Patrick Chappatte/PoliticalCartoons.com

The World Is Spiky

Globalization has changed the economic playing field, but hasn't leveled it

Ⓐ POPULATION
Urban areas house half of all the world's people, and continue to grow in both rich and poor countries.

PEAKS, HILLS, AND VALLEYS

When looked at through the lens of economic production, many cities with large populations are diminished and some nearly vanish. Three sorts of places make up the modern economic landscape. First are the cities that generate innovations. These are the tallest peaks; they have the capacity to attract global talent and create new products and industries. They are few in number, and difficult to topple. Second are the economic "hills"—places that manufacture the world's established goods, take its calls, and support its innovation engines. These hills can rise and fall quickly; they are prosperous but insecure. Some, like Dublin and Seoul, are growing into innovative, wealthy peaks; others are declining, eroded by high labor costs and a lack of enduring competitive advantage. Finally there are the vast valleys—places with little connection to the global economy and few immediate prospects.

The world, according to the title of the *New York Times* columnist Thomas Friedman's book, is flat. Thanks to advances in technology, the global playing field has been leveled, the prizes are there for the taking, and everyone's a player—no matter where on the surface of the earth he or she may reside. "In a flat world," Friedman writes, "you can innovate without having to emigrate."

Friedman is not alone in this belief: for the better part of the past century economists have been writing about the leveling effects of technology. From the invention of the telephone, the automobile, and the airplane to the rise of the personal computer and the Internet, technological progress has steadily eroded the economic importance of geographic place—or so the argument goes.

But in partnership with colleagues at George Mason University and the geographer Tim Gulden, of the Center for International and Security Studies, at the University of Maryland, I've begun to chart a very different economic topography. By almost any measure the international economic landscape is not at all flat. On the contrary, our world is amazingly "spiky." In terms of both sheer economic horsepower and cutting-edge innovation,

surprisingly few regions truly matter in today's global economy. What's more, the tallest peaks—the cities and regions that drive the world economy—are growing ever higher, while the valleys mostly languish.

The most obvious challenge to the flat-world hypothesis is the explosive growth of cities worldwide. More and more people are clustering in urban areas—the world's demographic mountain ranges, so to speak. The share of the world's population living in urban areas, just three percent in 1800, was nearly 30 percent by 1950. Today it stands at about 50 percent; in advanced countries three out of four people live in urban areas. Map A shows the uneven distribution

of the world's population. Five megacities currently have more than 20 million inhabitants each. Twenty-four cities have more than 10 million inhabitants, sixty more than 5 million, and 150 more than 2.5 million. Population density is of course a crude indicator of human and economic activity. But it does suggest that at least some of the tectonic forces of economics are concentrating people and resources, and pushing up some places more than others.

Still, differences in population density vastly understate the spikiness of the global economy; the continuing dominance of the world's most productive urban areas is astounding. When it comes to actual economic output, the ten largest U.S. metropolitan areas combined are behind only the United

SOURCE: CENTER FOR INTERNATIONAL EARTH SCIENCE INFORMATION NETWORK

OCTOBER 2005

Data source: Center for International Earth Science Information Network, Columbia University; and Centro Internacional de Agricultura Tropical. (Reprinted by permission of *The Atlantic Monthly*)

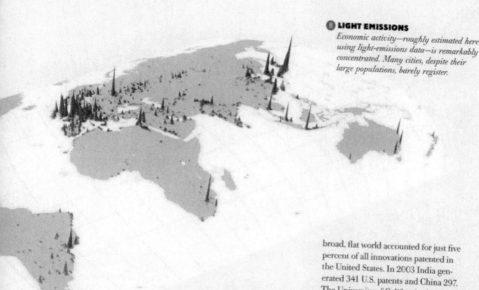

SOURCE: U.S. DEFENSE METEROLOGICAL SATELLITE PROGRAM

Economic activity—roughly estimated here using light-emissions data—is remarkably concentrated. Many cities, despite their large populations, barely register.

States as a whole and Japan. New York's economy alone is about the size of Russia's or Brazil's, and Chicago's is on a par with Sweden's. Together New York, Los Angeles, Chicago, and Boston have a bigger economy than all of China. If U.S. metropolitan areas were countries, they'd make up forty-seven of the biggest 100 economies in the world.

Unfortunately, no single, comprehensive information source exists for the economic production of all the world's cities. A rough proxy is available, though. Map B shows a variation on the widely circulated view of the world at night, with higher concentrations of light—indicating higher energy use and, presumably, stronger economic production—appearing in greater relief. U.S. regions appear almost Himalayan on this map. From their summits one might look out on a smaller mountain range stretching across Europe, some isolated peaks in Asia, and a few scattered hills throughout the rest of the world.

Population and economic activity are both spiky, but it's innovation—the engine of economic growth—that is most concentrated. The World Intellectual Property Organization recorded about 300,000 patents from resident inventors in more than a hundred nations in 2002 (the most recent year for which statistics are available). Nearly two thirds of them went to American and Japanese inventors. Eighty-five percent went to the residents of just five countries (Japan, the United States, South Korea, Germany, and Russia).

Worldwide patent statistics can be somewhat misleading, since different countries follow different standards for granting patents. But patents granted in the United States—which receives patent applications for nearly all major innovations worldwide, and holds them to the same strict standards—tell a similar story. Nearly 90,000 of the 170,000 patents granted in the United States in 2002 went to Americans. Some 35,000 went to Japanese inventors, and 11,000 to Germans. The next ten most innovative countries—including the usual suspects in Europe plus Taiwan, South Korea, Israel, and Canada—produced roughly 25,000 more. The rest of the

broad, flat world accounted for just five percent of all innovations patented in the United States. In 2003 India generated 341 U.S. patents and China 297. The University of California alone generated more than either country. IBM accounted for five times as many as the two combined.

This is not to say that Indians and Chinese are not innovative. On the contrary, AnnaLee Saxenian, of the University of California at Berkeley, has shown that Indian and Chinese entrepreneurs founded or co-founded roughly 30 percent of all Silicon Valley startups in the late 1990s. But these fundamentally creative people had to travel to Silicon Valley and be absorbed into its innovative ecosystem before their ideas became economically viable. Such ecosystems matter, and there aren't many of them.

Map C—which makes use of data from both the World Intellectual Property Organization and the U.S. Patent and Trademark Office—shows a world composed of innovation peaks and valleys. Tokyo, Seoul, New York, and San Francisco remain the front-runners in the patenting competition. Boston, Seattle, Austin, Toronto, Vancouver, Berlin, Stockholm, Helsinki, London, Osaka, Taipei, and Sydney also stand out.

Map D shows the residence of the 1,200 most heavily cited scientists in leading fields. Scientific advance is even more concentrated than patent

source: U.S. Defense Meterological Satellite Program. (Reprinted by permission of *The Atlantic Monthly*)

○C PATENTS
Just a few places produce most of the world's innovations. Innovation remains difficult without a critical mass of financiers, entrepreneurs, and scientists, often nourished by world-class universities and flexible corporations.

THE GEOGRAPHY OF INNOVATION

Commercial innovation and scientific advance are both highly concentrated—but not always in the same places. Several cities in East Asia—particularly in Japan—are home to prolific business innovation but still depend disproportionately on scientific breakthroughs made elsewhere. Likewise, some cities excel in scientific research but not in commercial adaptation. The few places that do both well are very strongly positioned in the global economy. These regions have little to fear, and much to gain, from continuing globalization.

production. Most occurs not just in a handful of countries but in a handful of cities—primarily in the United States and Europe. Chinese and Indian cities do not even register. As far as global innovation is concerned, perhaps a few dozen places worldwide really compete at the cutting edge.

Concentrations of creative and talented people are particularly important for innovation, according to the Nobel Prize–winning economist Robert Lucas. Ideas flow more freely, are honed more sharply, and can be put into practice more quickly when large numbers of innovators, implementers, and financial backers are in constant contact with one another, both in and out of the office. Creative people cluster not simply because they like to be around one another or they prefer cosmopolitan centers with lots of amenities, though both those things count. They and their companies also cluster because of the powerful pro-

ductivity advantages, economies of scale, and knowledge spillovers such density brings.

So although one might not *have* to emigrate to innovate, it certainly appears that innovation, economic growth, and prosperity occur in those places that attract a critical mass of top creative talent. Because globalization has increased the returns to innovation, by allowing innovative products and services to quickly reach consumers worldwide, it has strengthened the lure that innovation centers hold for our planet's best and brightest, reinforcing the spikiness of wealth and economic production.

The main difference between now and even a couple of decades ago is not that the world has become flatter but that the world's peaks have become slightly more dispersed—and that the world's hills, the industrial and service centers that produce mature products and support innovation centers, have proliferated and shifted. For the

better part of the twentieth century the United States claimed the lion's share of the global economy's innovation peaks, leaving a few outposts in Europe and Japan. But America has since lost some of those peaks, as such industrial-age powerhouses as Pittsburgh, St. Louis, and Cleveland have eroded. At the same time, a number of regions in Europe, Scandinavia, Canada, and the Pacific Rim have moved up.

The world today looks flat to some because the economic and social distances between peaks worldwide have gotten smaller. Connection between peaks has been strengthened by the easy mobility of the global creative class—about 150 million people worldwide. They participate in a global technology system and a global labor market that allow them to migrate freely among the world's leading cities. In a Brookings Institution study the demographer Robert Lang and the world-cities expert Peter Taylor identify a relatively small group of leading city-regions—London, New York, Paris, Tokyo, Hong Kong, Singapore, Chicago, Los Angeles, and San Francisco among them—that are strongly connected to one another.

But Lang and Taylor also identify a much larger group of city-regions that are far more locally oriented. People in spiky places are often more connected

OCTOBER 2005

SCIENTIFIC CITATIONS

The world's most prolific and influential scientific researchers overwhelmingly reside in U.S. and European cities.

to one another, even from half a world away, than they are to people and places in their veritable back yards.

The flat-world theory is not completely misguided. It is a welcome supplement to the widely accepted view (illustrated by the Live 8 concerts and Bono's forays into Africa, by the writings of Jeffrey Sachs and the UN Millennium project) that the growing divide between rich and poor countries is the fundamental feature of the world economy. Friedman's theory more accurately depicts a developing world with capabilities that translate into economic development. In his view, for example, the emerging economies of India and China combine cost advantages, high-tech skills, and entrepreneurial energy, enabling those countries to compete effectively for industries and jobs. The tensions set in motion as the playing field is leveled affect mainly the advanced countries, which see not only manufacturing work but also higher-end jobs, in fields such as software development and financial services, increasingly threatened by offshoring.

But the flat-world theory blinds us to far more insidious tensions among the world's growing peaks, sinking valleys, and shifting hills. The innovative, talent-attracting "have" regions seem increasingly remote from the talent-exporting "have-not" regions. Second-tier cities, from Detroit and Wolfsburg to Nagoya and Mexico City, are entering an escalating and potentially devastating competition for jobs, talent, and investment. And inequality is growing across the world and within countries.

This is far more harrowing than the flat world Friedman describes, and a good deal more treacherous than the old rich-poor divide. We see its effects in the political backlash against globalization in the advanced world. The recent rejection of the EU constitution by the French, for example, resulted in large part from high rates of "no" votes in suburban and rural quarters, which understandably fear globalization and integration.

But spiky globalization also wreaks havoc on poorer places. China is seeing enormous concentrations of talent and innovation in centers such as Shanghai, Shenzhen, and Beijing, all of which are a world apart from its vast,

impoverished rural areas. According to detailed polling by Richard Burkholder, of Gallup, average household incomes in urban China are now triple those in rural regions, and they've grown more than three times as fast since 1999; perhaps as a result, urban and rural Chinese now have very different, often conflicting political and lifestyle values. India is growing even more divided, as Bangalore, Hyderabad, and parts of New Delhi and Bombay pull away from the rest of that enormous country, creating destabilizing political tensions. Economic and demographic forces are sorting people around the world into geographically clustered "tribes" so different (and often mutually antagonistic) as to create a somewhat Hobbesian vision.

We are thus confronted with a difficult predicament. Economic progress requires that the peaks grow stronger and taller. But such growth will exacerbate economic and social disparities, fomenting political reactions that could threaten further innovation and economic progress. Managing the disparities between peaks and valleys worldwide—raising the valleys without shearing off the peaks—will be among the top political challenges of the coming decades. —*RICHARD FLORIDA*

Richard Florida, the author of The Flight of the Creative Class, *is the Hirst Professor of Public Policy at George Mason University.*

source: Michael Batty, Centre for Advanced Spatial Analysis, University College London (). (Reprinted by ission of *The Atlantic Monthly*)

ROBYN **MEREDITH** AND SUZANNE **HOPPOUGH**

Why Globalization Is Good

Robyn Meredith is author of the best-selling book *The Elephant and the Dragon: The Rise of India and China and What It Means for All of Us.* She and her colleague at *Forbes* magazine, Suzanne Hoppough, collaborated on the following excerpt from *The Elephant and the Dragon* and published it in *Forbes* on April 16, 2007.

A ragtag army of save-the-world crusaders has spent years decrying multinational corporations as villains in the wave of globalization overwhelming the Third World. This ominous trend would fatten the rich, further impoverish and oppress the poor, and crush local economies.

2 The business-bashing group Public Citizen argued as much in a proclamation signed by almost 1,500 organizations in 89 countries in 1999. Whereupon hundreds of protesters rioted outside a conference of the World Trade Organization in Seattle, shattering windows, blocking traffic, and confronting cops armed with tear gas and pepper spray. Six hundred people were arrested.

3 Cut to 2007, and the numbers are in: The protesters and do-gooders are just plain wrong. It turns out that globalization is good—and not just for the rich, but *especially* for the poor. The booming economies of India and China—the Elephant and the Dragon—have lifted 200 million people out of abject poverty in the 1990s as globalization took off, the International Monetary Fund says. Tens of millions more have catapulted themselves far ahead into the middle class.

4 It's remarkable what a few container ships can do to make poor people better off. Certainly more than $2 trillion of foreign aid, which is roughly the amount (with an inflation adjustment) that the U.S. and Europe have poured into Africa and Asia over the past half-century.

5 In the next eight years almost a billion people across Asia will take a Great Leap Forward into a new middle class. In China middle-class incomes are set to rise threefold, to $5,000, predicts Dominic Barton, a Shanghai managing partner for McKinsey & Co.

6 As the Chindia revolution spreads, the ranks of the poor get smaller, not larger. In the 1990s, as Vietnam's economy grew 6% a year, the number of people living in poverty (42 million) fell 7% annually; in Uganda, when GDP growth passed 3%, the number fell 6% per year, says the World Bank.

7 China unleashed its economy in 1978, seeding capitalism first among farmers newly freed to sell the fruits of their fields instead of handing the produce over to Communist Party collectives. Other reforms let the Chinese create 22 million new businesses that now employ 135 million people who otherwise would have remained peasants like the generations before them. Foreign direct investment, the very force so virulently opposed by the do-gooders, has helped drive China's gross domestic product to a more than tenfold increase since 1978. Since the reforms started, $600 billion has flooded into the country, $70 billion of it in the past year. Foreigners built hundreds

of thousands of new factories as the Chinese government built the coal mines, power grid, airports, and highways to supply them.

8   As China built infrastructure, it created Special Economic Zones where foreign companies willing to build modern factories could hire cheap labor, go years without paying any taxes, and leave it to government to build the roads and other infrastructure they needed. All of that, in turn, drove China's exports from $970 million to $974 billion in three decades. Those container loads make Americans better off, too. You can get a Chinese DVD at Walmart for $28, and after you do you will buy some $15 movies made in the U.S.A.

9   Per-person income in China has climbed from $16 a year in 1978 to $2,000 now. Wages in factory boomtowns in southern China can run $4 a day—scandalously low in the eyes of the protesters, yet up from pennies a day a generation ago and far ahead of increases in living costs. Middle-class Chinese families now own TVs, live in new apartments, and send their children to private schools. Millions of Chinese have traded in their bicycles for motorcycles or cars. McDonald's has signed a deal with Sinopec, the huge Chinese gasoline retailer, to build drive-through restaurants attached to gas stations on China's new roads.

10   Today 254 Starbucks stores serve coffee in the land of tea, including one at the Great Wall and another at the Forbidden Palace. (The latter is the target of protesters.) In Beijing 54 Starbucks shops thrive, peddling luxury lattes that cost up to $2.85 a cup and paying servers $6 for an 8-hour day. That looks exploitative until you peek inside a nearby Chinese-owned teahouse where the staff works a 12-hour day for $3.75. Says one woman, 23, who works for an international cargo shipper in Beijing: "My parents were both teachers when they were my age, and they earned 30 yuan [$3.70] a month. I earn 4,000 yuan ($500) a month, live comfortably, and feel I have better opportunities than my parents did."

11   Tony Ma, age 51, was an unwilling foot soldier in Mao's Cultural Revolution. During that dark period from 1966 to 1976 universities were closed, and he was sent at age 16 to work in a steel mill for $2 a month. He cut metal all day long for seven years and feared he might never escape. When colleges reopened, he landed a spot to study chemistry, transferred to the U.S., got a Ph.D. in biochemistry, and signed on with Johnson & Johnson at $45,000 a year. Later he returned to the land he fled and now works for B.F. Goodrich in Hong Kong. The young college grads in China today wouldn't bother immigrating to the U.S. for a job that pays $45,000, he says—because now they have better opportunities at home.

12   Capitalism alone, however, isn't enough to remake Third World economies—globalism is the key. A big reason India trails behind its bigger neighbor to the northeast in lifting the lower classes is that, even after embracing capitalism, it kept barriers to the flow of capital from abroad. Thus 77% of Indians live on $2 a day or less, the Asian Development Bank says, down only nine percentage points from 1990. A third of the population is illiterate. In 1980 India had more of its population in urban centers than China did (23% versus 20% for China). But by 2005 China had 41% in cities, where wages are higher; India's urbanites had grown to only 29%.

3   Freed of British colonial rule in 1947 and scarred by its paternalistic effects, India initially combined capitalism with economic isolationism. It thwarted foreign companies

intent on investing there and hampered Indian firms trying to sell abroad. This hurt Indian consumers and local biz: A $100 Microsoft operating system got slapped with duties that brought the price to $250 in India, putting imported software and computers further from reach for most people and businesses. Meanwhile, the government granted workers lavish job protections and imposed heavy taxes and regulations on employers. Government jobs usually were by rote and paid poorly, but they guaranteed lifetime employment. They also ensured economic stagnation.

14   Financial crisis struck in 1991. Desperate for cash, India flew a planeload of gold reserves to London and began, grudgingly, to open its economy. Import duties were lowered or eliminated, so India's consumers and companies could buy modern, foreign-made goods and gear. Overseas firms in many industries were allowed to own their subsidiaries in India for the first time since 1977. India all but banned foreign investment until 1991. Since then foreign companies have come back, but not yet on the scale seen in China. Foreign companies have invested $48 billion in India since 1991—$7.5 billion of that just in the last fiscal year—the same amount dumped into China every six weeks. By the mid-1990s the economy boomed and created millions of jobs.

15   By the late 1990s U.S. tech companies began turning to India for software design, particularly in the Y2K crunch. The Indians proved capable and cheap, and the much-maligned offshoring boom began. Suddenly Indian software engineers were programming corporate America's computers. New college graduates were answering America's customer service phone calls. Builders hired construction workers to erect new high-rise buildings suddenly in demand as American and European firms rushed to hire Indian workers. The new college hires, whose older siblings had graduated without finding a job, tell of surpassing their parents' salaries within five years and of buying cell phones, then motorcycles, then cars and even houses by the time they were 30. All of that would have been impossible had India failed to add globalization to capitalism.

16   Today, despite its still dilapidated airports and pothole-riddled highways, the lumbering Elephant now is in a trot, growing more than 7% annually for the last decade. In 2005, borrowing from the Chinese, India began a five-year, $150 billion plan to update its roads, airports, ports, and electric plants. India is creating free trade zones, like those in China, to encourage exports of software, apparel, auto parts and more. S. B. Kutwal manages the assembly line where Tata Motors builds Safari SUVs. He remembers how, in the 1980s, people waited five years to buy a scooter and cars were only for the rich. "Since we've liberated the economy, lots of companies have started coming into India," says Kutwal. "People couldn't afford cars then. Now the buying power is coming."

17   In Mumbai (formerly Bombay), Delhi, Bangalore, and other big cities, shopping malls have sprung up, selling everything from Levi's jeans to Versace. India still has raggedy street touts, but when they tap on car windows at stoplights, instead of peddling cheap plastic toys, they sell to the new India: copies of *Vogue* and *House & Garden* magazines. Western restaurants are moving in, too: Domino's Pizza and Ruby Tuesday's have come to India, and 107 McDonald's have sprung up, serving veggie burgers in the land where cattle are sacred.

18   None of this gives pause to an entity called International Forum on Globalization. The group declares that globalism's aim is to "benefit transnational corporations over workers; foreign investors over local businesses; and wealthy countries over developing nations. While promoters . . . proclaim that this model is the rising tide that will lift all boats, citizen movements find that it is instead lifting only yachts."

19   "The majority of people in rich and poor countries aren't better off" since the World Trade Organization formed in 1995 to promote global trade, asserts Christopher Slevin, deputy director of Global Trade Watch, an arm of Ralph Nader's Public Citizen. "The breadth of the opposition has grown. It's not just industrial and steel workers and people who care about animal rights. It includes high-tech workers and the offshoring of jobs, also the faith-based community."

20   While well-off American techies may be worried, it seems doubtful that an engineer in Bangalore who now earns $40,000 a year, and who has just bought his parents' house, wants to ban foreign investment.

21   Slevin's further complaint is that globalism is a creature of WTO, the World Bank and other unelected bodies. But no, the people do have a voice in the process, and it is one that is equivocal on the matter of free market capitalism. The Western World's huge agriculture subsidies—$85 billion or more annually, between the U.S., Japan, and the European Union—are decreed by democratically elected legislatures. The EU pays ranchers $2 per cow in daily subsidies, more than most Indians earn. If these farmers weren't getting handouts, and if trade in farm products were free, then poor farmers in the Third World could sell more of their output, and could begin to lift themselves out of poverty.

Sadanand Dhume

Slumdog Paradox

Sadanand Dhume is a writer who is based in Washington, D.C. Having lived in Asia from 1999 to 2004, he is an expert on Asian affairs and the author of *My Friend the Fanatic: Travels with a Radical Islamist*, a travel narrative about the rise of Muslim fundamentalism in Indonesia. His writing has been published in the *Washington Post, Forbes, Commentary,* and *YaleGlobal Online*, where the following essay appeared on February 9, 2009.

The unexpected international success of *Slumdog Millionaire* has pleased some Indians while provoking unusually strong protests from others. The critical and commercial success of the film, contrasted with sharp criticism and a lackluster run in Indian theaters, captures the inherent contradictions of an increasingly globalized country. India basks in the glow of international recognition, but resents the critical scrutiny that global exposure brings.

2   Not since Sir Richard Attenborough's *Gandhi* has a film about India captured the world's imagination as strongly as *Slumdog Millionaire*, director Danny Boyle's gritty yet uplifting drama about a boy from the slums of Mumbai who makes good as a game-show contestant on the Indian version of *Who Wants to Be a Millionaire*. The low-budget production—which cost $15 million to make, a pittance in Hollywood terms—has garnered both commercial and critical success, grossing $96 million world-wide as of February 1st, and picking up four Golden Globe awards and 10 Oscar nominations. In one among a raft of glow-ing reviews, the *Wall Street Journal*'s Joe Morgenstern hailed *Slumdog* as "the world's first globalized masterpiece."

3   In India, however, the response to the film has been ambiva-lent. Commercially, it has failed to replicate its American success. Despite a wave of publicity and an ambitious nationwide rollout, *Slumdog* is showing in half-empty theaters. It trails the box-office receipts of an obscure Hindi horror movie released the same day. And though some Indian reviewers praised the film for everything from inspired casting to an improbable Bollywoodish storyline, it also attracted its share of brickbats. On his blog, Bollywood star Amitabh Bachchan struck a populist note: "If SM projects India as [a] third-world, dirty, underbelly developing nation and causes pain and disgust among nationalists and patriots, let it be known that a murky underbelly exists and thrives even in the most developed nations." The critic Meenakshi Shedde dismissed the

Young Jamal (Ayush Mahesh Khedekar) runs through the alleys of Mumbai in a scene from *Slumdog Millionaire* (2008).

film as "a laundry list of India's miseries." Interviewed in the *Los Angeles Times*, film professor Shyamal Sengupta called the film "a white man's imagined India."

4   In many ways, *Slumdog Millionaire* is a metaphor for India in the age of globalization. The director, Danny Boyle, and screenwriter, Simon Beaufoy, are British. The male lead, Dev Patel, who plays the part of the quiz-show contestant Jamal, is a Gujarati whose family migrated to London from Nairobi. His love interest, Latika, is played by Freida Pinto, a Catholic girl from Mumbai, India's most cosmopolitan city. The novel upon which the film is loosely based, *Q and A,* was written by an Indian diplomat currently stationed in South Africa. The television game show *Who Wants to Be a Millionaire,* which supplies the film's narrative backbone, is another British creation. Adapted in more than 50 countries, the show is recognizable to audiences from Beijing to Buenos Aires.

5   The film's success also underscores India's emergence on the world stage. Indeed, the superficial similarities with Ang Lee's *Crouching Tiger, Hidden Dragon,* the 2001 blockbuster set in Qing dynasty China, are striking. Both films draw on the talents of a widespread diaspora: Michelle Yeoh, Dev Patel. Like *Crouching Tiger, Slumdog* taps into Western curiosity about a country whose weight is increasingly felt in ordinary lives. Service workers in the West worry about being "Bangalored," or losing their jobs to less expensive competitors in India. Credit-card and consumer-appliance users routinely deal with customer-service professionals in Gurgaon or Hyderabad. In America, one no longer has to live in a big city to be familiar with yoga or chicken tikka masala. An Indian company, Tata Motors, owns the iconic automobile brands Jaguar and Land Rover. India-born professionals helm Pepsi and Citibank. Salman Rushdie and Jhumpa Lahiri occupy a similarly exalted place in fiction. To sum up, it seems unlikely that a story set in the slums of Manila or Jakarta would find nearly as large an audience in Boston or Baton Rouge.

6   For India, one of the most autarkic and culturally inward-looking countries in Asia until the advent of economic reforms in 1991, the benefits of globalization are easily apparent. In purchasing power parity terms, per capita income more than doubled from $1,400 in 1991 to $3,800 in 2006. The ranks of the middle class, broadly defined, have swelled to more than 250 million people. More Indians buy cell phones each month than any other people.

7   The same story can be told on the corporate and macroeconomic level. Since liberalization, a dozen Indian firms—spanning banking, pharmaceuticals, software, and services—have listed on the New York Stock Exchange, and three on the technology-heavy NASDAQ. The United Nations Conference on Trade and Development estimates that a record $36.7 billion of foreign direct

investment flowed into India in 2008. Foreign-exchange reserves stand at a robust $250 billion.

8   There are less tangible changes as well. For generations after independence from Britain in 1947, more or less the only way for an Indian to make a mark on the world stage was to emigrate. A. R. Rahman, the Chennai-based composer of the *Slumdog* soundtrack, has not needed to change the color of his passport to snag a Golden Globe or multiple Oscar nominations. In a broader sense, the same holds true for many of the scientists and engineers who work for General Electric or Microsoft in Bangalore, or for the employees of a clutch of ambitious homegrown pharmaceutical companies with global ambition. India may not quite be center-stage—its contribution to world trade remains a slender 1.5 percent—but neither is it off-stage anymore. If an ambitious government target is met, the country's share of world trade will more than triple to 5 percent by 2020.

9   Notwithstanding the giant strides made over the past 18 years, Indian criticism of *Slumdog* also reveals the chasm between the country's self-perception and projection and any reasonable measure of its achievements. India may boast homegrown programs in space exploration and nuclear power, but—as a first time visitor to India immediately notices and as the film mercilessly reveals—it also struggles to provide its people with electricity, sanitation, and drinking water. About half of Indian

Jamal Malik (Dev Patel) appears on the game show *Who Wants to Be a Millionaire?* in a scene from *Slumdog Millionaire* (2008).

women are illiterate, a higher percentage than in Laos, Cambodia, or Myanmar. It is at number 122—between Nepal and Lesotho—on the World Bank index that measures ease of doing business, and 85 on the global corruption index maintained by the anti-graft NGO Transparency International. To put it bluntly, the squalor of the slums depicted in *Slumdog* is closer to reality than an elaborately choreographed Bollywood dance sequence shot on location in Switzerland.

10   To sum up, by jettisoning socialism and embracing globalization India has become more prosperous than at any time in more than six decades of independence. But the effects of failed policies pursued between 1947 and 1991 cannot be erased overnight. As *Slumdog* reveals, India is doing better than ever only when benchmarked against its own dismal past. When compared to the West, or to East Asian countries that have truly transformed themselves—Japan, Taiwan, and Korea—the gap between India's rhetoric and its reality remains jarring. *Slumdog* may wound national pride, but the answer is more openness not less. As long as chronic poverty remains a central fact of Indian life, the spotlight that globalization brings will shine on India's software success as well as on its slums.

ISSUE IN FOCUS

Immigration

In June 2007, a group called the Fair Immigration Reform Movement organized a march on Washington, D.C., to protest immigration laws that force families to live apart. By using the strollers and the posters, what values are the protesters appealing to?

Just about everyone can quote the famous words that Emma Lazarus wrote for the pedestal of the Statue of Liberty ("Give me / Your tired, your poor, your huddled masses yearning to breathe free, / The wretched refuse of your teeming shore. / Send these, the homeless, tempest-tost to me") because the United States prides itself on being a nation of immigrants. And recently we have made good on the promise: more than 10 percent

The Statue of Liberty

of our people, over 30 million in all (up from 10 million in 1970), were born in other countries. Indeed, according to the most recent census, one in five U.S. citizens was born either abroad or to foreign-born parents. Steady increases in legal immigration after World War II developed into a boom during the 1980s and 1990s in part because the 1965 Immigration Act (amended in 1990) looked favorably on the immigration of relatives of U.S. citizens; repealed quotas on immigrants from certain nations; and therefore encouraged immigration from Asia, Latin America, and Africa. As a result, in 2008 and 2009 well over a million people were still immigrating legally to the United States, despite the economic recession. (An estimated 11 million other people were residing here illegally.) While immigrants in the late nineteenth and early twentieth centuries mostly came from southern and central Europe, most of today's immigrants come from Mexico; the Caribbean islands; the former Soviet Union; and Asian nations such as China, Vietnam, the Philippines, and India. While earlier immigrants typically passed by the Statue of Liberty and were processed at Ellis Island before going on to northern cities, more than half of recent immigrants have been attracted to Florida, Texas, and California.

Nevertheless, there has also been a long history of resistance to immigration in the United States, dating at least to those who proudly enrolled in the Know Nothing political party of the 1840s and 1850s. Members of that political faction resisted the immigrants from Ireland and Germany who were arriving in waves, and they tended to blame all the nation's ills on immigration—crime, economic problems, and social stresses. The questions (and fears) raised by those early critics persist today, except that now they are raised in connection with Asians, Arabs, and Latin Americans. Just what are the social and economic effects of immigration? How quickly and how completely do immigrants become assimilated—learning the majority language, identifying themselves with American cultural values, and participating in American political life? What is our national responsibility to support, educate, and help assimilate immigrants? Do immigrants constitute a threat to the nation's economic well-being because they are commonly poor and less educated, because they take jobs away from native workers, and because they require expensive social services, such as welfare, education, and health? Or do immigrants actually increase the nation's wealth because they

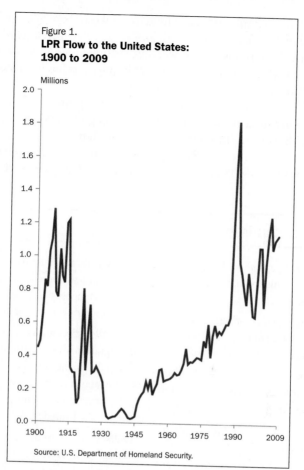

Figure 1.
**LPR Flow to the United States:
1900 to 2009**

Source: U.S. Department of Homeland Security.

Legal immigration, 1900–2009
Source: U.S. Department of Homeland Security

are highly motivated and because they supply labor to a perennially labor-hungry economy? Do immigrants endanger our democracy because they cling to their original national identities, are slow to learn English, and participate only fitfully in political life—or do immigrants enrich the nation with their values and beliefs, ideas and ideals, and hopes and hard work? Do immigrants pose a threat to national security?

This section provides diverse perspectives on immigration, as do selections included elsewhere in this text. Roy Beck's essay, an excerpt from his 1996 book *The Case Against Immigration*, represents the point of view of those who resist immigration on moral, economic, social, political, and environmental grounds. In "No Human Being Is Illegal," Mae Ngai (a professor of history at the University of Chicago, where she specializes in immigration studies) takes a balanced look at the stereotypes of immigrants in the United States. The essay, published in *Women's Studies Quarterly* in 2006, challenges readers to rethink the stereotypes we use to label immigrants and raises fundamental questions about what it means to participate in American society with and without the privilege of citizenship. The distinguished journalist Lance Morrow, writing in *Smithsonian* magazine in 2009, argues that symbolism associated with immigrants has been absolutely central to our national civic and political identity.

Finally, elsewhere in this book, you will find more voices in the serious debates that surround immigration. In "Crossing the Line" (page 176), Dan Stein argues that illegal immigrants are being dangerously welcomed when banks issue them credit cards. Responding to Stein, Gregory Rodriguez argues in "Illegal Immigrants—They're Money" (page 178) that people who have come

A Time Line on Immigration

1607. The first permanent English settlement at Jamestown, Virginia, is established.

1607–1776. "Open Door" era: individual colonies encourage immigration, restricting only criminals and "undesirables."

1776–1835. The "First Great Lull" in immigration: immigration numbers are low.

1808. Importation of slaves is halted.

1840s. Irish immigration (as a result of famine) initiates an era of mass immigration that lasts until World War I.

1875. The Supreme Court decides that immigration policy is the responsibility of the federal government, not the states.

1882–1917. Asian immigration is effectively interdicted. The 1882 Chinese Exclusion Act bars Chinese in particular.

1892. Ellis Island in New York Harbor becomes the leading entry point for immigrants.

1890–1920. A wave of immigration from southern and eastern Europe peaks at 1.3 million in 1907.

1921. Quotas are initiated to reduce immigration sharply and to make immigration reflect the established face of the American community (i.e., white and European).

1920–1945. Second "Great Lull" in immigration: more restrictive immigration policies, the effects of the Great Depression, and the Second World War limit the number of immigrants who settle in the United States.

1940s. Restrictions on Asian immigration are dropped.

1954. Operation Wetback effectively stops illegal immigration.

1965. The Immigration and Nationality Act increases immigration quotas, abolishes the principle of taking into account immigrants' national origins, and emphasizes family unification.

1986. The Immigration Reform and Control Act provides amnesty for many illegal immigrants.

1990s and 2000s. Immigration numbers increase substantially—for both legal and illegal immigrants.

Basic sources: Peter Brimelow, *Alien Nation; CQ Researcher*

Immigration Web Sites

You can learn more about immigration and read more arguments about it at a number of places on the World Wide Web. Here are a few:

The U. S. Department of Homeland Security, U.S. Citizenship and Immigration Services, administers and enforces U.S. immigration policy. For information check the Office of Immigration Statistics at uscis.gov/graphics/shared/statistics/index.htm.

For information about immigration from the **U.S. Census Bureau,** see www.census.gov/main/www/cen2000.html.

The Cato Institute offers demographic and economic statistics about immigrants: www. cato.org.

The Alexis de Tocqueville Institution works to increase public understanding of the cultural and economic benefits of immigration: www.adti.net.

The Center for Immigration Studies conducts research on the impact of immigration: www.cis.org.

The Federation for American Immigration Reform (FAIR) lobbies in favor of placing restrictions on immigration: www.fairus.org.

The National Council of La Raza lobbies on behalf of Latinos in the United States: www.nclr.org.

The National Immigration Forum builds public support for immigration: www.immigrationforum.org.

The Immigration History Research Center, based at the University of Minnesota, is a substantial resource on American immigration and ethnic history: www. ihrc.umn.edu.

to the United States to work should not be denied the opportunity for credit that other Americans enjoy. For a compelling narrative argument about brutalities associated with U.S. immigration policy, turn to Leslie Marmon Silko's "The Border Patrol State" (page 160), which relates the experience of being pulled over by the border police.

Silko's argument, which was written in 1994, gained new resonance in 2010, when the Arizona legislature passed a state law making it a crime to be in the United States illegally. Until that time, illegal immigration was considered a federal matter and enforcement was left to Washington; but the new Arizona law not only transformed police into border patrollers but also required immigrants—indeed, all citizens—to carry proof of their legal status, a requirement that angered even many conservatives (such as the U.S. Catholic bishops). The law also invited racial profiling by police who would have little reason to suspect illegality except for physical appearance. The outraged objections to this law—in June 2012 the Supreme Court upheld the legality of immigration status checks carried out by police but struck down three other provisions of the law—and the equally passionate defenses of it once again revealed how deeply divided Americans are over this important issue.

Waiting on the Mexican side of the Rio Grande

Roy Beck

A Nation of (Too Many) Immigrants?

Since 1970, more than 30 million foreign citizens and their descendants have been added to the local communities and labor pools of the United States.[1] It is the numerical equivalent of having relocated within our borders the entire present population of all Central American countries.

Demographic change on such a massive scale—primarily caused by the increased admission of legal immigrants—inevitably has created winners and losers among Americans. Based on opinion polls, it appears that most Americans consider themselves net losers and believe that the United States has become "a nation of too many immigrants." What level of immigration is best for America, and of real help to the world? Although we often hear that the United States is a nation of immigrants, we seldom ask just what that means. It can be difficult to ask tough questions about immigration when we see nostalgic images of Ellis Island, recall our own families' coming to America, or encounter a new immigrant who is striving admirably to achieve the American dream.

But tough questions about immigration can no longer be avoided as we enter a fourth decade of unprecedentedly high immigration and struggle with its impact on job markets, on the quality of life and social fabric of our communities, and on the state of the environment.

Efforts to discuss these questions alarm some business interests and others who support high immigration. They often express shock that Americans could consider violating what they claim to be the country's tradition of openness by cutting immigration. But they misunderstand U.S. history. It is the high level of immigration during the last three decades that has violated our immigration tradition. The anti-immigration tenor of the times is not nearly so much because Americans have changed as that immigration has changed.

Over the long span of history from the founding of the nation in 1776 until 1965, immigration varied widely but averaged around 230,000 a year. This was a phenomenal flow into a single country, unmatched in world history. It should be noted that during large parts of that period, the United States—with vast expanses of virtually open land—was much better able than today to handle 230,000 newcomers annually. Suddenly in the 1970s and 1980s, at the very time that the majority of Americans were coming to the conclusion that the U.S. population had grown large enough, immigration soared above American tradition, averaging more than 500,000 a year. And it has been running around 1 million a year during the 1990s.

Until recently, policymakers and politicians of every stripe had ignored what public opinion polls found to be the public's growing dissatisfaction with the abnormally high level of immigration. Majority public opinion can be shallow, fleeting, and wrong, but an honest look at major trends during the recent mass immigration shows that ordinary Americans' concerns can hardly be dismissed as narrow and unenlightened:

- Whole industries in the 1970s and 1980s reorganized to exploit compliant foreign labor, with the result that conditions have deteriorated for all workers in those industries.
- Long trends of rising U.S. wages have been reversed.
- Poverty has increased.
- The middle-class way of life has come under siege; income disparities have widened disturbingly.
- Aggressive civil rights programs to benefit the descendants of slavery have been watered down, co-opted, and undermined because of the unanticipated volume of new immigration. A nearly half-century march of economic progress for black Americans has been halted and turned back.
- The culture—and even language—of many local communities has been transformed against the wishes of their native inhabitants. Instead of spawning healthy diversity, immigration has turned many cities into caldrons of increased ethnic tension and divisiveness.

- A stabilizing U.S. population with low birth rates (like other advanced nations) has become the most rapidly congesting industrialized nation in the world (resembling trends in Third World countries). Vast tracts of remaining farmland, natural habitat, and ecosystems have been destroyed to accommodate the growing population. Environmental progress has been set back by the addition of tens of millions of new polluters.

- Numerous organized crime syndicates headquartered in the new immigrants, home countries have gained solid beachheads of operations. Law enforcement agencies have been confounded just as they thought they were near victory over the crime organizations that other ethnic groups had brought with them during the Great Wave.

It is common when discussing those negative trends to focus on individual immigrants' skills, education, and morals, their country of origin, culture, and race. If one side points out that some immigrants are prone to crime and destructive behavior, others note that most immigrants arrive with high motives, good character, and laudable behavior. Some observers fear that the volume of non-European immigration threatens to swamp America's cultural heritage; others welcome an ever more multicultural society. Nonetheless, the chief difficulties that America faces because of current immigration are not triggered by *who* the immigrants are but by *how many* they are.

The task before the nation in setting a fair level of immigration is not about race or some vision of a homogeneous white America; it is about protecting and enhancing the United States' unique experiment in democracy for all Americans, including recent immigrants, regardless of their particular ethnicity. It is time to confront the true costs and benefits of immigration numbers, which have skyrocketed beyond our society's ability to handle them successfully.

The cumulative effect of years of high immigration has taken a while for Americans to comprehend. But in the 1990s, many Americans have awakened to a rather startling realization: The unrelenting surge of immigration above traditional levels is transforming communities throughout the United States into something their residents often don't like or quite recognize as their own.

The unprecedented flow of immigration has dramatically reshaped the social and ecological landscape up and down America's coasts, and it has spilled over into the hinterlands, carving new economic and cultural channels in the Ozarks Hills, Wisconsin's little northwoods cities, Atlanta's outlying towns, the Rocky Mountains, and the Kansas-Nebraska-Iowa plains. Millions of new immigrants now pulse through the economic arteries of most urban areas, from New York City to Dodge City, and of an increasing number of non-urban regions, from North Carolina fishing villages to North Arkansas mountain hamlets.

None of this has been inevitable. Legal immigration into this country has quadrupled over the traditional American level for only one reason: Congress and the president made it happen.

Legal immigration could be stopped with a simple majority vote of Congress and a stroke of the president's pen. . . . Or it could be increased just as quickly. The volume of legal immigration is entirely at the discretion of Washington.

Nobody ever intended for such an onslaught when the immigration laws were changed in 1965; the huge increase in numbers was an accident. But for nearly three decades during various efforts to control illegal immigration, Congress stood by as the much larger legal immigration soared ever upward and as citizen opposition rose correspondingly.

Finally in 1993 and 1994, a few lawmakers of both parties—but outside their parties' leadership—proposed major cutbacks (of two-thirds to three-fourths) in annual legal immigration. They shocked everybody, including themselves, by drawing almost 100 supporters from among the 535 members of Congress.

Then, in 1995, more modest reductions (of about one-third) were proposed independently by two key Republican subcommittee chairmen, Senator Alan Simpson of Wyoming and Representative Lamar Smith of Texas, and by a bi-partisan federal commission led by former Democratic congresswoman Barbara Jordan. President Bill Clinton endorsed the concept. The emerging centrist consensus, however, quickly drew strong opposition from several top Republican congressional leaders (especially free-market libertarians) and from the Democrats' liberal wing, all of whom wished to protect current high immigration levels or increase them.

The United States entered 1996 with Congress assessing the effects of the unprecedented foreign influx of the last thirty years and trying to determine how drastically annual immigration should be cut.

Despite the loud outcry from immigration advocates that something draconian was being considered, a one-third reduction would leave legal admissions still near the level of the 1880–1924 Great Wave. Even after a one-third cut in 1996, the number of immigrants would be triple the average who entered during America's golden immigration era between 1925 and 1965. In that time of far lower immigration, immigrants enjoyed more popularity and a higher and quicker success rate than at any other time in American history.

Given the three decades of inertia that had made any rollback seem impossible, the leaders who proposed cutting legal immigration by around one-third have to be lauded. But they have approached the issue by starting with the current unprecedented immigration peak, determining that it is harmful to the country, and then asking what can be cut. If instead they were designing immigration policy based on what is best for the American people, they would start at zero and ask what level of immigration actually is needed by the nation. The final number in that exercise would be far lower—and far closer to what the American people most desire.

The country's grateful reaction to a cut of merely one-third might be similar to that of residents of a Mississippi River town after a flood has crested in the upstairs bedroom and then receded to the living room downstairs: "Conditions are improved, but we're still flooded."

This self-inflicted flooding of the past three decades has undercut ambitious efforts during the same period to create a society of more fairness and opportunity for all Americans. Strong evidence amasses that the levels of immigration after 1965 have eroded the country's ability to achieve some of its most cherished goals. Many politicians and pundits have said it is hyperbolic to suggest that the single phenomenon of renewed mass immigration could so negatively affect the country. But major demographic upheavals, like the Baby Boom after World War II, touch every aspect of a nation's life and reverberate for decades. Certainly, the more than 30 million people added by immigration policy during the last three decades qualify as a major demographic phenomenon.

There have been many impediments to reaching some of our nation's highest goals. Immigration has not been the only cause—and not usually the major cause—of various societal problems. But research from numerous sources converges to show that the new massive volume of immigration has played an important "spoiler" role in efforts to reach at least four of America's goals: (1) a middle-class society; (2) equal opportunity for the descendants of slavery; (3) harmonious and safe communities; and (4) a protected and restored natural environment. . . .

A Middle-Class Society

Today, Americans live in a society of widening economic disparity, with an increasing gulf between poor and rich, and fewer and fewer people in the middle class. This is a reversal of our egalitarian dreams of a society in which all who were willing could find a job, and in which even those who performed the lower-skilled tasks needed by society would earn an income that could support a family in modest dignity.

The Council of Economic Advisors told the president in 1993 that "immigration has increased the relative supply of less educated labor and appears to have contributed to the increasing inequality of income. . . . [author's ellipses]"[2] That was consistent with a United Nations report on the effect of immigration on the industrialized nations. It concluded that immigration reinforces existing gaps between rich and poor.[3]

Nonetheless, immigration definitely brings some benefits to a nation. In fact, most Americans may have benefited as consumers because the immigrants have kept the price of labor lower, which may have led to lower prices than otherwise would have occurred. But consumers also tend to be laborers drawing those depressed wages. According to the UN report, it is only for the upper crust that the financial benefits of immigration tend to outweigh the losses. And that serves to increase income disparity.

Who wins and who loses? A glance through the roster of immigration winners quickly finds business owners who have followed a low-wage labor strategy. Land developers, real estate agents, home mortgage officials, and others who tend to profit from population growth are winners. Owners of high-tech industries have lowered their costs by importing skilled immigrants who will work at lower wages than college-educated Americans. People who can afford nannies, gardeners, and housekeepers have benefited from lower costs. Americans who prize cultural diversity are among the non-financial winners. Others have won by having the security, prestige, or pay of their jobs enhanced by the high immigrant flow. That would include immigration lawyers, refugee resettlement agency personnel, officials of immigrant-advocacy groups, and educators and other social services employees who work with immigrants.

Unfortunately, the roster of immigration losers is much larger and includes some of America's most vulnerable citizens: poor children, lower-skilled workers, residents of declining urban communities, large numbers of African Americans, the unskilled immigrants who already are here and face the most severe competition from new immigrants, and even some of America's brightest young people, who lose opportunities to pursue science-based careers because of some corporations' and universities' preferences for foreign scientists and engineers.

Also among the losers from immigration are all Americans who prefer to live in a more middle class and less economically polarized society. Under low-immigration conditions from 1925 to 1965, the United States enjoyed increasing egalitarianism. But by the middle of the 1980s, it had a larger gap between the rich and poor than could be found in any other major industrialized nation, according to the U.S. Census Bureau. Nearly every community receiving substantial numbers of immigrants has experienced increased disparities among its population and diminished cohesiveness. Even many Americans who would gain financially from high immigration into their community have come to oppose it because of the changes it would bring; they don't want to create a community of rising disparities, even if they would make more money. Consider the recent examples of Clay County, Alabama, and Clay County, Iowa.

In Alabama, the county chamber of commerce helped organize business, civic, and educational leaders in 1995 to discourage an Arkansas corporation from using immigrant labor to expand its existing poultry-processing operations in rural Clay County. Asked if it wasn't a little strange to have a chamber of commerce opposing local economic and population growth, executive director Carolyn Dunagan said: "I don't know about other places, but here when it comes to a choice between quality of life and growth, quality of life is the most important." The Clay County leaders acted out of two primary concerns: (1) The importation of immigrants likely would hurt the county's black workers, harming their already modest economic position; and (2) the impoverished, Deep South county was having enough trouble trying to create a cohesive culture out of its black and white residents, without adding foreign cultures and languages into the mix and contributing to a population growth unlikely to pay its own way.

Mayor Irving Thompson of Ashland, the county seat, told me that many townspeople believed the corporation was preparing to recruit immigrant workers in response to recent protests by local black employees over working conditions. "The fear," high school history teacher Mark Tucker said, "is that the next time black workers walk out over a labor problem, they'll be replaced by Third World workers." It is not a frivolous fear; replacing black employees—more than any other Americans—with foreign workers has become somewhat commonplace around the country under Washington's expanded immigration programs.

In Clay County, Iowa, the economic enticements were greater. An outside corporation sought a zoning change to allow it to start up operations in an abandoned plant in Spencer, the county seat. An enraged citizenry crowded into the high school fieldhouse in an emotional demonstration before the city council, winning unanimous approval to block the corporation.

Why would they kiss good-bye 350 new industrial jobs for the city of 11,000? In a word: immigration. The proposed operation was in an industry with a long track record of drawing foreign workers. Local advocates for the new jobs accused opponents of being racist. Opponents, though, noted that the community had freely embraced refugees over the years, and that their concern about an influx of foreign workers was that the experience of other cities showed an unacceptable change in a previously egalitarian way of life.

The most telling reason Spencer citizens gave for blocking the new jobs was: "We don't want to become another Storm Lake."

Until the 1980s, Storm Lake—less than an hour's drive to the south—had been like a twin to Spencer: neighboring agricultural county seat, same size, similar history and economy, a shared bucolic, safe, midwestern lifestyle with excellent schools, and the same epic prairie sky of uninhibited expressiveness. But a corporation similar to the one just blocked in Spencer moved into Storm Lake and immediately began attracting foreign workers. The steady flow soon turned Storm Lake into one of the scores of new immigration hubs created by federal immigration mandates since 1965.

The unrequested changes to life in Storm Lake followed patterns similar to those in many new-immigration cities. Overnight, Storm Lake schools were dealing with the cultural ramifications of a student body that now is one-fifth immigrant (predominantly Laotian and Mexican) and with the challenges of teaching in different languages. New facilities have been needed to handle the growing population of high-fertility foreign families with their low incomes and low tax payments. Some Storm Lake residents have lost their jobs to immigrants; more have seen their wages depressed because of the loosening of the labor market and the immigrants' lower expectations. The immigrants have tended to occupy housing units in higher densities than natives and have settled in enclaves, changing the character of neighborhoods and causing some elementary schools to be disproportionately filled with newcomers. For the first time, parts of town became undesirable in the real estate market based on which schools had high populations of students who didn't speak English. A community, which previously had little reason to think in terms of haves and have-nots, became a starkly stratified society.

Especially unsettling—but to be expected in a community of wide disparities, transience, and separate cultures—has been the deterioration in Storm Lake residents' sense of safety. The crime rate soared above that of the rest of Iowa. It is four times higher than crime in Spencer, its former twin.

To a visitor from a coastal city, where the national trend toward economic stratification has been visible longer, Storm Lake still can seem like a delightful place to live. But to those who knew the city before, the changes have been difficult to accept. "It breaks my heart to see what has become of my hometown," said Mary Galik, a Storm Lake native who moved to Spencer.

Given a choice, there was nothing about the creation of sharp disparities in the Storm Lake population that Spencer's citizens wanted to risk duplicating. Even main street merchants did not oppose efforts to block the new industry. As business owners, they favored the new plant because it would have increased their retail sales, explained Bob Rose, program manager of the merchants' economic growth organization. But as parents and grandparents, the merchants did not look favorably on economic development that might endanger what they saw as Spencer's special midwestern small-town culture and quality of life.

Nationally during the last two decades of high immigration, the richest 20 percent of Americans have enjoyed some economic improvement and the richest 1 percent have reaped strong increases of income. But the average wage for most American groups has declined.

No scholar suggests that increased immigration is the chief culprit in America's overall decline in wages. The economist Paul Krugman, of Stanford University, says the obvious central cause of the disappointing economic conditions for the American majority since 1973 is the drastic drop in the rate of growth in output (productivity) per worker. But the experts are uncertain about precisely why productivity growth has dropped so low and stayed there.[4] Clearly, though, Congress picked a terribly inappropriate period of U.S. history to be increasing the number of U.S. workers through immigration.

At the same time immigration was snowballing in the 1970s, the labor market was being flooded with baby boomers who were reaching employment age and with a big increase in married women seeking jobs. Based on recent research by several economists, it would appear that the big increases in the labor supply probably contributed to the drop in productivity growth, and definitely worked against efforts to improve it after it did drop.

Research by the economist Paul Romer explains that the problem with a large increase in the number of workers is that it tends to result in a lower amount of capital investment per worker. It is the capital investment per worker, along with technology, that is the most important ingredient in increasing per capita output, according to Romer's study, published in the authoritative National Bureau of Economic Research journal. Thus, immigration during the last two decades, by greatly increasing the labor supply, would seem to be undermining capital investment per worker, the very process that could send wages upward again.

Romer's research flies in the face of today's immigration advocates, who insist that the federal government must continue to run a high-immigration program in order to boost the economy. Adding workers usually *does* increase the nation's overall economic output, but not by enough to improve the circumstances of the average worker. "In fact, what the data suggest is that labor productivity responds quite negatively to increases in the labor force," Romer maintains. Looking across American history, Romer found that when the growth in number of workers went up (through high immigration and fertility), there was a decline in the growth of per capita output—just as has occurred during this latest time of high immigration and depressed wages.[5]

Studies by Harvard's Jeffrey G. Williamson have found that during those same periods of high immigration, the United States became less of a middle-class society and experienced its highest degree of economic disparity—just as is happening during the current period of high immigration.[6]

It isn't difficult to see how an abundant supply of new foreign workers could retard wage increases. U.S. Secretary of Labor Robert B. Reich fretted in 1994 that constant supplies of foreign labor have enticed many employers to continue relying on low-paid, low-skilled jobs, instead of making technological improvements and then training workers for more productive, higher-paying jobs.[7]

A U.S. Bureau of Labor Statistics study concluded that immigration was responsible for roughly half the decline in real wages for native-born high school dropouts in the fifty largest metropolitan areas during the 1980s. The study found that immigration accounted for 20 to 25 percent of the increase in the wage gap between low-skill and high-skill workers.[8] And economists Timothy J. Hatton and Jeffrey G. Williamson declared in 1994 that all standard mainstream economic models predict migration will tend to lower wages where immigrants settle.[9]

Because the United States has had a surplus of workers, even the profits of the small recent growth in per capita productivity have not been passed on to the workers. Krugman has noted that when the number of workers surges, "the way that a freely functioning labor market ensures that almost everyone who wants a job gets one is by allowing wage rates to fall, if necessary, to match demand to supply." Most of the profits from recent increased productivity have gone to Americans in the top 1 percent of income.[10] According to the research of immigrant economist George Borjas, high immigration during the 1980s helped facilitate a massive redistribution of wealth—more than $100 billion a year—from American workers to the upper class.[11]

The trend in this country during the previous decades of low immigration had long been toward higher wages, less poverty, and a larger middle class. Beginning with the shortage of workers during World War II, more and more Americans found that the toil of their labor earned them middle-class status. The number of Americans in poverty declined for decades. That happy circumstance came to a halt in 1973. Except for minor variations, the number of impoverished Americans has been increasing ever since.

The United States now routinely violates what Washington policy analyst Norman Ornstein has concluded is an implicit, national bipartisan compact. In words similar to Bill Clinton's during his first presidential campaign, Ornstein says the compact holds that "if people play by the rules, working hard and doing their jobs, they will not have to live in poverty."[12] But his contention has become increasingly difficult to uphold as inflation-adjusted wages have declined for Americans without college degrees and even many with degrees.

What to do about the millions of Americans mired in poverty or struggling just above it? "The best way to help these young unskilled workers is through supply-side interventions," maintains labor professor Robert M. Hutchens of Cornell University. Initiatives that limit immigration of workers "can promote an environment where academic underachievers have at least some opportunity for upward mobility," he adds.[13]

No studies suggest that halting immigration would immediately put middle-class wages into the pockets of a large percentage of today's poor. But America's poor and its working class are not among the net winners of an immigration policy that brings in people who can compete directly with them in the job market. If the nation desires a return to a more middle-class economy, it is difficult to understand why its government would allow more than a nominal flow of immigrants at this time. . . .

---

[1]Total immigration-related population growth was calculated in a three-step process: (1) Demographer Leon Bouvier determined the 1995 population of 1970-stock Americans (those who were in the country in 1970, plus their descendants, minus all deaths of the two groups by 1995). (2) The U.S. Census Bureau estimated the total U.S. population in 1995. The total included both 1970-stock Americans and post-1970 immigrants and their descendants. (3) I merely subtracted the 1970-stock American population from the U.S. total population to determine the segment of total population that can be attributed to post-1970 legal and illegal immigrants, plus their descendants. See Roy Beck, "Immigration: No. 1 in U.S. Growth," *The Social Contract* (Winter 1991-92).

[2]Council of Economic Advisors, *1993 Annual Report to the President* (4 February 1994).

[3]United Nations Population Fund, *State of the World Population 1993* (New York: United Nations Population Fund, 1993).

[4]Paul Krugman, *Peddling Prosperity: Economic Sense and Nonsense in the Age of Diminished Expectations* (New York: W. W. Norton & Co., 1994).

[5]Paul Romer, "Crazy Explanations for the Productivity Slowdown," *Macroeconomics Annual* (Cambridge, MA: National Bureau of Economic Research, 1987), pp. 181–183.

[6]Jeffrey Williamson, *Inequality, Poverty and History: The Kuznets Memorial Lectures* (Cambridge, MA: Blackwell, 1991).

[7]Roberto Suro, "Immigrants Crowd Labor's Lowest Rung," *The Washington Post*, 13 September 1994.

[8]David A. Jaeger, "Skill Differences and the Effect of Immigrants on the Wages of Natives," Bureau of Labor Statistics Working Paper No. 273 (U.S. Department of Labor, December 1995).

[9]Timothy J. Hatton and Jeffrey G. Williamson, "International Migration

1850–1939: An Economic Survey," in *Migration and the International Labor Market 1850–1939,* Hatton and Williamson, eds. (New York: Routledge, 1994), p. 19.

[10]Krugman, *Peddling Prosperity,* pp. 124, 137–138.

[11]George J. Borjas, "Know the Flow," *National Review,* vol. XLVII (17 April 1995): 49.

[12]Norman Ornstein, "Can America Afford $5.15 An Hour?" *The Washington Post,* 12 February 1995, p. C1.

[13]Robert M. Hutchens, *A Path to Good Jobs? Unemployment and Low Wages: The Distribution of Opportunity for Young Unskilled Workers.* Public Policy Brief No. 11 (Annandale-on-Hudson, NY: The Jerome Levy Economics Institute, 1994).

Wiley Miller has been writing *Non Sequitur* since 1991 and has won four National Cartoonist Society awards. This cartoon appeared in 2002.

Mae M. Ngai

No Human Being Is Illegal

Like abortion and guns, immigration has emerged as a hot-button issue in American politics. Because immigration involves concerns in different registers, economic and cultural, it is strangely and perhaps uniquely misaligned in traditional partisan terms (Wong 2006; Zolberg 2006). President Bush cannot manage the split in his own party, between those Republicans who want to exploit immigrants and those who want to expel them. Among Democratic voters, some support cultural diversity and inclusion while others worry that cheaper immigrant labor depresses domestic wages. Political consultants, sensing a no-win situation, are advising Democrats with presidential aspirations to stay clear of the issue altogether.

2   The lack of partisan coherence, however, does not explain why immigration evokes such heated debate. There is a dimension to the debate that seems irrational, impervious to arguments involving empirical data, historical experience, or legal precedent. This was brought home to me after I wrote an op-ed in a major newspaper about how, during the first half of the twentieth century, the U.S. government legalized tens of thousands of illegal European immigrants (Ngai 2006). I received postcards with invectives like, "stupid professor!" I faced similar hostility during a live call-in show on public radio. Confronted with ranting about how immigrants are bad for the United States, I wanted to counter that immigrants are good for the United States. At one level, negative generalizations about immigrants can be refuted point by point: they do not hurt the economy, they expand it; they are more law abiding than the native-born population; they want to learn English and their children all do (Smith and Edmonston 1997; Alba and Nee 2003).

3   But this approach is risky. Generalizations reproduce stereotypes and efface the complexity and diversity of immigrant experience. As Bonnie Honig (2001) has argued, xenophilia is the flip side of xenophobia. In both cases citizens use "immigrants" as a screen onto which they project their own aspirations or frustrations about American democracy. Casting immigrants as bearers of the work ethic, family values, and consensual citizenship renews the tired citizen's faith-liberal capitalism. But when the immigrants disappoint or when conditions change, they become easy scapegoats.

4   As Honig suggests, this kind of immigration discourse is an exercise in nationalism. In an important sense, "Are immigrants good or bad for us?" is the wrong question. It takes as its premise that immigrants are not part of "us." The idea falsely posits that non-citizens are not part of American society and leaves them out of the discussion. The mass demonstrations of Mexicans and other immigrants last spring were significant because they showed that immigrants are no longer content to be the object of discussion but have emerged as subjects with voice and agency. It was particularly noteworthy but perhaps not surprising that so many of the participants were female, from older hotel workers to high school students, giving lie to the

stereotypes that the "illegal alien" is a solo male laborer or that immigrants are meek. Undocumented immigration involves men, women, and families, and they are all standing up.

5   Further, the question assumes that "we" (the United States, defined by its citizens) have a singular interest above and against the interests of "them" (all non-citizens and the foreign countries from whence they came). To be sure, while human migration is as old as human history, immigration and naturalization are modern phenomena, part of the international system based on nation-states that was consolidated in the period between the late nineteenth century and World War I. In this system, sovereign nations assert their absolute right to determine, in the first instance, who shall be admitted to territory and membership and who shall not.

6   In the United States, immigration was not regulated by the federal government until after the civil war, and not until the late 1880s and 1890s did the U.S. Supreme Court invoke the sovereign principle as the basis for immigration policy. Before that, it considered immigration part of the commerce clause of the Constitution; as laborers, immigrants were easily imagined as "articles of commerce" (Bilder 1996).

7   But Chinese exclusion, first legislated in 1882, required the Court to justify why some laborers were desired and others were not. Was the claim that Chinese were racially inassimilable an acceptable reason? The Court said yes; in fact, it said that Congress did not have to justify itself in terms of the Constitution. In the Chinese Exclusion Case (130 U.S. 518 [1889]) the Court recognized Congress's plenary, or absolute power to regulate immigration as part of its authority over foreign relations, in the same realm as declaring war and making treaties. "Aliens enter and remain in the United States only with the license, permission, and sufferance of Congress," it opined (Fong Yue Ting v. U.S., 149 U.S. 698 [1893]). To this day the plenary power doctrine over immigration stands.

8   American political culture has thoroughly normalized the primacy of national sovereignty in immigration affairs, and with important consequences. Nationalism generates the view that immigration is a zero-sum game among competitive nation-states. Americans like to believe that immigration to the United States proves the superiority of liberal capitalism, that "America" is the object of global envy; we resist examining the role that American world power has played in global structures of migration, including the gendered dimensions of migrant exploitation. Increasing numbers of women from the global south are leaving their families behind as they migrate to the affluent countries to work as caretakers for other people's children, as hotel-room cleaners, or as indentured sex-workers. We prefer to ignore these realities and to think, instead, that our immigration policy is generous—indeed, too generous, as we also resent the demands made upon us by others and we think we owe outsiders nothing (Ngai 2004).

9   The emphasis on national sovereignty is the basis for the alarm that we've "lost control" of the border and for the draconian proposals against unauthorized immigration: more fencing, criminalization of the undocumented and those who hire or assist them, mass deportations. But many liberals who are sympathetic to Mexican immigrants also want "something done" to stop illegal immigration, although few would actually support turning the entire country into a police state, which is what would be necessary to truly seal the border from unauthorized entry. The cost of viewing sovereignty as the exclusive grounds for immigration policy is that we push to the margins other considerations,

such as human rights and global distributive justice. The current debate over immigration policy reform reminds us that sovereignty is not just a claim to national right; it is a theory of power (Carens 1998).

10   Just two months before September 11, 2001, it will be recalled, President Bush announced his intention to legalize undocumented Mexican immigrants and institute a guest-worker program that would offer a path to permanent residency and citizenship. In its details it was not particularly generous and it faced a complex process of legislative negotiation, as have all efforts to reform the immigration laws. But it did not provoke the kind of emotional controversy that we hear today.

11   However, after 9/11 the immigration issue disappeared from the Washington scene. It resurfaced a couple of years ago, with Bush's proposal receiving support from then-president of Mexico, Vicente Fox. But only in the last year has it become an explosive issue in national politics, with vociferous rhetoric like "stop the invasion" and "no amnesty for lawbreakers." It seems no accident that immigration restriction has moved to the fore as public disaffection with the war in Iraq grows. According to Republican strategist Don Allen, immigration is an issue that "gets us talking about security and law and order" (Hulse 2006). House majority leader Dennis Hastert deploys flexible rhetoric of popular sovereignty most succinctly: "We're at war. Our borders are a sieve" (Swarns 2006). Whether mongering terrorism and illegal immigration will result in greater mass support for U.S. wars against both will succeed remains to be seen. But the very connections made between them suggest broad ground for oppositional action.

WORKS CITED

Alba, Richard, and Victor Nee. 2003. *Remaking the American Mainstream.* Cambridge: Harvard University Press.

Bilder, Mary Sarah. 1996. "The Struggle over Immigration: Indentured Servants, Slaves, and Articles of Commerce," *Missouri Law Review.*

Carens, Joseph. 1998. "Aliens and Citizens: The Case for Open Borders," in *The Immigration Reader: America in Multidisciplinary Perspective,* ed. David Jacobson. Malden, MA: Blackwell Publications.

Honig, Bonnie. 2001. *Democracy and the Foreigner.* Princeton: Princeton University Press.

Hulse, Carl. 2006. "In Bellweather District, GOP Runs on Immigration," *New York Times,* September 6, A1.

Ngai, Mae M. 2004. *Impossible Subjects: Illegal Aliens and the Making of Modern America.* Princeton: Princeton University Press.

———. 2006. "How Granny Got Legal." *Los Angeles Times,* May 18.

Smith, James P., and Barry Edmonston, eds. 1997. *The New Americans: Economic, Demographic, and Fiscal Effects of Immigration.* Washington, DC: National Academy Press.

Swarns, Rachel. 2006. "Immigration Overhaul Takes a Backseat as Campaign Season Begins," *New York Times,* September 8, A1.

Wong, Carolyn. 2006. *Lobbying for Inclusion.* Stanford: Stanford University Press.

Zolberg, Aristide. 2006. *A Nation by Design.* New York: Russell Sage Foundation; Cambridge: Harvard University Press. ■

This tower, near Arivaca, Arizona, is one of many equipped with radar and cameras designed to detect people entering the United States illegally. The tower and the fence (in the background) are designed to discourage illegal immigrants: What feelings does the image of this surveillance technology and the desert sunset evoke?

LANCE **MORROW**

Cowboys and Immigrants

A t Fort Clark in West Texas one night in the 1870s, my great-grandmother Ella Mollen Morrow was asleep in the officers' quarters. Her husband, Maj. Albert Morrow, was several days' ride away, on patrol with his troop of Fourth U.S. Cavalry. A soldier, probably drunk, crawled into the house through a window. My great-grandmother heard him. She took up a Colt .44 revolver and warned him to get out. He kept coming at her. She warned him again. The man kept coming.

She shot him—"between the eyes," as a family history said, adding, "No inquiry was held, or deemed necessary."

That was the frontier, all right, and I confess that during the presidential campaign last fall, Sarah Palin—moose hunter, wilderness mom—stirred, for a moment anyway, a genetic current of admiration in my heart. It was an atavistic memory of Ella, of her self-sufficient smoking pistol and its brisk frontier justice, which, on that night in West Texas, pre-emptively brought the bad guy down, dead at her feet. No nonsense.

At the time, the McCain-Obama campaign seemed a clash of neat American opposites. John McCain (maverick, ex-fighter pilot, military hero, senator from Geronimo country), with his sidekick Palin (chirpy backwoods deadeye), worked the Frontier story line. Barack Obama came onstage as apotheosis, the multiracial, multicultural evolution of what Ellis Island promised to the Nation of Immigrants long ago.

John Wayne in a scene from *The Searchers* (1956), directed by John Ford, a film widely considered to be one of the greatest Westerns of all time.

5   But in the evolving financial shambles of the months since the election, the conflict between these mystic poles of American history appeared to vanish, or to dissolve in a chaotic nonideological synthesis. Both Ellis Island and the Frontier hated Wall Street, just as passengers in steerage and passengers in first-class unite in despising icebergs. And amid the great federal bailouts, *Newsweek* proclaimed, "We Are All Socialists Now."

6   I wonder. The Frontier and Ellis Island are myths of origin, alternate versions of the American Shinto. They're not likely to disappear anytime soon.

7   The two myths are sentimental and symbolic categories, no doubt—ideas or mere attitudes more than facts: facets of human nature. (Quite often, when given a hard look, myths fall apart: the historical frontier, for example, was demonstrably communitarian as well as individualist.) But like the philosopher Isaiah Berlin's Hedgehog and

Emma Lazarus

The New Colossus

Emma Lazarus (1849–1887) wrote poetry and essays on a wide variety of topics. Her works were published in the best-known magazines of her time, and she became an influential figure in the rapidly changing New York art scene. She was born into a well-established Jewish family in New York City, was well educated, and worked to improve the conditions of Jews both at home and abroad by establishing programs to educate new immigrants and by founding the Society for the Improvement and Colonization of Eastern European Jews. Her most famous sonnet, reprinted here, was written in 1883 to help raise money for the Statue of Liberty Pedestal, and in 1903 it was engraved on a tablet within the pedestal on which the Statue of Liberty now stands.

Fox or literary critic Philip Rahv's Paleface and Redskin, they offer convenient bins in which to sort out tendencies.

Both myths owe something of their vividness to Hollywood—one to the films of John Ford and John Wayne, for example, and the other to Frank Capra's parables of the common man. The Frontier is set on the spacious Western side of American memory—a terrain whose official masculinity made my great-grandmother's, and Palin's, Annie Oakley autonomies seem somehow bracing. On the other side (diverse, bubbling away in the "melting pot," vaguely feminine in some *gemütlich* nurturing sense) lies Ellis Island. If Frontier dramas call for big skies, open space and freedom, Ellis Island's enact themselves in cities; their emphasis is human, sympathetic, multilingual, and noisy, alive with distinctive cooking smells and old-country customs. The Frontier is big, open-ended, physically demanding, silent.

This bifurcation of American consciousness occurred with a certain chronological neatness—a development "unforeseen, though not accidental," as Trotsky might have said, working his eyebrows. Ellis Island opened for business in 1892 as the gateway for the first of some 12 million immigrants. One year later, the historian Frederick Jackson Turner delivered his "frontier thesis" before the American Historical Society at the World's Columbian Exposition in Chicago. When the Pacific Ocean halted the American frontier on the West Coast, Turner argued, the distinctive urgencies of American destiny closed down. But at just that moment, the East Coast opened up to a powerful flow of new immigrant energies.

In the years 1889–96, the gun-toting ranchman-intellectual Theodore Roosevelt published his four-volume history, *The Winning of the West*. The evolution of the Frontier mythology was in some ways an instinctive reaction against all those foreigners. Ellis Island made the Frontier feel claustrophobic, just as the arrival of sodbusters with their plows and fences would incense the free-range cattle people.

Starting with Teddy Roosevelt, these two American archetypes have reappeared from time to time as presidential styles and ideological motifs. T.R., the sickly New York City boy who repaired health and heart in the Dakota Badlands, was the first modern Frontier president. His dramatization of Frontier attitude occurred at the moment of the Spanish-American War, of Senator Albert Beveridge's triumphal jingo

> Not like the brazen giant of Greek fame,
> With conquering limbs astride from land to land;
> Here at our sea-washed, sunset gates shall stand
> A mighty woman with a torch, whose flame
> 5   Is the imprisoned lightning, and her name
> Mother of Exiles. From her beacon-hand
> Glows world-wide welcome; her mild eyes command
> The air-bridged harbor that twin cities frame.
> "Keep, ancient lands, your storied pomp!" cries she
> 10   With silent lips. "Give me your tired, your poor,
> Your huddled masses yearning to breathe free,
> The wretched refuse of your teeming shore.
> Send these, the homeless, tempest-tost to me,
> I lift my lamp beside the golden door!"

about "The March of the Flag." In 1899, sixteen of Teddy's Rough Riders joined Buffalo Bill Cody's touring Wild West show. Gaudy Wild Bill in fringed buckskins told an audience at the Trans-Mississippi Exposition in Omaha: "The whistle of the locomotive has drowned the howl of the coyote; the barb-wire fence has narrowed the range of the cow-puncher; but no material evidence of prosperity can obliterate our contribution to Nebraska's imperial progress."

12   But in Frontier rhetoric there was often a paradoxical note of elegy and loss, as if the toughest place and moment of the American story was also the most transient, most fragile. By 1918, the Old Bull Moose, reconciled to the Republican Party, was condemning the "social system . . . of every man for himself" and calling for worker's rights, public housing, and day care for the children of mothers working in factories. In nine months, he was dead.

13   The other Roosevelt, T.R.'s cousin Franklin, became the first Ellis Island president. He came to office not at a moment when America had seemed to triumph, but when it had seemed to fail. In myth, if not in fact, the Frontier sounded the bugle—cavalry to the rescue. Ellis Island's narrative began with Emma Lazarus' disconcerting, hardly welcoming phrases of abjection—"your tired, your poor . . . the wretched refuse . . . " Its soundtrack was the street sounds of the *pluribus*.

14   One of the things that made Lyndon Johnson interesting was that he so thoroughly embodied both the Frontier and Ellis Island—and tried to enact both, in the Great Society and in Vietnam. Perhaps it was the conflict between the two ideals that brought him down. A son of the Texas hill country, with its lingering folklore of the Alamo and of long-ago massacres under the Comanche moon, Johnson was also a New Deal Democrat and FDR protégé with all the activist-government Ellis Island instincts. In an interplay of Ellis and the Frontier, he actually tried to bomb Ho Chi Minh into submission while offering to turn Vietnam into a Great Society, full of New Deal projects (dams and bridges and electrification), if only Uncle Ho would listen to reason.

Thomas Bailey Aldrich

The Unguarded Gates

Thomas Bailey Aldrich (1836–1907) provides a poetic argument from the same time period as Emma Lazarus (his poem was published in 1895—two years after hers), but with a more guarded viewpoint. Aldrich was a prominent and prolific New England writer originally from Portsmouth, New Hampshire; his 1883 book An Old Town by the Sea *was an important regional book. Aldrich's 1870 novel* Story of a Bad Boy *served as one inspiration for Mark Twain's* Tom Sawyer.

Wide open and unguarded stand our gates.
And through them press a wild, a motley throng—
Men from the Volga and the Tartar steppes,
Featureless figures of the Hoang Ho,
5   Malayan, Seythian, Teuton, Kelt, and Slav,
Flying the Old World's poverty and scorn;

15   At the Democratic National Convention in 1984, the perfect Ellis Island man, Gov. Mario Cuomo of New York, conjured up a sweet America that originated in sepia photographs of ships arriving in New York Harbor, the vessels' rails crowded with the yearning faces of people from a dozen countries over there, at the instant of their rebirth, their entry into the American alchemy that would transform them and their children forever. "We speak for the minorities who have not yet entered the mainstream," this son of Italian immigrants proclaimed. "We speak for ethnics who want to add their culture to the magnificent mosaic that is America." He called up Ellis Island that summer of 1984 at the same moment Ronald Reagan of California convinced Americans that they were tall in the saddle again, riding into the sunshine of a new morning in America. The Frontier won that round, by a landslide.

16   Reagan personified the cowboy universe that sees itself as self-reliant, competent, freedom-loving, morally autonomous, responsible. He owned a ranch and wore cowboy clothes, and in the Oval Office he displayed a passel of sculptures of cowboys and Indians and bucking broncos. In Reagan's exercise room in the family quarters of the White House, his wife, Nancy, had hung a favorite Reagan self-image, a framed photograph showing him in bluejeans and work shirt and shield-size belt buckle and a well-aged, handsomely crushed white cowboy hat: Reagan's eyes crinkle at the far horizon. The photo watched from the wall as President Reagan pumped iron.

17   George W. Bush put himself in the Reagan mold. Barack Obama's victory represented, among other things, a repudiation of the Frontier style of Bush and Dick Cheney, in favor of an agenda arising from the Ellis Island point of view, with its emphasis on collective social interests, such as health care and the environment. A civic paradigm seemed to have shifted, and a generational paradigm as well.

18   And yet the future (Obama's hopeful young constituency) found itself boomeranged back to the Great Depression. The simultaneous arrival of Obama and bad financial times elicited perhaps too many articles about Franklin Roosevelt and the New

> These bringing with them unknown gods and rites,
> Those tiger passions, here to stretch their claws.
> In street and alley what strange tongues are these.
> 10 Accents of menace alien to our air,
> Voices that once the tower of Babel knew!
> O, Liberty, white goddess, is it well
> To leave the gate unguarded? On thy breast
> Fold sorrow's children, soothe the hurts of fate,
> 15 Lift the downtrodden, but with the hand of steel
> Stay those who to thy sacred portals come
> To waste the fight of freedom. Have a care
> Lest from thy brow the clustered stars be torn
> And trampled in the dust. For so of old
> 20 The thronging Goth and Vandal trampled Rome,
> And where the temples of the Caesars stood
> The lean wolf unmolested made her lair. ∎

Deal. Implicitly, George W. Bush and the Frontier way of doing things seem as discredited today as Herbert Hoover seemed in 1933.

19   *Newsweek*'s proclamation notwithstanding, my guess is that the categories of Ellis Island and the Frontier persist—but now, like so much else, have been globalized. In the 21st century, the division between the two mind-sets projects itself into McLuhan's misnamed "global village," which, more accurately, has become a planetary megacity with some wealthy neighborhoods (now not as wealthy as they thought they were) and vast slum districts—a megacity without police force or sanitation department. The messy municipal planet remains in many ways a frontier, a multicultural Dodge City or Tombstone (lawless, with shooting in the streets, dangerous with terrorism and nuclear possibilities, not a fit place for women and children) that has an Ellis Island aspiration to survive and prosper as the family of man.

20   The Frontier and Ellis Island analyze problems in different ways and arrive at different decisions. The Frontier assumes the drunken soldier is a rapist or murderer and shoots him between the eyes. Ellis Island may see him as a confused fool and hope to talk him into a cup of coffee and a 12-step program. Roughly the same choices present themselves to a president: the planet is the Frontier; the planet is Ellis Island. Genius is the ability to hold two contradictory truths in the mind at the same time without going crazy.

Immigrant families on Ellis Island, 1900, waiting for a ferry to Manhattan.

FROM READING TO WRITING

1. Analyze the argument by Gitlin, Carlson, Ngai, or Morrow: how is that argument the product of its audience and purpose? How would the argument be presented differently if it were directed to a different readership or published in a different forum? How would the argument be different if it were rewritten on this very day? (See Chapter 5 for advice on rhetorical analysis.)

2. Examine the various photos, charts, and other illustration that accompany the selections in this chapter. What visual argument does each one make? (See Chapter 6 for guidance on analyzing visuals.)

3. Write your own argument about some aspect of globalization. Do you see its effects on your campus and in your community? How has immigration affected your community and your university?

4. Propose your own solution to a problem associated with globalization or immigration. (See Chapter 13 for advice on writing proposals.)

5. Is there a current proposal being considered in Washington to address illegal immigration? Write an essay in support or opposition to the legislation.

6. Or write an essay refuting the argument of someone who is proposing or supporting the legislation. (See Chapter 12 for advice on writing rebuttals.) Consider whether you wish to show the weaknesses in that other argument, or whether you wish to counterargue, or whether you want to do both.

7. Are you an immigrant yourself, or the child (or grandchild) of an immigrant parent or two? Write a narrative argument related to immigration or globalization that is based on, and generalizes from, your own experiences. (See Chapter 11 for advice on writing narrative arguments.)

8. What exactly is "globalization," anyway? Write an essay that defines the term in such a way that persuades readers to sympathize with it—or to oppose it. (See Chapter 8 for advice on writing definition arguments.)

9. Evaluate immigration or globalization, using data from secondary research (or your personal observations) to support your conclusions.

25 | Science and Ethics

The Ethics of Science and Technology

How does the Nuvo robot's appearance meet—or not meet—your notions of what a household robot might look like? What are some of the ethical concerns associated with having robots "living" in the home?

Item: In November 2004, couples with a family history of cancer were given an unusual permission by the Human Fertilization and Embryology Authority in Great Britain—they were allowed to select for human fertilization embryos free of cancer-causing genes. Critics immediately complained about this effort to create "designer babies." They drew comparisons with Adolph Hitler's interest in creating a "super-race" of genetically enhanced Aryans and raised concerns about the possibility that "better" human beings might have advantages over "natural" people.

Item: Early in 2005 in the United States, members of the National Academy of Sciences were finishing a recommendation report on the legal and ethical status of "chimeras"— hybrid creatures created by implanting one animal's stem cells into the fetal matter of a different species. Several living creatures have been "invented" and patented in recent years, raising the question of the possibility of others—mice with human brains? Pigs bioengineered to produce human blood? Or even a genetically plausible hybrid between humans and chimpanzees?

Item: One Thanksgiving Day, teenager Shawn Woolley committed suicide after (his mother claims) weeks of 12-hour stints playing the online role-playing game EverQuest addled his neurochemical condition. Do electronically mediated experiences like playing EverQuest—not to mention similar experiences that may soon make the transition from science fiction to reality— have mind-and-body effects on the human condition? What about the widespread use of Prozac and other mind-altering drugs: do they threaten to change our sense of what human

> "Twenty-first century technologies—genetics, nanotechnology, and robotics—are so powerful they can spawn whole new classes of accidents and abuses."
>
> —BILL JOY, SUN MICROSYSTEMS

nature is at its core? No wonder science fiction movies and narratives are so popular—characters like the Terminator (hybrids of human and nonhuman) seem possible in the not-so-very-distant future.

These three items, brought to our attention by Jeffrey Pruchnic, highlight some of the ethical issues related to science and technology that people are grappling with these days. Science and technology, as central enterprises in our culture, have always raised difficult moral and ethical questions. Science fiction stories and films have frequently addressed those same questions. Whether it is environmental protection (the subject of Chapter 22), medicine, genetic engineering (including stem cell research and cloning), animal rights, the teaching of evolution, computer technologies, space exploration, or military weapons technology, science and technology command our attention and our committed arguments because they challenge our assumptions about what is possible and push the limits of what we think of as ethical.

Contemporary Arguments

Many new technologies are calling into question "the nature of nature," including our human nature. Is the natural world really "natural" when genetic engineers construct new species of plants and animals? And what are we to make of scientific developments that offer the potential for tremendous human benefits if they also have the potential to change our very human natures? Here we include arguments on four especially important and compelling developments related to science and human nature.

The first is robotics. According to Bill Gates, robots have the potential to become as ubiquitous as computers—although he acknowledges that there are as many naysayers about today's robotics developments as there once were about the possibilities of bringing computers into nearly every home. In "A Robot in Every Home," Gates discusses the potential for robotics with enthusiasm, but detractors (represented here by Paul Marks) are raising questions about the ethics of replacing humans and human labor with robots and robotic labor. The rise of robotics lends an almost science-fiction quality to technology and gives rise in the popular imagination to sci-fi's greatest dreams and fears. Will robots turn on their creators, as Frankenstein turned on his? Or will they remain friendly as pets, like C3PO and R2D2?

The second new technology under watch is nanotechnology. MIT researcher K. Eric Drexler coined the term because *nano* literally means "one billionth": nanotechnology refers to the science of creating molecule-sized materials and machines. Occupying the space between biology and engineering, nanotechnologists promise to create new things that fundamentally change the ways we work and live. As *Spiderman, Star-Trek: The Next Generation,* and popular magazines such as *Forbes* and *Wired* all indicate, nanotechnology promises to be the Next Big Thing. Nano skin creams are on the market, nano-enhanced tennis balls are used in the Davis Cup, and microscopic silicon chips run computer games. More important, nanotechnologists are developing micromachines that might radically improve water quality, benefit agriculture, clean up toxic waste, or make obsolete our reliance on oil by improving the efficiency of solar power. Others might enter the human body to repair tissue. Nanomaterials hundreds of times stronger than steel might make possible ten-pound automobiles or airplanes.

But is nanotechnology safe? Could dangerous nanoparticles escape and cause great damage? And what about nanotechnology's implications for the way human beings think of themselves? Will nanotechnology widen the gap between haves and have-nots around the globe? Those very serious questions are raised here in an essay by Bill Joy and in an interview with Ralph C. Merkle.

Third, we invite you to meditate on medical ethics. How do we ethically balance the risks and responsibilities of tampering with the "natural"? No doubt you have read and heard a great deal about stem cell research because of highly publicized appeals on its behalf by very public people: Michael J. Fox (who suffers from Parkinson's disease); Christopher Reeve (who suffered paralyzing, ultimately fatal spine damage in a horseback riding accident); Nancy Reagan (who cared for former president Ronald Reagan during his battle with Alzheimer's); former Senator Arlen Specter (who suffers from cancer); and, at the Democratic National Convention in 2004, the ex-president's son, Ron Reagan. All these people advocate stem cell research.

Savage Chickens   by Doug Savage

New scientific advances are creating new ethical issues for consideration. What are the ethical consequences of pursuing genetic engineering or creating robots with humanlike intelligence?

Savage Chickens copyright © 2009 Doug Savage

And yet there are many others who find stem cell research to be dangerous and/or unethical, and who find claims of potential miracle cures to be highly exaggerated (and sometimes motivated by the prospect of grant money). Some opponents fear that stem cell research, if approved, would lead to and encourage cloning or the use of aborted fetal tissue—or perhaps even to planned pregnancies and subsequent abortions designed to create the necessary stem cells. If opponents of stem cell research lack high-profile advocates like Fox and the Reagans, they do not lack in fervor and organization. The images and words that follow give you a glimpse of some of the arguments, visual and verbal, that recur in the debate over stem cell research. In addition to photos and cartoons, we include Ron Reagan's highly publicized speech at the 2004 Democratic National Convention and a response to it by Richard M. Doerflinger, an advocate for prolife issues employed by the United States Conference of Catholic Bishops. And we offer a controversial proposal by Sally Satel to permit—under controlled conditions—citizens to sell their organs to people waiting for transplants.

Finally, we close with an Issue in Focus, on genetically modified food—the fourth science-and-ethics controversy represented here. Perhaps you too have personal, moral, religious, or occupational reasons to be concerned about one or another of these controversies. Read the selections that follow with care—and then develop and express your own considered views.

BILL **JOY**

Why the Future Doesn't Need Us

Bill Joy is a cofounder of Sun Microsystems and was the chief scientist there until 2003. He played a major role in developing an early form of UNIX, a computer operating system, as well as other computer technologies, such as the JAVA programming language. "Why the Future Doesn't Need Us" appeared in the April 2000 issue of *Wired* magazine, a monthly periodical that covers cultural, political, and economic impacts of technology. The article, which expresses a surprisingly critical position on technology, created a large stir—see the interview with Ralph C. Merkle that follows this selection by Bill Joy.

From the moment I became involved in the creation of new technologies, their ethical dimensions have concerned me, but it was only in the autumn of 1998 that I became anxiously aware of how great are the dangers facing us in the 21st century. I can date the onset of my unease to the day I met Ray Kurzweil, the deservedly famous inventor of the first reading machine for the blind and many other amazing things.

Ray and I were both speakers at George Gilder's Telecosm conference, and I encountered him by chance in the bar of the hotel after both our sessions were over. I was sitting with John Searle, a Berkeley philosopher who studies consciousness. While we were talking, Ray approached and a conversation began, the subject of which haunts me to this day.

I had missed Ray's talk and the subsequent panel that Ray and John had been on, and they now picked right up where they'd left off, with Ray saying that the rate of improvement of technology was going to accelerate and that we were going to become robots or fuse with robots or something like that, and John countering that this couldn't happen, because the robots couldn't be conscious.

4   While I had heard such talk before, I had always felt sentient robots were in the realm of science fiction. But now, from someone I respected, I was hearing a strong argument that they were a near-term possibility. I was taken aback, especially given Ray's proven ability to imagine and create the future. I already knew that new technologies like genetic engineering and nanotechnology were giving us the power to remake the world, but a realistic and imminent scenario for intelligent robots surprised me.

5   It's easy to get jaded about such breakthroughs. We hear in the news almost every day of some kind of technological or scientific advance. Yet this was no ordinary prediction. In the hotel bar, Ray gave me a partial preprint of his then-forthcoming book *The Age of Spiritual Machines,* which outlined a utopia he foresaw—one in which humans gained near immortality by becoming one with robotic technology. On reading it, my sense of unease only intensified; I felt sure he had to be understating the dangers, understating the probability of a bad outcome along this path.

6   I found myself most troubled by a passage detailing a *dys*topian scenario:

> First let us postulate that the computer scientists succeed in developing intelligent machines that can do all things better than human beings can do them. In that case presumably all work will be done by vast, highly organized systems of machines and no human effort will be necessary. Either of two cases might occur. The machines might be permitted to make all of their own decisions without human oversight, or else human control over the machines might be retained.
>
> If the machines are permitted to make all their own decisions, we can't make any conjectures as to the results, because it is impossible to guess how such machines might behave. We only point out that the fate of the human race would be at the mercy of the machines. It might be argued that the human race would never be foolish enough to hand over all the power to the machines. But we are suggesting neither that the human race would voluntarily turn power over to the machines nor that the machines would willfully seize power. What we do suggest is that the human race might easily permit itself to drift into a position of such dependence on the machines that it would have no practical choice but to accept all of the machines' decisions. As society and the problems that face it become more and more complex and machines become more and more intelligent, people will let machines make more of their decisions for them, simply because machine-made decisions will bring better results than man-made ones. Eventually a stage may be reached at which the decisions necessary to keep the system running will be so complex that human beings will be incapable of making them intelligently. At that stage the machines will be in effective control. People won't be able to just turn the machines off, because they will be so dependent on them that turning them off would amount to suicide.
>
> On the other hand it is possible that human control over the machines may be retained. In that case the average man may have control over certain private machines of his own, such as his car or his personal computer, but control over large systems of machines will be in the hands of a tiny elite—just as it is today, but with two differences. Due to improved techniques the elite will have greater control over the masses; and because human work will no longer be necessary the masses will be superfluous, a useless burden on the system. If the elite is ruthless they may simply decide to exterminate the mass of humanity. If they are humane they may use

propaganda or other psychological or biological techniques to reduce the birth rate until the mass of humanity becomes extinct, leaving the world to the elite. Or, if the elite consists of soft-hearted liberals, they may decide to play the role of good shepherds to the rest of the human race. They will see to it that everyone's physical needs are satisfied, that all children are raised under psychologically hygienic conditions, that everyone has a wholesome hobby to keep him busy, and that anyone who may become dissatisfied undergoes "treatment" to cure his "problem." Of course, life will be so purposeless that people will have to be biologically or psychologically engineered either to remove their need for the power process or make them "sublimate" their drive for power into some harmless hobby. These engineered human beings may be happy in such a society, but they will most certainly not be free. They will have been reduced to the status of domestic animals.[1]

7   In the book, you don't discover until you turn the page that the author of this passage is Theodore Kaczynski—the Unabomber. I am no apologist for Kaczynski. His bombs killed three people during a 17-year terror campaign and wounded many others. One of his bombs gravely injured my friend David Gelernter, one of the most brilliant and visionary computer scientists of our time. Like many of my colleagues, I felt that I could easily have been the Unabomber's next target.

8   Kaczynski's actions were murderous and, in my view, criminally insane. He is clearly a Luddite, but simply saying this does not dismiss his argument; as difficult as it is for me to acknowledge, I saw some merit in the reasoning in this single passage. I felt compelled to confront it.

9   Kaczynski's dystopian vision describes unintended consequences, a well-known problem with the design and use of technology, and one that is clearly related to Murphy's law—"Anything that can go wrong, will." (Actually, this is Finagle's law, which in itself shows that Finagle was right.) Our overuse of antibiotics has led to what may be the biggest such problem so far: the emergence of antibiotic-resistant and much more dangerous bacteria. Similar things happened when attempts to eliminate malarial mosquitoes using DDT caused them to acquire DDT resistance; malarial parasites likewise acquired multi-drug-resistant genes.[2]

10   The cause of many such surprises seems clear: The systems involved are complex, involving interaction among and feedback between many parts. Any changes to such a system will cascade in ways that are difficult to predict; this is especially true when human actions are involved.

11   I started showing friends the Kaczynski quote from *The Age of Spiritual Machines;* I would hand them Kurzweil's book, let them read the quote, and then watch their reaction as they discovered who had written it. At around the same time, I found Hans Moravec's book *Robot: Mere Machine to Transcendent Mind.* Moravec is one of the leaders in robotics research, and was a founder of the world's largest robotics research program, at Carnegie Mellon University. *Robot* gave me more material to try out on my friends—material surprisingly supportive of Kaczynski's argument. For example:

Biological species almost never survive encounters with superior competitors. Ten million years ago, South and North America were separated by a sunken Panama isthmus. South America, like Australia today, was populated by marsupial mammals, including pouched equivalents of rats, deers, and tigers. When the isthmus connecting North and South America rose, it took only a few thousand years for the northern placental species, with slightly more effective metabolisms and reproductive and nervous systems, to displace and eliminate almost all the southern marsupials.

In a completely free marketplace, superior robots would surely affect humans as North American placentals affected South American marsupials (and as humans have affected countless species). Robotic industries would compete vigorously among themselves for matter, energy, and space, incidentally driving their price beyond human reach. Unable to afford the necessities of life, biological humans would be squeezed out of existence.

There is probably some breathing room, because we do not live in a completely free marketplace. Government coerces nonmarket behavior, especially by collecting taxes. Judiciously applied, governmental coercion could support human populations in high style on the fruits of robot labor, perhaps for a long while.

12   A textbook dystopia—and Moravec is just getting wound up. He goes on to discuss how our main job in the 21st century will be "ensuring continued cooperation from the robot industries" by passing laws decreeing that they be "nice,"[3] and to describe how seriously dangerous a human can be "once transformed into an unbounded superintelligent robot." Moravec's view is that the robots will eventually succeed us—that humans clearly face extinction.

13   I decided it was time to talk to my friend Danny Hillis. Danny became famous as the cofounder of Thinking Machines Corporation, which built a very powerful parallel supercomputer. Despite my current job title of Chief Scientist at Sun Microsystems, I am more a computer architect than a scientist, and I respect Danny's knowledge of the information and physical sciences more than that of any other single person I know. Danny is also a highly regarded futurist who thinks long-term: four years ago he started the Long Now Foundation, which is building a clock designed to last 10,000 years, in an attempt to draw attention to the pitifully short attention span of our society.

14   So I flew to Los Angeles for the express purpose of having dinner with Danny and his wife, Pati. I went through my now-familiar routine, trotting out the ideas and passages that I found so disturbing. Danny's answer—directed specifically at Kurzweil's scenario of humans merging with robots—came swiftly, and quite surprised me. He said, simply, that the changes would come gradually, and that we would get used to them.

15   But I guess I wasn't totally surprised. I had seen a quote from Danny in Kurzweil's book in which he said, "I'm as fond of my body as anyone, but if I can be 200 with a body of silicon, I'll take it." It seemed that he was at peace with this process and its attendant risks, while I was not.

16   While talking and thinking about Kurzweil, Kaczynski, and Moravec, I suddenly remembered a novel I had read almost 20 years ago—*The White Plague,* by Frank Herbert—in which a molecular biologist is driven insane by the senseless murder of his family. To seek revenge he constructs and disseminates a new and highly contagious plague that kills widely but selectively. (We're lucky Kaczynski was a mathematician, not a molecular biologist.) I was also reminded of the Borg of *Star Trek,* a hive of partly biological, partly robotic creatures with a strong destructive streak. Borg-like disasters are a staple of science fiction, so why hadn't I been more concerned about such robotic dystopias earlier? Why weren't other people more concerned about these nightmarish scenarios?

17   Part of the answer certainly lies in our attitude toward the new—in our bias toward instant familiarity and unquestioning acceptance. Accustomed to living with almost routine scientific breakthroughs, we have yet to come to terms with the fact that the most compelling 21st-century technologies—robotics, genetic engineering, and nanotechnology—pose a different threat than the technologies that have come before. Specifically, robots, engineered organisms, and nanobots share a dangerous amplifying factor: They can self-replicate. A bomb is blown up only once—but one bot can become many, and quickly get out of control.

18   Much of my work over the past 25 years has been on computer networking, where the sending and receiving of messages creates the opportunity for out-of-control replication. But while replication in a computer or a computer network can be a nuisance, at worst it disables a machine or takes down a network or network service. Uncontrolled self-replication in these newer technologies runs a much greater risk: a risk of substantial damage in the physical world.

19   Each of these technologies also offers untold promise: the vision of near immortality that Kurzweil sees in his robot dreams drives us forward; genetic engineering may soon provide treatments, if not outright cures, for most diseases; and nanotechnology and nanomedicine can address yet more ills. Together they could significantly extend our average life span and improve the quality of our lives. Yet, with each of these technologies, a sequence of small, individually sensible advances leads to an accumulation of great power and, concomitantly, great danger.

20   What was different in the 20th century? Certainly, the technologies underlying the weapons of mass destruction (WMD)—nuclear, biological, and chemical (NBC)—were powerful, and the weapons an enormous threat. But building nuclear weapons required, at least for a time, access to both rare—indeed, effectively unavailable—raw materials and highly protected information; biological and chemical weapons programs also tended to require large-scale activities.

21   The 21st-century technologies—genetics, nanotechnology, and robotics (GNR)—are so powerful that they can spawn whole new classes of accidents and abuses. Most dangerously, for the first time, these accidents and abuses are widely within the reach of individuals or small groups. They will not require large facilities or rare raw materials. Knowledge alone will enable the use of them.

22   Thus we have the possibility not just of weapons of mass destruction but of knowledge-enabled mass destruction (KMD), this destructiveness hugely amplified by the power of self-replication.

23   I think it is no exaggeration to say we are on the cusp of the further perfection of extreme evil, an evil whose possibility spreads well beyond that which weapons of mass destruction bequeathed to the nation-states, on to a surprising and terrible empowerment of extreme individuals.

II

4   Nothing about the way I got involved with computers suggested to me that I was going to be facing these kinds of issues.

5   My life has been driven by a deep need to ask questions and find answers. When I was 3, I was already reading, so my father took me to the elementary school, where I sat on the principal's lap and read him a story. I started school early, later skipped a

grade, and escaped into books—I was incredibly motivated to learn. I asked lots of questions, often driving adults to distraction.

26   As a teenager I was very interested in science and technology. I wanted to be a ham radio operator but didn't have the money to buy the equipment. Ham radio was the Internet of its time: very addictive, and quite solitary. Money issues aside, my mother put her foot down—I was not to be a ham; I was antisocial enough already.

27   I may not have had many close friends, but I was awash in ideas. By high school, I had discovered the great science fiction writers. I remember especially Heinlein's *Have Spacesuit Will Travel* and Asimov's *I, Robot,* with its Three Laws of Robotics. I was enchanted by the descriptions of space travel, and wanted to have a telescope to look at the stars; since I had no money to buy or make one, I checked books on tele-scope-making out of the library and read about making them instead. I soared in my imagination.

28   Thursday nights my parents went bowling, and we kids stayed home alone. It was the night of Gene Roddenberry's original *Star Trek,* and the program made a big impression on me. I came to accept its notion that humans had a future in space, West-ern-style, with big heroes and adventures. Roddenberry's vision of the centuries to come was one with strong moral values, embodied in codes like the Prime Directive: to not interfere in the development of less technologically advanced civilizations. This had an incredible appeal to me; ethical humans, not robots, dominated this future, and I took Roddenberry's dream as part of my own.

29   I excelled in mathematics in high school, and when I went to the University of Michigan as an undergraduate engineering student I took the advanced curriculum of the mathematics majors. Solving math problems was an exciting challenge, but when I discovered computers I found something much more interesting: a machine into which you could put a program that attempted to solve a problem, after which the machine quickly checked the solution. The computer had a clear notion of correct and

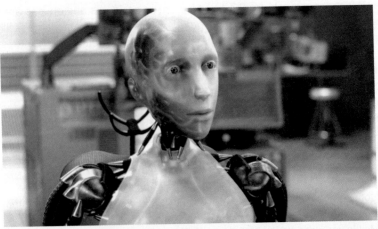

Science fiction has long toyed with the question of what will happen if robots advance to human (or even above human) reasoning ability. In this film still from *I, Robot,* we see Sonny, a robot with both intelligence and free will.

incorrect, true and false. Were my ideas correct? The machine could tell me. This was very seductive.

30   I was lucky enough to get a job programming early supercomputers and discovered the amazing power of large machines to numerically simulate advanced designs. When I went to graduate school at UC Berkeley in the mid-1970s, I started staying up late, often all night, inventing new worlds inside the machines. Solving problems. Writing the code that argued so strongly to be written.

31   In *The Agony and the Ecstasy,* Irving Stone's biographical novel of Michelangelo, Stone described vividly how Michelangelo released the statues from the stone, "breaking the marble spell," carving from the images in his mind.[4] In my most ecstatic moments, the software in the computer emerged in the same way. Once I had imagined it in my mind I felt that it was already there in the machine, waiting to be released. Staying up all night seemed a small price to pay to free it—to give the ideas concrete form.

32   After a few years at Berkeley I started to send out some of the software I had written—an instructional Pascal system, Unix utilities, and a text editor called vi (which is still, to my surprise, widely used more than 20 years later)—to others who had similar small PDP-11 and VAX minicomputers. These adventures in software eventually turned into the Berkeley version of the Unix operating system, which became a personal "success disaster"—so many people wanted it that I never finished my PhD. Instead I got a job working for Darpa putting Berkeley Unix on the Internet and fixing it to be reliable and to run large research applications well. This was all great fun and very rewarding. And, frankly, I saw no robots here, or anywhere near.

33   Still, by the early 1980s, I was drowning. The Unix releases were very successful, and my little project of one soon had money and some staff, but the problem at Berkeley was always office space rather than money—there wasn't room for the help the project needed, so when the other founders of Sun Microsystems showed up I jumped at the chance to join them. At Sun, the long hours continued into the early days of workstations and personal computers, and I have enjoyed participating in the creation of advanced microprocessor technologies and Internet technologies such as Java and Jini.

34   From all this, I trust it is clear that I am not a Luddite. I have always, rather, had a strong belief in the value of the scientific search for truth and in the ability of great engineering to bring material progress. The Industrial Revolution has immeasurably improved everyone's life over the last couple hundred years, and I always expected my career to involve the building of worthwhile solutions to real problems, one problem at a time.

35   I have not been disappointed. My work has had more impact than I had ever hoped for and has been more widely used than I could have reasonably expected. I have spent the last 20 years still trying to figure out how to make computers as reliable as I want them to be (they are not nearly there yet) and how to make them simple to use (a goal that has met with even less relative success). Despite some progress, the problems that remain seem even more daunting.

36   But while I was aware of the moral dilemmas surrounding technology's consequences in fields like weapons research, I did not expect that I would confront such issues in my own field, or at least not so soon.

Perhaps it is always hard to see the bigger impact while you are in the vortex of a change. Failing to understand the consequences of our inventions while we are in the rapture of discovery and innovation seems to be a common fault of scientists and technologists; we have long been driven by the overarching desire to know that is the nature of science's quest, not stopping to notice that the progress to newer and more powerful technologies can take on a life of its own.

I have long realized that the big advances in information technology come not from the work of computer scientists, computer architects, or electrical engineers, but from that of physical scientists. The physicists Stephen Wolfram and Brosl Hasslacher introduced me, in the early 1980s, to chaos theory and nonlinear systems. In the 1990s, I learned about complex systems from conversations with Danny Hillis, the biologist Stuart Kauffman, the Nobel-laureate physicist Murray Gell-Mann, and others. Most recently, Hasslacher and the electrical engineer and device physicist Mark Reed have been giving me insight into the incredible possibilities of molecular electronics.

In my own work, as codesigner of three microprocessor architectures—SPARC, picoJava, and MAJC—and as the designer of several implementations thereof, I've been afforded a deep and firsthand acquaintance with Moore's law. For decades, Moore's law has correctly predicted the exponential rate of improvement of semiconductor technology. Until last year I believed that the rate of advances predicted by Moore's law might continue only until roughly 2010, when some physical limits would begin to be reached. It was not obvious to me that a new technology would arrive in time to keep performance advancing smoothly.

But because of the recent rapid and radical progress in molecular electronics—where individual atoms and molecules replace lithographically drawn transistors—and related nanoscale technologies, we should be able to meet or exceed the Moore's law rate of progress for another 30 years. By 2030, we are likely to be able to build machines, in quantity, a million times as powerful as the personal computers of today—sufficient to implement the dreams of Kurzwell and Moravec.

As this enormous computing power is combined with the manipulative advances of the physical sciences and the new, deep understandings in genetics, enormous transformative power is being unleashed. These combinations open up the opportunity to completely redesign the world, for better or worse: The replicating and evolving processes that have been confined to the natural world are about to become realms of human endeavor.

In designing software and microprocessors, I have never had the feeling that I was designing an intelligent machine. The software and hardware is so fragile and the capabilities of the machine to "think" so clearly absent that, even as a possibility, this has always seemed very far in the future.

But now, with the prospect of human-level computing power in about 30 years, a new idea suggests itself: that I may be working to create tools which will enable the construction of the technology that may replace our species. How do I feel about this? Very uncomfortable. Having struggled my entire career to build reliable software systems, it seems to me more than likely that this future will not work out as well as some people may imagine. My personal experience suggests we tend to overestimate our design abilities.

44   Given the incredible power of these new technologies, shouldn't we be asking how we can best coexist with them? And if our own extinction is a likely, or even possible, outcome of our technological development, shouldn't we proceed with great caution?

Notes

[1] The passage Kurzweil quotes is from Kaczynski's "Unabomber Manifesto," which was published jointly, under duress, by the *New York Times* and the *Washington Post* to attempt to bring his campaign of terror to an end. I agree with David Gelernter, who said about their decision:

"It was a tough call for the newspapers. To say yes would be giving in to terrorism, and for all they knew he was lying anyway. On the other hand, to say yes might stop the killing. There was also a chance that someone would read the tract and get a hunch about the author; and that is exactly what happened. The suspect's brother read it, and it rang a bell.

"I would have told them not to publish. I'm glad they didn't ask me. I guess."

(*Drawing Life: Surviving the Unabomber.* Free Press, 1997: 120.)

[2] Garrett, Laurie. *The Coming Plague: Newly Emerging Diseases in a World Out of Balance.* Penguin, 1994: 47–52, 414, 419, 452.

[3] Isaac Asimov described what became the most famous view of ethical rules for robot behavior in his book *I, Robot* in 1950, in his Three Laws of Robotics: 1. A robot may not injure a human being, or, through inaction, allow a human being to come to harm. 2. A robot must obey the orders given it by human beings, except where such orders would conflict with the First Law. 3. A robot must protect its own existence, as long as such protection does not conflict with the First or Second Law.

[4] Michelangelo wrote a sonnet that begins:

> Non ha l' ottimo artista alcun concetto
> Ch' un marmo solo in sʃl non circonscriva
> Col suo soverchio; e solo a quello arriva
> La man che ubbidisce all' intelleto.

Stone translates this as:

> The best of artists hath no thought to show
> which the rough stone in its superfluous shell
> doth not include; to break the marble spell
> is all the hand that serves the brain can do.

Stone describes the process: "He was not working from his drawings or clay models; they had all been put away. He was carving from the images in his mind. His eyes and hands knew where every line, curve, mass must emerge, and at what depth in the heart of the stone to create the low relief."

(*The Agony and the Ecstasy.* Doubleday, 1961: 6, 144.)

Ralph C. Merkle

Nanotechnology: Designs for the Future

Ubiquity is a Web-based publication of the Association for Computing Machinery focusing on a variety of issues related to the information technology industry. In 2000, *Ubiquity* interviewed Ralph C. Merkle, a former research scientist at Xerox Parc; advisor at the Foresight Institute; and at the time a nanotechnology theorist at Zyvex, a nanotechnology research and development company. Merkle's main research interests are nanotechnology (also called molecular manufacturing), cryptography, and cryonics. He served as executive editor of the journal *Nanotechnology* for several years. In 1998, Merkle won the Feynman Prize in *Nanotechnology* for his theoretical work. As you will see, the interview excerpted below is partly in response to Bill Joy's "Why the Future Doesn't Need Us," the first selection in this chapter.

UBIQUITY: Bill Joy's recent *Wired* article on the perils of today's advanced technologies—including nanotechnology—has certainly received a lot of attention, and we did a follow-up interview with him in *Ubiquity*. What are your thoughts on that subject?

2 RALPH C.: Well, certainly the idea that nanotechnology would raise concerns
MERKLE: is something that actually was a major impetus for the founding of the Foresight Institute back in 1986—and by 1989, Foresight had its first technical conference on nanotechnology, and in fact Bill Joy spoke at that meeting. So one of the things that's a bit surprising is that Bill's concerns about nanotechnology seem to be quite recent—just the last year or two—even though the understanding that this particular technology was going to be very powerful and would raise significant concerns has been around for at least a couple of decades.

3 UBIQUITY: Why don't you take a moment now to tell us about the Foresight Institute?
4 MERKLE: The Foresight Institute (www.foresight.org/guidelines/index.html) was created primarily to guide the development of nanotechnology, and it was founded in large part because, when you look at where the technology is going, you reach the conclusion that, though it has great potential for good, there are also some concerns which need to be addressed. We've been having a series of gatherings at Foresight now for some years where Senior Associates (people who have pledged to support the Foresight Institute) can get together informally and off the record and discuss the various issues.

5 UBIQUITY: What are the meetings like?
6 MERKLE: The most recent gathering had over 250 people—including Bill Joy, as a matter of fact—and one of the sessions was a discussion of the Foresight guidelines for safe development of nanotechnology. A year and a half ago we had a workshop where we discussed the guidelines and

worked out an initial draft, which was discussed at the 1999 gathering at Foresight, and then further modified and updated and then discussed again at the most recent gathering.

UBIQUITY: What do you think would explain the sudden increase of concern about this?

MERKLE: Well, I can't really address the specifics of Bill Joy's situation. I do know that nanotechnology is an idea that most people simply didn't believe, even though the roots of it go back to a lecture by Richard Feynman in 1959 (www.zyvex.com/nanotech/feynman.html). That was a very famous talk in which he basically said the laws of physics should allow us to arrange things molecule by molecule and even atom by atom, and that at some point it was inevitable that we would develop a technology that would let us do this. I don't think that it was taken very seriously at that time, but as the years progressed it gradually began to be more accepted. If you think the technology is infeasible, you don't worry about what it might do and what its potential is. However, as you begin to internalize the fact that this technology is going to arrive and that we are going to have a very powerful manufacturing technology that will let us build a wide range of remarkable new products, then one of the things that arises is a concern that this new set of capabilities could create new problems, new concerns, and that these should be addressed.

UBIQUITY: But not the way Bill Joy is addressing them?

MERKLE: One of the things about Bill Joy's original article that concerned me is that he was calling for a relinquishment, as he put it, of research—and I think that's a *very* foolish strategy. If you look at the various strategies available for dealing with a new technology, sticking your head in the sand is not the most plausible strategy and in fact actually makes the situation more dangerous.

UBIQUITY: Why so?

MERKLE: For at least three reasons. The first, of course, is that we need to have a collective understanding of the new technology in order to ensure that we develop it appropriately. The second reason is that the new technologies that we see coming will have major benefits, and will greatly alleviate human suffering. The third reason is that, if we attempt to block the development of new technology, if we collectively try and say, "These technologies are technologies that are not meant for humans to understand," and we try to back away from them, what we effectively have done is not to block the technologies, we have simply ensured that the most responsible parties will not develop them.

UBIQUITY: So you think "relinquishment" is exactly the wrong strategy.

MERKLE: Right. Those people who pay no attention to a call for relinquishment, and in particular those people who are least inclined to be concerned about safe development will, in fact, be the groups that eventually develop the technology. In other words, a relinquishment of the new technology, unless it is absolutely 100 percent effective, is not effective at all. If it's 99.99 percent effective, then you simply ensure that the .01 percent who pays no attention to such calls for relinquishment is the group that will develop it. And that actually creates a worse outcome than if the responsible players move forward and develop the technology with the best understanding that they have and the best efforts to ensure that the technology is developed in a safe and responsible fashion.

15 UBIQUITY: Let's go back to the second reason and expand on that to the extent of enumerating what you consider are the most prominent hopes that it offers.

16 MERKLE: Well, certainly what we see today is an entire planet, which has many limitations. I'm not quite sure how to express it, but certainly if you look at the human condition today, not everyone is well fed. Not everyone has access to good medical care. Not everyone has the basics—the physical basics that provide for a healthy and a happy life. And clearly, if you have a lower cost manufacturing technology, which can build a wide range of products less expensively, it can build, among other things, better medical products. Disease and ill health are caused largely by damage at the molecular and cellular level, yet today's surgical tools are too large to deal with that kind of problem. A molecular manufacturing technology will let us build molecular surgical tools, and those tools will, for the first time, let us directly address the problems at the very root level. So today we see a human population of over six billion people, many of whom have serious medical conditions, which either can't be treated or cannot be treated economically. In other words, we don't have the resources to effectively treat all the conditions that we see. If we can reduce the cost and improve the quality of medical technology through advances in nanotechnology, then we can more widely address the medical conditions that are prevalent and reduce the level of human suf-

This robot, an example of nanotechnology in medicine, is removing plaque from a diseased blood vessel.

fering. (See www.foresight.org/Nanomedicine for more information about medical applications.)

UBIQUITY: And besides the opportunities in medicine? What else?

MERKLE: On another level, food; the simple process of feeding the human population. Today because of technological limits there is a certain amount of food that we can produce per acre. If we were to have intensive greenhouse agriculture, which would be something we could do economically, if we could economically manufacture the appropriate computer controlled enclosures that would provide protection and would provide a very controlled environment for the growth of food we could have much higher production. It looks as though yields of over 10 times what we can currently grow per acre are feasible if you control, for example, the CO_2 concentration, the humidity, the temperature, all the various factors that plants depend on to grow rapidly. If we control those, if we make those optimal for the growth of various crops then we can grow more per acre. And furthermore, we can grow it less expensively because molecular manufacturing technology is inherently low cost, and therefore it will let us grow more food more easily.

UBIQUITY: What are the implications?

MERKLE: The first is that it makes food less expensive. The second is that many of the people in the world today who are starving are not starving because there is an inherent inability to produce food, they are starving because they are caught in the middle of political fights and blockades that have been used as political weapons. As a consequence, food is available but it cannot be shipped into an area and so the people in that area suffer the consequences. However, if you have a distributed manufacturing technology, one of the great advantages is that it should let us have a much lower cost infrastructure. In other words, today manufacturing takes place in very large facilities. If you want to build, for example, a computer chip, you need a giant semiconductor fabrication facility. But if you look at nature, nature can grow complex molecular machines using nothing more than a plant.

UBIQUITY: Example?

MERKLE: Well, a potato, for example, can grow quite easily on a very small plot of land. With molecular manufacturing, in a similar fashion, we'll be able to have distributed manufacturing, which will permit manufacturing at the site using technologies that are low cost and easily available once the core technology has been developed. And as a consequence, you would have people able to build low-cost greenhouse agriculture tools even if there were a blockade because the manufacturing facilities would be widely distributed, and therefore they could avoid the blockade by simply making what they need inside the blockaded region using cheap raw materials and sunlight.

UBIQUITY: And if nanotechnology did so much for people's health and food production, what would it do, do you suppose, for their current economic institution? Would it transition to large-scale nanotechnology? Have unintended consequences in terms of disrupting the economy?

24   MERKLE: I think we would see changes in the economy. Previous technologies have made major changes. Old companies that have had major advantages in the past certainly find those advantages go away. Certainly as manufacturing becomes less expensive, then today's major manufacturing companies would find that they would be at a disadvantage in the future. Other companies that are producing intellectual products, software companies or companies that are not dealing with material objects—banks and financial institutions, for example—fundamentally are dealing with a flow of information so would be relatively less affected. I think you would see some major shifts in the economy in that manufacturing companies would find that what they were doing was either greatly changed or outright replaced. As in any technological revolution, there will be winners and losers. On balance, everyone will come out ahead, although there will be specific instances where particular companies will have major problems, and in fact, will simply not be able to cope with a new environment and presumably suffer the consequences.

25   UBIQUITY: What about the competition between different countries? Would, for example, the severely underdeveloped countries have an ability to do very rapid catch-up?

26   MERKLE: Yes. I think they would. Also, you have to remember that we are looking at a future where to a first approximation everyone is wealthy. Now, there are certain things that are inherently scarce. For example, there is only a certain amount of beachfront property in California. It is going to be scarce, it is going to be expensive, and only a small percentage of the population will be able to afford it. But if you look at other material possessions—housing or electronics—you find that the only limitation is our ability to manufacture them inexpensively. So the first approximation in this future that we're looking at is that everyone will be physically well off. They will have a great abundance in material goods, and as a consequence, I think that will soften and ease some of the conflicts that we see now. One of the issues facing us today is that there are countries where there is a serious lack of resources, the standards of living are very low, and as a consequence this creates a fundamental unease and discomfort in entire populations. If you have a higher standard of living, at least that source of conflict will be greatly reduced. Now, as we all know, there are many potential sources of conflict in the world, but even easing some of them will be very helpful.

27   UBIQUITY: Give us an example of a product that would be improved using molecular manufacturing?

28   MERKLE: The answer that comes most readily to mind is diamonds. Diamond has a better strength-to-weight ratio than steel or aluminum. Its strength-to-weight ratio is more than 50 times that of steel or aluminum alloy. So, it's much stronger and much lighter. If we had a shatterproof variant of diamond, we would have a remarkably light and strong material from which

to make all of the products in the world around us. In particular, aerospace products—airplanes or rockets—would benefit immensely from having lighter, stronger materials. So one of the things that we can say with confidence is that we will have much lighter, much stronger materials, and this will reduce the cost of air flight, and it will reduce the cost of rockets. It will let us go into space for literally orders of magnitude lower cost.

29 UBIQUITY: Has NASA shown any interest in this?

30 MERKLE: Needless to say, they are pursuing research in nanotechnology with the idea of having lighter, stronger materials as one of the significant objectives. There is a whole range of other capabilities, of course, that would be of interest in NASA. For example, lighter computers and lighter sensors would let you have more function in a given weight, which is very important if you are launching things into space, and you have to pay by the pound to put things there.

31 UBIQUITY: Are there any other areas that would be significantly affected by nanotechnology?

32 MERKLE: The other area is in advanced computer technology. The computer hardware revolution has been continuing with remarkable steadiness over the last few decades. If you extrapolate into the future you find that, in the coming decades, we'll have to build molecular computers to keep the computer hardware revolution on track. Nanotechnology will let us do that, and it will let us build computers that are incredibly powerful. We'll have more power in the volume of a sugar cube than exists in the entire world today.

33 UBIQUITY: Can you put any kind of timeframe on that?

34 MERKLE: We're talking about decades. We're not talking about years; we're not talking about a century. We're talking decades—and probably not many decades.

BILL **GATES**

A Robot in Every Home

From 1995 to 2009, Bill Gates had been ranked by *Forbes* magazine as the richest person in the world (he has now "fallen" to number 2). Best known for his role with Microsoft, the company he cofounded with Paul Allen, Gates now serves as the primary stockholder for that corporation. He spends most of his time doing philanthropic work with the Gates Foundation, which he and his wife, Melinda, founded in 2000. In "A Robot in Every Home," which first appeared in the December 2006 issue of *Scientific American*, Gates waxes enthusiastic and optimistic about the prospect of bringing robotics into every American household—much as Microsoft did with personal computers.

Imagine being present at the birth of a new industry. It is an industry based on groundbreaking new technologies, wherein a handful of well-established corporations sell highly specialized devices for business use and a fast-growing number of start-up companies produce innovative toys, gadgets for hobbyists and other interesting niche products. But it is also a highly fragmented industry with few common standards or platforms. Projects are complex, progress is slow, and practical applications are relatively rare. In fact, for all the excitement and promise, no one can say with any certainty when—or even if—this industry will achieve critical mass. If it does, though, it may well change the world.

2   Of course, the paragraph above could be a description of the computer industry during the mid-1970s, around the time that Paul Allen and I launched Microsoft. Back then, big, expensive mainframe computers ran the back-office operations for major companies, governmental departments and other institutions. Researchers at leading universities and industrial laboratories were creating the basic building blocks that would make the information age possible. Intel had just introduced the 8080 microprocessor, and Atari was selling the popular electronic game Pong. At homegrown computer clubs, enthusiasts struggled to figure out exactly what this new technology was good for.

3   But what I really have in mind is something much more contemporary: the emergence of the robotics industry, which is developing in much the same way that the computer business did 30 years ago. Think of the manufacturing robots currently used on automobile assembly lines as the equivalent of yesterday's mainframes. The industry's niche products include robotic arms that perform surgery, surveillance robots deployed in Iraq and Afghanistan that dispose of roadside bombs, and domestic robots that vacuum the floor. Electronics companies have made robotic toys that can imitate people or dogs or dinosaurs, and hobbyists are anxious to get their hands on the latest version of the Lego robotics system.

4   Meanwhile some of the world's best minds are trying to solve the toughest problems of robotics, such as visual recognition, navigation and machine learning. And they are succeeding. At the 2004 Defense Advanced Research Projects Agency (DARPA) Grand Challenge, a competition to produce the first robotic vehicle capable of navigating autonomously over a rugged 142-mile course through the Mojave Desert, the top competitor managed to travel just 7.4 miles before breaking down. In 2005, though, five vehicles covered the complete distance, and the race's winner did it at an average speed of 19.1 miles an hour. (In another intriguing parallel between the robotics and computer industries, DARPA also funded the work that led to the creation of Arpanet, the precursor to the Internet.)

5   What is more, the challenges facing the robotics industry are similar to those we tackled in computing three decades ago. Robotics companies have no standard operating software that could allow popular application programs to run in a variety of devices. The standardization of robotic processors and other hardware is limited, and very little of the programming code used in one machine can be applied to another. Whenever somebody wants to build a new robot, they usually have to start from square one.

6   Despite these difficulties, when I talk to people involved in robotics—from university researchers to entrepreneurs, hobbyists and high school students—the level of excitement and expectation reminds me so much of that time when Paul Allen and I

looked at the convergence of new technologies and dreamed of the day when a computer would be on every desk and in every home. And as I look at the trends that are now starting to converge, I can envision a future in which robotic devices will become a nearly ubiquitous part of our day-to-day lives. I believe that technologies such as distributed computing, voice and visual recognition, and wireless broadband connectivity will open the door to a new generation of autonomous devices that enable computers to perform tasks in the physical world on our behalf. We may be on the verge of a new era, when the PC will get up off the desktop and allow us to see, hear, touch and manipulate objects in places where we are not physically present.

From Science Fiction to Reality

7   The word "robot" was popularized in 1921 by Czech playwright Karel Capek, but people have envisioned creating robot-like devices for thousands of years. In Greek and Roman mythology, the gods of metalwork built mechanical servants made from gold. In the first century A.D., Heron of Alexandria—the great engineer credited with inventing the first steam engine—designed intriguing automatons, including one said to have the ability to talk. Leonardo da Vinci's 1495 sketch of a mechanical knight, which could sit up and move its arms and legs, is considered to be the first plan for a humanoid robot.

8   Over the past century, anthropomorphic machines have become familiar figures in popular culture through books such as Isaac Asimov's *I, Robot*, movies such as *Star Wars* and television shows such as *Star Trek*. The popularity of robots in fiction indicates that people are receptive to the idea that these machines will one day walk among us as helpers and even as companions. Nevertheless, although robots play a vital role in industries such as automobile manufacturing—where there is about one robot for every 10 workers—the fact is that we have a long way to go before real robots catch up with their science-fiction counterparts.

9   One reason for this gap is that it has been much harder than expected to enable computers and robots to sense their surrounding environment and to react quickly and accurately. It has proved extremely difficult to give robots the capabilities that humans take for granted—for example, the abilities to orient themselves with respect to the objects in a room, to respond to sounds and interpret speech, and to grasp objects of varying sizes, textures and fragility. Even something as simple as telling the difference between an open door and a window can be devilishly tricky for a robot.

10   But researchers are starting to find the answers. One trend that has helped them is the increasing availability of tremendous amounts of computer power. One megahertz of processing power, which cost more than $7,000 in 1970, can now be purchased for just pennies. The price of a megabit of storage has seen a similar decline. The access to cheap computing power has permitted scientists to work on many of the hard problems that are fundamental to making robots practical. Today, for example, voice-recognition programs can identify words quite well, but a far greater challenge will be building machines that can understand what those words mean in context. As computing capacity continues to expand, robot designers will have the processing power they need to tackle issues of ever greater complexity.

11   Another barrier to the development of robots has been the high cost of hardware, such as sensors that enable a robot to determine the distance to an object as well as motors and servos that allow the robot to manipulate an object with both strength and

delicacy. But prices are dropping fast. Laser range finders that are used in robotics to measure distance with precision cost about $10,000 a few years ago; today they can be purchased for about $2,000. And new, more accurate sensors based on ultrawide-band radar are available for even less.

12   Now robot builders can also add Global Positioning System chips, video cameras, array microphones (which are better than conventional microphones at distinguishing a voice from background noise) and a host of additional sensors for a reasonable expense. The resulting enhancement of capabilities, combined with expanded processing power and storage, allows today's robots to do things such as vacuum a room or help to defuse a roadside bomb—tasks that would have been impossible for commercially produced machines just a few years ago.

A BASIC Approach

13   In February 2004 I visited a number of leading universities, including Carnegie Mellon University, the Massachusetts Institute of Technology, Harvard University, Cornell University and the University of Illinois, to talk about the powerful role that computers can play in solving some of society's most pressing problems. My goal was to help students understand how exciting and important computer science can be, and I hoped to encourage a few of them to think about careers in technology. At each university, after delivering my speech, I had the opportunity to get a firsthand look at some of the most interesting research projects in the school's computer science department. Almost without exception, I was shown at least one project that involved robotics.

14   At that time, my colleagues at Microsoft were also hearing from people in academia and at commercial robotics firms who wondered if our company was doing any work in robotics that might help them with their own development efforts. We were not, so we decided to take a closer look. I asked Tandy Trower, a member of my strategic staff and a 25-year Microsoft veteran, to go on an extended fact-finding mission and to speak with people across the robotics community. What he found was universal enthusiasm for the potential of robotics, along with an industry-wide desire for tools that would make development easier. "Many see the robotics industry at a technological turning point where a move to PC architecture makes more and more sense," Tandy wrote in his report to me after his fact-finding mission. "As Red Whittaker, leader of [Carnegie Mellon's] entry in the DARPA Grand Challenge, recently indicated, the hardware capability is mostly there; now the issue is getting the software right."

15   Back in the early days of the personal computer, we realized that we needed an ingredient that would allow all of the pioneering work to achieve critical mass, to coalesce into a real industry capable of producing truly useful products on a commercial scale. What was needed, it turned out, was Microsoft BASIC. When we created this programming language in the 1970s, we provided the common foundation that enabled programs developed for one set of hardware to run on another. BASIC also made computer programming much easier, which brought more and more people into the industry. Although a great many individuals made essential contributions to the development of the personal computer, Microsoft BASIC was one of the key catalysts for the software and hardware innovations that made the PC revolution possible.

16   After reading Tandy's report, it seemed clear to me that before the robotics industry could make the same kind of quantum leap that the PC industry made 30 years

ago, it, too, needed to find that missing ingredient. So I asked him to assemble a small team that would work with people in the robotics field to create a set of programming tools that would provide the essential plumbing so that anybody interested in robots with even the most basic understanding of computer programming could easily write robotic applications that would work with different kinds of hardware. The goal was to see if it was possible to provide the same kind of common, low-level foundation for integrating hardware and software into robot designs that Microsoft BASIC provided for computer programmers.

17   Tandy's robotics group has been able to draw on a number of advanced technologies developed by a team working under the direction of Craig Mundie, Microsoft's chief research and strategy officer. One such technology will help solve one of the most difficult problems facing robot designers: how to simultaneously handle all the data coming in from multiple sensors and send the appropriate commands to the robot's motors, a challenge known as concurrency. A conventional approach is to write a traditional, single-threaded program—a long loop that first reads all the data from the sensors, then processes this input and finally delivers output that determines the robot's behavior, before starting the loop all over again. The shortcomings are obvious: if your robot has fresh sensor data indicating that the machine is at the edge of a precipice, but the program is still at the bottom of the loop calculating trajectory and telling the wheels to turn faster based on previous sensor input, there is a good chance the robot will fall down the stairs before it can process the new information.

18   Concurrency is a challenge that extends beyond robotics. Today as more and more applications are written for distributed networks of computers, programmers have struggled to figure out how to efficiently orchestrate code running on many different servers at the same time. And as computers with a single processor are replaced by machines with multiple processors and "multicore" processors—integrated circuits with two or more processors joined together for enhanced performance—software designers will need a new way to program desktop applications and operating systems. To fully exploit the power of processors working in parallel, the new software must deal with the problem of concurrency.

19   One approach to handling concurrency is to write multi-threaded programs that allow data to travel along many paths. But as any developer who has written multi-threaded code can tell you, this is one of the hardest tasks in programming. The answer that Craig's team has devised to the concurrency problem is something called the concurrency and coordination runtime (CCR). The CCR is a library of functions—sequences of software code that perform specific tasks—that makes it easy to write multithreaded applications that can coordinate a number of simultaneous activities. Designed to help programmers take advantage of the power of multicore and multiprocessor systems, the CCR turns out to be ideal for robotics as well. By drawing on this library to write their programs, robot designers can dramatically reduce the chances that one of their creations will run into a wall because its software is too busy sending output to its wheels to read input from its sensors.

0   In addition to tackling the problem of concurrency, the work that Craig's team has done will also simplify the writing of distributed robotic applications through a technology called decentralized software services (DSS). DSS enables developers to create applications in which the services—the parts of the program that read a sensor, say, or

control a motor—operate as separate processes that can be orchestrated in much the same way that text, images and information from several servers are aggregated on a Web page. Because DSS allows software components to run in isolation from one another, if an individual component of a robot fails, it can be shut down and restarted—or even replaced—without having to reboot the machine. Combined with broadband wireless technology, this architecture makes it easy to monitor and adjust a robot from a remote location using a Web browser.

21   What is more, a DSS application controlling a robotic device does not have to reside entirely on the robot itself but can be distributed across more than one computer. As a result, the robot can be a relatively inexpensive device that delegates complex processing tasks to the high-performance hardware found on today's home PCs. I believe this advance will pave the way for an entirely new class of robots that are essentially mobile, wireless peripheral devices that tap into the power of desktop PCs to handle processing-intensive tasks such as visual recognition and navigation. And because these devices can be networked together, we can expect to see the emergence of groups of robots that can work in concert to achieve goals such as mapping the seafloor or planting crops.

22   These technologies are a key part of Microsoft Robotics Studio, a new software development kit built by Tandy's team. Microsoft Robotics Studio also includes tools that make it easier to create robotic applications using a wide range of programming languages. One example is a simulation tool that lets robot builders test their applications in a three-dimensional virtual environment before trying them out in the real world. Our goal for this release is to create an affordable, open platform that allows robot developers to readily integrate hardware and software into their designs.

Robots like this vacuum by IRobot are already in use in households around the world.

Should We Call Them Robots?

23 How soon will robots become part of our day-to-day lives? According to the International Federation of Robotics, about two million personal robots were in use around the world in 2004, and another seven million will be installed by 2008. In South Korea the Ministry of Information and Communication hopes to put a robot in every home there by 2013. The Japanese Robot Association predicts that by 2025, the personal robot industry will be worth more than $50 billion a year worldwide, compared with about $5 billion today.

24   As with the PC industry in the 1970s, it is impossible to predict exactly what applications will drive this new industry. It seems quite likely, however, that robots will play an important role in providing physical assistance and even companionship for the elderly. Robotic devices will probably help people with disabilities get around and extend the strength and endurance of soldiers, construction workers and medical professionals. Robots will maintain dangerous industrial machines, handle hazardous materials and monitor remote oil pipelines. They will enable health care workers to diagnose and treat patients who may be thousands of miles away, and they will be a central feature of security systems and search-and-rescue operations.

25   Although a few of the robots of tomorrow may resemble the anthropomorphic devices seen in *Star Wars*, most will look nothing like the humanoid C-3PO. In fact, as mobile peripheral devices become more and more common, it may be increasingly difficult to say exactly what a robot is. Because the new machines will be so specialized and ubiquitous—and look so little like the two-legged automatons of science fiction—we probably will not even call them robots. But as these devices become affordable to consumers, they could have just as profound an impact on the way we work, communicate, learn and entertain ourselves as the PC has had over the past 30 years.

Paul Marks

Armchair Warlords and Robot Hordes

Paul Marks is a technology correspondent for *New Scientist*, an international weekly science magazine and Web site that covers issues in science and technology. In 2007, Marks won the BT IT Security Journalist of the Year Award. His portfolio included the article below, published in *New Scientist* on October 28, 2006, which examines the development of lethal robot soldiers and the risks attached to their use.

It sounds like every general's dream: technology that allows a nation to fight a war with little or no loss of life on its side. It is also a peace-seeking citizen's nightmare. Without the politically embarrassing threat of soldiers returning home in flag-wrapped coffins, governments would find it far easier to commit to military action. The consequences for countries on the receiving end—and for world peace—would be immense.

2   This is not a fantasy scenario. Over the coming years, the world's most powerful military machine, the U.S. Department of Defense, aims to replace a large proportion of its armed vehicles and weaponry with robotized technologies. By 2010, a third of its "deep-strike" aircraft will be unmanned aerial vehicles (UAVs), according to a Congressional Research Service report issued in July (http://tinyurl.com/yafoht). In a further five years a similar proportion of the U.S. army's ground combat vehicles will be remote-controlled robots varying in size from supermarket carts to trucks. The U.S. navy, too, will have fleets of uncrewed boats and submarines.

3   The U.S. military is already using robots in various roles. In November 2002, for example, an armed UAV destroyed a car in Yemen carrying the suspected chief of Al-Qaida in that country, killing him and five others. In Iraq and Afghanistan, robots are proving highly successful in neutralizing roadside bombs and other small-scale explosives.

4   This is only the start. One of the next steps is to give robotic ground vehicles the attack power of UAVs, arming them with weapons such as machine guns, grenade launchers and anti-tank rockets (*New Scientist,* 21 September, p. 28). They could then be sent into places that were particularly dangerous for troops, such as booby-trapped or ambush-vulnerable buildings.

5   After that the plan is to take things to a whole new level, with unmanned planes and ground robots able to communicate with each other and act in concert. A reconnaissance UAV could signal swarms of robots to attack an enemy position, for example, or an unmanned ground vehicle might call in an air strike from UAVs.

6   All uncrewed vehicles are remote-controlled at present, but the Pentagon's Office of Naval Research is planning to develop technology that it hopes will enable a robot to determine whether a person it comes across is a threat, using measures such as the remote sensing of their heartbeat—though whether these kinds of methods can be made reliable is highly questionable.

7   "Teleoperation [remote control] is the norm, but semi-autonomous enhancements are being added all the time," says Bob Quinn of Foster-Miller, a technology firm in Waltham, Massachusetts, owned by the UK defense research company Qinetiq. Foster-Miller, like its main rival iRobot, was set up by roboticists from the Massachusetts Institute of Technology. The company's armed robot, dubbed Swords, has just received U.S. army safety certification. Nevertheless, doubts remain over how reliable armed robotic devices will be, especially if they end up operating autonomously. What happens when the software fails?

8   Such fears have persuaded the military to go slow on the use of autonomous weaponry. An early version of one of Foster-Miller's robots was designed to de-mine beaches autonomously

but was later converted to remote control at the navy's request. It is feasible that as safety concerns are addressed, autonomous devices will become increasingly popular, though experts in robotics point out that might be a long time away. An armed robot will not only need to be fail-safe, it must also be able to identify friend and foe just as well as a soldier.

9   Despite these fears, the rise of armed robots seems inevitable. Quinn tells the story of a group of U.S. marines impressed by a Swords robot armed with a machine gun being tested at a U.S. army base. "If they could have, they would have put that robot in their trunk, because they were off to Ramadi, Iraq, and they wanted that robot to [help them] stay alive. When you see that passion, I have no philosophical problems about this technology whatsoever," he says.

10   Outside the military, however, plenty of people beg to differ. Ultimately, these developments will allow the U.S., as well as several NATO countries that are also keen on the technology, to fight wars without suffering anywhere near as many casualties. The idea that warfare can be "clinical" has been found wanting time and again in recent years—think of the current conflicts in Iraq and Afghanistan, and Israel's recent bombardment of Lebanon—but there's no question that reliable autonomous robots deployed on a large scale could make fighting wars a great deal less risky for those that own them.

11   And therein lies the great danger. What are the chances of a less violent world when the powerful nations can make their mark on the less powerful at the flick of a switch? As Quinn puts it: "We are not trying to create a level battlefield here, we are trying to do the opposite: create a very un-level battlefield."

Sally Satel

Organs for Sale

Sally Satel is a practicing psychiatrist, lecturer at the Yale University School of Medicine, and resident scholar at the American Enterprise Institute for Public Policy Research, a nonpartisan, nonprofit institution committed to research and education on issues of government, politics, economics, and social welfare. Her work focuses on mental health policy and political trends in medicine. She is the author of several books, including *When Altruism Isn't Enough: The Case for Compensating Kidney Donors*. Her argument below appeared in the *Journal of the American Enterprise Institute* on October 14, 2006.

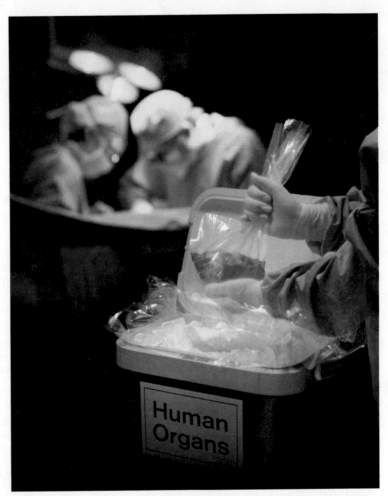

How should we resolve the ever-increasing demand for organs to aid those in need of transplants?

A year ago, I was searching the Internet for something rare and valuable: a human kidney. In August 2004, I learned I had end-stage renal disease and would need a transplant. At the time, my prospects for a donation from family or friends looked bleak, and I would soon have to begin dialysis. I would be hooked up to a machine three days a week for four hours at a time. This would continue for at least five years—the time it would take for a kidney from a deceased donor to become available. Even with dialysis, the kidneys of many sick people deteriorate so quickly that time runs out. An average of 11 Americans die each day waiting for a renal transplant.

2   Waiting for a kidney from a deceased donor is such a risky business that some people try publicly to convince strangers to give them live organs. Some put up billboards ("I NEED A KIDNEY, CAN YOU HELP? Call . . . "), start websites (GordyNeedsAKidney.org, whose opening page carries the plaintive headline, "Please

Help Our Dad"), or go overseas to become "transplant tourists" on the Chinese black market with the frightful knowledge that the organ they get will almost surely come from an executed political prisoner. The desperation, as I found myself, is perfectly understandable. I have no siblings. Several friends said they would look into it—donors don't need to be genetically related—but they turned out to have disqualifying medical problems or spouses who objected, or they grew scared.

3   Last fall, I turned to a website called MatchingDonors.com—which "matches" mostly prospective kidney donors with recipients—and quickly found a prospective donor. But six weeks later, he changed his mind. Then my wonderful friend Virginia Postrel came along. We are both healthy after a transplant operation on March 4 at the Washington Hospital Center. If Virginia had not donated her kidney, I could have languished on dialysis for years. Indeed, when I joined the national queue in January 2005, there were about 60,000 other people ahead of me, according to the nonprofit United Network for Organ Sharing (UNOS), which maintains the list under a monopoly contract with the federal government.

4   Today, there are 67,600 people waiting for a posthumous kidney. In big cities, where the ratio of needy patients to available organs is highest, the wait—spent on dialysis, a procedure that circulates your blood through a machine that purifies it and returns it to your body—is up to eight years. Last year, only 16,470 people received kidneys; roughly half of the donors were deceased, and half were living. Meanwhile, 4,100 died waiting. By 2010, the wait will be at least ten years, exceeding the average length of time that adults on dialysis survive.

5   Despite decades of public education about the virtues of donating organs at death, the level of such gifts has remained disappointingly steady. Only about one-third of Americans have designated themselves as donors on their driver's licenses or on state-run donor registries. For the rest, the decision to donate organs will fall to family members, who about half the time deny the requests of hospitals. More important, however, is that very few of the Americans who die, perhaps 13,000 a year (or less than 1 percent of all deaths), possess organs healthy enough for transplanting—so even if every family consented, the need for thousands of kidneys would go unmet.

6   The chasm between the number of available kidneys and the number of people needing one will widen each year. This is due to our misplaced faith in the power of altruism. The "transplant community," as it is called—organizations that encourage funding and gifts of organs, and many surgeons and nephrologists—expects people, both living donors and loved ones of the deceased, to give a body part and to receive nothing in return. In fact, it is illegal in the United States to receive money or anything of value ("valuable consideration") in exchange for an organ, a principle set down by Congress in 1984 in the National Organ Transplantation Act.

7   Don't get me wrong. Altruism is a beautiful thing—it's the reason I have a new kidney—but altruism alone cannot resolve the organ shortage. For that reason, more and more physicians, ethicists, economists, and legal scholars are urging the legalization of payments for organs in order to generate more kidneys for transplantation. One doesn't need to be Milton Friedman to know that a price of zero for anything virtually guarantees its shortage.

"Is it wrong for an individual . . . who wishes to utilize part of his body for the benefit of another [to] be provided with financial compensation that could obliterate a life of destitution for the individual and his family?" asked Dr. Richard Fine, president of the American Society of Transplantation, in his address to the World Transplant Congress this year. Supporters of experimenting with a market for organs encounter an array of objections, theoretical and practical. One popular argument, first advanced by Richard M. Titmuss, professor of social administration at the London School of Economics, is that altruism is the sole legitimate impulse behind organ donation. In 1971, Titmuss, a dedicated socialist and member of the Fabian Society, published *The Gift Relationship: From Human Blood to Social Policy*, which rapidly became a U.S. bestseller. He argued that altruistic acts are among the most sensitive indicators of the quality of human relationships and values in a society. Capitalism, on the other hand, is morally bankrupt.

This ethic is very much alive among the bureaucrats that run the United Network for Organ Sharing, which manages the transplant list. "Organ transplantation is built upon altruism and public trust. If anything shakes that trust, then everyone loses," says the UNOS website. Yet the trust is already badly rattled. "The current system has degenerated into an equal opportunity to die on the waiting list," observes nephrologist Benjamin Hippen, who advocated compensating donors (or perhaps they should be called "vendors") before the President's Council on Bioethics this summer.

10   Another theoretical objection to compensating donors is the notion that it will "commodify" the body and thus dehumanize the rest of us, let alone the person who gives his kidney in exchange for "valuable consideration." Yet with proper respect for donors and informed consent, it strikes me that careful engagement in financial arrangements is far less distasteful than allowing people to suffer and die. These are not abstract people, mind you, like the ones who may well be helped by stem cell discoveries years down the road, but live humans like the 49-year-old former secretary from the Pentagon I met last summer. For four years now, every Monday, Wednesday, and Friday, she has been sitting in Chair No. 7 in the dialysis center a few blocks from our offices.

11   Others go so far as to reject the very premise that saving lives is a paramount goal of medicine. "If we turn organ procurement into a crusade, we make of death simply a problem to be solved rather than an event to be endured as best we can, with whatever resources of mind and spirit are available to us,"[1] says Gilbert Meilaender, professor of theological ethics at Valparaiso University and a member of the President's Council on Bioethics. Now, it is one thing to question whether we should prolong the life of a vegetative patient, but quite another to abandon treatments for renal failure under circumstances in which a well-established remedy (transplantation) already exists—a remedy whose economic cost to society is lower than the cost of the less effective alternative, dialysis.

12   This is a good time to point out that the live donor—or vendor—of a kidney is exposed to only minor risks, the most significant being those associated with anesthesia and surgery itself—0.03% mortality—comparable to any other operation. Because the surgery is done using a laparoscopic approach, the visible scar is only 2 to 3 inches long. My donor, Virginia, was out of the hospital in three days and back to writing her magazine column a week later.

13   Long-term risks are also low. Typical is a 1997 study from Norway that followed 1,332 kidney donors for an average of 32 years. It found no difference in mortality rates between people who give kidneys and the general population. A 25-year follow-up of

70 donors conducted by the Cleveland Clinic found that the renal function is "well preserved" and that the overall incidence of hypertension was comparable to that of non-donors. The truth is that a normal person can get along perfectly well with one kidney. The risk a donor runs is that his single functioning kidney will become diseased or injured, and he'll need a transplant himself—a highly unlikely event.

14   Perhaps the most vocal critic of compensating donors is the National Kidney Foundation. It is offended by the idea that a donor might benefit in ways other than the psychic reward of pure giving. States NKF chairman Charles Fruit, "Families decide to donate the organs of a loved one for altruistic reasons. Payment is an affront to those who have already donated."[2] Virginia, a take-no-prisoners journalist, responded pointedly to Fruit on her website, <www.dynamist.com>, "The argument that paying organ donors is 'an affront' to unpaid donors is disgusting. Are unpaid donors giving organs to save lives or just to make themselves feel morally superior? Even in the latter case, they shouldn't care if *other* people get paid."

15   In the end, moral objections such as these put us at a standoff. I doubt I could change the mind of Professor Meilaender, who sincerely believes that organ donation violates what it means to be human. And there's nothing he can say to dissuade me from believing that free, informed, and willing individuals should be able to participate in a regulated exchange involving valuable consideration. Thus, the meaningful question becomes how both sides can honor their moral commitments.

16   The best answer is by creating a market arrangement to exist in parallel with altruistic giving. Within such a framework, any medical center or physician who objects to the practice of compensating donors can simply opt out of performing transplants that use such organs. Recipients on the list are free to turn down a paid-for organ and wait for one given altruistically. Choice for all—donors, recipients, and physicians—is enhanced. And it is choice in the greater service of diminishing sickness and death. Paradoxically, the current system based on altruism-or-else undermines the individual autonomy that is at the heart of the most widely held values in bioethics.

17   Not all objections to donor compensation, however, are abstract. A common concern is the potential for exploiting donors—especially low-income donors, who, as the critics reasonably claim, will be the most likely to find incentives attractive. Without question, protecting donors is enormously important. That is why any plan for compensation should be regulated. Potential donors must receive education about what it means to donate a kidney and the risks they run. They must undergo careful medical and psychological screening and receive quality follow-up care.

18   Critics often point to the horror stories from transplant black markets overseas and hold them up as cautionary tales. But the catastrophists have it exactly backward. It is when payment is not an above-board part of the medical system that black markets lead to minimal education of prospective donors, poor post-operative and follow-up care, and failure to honor agreements for payment.

19   Finally, some critics argue we have no evidence that an incentive system would work. True. So we need experimentation. Frankly, I don't know what the perfect kidney market would look like, but let's assume that Congress makes a bold and common-sense move and amends current law to permit the exchange of money or something of value for a kidney. Here are several alternative market systems:

1. A FORWARD MARKET FOR CADAVER ORGANS:

Economist Lloyd Cohen proposed one of the first market-based models to increase the number of cadaver organs. Potential donors would either (1) be paid a small amount today by the government or insurance companies to join the current donor registry, or (2) register today in return for the possibility of a much larger payment to their estates should the organs be used at death.

The advantage of such a forward-looking approach is that the decision-making burden is taken off family members at a painful time—when they are sitting in the emergency room learning that someone they love is now brain-dead. And, of course, there is no worry of exploiting the donor. A forward market could also help satisfy the 23,000 people waiting for livers, hearts, and lungs.

But deceased donors cannot meet the need for kidneys. In addition, kidneys from live donors are healthier than those obtained after death and survive, typically, for 10 to 20 years (or one-third longer). Thus, to mitigate the shortage of kidneys, we must consider offering incentives to people amenable to relinquishing one while they are alive.

2. THE CENTRALIZED SINGLE COMPENSATOR:

In this approach, the federal government or a designated agency acts as the only authority with the power to buy and allocate organs for transplants. As is currently the case with cadaver organs, kidneys obtained through compensated donors would be matched with the next best candidate waiting on the national list.

Under this scheme, Medicare would underwrite the incentives in light of the fact that it already pays for dialysis treatment under the 1972 End Stage Renal Disease (ESRD) amendment to the Social Security Act. This entitlement provides care for Americans with terminal renal failure regardless of age if they have met required work credits for Social Security. Last year, the ESRD program spent about $16 billion on dialysis, or about $66,000 per patient annually. Since a 35-year-old spends about nine years on dialysis, the total cost is around $600,000; for a 64-year-old, about four years at $300,000. Compare these expenses with the cost of a transplant operation—approximately $75,000 in all for the one-time cost of the surgeries and hospital stays of the donor and recipient, plus the first year of follow-up medical care (including medicine).

In most cases, these savings would easily pay for a lifetime supply of the expensive immunosuppressant drugs to prevent rejection of the new kidney. The drugs cost $15,000 to $20,000 a year, and every recipient must take them every day for life. Medicare pays for transplant surgery but stops reimbursing for the drugs, at 80 percent of full price, three years post-transplant if the patient goes back to work.

What kinds of compensation should be offered? A reasonable case could be made for an outright payment—after all, it is hard to argue that an individual is competent enough to sell an organ yet unfit to manage the money he receives in exchange for it—but I am partial to a compromise approach in order to defuse those who say that people will sell their organs for quick cash or use it to buy something frivolous. For example, the donor could choose from a menu of options, including a deposit to a 401(k) retirement plan, tax credits, tuition vouchers for the donor's children, long-term nursing care, family health coverage, life and nonfatal injury insurance, a charitable contribution in the donor's name, or cash payments stretched over time.

Donor protection is the linchpin of any compensation model. Standard guidelines for physical and psychological screening, donor education, and informed consent could be formulated by a medical organization, such as the American Society of Transplant Surgeons, or another entity designated by the federal Department of Health and Human Services. A "waiting period" of three to six months could be built in to ensure the prospective donor has ample time to think it through. Monitoring donor health post-transplant is important as well. One idea is to provide lifetime health insurance, through Medicare or a private insurer for the donor. He would receive annual physicals, routine medical screening, and long-term follow-up in addition to standard health coverage. A federally sponsored registry of donors could help us study long-term outcomes for donors and vendors and take steps to remedy physical or psychological difficulties that arise.

3. MULTIPLE COMPENSATORS:

In this scheme, donors, compensators (that is, the entities that pay for the transplants), and medical centers (that perform them) would be coordinated with one another through an intermediary broker. Medicare would be one of several possible compensators, along with private insurers, charitable foundations, or a fund established perhaps through a surcharge added to the cost paid by insurers and foundations.

4. PRIVATE CONTRACTS:

The easiest way to start a market for organs is simply to change the law to allow someone who needs an organ and someone who wants to sell one to make their own arrangements through contract—as infertile couples currently do with surrogate mothers. But such a system would inevitably attract criticism because it appears to favor well-off sick people over poor.

While private contracts may seem unfair because only those with means will be able to purchase directly, poor people who need kidneys would be no worse off—and, very likely, considerably better off—than under the current system. First, a stranger interested in selling a kidney is unlikely to give it away for free to the next person on the list (only 88 donors last year made such anonymous gifts); thus, few poor people would be deprived of kidneys they would otherwise have gotten voluntarily. Second, anyone who gets a kidney by contract is removed from the waiting list, and everyone behind him benefits by moving up. Third, private charities could offer to help subsidize the cost for a needy patient or pay outright.

These broad proposals, and variants on them, need considerable elaboration. Many questions remain: How would prices be determined? Would each available kidney be allotted to the next well-matched person on the list? Or should living organs be preferentially allocated to the healthiest people on the list—that is, those who will get the most "life" out of the organ? Could noncitizens be paid donors? Also, could people have a say in who would receive their kidneys? As it currently stands, most living donors give altruistically because they are trying to help a friend or relative, not a stranger. But it is surely possible that the decision of an ambivalent friend could tip in the direction of giving with the promise of compensation. And since each patient on dialysis is functionally "attached" to a Medicare entitlement, perhaps the recipient could direct a portion of "his" Medicare allotment to his friend as payment.

There is no denying the political and practical challenges that come with introducing payment into a 20-year-old scheme built on the premise that generosity is the only legitimate motive for giving. Yet as death and suffering mount, constructing a market-based incentive program to increase the supply of transplantable organs has become a moral imperative. Its architects must give serious consideration to principled reservations and to concerns about donor safety, but repugnance and caution are not in themselves arguments against innovation. They are only reasons for vigilance and care.

Notes

[1] Gilbert Meilaender, "Gifts of the Body," *New Atlantis*, Number 13 (Summer 2006): 25–35.

[2] Letters in response to Richard Epstein, "Kidney Beancounters," *Wall Street Journal*, May 15, 2006 (May 26, 2006). ■

Ron Reagan

Speech at the Democratic National Convention, July 27, 2004

Ron Reagan is the son of the fortieth president of the United States. In August 1994, at the age of 83, President Reagan was diagnosed with Alzheimer's disease, an incurable neurological disorder that destroys brain cells, and he died of the disease in June 2004. A few months later, on July 27, Ron Reagan offered the following speech to the delegates to the Democratic National Convention and to the millions of Americans watching on television. It was countered the next day by Richard Doerflinger, whose piece follows this one.

Good evening, ladies and gentlemen.

2   A few of you may be surprised to see someone with my last name showing up to speak at a Democratic Convention. Apparently some of you are not. Let me assure you, I am not here to make a political speech and the topic at hand should not—must not—have anything to do with partisanship.

3   I am here tonight to talk about the issue of research into what may be the greatest medical breakthrough in our or any lifetime: the use of embryonic stem cells—cells created using the material of our own bodies—to cure a wide range of fatal and debilitating illnesses: Parkinson's disease, multiple sclerosis, diabetes, lymphoma, spinal cord injuries, and much more.

4   Millions are afflicted. And every year, every day, tragedy is visited upon families across the country, around the world. Now, it may be within our power to put an end to this suffering. We only need to try.

5   Some of you already know what I'm talking about when I say embryonic stem cell research. Others of you are probably thinking, that's quite a mouthful. Maybe this is a good time to go for a tall cold one. Well, wait a minute, wait a minute.

6   Let me try and paint as simple a picture as I can while still doing justice to the science, the incredible science involved. Let's say that ten or so years from now you are diagnosed with Parkinson's disease. There is currently no cure, and drug therapy, with its attendant side-effects, can only temporarily relieve the symptoms.

7   Now, imagine going to a doctor who, instead of prescribing drugs, takes a few skin cells from your arm. The nucleus of one of your cells is placed into a donor egg whose own nucleus has been removed. A bit of chemical or electrical stimulation will encourage your cell's nucleus to begin dividing, creating new cells which will then be placed into a tissue culture. Those cells will generate embryonic stem cells containing only your DNA, thereby eliminating the risk of tissue rejection. These stem cells are then driven to become the very neural cells that are defective in Parkinson's patients. And finally, those cells—with your DNA—are injected into your brain where they will replace the faulty cells whose failure to produce adequate dopamine led to the Parkinson's disease in the first place.

8   In other words, you're cured.

9   And another thing, these embryonic stem cells, they could continue to replicate indefinitely and, theoretically, can be induced to recreate virtually any tissue in your body.

10   How'd you like to have your own personal biological repair kit standing by at the hospital? Sound like magic? Welcome to the future of medicine.

11   Now by the way, no fetal tissue is involved in this process. No fetuses are created, none destroyed. This all happens in the laboratory at the cellular level.

12   Now, there are those who would stand in the way of this remarkable future, who would deny the federal funding so crucial to basic research. They argue that interfering with the development of even the earliest stage embryo, even one that will never be implanted in a womb and will never develop into an actual fetus, is tantamount to murder.

13   A few of these folks, needless to say, are just grinding a political axe and they should be ashamed of themselves. But many are well-meaning and sincere. Their belief is just that, an article of faith, and they are entitled to it. But it does not follow that the theology of a few should be allowed to forestall the health and well-being of the many.

14   And how can we affirm life if we abandon those whose own lives are so desperately at risk? It is a hallmark of human intelligence that we are able to make distinctions.

15   Yes, these cells could theoretically have the potential, under very different circumstances, to develop into human beings—that potential is where their magic lies. But they are not, in and of themselves, human beings. They have no fingers and toes, no brain or spinal cord. They have no thoughts, no fears. They feel no pain.

16   Surely we can distinguish between these undifferentiated cells multiplying in a tissue culture and a living, breathing person—a parent, a spouse, a child.

17   I know a child—well, she must be 13 now so I guess I'd better call her a young woman. She has fingers and toes. She has a mind. She has memories. She has hopes. She has juvenile diabetes. Like so many kids with this disease, she's adjusted amazingly well. The insulin pump she wears—she's decorated hers with rhinestones. She

Actor Michael J. Fox, who was diagnosed in 1991 with Parkinson's disease, spoke at the Bio International Convention in 2007. Fox appealed to scientists and investors to aggressively translate scientific research into creative treatments for debilitating diseases, including Parkinson's.

can handle her own catheter needle. She's learned to sleep through the blood drawings in the wee hours of the morning.

18   She's very brave. She is also quite bright and understands full well the progress of her disease and what that might ultimately mean: blindness, amputation, diabetic coma. Every day, she fights to have a future.

19   What excuse will we offer this young woman should we fail her now? What might we tell her children? Or the millions of others who suffer? That when given an opportunity to help, we turned away? That facing political opposition, we lost our nerve? That even though we knew better, we did nothing?

20   And, should we fail, how will we feel if, a few years from now, a more enlightened generation should fulfill the promise of embryonic stem cell therapy? Imagine what they would say of us who lacked the will.

21   No, we owe this young woman and all those who suffer—we owe ourselves—better than that. We are better than that. We are a wiser people, a finer nation.

22   And for all of us in this fight, let me say: we will prevail. The tide of history is with us. Like all generations who have come before ours, we are motivated by a thirst for knowledge and compelled to see others in need as fellow angels on an often difficult path, deserving of our compassion.

23   In a few months, we will face a choice. Yes, between two candidates and two parties, but more than that. We have a chance to take a giant stride forward for the good of all humanity. We can choose between the future and the past, between reason and ignorance, between true compassion and mere ideology.

24   This—this is our moment, and we must not falter.

25   Whatever else you do come November 2, I urge you, please, cast a vote for embryonic stem cell research.

26   Thank you for your time.

Richard M. Doerflinger

Don't Clone Ron Reagan's Agenda

Richard M. Doerflinger is the Secretariat on Pro-life Activities for the United States Conference of Catholic Bishops. In 2009 Doerflinger was awarded an inaugural Life Prize by the Gerard Health Foundation for his work in "preserving and upholding the sanctity of human life" in areas such as public advocacy, legal action, and outreach. A specialist in bioethics, biotechnology, and public policy, he wrote the essay that follows on July 28, 2004, in response to the previous essay in this chapter, by Ron Reagan.

Ron Reagan's speech at the Democratic convention last night was expected to urge expanded funding for stem cell research using so-called "spare" embryos—and to highlight these cells' potential for treating the Alzheimer's disease that took his father's life.

2   He did neither. He didn't even mention Alzheimer's, perhaps because even strong supporters of embryonic stem cell research say it is unlikely to be of use for that disease. (Reagan himself admitted this on a July 12 segment of MSNBC's *Hardball*.) And he didn't talk about current debates on funding research using existing embryos. Instead he endorsed the more radical agenda of human cloning—mass-producing one's own identical twins in the laboratory so they can be exploited as (in his words) "your own personal biological repair kit" when disease or injury strikes.

3   Politically this was, to say the least, a gamble. Americans may be tempted to make use of embryos left over from fertility clinics, but most polls show them to be against human cloning for any purpose. Other advanced nations—Canada, Australia, France, Germany, Norway—have banned the practice completely, and the United Nations may approve an international covenant against it this fall. Many groups and individuals who are "pro-choice" on abortion oppose research cloning, not least because it would require the mass exploitation of women to provide what Ron Reagan casually calls "donor eggs." And the potential "therapeutic" benefits of cloning are even more speculative than those of embryonic stem cell research—the worldwide effort even to obtain viable stem cells from cloned embryos has already killed hundreds of embryos and produced exactly one stem cell line, in South Korea.

4   But precisely for these reasons, Ron Reagan should be praised for his candor. The scientists and patient groups promoting embryonic stem cell research know that the current debate on funding is a mere transitional step. For years they have supported the mass manufacture of human embryos through cloning, as the logical and necessary goal of their agenda, but lately they have been coy about this as they fight for the more popular slogan of "stem cell research." With his speech Reagan has removed the mask, and allowed us to debate what is really at stake.

5   He claimed in his speech, of course, that what is at stake in this debate is the lives of millions of patients with devastating diseases. But by highlighting Parkinson's disease and juvenile diabetes as two diseases most clearly justifying the move to human cloning, he failed to do his homework. These are two of the diseases that pro-cloning scientists now admit will probably *not* be helped by research cloning.

6   Scottish cloning expert Ian Wilmut, for example, wrote in the *British Medical Journal* in February that producing genetically matched stem cells through cloning is probably quite unnecessary for treating any neurological disease. Recent findings suggest that the nervous system is "immune privileged," and will not generally reject stem cells from a human who is genetically different. He added that cloning is probably useless for auto-immune diseases like juvenile diabetes, where the body mistakenly rejects its own insulin-producing cells as though they were foreign. "In such cases," he wrote, "transfer of immunologically identical cells to a patient is expected to induce the same rejection."

7   Wilmut's observations cut the ground out from under Ron Reagan's simple-minded claim that cloning is needed to avoid tissue rejection. For some diseases, genetically matched cells are unnecessary; for others, they are useless, because they only replicate the genetic profile that is part of the problem. (Ironically, for Alzheimer's both may be true—cloning may be unnecessary to avoid tissue rejection in the brain, and useless because the cloned cells would have the same genetic defect that may lead to Alzheimer's.) Reagan declared that this debate requires us to "choose between . . . reason and ignorance," but he did not realize which side has the monopoly on ignorance.

8   That ignorance poses an obstacle to real advances that are right before our eyes. Two weeks before Ron Reagan declared that a treatment for Parkinson's may arrive "ten or so years from now," using "the material of our own bodies," a Parkinson's patient and his doctor quietly appeared before Congress to point out that this has already been done. Dennis Turner was treated in 1999 by Dr. Michel Levesque of Cedars-Sinai Medical Center in Los Angeles, using his own adult neural stem cells. Dr. Levesque did not use the Rube Goldberg method of trying to turn those cells into a cloned embryo and then killing the embryo to get stem cells—he just grew Turner's own adult stem cells in the lab, and turned them directly into dopamine-producing cells. And with just one injection, on one side of Turner's brain, he produced an almost complete reversal of Parkinson's symptoms over four years.

9   Turner stopped shaking, could eat without difficulty, could put in his own contact lenses again, and resumed his avocation of big-game photography—on one occasion scrambling up a tree in Africa to escape a charging rhinoceros.

10   Amazingly, while this advance has been presented at national and international scientific conferences and featured on ABC-TV in Chicago, the scientific establishment supporting embryonic stem cell research has almost completely ignored it, and most news media have obediently imposed a virtual news blackout on it. That did not change even after the results were presented to the Senate Commerce Subcommittee on Science, Technology and Space this month. Pro-cloning Senators on the panel actually seemed angry at the witnesses, for trying to distract them from their fixation on destroying embryos.

11   Turner also testified that his symptoms have begun to return, especially arising from the side of his brain that was left untreated, and he would like to get a second treatment. For that he will have to wait. Dr. Levesque has received insufficient appreciation and funding for his technique, and is still trying to put together the funds for broader clinical trials—as most Parkinson's foundations and NIH peer reviewers look into the starry distance of Ron Reagan's dreams about embryonic stem cells.

12   But hey, who cares about real Parkinson's patients when there's a Brave New World to sell? ∎

ED FISCHER

Good news! Some of you may be saved... until the stem cells run out, of course...

debilitating diseases

Is stem cell research ethical?

www.CartoonStock.com

ISSUE IN FOCUS

Is Genetically Modified Food a Boon or a Risk?

Each month, the United States Food and Drug Administration lists on its Web site its latest "food alerts": foods recalled by sellers because of fears about their safety. In the first two weeks of May 2010 alone, the FDA alerted Americans to concerns about certain apricots, breads, sunflower seeds, cheeses, lettuce, bread, and Amish pumpkin butter.

In one sense, fears about food safety have been around since time immemorial; ever since the Garden of Eden, consumers have worried about what they were putting into their mouths. Nevertheless, out of necessity early humans began experimenting with various species to tame for agricultural purposes so that today, just over 100 crop species are grown intensively around the world, and only a handful of these supply us with most of what we now eat. Through a process of trial and error, farmers and scientists developed processes of selection and cross-breeding (or "hybridization") to combine desirable traits from several varieties into elite cross-bred species. When desired characteristics were unavailable in the crop species, farmers introduced genes from wild species into the cultivated plants. The result, as in the case of corn and dairy cows, is the production of highly productive food species that people born two centuries ago could not have envisioned.

And so in a sense the modern use of gene transfer techniques in the development of genetically modified (GM) crops is but a logical extension of a practice that has existed in agriculture for thousands of years. While GM crops are initially more costly to produce, they eventually save farmers money due to the efficiencies created by greater yields and resistance to insects. Biotechnology, its proponents maintain, further benefits our food supply because genetic modification reduces harmful toxic compounds that exist either naturally or unnaturally in the food we eat. Biotechnology may also allow farmers to produce plants that are tolerant to low temperatures, that thrive in poor soil conditions, and that have a longer shelf-life—all of which could benefit the world's hungry.

And yet modern GM processes are decidedly different from their forebears. While the development of new cultivars through classical breeding processes generally takes ten to fifteen years, changes from new gene transfer methods can occur within one generation; and while traditional cross-breeding transfers genes only between similar plants, modern bioengineering can isolate a gene from one type of organism and combine it with the DNA of dissimilar species. Given what is still unknown about the effects of such rapid and dramatic transformation, critics express concern over the rapidity with which GM foods are spreading across the globe. Critics of GM also worry about losses of crop biodiversity—essential for species resilience and the health of surrounding ecosystems—as the popularity of high-yielding varieties limits the genetic variation found in major crops. Should not new species be tested carefully over a long period of time in order that potential risks to health, safety, society, and the environment can be fully assessed?

In the following pages, we present several arguments related to genetically modified food. Mark Anslow, writing in March 2008 for The *Ecologist* (a British publication that promotes ecologically conscious living), summarizes the case against GM foods in his "Ten Reasons Why GM Won't Feed the World." His suspicions are supported by a 2004 argument by Jeffrey Smith (author of *Genetic Roulette: The Documented Health Risks of Genetically Engineered Foods*), who contends that GM foods are influencing behavior; and by a 2009 argument by Ben Burkett, an African American farmer from Mississippi who is president of the National Family Farm. (The cover of this book also offers a visual argument related to GM.)

By contrast, James Freeman defends GM in an essay that originally appeared in *USA Today* in February 2000. Freeman maintains that biotechnology is nothing more than a highly developed breeding tool, and he labels its opponents "scare mongers" with a limited understanding of the realities of biotechnology and its benefits. Freeman's views are reinforced by James McWlliams, an environmentalist and proponent of natural and organic foods who nevertheless supports (cautiously) the development of genetically modified foods. In his essay, which was

How was your food grown? If you are living in the United States, it is likely that you are consuming genetically modified foods on a regular basis.

published in the online magazine *Slate* in 2009, McWilliams offers the possibility that genetically modified foods can benefit the environment. Finally, we offer Gregory Jaffe's advice on how to "Lessen the Fear of Genetically Engineered Crops." An expert on consumer issues relating to agricultural biotechnology, Jaffe suggests in his essay (which appeared August 8, 2001 in the *Christian Science Monitor*) that "sensible measures" must be developed to ensure that GM foods are safe for public consumption.

So in the end is it ethical and practical for scientists to modify living organisms, to tamper with the food supply? Is the genetic modification of crops inherently hazardous? Could we unwittingly be making our foods and our world unsafe? And what about the long-term consequences of producing and consuming GM foods? Do GM crops affect the environment or the wild ecosystem, reducing crop biodiversity and the persistence of beneficial insects? (Some suspect that the revered monarch butterfly is being compromised by new varieties of corn.) Could new crops lead to the development of noxious "superweeds"? And what about genetic pollution? Should we be concerned that GM genes might be transferred to other organisms, even to humans and other animals? How can scientists allay public concerns considering the complexities of the issues involved?

MARK ANSLOW

Ten Reasons Why GM Won't Feed the World

G enetic modification can't deliver a safe, secure future food supply. Here's why.

1. Failure to deliver

2   Despite the hype, genetic modification consistently fails to live up to industry claims. Only two GM traits have ever made it to market: herbicide resistance and BT toxin expression (see below). Other promises of genetic modification have failed to materialize. The much vaunted GM "golden rice"—hailed as a cure to vitamin A deficiency—has never made it out of the laboratory, partly because in order to meet recommended levels of vitamin A intake, consumers would need to eat 12 bowls of the rice every day.[1] In 2004, the Kenyan government admitted that Monsanto's GM sweet potatoes were no more resistant to feathery mottle virus than ordinary strains, and in fact produced lower yields.[2] And in January 2008, news that scientists had modified a carrot to cure osteoporosis by providing calcium had to be weighed against the fact that you would need to eat 1.6 kilograms of these vegetables each day to meet your recommended calcium intake.[3]

2. Costing the Earth

3   GM crops are costing farmers and governments more money than they are making. In 2003, a report by the Soil Association estimated the cost to the US economy of GM crops at around $12 billion (£6 billion) since 1999, on account of inflated farm subsidies, loss of export orders, and various seed recalls.[4] A study in Iowa found that GM soybeans required all the same costs as conventional farming but, because they produced lower yields (see below), the farmers ended up making no profit at all.[5] In India, an independent study found that BT cotton crops were costing farmers 10 per cent more than non-BT variants and bringing in 40 per cent lower profits.[6] Between 2001 and 2005, more than 32,000 Indian farmers committed suicide, most as a result of mounting debts caused by inadequate crops.[7]

3. Contamination and gene escape

4   No matter how hard you try, you can never be sure that what you are eating is GM-free. In a recent article, the *New Scientist* admitted that contamination and cross-fertilization between GM and non-GM crops "has happened on many occasions already."[8] In late 2007, U.S. company Scotts Miracle-Gro was fined $500,000 by the U.S. Department of Agriculture when genetic material from a new golf-course grass was found in native grasses as far away as 13 miles away from the test sites, apparently released when freshly cut grass was caught and blown by the wind.[9] In 2006, an analysis of 40 Spanish

conventional and organic farms found that eight were contaminated with GM corn varieties, including one farmer whose crop contained 12.6 per cent GM plants.

4. Reliance on pesticides

Far from reducing dependency on pesticides and fertilizers, GM crops frequently increase farmers' reliance on these products. Herbicide-resistant crops can be sprayed indiscriminately with weedkillers such as Monsanto's Roundup because they are engineered to withstand the effect of the chemical. This means that significantly higher levels of herbicide are found in the final food product, however, and often a second herbicide is used in the late stages of the crop to promote "dessication," or drying, meaning that these crops receive a double dose of harmful chemicals.[10] BT maize, engineered to produce an insecticidal toxin, has never eliminated the use of pesticides,[11] and because the BT gene cannot be switched off, the crops continue to produce the toxin right up until harvest, reaching the consumer at its highest possible concentrations.[12]

5. Frankenfoods

Despite the best efforts of the biotech industry, consumers remain staunchly opposed to GM food. In 2007, the vast majority of 11,700 responses to the government's consultation on whether contamination of organic food with traces of GM crops should be allowed were strongly negative. The British government's own "GM Nation" debate in 2003 discovered that half of its participants "never want to see GM crops grown in the United Kingdom under any circumstances," and 96 per cent thought that society knew too little about the health impacts of genetic modification. In India, farmers' experience of BT cotton has been so disastrous that the Maharashtra government now advises that farmers grow soybeans instead. And in Australia, over 250 food companies lodged appeals with the state governments of New South Wales and Victoria over the lifting of bans against growing GM canola crops.[13]

6. Breeding resistance

Nature is smart, and there are already reports of species emerging that are resistant to GM crops. This is seen in the emergence of new "superweeds" on farms in North America—plants that have evolved the ability to withstand the industry's chemicals. A report by the conservation body English Nature (now Natural England), in 2002, revealed that oilseed rape plants that had developed resistance to three or more herbicides were "not uncommon" in Canada.[14] The superweeds had been created through random crosses between neighboring GM crops. In order to tackle these superweeds, Canadian farmers were forced to resort to even stronger, more toxic herbicides.[15] Similarly, pests (notably the diamondback moth) have been quick to develop resistance to BT toxin, and in 2007 swarms of mealy bugs began attacking supposedly pestresistant Indian cotton.

7. Creating problems for solutions

Many of the so-called "problems" for which the biotechnology industry develops "solutions" seem to be notions of PR rather than science. Herbicide-resistance was sold under the claim that because crops could be doused in chemicals, there would be much less need to weed mechanically or plough the soil, keeping more carbon and nitrates under the surface. But a new long-term study by the U.S. Agricultural Research Service has shown that organic farming, even with ploughing, stores more carbon than the GM crops save.[16] BT cotton was claimed to increase resistance to pests, but farmers in East Africa discovered that by planting a local weed amid their corn crop, they could lure pests to lay their eggs on the weed and not the crop.[17]

8. Health risks

9   The results of tests on animals exposed to GM crops give serious cause for concern over their safety. In 1998, Scottish scientists found damage to every single internal organ in rats fed blight-resistant GM potatoes. In a 2006 experiment, female rats fed on herbicide-resistant soybeans gave birth to severely stunted pups, of which half died within three weeks. The survivors were sterile. In the same year, Indian news agencies reported that thousands of sheep allowed to graze on BT cotton crop residues had died suddenly. Further cases of livestock deaths followed in 2007. There have also been reports of allergy-like symptoms among Indian laborers in BT cotton fields. In 2002, the only trial ever to involve human beings appeared to show that altered genetic material from GM soybeans not only survives in the human gut, but may even pass its genetic material to bacteria within the digestive system.[18]

9. Left hungry

10   GM crops have always come with promises of increased yields for farmers, but this has rarely been the case. A three-year study of 87 villages in India found that non-BT cotton consistently produced 30 per cent higher yields than the (more expensive) GM alternative.[19] It is now widely accepted that GM soybeans produce consistently lower yields than conventional varieties. In 1992, Monsanto's own trials showed that the company's Roundup Ready soybeans yield 11.5 per cent less on harvest. Later Monsanto studies went on to reveal that some trials of GM canola crops in Australia actually produced yields 16 per cent below the non- GM national average.[20]

10. Wedded to fertilizers and fossil fuels

11   No genetically modified crop has yet eliminated the need for chemical fertilizers in order to achieve expected yields. Although the industry has made much of the possibility of splicing nitrogen-fixing genes into commercial food crops in order to boost yields, there has so far been little success. This means that GM crops are just as dependent on fossil fuels to make fertilizers as conventional agriculture. In addition to this, GM traits are often specifically designed to fit with large-scale industrial agriculture. Herbicide resistance is of no real benefit unless your farm is too vast to weed mechanically, and it presumes that the farmers already farm in a way that involves the chemical spraying of their crops. Similarly, BT toxin expression is designed to counteract the problem of pest control in vast monocultures, which encourage infestations.

12   In a world that will soon have to change its view of farming—facing as it does the twin challenges of climate change and peak oil—GM crops will soon come to look like a relic of bygone practices.

References

[1] http://www.gmwatch.org/archive2.asp?arcid=8521

[2] http://www.greens.org/s-r/35/35-03.html

[3] *Telegraph*, 14th January 2008, http://tinyurl.com/38e2rp

[4] Soil Association, 2007, http://tinyurl.com/33bfuh

[5] http://ianrnews.unl.edu/static/0005161.shtml

[6] http://www.i-sis.org.uk/IBTCF.php

[7] *Indian Muslims*, 20th November 2007, http://tinyurl.com/2u7wy7

[8] *New Scientist*, "Genes for Greens," 5th January 2007, Issue 2637, Vol 197

[9] http://gmfoodwatch.tribe.net/thread/a1b77b8b-15f5-4f1d-86df-2bbca5aaec70

[10] http://www.prospect-magazine.co.uk/article_details.php?id=9927

[11] http://www.btinternet.com/~nlpWESSEX/Documents/usdagmeconomics.htm

[12] http://www.prospect-magazine.co.uk/article_details.php?id=9927

[13] http://www.indybay.org/newsitems/2007/11/27/18463803.php

[14] http://www.english-nature.org.uk/pubs/publication/PDF/enrr443.pdf

[15] *Innovations Report*, 20th June 2005, http://tinyurl.com/3axmln

[16] http://www.gmwatch.org/archive2.asp?arcid=8658

[17] http://www.i-sis.org.uk/GMcropsfailed.php

[18] All references from "GM Food Nightmare Unfolding in the Regulatory Sham," by Mae-Wan Ho, Joe Cummins, and Peter Saunders, ISIS report.

[19] http://www.i-sis.org.uk/IBTCF.php

[20] http://www.gmwatch.org/archive2.asp?arcid=8558

James Freeman

You're Eating Genetically Modified Food

There's no escape. You are consuming mass quantities of genetically modified food. The milk on your Cheerios this morning came from a genetically modified cow, and the Cheerios themselves featured genetically modified whole grain goodness. At lunch you'll enjoy french fries from genetically modified potatoes and perhaps a bucket of genetically modified fried chicken. If you don't have any meetings this afternoon, maybe you'll wash it all down with the finest genetically modified hops, grains, and barley, brewed to perfection—or at least to completion if you're drinking Schaefer.

Everything you eat is the result of genetic modification. When a rancher in Wyoming selected his stud bull to mate with a certain cow to produce the calf that ultimately produced the milk on your breakfast table, he was manipulating genes. Sounds delicious, doesn't it? Sorry, but you get the point.

Long before you were ever born, farmers were splicing genes and manipulating seeds to create more robust plants. Genetic modification used to be called "breeding," and people have been doing it for centuries. Thomas Jefferson did it at Monticello, as he experimented in his gardens with literally hundreds of varieties of fruits and vegetables. (Hmm, Thomas Jefferson and genes. . . . This column is going to disappoint a lot of people doing Web searches.)

Anyway, to return to the topic at hand, breeding isn't a scary word, so people who oppose technology call it "genetic modification." They want to cast biotechnology, which is just a more precise and effective breeding tool, as some kind of threat to our lives, instead of the blessing that it is.

Have you ever seen corn in its natural state without genetic modification? It's disgusting. We're talking about that nasty, gnarled, multi-colored garbage used as ornamentation in Thanksgiving displays. The fear mongers should eat that the next time they want to criticize technology. In fact, the fear mongers are waging a very successful campaign against biotechnology, especially in Europe where they've lobbied to limit the availability of "genetically modified" foods. Even in the United States, where we generally embrace technology and its possibilities, the fear is spreading—not because of some horrible event related to the food supply, but because of more aggressive spinning of the media. In fact, you've been enjoying foods enhanced by biotechnology for most of the last decade. And the news is all good—lower prices and more abundant food.

As for the future, the potential to eliminate human suffering is enormous. Right now, according to the World Health Organization, more than a million kids die every year because they lack vitamin A in their diets. Millions more become blind. WHO estimates that more than a billion people suffer from anemia, caused by iron deficiency. What if we could develop rice or corn plants with all of the essential vitamins for children? Personally, I'd rather have an entire day's nutrition bio-engineered into a Twinkie or a pan pizza, but I recognize the benefits of more-nutritious crops. Reasonable people can disagree on the best applications for this technology.

Still, the critics want to talk about the dangers of genetically modified crops. The Environmental Protection Agency wants to regulate the use of certain bio-engineered corn seeds because they include a resistance to pests. Specifically, the seeds are bred to include a toxin called BT that kills little creatures called corn borers, so farmers don't need to spray pesticides. Turns out, according to the EPA, that the toxin in the corn can kill monarch butterflies, too. The butterflies don't eat corn, but the EPA is afraid that the corn pollen will blow over and land on a milkweed and stick to it and then confused monarch caterpillars will inadvertently eat the pollen. Not exactly the end of the world, but it sounds bad—until you consider the alternatives. According to Professor Nina Fedoroff, "A wide-spectrum pesticide sprayed from a plane is going to kill a lot more insects than will be killed by an in-plant toxin."

Of course, the anti-tech crowd will say that they don't like pesticides either. They promote organic farming—meaning we use more land to produce our food and we clear more wilderness. We also pay more for food, since we're not using the efficiencies that come from technology. Maybe that's not a problem for you or me, but it's bad news for those millions of malnourished kids around the world. Says Fedoroff, "I think that most inhabitants of contemporary urban societies don't have a clue about how tough it is to grow enough food for the human population in competition with bacteria, fungi, insects, and animals and in the face of droughts, floods, and other climatic variations." That may be true, but I do think that most Americans understand the positive impact of technology. And that's why they'll ultimately reject the scare campaign against biotechnology.

Jeffrey Smith

Another Reason for Schools to Ban Genetically Engineered Foods

Before the Appleton, Wisconsin high school replaced their cafeteria's processed foods with wholesome, nutritious food, the school was described as out-of-control. There were weapons violations, student disruptions, and a cop on duty full-time. After the change in school meals, the students were calm, focused, and orderly. There were no more weapons violations, and no suicides, expulsions, dropouts, or drug violations. The new diet and improved behavior has lasted for seven years, and now other schools are changing their meal programs with similar results.

2   Years ago, a science class at Appleton found support for their new diet by conducting a cruel and unusual experiment with three mice. They fed them the junk food that kids in other high schools eat everyday. The mice freaked out. Their behavior was totally different than the three mice in the neighboring cage. The neighboring mice had good karma; they were fed nutritious whole foods and behaved like mice. They slept during the day inside their cardboard tube, played with each other, and acted very mouse-like. The junk food mice, on the other hand, destroyed their cardboard tube, were no longer nocturnal, stopped playing with each other, fought often, and two mice eventually killed the third and ate it. After the three month experiment, the students rehabilitated the two surviving junk food mice with a diet of whole foods. After about three weeks, the mice came around.

3   Sister Luigi Frigo repeats this experiment every year in her second grade class in Cudahy, Wisconsin, but mercifully, for only four days. Even on the first day of junk food, the mice's behavior "changes drastically." They become lazy, antisocial, and nervous. And it still takes the mice about two to three weeks on unprocessed foods to return to normal. One year, the second graders tried to do the experiment again a few months later with the same mice, but this time the animals refused to eat the junk food.

4   Across the ocean in Holland, a student fed one group of mice genetically modified (GM) corn and soy, and another group the non-GM variety. The GM mice stopped

playing with each other and withdrew into their own parts of the cage. When the student tried to pick them up, unlike their well-behaved neighbors, the GM mice scampered around in apparent fear and tried to climb the walls. One mouse in the GM group was found dead at the end of the experiment.

5   It's interesting to note that the junk food fed to the mice in the Wisconsin experiments also contained genetically modified ingredients. And although the Appleton school lunch program did not specifically attempt to remove GM foods, it happened anyway. That's because GM foods such as soy and corn and their derivatives are largely found in processed foods. So when the school switched to unprocessed alternatives, almost all ingredients derived from GM crops were taken out automatically.

6   Does this mean that GM foods negatively affect the behavior of humans or animals? It would certainly be irresponsible to say so on the basis of a single student mice experiment and the results at Appleton. On the other hand, it is equally irresponsible to say that it doesn't.

7   We are just beginning to understand the influence of food on behavior. A study in *Science* in December 2002 concluded that "food molecules act like hormones, regulating body functioning and triggering cell division. The molecules can cause mental imbalances ranging from attention-deficit and hyperactivity disorder to serious mental illness." The problem is we do not know which food molecules have what effect. The bigger problem is that the composition of GM foods can change radically without our knowledge.

8   Genetically modified foods have genes inserted into their DNA. But genes are not Legos; they don't just snap into place. Gene insertion creates unpredicted, irreversible changes. In one study, for example, a gene chip monitored the DNA before and after a single foreign gene was inserted. As much as 5 percent of the DNA's genes changed the amount of protein they were producing. Not only is that huge in itself, but these changes can multiply through complex interactions down the line.

9   In spite of the potential for dramatic changes in the composition of GM foods, they are typically measured for only a small number of known nutrient levels. But even if we *could* identify all the changed compounds, at this point we wouldn't know which might be responsible for the antisocial nature of mice or humans. Likewise, we are only beginning to identify the medicinal compounds in food. We now know, for example, that the pigment in blueberries may revive the brain's neural communication system, and the antioxidant found in grape skins may fight cancer and reduce heart disease. But what about other valuable compounds we don't know about that might change or disappear in GM varieties?

10   Consider GM soy. In July 1999, years after it was on the market, independent researchers published a study showing that it contains 12–14 percent less cancer-fighting phytoestrogens. What else has changed that we don't know about? [Monsanto responded with its own study, which concluded that soy's phytoestrogen levels vary too much to even carry out a statistical analysis. They failed to disclose, however, that the laboratory that conducted Monsanto's experiment had been instructed to use an obsolete method to detect phytoestrogens—one that had been replaced due to its highly variable results.]

11   In 1996, Monsanto published a paper in the *Journal of Nutrition* that concluded in the title, "The composition of glyphosate-tolerant soybean seeds is equivalent to that of conventional soybeans." The study only compared a small number of nutrients and

a close look at their charts revealed significant differences in the fat, ash, and carbohydrate content. In addition, GM soy meal contained 27 percent more trypsin inhibitor, a well-known soy allergen. The study also used questionable methods. Nutrient comparisons are routinely conducted on plants grown in identical conditions so that variables such as weather and soil can be ruled out. Otherwise, differences in plant composition could be easily missed. In Monsanto's study, soybeans were planted in widely varying climates and geography.

12   Although one of their trials *was* a side-by-side comparison between GM and non-GM soy, for some reason the results were left out of the paper altogether. Years later, a medical writer found the missing data in the archives of the *Journal of Nutrition* and made them public. No wonder the scientists left them out. The GM soy showed significantly lower levels of protein, a fatty acid, and phenylalanine, an essential amino acid. Also, toasted GM soy meal contained nearly twice the amount of a lectin that may block the body's ability to assimilate other nutrients. Furthermore, the toasted GM soy contained as much as seven times the amount of trypsin inhibitor, indicating that the allergen may survive cooking more in the GM variety. (This might explain the 50 percent jump in soy allergies in the UK, just after GM soy was introduced.)

13   We don't know all the changes that occur with genetic engineering, but certainly GM crops are not the same. Ask the animals. Eyewitness reports from all over North America describe how several types of animals, when given a choice, avoided eating GM food. These included cows, pigs, elk, deer, raccoons, squirrels, rats, and mice. In fact, the Dutch student mentioned above first determined that his mice had a two-to-one preference for non-GM before forcing half of them to eat only the engineered variety.

14   Differences in GM food will likely have a much larger impact on children. They are three to four times more susceptible to allergies. Also, they convert more of the food into body-building material. Altered nutrients or added toxins can result in developmental problems. For this reason, animal nutrition studies are typically conducted on young, developing animals. After the feeding trial, organs are weighed and often studied under magnification. If scientists used mature animals instead of young ones, even severe nutritional problems might not be detected. The Monsanto study used mature animals instead of young ones.

15   They also diluted their GM soy with non-GM protein 10- or 12-fold before feeding the animals. And they never weighed the organs or examined them under a microscope. The study, which is the only major animal feeding study on GM soy ever published, is dismissed by critics as rigged to avoid finding problems.

16   Unfortunately, there is a much bigger experiment going on—an uncontrolled one which we are all a part of. We're being fed GM foods daily, without knowing the impact of these foods on our health, our behavior, or our children. Thousands of schools around the world, particularly in Europe, have decided not to let their kids be used as guinea pigs. They have banned GM foods.

17   The impact of changes in the composition of GM foods is only one of several reasons why these foods may be dangerous. Other reasons may be far worse (see www.seedsofdeception.com). With the epidemic of obesity and diabetes and with the results in Appleton, parents and schools are waking up to the critical role that diet plays. When making changes in what kids eat, removing GM foods should be a priority.

James E.
McWilliams

The Green Monster: Could Frankenfoods Be Good for the Environment?

I'm sitting at my desk examining a $10.95 jar of South River Miso. The stuff is delicious, marked by a light, lemony tang. The packaging, by contrast, is a heavy-handed assurance of purity. The company is eager to tell me that the product I've purchased is certified organic, aged for three weeks in wood (sustainably harvested?), unpasteurized, made with "deep well water," hand-crafted, and—the designation that most piques my interest—*GMO free*.

2   GMO refers to "genetically modified organisms." A genetically modified crop results from the laboratory insertion of a gene from one organism into the DNA sequence of another in order to confer an advantageous trait such as insect resistance, drought tolerance, or herbicide resistance. Today almost 90 percent of soy crops and 80 percent of corn crops in the United States sprout from genetically engineered seeds. Forty-five million acres of land worldwide contain genetically engineered crops. From the perspective of commercial agriculture, the technology has been seamlessly assimilated into traditional farming routines.

3   From the perspective of my miso jar, however, it's evident that not all consumers share the enthusiasm. It's as likely as not that you know GMOs by their stock term of derision: *Frankenfoods*. The moniker reflects a broad spectrum of concerns: Some anti-biotech activists argue that these organisms will contaminate their wild cousins with GM pollen and drive native plants extinct. Others suggest that they will foster the growth of "superweeds"—plants that develop a resistance to the herbicides many GMOs are engineered to tolerate. And yet others fear that genetic alterations will trigger allergic reactions in unsuspecting consumers. Whether or not these concerns collectively warrant a ban on GMOs—as many (most?) environmentalists would like to see—is a hotly debated topic. The upshot to these potential pitfalls, however, is beyond dispute: A lot of people find this technology to be creepy.

4   Whatever the specific cause of discontent over GM crops, popular resistance came to a head in 2000, when the National Organic Program solicited public input on the issue of whether they should be included. In response, sustainable-food activists deluged officials with a rainforest's worth of letters—275,000, to be exact—beating the measure into oblivion. Today, in the same spirit, environmentalists instinctively deem GMOs the antithesis of environmental responsibility.

5   Many scientists, and even a few organic farmers, now believe the 2000 rejection was a fatal rush to judgment. Most recently, Pamela Ronald, a plant pathologist and chair of the Plant Genomics Program at the University of California-Davis, has declared herself one such critic. In *Tomorrow's Table: Organic Farming, Genetics, and the Future of Food*, she argues that we should, in fact, be actively merging genetic engineering and organic farming to achieve a sustainable future for food production. Her research—which she conducts alongside her husband, an organic farmer—explores genetically engineered crops that, instead of serving the rapacity of agribusiness, foster the fundamentals of sustainability. Their endeavor, counterintuitive as it seems, points to an emerging green biotech frontier—a hidden realm of opportunity to feed the world's impending 9 billion a diet produced in an environmentally responsible way.

6   To appreciate how "responsible genetic modification" isn't an oxymoron, consider grass-fed beef. Cows that eat grass are commonly touted as the sustainable alternative to feedlot beef, a resource-intensive form of production that stuffs cows with a steady diet of grain fortified with antibiotics, growth hormones, steroids, and appetite enhancers that eventually pass through the animals into the soil and water. One overlooked drawback to grass-fed beef, however, is the fact that grass-fed cows emit four times more methane—a greenhouse gas that's more than 20 times as powerful as carbon dioxide—as regular, feedlot cows. That's because grass contains lignin, a substance that triggers a cow's digestive system to secrete a methane-producing enzyme. An Australian biotech company called Gramina has recently produced a genetically modified grass with lower amounts of lignin. Lower amounts of lignin mean less methane, less methane means curbed global warming emissions, and curbed emissions means environmentalists can eat their beef without hanging up their green stripes.

7   Another area where sustainable agriculture and genetic modification could productively overlap involves nitrogen fertilizer. A plant's failure to absorb all the nutrients from the fertilizer leads to the harmful accumulation of nitrogen in the soil. From there it leaches into rivers and oceans to precipitate dead zones so choked with algae that other marine life collapses. In light of this problem, Syngenta and other biotech companies are in the process of genetically engineering crops such as potatoes, rice, and wheat to improve their nitrogen uptake efficiency in an effort to diminish the negative consequences of nitrogen fertilization. Early results suggest that rice farmers in Southeast Asia and potato farmers in Africa might one day have the option of planting crops that mitigate the harmful effects of this long-vilified source of agricultural pollution.

8   Animals, of course, are just as modifiable as plants. Livestock farmers have been genetically tinkering with their

beasts for centuries through the hit-or-miss process of selective breeding. They've done so to enhance their animals' health, increase their weight, and refine their fat content. Breeding animals to reduce environmental impact, however, hasn't been a viable option with the clunky techniques of conventional breeding. But such is not the case with genetic engineering.

9   Case in point: Canadian scientists have recently pioneered the "enviropig," a genetically modified porker altered to diminish the notoriously high phosphorous level of pig manure by 60 percent. Like nitrogen, phosphorous runoff is a serious pollutant with widespread downstream consequences. But with the relatively basic insertion of a gene (from E. coli bacteria) that produces a digestive enzyme called phytase, scientists have provided farmers with yet another tool for lessening their heavy impact on the environment.

10   When commercial farmers hear about GM grass, increased nitrogen uptake, and cleaner pigs, they're excited. And when they hear about other products in the works—genetically modified sugar beets that require less water and have higher yields than cane sugar; a dust made from genetically modified ferns to remove heavy metals from the soil; genetically modified and *edible* cotton seeds that require minimal pesticide use—they're also excited. And they're excited not only because these products have the potential to streamline production, but also because GM technology allows them to play a meaningful role in reducing their carbon footprint.

11   However, with the exception of the modified sugar beets, the GMOs mentioned in this article are not currently on the market. The cutting-room floors of research laboratories all over the world, in fact, are littered with successful examples of genetically engineered products that have enormous potential to further the goals of sustainable agriculture. Demand for these products remains high among farmers—it almost always does—but food producers fear the bad publicity that might come from anti-GMO invective.

12   Given the potential of these products to reduce the environmental impact of farming, it's ironic that traditional advocates for sustainable agriculture have led a successful campaign to blacklist GMOs irrespective of their applications. At the very least, they might treat them as legitimate ethical and scientific matters deserving of a fair public hearing. Such a hearing, I would venture, would not only please farmers who were truly concerned about sustainability, but it would provide the rest of us—those of us who do not grow food for the world but only think about it—a more accurate source of scientific information than the back of a miso jar.

How effective is the illustration in conveying a point of view on the genetic modification of livestock? Why?

Ben Burkett

Green Revolution a Failure in Africa

The global food crisis and how to stop hunger from escalating in the midst of the current economic crisis will be the subject of a recent G8 meeting of Agricultural ministers in Treviso, Italy. For now, the G8 and the United States continue to advocate the same disastrous policies that got us into the current mess where 1 billion people lack access to adequate food. U.S. agriculture secretary Tom Vilsack has said that biotechnology is necessary to address hunger while the U.S. Senate Foreign Relations Committee recently approved without much public debate the "Global Hunger Security Act" sponsored by Senators Bob Casey and Richard Lugar, that for the first time would mandate the U.S. to fund genetic engineering projects in foreign agriculture research. Meanwhile, the Gates Foundation has billions invested in the "Alliance for a Green Revolution in Africa."

2   As an African American farmer from Mississippi who has visited and traveled to Africa many times, I am stunned that the

real solutions continue to be ignored. We face multiple crises—financial, climate, energy, and water. Business as usual will not solve our global hunger crisis. More expensive genetically modified seeds, pesticides, and chemical-intensive practices won't help the hungry and will only allow more profits and control for seed companies like Monsanto and Syngenta.

3   While the G8 calls for more "free trade" in agriculture and more biotechnology, groundbreaking scientific reports and actions at the United Nations are actively calling for a different vision of agriculture. This would be based on agroecological methods that respect our planet's resources and provide a decent living for family farmers. In 2008, the International Assessment of Agricultural Knowledge, Science and Technology for Development (IAASTD), backed by United Nations agencies, the World Bank, and over 400 contributing scientists from 80 countries found that the most promising solutions to the world's food crisis include investing in agroecological research, extension, and farming. The Congress and Obama Administration need to take a serious look at the IAASTD report before funneling scarce resources into another Green Revolution in Africa.

4   Past public-private partnerships in Africa have proven to be failures, such as the 14-year project between Monsanto, USAID, and the Kenyan Agricultural Research Institute to engineer a virus-resistant sweet potato. The GM sweet potato failed to show any resistance to the virus while local varieties actually outperformed the GM variety in field trials. The U.S. approach to helping Africa should not be a top-down process that excludes the voices of African farmers who have the knowledge of their land and what food to grow.

5   The UN is helping to move the discussion towards "food sovereignty" by appointing a Special Rapporteur on the "Right to Food," and convening a Panel on the Right to Food. I was privileged to hear General Coordinator of La Via Campesina Henry Saragih of Indonesia and Professor Olivier De Schutter before the United Nations General Assembly. De Schutter said, "the right to food is not simply about more production, but about distribution and access. While high food prices are bad for consumers, so too are depressed prices for farmers who can't make a living. De Schutter pointed out that 60% of hungry people in the world are small farmers, pastoralists, fisherfolk, and others who make a living off the land. An additional 20% are landless agriculture workers."

6   A "right to food" framework therefore goes deeper than simply the misguided obsession with yields and productivity, and more fundamentally towards questions regarding democracy and access to resources, including land, water and credit. A recent re-

port by Union of Concerned Scientists titled "Failure to Yield: Evaluating the Performance of Genetically Engineered Crops," showed that despite 20 years of research and 13 years of commercialization, genetic engineering has failed to significantly increase U.S. crop yields while only driving up costs for farmers. In comparison, traditional breeding continues to deliver better results. The scientific research and renewed focus on the "right to food" exposes why we must move away from Green Revolution monoculture practices and instead embrace ecologically sound practices, more equitable trade rules and local food distribution systems to empower family farmers. Now the governments of the world and the Gates Foundation need to finally get the message as well.

GREGORY **JAFFE**

Lessen the Fear of Genetically Engineered Crops

Protesters carrying signs stating "Biocide is Homicide" and shouting concerns about the risks of eating genetically engineered foods recently demonstrated outside the biotechnology industry's annual convention. Inside the convention center, industry extolled the safety of genetically engineered foods and the benefits of future crops like "golden rice."

Neither corporate hyperbole nor radical slogans do much to inform the public. What is needed is the shaping of sensible measures to ensure that genetically engineered foods are safe. The first few first engineered crops are already providing remarkable benefits. Cotton modified to kill insects has greatly diminished farmers' use of toxic insecticides, thereby reducing costs, increasing yields, and, presumably, reducing harm to nontarget species. Likewise, biotech soybeans facilitate no-till farming, which reduces soil erosion and water pollution.

Despite such benefits, agricultural biotechnology is under siege for reasons good and bad. Activists have burned fields and bombed labs. Farmers will not plant genetically engineered sweet corn, sugar beets, and apples, for fear of consumer rejection. And countries in Europe and Asia refuse to import U.S.-grown genetically engineered crops. Some countries now require labeling of foods containing engineered ingredients. Those requirements have spurred food processors, who want to avoid negative-sounding labels, to eliminate bioengineered ingredients.

Buffeted by the polarized debate, many Americans oppose biotech foods, in part because farmers and seed companies get the benefits while consumers bear the risk. If anti-genetically engineered sentiment increases, U.S. farmers may be forced to forgo the advantages of engineered crops. And most public and private investment in agricultural biotechnology would dry up.

5   To reap the benefits of agricultural biotechnology, minimize the risks, and boost public confidence, the U.S. must upgrade its flawed regulatory system. Currently, the Food and Drug Administration (FDA) does not formally approve any genetically engineered crops as safe to eat. Instead, it reviews safety data provided voluntarily by seed companies. That consultation process, which the FDA admits is "not a comprehensive scientific review of the data," culminates with the FDA stating only that it has "no further questions . . . at this time." Although no health problems with genetically engineered crops have been detected, that industry-driven process is weak insurance. The recent FDA proposal requiring a formal notification before marketing a biotech food is an improvement.

6   All biotech foods should go through a mandatory approval process with specific testing and data requirements. The National Academy of Sciences should be commissioned to recommend a precise method of assessment.

7   Genetically engineered crops also raise environmental concerns. They could lead to pesticide-resistant insects and weeds and might contaminate plants that are close relatives of the crops. To safeguard our ecosystem, the current laws need fixing. Congress should close regulatory gaps to ensure that all future applications of biotechnology, ranging from fast-growing fish to corn plants that produce industrial chemicals, receive thorough environmental reviews. Also, the Environmental Protection Agency must enforce restrictions it has imposed on bioengineered crops to help prevent emergence of insecticide-resistant pests.

8   Although strong regulations would minimize environmental and safety risks, nothing would boost public confidence more than engineered products that benefit consumers. No beneficial products currently exist.

9   Worldwide acceptance of biotechnology will occur only when other countries reap benefits from this technology. Instead of spending millions of dollars on feel-good advertising campaigns, the biotech industry should train developing-country scientists and fund research in those countries. Companies—and universities—should donate patented crops and processes to developing countries. Agricultural biotechnology is not a panacea for all agricultural problems here or abroad, nor is it free from risk. But, with adequate safeguards, it could provide tremendous benefits for an ever-populous, pesticide-drenched, and water-deficient globe.

FROM READING TO WRITING

1. In this section, you read Bill Joy's written argument for caution in the development of new nanotechnologies, followed by Merkle's reaction to Joy's piece, which takes place in the form of an interview. Conduct a rhetorical analysis of these two forms of argumentation: What are some of the rhetorical differences between arguing through a written essay versus speaking out via a moderated verbal dialogue? Consider questions of audience, the process of argument construction, ethos, rhetorical impact, and so on.

2. In his essay, Bill Gates writes glowingly of the potential for robots to benefit human society. Yet, as you have also seen (in the arguments put forth by Joy and Marks), robots are not without their critics. Exactly what is a robot, anyway? What differentiates robots from other machines? Write an essay that shows your attitude toward robots by defining them in a particular way. (For advice on writing definitions, see Chapter 8.)

3. One of the major methods for convincing people of the need for organ donor compensation or stem cell research is the use of personal examples—narratives—about people who might benefit. Beginning from your own informed beliefs, write a story that illustrates your position on a particular scientific issue—stem cell, organ donation, genetically modified foods, or some other controversial process or technology. If possible, draw from your personal experience with the subject at hand. (For advice on narrative arguments, see Chapter 11.)

4. Conduct a rhetorical analysis of the arguments of Ron Reagan. How is his speech a product of the particular rhetorical situation that he found himself in: in front of the Democratic National Convention, a few weeks after the death of his Republican father, and before a national television audience? How might he have presented his argument if he had appeared before Republicans, or if his speech had not been televised? Do you agree with Reagan's assertion that his speech is not political? (See Chapter 5 for advice on rhetorical analysis.)

5. Evaluate—on the basis of practicality, ethics, or esthetics (or all of them)—one of the scientific processes or technologies discussed in this chapter. (See Chapter 10 for information on how evaluation arguments work.)

6. Based on the guidelines in Chapter 13, write a proposal argument that defends or undermines the practice of genetic modification of food crops *from a human rights perspective*. Is genetic engineering the solution to world hunger (or at least a part of that solution)? Or will it only exacerbate the existing polarization between the "haves" and the "have-nots?" Conduct your own research prior to constructing your argument.

26 | Privacy

New Challenges to Personal Privacy

How does a new bathroom design, like this colored glass structure in the middle of an apartment, reflect (or push for) new attitudes about privacy?

The Dog Poop Girl (as she came to be known) was riding the subway in Seoul, South Korea, one day when her dog decided to "take care of business." According to a *Washington Post* story written by Jonathan Krim on July 7, 2005, the woman (a university student) made no move to clean up the mess, so fellow passengers grew agitated. One of them recorded the scene on a cell phone camera and then posted photos on a Web site. Web surfers came upon the photos and began referring to her as Dog Poop Girl. One thing led to another, and soon her privacy was completely gone: people revealed her true name, began asking for and sharing more information about her, launched blogs commenting about her and her relatives, and generally crackled with gossip about her and her behavior. Ultimately she became the subject of sermons and online discussions, and her story made the national news. In humiliation, Dog Poop Girl withdrew from her university.

According to an American Civil Liberties Union (ACLU) Web posting in May 2010, the Department of Justice was seeking to obtain the contents of a Yahoo! e-mail account without the e-mailer's permission and without a search warrant. Government investigators in the process of building a criminal case were maintaining that because the Yahoo! e-mail had been accessed by the user, it no longer qualified as "in electronic storage" (protected as private property under the Stored Communications Act). But Yahoo! asked a federal court judge to block the government attempt, and the company was supported by the ACLU, the Electronic Frontier Foundation (EFF), Google, and many other public interest organizations. "The government is trying to evade federal privacy law and the Constitution," said EFF Senior Staff Attorney Kevin Bankston. "The Fourth Amendment protects these stored e-mails, just like it does our private papers. We all have a reasonable expectation of privacy in the contents of our e-mail accounts, and the government should have to make a show-

> "You have zero privacy now—get over it."
>
> —Scott McNealy, CEO of Sun Microsystems

ing of probable cause to a judge before it rifles through our private communications."

A third incident was reported by Felisa Cardona in the *Denver Post* on August 2, 2005. A computer security breach at the University of Colorado left 29,000 students and 7,000 faculty and staff vulnerable to identity theft. It seems that hackers attacked the university computers in order to gain access to the Buff One ID card used by many students and staff. Though no information seems to have been used as a result of this attack, 6,000 students had to be issued new cards in order to gain access to their dorms. Moreover, after the incident, Colorado officials decided to stop using Social Security number identifications, and many other universities have done the same because they too have been targeted by identity thieves.

These three incidents illustrate some of the new challenges to personal privacy that have been raised in response to technology developments and concerns about secu-

A biometric measuring instrument at Busch Gardens helps staff make sure the same person uses the same ticket each day.

rity that are one legacy of the September 11, 2001, attacks. There is no doubt that electronic technologies have given people a new degree of personal freedom: hand-held computers, cell phones, e-mail, and Web shopping are now routine time-savers. But there is also no doubt that a price has been paid for that freedom: That price is the surveillance side of the Internet and other technologies. In the wake of September 11, other terrorist attacks, and the increased attention to security that has ensued, privacy issues have been an increasing concern in American life. Law enforcement officials seek access to information about potential conspiracies, parents are placing devices on their children in order to keep tabs on their whereabouts, and businesses increasingly gather information about people to individualize marketing campaigns, keep an eye out for good (and bad) credit risks, and customize customers. (Businesses and police also increasingly spy on their own employees.)

One emerging technology—biometrics—measures physical and behavioral data, such as fingerprints or keystroke patterns, in order to identify individual human beings. Biometric recognition provides a deeply personalized means of identification that enhances security, say its supporters, but a national biometric database also raises questions of privacy, say its detractors. What would it mean in terms of national security and surveillance to store citizens' inherently unique characteristics in a nationwide database?

And when is freedom too much freedom? If bloggers act as a posse, tracking down criminals and turning them over to law enforcement, is that appropriate action or vigilante action? What about efforts to replicate what was done to the Dog Poop Girl? Should laws prevent people from publicizing and branding people who seem undesirable? Is too much sharing going on via Facebook? Should people who wish to share secrets—whether the secrets are true or not—have the anonymity and apparent protection afforded by the Internet? Must e-mail users simply accept as a fact of life that they are bombarded by hundreds of unauthorized, unsolicited spam messages? And what are the limits of what government officials should be able to do to inspect the personal records of citizens?

Contemporary Arguments

Is it possible, in other words, to have both security and freedom in the United States? What is the proper balance of the two?

On the one hand, some people support a national ID card (like those already used, incidentally, in several European nations) or sign up for in-vehicle security systems such as OnStar (always on the watch!) as a safety feature. They root for police to pursue potential terrorists, they use E-ZPass without giving a thought to the fact that they are giving out their whereabouts, they approve when cameras are mounted to watch over high-crime areas, they wink when Internet service providers disclose customer records to government agents if they feel that a crime is being committed, and they appreci-ate being notified that convicted felons have moved into the neighbor-hood. On the other hand, they also protest when police use wiretaps without explicit legal permission, worry about the ability of global positioning systems to snoop on people from satellites (especially by zeroing in on cell phones or implanted homing devices), and protest when roving surveillance cameras are mounted in stores and at street corners, in public parks and on school playgrounds.

Everyone these days seems to be monitored or monitoring. Online data collectors record which Web sites people visit; airlines record data on people's travels; companies routinely perform background checks on potential employees; bus and train companies check passenger lists against records of "suspicious" characters;

While surveillance cameras may be designed to provide security, the devices may also intrude on individuals' privacy, even without their knowledge.

businesses seek to develop systems that can deliver customized marketing informa-tion to particular households and commuters; and supermarkets record purchases in order to fine-tune their stocking patterns. In the future, some say, we can look forward to smart cars, smart airports, smart TVs, smart credit cards, and smart homes—all designed to give us certain freedoms, if at the price of losing some of our privacy.

The arguments in this chapter discuss all these questions related to privacy. Adam Penenberg's "The Surveillance Society" overviews the brave new world that is now developing (for better or for worse), and the selections that follow argue about aspects of technology that undermine our privacy. Robert Cringely sounds an alert about Facebook. Jonathan Locker worries about OnStar. Dahlia Lithwick questions the ethics of sexting. Jay Stanley (speaking for the American Civil Liber-ties Union) contends than body searches of airline passengers are neither effective nor constitutional. And Adam Cohen makes a plea for citizens to be able to walk down the street without being monitored by cameras—to be able to enjoy what he calls "locational privacy." These are just a small sample of the issues that are fac-ing Americans as it becomes easier and easier for us to watch each other.

Because the emerging field of biometrics effectively illustrates the tensions between protection and privacy, we look in detail at this emerging technology in the Issue in Focus. The selections reproduced there describe the technologies (such as signature analysis, keystroke patterns, and vein biometric systems) and dramatize the excitement—and the fears—that accompany them. On one hand, biometric technologies hold out the promise of improved crime fighting and na-tional security. On the other, such technologies inevitably encroach on individu-als' privacy and may even open the door to DNA identify theft. What price are we willing to pay for privacy (or security)? At what point does it make sense to forfeit private information for protection and convenience?

ADAM PENENBERG

The Surveillance Society

Adam L. Penenberg's Web site indicates that he is assistant director of the Business and Economic Program at New York University. He is the author of several books, including *Spooked: Espionage in Corporate America* and *Viral Loop: From Facebook to Twitter, How Today's Smartest Businesses Grow Themselves*. Formerly senior editor at *Forbes*, Penenberg is now a contributing writer to *Fast Company* and has also written for *Inc.*, the *New York Times*, *Slate*, *Playboy*, *Mother Jones*, and *Wired*, in which the following article appeared in December 2001, shortly after 9-11.

Within hours of the attacks on the World Trade Center and the Pentagon, as federal officials shut down airports and U.S. strategists began plotting a military response, Attorney General John Ashcroft was mobilizing his own forces. In meetings with top aides at the FBI's Strategic Information and Operations Center—during which the

Surveillance cameras have become a part of the urban landscape.

White House as well as the State and Defense departments dialed in via secure video-conference—Ashcroft pulled together a host of antiterrorism measures. Days later, the attorney general sent to Capitol Hill a bill (the Patriot Act) that would make it easier for the government to tap cell phones and pagers, give the Feds broad authority to monitor email and Web browsing, strengthen money-laundering laws, and weaken immigrants' rights. There were whispers of a national identity card and of using face-recognition software and retinal scans at airports and in other public spaces. And high above it all would sit an Office of Homeland Security, run by former Pennsylvania Governor Tom Ridge, who would report directly to the Oval Office.

2   Such talk usually generates fractious debate between privacy hawks and security hounds. By now, most of us can recite the familiar *Nightline* arguments and counterarguments. But this time the acrimony has been muted. The terrorist assault on America shifted the balance between privacy and security. What was considered Orwellian one week seemed perfectly reasonable—even necessary—the next. Politicians who routinely clash were marching in lockstep. "When you're in this type of conflict—when you're at war—civil liberties are treated differently," said Senate Republican Trent Lott. "This event will change the balance between freedom and security," echoed House Democrat Richard Gephardt. "There's a whole range of issues that we're going to be grappling with in the next month that takes us to this basic trade-off."

3   Almost immediately, there were unmistakable signs that new surveillance tools would be a linchpin in the war on terrorism. The FBI met with AOL, EarthLink, and other large ISPs, and there was renewed talk of using DCS 1000 to let the FBI monitor email traffic. Visionics—a maker of face-recognition software used in surveillance cameras in London and Tampa, Florida, and in the databases of close to a dozen state law enforcement agencies—reported that its switchboards were jammed. The stock prices of some companies in the security business spiked as the rest of the market crumbled.

4   But truth be told, the U.S. was embracing the Surveillance Society well before September 11. In the name of safety, we have grown increasingly comfortable with cameras monitoring us whenever we stop to buy a Slurpee, grab cash from an ATM, or park in a downtown lot. And in the name of convenience, we've happily accepted a range of products and services, from cell phones to credit cards to Web browsers, that make our lives easier and have the secondary effect of permitting us to be tracked. They're not spy technologies—but they might as well be.

5   Americans don't seem to be spooked by these incursions. "Apparently, consumers don't feel their privacy is threatened," says Barbara Bellissimo, owner of a now-defunct dotcom that offered anonymous Web browsing. "That's why there are no profitable privacy companies." (It might also be why millions of Americans watch reality-based television shows like *Survivor* that package round-the-clock surveillance as entertainment.)

6   Just how vast is the new surveillance world? Let's start with cameras. More than 60 communities in a dozen states have set up traffic-light cameras that ticket drivers for running red lights or speeding. Casinos in Las Vegas zoom in on the cards we hold at the blackjack table. Cameras are mounted on police cars, they hang from trees in public parks, they're affixed to the walls in sports stadiums and shopping malls. David Brin, author of *The Transparent Society,* postulates a "Moore's law of cameras." He sees them roughly "halving in size, and doubling in acuity and movement capability and sheer numbers, every year or two."

7   The surveillance net also has a digital arm. With computers home to the data entrails of half a billion bank accounts, just as many credit card accounts, and hundreds of millions of medical claims, mortgages, and retirement funds, there exists a significant cache of online data about each of us.

8   Then there's the matter of monitoring our daily travels. Debit cards like New York's E-ZPass deduct a fee as commuters zip through tollbooths *and* track our comings and goings on the road; transit cards chart riders' subway journeys; employee ID cards can show when we arrived at work, when we left, and where we went within the office complex. Phone cards mark who we call and, often, from where. Credit card records etch us in time and space more reliably than any eyewitness. So do airline tickets—even if you pay cash. And as for the cell phone: "If you turn it on, you can be tracked," says Jim Atkinson, a countersurveillance expert who is president of Granite Island Group in Gloucester, Massachusetts.

9   OnStar, GM's onboard communications system, offers a GPS service to its 1.5 million customers. That means that at any given moment, OnStar can locate each of those 1.5 million cars. (OnStar will track a car only at the request of the driver or, in some instances, the police; the company keeps no historical database of car locations, though if it had the inclination—or was pressured—to gather and store reams of data, it could.) Mercedes' TeleAid and Ford's Wingcast provide similar services. As does

AirIQ, which Hertz, Avis, and Budget use for their premium fleets: If a car is abandoned, AirIQ can locate it; if it's stolen, the company can disable its motor.

10   For now, the information about each of us resides in dozens of separate databases owned by the credit card companies and the phone carriers, the rental car agencies and police departments, the ISPs and the IRS. But the aftermath of September 11 could change all that by creating in many of us an appetite for information and a willingness to be monitored. And this raises a disquieting possibility: Will the disparate elements of our surveillance society be assembled into a surveillance web? Will the private companies and the government agencies come together to create a superdatabase accessible to . . . who? Will it strip us not just of personal privacy—we seem resigned, even OK, with that—but of public anonymity?

11   Worrying is a waste of time. Surveillance is here. It was inevitable. But the surveillance state is not.

12   A few days after September 11, Akram Jaber was driving his Chevy Suburban over the pothole-strewn streets of Chicago's south side. With his 15-month-old son in the backseat, he was heading to the liquor store he owns to lock up for the night. A battered Chevy Caprice sped by, then stopped in front of him at a red light. Two men emerged; one pointed a gun at Jaber. "Take it easy," Jaber called out. "I have my son in the car." He left the keys in the ignition, unhitched his son, and turned over the $50,000 vehicle.

13   As the carjackers sped away, Jaber whipped out his cell phone to dial 911. Then he called an operator at OnStar. (He had been paying $16.95 a month for the basic Safety & Security plan: roadside and emergency assistance, remote lock and unlock, and stolen vehicle tracking.) He gave his name, license plate number, and four-digit PIN. The operator called Jaber's vehicle and requested GPS data, then updated the car's position by pinging it every minute. The operator relayed the car's heading to the police officer on the scene, who forwarded it to a dispatcher. Within minutes, officers swooped in on the vehicle and arrested the men. "The police were amazed at how easy it was," say Jaber, who himself was awfully pleased.

14   What's really amazing is just how many similar tools are becoming available to law enforcement. A suspect's alibi can be checked out by looking at the location data trail created by use of his tollbooth pass, transit card, or credit card. Surveillance cameras capture images that authorities can cross-check against a database of criminals through the use of face-recognition software. And cell phones have become the digital equivalent of Hansel and Gretel's bread crumbs.

15   When a cell phone is turned on, it broadcasts an identification number to the closest antennas, which allow the carrier to chart its customers. It's a simple matter—known as triangulation—to track the signal as it arrives at different towers, then calculate the location of the phone based on time differences. The police have taken full advantage of this tracking trick, though—technically, at least—they need a court order to access the information. Earlier this year, Timothy Crosby, 40, was busted for raping and robbing a Brooklyn woman after the police located him by homing in on his cell phone signal. In November 2000, authorities pursued Kofi Apea Orleans-Lindsay for allegedly killing a Maryland state trooper during a buy-and-bust operation. Police used cell data to track Orleans-Lindsay to Brooklyn, where they arrested him.

16   Then there was the case of Christopher Stewart, a New York subway employee whose alibi in the March slaying of his ex-girlfriend crumbled when police subjected his

MetroCard transit pass to detailed analysis (MetroCard use can be traced by a serial number). Stewart had claimed he was boarding a Staten Island ferry at the time she was killed. But data from the MetroCard, still in his possession, had him exiting a subway station near the crime scene just before the murder. He was arrested and indicted by a grand jury. MetroCard records were also used against Marco Valencia, who was charged in the December 1999 assault and robbery of a supermarket manager in Manhattan. Valencia claimed he was in Staten Island, but his MetroCard told a different tale, and when confronted, he pleaded guilty.

17   In light of the way cell phones and transit cards are being used to track criminals, video cameras seem remarkably, well, obvious. But they're a cornerstone of the surveillance society, and they've proved an important weapon in law enforcement's arsenal. Prior to September 11, such cameras stirred up controversy. When the Tampa Police Department installed face-recognition software in its network last June, the public was outraged, and House majority leader Dick Armey joined with civil rights groups to protest. There was similar push-back in Britain in 1996, when authorities installed 300 cameras in the East London neighborhood of Newham in an effort to gather intelligence on suspected IRA bombings. The cameras didn't help much in the fight on terrorism, but overall crime rates fell 30 percent after they were deployed, according to city figures. Crime dropped an additional 34 percent in 1998, after the cameras were equipped with Visionic's face-recognition software. Last year, illegal activities in surrounding areas increased between 10 and 20 percent, but Newham's inched up less than half a percent. The program has been so successful that Visionics has been retained to hook up closed-circuit TV cameras in five more nearby London neighborhoods.

18   Although face-recognition surveillance systems are not foolproof, most Brits now view "spy" cameras as a part of everyday life, and polls indicate a majority of citizens support their use. England already boasts about 1.5 million police surveillance cameras—more than any other country—and the government plans to double that number within three years. With so many cams, the average city denizen can expect to be taped every five minutes, according to *The Times* of London.

19   Even as new surveillance technologies increase the amount of information available about each of us, there's something reassuring in the fact that this data is extremely far-flung. It would, today, take a considerable amount of sleuthing and multiple search warrants for anyone—individuals, private companies, public agencies—to aggregate the fruits of the surveillance web in any useful way.

20   But there are signs that in the future it might be much easier to access disparate data about individuals—where they've been, what they bought, who they were with, what they were wearing, who they called, what Web sites they visited, what they wrote in email. After all, the information exists, and from a technical perspective, it's easy to tap (cell phones, credit cards, ATMs, tollbooth passes—all are part of the same bitstream of 0s and 1s). The legal protections that might have prevented access to this data are eroding. And as the line between the public and private sectors blurs, the data will likely flow in ways it never has before.

21   So what do we get? Think of all these factoids residing not in some static database but in a dynamic environment in which strands of information can be pulled together from a huge variety of sources based on a user's request. It's not Microsoft Outlook, it's Google. In fact, researchers at Applied Systems Intelligence in Roswell,

Georgia, are working on just such software. Called Karnac (Knowledge Aided Retrieval in Activity Context), the program would scan everything from gun registrations and credit card records to newspapers and Web sites. While Karnac or a similar program may be a long way off, more modest developments provide a glimpse into where we could be headed. In the weeks following the attacks, airport authorities hatched plans for security systems that would link biometric techniques like iris scans with a government database of known or suspected terrorists. Such systems could easily migrate to other public spaces, motivated by a concern for community safety and a desire to catch criminals.

22   Eventually, surveillance cameras in every mom-and-pop store could use face-recognition software and network databases to link you to your Social Security number, consumer profile, credit report, home and work addresses, and criminal and driving records. Networked street cams could track your location—and keep the digital footage on file.

23   The gated communities of tomorrow will be monitored by cameras, motion detectors, and sensors of all kinds embedded in the walls, floors—every surface. Such systems, hyped as smart-house technologies, are already in beta at universities and corporate labs across the country. Tools such as Bluetooth and 802.11 will turn every object and street corner into a node of the wireless Web, aware of and communicating with the Net-connected PDA and cell of every passerby. Like transit cards and toll-booth passes, the wireless Web isn't a surveillance technology per se, but it will have that effect.

24   Look out a few more years and nano-cameras as small as grains of sand will create a world in which the wind has eyes. Fingerprint-scanning doorknobs and steering wheels could know their users by touch.

25   There will be limits, of course—legal mechanisms like search warrants that protect individuals from undue surveillance. But those safeguards will change with the times. In an effort to bring wiretapping laws into the cellular age, Attorney General Ashcroft proposed—and Congress approved—"roving wiretaps" to give the government authority to monitor a suspect's calls from any phone and any jurisdiction. As communications technologies continue to multiply and blur, it will be increasingly difficult to say where the telephone network ends and the Web begins. Cell phones send messages to pagers. Cars log on to the Internet. The search warrants of the surveillance era will need to span multiple technologies and will likely be written with increasingly broad language.

26   If all this raises the specter of Big Brother, well, that's understandable. But it's also wrong. Even as we trade privacy for security and convenience, we're hardly headed toward totalitarianism. Orwell's greatest error, says Peter Huber, author of *Orwell's Revenge,* was his view that the government had a monopoly on surveillance technologies. Says Huber: "If the Thought Police use telescreens, so can others—that's just the way telescreens work, if they work at all."

27   Indeed, citizens have already learned to use surveillance tools to keep government accountable. When motorist Rodney King was beaten by Los Angeles police officers in 1991, a bystander caught the incident on video. Though the subsequent trial ended in acquittal of the officers, it proved the potency of videotape as evidence.

"Video cameras create a potential counterbalance—a kind of ombudsman," says Sam Gregory, a program coordinator for Witness, a New York nonprofit that lends video equipment to human rights activists around the world. "They let citizens protect themselves and hold the state accountable." Recent projects sponsored by Witness include *Operation Fine Girl,* which documents rape as a weapon of war in Sierra Leone, and *Behind the Labels,* an exposé of the clothing-industry sweatshops in Saipan.

28   In Orange County, California, the sheriff's department mounted video cameras on its patrol cars with the idea that footage of arrests could be used to protect against false accusations of excessive force. Not surprisingly, those tapes have been used against the police officers themselves. In June, Robert Delgiudice, who was beaten by police for resisting arrest, had his case dismissed when the video showed that the officer had lied in his police report and preliminary hearing testimony. (Delgiudice is now planning a civil suit.) As Don Landis Jr., the Orange County deputy public defender who argued Delgiudice's case, puts it: "The cameras bring accountability."

29   They also bring transparency, which is almost always a good thing. An antidote to corruption, it keeps financial markets strong, governments honest, and corporations accountable. In public institutions and on city streets, the more transparency the better. Sometimes the reverse is true: The darkness of privacy is essential to the conversations between doctor and patient, to the personal information sent by letter, and to the things we do and say within our bedrooms. In those cases, privacy must be staunchly defended.

30   "Just about the only Fourth Amendment concern that the Supreme Court protects, year after year, decision after decision, is a U.S. citizen's privacy in his own home," says Landis. Earlier this year, the court upheld this principle again, deciding that the police in Florence, Oregon, had violated the Fourth Amendment when, without a warrant, they used thermal imaging technology to detect the heat lamps inside the house of a man they suspected of growing marijuana. Any technology that enables law enforcement to see or hear through walls, the court decreed, required a search warrant; without a warrant, the practice amounted to an unreasonable search.

31   The Constitution itself, therefore, stands in the way of Big Brother. OK, privacy is eroding. But liberty, and the safeguards inherent in due process, remain strong. The government can collect megabytes of information about us, but where and when they do and how that information is used is still subject to the laws designed to keep the state from abusing its power. And of course, even as Congress and the judicial system struggle to maintain the balance of privacy and security, citizens will continue to take technology into their own hands.

32   "Look at all the cameras and cell phones, a gazillion of them, that documented everything on September 11," says David Brin. "The powers of vision and information are expanding exponentially in the hands of the people, far faster than they are being acquired by government." In the long run, Brin predicts, it will be people—empowered by the surveillance web—who thwart the thugs, the tyrants, and even the terrorists.

Mike Luckovich's Pulitzer Prize–winning political cartoons appear in the *Atlanta Journal-Constitution* and are frequently reprinted. This one appeared first on May 27, 2010, just after Facebook founder Mark Zuckerberg announced that he was taking steps, in response to criticism, to protect the privacy of Facebook participants.

By permission of Mike Luckovich and Creators Syndicate, Inc.

Robert X. Cringely

Facebook Puts Your Privacy on Parade

From 1987 to 1995 Robert X. Cringely wrote the "Notes from the Field" column in *InfoWorld*, a weekly computer trade newspaper. More recently, his writing has appeared in the *New York Times*, *Newsweek*, *Forbes*, *Upside*, *Success*, and *Worth*, among other publications. The argument printed here originally appeared on InfoWorld's Web site in January 2010. In May 2010, Facebook responded to its critics by altering its privacy controls (see the cartoon above), but the criticism has not stopped.

Once again Facebook is involved in a privacy imbroglio, and once again it's because boy-founder Mark Zuckerberg opened his yap and stuck his Keds-clad foot inside.

2   Last week at The Crunchies, the annual awards party thrown by TechCrunch doyenne Michael Arrington, Zuckerberg got on stage briefly and made the following statement (per Gawker):

When I got started in my dorm room at Harvard, the question a lot of people asked was "why would I want to put any information on the Internet at all? Why would I want to have a website?"

And then in the last 5 or 6 years, blogging has taken off in a huge way and all these different services that have people sharing all this information. People have really gotten comfortable not only sharing more information and different kinds, but more openly and with more people. That social norm is just something that's evolved over time.

We view it as our role in the system to constantly be innovating and be updating what our system is to reflect what the current social norms are.

So now, a lot of companies would be trapped by the conventions and their legacies of what they've built, [and so] doing a privacy change for 350 million users is not the type of thing that a lot of companies would do. But we viewed that as a really important thing, to always keep a beginner's mind and think: what would we do if we were starting the company now, and starting the site now, and we decided that these would be the social norms now and we just went for it.

3   Allow me to translate. By "innovating and updating" his system, Zuckerberg means the modifications to user privacy settings Facebook unveiled a few weeks ago that made Facebookers' information more easily accessible by Google et al. by default. And by "current social norms," Zuckerberg means "stuff we think we can get away with today that we couldn't get away with three or four years ago."

Facebook.com founder Mark Zuckerberg at the company's Palo Alto, California, headquarters.

4   Interestingly, after Facebook's default settings changed, Zuckerberg's personal profile went from being virtually inaccessible (unless you were the CEO's friend) to nearly wide open, allowing any Facebooker to view the 290 photos he'd posted. These included several of Zucky the Party Animal (the worst of which Gawker happily scooped up and republished). A couple of days later those photos were mysteriously inaccessible again.

5   So much for social norms.

6   After those changes, ten privacy groups banded together and filed a protest with the FTC about Facebook's sudden open-book privacy policy. In response, Facebook also made a few small tweaks to restore some (but not all) of its previous privacy settings.

7   Zuckerberg's comments last week just re-ignited the Facebook privacy debate, including the inevitable responses from knuckleheads like Arrington "that privacy is already really, really dead. . . . We don't really care about privacy anymore. And Facebook is just giving us exactly what we want." (There is, however, no truth to the rumor that Zuckerberg is planning to publish nude pix of himself on his profile as part of Facebook's new "bare it and share it" campaign.)

8   It's almost always the case that people who like to say "privacy is dead, get over it," (a) have a financial interest in buying and selling personal information, and (b) guard their own personal information zealously, even if they live otherwise very public lives. For example: I'm still waiting for Arrington to share his Social Security number with the world, like the Lifelock CEO he seems to like so much, or to post pix from his vacation at that nudist colony (I'm making that last bit up—I hope). Even if he did, that doesn't mean other people should.

9   People may not give a damn about some kinds of personal information, but they care a great deal about other information. The stuff they care about just varies from person to person. In fact, it's usually the most public of us that have the greatest need for privacy. Exotic dancers may take their clothes off in public (or on MySpace), but they don't usually use their real names or broadcast their home address. Their bodies may be public, but not their identities.

10   Likewise, just because women shared their bra colors on Facebook to raise awareness of breast cancer doesn't mean they want to share that information with the marketers at Victoria's Secrets. (Facebook is not explicitly doing this, but opening up people's status updates to searches makes that possible.)

11   I think people want the ability to easily control what information is and isn't private. While Facebook offers a lot of control—you

might even say a confusing amount for most people—it's still doing its best to encourage you to share early and often. If you can't easily determine how someone wants a particular piece of information to be treated, you should assume it is private, not that they want to share it with the world. The latter is the assumption Facebook is making and Zuckerberg was defending.

12   What people really want is not what Facebook is giving us. As Read Write Web's Marshall Fitzpatrick points out, Facebook's popularity stems in part from how carefully it protected its members' information—at first limiting access to college students, then just to your networks of friends. Now it seems to have forgotten all of that, to its detriment.

13   Why? In a word, money. You can't easily monetize data that's private. The more data you can share with the world, the more revenue you can generate. Facebook isn't trying to give users what they want or to conform with "social norms." It's trying to make a buck out of each and every one of its 350 million users, over and over again. Nothing wrong with that, except perhaps how you go about it.

Jonathan
Locker

OnStar: Big Brother's Eye in the Sky

Jonathan I. Locker contributed the following article to the Web site "The Truth About Cars," which presents automotive news, reviews, and editorials. The article appeared February 14, 2008.

Ever since the Model T hit the silver screen, evading the long arm of the law has been a cinematic theme. From the General Lee locomotive outrunning Boss Hogg, to Smokey being outwitted by Burt Reynolds' mustache, the public imagination has always associated fast cars with police pursuit. While the majority of motorists would never dream of trying to outrun the long arm of the law, soon, they won't have to. It'll be resting on their shoulder.

2   Consider OnStar.

3   OnStar is a telemetry system providing a central data bank with real-time data on virtually every system in your car, including GPS. OnStar's computer knows where you were, when you were there, and how fast you went. It knows if and when you applied the brakes, if and when the air bags deployed, and what speed you were going at the time. It knows if and when your car was

serviced. OnStar operators can determine if you have a passenger in the front seat (airbag detection). All interactions with OnStar's operators are automatically recorded (hence the commercials). By the same token, under certain conditions, OnStar can switch on your GM car's microphone remotely and record any and all sounds within the vehicle (i.e., conversations).

4   But wait, there's more. As of 2009, customers who upgrade to OnStar's "Safe & Sound" plan automatically receive the "Stolen Vehicle Slowdown" service. (Yes, it's an "opt out" deal.) If the OnStar-equipped vehicle is reported stolen and law enforcement has "established a clear line of sight of the stolen vehicle," the police may ask OnStar to slow it down remotely.

5   Many customers find OnStar immensely reassuring; it's their guardian e-angel. No question: OnStar has saved lives and provided its customers with valuable services. Otherwise, they wouldn't be in business.

6   But what if the police are investigating a crime. They ask OnStar where your car was on a certain date and time, to corroborate an alibi. Or what if you're in a crash and the other guy's attorney would like to know how fast you were driving when you ran the red light? Would OnStar surrender the information? GM notes that "OnStar is required to locate the car to comply with legal requirements, including valid court orders showing probable cause in criminal investigations." And OnStar may use gathered information to "protect the rights, property, or safety of you or others."

7   Imagine the following scenario. The FBI shows up at OnStar master command and tells them your car's been stolen by a terrorist, who may be using it to commit a crime at this very moment. Contacting the owner is out of the question; the owner may also be a terrorist. What does OnStar do? They cooperate with the FBI and give them everything they've got on your car. No warrant needed and no notification to you. Hell, you may not even have the service enabled. In other words, you not only have to trust OnStar to protect your privacy, you have to trust the police not to ask the questions in the first place.

8   The Constitution of the United States protects us from the heavy hand of government. However, when it comes to protection from private entities, it does little. Into this void, multiple privacy laws have entered, creating a farrago of local, state, and federal laws which provide limited and haphazard protection to citizens. Whatever privacy protection these laws provide are usually nullified when companies violate them in "good faith" (e.g., while assisting the authorities).

9   So who is going to stop the government from monitoring your car? The Bill of Rights protects you from an unreasonable search and seizure; the government cannot take what belongs to you without a warrant. OnStar can owns the information they collect about your car. In short, there is nothing to stop the police or OnStar from using the information you paid for against you.

10   And the next step is even more insidious. Imagine GPS speed limiters which only allow you to go the speed limit based upon a map uploaded into your car's navigation system. Now Sammy Hagar will only be driving 55 no matter how hard he stomps on the go pedal. This is the ultimate assault on pistonheads. The only place where driving will be fun will be on the track—if OnStar and/or the car's manufacturer (e.g., the Japanese GT-R) let you.

11   There's only one sensible response to this trend: boycott vehicles equipped with OnStar, even if you don't sign up for the service. (Remember: it can be remotely enabled.) If customers actively avoid vehicles that spy on them, manufacturers will have to stop installing the monitoring software and hardware. And law enforcement agencies and prosecutors will have to get their information and apprehend criminals the old-fashioned way: through legally-sanctioned police work.

12   In short, I don't buy OnStar, and neither should you.

DAHLIA LITHWICK

Teens, Nude Photos and the Law

Dahlia Lithwick is a contributing editor at *Newsweek* and senior editor at *Slate*, an online current affairs and culture magazine, for which she writes "Supreme Court Dispatches" and "Jurisprudence." Her work has also appeared in the *New Republic*, *ELLE*, the *New York Times*, the *Ottawa Citizen*, and the *Washington Post*. A product of Stanford University's law school, Lithwick worked for a family law firm and clerked for Judge Procter Hug on the United States Court of Appeals for the Ninth Circuit, before turning to a career as a writer. The following article appeared in *Newsweek* in February 2009.

A sk yourself: should the police be involved when tipsy teen girls e-mail their boyfriends naughty Valentine's Day pictures?

2   Say you're a middle-school principal who confiscated a cell phone from a 14-year-old boy, only to discover that it contains a nude photo of his 13-year-old girlfriend. Do you (a) call the boy's parents in despair; (b) call the girl's parents in despair; or (c) call the police? More and more, the answer is (d) all of the above. Which could result in criminal charges for both of your students, and their eventual designation as

sex offenders. "Sexting" is the clever new name for the act of sending, receiving, or forwarding naked photos via your cell phone, and I wasn't fully convinced that America was facing a sexting epidemic, as opposed to a journalists-writing-about-sexting epidemic, until I saw a new survey done by the National Campaign to Prevent Teen and Unplanned Pregnancy. One teenager in five reported having sent or posted naked photos of themselves. Whether all this reflects a new child-porn epidemic, or is just a new iteration of the old teen narcissism epidemic, remains unclear.

3   Last month, three girls (ages 14 or 15) in Greensburg, Pa., were charged with disseminating child pornography for sexting their boyfriends. The boys who received the images were charged with possession. A teenager in Indiana faces felony obscenity charges for sending a picture of his genitals to female classmates. A 15-year-old girl in Ohio and a 14-year-old girl in Michigan were charged with felonies for sending nude images of themselves to classmates. Some of these teens have pleaded guilty to lesser charges. Others have not. If convicted, these young people may have to register as sex offenders, in some cases for a decade or two. Similar charges have been brought in cases reported in Alabama, Connecticut, Florida, New Jersey, New York, Pennsylvania, Texas, Utah, and Wisconsin.

4   Want one quick clue that the criminal-justice system is probably not the best venue for addressing sexting? A survey of the charges brought in these cases reflects that—depending on the jurisdiction—prosecutors have charged the senders of smutty photos, the recipients of smutty photos, those who save the smutty photos, and the hapless forwarders of smutty photos with the same crime: child pornography. Who is the victim here? Everybody and nobody.

5   There may be an argument for police intervention in cases that involve a genuine threat or cyberbullying, such as a recent Massachusetts incident in which the picture of a naked 14-year-old girl was allegedly sent to more than 100 cell phones, or a New York case involving a group of boys who turned a nude photo of a 15-year-old girl into crude animations and PowerPoint presentations. But ask yourself whether those cases are the same as the cases in which tipsy teen girls send their boyfriends naughty Valentine's Day pictures.

6   The argument for hammering every such case seems to be that sending naked pictures might have serious consequences, so let's charge these kids with felonies, which will surely have serious consequences. In the Pennsylvania case a police captain explained that the charges were brought because "it's very dangerous. Once it's on a cell phone, that cell phone can be put on the Internet where everyone in the world can get access to that juvenile picture." The argument that we must prosecute kids as the producers and purveyors of kiddie porn because they are too dumb to understand that their seemingly innocent acts can harm them goes beyond paternalism. Child-pornography laws intended to protect children should not be used to prosecute and then label children as sex offenders. We seem to forget that kids can be as tech-savvy as Bill Gates but as gullible as Bambi. Even in the age of the Internet, young people fail to appreciate that naked pictures want to roam free.

7   The real problem with criminalizing teen sexting as a form of child pornography is that the great majority of these kids are not predators. They just think they're being brash and sexy. And while some of the reaction to sexting reflects legitimate concerns about children as sex objects, some also perpetuates legal stereotypes and fallacies.

A recent *New York Times* article quotes the Family Violence Prevention Fund, a non-profit domestic-violence-awareness group, as saying that the sending of nude pictures, even if done voluntarily, constitutes "digital dating violence." But do we truly believe that one in five teens is participating in an act of violence? Experts insist the sexting trend hurts teen girls more than boys, fretting that they feel "pressured" to take and send naked photos. Paradoxically, the girls in the Pennsylvania case were charged with "manufacturing, disseminating, or possessing child pornography" while the boys were merely charged with possession. If the girls are the real victims, why are we treating them more harshly than the boys?

8   Judging from the sexting prosecutions in Pennsylvania, Ohio, and Indiana this year, it's clear that the criminal-justice system is too blunt an instrument to resolve a problem that reflects more about the volatile combination of teens and technology than about some national cybercrime spree. Parents need to remind their teens that a dumb moment can last a lifetime in cyberspace. But judges and prosecutors need to understand that a lifetime of cyberhumiliation shouldn't be grounds for a lifelong real criminal record.

Jay Stanley

ACLU Opposes Body Cavity Searches for Airline Passengers

Jay Stanley works for the American Civil Liberties Union (ACLU) Technology and Liberty Program, and he especially writes and speaks about privacy issues related to technology. He is the coauthor of *Bigger Monster, Weaker Chains: The Growth of an American Surveillance Society*, an ACLU report examining how the government infringes on people's privacy. The following statement was published on the ACLU site December 31, 2009, in response to calls for increased screenings at U.S. airports.

Okay, so no one is explicitly calling for body cavity searches for all airline travelers—yet. But the logic of those pushing for body scanners for all airline passengers, and criticizing the ACLU for opposing that, leads to the inescapable conclusion that these critics would support such a policy.

2   Consider:

1. When Richard Reid brought explosives onto an airliner hidden in his shoes, the authorities began making everyone remove their shoes. When security experts and other critics pointed out that this was "silly security," defenders argued that we must put up with it in order to block that particular kind of plot.

2. Now that a disturbed person has brought explosives onto an airliner in his underwear, panicked voices want the TSA to essentially view naked pictures of every passenger who boards an airline—that's up to 2.5 million people per day on domestic flights alone. When the ACLU and members of Congress object, critics cry that we must abandon our personal dignity and privacy in order to block that particular kind of plot.

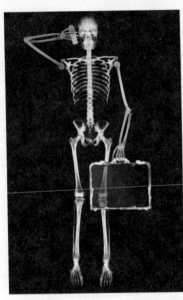

How much should airport scanners be able to reveal? Are full-body scanners, which reveal far more than this x-ray scan, ethical?

3. It is far from clear that body scanners will, as so many people seem to be assuming, detect explosives concealed the way that Umar Farouk Abdulmutallab concealed them. Some experts have said plastic explosives can be concealed against the human body. It's not clear how good scanner operators would have been at detecting the "anatomically congruent" explosives Abdulmutallab hid in his underwear (let alone how consistently effective bored operators would be if these $200,000 machines were placed at every screening station in every airport for 2.5 million people a day).

4. However, if terrorists even *perceive* that scanners will work, they take the next logical step and conceal explosives in their body cavities. Al Qaeda has already used this technique; in September a suicide bomber stowed a full pound of high explosives and a detonator inside his rectum, and attempted to assassinate a Saudi prince by blowing himself up. (The prince survived.)

3 So it seems that when the next terrorist tries to blow up an airliner using this technique, all the usual jittery voices surely will once again say that we must abandon our personal dignity and privacy in order to block that particular kind of plot. So we'd just like to get ahead of the game and state right now that the ACLU will be opposed to that.

4 Of course, even if body cavity searches for all were made policy, terrorists would probably shift their efforts to just hiding explosives in their carryon baggage, and the TSA's level of success in catching contraband has always been, shall we say, mixed. And reliably catching every possible means of hiding 50 grams of

explosives is probably impossible given the millions of people who fly each day.

5   Yes, the government must zealously work to make us as safe as possible and must take every reasonable step to make sure security breaches like the ones that led to the Christmas Day attempted attack are not repeated. But we need to act wisely. That means not trading away our privacy for ineffective policies. We should be investing in developing technologies such as trace portal detectors (a.k.a. "puffer machines") that provide a layer of security without invading privacy, and in developing competent law enforcement and intelligence agencies that will stop terrorists *before* they show up at the airport.

6   Ultimately, it is up to the American people to figure out just how much privacy they want to abandon to block a few particular means of carrying out terrorist attacks. The ACLU represents those who value privacy in this debate. But when Americans make that decision, they should do so with their eyes wide open, without any illusions that this will prevent all attacks on airliners, much less attacks on shopping malls or all the infinite number of other plots and targets that terrorists could come up with if they are not stopped by competent law enforcement and intelligence agencies.

ADAM **COHEN**

A Casualty of the Technology Revolution: "Locational Privacy"

Adam Cohen is a member of the *New York Times* editorial board; before that he was a senior writer at *Time*. Since he holds a law degree, he naturally writes on legal issues, particularly when they involve technology. Among other things, he is the author of *Nothing to Fear: FDR's Inner Circle* and *American Pharaoh: Mayor Richard J. Daley*. The editorial printed below was published by the *New York Times* in September 2009.

When I woke up the other day, I went straight to my computer to catch up on the news and to read e-mail. About 20 minutes later, I walked half a block to the gym, where I exercised for 45 minutes. I took the C train to The New York Times building, and then at the end of the day, I was back on the C train. I had dinner on my friends' (Elisabeth and Dan's) rooftop, then walked home seven blocks.

2   I'm not giving away any secrets here—nothing I did was secret to begin with. Verizon online knows when I logged on, and New York Sports Club knows when I swiped my membership card. The M.T.A. could trace (through the MetroCard I bought with a credit card) when and where I took the subway, and *The Times* knows when I used my ID to enter the building. AT&T could follow me along the way through my iPhone. There may also be videotape of my travels, given the ubiquity of surveillance cameras in New York City. There are thousands of cameras on buildings and lampposts around Manhattan, according to the New York Civil Liberties Union, many near my home and office. Several may have been in a position to film my dinner on Elisabeth and Dan's roof.

3   A little-appreciated downside of the technology revolution is that, mainly without thinking about it, we have given up "locational privacy." Even in low-tech days, our movements were not entirely private. The desk attendant at my gym might have re-called seeing me, or my colleagues might have remembered when I arrived. Now the information is collected automatically and often stored indefinitely.

Location-aware cell phones, iPads, and other mobile devices make it easy for anyone to track your location and movements. Privacy advocates are concerned; are you?
© 2010 Google-Map Data © Google, Sanborn

4   Privacy advocates are rightly concerned. Corporations and the government can keep track of what political meetings people attend, what bars and clubs they go to, whose homes they visit. It is the fact that people's locations are being recorded "perva-sively, silently, and cheaply that we're worried about," the Electronic Frontier Foundation said in a recent report.

5   People's cellphones and E-ZPasses are increasingly being used against them in court. If your phone is on, even if you are not on a call, you may be able to be found (and perhaps picked up) at any hour of the day or night. As disturbing as it is to have your private data breached, it is worse to think that your physical location might fall into the hands of people who mean you harm.

6   This decline in locational privacy, from near-absolute to very little in just a few years, has not generated much outrage, or even discussion. That is partly because so much of it is a side-effect of technology that people like. Drivers love E-ZPasses. G.P.S. enables all sorts of cool smart phone applications, from driving directions and find-a-nearby-restaurant features to the ever-popular "Take Me to My Car."

7   And people usually do not know that they are being monitored. The transit authority does not warn buyers that their MetroCards track their subway use (or that the police have used the cards in criminal investigations). Cameras that follow people on the street are placed in locations that are hard to spot. It is difficult for cellphone users to know precisely what information their devices are sending about their current location, when they are doing it, and where that information is going. Some privacy advocates were upset by recent reports that the Palm Pre, which has built-in G.P.S., has a feature that regularly sends its users' location back to Palm without notifying them at the time.

8   What can be done? As much as possible, location-specific information should not be collected in the first place, or not in personally identifiable form. There are many ways, as the Electronic Frontier Foundation notes, to use cryptography and anonymization to protect locational privacy. To tell you about nearby coffee shops, a cellphone application needs to know where you are. It does not need to know who you are.

9   In addition, when locational information is collected, people should be given advance notice and a chance to opt out. Data should be erased as soon as its main purpose is met. After you pay your E-ZPass bill, there is no reason for the government to keep records of your travel.

10   The idea of constantly monitoring the citizenry's movements used to conjure up images of totalitarian states. Now, technology does the surveillance—generally in the name of being helpful. It's time for a serious conversation about how much of our privacy of movement we want to give up.

ISSUE IN FOCUS

BIOMETRICS: Measuring the Body for Identity

The 1997 film *Gattaca,* starring Ethan Hawke and Uma Thurman, features the supposedly futuristic plot of a "natural" man stealing genetic information to pose as an elite citizen—someone who was genetically engineered before birth. Using stolen biometric identifiers, Hawke's character poses as another person, but the

Tom Cruise in *Minority Report* (2002)

film's final message just may be that the "natural" man still triumphs: spirit trumps technology. Another more recent film, *Minority Report* (2002), starring Tom Cruise, also involves biometric technologies. Cruise's character takes someone else's retinas in order to clear his name of a crime he supposedly commits in the future. Like *Gattaca*, *Minority Report* employs futuristic biometric technologies that today are not entirely feasible but are no longer beyond the realm of possibility. Indeed, both films characterize the possibilities—fascinating and frightening—of biometrics that no longer belong exclusively to the realm of science fiction.

2   Biometrics encompasses a variety of identification strategies. You've seen them on TV shows like *CSI* and *NCIS*. Biometric devices can record physical characteristics such as irises, retinas, fingerprints, hands, knuckles, palms, veins, faces, DNA, sweat, pores, lips, odors, and voices. In addition, biometric technologies can analyze human behavior patterns such as signatures, keyboard keystroke patterns, and gaits. Some of these technologies are more advanced and more feasible than others, but the goal of biometrics is to conclusively determine individual identity and thus remove the element of human error that comes with lost, stolen, hacked, copied, or shared passwords and tokens. Biometrics helps us bypass these pitfalls by securing data that belongs exclusively to one person—since that data is actually part of the person.

3   There are more everyday problems with biometrics than *CSI* and *NCIS*, *Gattaca,* and *Minority Report* suggest. For one thing, in large-scale uses of biometrics, there are likely to be portions of the population for whom some facets

of the technology simply don't work, as well as small percentages of overlap that make identity difficult to determine. In addition to concerns about the cleanliness and safety of the machinery used to collect and measure biometric data, some detractors raise concerns about security and privacy: if biometric data are stolen, individuals can be permanently vulnerable because, unlike passwords and tokens, biometric information is difficult, if not impossible, to change. Furthermore, biometrics incites fears that individuals who protect valuable property with biometrics might be physically harmed or endangered if someone tries to steal the property. These concerns about biometrics extend beyond the cost and logistics to the ways in which we use, store, and manipulate our bodies for security's sake.

4   The reading selections in this section describe the range of types and uses of biometrics and argue about advantages and disadvantages that accompany this emerging technology. Because biometric recognition technologies effectively illustrate the tensions between protection and privacy, we include images and articles that dramatize the excitement and fear surrounding them.

5   The section opens with an article by Steven C. Bennett, a partner in a law firm who teaches a course in privacy law at Hunter College. He gives an even-handed discussion of the pros and cons of biometric technologies and goes on to argue that the biometrics industry should set standards that protect the privacy of individuals. Less even-handed is a page from the FBI Web site, which extols the benefits of these technologies. Paul Saffo, Managing Director of Foresight at Discern Analytics and teacher at Stanford, is a writer whose essays have appeared in *Fortune,* the *Harvard Business Review,* the *Los Angeles Times, Newsweek,* the *New York Times,* the *Washington Post,* and *Wired.* He explains the not-so-science-fiction possibility of DNA identity theft and cautions against blind faith in biometrics. We conclude with Ben Goldacre lamenting "the biometric blues"; a physician and medical researcher in Britain, Goldacre contributes frequently to the British national newspaper the *Guardian*—especially in a regular column entitled "Bad Science."

6   As you read and analyze the texts and images, consider the desirability of biometrics—a technology that started as science fiction but has been studied and advanced by the U.S. military in efforts to secure the nation and catch terrorists. What about this technology captivates our imaginations in so many different ways? What balance are we willing to strike between personal privacy and national security, or even personal protection? How does biometrics alter our sense of ourselves as unique individuals—both in terms of what information we would share publicly and in terms of identity theft? These selections introduce you to a complex and significant technological advance, and they can prompt further thinking, reading, research, and writing as you enter this important contemporary debate about security and privacy.

STEVEN C. **BENNETT**

Privacy Implications of Biometrics

roadly speaking, biometrics is a term for any measurement of individuals used either to identify or authenticate their claimed identity. Fingerprints and wanted posters, for example, are well-established biometric methods used by law enforcement to track down, identify, and authenticate suspects. Modern information technology has added a number of new machine-based identification techniques, such as facial scanning and recognition, and improved the older techniques. These mechanical innovations offer a host of benefits, chiefly speed, efficiency, and vast analytical power. Several nations, including the United States and most of Europe, have begun to take advantage of the security benefits of these advances by issuing passports and other forms of identification encoded with biometric information. With such benefits, however, may come significant risks to the privacy and data security rights of consumers, workers, and citizens at large. The development of "best practices" in managing the use of biometrics is essential to strike an appropriate balance, ensuring proper use of these techniques and safeguards against abuse. If industry does not develop and follow such guidelines, more stringent regulations may be imposed.

2   A prime example of both the potential benefits and the threats of rapidly evolving biometric technology appears in the use of facial scanning technology at several recent NFL Superbowls. Before the 2001 Superbowl in Tampa, over 30 closed-circuit television cameras were installed to monitor the crowd and compare images of spectators to images of known criminals. Approximately 20 matches were made, several during the game. There was a widespread outcry, including dramatic media accounts labeling the game the "Snooper Bowl," disparaging the Orwellian overtones, after this use of biometrics became public knowledge. These complaints were muted at the New Orleans Superbowl in 2002, perhaps as a consequence of the September 11th attacks. Nonetheless, the use of facial recognition technology during the Superbowl has since been abandoned.

WHAT IS BIOMETRICS?

3   Essentially, biometrics is the use of human physical characteristics as identifiers. While any trait can be used, several specific types have proven to be most useful. The three most common genres of biometric identifiers are appearance, physiography, and bio-dynamics. Physical appearance is primarily judged through the use of photographs or other still images, but can also be validated through written descriptions of an individual's height, weight, coloration, hair, and visible markings. Physiography, on the other hand, requires some form of measurement—such as fingerprints, dental measurements, optical scans of the retina or iris, hand geometry, or DNA testing. As opposed to these two static characteristics, bio-dynamics measures patterned active behavior— voice fluctuation, keystroke tendencies, manner of writing a signature, and habituated body signals such as gait.

4   To perform the task of identification or authentication, biometrics relies on the comparison of live data supplied—voluntarily or not—by the subject to a dataset or template containing pre-existing information. The prime difference between the objectives of identification and authentication lies in the scope of pre-existing information required for each

task. Identification can assign a name or other value to a previously anonymous person by comparing the live data to a large number of samples, a "1:N search," to determine whether there is a match. Authentication, on the other hand, merely requires confirmation that individuals are who they claim to be. The comparison, then, is between the live data and previously supplied data from a single individual, or a "1:1 search." Both searches can either be positive or negative; they can ensure either that a person is already within the database and permitted access (positive) or, as in the Superbowl example, that a person is not within a database and therefore permitted access (negative).

5   Basic forms of biometrics are all around us. The typical driver's license or state identification card, for example, contains a photograph and some form(s) of physical description (such as height and eye color). The license often also contains a sample signature from the individual; and the individual's address. All of these, in some ways, are forms of biometrics:

- The photograph may be compared to the individual carrying the license;
- The physical characteristics described on the license may also be compared to those of the individual;
- The individual may be asked for a signature sample, and that sample compared to the license sample;
- The individual may be asked to recall (unaided) his or her address, and that answer compared to the license information.

What Is Different About Machine Biometrics?

6   Biometrics standing alone are just characteristics; they neither protect nor threaten individual privacy. As the license example suggests, the use of biometrics has been accepted and commonplace for over 100 years. It is how biometric technologies are used that determines their effect on privacy. The rise of mechanical biometric technology, especially computers and computerized databases, and the consequent automation of the identification process have radically increased both the ability to identify individuals biometrically and the potential for abuse of biometrics. These changes extend to almost every aspect of biometrics—data capture, analysis, communication, and storage—and must be understood before analyzing their implications for privacy and data security rights of individuals.

Data Capture

7   Technological advances now allow for involuntary or unknowing capture of biometric characteristics. The Superbowl provides an example—if the security firm had chosen to store the captured images rather than merely test and destroy them, it would have created the possibility for biometric identification of all who attended the game. Even when the submission of information is voluntary, many biometrics are very difficult for a human to gather unaided. For example, scanning the retina of the human eye requires light-producing and magnification devices, and meaningful analysis of the results requires imaging and comparison technology. These techniques, however, may offer highly individualized identification when used properly. Even biometric methods that can be performed competently by humans (such as fingerprint or hand shape identification) can be greatly improved through machine operation.

Data Analysis

8   Though Moore's law of increasing computer capacity is only observational, the exponential growth of computing power has allowed for ever more rapid identification searches, even as databases expand. Fingerprinting technology provides the perfect lens through which to view this growth. Originally, fingerprinting could only be used to authenticate the identity of criminals who had left their prints at a crime scene, noting any 1:1 matches. Gradually, a classification system (the Henry system) developed, which allowed for identification searches, but these searches required significant amounts of time to perform. By 1971, the FBI possessed over 200 million paper fingerprint files, including records on 30 million criminals, and J. Edgar Hoover had unsuccessfully promoted universal fingerprinting. The true technological shift, however, came in the 1990s, when new fingerprint scanners cut the time to identify prints from months to hours.

Data Communication

9   Many forms of biometrics were impossible to communicate until recently. Before the creation of reasonably high quality photographs and copies, accurate re-creation of most biometrics via transmission was impossible. The year 1924 witnessed the first transmission of fingerprints from Australia to Scotland Yard via telegraph. Since then, modern communication has dramatically enhanced the efficiency of biometrics. Just as computational analysis has followed the predictions of Moore's law, so too the field of communications has lived up to the even more aggressive predictions of the "Photon Law"—that bandwidth will more than double every year. As bandwidth increases, more biometrics can be transmitted, and data transfer is faster. This allows for linkage of varied biometric data sets, as well as non-biometric information.

Data Storage

10   Finally, the ability to reduce biometrics to electronic datasets of relatively small size has allowed for construction of large, searchable electronic databases. As a result of the falling costs of electronic data storage and the rising ability to transmit that data rapidly across long distances, technological shifts have allowed for creation of massive interlinked databases of biometric information. The FBI's Integrated Automated Fingerprint Identification System ("IAFIS") is the largest biometric database in the world, containing the fingerprints and related criminal history of over 47 million individuals. Remote electronic submissions for criminal inquiries can receive a response from IAFIS within two hours. The IAFIS data illustrate a final observational law of technology, Metcalfe's law, which states that the power of a network increases (exponentially, though this value is debated) as every node is added. Thus, the ability to integrate and store information from many different databases dramatically increases the value of biometric data.

THE VALUE OF MACHINE BIOMETRICS

11   The efficiency gained from mechanization of biometrics is clear. Fingerprint searches that a decade ago took three months to complete now can be completed in under two hours. Biometrics also has an intrinsic value in its ability to function as

(potentially) the most effective security safeguard, restricting access to sensitive information or physical areas. To secure such access, authorization (or identity) must be validated. The rise in identity theft demonstrates the weakness of validating systems based purely on possession of particular information about the individual. These faults have caused many in business to turn to biometrics as a more secure method of identifying or authenticating individuals.

12   In response to digital hackers, many password systems now require frequent changes or the use of special symbols and non-repetitive character strings. These shifts, designed to protect security, tend instead to undermine it as users often write their passwords on a sticky note by their desks. Relying on access cards is equally problematic—such cards can be lost, stolen, or left right by the computer to which they provide access. A recent survey, moreover, found that 70 percent of Americans, in response to an unsolicited email or phone call, would share information such as an account number, or provide the answer to a security code question. A majority also indicated they would not want their accounts locked after three failed attempts to verify the identity of someone trying to gain access. More than two-thirds of respondents in this survey were open to using biometric technologies—they want technology that is as secure as it is convenient.

13   The weaknesses and security lapses in other validation mechanisms have increasingly caused industry innovators to turn to biometrics. Banco Azteca was created in 2001 by the massive Grupo Elektra, to target the previously untapped 70 percent of Mexico's population that did not use banks at all. One of the problems the new bank confronted in enrolling customers in underserved communities was the lack of any form of secure identification papers, driver's licenses, or the like. In response, the bank turned to biometrics and fingerprint scans. Over seven million Banco Azteca customers have enrolled in the biometric identification program; more than 75 percent of the bank's business comes from customers who have dealt with a bank for the first time due to this program.

HOW CAN MACHINE BIOMETRICS THREATEN PRIVACY?

14   Although biometrics techniques may provide new opportunities for security, these techniques also present the potential for abuse. Biometric information is inherently linked to individuality and functions as a unique identifier in a way that would make its loss irreplaceable. The potentially unrestrained scope of data collecting, sharing, linking, and warehousing also may invite misuse. Finally, the potential for pervasive monitoring of movement and activities may chill discourse and protest.

15   Identity theft in a biometric world may be particularly problematic. When a check is lost or stolen, one immediately requests a stop payment order. When a credit card is taken, one calls the company to freeze the account and order a new card. What does one do when biometric information is stolen? Once biometric information is reduced to electronic data, that data can be captured or altered by hackers. Hackers can then reproduce the data in a way that convinces biometric scanners that they are authorized, and thereby gain access to supposedly secure information or locations. Essentially, biometrics are the equivalent of a PIN that is impossible to change. The theft of biometric information amounts to permanent identity theft, and thus may be extremely difficult to counteract.

16   Use of biometrics also risks the problem of data creep, in which information given voluntarily to one recipient for one purpose may be transferred, without permission or knowledge, to another recipient, linked with other data, or applied to a new purpose. The average American's personal information is now available in approximately 50 different commercial databases. Linkage of such information could permit discrimination based on physical characteristics that might otherwise remain unknown.

17   Followed to its logical extreme, moreover, the linkage of digital images into a single database with facial recognition technology would permit the tracking of everyone's movements. The possibility of such tracking, however remote, epitomizes the threat that widespread use of biometrics poses for personal privacy. If an organization or government can monitor movement and actions, it could discriminate against individuals based on their associations. As anonymous behavior becomes less possible, dissent may be suppressed.

WHAT FORM OF REGULATION IS APPROPRIATE?

18   Individual autonomy is the cornerstone of the American legal and social structure. The free flow of information, however, is equally essential to a functioning democracy. The challenge of regulating biometrics lies in resolving the tension between the rights to privacy, free speech, and information security.

19   Americans generally disfavor broad government regulation of industry practices regarding personal information. Congress prefers to rely on industry self-regulation when possible. Nevertheless, the government will step in to regulate a market when the market clearly has failed to provide adequate safeguards. Notable examples of such government intervention include the Child Online Protection Act, the Graham-Leach-Bliley Act, and the Health Insurance Portability and Accountability Act. If the biometrics industry wishes to avoid potentially strict sector-specific government regulations, it must self-regulate, to harmonize the tensions between the fundamental benefits of biometrics while limiting the potential for abuse. In establishing such best practices, the industry must proceed from two basic principles: notice and security.

Notice

20   Individuals must know when data collection occurs. A notice requirement recognizes the importance of individual autonomy and enables people to choose whether to participate. Notice, however, means more than simply saying "surveillance cameras are in use," when police apply facial recognition software at the Superbowl. When any biometric system is used, there should ideally be an open statement of its scope, purpose, function, and application, including the system's potential uses. The evaluation of potential uses is beneficial because biometric systems rarely threatens abuse in themselves. The true threat to privacy comes from the mission creep permitted by latent capabilities. Biometric systems should be narrowly tailored to the job they are to perform. Participation, if at all possible, should be optional. Any change in scope once in use should have the same public disclosure, and participants should be given the option to unenroll from the system.

21   While enrolled within a system, participants should be able to access and correct their personal information contained within the system. Failure to provide for access and correction will increase error in the program and may violate privacy principles.

22   The final notice element of a good self-regulatory program is third-party oversight. Some independent oversight should be implemented to ensure conformity with "best practices," and to suggest other improvements. Periodic audits of the scope and operation of the system coupled with public disclosure of the results of the audits may provide particular deterrence against abuse.

Security

23 To ensure adequate security of biometric information requires both limits on construction of system capabilities as well as protections for data use. System operators should inform participants of the different security measures a biometric identification system will undertake.

24   Data collected should be protected by techniques such as encryption, data hashing, and the use of closed networks and secure facilities. Wireless transmissions of data, even when encrypted, should be avoided. To the extent possible, data should not be stored in a warehouse or database but rather with the individual participant, by means of an encrypted smart card. If storage is necessary, the initial collection of biometric data should be used to generate templates of authorized people and not linked to any one individual.

Government Oversight

25 If the biometrics industry establishes adequate notice and security practices, it may avoid potentially more restrictive governmental regulations. Some system of enforcement of best practice principles may be necessary. The Federal Trade Commission's power to prosecute unfair, deceptive, or fraudulent business activities may help prevent violations of security procedures or unannounced expansions of a biometric system's purview. The FTC already leads in the data protection field, having developed its own set of information practice principles.

WHAT IS THE FUTURE OF BIOMETRICS?

26 A decade ago, Bill Gates forecast that biometrics would be among "the most important IT innovations of the next several years." Technological innovation has dramatically increased the breadth, depth, and speed with which disparate data sets can be connected and analyzed. Recent developments demonstrate the widespread growth and potential power of biometrics. Use of this technology will certainly continue to grow in the next decade. Taken on its own, biometrics is neither a friend nor a foe to privacy rights; their relationship depends on the manner in which the technology is used.

27   If the biometrics industry wishes to maintain its current flexibility and avoid overly stringent regulations, it must respond to the potential threats to privacy by formulating and adopting best practice principles, keeping in mind the essential need for notice and security. Such self-regulation in managing the use of biometrics will allow the market to strike an appropriate balance between the rights to privacy, free speech, and effective use of information technology.

PAUL SAFFO

A Trail of DNA and Data

2   If you're worried about privacy and identity theft, imagine this:

3   The scene: Somewhere in Washington. The date: April 3, 2020.
You sit steaming while the officer hops off his electric cycle and walks up to the car window. "You realize that you ran that red light again, don't you, Mr. Witherspoon?" It's no surprise that he knows your name; the intersection camera scanned your license plate and your guilty face, and matched both in the DMV database. The cop had the full scoop before you rolled to a stop.

4   "I know, I know, but the sun was in my eyes," you plead as you fumble for your driver's license.

5   "Oh, don't bother with that," the officer replies, waving off the license while squinting at his hand-held scanner. Of course. Even though the old state licensing system had been revamped back in 2014 into a "secure" national program, the new licenses had been so compromised that the street price of a phony card in Tijuana had plummeted to five euros. In frustration, law enforcement was turning to pure biometrics.

6   "Could you lick this please?" the officer asks, passing you a nanofiber blotter. You comply and then slide the blotter into the palm-sized gizmo he is holding, which reads your DNA and runs a match against a national genomic database maintained by a consortium of drug companies and credit agencies. It also checks half a dozen metabolic fractions looking for everything from drugs and alcohol to lack of sleep.

7   The officer looks at the screen, and frowns, "Okay. I'll let you off with a warning, but you really need more sleep. I also see that your retinal implants are past warranty, and your car tells me that you are six months overdue on its navigation firmware upgrade. You really need to take care of both or next time it's a ticket."

8   This creepy scenario is all too plausible. The technologies described are already being developed for industrial and medical applications, and the steadily dropping cost and size of such systems will make them affordable and practical police tools well before 2020. The resulting intrusiveness would make today's system of search warrants and wiretaps quaint anachronisms.

9   Some people find this future alluring and believe that it holds out the promise of using sophisticated ID techniques to catch everyone from careless drivers to bomb-toting terrorists in a biometric dragnet. We have already seen places such as Truro, Mass., Baton Rouge, La. and Miami ask hundreds or thousands of citizens to submit to DNA mass-testing to catch killers. Biometric devices sensing for SARS symptoms are omnipresent in Asian airports. And the first prototypes of systems that test in real time for SARS, HIV and bird flu have been deployed abroad.

10   The ubiquitous collection and use of biometric information may be inevitable, but the notion that it can deliver reliable, theft-proof evidence of identity is pure science fiction. Consider that oldest of biometric identifiers—fingerprints. Long the exclusive domain of government databases and FBI agents who dust for prints at crime scenes,

fingerprints are now being used by electronic print readers on everything from ATMs to laptops. Sticking your finger on a sensor beats having to remember a password or toting an easily lost smart card.

11   But be careful what you touch, because you are leaving your identity behind every time you take a drink. A Japanese cryptographer has demonstrated how, with a bit of gummi bear gelatin, some cyanoacrylic glue, a digital camera and a bit of digital fiddling, he can easily capture a print off a glass and confect an artificial finger that foils fingerprint readers with an 80 percent success rate. Frightening as this is, at least the stunt is far less grisly than the tale, perhaps apocryphal, of some South African crooks who snipped the finger off an elderly retiree, rushed her still-warm digit down to a government ATM, stuck it on the print reader and collected the victim's pension payment. (Scanners there now gauge a finger's temperature, too.)

12   Today's biometric advances are the stuff of tomorrow's hackers and clever crooks, and anything that can be detected eventually will be counterfeited. Iris scanners are gaining in popularity in the corporate world, exploiting the fact that human iris patterns are apparently as unique as fingerprints. And unlike prints, iris images aren't left behind every time someone gets a latte at Starbucks. But hide something valuable enough behind a door protected by an iris scanner, and I guarantee that someone will figure out how to capture an iris image and transfer it to a contact lens good enough to fool the readers. And capturing your iris may not even require sticking a digital camera in your face—after all, verification requires that the representation of your iris exist as a cloud of binary bits of data somewhere in cyberspace, open to being hacked, copied, stolen and downloaded. The more complex the system, the greater the likelihood that there are flaws that crooks can exploit.

13   DNA is the gold standard of biometrics, but even DNA starts to look like fool's gold under close inspection. With a bit of discipline, one can keep a card safe or a PIN secret, but if your DNA becomes your identity, you are sharing your secret with the world every time you sneeze or touch something. The novelist Scott Turow has already written about a hapless sap framed for a murder by an angry spouse who spreads his DNA at the scene of a killing.

14   The potential for DNA identity theft is enough to make us all wear a gauze mask and keep our hands in our pockets. DNA can of course be easily copied—after all, its architecture is designed for duplication—but that is the least of its problems. Unlike a credit card number, DNA can't be retired and swapped for a new sequence if it falls into the hands of crooks or snoops. Once your DNA identity is stolen, you live with the consequences forever.

15   This hasn't stopped innovators from using DNA as an indicator of authenticity. The artist Thomas Kinkade signs his most valuable paintings with an ink containing a bit of his DNA. (He calls it a "forgery-proof DNA Matrix signature.") We don't know how much of Tom is really in his paintings, but perhaps it's enough for forgers to duplicate the ink, as well as the distinctive brush strokes.

16   The biggest problem with DNA is that it says so much more about us than an arbitrary serial number does. Give up your Social Security number and a stranger can inspect your credit rating. But surrender your DNA and a snoop can discover your in-

nermost genetic secrets—your ancestry, genetic defects and predispositions to certain diseases. Of course we will have strong genetic privacy laws, but those laws will allow consumers to "voluntarily" surrender their information in the course of applying for work or pleading for health care. A genetic marketplace not unlike today's consumer information business will emerge, swarming with health insurers attempting to prune out risky individuals, drug companies seeking customers and employers managing potential worker injury liability.

17   Faced with this prospect, any sensible privacy maven would conclude that DNA is too dangerous to collect, much less use for a task as unimportant as turning on a laptop or working a cash machine. But society will not be able to resist its use. The pharmaceutical industry will need our DNA to concoct customized wonder drugs that will fix everything from high cholesterol to halitosis. And crime fighters will make giving DNA information part of our civic duty and national security. Once they start collecting, the temptation to use it for other purposes will be too great.

18   Moreover, snoops won't even need a bit of actual DNA to invade our privacy because it will be so much easier to access its digital representation on any number of databanks off in cyberspace. Our Mr. Witherspoon will get junk mail about obscure medical conditions that he's never heard of because some direct marketing firm "bot" will inspect his digital DNA and discover that he has a latent disease or condition that his doctor didn't notice at his annual checkup.

19   It is tempting to conclude that Americans will rise up in revolt, but experience suggests otherwise. Americans profess a concern for privacy, but they happily reveal their deepest financial and personal secrets for a free magazine subscription or cheesy electronic trinket. So they probably will eagerly surrender their biometric identities as well, trading fingerprint IDs for frequent shopper privileges at the local supermarket and genetic data to find out how to have the cholesterol count of a teenager.

20   Biometric identity systems are inevitable, but they are no silver bullet when it comes to identity protection. The solution to identity protection lies in the hard work of implementing system-wide and nationwide technical and policy changes. Without those changes, the deployment of biometric sensors will merely increase the opportunities for snoops and thieves—and escalate the cost to ordinary citizens.

21   It's time to fix the problems in our current systems and try to anticipate the unique challenges that will accompany the expanded use of biometrics. It's the only way to keep tomorrow's crooks from stealing your fingers and face and, with them, your entire identity.

FBI

Using Technology to Catch Criminals

The FBI's enthusiasm for biometric technologies is reflected on its Web site. The page shown here was posted on December 27, 2005.

Home | Site Map | FAQs

FEDERAL BUREAU OF INVESTIGATION

Celebrating a Century 1908-2008

SEARCH

Contact Us
- Your Local FBI Office
- Overseas Offices
- Submit a Crime Tip
- Report Internet Crime
- More Contacts

Learn About Us
- Quick Facts
- What We Investigate
- Natl. Security Branch
- Information Technology
- Fingerprints & Training
- Laboratory Services
- Reports & Publications
- History
- More About Us

Get Our News
- Press Room
- E-mail Updates
- News Feeds

Be Crime Smart
- Wanted by the FBI
- More Protections

Use Our Resources
- For Law Enforcement
- For Communities
- For Researchers
- More Services

Visit Our Kids' Page

Apply for a Job

Headline Archives

USING TECHNOLOGY TO CATCH CRIMINALS
Fingerprint Database "Hits" Felons at the Border

12/27/05

A CBP officer takes a passenger's fingerprint scan to compare with the IAFIS database.

When U.S. Customs and Border Protection installed technology that can quickly check the fingerprints of illegal immigrants against the FBI's massive biometric database, its chief called the measure "absolutely critical."

"This technology helps...shed light on those with criminal backgrounds we could never have identified before," Commissioner Robert C. Bonner said in a press statement in October, a month after our Integrated Automated Fingerprint Identification System (IAFIS) became fully available in all 136 border patrol stations.

A very bright light, it turns out. Since last September, IAFIS has returned "hits" on 118,557 criminal subjects who were trying to enter this country illegally, according to Customs and Border Protection officials.

Many of the "hits"—a match of an individual's 10 fingerprints—led to arrests of dangerous criminal suspects, including:

- 460 individuals for homicide
- 155 for kidnapping
- 599 for sexual assault
- 970 for robbery
- 5,919 for assault
- 12,077 for drug-related charges

Border Patrol officials began using our biometric tool in the summer of 2001, connecting two of their facilities in San Diego to our Criminal Justice Information Services Division facility in Clarksburg, West Virginia. Congress sought the deployment to supplement the Border Patrol's 10-year-old biometric database called IDENT, which relies on matching an individual's index fingers, rather than the comprehensive 10-finger prints made by IAFIS.

With IAFIS in place, Border Patrol agents can simultaneously check IDENT's specialized databases and IAFIS's 49 million sets of prints.

Voice Verification for Transactions

VoiceVerified's patent-pending Point Service Provider (PSP) platform uses voice verification to help businesses secure remote transactions, protect consumer data, and combat identity fraud. During the verification process, a user is prompted to repeat five random numeric digits to create a voice sample that is compared to a previously enrolled voiceprint to determine a match.

Somerset, Pa.–based Somerset Trust has purchased the PSP to secure wire transfers, and the bank envisions future usage across all banking services requiring multifactor authentication. VoiceVerified is currently in discussions with several other financial institutions as banks seek to comply with the Federal Financial Institutions Examination Council's recent guidelines advocating multifactor user authentication during electronic transactions.

BEN **GOLDACRE**

Now for ID Cards—and the Biometric Blues

Sometimes just throwing a few long words about can make people think you know what you're talking about. Words like "biometric."

2   When Alistair Darling was asked if the government will ditch ID cards in the light of this week's data crack-up, he replied: "The key thing about identity cards is, of course, that information is protected by personal biometric information. The problem at present is that, because we do not have that protection, information is much more vulnerable than it should be."

3   Yes, that's the problem. We need biometric identification. Fingerprints. Iris scans. Gordon Brown says so too: "What we must ensure is that identity fraud is avoided, and the way to avoid identity fraud is to say that for passport information we will have the biometric support that is necessary."

4   Tsutomu Matsumoto is a Japanese mathematician, a cryptographer who works on security, and he decided to see if he could fool the machines which identify you by your fingerprint. This home science project costs about £20. Take a finger and make a cast with the moulding plastic sold in hobby shops. Then pour some liquid gelatin (ordinary food gelatin) into that mould and let it harden. Stick this over your finger pad: it fools fingerprint detectors about 80% of the time. The joy is, once you've fooled the machine, your fake fingerprint is made of the same stuff as fruit pastilles, so you can simply eat the evidence.

5   But what if you can't get the finger? Well, you can chop one off, of course—another risk with biometrics. But there is an easier way. Find a fingerprint on glass. Sorry, I should have pointed out that every time you touch something, if your security systems rely on biometric ID, then you're essentially leaving your pin number on a post-it note.

6   You can make a fingerprint image on glass more visible by painting over it wit. some cyanoacrylate adhesive. That's a posh word for superglue. Photograph that with a digital camera. Improve the contrast in a picture editing program, print the image on to a transparency sheet, and then use that to etch the fingerprint on to a copper-plated printed circuit boar. (It sounds difficult, but you can buy a beginner's etching set for about for £10.) This gives an image with some three-dimensional relief. You can now make your gelatin fingerpad using this as a mould.

7   Should I have told you all that, or am I very naughty? Yes to both.

8   It's well known that security systems which rely on secret methods are less secure than open systems, because the greater the number of people who know about the system, the more people there are to spot holes in it, and it is important that there are no holes. If someone tells you their system is perfect and secret, that's like quacks who tell you their machine cures cancer but they can't tell you how. Open the box, quack. In fact you might sense that the whole field of biometrics and ID is rather like medical quackery: as usual, on the one hand we have snake oil salesmen promising the earth, and on the other a bunch of humanities graduates who don't understand technology, science, or even human behaviour: buying it; bigging it up; thinking it's a magic wand.

9   But it's not. Leaks occur not because of unauthorized access, and they can't be stopped with biometrics; they happen because of authorized access, often ones which are managed with contemptible, cavalier incompetence. The damaging repercussions will not be ameliorated by biometrics.

10   So will biometrics prevent ID theft? Well, it might make it more difficult for you to prove your innocence. And once your fingerprints are stolen, they are harder to replace than your pin number. But here's the final nail in the coffin. Your fingerprint data will be stored in your passport or ID card as a series of numbers, called the "minutiae template." In the new biometric passport with its wireless chip, remember, all your data can be read and decrypted with a device near you, but not touching you.

11   What good would the data be, if someone lifted it? Not much, insisted Jim Knight, the minister for schools and learners, in July: "It is not possible to recreate a fingerprint using the numbers that are stored. The algorithm generates a unique number, producing no information of any use to identity thieves." Crystal clear, Jim.

12   Unfortunately, a team of mathematicians published a paper in April this year, showing that they could reconstruct a fingerprint from this data alone. In fact, they printed out the images they made, and then—crucially, completing the circle—used them to fool fingerprint readers.

3   Ah biometrics. Such a soothingly technical word. Repeat it to yourself.

Fujitsu Computer Products of America recently launched its palm vein authentication device that captures a person's palm vein pattern and checks it against a preregistered palm vein pattern from that individual. The device offers users a high level of accuracy and security. It is in use at some of Asia's leading financial institutions.

. Examine the outcries of biometrics critics and consider writing a rebuttal of one or more of their arguments. (Consult Chapter 12 on writing a rebuttal.)

2. In a causal argument (see Chapter 9), consider how the technological age in which we live exacerbates issues of privacy.

3. Evaluate any one of the technologies described in this chapter, on the basis of practicality and/or constitutional principles. Has this technology actually helped in the war on terrorism? Has it actually led to significant privacy violations? (See Chapter 10 for advice on evaluation.)

4. Consider popular portrayals of security technologies and biometrics (like those in *CSI* or *NCIS*). Why are these technologies so fascinating within the realm of science fiction? What qualities do these popular versions exaggerate, and why? What effect might these popular images have on viewers' opinions of real-life technologies, and why?

5. Analyze the visual images associated with this issue, building on Chapter 6 of this text. What is the nature of the arguments made in these visuals? How do they work to persuade an audience?

6. Write a narrative argument (such as the ones described in Chapter 11) that contributes to the debates represented in this chapter. How does a single incident—drawn from the news, an interview, or your own experience—contribute to this conversation? Alternatively, write a short story portraying the issue with a science fiction or futuristic slant.

27 | Regulating Substances, Regulating Bodies

Private Bodies, Public Controls

Regulation is often about deciding where lines may be crossed—and where they should not be crossed. How would we decide which burgers or fries (if any) should be regulated?

The U.S. prison population—now at 2.3 million, the Justice Department reported in 2008—has more than quadrupled since the early 1980s, which means that our nation now has the highest rate of incarceration in the world. Although only 4 percent of the world population is in the United States, the United States has a quarter of the entire world's prison population, and 1 in every 31 American adults is now in prison, on probation, or on parole. A great many of those in prison are nonviolent drug offenders, usually small-timers who need help with their own addictions. In the late 1980s, in the face of a cocaine epidemic that was ravaging the nation's cities and claiming the lives of citizens as prominent as Boston Celtics first-round draftee Len Bias, legislators and law enforcement agents cracked down by instituting mandatory minimum sentences. Because people who inform on others can often secure reduced sentences, small-time drug violators often get stiffer sentences than major dealers. According to *Newsweek,* 6 percent of inmates in state prisons in 1980 were there for drug violations; in 1996 the figure was 23 percent. In 1980, 25 percent of inmates in federal prisons were drug violators, while in 2005 the figure had risen to over 60 percent.

Should we be so hard on drug dealers and abusers? Is the state and federal governments' "war on drugs" going so poorly that it should be abandoned? Many people think so. Critics call attention not only to the figures on incarceration but also to the other social costs associated with strict drug laws. For example, many addicts resist treatment because they fear punishment; instead, they commit crimes to support their bad habits. Widespread urine testing and seizures of drug-related property have threatened basic civil rights and undermined respect for police.

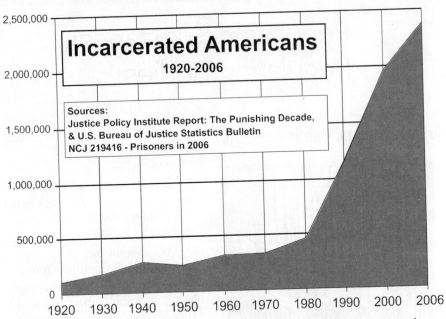

Number of inmates in U.S. prisons, 1920 to 2006. The number of inmates in U.S. prisons has more than quadrupled since the early 1980s.

Extensions of the drug war have led to conflicts with other nations where drugs are produced. Moreover, if drugs were considered a medical and social problem rather than a criminal one, citizens could be helped rather than sent to prison. Needle-exchange programs could help check the spread of AIDS by reducing the incidence of shared needles. Recognizing that illegal drugs often are no worse and no better than alcohol (legal since the disastrous 1920s experiment known as Prohibition), Californians voted to legalize marijuana use for cancer and AIDS patients. Many people, drawing from the experiences of other nations, are now calling for moves to decriminalize some kinds of drug use, or at least to reduce penalties and increase treatment. In other words, the war on drugs might be maintained—but without quite so much prison warehousing.

On the other hand, many people argue for a continuing hard line on drugs (including alcohol) because of the damage that illegal drugs do. They point to the health risks and social costs—to early deaths, lost work days, rapes and assaults and broken lives attributable to substance abuse. In the tradition of Carry Nation and other temperance warriors who successfully lobbied for prohibition

An estimated 80–100 million Americans have tried marijuana.

Of every one hundred people who have smoked marijuana, twenty-eight have tried cocaine—but only one uses cocaine weekly.

of alcohol in the 1920s, they have evidence that drug use (especially cocaine use) has decreased during the years of the war on drugs, that marijuana may be a "gateway drug" to more dangerous substances (because marijuana smokers are far more likely to try other drugs, such as cocaine), and that the war on drugs is worth waging for all sorts of other reasons.

Advocates of a hard line on drugs sometimes take on not only drug kingpins but also others—alcohol producers, Big Tobacco, performance-enhancing drug users. For example, they promote stiff taxes on cigarettes and alcohol on the grounds that making harmful substances expensive discourages use and pays for the social costs involved. And they are often proponents of testing athletes for the use of unfair and dangerous performance-enhancing substances, such as steroids (which promote muscle growth but have harmful side effects), synthetic forms of testosterone (for which 2006 Tour de France winner Floyd Landis tested positive, causing him to be stripped of his title), and creatine (a dietary supplement that many athletes feel helps their training). They point to the popularity of such substances among young people. They also work to combat binge drinking on campuses because they see it as a frightening epidemic that encourages date rape, promotes vandalism, and otherwise ruins or undermines the lives of countless college students.

Reformer Carry Nation holding the weapons of her trade: a hatchet for destroying liquor containers and a copy of the Bible

Contemporary Arguments

Should certain substances be regulated—and, if so, which ones? Is substance abuse a victimless crime that we have to live with in order to preserve a free society? Is education the only proper approach to the problem? If not, what exactly should be done about obesity, about various drugs, alcohol, and tobacco, and about other controversial and harmful substances and practices? Just how should we weigh the risks of obesity and of drug and alcohol use against the costs of overzealous law enforcement and other means of social control?

The essays in this section provide a number of perspectives on public control over private bodies. Consider, for instance, the debate between Joe Klein and Bernadine Healy concerning the legalization of marijuana. Each writer looks at the legalization and criminalization of marijuana from a different perspective and with a different ultimate proposal. Then consider the argument about steroid use that follows: celebrated baseball analyst Bill James asks on his Web site whether our collective condemnation of performance enhancing drugs (PEDs) will soften in the coming years, offering his own perspective on the dangers posed by PEDs and the issues of fairness and consequence that are raised when professional athletes use such substances. Where exactly should lines be drawn between personal freedom—what we choose to do with our own bodies—and government intervention on behalf of health and public safety? That question underlies the other arguments about body weight and body image, controlling tobacco, and disability. Three items in particular take up matters related to obesity: How serious is the "obesity crisis"? What are the causes of and cures for obesity? And how should this health problem be addressed? We conclude the chapter with an Issue in Focus that has particular relevance: What, if anything, should be done to regulate excessive and dangerous alcohol consumption by college students?

Finally, consider as you read this chapter how visuals can serve

When Barry Bonds hit his 756th Major League Baseball home run on August 7, 2007, he broke the all-time record held by Henry Aaron. Although Bonds has never failed an official steroid test, he has been implicated frequently in the taking of steroids, and his home run record is embroiled in controversy. Other prominent players, most famously Roger Clemens and Alex Rodriguez, also have been implicated.

to regulate bodies indirectly, both through the ideals that are presented and the concepts and values that are omitted. Photos, cartoons, ads, and other visuals in this chapter suggest that our identifications with certain body types can influence our behaviors; that argument also applies to television shows and movies. These issues concerning written and visual arguments arise especially in the essays by Terrence Rafferty (on film and body image), Rebecca Traister (on the Dove Campaign for Real Beauty), and James Hibberd (on the employment of college students as "beer boys" and girls).

JOE KLEIN

Why Legalizing Marijuana Makes Sense

Joe Klein (born 1946) is journalist, a member of the Council on Foreign Relations, and a former Guggenheim Fellow. He has been a contributor to *Time* since 2003 and has also been published in the *New Republic*, the *New York Times*, the *Washington Post*, and *Rolling Stone*. He is the author of *Primary Colors*, an "anonymously" written exposé novel about Bill Clinton's first presidential campaign that later became a movie, as well as a follow-up entitled *Running Mate*. He contributed the following article to *Time* in April 2009.

For the past several years, I've been harboring a fantasy, a last political crusade for the baby-boom generation. We who started on the path of righteousness, marching for civil rights and against the war in Vietnam, need to find an appropriately high-minded approach to life's exit ramp. In this case, I mean the high-minded part literally. And so, a deal: give us drugs, after a certain age—say, 80—all drugs, any drugs we want. In return, we will give you our driver's licenses. (I mean, can you imagine how terrifying a nation of decrepit, solipsistic 90-year-old boomers behind the wheel would be?) We'll let you proceed with your lives—much of which will be spent paying for our retirement, in any case—without having to hear us complain about our every ache and reflux. We'll be too busy exploring altered states of consciousness. I even have a slogan for the campaign: "Tune in, turn on, drop dead."

2   A fantasy, I suppose. But beneath the furious roil of the economic crisis, a national conversation has quietly begun about the irrationality of our drug laws. It is going on in state legislatures, like New York's, where the draconian Rockefeller drug laws are up for review; in other states, from California to Massachusetts, various forms of marijuana decriminalization are being enacted. And it has reached the floor of Congress, where Senators Jim Webb and Arlen Specter have proposed a major prison-reform package, which would directly address drug-sentencing policies.

3   There are also more puckish signs of a zeitgeist shift. A few weeks ago, the White House decided to stage a forum in which the President would answer questions submitted by the public; 92,000 people responded—and most of them seemed obsessed with the legalization of marijuana. The two most popular questions about "green jobs and energy," for example, were about pot. The President dismissed the

outpouring—appropriately, I guess—as online ballot-stuffing and dismissed the legalization question with a simple: "No."

This was a rare instance of Barack Obama reacting reflexively, without attempting to think creatively, about a serious policy question. He was, in fact, taking the traditional path of least resistance: an unexpected answer on marijuana would have launched a tabloid firestorm, diverting attention from the budget fight and all those bailouts. In fact, the default fate of any politician who publicly considers the legalization of marijuana is to be cast into the outer darkness. Such a person is assumed to be stoned all the time, unworthy of being taken seriously. Such a person would be lacerated by the assorted boozehounds and pill poppers of talk radio. The hypocrisy inherent in the American conversation about stimulants is staggering.

But there are big issues here, issues of economy and simple justice, especially on the sentencing side. As Webb pointed out in a cover story in *Parade* magazine, the U.S. is, by far, the most "criminal" country in the world, with 5% of the world's population and 25% of its prisoners. We spend $68 billion per year on corrections, and one-third of those being corrected are serving time for nonviolent drug crimes. We spend about $150 billion on policing and courts, and 47.5% of all drug arrests are marijuana-related. That is an awful lot of money, most of it nonfederal, that could be spent on better schools or infrastructure—or simply returned to the public.

At the same time, there is an enormous potential windfall in the taxation of marijuana. It is estimated that pot is the largest cash crop in California, with annual revenues approaching $14 billion. A 10% pot tax would yield $1.4 billion in California alone. And that's probably a fraction of the revenues that would be available—and of the economic impact, with thousands of new jobs in agriculture, packaging, marketing and advertising. A veritable marijuana economic-stimulus package!

So why not do it? There are serious moral arguments, both secular and religious. There are those who believe—with some good reason—that the accretion of legalized vices is debilitating, that we are a less virtuous society since gambling spilled out from Las Vegas to "riverboats" and state lotteries across the country. There is a medical argument, though not a very convincing one: alcohol is more dangerous in a variety of ways, including the tendency of some drunks to get violent. One could argue that the abuse of McDonald's has a greater potential healthcare cost than the abuse of marijuana. (Although it's true that with legalization, those two might not be unrelated.) Obviously, marijuana can be abused. But the costs of criminalization have proved to be enormous, perhaps unsustainable. Would legalization be any worse?

In any case, the drug-reform discussion comes just at the right moment. We boomers are getting older every day. You're not going to want us on the highways. Make us your best offer.

Bernadine Healy

Legalize Marijuana? Obama Was Right to Say No

Dr. Bernadine Healy (born 1944), a cardiologist, formerly headed the National Institutes of Health (NIH) and was once president of the American Red Cross. Currently she is health editor and columnist for *U.S. News & World Report.* The following column appeared February 4, 2009, on the *U.S. News* Web site.

Puff the Magic Dragon—in his naughtier incarnation—bit the dust when President Barack Obama recently made it clear that he is against legalizing marijuana. His message was delivered on his website, Change.gov, even before he placed his hand on the Lincoln Bible. Astonishingly, legalization of marijuana ranked as Priority No. 1 for the new administration among the thousands of possible actions voted upon on the website by the public—yes, even above stem cell research, the war in Iraq, and Wall Street bailouts. Obama's prompt no to the query "Will you consider legalizing marijuana so that the government can regulate it, tax it, put age limits on it, and create millions of new jobs and create a billion-dollar industry right here in the U.S.?" dashed the hopes of many who thought our young, hip, new president—who long ago dabbled in the stuff and, by his own admission, inhaled—would come to marijuana's rescue.

2   Listen to the president's inauguration speech, and it seems clear why he's unwilling. In a "new era of responsibility," somehow a fat new billion-dollar U.S. marijuana industry doesn't quite square with a world that almost universally outlaws the stuff. Making weed as accessible to our children as cigarettes doesn't fit with Obama's words to parents about nurturing their children, as he and Michelle so sweetly do their own little girls. And it would be the antithesis of the inaugural pledge he made to respect science.

3   Scientific research from the National Institute on Drug Abuse and elsewhere leaves little doubt that marijuana abuse is bad for brains, particularly younger ones. The psychoactive chemical in weed, THC (short for delta-9-tetrahydrocannabinol), binds to a class of receptors known as cannabinoids that are dense on neurons in brain areas associated with thinking, memory, concentration, sensation, time perception, and emotions like fear, anxiety, and pleasure. Once THC has delivered its buzz, it hangs around for days, if not many weeks, accumulating with regular use. The lingering chemical makes drug testing possible long after the last

puff, and it also means that weekend joints carry a low-grade marijuana haze into the next week, perhaps contributing to marijuana's so-called amotivational syndrome.

4   Researchers remain unsure whether the residual effects of cannabis on intellectual performance, attention span, and learning ability now identified in users (including college students) represent lingering drug, withdrawal symptoms, or toxic damage. Evidence is accumulating, however, that heavy drug use is associated with lasting damage. Just published in the journal *Pediatrics* is a preliminary study of young men who had been heavy marijuana users starting in their early teens. MRI scans showed disrupted neural development in the brain areas that influence memory, attention, and high level decision making, areas known to develop and mature during adolescence.

5   As for marijuana's association with anxiety, depression, and suicidal or even psychotic thinking, it's hard to say whether the mental disturbances are caused by the drug or are the trigger for its use in those already struggling with a mental illness. But however it's argued, academic stars are rarely potheads, and regular exposure to this powerful psychoactive drug is a nasty idea for developing young minds trying to study hard, mature emotionally, and get started in life.

6   Moreover, contrary to popular thought, NIDA stresses that marijuana can be physiologically and psychologically addictive. And Australian scientists recently reported that cannabis junkies hooked for more than 10 years develop brain injury. Compared with matched controls, users in this relatively small but provocative study scored lower on mental health and cognitive performance measures, and their MRI scans showed brain shrinkage in regions targeted by cannabis. Face it: Were the crude, dried, ground weed reviewed by the Food and Drug Administration for safety, it would flunk on its brain effects alone.

7   Yet cannabis has adverse effects on more than the brain. The heart is stressed by marijuana, which for one thing elevates serum triglycerides that bring coronary disease risk. Marijuana is a serious respiratory irritant that serves up more carcinogenic hydrocarbons than tobacco smoke. When pregnant women smoke, the drug gets into the fetus; in nursing mothers, it enters breast milk. And in the cannabis-receptor-laden testicles, there is growing evidence from the laboratory and in humans that THC causes mutant sperm, which among other things can't swim right—thus impairing male fertility, at least while the male and his sperm are under the influence.

8   Clearly, legalization of medical marijuana use is a more persuasive battle cry than that of recreational highs. The FDA has al-

ready approved synthetic THC in pill and suppository form to stimulate appetite (the marijuana "munchies") and to ease the nausea of chemotherapy in seriously ill or terminal patients. Anti-inflammatory and pain-perception benefits may be important as well.

9   All that said, the science remains immature and stymied by ideological and moral objections, at a time when there is much to be learned both about a drug that's so commonly used and about the body's own natural and still-mysterious cannabinoid receptor network. In the spirit of honoring science and an open mind, such work should be pursued—and, I might add, compassion and consideration afforded the sick and dying who use marijuana under a doctor's care.

10   As for the rest of society, arguments for legalization will rage: End the criminal underground that prohibition fosters; let adults be free to grow and smoke whatever they wish; or, lamely, pot's no worse than other—legal—vices. But as I see it, in an age of responsibility, protecting our young people's health is the stronger imperative and should rightfully keep policymakers from cozying up to this brain-toxic drug.

Bill James

Cooperstown and the 'Roids

Bill James (born 1949) is one of the most influential people in baseball history—though he never played the game professionally. A statistician who has brought social science methods, an open mind, and excellent writing ability to the study of professional baseball, James since the late 1970s has written many books and articles about baseball history and the performance of baseball players and teams. As a result of his work and the work of like-minded individuals affiliated with the Society for American Baseball Research, people now consider ballpark factors when they evaluate players, newspapers publish "onbase plus slugging percentages" as well as batting averages, and teams look at hard numbers (not just what they see with the naked eye) when they evaluate prospects. Amazingly, *Time* named him one of the one hundred most influential people in the world in 2006. James now serves as an adviser to the Boston Red Sox and maintains a Web site, billjamesonline.com, where the essay below appeared in July 2009.

For the last ten years or so people have been asking me to comment on the issue of steroids and the Hall of Fame. To this point I have resisted addressing these questions, arguing—as I do with the Hall of Fame status of active players—that there is nothing to be gained by trying to guess where objects still in motion will eventually land. With the passage of time the dust will settle, and we will see the issue more clearly.

2   After ten years, however, the dust does not seem to be settling very rapidly. There seem to be as many different and contradictory opinions on the issue now as there were five or eight years ago. We are all tired of arguing about it, but we still don't agree. In any case, I am finally ready to say what I have to say about it. It is my opinion that, in time, the use of steroids or other Performance Enhancing Drugs will mean virtually nothing in the debate about who gets into the Hall of Fame and who does not.

3   The process of arriving at this conclusion began when I was studying aging patterns in the post-steroid era. One of the characteristics of the steroid era was that we had several dozen players who continued to improve beyond the normal aging time frame, so that many of them had their best seasons past the age of 32. This is historically not normal. In the post-steroid era we are returning to the historic norm in which players hit a wall sometime in their early thirties. But what does this mean?

4   It means that *steroids keep you young.* You may not like to hear it stated that way, because steroids are evil, wicked, mean and nasty and youth is a good thing, but . . . that's what it means. Steroids help the athlete resist the effects of aging.

5   Well, if steroids help keep you young, what's wrong with that?

6   What's wrong with that is that steroids may help keep players "young" at some risk to their health, and the use of steroids by athletes may lead non-athletes to risk their health as well. But the fact is that, with time, the use of drugs like steroids will not disappear from our culture. It will, in fact, grow, eventually becoming so common that it might almost be said to be ubiquitous. *Everybody wants to stay young.* As we move forward in time, more and more people are *going* to use more and more drugs in an effort to stay young. Many of these drugs are going to be steroids or the descendants of steroids.

7   If we look into the future, then, we can reliably foresee a time in which *everybody is going to be using steroids* or their pharmaceutical descendants. We will learn to control the health risks of these drugs, or we will develop alternatives to them. Once that happens, people will start living to age 200 or 300 or 1,000, and

doctors will begin routinely prescribing drugs to help you live to be 200 or 300 or 1,000. If you look into the future 40 or 50 years, I think it is quite likely that every citizen will routinely take anti-aging pills every day.

8   How, then, are those people of the future—who are taking steroids every day—going to look back on base-ball players who used steroids? They're going to look back on them as pioneers. They're going to look back at it and say "So what?"

9   The argument for discriminating against PED users rests upon the assumption of the moral superiority of non-drug users. But in a culture in which *everyone* routinely uses steroids, that argument cannot possibly prevail. You can like it or you can dislike it, but your grandchildren are going to be steroid users. Therefore, they are very likely to be people who do not regard the use of steroids as a moral failing. They are more likely to regard the banning of steroids as a bizarre artifice of the past.

10   Let us suppose that I am entirely wrong about all of that; let us suppose that our grandchildren do *not* wind up regularly ingesting chemicals to extend their youth. I would still argue that, in the long run, the use of steroids will eventually become a non-issue in who gets into the Hall of Fame.

11   My second argument is this:

1. Eventually, *some* players who have been associated with steroids are going to get into the Hall of Fame. This is no longer at issue. One cannot keep Barry Bonds, Roger Clemens, A-Rod, Manny Ramirez, Mark McGwire, Sammy Sosa and all of the others out of the Hall of Fame forever. *Some* of them have to get in. If nothing else, somebody will eventually get in and *then* acknowledge that he used steroids.

2. Once *some* players who have been associated with steroids are in the Hall of Fame, the argument against the others will become un-sustainable.

12   When the time comes at which two or three or four players are in the Hall of Fame who have acknowledged some steroid use, the barrier to other steroid users rests upon some sort of balancing test. Did this player use *too many* steroids to be considered legitimate? Is his career a creation of the steroids? Would he have been a Hall of Fame player without the steroids?

13   I am not suggesting that it is inappropriate for any one sportswriter or any one Hall of Fame voter to balance these considerations as best he can. But one does not build a house upon a well-balanced rock. The way that each sportswriter looks at these

issues is going to be different from the way that each other looks at them. There can only be a consensus on one of two positions:

a. that steroid users should not be in the Hall of Fame,

or

b. that steroid use is not an issue in the debate.

14   Between the two extreme positions, it becomes a fluid discussion. Once we move away from the one extreme, in my view, we will begin to drift inevitably toward the other.

15   I would liken this to attitudes about sexuality and television. At one point there was a firm consensus that there was no place for sex on TV. Married couples, on TV, slept in twin beds. The first departures from this firm position were small and insignificant . . . PBS specials on prostitution, chewing gum and soft drink commercials that pushed the boundaries of "taste", and edited-for-TV movies that were not quite as edited as they would have been a few years ago. Once there was no longer a firm consensus at an extreme position, there was a fluid standard that moved inevitably toward more and more openness about sexuality.

16   I will note that this happened without the consent and without the approval of most of the American public. It was never true that *most* people wanted to see more sex on TV. Probably it was generally true that most Americans disliked what they regarded as the erosion of standards of decency. But it was always true that *some* people wanted to see more sex on TV, and that was all that mattered, because that created a market for shows that pushed the envelope, and thus eroded the barriers. It was like a battle line that disintegrated once the firing started. The importance of holding the battle line, in old-style military conflict, was that once the line was breached, there was no longer an organized point of resistance. Once the consensus against any sexual references on TV was gone, there was no longer any consensus about what the standards should be—thus, a constant moving of the standards.

17   I think the same thing will happen here: Once there is no longer a firm consensus against steroid users in the Hall of Fame, there will be a fluid situation which moves inevitably in the direction of more and more inclusiveness. It is not necessary that people approve of this movement in principle. It is only necessary that there be advocates for those who are still on the outside looking in . . . for Sammy Sosa, let's say, and Manny Ramirez. And there is no question that there will be those advocates.

18   Third argument. History is forgiving. Statistics endure.

19   At the time that Dick Allen left the major leagues, virtually no one thought of him as a Hall of Fame player. In his first year of

eligibility for the Hall of Fame, he received the support of a little less than 4% of the voters. In his fifteen years of eligibility for BBWAA selection, he never reached 20% in the voting.

20   Dick Allen did not have imaginary sins or imaginary failings as a player. He had very real offenses. But as time passes, the details of these incidents (and eventually the incidents themselves) are forgotten, and it becomes easier for Allen's advocates to re-interpret them as situations in which Allen was the victim, rather than the aggressor or offender. The people who were there die off. A certain number of people want to play the role of Dick Allen's ad-vocate. No one—including me—wants to play the role of persistently denigrating Dick Allen; in fact, I'm pretty sure you can go to hell for that. People who were friends of Dick Allen speak up; the dozens or hundreds of exteammates who despised Dick Allen keep silent, or speak of him as well as they can manage.

21   For very good reasons, we do not nurture hatred. We let things pass. This leads history to be forgiving. Perhaps it is right, perhaps it is wrong, but that is the way it is. Sometime between 2020 and 2030, Dick Allen will be elected to the Hall of Fame.

22   The same thing has happened, more slowly, with the Black Sox. In 1950 no one thought Joe Jackson should be in the Hall of Fame. Now it is a common opinion—perhaps a majority opinion—that he should. People question whether he "really" did the things that he clearly admitted doing. His virtues are celebrated; his sins are minimized. Perhaps this is right; perhaps it is wrong. It is the way of history.

23   History will rally on the side of the steroid users in the same way that it has rallied on the side of Dick Allen, Joe Jackson, Orlando Cepeda, Hack Wilson and many others. But with the steroid users, we are not talking about a single isolated "offender", but about a large group of them, representing the bulk of the domi-nant players of their generation. The forces that push for their acceptance will get organized much more quickly and will move with much greater force. This, in my view, will make the use of steroids a non-factor in Hall of Fame discussions within 30 to 40 years.

24   Fourth argument. Old players play a key role in the Hall of Fame debate. It seems unlikely to me that aging ballplayers will di-vide their ex-teammates neatly into classes of "steroid users" and "non-steroid users."

25   One of the key reasons that Dick Allen will eventually be in the Hall of Fame is that one of his ex-teammates—Goose Gossage—feels strongly that he should be, and is outspoken on this issue. Goose Gossage is now a Hall of Famer. His voice carries weight.

26   Eventually, younger players who were teammates of Mark McGwire, Sammy Sosa, A-Rod and Roger Clemens are going to be in the Hall of Fame. Andy Pettitte is probably going to be in the Hall of Fame. When he is in the Hall of Fame—if he gets there before Roger—he is *going* to speak up for Roger Clemens. Hell, somebody might even speak up for Barry Bonds.

27   Once this happens, it will erode the prejudice against steroid users in the Hall of Fame, to the extent that that prejudice might otherwise exist. *You* might choose to divide the world of baseball players into steroid users and non-steroid users, but this is not a division that makes intuitive sense when you know the people involved. Therefore, this is not the division that will ultimately endure, once the long historical sorting-out process that makes Goose Gossage relevant and Lindy McDaniel irrelevant has run its course.

28   I have a fifth argument here, but before I get to that, let me speak for a moment on the other side of the issue. Let us adopt, as the face of the non-steroid user, Will Clark. Will Clark and Rafael Palmeiro were college teammates, and apparently were not the best of friends. As players they were rivals. Texas had Palmeiro (1989-1993) and then had Clark (1994-1998), while Palmeiro went to Baltimore. After the 1998 season the Orioles—then a strong franchise—signed Clark, while Palmeiro went back to the Rangers. Later on Palmeiro went back to the Orioles, so that both the Rangers and the Orioles had Palmeiro, then Clark, then Palmeiro. There was always a debate about which was the better player.

29   I've always been a great admirer of Will Clark, who I think was a great player and is a historically under-rated player in part because his numbers are dimmed by comparison to the steroid-inflated numbers that came just after him. Will Clark, in the pre-steroid era, was a much better player than Palmeiro, although Palmeiro was good. Palmeiro, as we entered the steroid era, gradually pulled ahead of Clark. I have no idea whether Will Clark ever used steroids or not, but let us use Will Clark as the face of the player who chose *not* to use steroids in order to stay in the game, the player who chose the natural route and suffered the consequences of that.

30   Is it fair to Will Clark to compare him to players who chose to cheat in order to move beyond that level? No, it is not. Absolutely, it is not. But the critical issue is, Is this cheating? If you choose to regard it as cheating, if you choose not to support the Hall of Fame candidacy of a steroid user because you regard it as cheating, I would not argue with you. I think that Will Clark has a perfect right to feel that he was cheated out of a fair chance to compete for honors in his time, and, if you choose to look at it

from the standpoint of Will Clark, I don't think that you are wrong to do so.

31   But at the same time, I do not believe that history will look at this issue from the standpoint of Will Clark. I don't see how it can. What it seems to me that the Will Clark defenders have not come to terms with is the breadth and depth of the PED problem, which began in the 1960s and expanded without resistance for almost 40 years, eventually involving generations of players. It seems to me that the Will Clark defenders are still looking at the issue as one of "some" players gaining an advantage by using Performance Enhancing Drugs. But it wasn't really an issue of *some* players gaining an advantage by the use of Performance Enhancing Drugs; it is an issue of *many* players using Performance Enhancing drugs in competition with one another. Nobody knows how many. It would be my estimate that it was somewhere between 40 and 80%.

32   The discrimination against PED users in Hall of Fame voting rests upon the perception that this was *cheating.* But is it cheating if one violates a rule that nobody is enforcing, and which one may legitimately see as being widely ignored by those within the competition?

33   It seems to me that, at some point, this becomes an impossible argument to sustain—that all of these players were "cheating," in a climate in which most everybody was doing the same things, and in which there was either no rule against doing these things or zero enforcement of those rules. If one player is using a corked bat, like Babe Ruth, clearly, he's cheating. But if 80% of the players are using corked bats and no one is enforcing any rules against it, are they all cheating? One better: if 80% of the players are using corked bats and it is unclear whether there are or are not any rules against it, is that cheating?

34   And . . . was there really a rule against the use of Performance Enhancing Drugs? At best, it is a debatable point. The Commissioner issued edicts banning the use of Performance Enhancing Drugs. People who were raised on the image of an all-powerful commissioner whose every word was law are thus inclined to believe that there was a rule against it.

35   But "rules," in civilized society, have certain characteristics. They are agreed to by a process in which all of the interested parties participate. They are included in the rule book. There is a process for enforcing them. Someone is assigned to enforce the rule, and that authority is given the powers necessary to enforce the rule. There are specified and reasonable punishments for violation of the rules.

36   The "rule" against Performance Enhancing Drugs, if there was such a rule before 2002, by-passed all of these gates. It was never

agreed to by the players, who clearly and absolutely have a right to participate in the process of changing any and all rules to which they are subject. It was not included in any of the various rule books that define the conduct of the game from various perspectives. There was no process for enforcing such a rule. The punishments were draconian in theory and non-existent in fact.

37   It seems to me that, with the passage of time, more people will come to understand that the commissioner's periodic spasms of self-righteousness do not constitute baseball law. It seems to me that the argument that it is cheating must ultimately collapse under the weight of carrying this great contradiction—that 80% of the players are cheating against the other 20% by violating some "rule" to which they never consented, which was never included in the rule books, and for which there was no enforcement procedure. History is simply *not* going to see it that way.

38   The end of the day here is about the year 2040, perhaps 2050. It will come upon us in a flash. And, at the end of the day, Mark McGwire is going to be in the Hall of Fame, and Roger Clemens, and Sammy Sosa, and Rafael Palmeiro, and probably even Barry Bonds. I am not especially advocating this; I simply think that is the way it is. I only hope that, when all of these players are enshrined, they will extend a hand up to a few players from the Will Clark division of the game.

Star MLB pitcher Roger Clemens and others are sworn in prior to their testimony before the U.S. House Oversight and Government Reform Committee investigation into allegations of widespread performance-enhancing drug use in Major League Baseball.

Oscar Pistorius, a world-class athlete who runs on J-shaped prosthetic legs, won the right to participate in the 2012 London Olympics as a member of the South African team. Yet controversy surrounding the decision did not abate. Some felt the sprinter's carbon-fiber prostheses gained him an advantage. Others simply felt Olympic athletes should rely solely on their own innate talents to compete. Despite progress in eliminating barriers to full participation in society for disabled people, questions remain. How far should society go—and at what cost—to accommodate people with disabilities? And how true is the adage of disabilities advocates that "Attitudes are the real disability"?

TERRENCE **RAFFERTY**

Kate Winslet, Please Save Us!

Brooklyn native Terrence Rafferty is a film critic whose articles have appeared in the *Atlantic*, the *Village Voice, Film Quarterly*, the *New York Times*, and many other publications. He also has been the "critic-at-large" for *GQ* (short for *Gentleman's Quarterly*), a fashion and culture magazine geared to young professional men. *GQ* carried the following argument in May 2001. Do you think the argument would have been constructed differently if it had been published elsewhere?

When I go to the movies these days, I sometimes find myself gripped by a very peculiar sort of nostalgia: I miss flesh. I see skin, I see bones, I see many rocklike outcroppings of muscle, but I rarely see, in the angular bodies up there on the screen—either the hard, sculpted ones or the brittle, anorexic ones—anything extra, not even a hint of the soft layer of fatty tissue that was once an essential component of the movies' romantic fantasy, the cushion that made encounters between the sexes seem like pleasant, sensual experiences rather than teeth-rattling head-on collisions. The sleek form-follows-function physiques of today's film stars suggest a world in which power and brutal efficiency are all that matter, in the bedroom no less than in the pitiless, sun-seared arena of Gladiator. This may well be an accurate reflection of our anxious time, but it's also mighty depressing. When I come out of the multiplex now, I often feel like the archetypal ninety-eight-pound weakling in the old Charles Atlas ads—like big bullies have been kicking sand in my face for two hours. And that's just the women.

Kate Moss, waiflike

2   This is a touchy area, I realize. Where body type is concerned, an amazingly high percentage of social and cultural commentary is fueled by simple envy, resentment of the young and the buff. A few years ago, when Calvin Klein ads featuring the stunning, wai-flike Kate Moss appeared on the sides of New York City buses, they were routinely defaced with bitter-sounding graffiti—FEED ME was the most popular—which was, you had to suspect, largely the product of women who were enraged by her distinctive beauty. (Men, to my knowledge, had few complaints about having to see Moss in her underwear whiz past them on Madison Avenue.) Protesters insisted that images such as those in the Klein ads promote eating disorders in impressionable teenage girls. Maybe that's so—I don't have the statistics—but the sheer violence of the attacks on Moss, along with the fact that they seemed to be directed more at the model herself than at the marketing wizards who exploited her, strongly suggested another, less virtuous agenda. The taste of sour grapes was unmistakable.

3   I happened to think Moss looked great—small, but well-proportioned, and mercifully lacking the ropy musculature that had begun to creep into pop-culture images of femininity, in the cunning guise of "empowerment." The Bionic Woman could only dream of the bulging biceps sported by Linda Hamilton in *Terminator 2: Judgment Day* (1991); and Ginger Rogers, even when she was struggling to match steps with Astaire, never had the calf muscles of the mighty Madonna. (Nor would she have wanted them: She was a dancer and not, like Mrs. Ritchie or any of her brood of MTV chicks, a kinky aerobics instructor.) It's understandable, I suppose, that women might have felt the impulse to bulk up during the might-makes-right regimes of Ronald Reagan and George Herbert Walker Bush, when the rippling behemoths of machismo, Arnold and Sly, ruled the screen; in that context, working on one's abs and pecs could be considered a prudent strategy of self-defense. But the arms buildup in the Cold War between the sexes was not a pretty sight. Applied to sex, the doctrine of Mutually Assured Destruction is kind of a bummer. The wages of sinew is the death of romance.

4   At least that's how it looks to people of my generation, whose formative years were the '60s, and to many of Moss's generation (the one commonly designated "X"), who in their youth embraced, for a while, the antipower aesthetic of grunge. What we oversaturated pop-culture consumers consider attractive— i.e., what's sexy in the

opposite gender and worth aspiring to in one's own—usually develops in adolescence, as the relevant body parts do, and doesn't change much thereafter. For men older than I am, the perfect woman might have been Sophia Loren or Elizabeth Taylor or Marilyn Monroe or Rita Hayworth or the wartime pinup Betty Grable or (reaching back to the hugely eroticized flapper era) the original It girl, Clara Bow. And for them, the image of the ideal masculine self might have been Cary Grant or Clark Gable or Henry Fonda or Gary Cooper or even, for the less physically prepossessing—OK, shorter—guys, Cagney or Bogart or Tracy. By the time the '60s rocked and rolled into history, some subtle transformations had occurred, primarily in female sexual iconography. While the male stars of that decade remained more or less within the range of body types of their predecessors—Steve McQueen and Sean Connery might have looked a bit more athletic than the old norms demanded, but they wouldn't qualify as hard-bodies by today's standards—the shape of desirability in women distinctly altered, to something less voluptuous and more elongated. The fashions of the era tended to shift the erotic focus southward, from the breasts and the hips down to the legs, which, in a miniskirt, did rather overwhelm all other possible indicators of a woman's sexual allure. Although smaller-chested, leaner-hipped women, such as Julie Christie, stole some thunder from the conspicuously curvaceous, a certain amount of flesh was still required. Minis didn't flatter skinny legs any more than they did chubby ones.

5   So there was, to the avid eyes of teenage boys like me, a fine balance struck in the body aesthetic of the '60s, between, so to speak, length and width, Giacometti and Rubens. And muscles weren't part of the equation. He-men such as Steve Reeves—whose 1959 *Hercules,* a cheap Italian import initiated a spate of "sword and sandal" epics—seemed, to both sexes, ridiculous, vain rather than truly manly. (It's worth noting that in those days it was widely perceived that the primary market for body-building magazines was gay men.) And women? Forget it. The epitome of the muscular gal was the Russian or East German Olympic athlete, an Olga or a Helga, whose gender identity was frequently, and often justly, a matter of some dispute. There's an echo of that attitude in Ridley Scott's 1997 *G.I. Jane,* in which a feminist senator played by Anne Bancroft, trying to select a candidate for the first woman to undergo Navy SEAL training, summarily dismisses several of the beefier applicants on the grounds of ambiguous sexuality. She settles on Demi Moore, who is slender and pretty and, on the evidence of a spectacularly obvious boob job, unquestionably straight.

6   But bodies like Moore's puzzle me. What, exactly, is the empowering element here—the iron she's pumped or the silicone that's been pumped into her chest? My number one teenage crush, Diana Rigg, didn't need either in order to be wholly convincing as kick-ass secret agent Emma Peel in the TV series *The Avengers.* Paired with a dapper male partner, John Steed (played by Patrick Macnee), Mrs. Peel was not only fully empowered but was also by far the more physically active of the two. In her mod pantsuits and go-go boots, she did most of the actual fighting in the kung fu-ish battles that climaxed virtually every episode, while Steed, perhaps mindful of potential damage to his impeccably cut Pierre Cardin suits, generally limited his martial activity to an occasional deft thrust with the umbrella.

7   Maybe if I'd come of age with visions of Madonna dancing in my head, I might find GI Demi devastatingly sexy rather than grotesque, but, objectively, I think the idea that women's power depends on either sculpted muscles or gigantic, orblike

breasts (much less both) smacks of desperation. Mrs. Peel wielded her power so coolly, so confidently, and clearly never felt the need to enhance it by strenuous training or expensive medical procedures. Comfort in one's own skin is always appealing, which is probably why, in this sweating, striving, aggressively self-improving era, I find bodies as diverse as Kate Moss's and Kate Winslet's mighty attractive. It's not the body type per se—neither the frail Kate nor the ampler one precisely conforms to my Riggian ideal—but a woman's attitude toward her body that makes her sexy.

Kate Winslet from *Titanic* days

8   What's unnerving about today's popculture images of women is how extreme they are—and how much emphasis they place on the *effort* required to correct nature, to retard the aging process, to be all that you can be (and not, God forbid, simply what you are). The ethic of progress through hard work and technology is deeply ingrained in our society, as is the democratic notion that everyone should be whatever he or she wants to be— a noble idea that gets a tad problematic when what everyone wants to be is a star. And every star wants to be a bigger star. As a result, we're seeing, in the movies and on television and in the pages of fashion magazines, increasingly bizarre manifestations of our paradoxical collective need to feel unique and, more, admired. Being really fat, for example, can confer on a person a certain distinction, but not the kind most of us yearn for. (In the old days, for men, a degree of heft often indicated prosperity; the movies embodied their image of financial success in portly figures such as Eugene Pallette and Edward Arnold. No more.) To stand out on the runway these days, a model has to be significantly gaunter—and younger—than even the FEED ME–era Moss. And to make her mark on the screen, an actress has several equally grueling options: starve herself skeletal, go to the gym and get muscular, or—sometimes in perverse combination with one of the previous—have her breasts inflated surgically. In each case, the result is a wild exaggeration of what would be, in moderation, a desirable quality: slimness, fitness or voluptuousness. When I look at women in the movies now, I often feel as if I were gazing not at real people but at cartoon characters—Olive Oyl, Popeye (in drag) and Jessica Rabbit.

9   Of course, there are exceptions: the spectacular Winslet; the cherubic and blissfully unself-conscious Drew Barrymore; the graceful, athletic Asian stars Michelle Yeoh and Maggie Cheung; and (no epithet necessary) Julia Roberts. But too many of the screen's great beauties have been developing a lean and hungry look in recent years. They've felt the burn, and something more than body fat appears to have been eliminated—a certain amount of joy seems to have melted away at the same time. Clearly, we live in extraordinarily ruthless and competitive times; and popular culture is bound

to reflect that condition, but I can't think of another age in which the competitive anxieties of the performers themselves were so mercilessly exposed to the public's view. When tough, chunky guys like Cagney squared off against one another in a boxing ring or on the mean streets of New York or Chicago, you sensed that the survival of an entire community of immigrants was at stake; you could see it in every movement of their squat brawler's bodies. And when the Depression was over, those fierce small men just about vanished from the movies, giving way to their larger, better-nourished children, who left the field, in turn, to generations who would be conscious of their bodies without having nearly as much use for them as their ancestors had had. What's at stake for today's action heroes and heroines, all pumped up with no place to go except to the "explosive" climax of a fanciful plot? The steroidal action pictures of the '80s and '90s created a race of pointless Supermen. Everyone in the audience was in on the joke: Bruce Willis and Tom Cruise and Nicolas Cage and Keanu Reeves didn't bulk up to save the world or any recognizable part of it; they did it because starring in an action franchise was, and remains, a surefire means of moving up the Hollywood ladder.

10 As the historian Lynne Luciano points out in her useful new book, *Looking Good: Male Body Image in America,* in a white-collar, service economy all most of us do with our bodies is compare them with everybody else's. We look, we admire, we envy, we check the mirror, we get dissatisfied, we go back to the old drawing board (the gym, the plastic surgeon, Jenny Craig, whatever). And this strikes many as perfectly reasonable and natural: You have to keep an edge, and you have to *work* on it. Constant vigilance is required for both men and women, and folks are starting to look a little haggard. This applies even to the beautiful people of the silver screen. We can see the strain as they try to hang on to their precarious positions, like Tom Cruise at the beginning of *M.I.2.* And who, aside from the stars themselves, their families and their agents, could possibly care?

11 I haven't used the word *narcissism* yet, and it's long overdue. The unseemly vanity once ascribed to poor Steve Reeves has become the norm in Hollywood, which, kind of hilariously, apparently believes that we're so vain we probably think their movies are about us. I can't come up with another explanation for berserk pictures like David Fincher's *Fight Club* (1999), in which Edward Norton, as a harried white collar Everyman, takes as his guru and alter ego an alarmingly buff *Übermensch* played by Brad Pitt. If the weak box-office returns are any indication, *Fight Club* did not strike the deep chord in the hearts of American men that its makers evidently thought it would, and, to add insult to injury, the picture didn't even provoke the "controversy" that might have validated the artists' sense of their own fearlessness and edginess. The whole spectacle was simply self-important and silly—as silly as *Hercules* and, because no one involved seemed to recognize it, then some.

12 It's time to stop the madness. Sure, we viewers are stressed-out and perhaps slightly self-absorbed, but more of us than Hollywood thinks have some perspective on the absurdities of our lives and the inanities of our culture. Fewer of us than the studios imagine actually believe that a diet or a set of weights or silicone implants will change our lives, even if every movie star worth his or her (pardon the expression) salt apparently does believe it. That's their business, and, as we know—though Hollywood has obviously forgotten— there's *no* business like show business. The feral, predatory creatures prowling across the screen for our amusement are in a world of their own. And although they carry themselves as if they

were wolves, magnificent in their power, they're really just coyotes, roaming the hills restlessly for scraps and deluding themselves even more doggedly than Chuck Jones's indefatigable Wile E. At least he knew what he was.

13   In a sense, body image represents the final frontier of postmodernism, the only area as yet untouched by our culture's pervasive irony. It would be useful, I think, for moviemakers to drop the pretense that entertainment is a life-and-death struggle, which only the strong survive. The stars of earlier eras, with their variety of unapologetically eccentric physiques, understood it was all a lovely con, a game played for pleasure: That's what those discreet little layers of flesh ultimately meant. But what would it take, I wonder, to make today's hardbodies lighten up and laugh at their own desperate exertions or, failing that, merely stop gazing out at us cowed viewers as if they were dying to beat the crap out of us? I don't know, but I suspect that cranky magazine columns won't do the job. A higher power will have to be invoked. Mrs. Peel, you're needed.

Rebecca Traister

"Real Beauty"—Or Really Smart Marketing?

Rebecca Traister is staff writer for the "Life" section of *Salon*, the online news and culture journal that carried the following article in 2005. Her work typically considers issues related to women, gender, and power and has been published in a variety of publications, including *ELLE*, the *New York Times*, *Vogue*, and the *Nation*.

The words appear slowly, against the familiar powder-blue shape of the bird in flight—the Dove soap symbol—like soothing, watery poetry:

> *For too long*
> *beauty has been defined by narrow, stifling sterotypes [sic].*
> *You've told us it's time to change all that. We agree.*
> *Because we believe real beauty comes*
> *In many shapes, sizes and ages.*
> *It is why we started the Campaign for Real Beauty.*
> *And why we hope you'll take part.*

2   This is the lilting intro to the Web site that Dove has dedicated to its "Real Beauty" advertising campaign, for which it has picked six women who are not professional models—each beautiful, but

broader than Bundchen, heftier than an Olsen twin—to model in bras and panties.

3   The campaign is massive; these six broads are currently featured in national television and magazine ads, as well as on billboards and the sides of buses in urban markets like Boston, Chicago, Washington, Dallas, Los Angeles, Miami, New York, and San Francisco. And they've made quite an impact. Apparently, this public display of non-liposuctioned thighs is so jaw-droppingly revelatory that recent weeks have seen the Real Beauty models booked on everything from "The Today Show" to "The View" to CNN.

4   All the hoopla is precisely what Dove expected. According to a press release, Dove wants "to make women feel more beautiful every day by challenging today's stereotypical view of beauty and inspiring women to take great care of themselves." The use of "real women" (don't think too hard about the Kate Mosses of the world losing their status as biological females here) "of various ages, shapes and sizes" is designed "to provoke discussion and debate about today's typecast beauty images."

5   It's a great idea—a worthy follow-up to Dove's 2004 campaign, which featured women with lined faces, silver hair and heavy freckles, and asked questions like, "Wrinkled? Or Wonderful?" and also got a lot of attention, including a shout-out on the "Ellen DeGeneres Show."

6   As Stacy Nadeau, one of the Real Beauty models and a full-time student from Ann Arbor, Mich., says on the campaign Web site, "I have always been a curvier girl and always will be. I am proud of my body and think all women should be proud of theirs too. This is my time to encourage and help women feel great about themselves, no matter what they weigh or look like. Women have surrendered to diets and insane eating habits to live up to social stereotypes for too long. It's time that all women felt beautiful in their own skin."

7   But let's hope that skin doesn't have any cellulite. Because no one wants to look at a cottage-cheesy ass.

8   That's right. The one little wrinkle—so to speak—in this you-go-grrl stick-it-to-the-media-man empowerment campaign is that the set of Dove products that these real women are shilling for is *cellulite firming cream*. Specifically, Dove's new "Intensive Firming Cream," described as "a highly effective blend of glycerin, plus seaweed extract and elastin peptides known for their skin-firming properties." It's supposed "to work on problem areas to help skin feel firmer and reduce the appearance of cellulite in two weeks." There are also the Intensive Firming Lotion and the Firming Moisturizing Body Wash, which do pretty much the same thing.

9   The ad copy on the posters—in which the women stand alone, often looking over their rounded backsides—is composed of sing-it-sister lines like "Let's face it, firming the thighs of a size 2 supermodel is no challenge" and "New Dove Firming. As tested on real curves."

10   Meanwhile, on its Web site, Dove encourages us to get behind something called "The Dove Self-Esteem Fund," which involves a partnership with the Girl Scouts (and a program called *uniquely ME!*). It is supposed to help "girls to overcome life damaging hang-ups by putting beauty into perspective." Yes, when I think of putting beauty in perspective for girls, mostly I think of suggesting that they shell out for three separately sold products that will temporarily make it appear that they have less cellulite.

11   It's not that I have anything against firming cream. By all means, sell firming cream! Go ahead! I'm even prepared to believe that it may be a useful tool for women who truly are plagued by their cellulite and are thankful to have a product that can help them combat it. I also understand that companies sell stuff. They advertise, they flog product; thus is life and business.

12   But as long as you're patting yourself on the back for hiring real-life models with imperfect bodies, thereby "challenging today's stereotypical view of beauty and inspiring women to take great care of themselves," why ask those models to flog a cream that has zero health value and is just an expensive and temporary Band-Aid for a "problem" that the media has told us we have with our bodies. Incidentally, cellulite isn't even a result of being overweight! It's the result of cellular changes in the skin. Skinny people have cellulite. Old people have cellulite. Young people have cellulite. Gwyneth Paltrow has cellulite. All God's children have cellulite.

13   Why not run an ad that proclaims, "Cellulite: Uniquely MINE!"

14   Or, more realistically, why aren't these women selling shampoo? Or soap? Or moisturizer?

15   Stacie Bright, a spokeswoman for Unilever, Dove's parent company, emphasized that this campaign "is for women of all shapes and sizes, and a lot of women want firming products. It's about feeling good about yourself. And that's about bringing products that matter to women." Pressed on the inconsistency of having women who feel good about themselves sell a product that makes a lot of us feel bad about ourselves, Bright replied, "Let's face it, if you had a firming product, and you had a size 2 woman selling it, that would really be the contradiction."

16   Clearly the idea behind the campaign is a smart, worthwhile and rational one. It does feel refreshingly non-self-loathing to log

on to the Dove site and hear the models saying things like "I love these big ol' hips" and "I don't think about being slim." It's a little ray of sanity in this anorexic world. But it's also a business proposition and an advertising campaign. And doing something radically different—like presenting female consumers with models who actually resemble human beings they've met—is getting these products a lot of coveted attention. In fact, Dove may have tapped a zeitgeist vein, since the sport of lashing out at manipulated images of female beauty seems to be enjoying a bit of a vogue right now.

17   This spring, Oscar-winning actress Cate Blanchett spoke in interviews about her horror at the Botox craze. "I look at people sort of entombing themselves and all you see is their little pinholes of terror," said the actress. "And you think, Just live your life—death is not going to be any easier just because your face can't move." Blanchett also said that she thinks "that women and their vulnerabilities are played on in the cosmetic industry. . . . Women are encouraged to be terrified of aging." In this month's *Vogue*, Kate Winslet says of her battle with the press over her normal weight, "I'm relatively slim, I eat healthily, I keep fit. . . . I couldn't be 105 pounds even if I tried, and I really don't want to be 105 pounds."

18   And in just over a week, Bath and Body Works in association with American Girl dolls, will launch a line of "Real Beauty Inside and Out" personal care products "designed to help girls ages 8 to 12 feel—and be—their best." The line will include body lotions, splashes, soaps and lip balms, all dressed up in girl-friendly "hues of berry" and each arriving with an inspirational message like "Real beauty means no one's smile shines exactly like yours," "Real beauty is helping a friend," or "Real beauty is trusting in yourself."

19   It's a great gimmick—one that few of us can take issue with. But just like Dove's "love your ass but not the fat on it" campaign, much of this stuff prompts grim questions about whether it's even possible to break the feel-bad cycle of the beauty industry. Blanchett, after all, recently signed on as spokeswoman for SK-II line of cosmetics. And while it's all well and good to tell 8-year-old girls that real beauty is about trust, it's sort of funny to think about doing it while selling them minty lip shine or fruit-scented "My Way Styling Gel" for eight bucks a pop.

20   Let them be. After all, they have decades ahead of them in which to worry about eradicating the cellulite from their really beautiful curves.

The two visual arguments on this page, produced by an organization called Consumer Freedom, ridicule the idea that American corporations might be responsible for obesity.

David
Edelstein

Up in Smoke: Give Movies with Tobacco an Automatic 'R'

David Edelstein, an occasional playwright, is a film critic for *New York* magazine and National Public Radio's *Fresh Air*, as well as an occasional commentator on *CBS Sunday Morning*. His work has also appeared in the *Village Voice, Rolling Stone, Slate*, and the *New York Times*. The following blog post appeared on *New York* magazine's Web site in January 2010 as a response to a January 5 *New York Times* article by A. O. Scott called "Movies and Vice" that concluded, "Tobacco use is part of history—of movie history in particular. And in the course of that history lighting up has acquired connotations of individualism, rebellion, sophistication and sex that will be hard to eradicate even as they become increasingly shrouded in nostalgia."

A. O. Scott's meditation on tobacco in movies is a savvy piece of hipsterism: admit that smoking is bad but argue that anti-vice cultural crusaders are worse, and end with the hope that cigarettes will someday be akin to "time travel, or slapstick, or a mad drive to the airport to stop the one you love from getting on that plane—something that only happens in the movies." Those comparisons are facetious, of course. It's unlikely we'll see time travel in our lifetime; pratfalls in the real world are involuntary; and no one has to race to the airport in an era when anti-terrorist screenings hold passengers up for hours. Smoking, on the other hand, is a choice, and one that's deeply responsive to social cues. That's why tobacco companies pay millions to studios to have glamorous actors light up and strike sultry poses. In Scott's nicotine-fueled brain he knows this, but he doesn't want to sound like a bluestocking.

2   Over the years, I've gotten a lot of e-mails from anti-smoking groups demanding either a ban on cigarettes in movies or an automatic "R" rating when a character uses tobacco. My first response is indignation at the "nanny state." I remember how, more than two decades ago, I was forbidden from mentioning smoking in a profile I did in the late *Mirabella* on Jan Hooks, who chain-smoked through our two interviews. I loved her—but I also could see by how she smoked that she was very, very high-strung. It was an important detail, except that editor Grace Mirabella's husband, Dr. William Cahan, was an anti-tobacco crusader, and no mention of cigarettes was allowed in the magazine, ever. I fought and fought and finally, *finally* Mirabella yielded—but only if I wrote something like, "Her yellow-stained fingers trembling, she nervously inserted another death stick between her brown, misshapen teeth." I was furious. I still am.

3   On the other hand, editors at a well-known music publication that same year told me that no anti-smoking references would ever appear in their magazine: Tobacco companies paid big bucks for ads on the back cover and to sponsor the regular live-performance centerpiece. Against such vast financial resources, anti-smoking crusaders had no leverage. In the end, it was only the dread "nanny state" that could keep tobacco ads away from the young and impressionable.

4   These days, I don't believe that the anti-smoking crusaders are so out of line, at least in their demand that movies with cigarettes get an automatic "R" rating. No, that doesn't mean we expunge smoking from movies already made. We just make it tougher for new films with cigarette use to influence kids. Just as important, when tobacco companies pay to put their wares in a film, that information needs to appear in the credits— *prominently*. It's one thing when everyone lights up in *Good Night and Good Luck*, in which the ubiquitous tobacco smoke evokes the era better than anything onscreen. (Too bad there was no list at the end of all the characters' real-life counterparts who died of lung cancer or associated heart disease.) It's another when cigarettes are a product placement akin to Cheerios or Apple computers.

5   This isn't an easy call. I treasure the image of William Powell and Myrna Loy attempting to out-drink one another in *The Thin Man*—I think of it often as I order my fourth or fifth whiskey. Somewhere, I still have a poster of Cheech and Chong in *Up in Smoke*, which probably retains the aroma of the bong that sat proudly beneath it in my dorm room. And damn if Bogie and Belmondo aren't still the apogee of cool. Scott is dead right in arguing that vice in movies can be very entertaining. But for our kids' sake, let's treat the addiction to deadly chemicals *as* a vice and not as a normal, healthy part of everyday life.

6   *Update*: Some people have written to accuse me of having a double standard, and to say that, if one follows my logic, kids should no longer be exposed to drinking, overeating, brutally killing people, or anything that might corrupt our little angels. And then, of course, as one correspondent put it, "Our movies would be a little less true." I happen to believe that glamorizing the act of sucking tar and nicotine into one's lungs results in images a lot less true than, say, skeletal lung-cancer patients dissolving from the inside out in an Intensive Care Unit. But let's leave that aside. I'm not arguing that smoking should be banned from movies or *always* associated onscreen with delinquency or death. I enjoy movies about people doing things that might not be good for them, whether it's lighting up or shooting up or crashing cars or screwing sheep. Let's have a cinema for grown-ups that depicts anything and everything, healthy and unhealthy. But let's also keep tobacco companies and the greedheads who take their money from bombarding kids with the message that smoking is what cool people do.

Tony Newman

Criminalizing Smoking Is Not the Answer: Bans on Cloves and Outdoor Smoking Will Backfire!

Tony Newman is the director of media relations at the Drug Policy Alliance Network, which promotes policy alternatives to the War on Drugs. Before joining the organization, he was media director for the human rights organization Global Exchange and cofounded the public relations firm Communication Works. The following article appeared in September 2009 on *the Huffington Post*, an Internet newspaper known for a slightly left-of-center political stance.

The war on cigarettes is heating up. This week a new federal ban went into effect making flavored cigarettes and cloves illegal. The new regulation halted the sale of vanilla and chocolate cigarettes that anti-smoking advocates claim lure young people into smoking. This ban is the first major crackdown since Congress passed a law in June giving the Food and Drug Administration the authority to regulate tobacco. There is already talk of banning Menthol cigarettes next.

2   Meanwhile, another major initiative to limit smoking wafted out of New York City last week. A report to Mayor Michael Bloomberg from the city's Health Commissioner called for a smoking ban at city parks and beaches to help protect citizens from the harms of second hand smoke. To his credit, Bloomberg rejected this measure citing concern over stretched city and police resources.

3   While I support many restrictions on public smoking, such as at restaurants and workplaces, and I appreciate public education campaigns and efforts aimed at discouraging young people from smoking, I believe the outdoor smoking ban and prohibition of cloves and possibly Menthols will lead to harmful and unintended consequences. All we have to do is look at the criminalization of other drugs, such as marijuana, to see some of the potential pitfalls and tragedies.

4   Cities across the country—from New York to Santa Cruz, California—are considering or have already banned smoking at parks and beaches. I am afraid that issuing tickets to people for smoking outdoors could easily be abused by overzealous law enforcement.

5   Let's look at how New York handles another "decriminalized" drug in our state, marijuana. Despite decriminalizing marijuana more than 30 years ago, New York is the marijuana arrest capital of the world. If possession of marijuana is supposed to be decriminalized in New York, how does this happen? Often it's because, in the course of interacting with the police, individuals are

asked to empty their pockets, which results in the pot being "open to public view"—which is, technically, a crime.

6   More than 40,000 people were arrested in New York City last year for marijuana possession, and 87 percent of those arrested were black or Latino, despite equal rates of marijuana use among whites. The fact is that blacks and Latinos are arrested for pot at much higher rates in part because officers make stop-and-frisk searches disproportionately in black, Latino and low-income neighborhoods.

7   Unfortunately, when we make laws and place restrictions on both legal and illegal drugs, people of color are usually the ones busted. Drug use may not discriminate, but our drug policies and enforcement do.

8   Now let's look at the prohibition of cloves and other flavored cigarettes. When we prohibit certain drugs, it doesn't mean that the drugs go away and people don't use them; it just means that people get their drugs from the black market instead of a store or deli. We've been waging a war on marijuana and other drugs for decades, but you can still find marijuana and your drug of choice in most neighborhoods and cities in this country.

9   For many people, cloves or Menthols are their smoke of choice. I have no doubt that someone is going to step in to meet this demand. What do we propose doing to the people who are caught selling illegal cigarettes on the street? Are cops going to have to expend limited resources to enforce this ban? Are we going to arrest and lock up people who are selling the illegal cigarettes? Prisons are already bursting at the seams (thanks to the drug laws) in states across the country. Are we going to waste more taxpayer money on incarceration?

10   The prohibition of flavored cigarettes also moves us another step closer to total cigarette prohibition. But with all the good intentions in the world, outlawing cigarettes would be just as disastrous as the prohibition of other drugs. After all, people would still smoke, just as they still use other drugs that are prohibited, from marijuana to cocaine. But now, in addition to the harm of smoking, we would find a whole range of "collateral consequences," such as black market-related violence, that crop up with prohibition.

11   Although we should celebrate our success curbing cigarette smoking and continue to encourage people to cut back or give up cigarettes, let's not get carried away and think that criminalizing smoking is the answer.

12   We need to realize that drugs, from cigarettes to marijuana to alcohol, will always be consumed, whether they are legal or illegal. Although drugs have health consequences and dangers, making them illegal—and keeping them illegal—will only bring additional death and suffering.

A great many ads are distributed these days in an effort to discourage smoking. This ad was created in 2012 by the New York State Department of Health. What kind of audience is it designed to influence?

Garry Trudeau (born 1948) won the Pulitzer Prize in 1975 for his comic strip *Doonesbury*. The strip published here appeared in January 2002.

Doonesbury *copyright © 2002 G. B. Trudeau. Reprinted with permission of Universal Uclick. All rights reserved.*

JORDAN RUBIN

Beware of Saturday Morning Cartoons

Jordan Rubin, who has made a career out of advocating for healthier nutrition, gained his inspiration from biblical texts. Host of a weekly television show, motivational speaker, writer, and entrepreneur, he founded Garden of Life, a health and wellness company that distributes natural foods, healthy supplements, and educational materials. In 2004 he published *The Maker's Diet* (also known as "the Bible diet"), and he has written many other books and articles promoting his views on healthy nutrition. The following article appeared in 2011 as a blog entry on the Web site *Raw Vitamins*, which offers advice about healthy nutrition, especially natural and organic foods.

The influence of media is nothing new, and most of us could not imagine life without today's technology. There's a down side, though, and perhaps the greatest negative impact is that the media is used to market unhealthy foods, drinks, and lifestyles to our kids. Case in point: 70 percent of polled six-to-eight-year-olds who watch a lot of television believe that fast foods are more nutritious than healthy, home-cooked foods.

2   It's no wonder kids think that way. Studies show that ads targeted to kids 12 and under lead them to request and consume high-calorie, low-nutrient products such as soft drinks, sweets, salty snacks, and fast food—adding up to more than one-third of their daily calories. Our kids are listening, watching, and believing the ads—and getting fat in the process. According to the Centers for Disease Control (CDC), the proportion of overweight children ages 6–11 has more than doubled, and the rate for adolescents has tripled since 1980. This development often sets them up for a lifetime of being overweight since around 80 percent of overweight adolescents become obese adults.

3   Looking back, it all began in the 1960s when marketers targeted children as a separate demographic category, prompting advertisers to move on this lucrative new market. In the 1970s, children were viewing an average of 20,000 TV commercials a year. By the late 1970s, research indicated that children could not distinguish between television programs and commercials, and they had little to no understanding of ads' persuasive intentions—making them especially vulnerable to ads' claims and appeals. In 1978, the Federal Trade Commission attempted to ban TV commercials aimed at youngsters—to no avail.

4   When cable channels exploded in the 1990s, opportunities to advertise directly to children expanded as well. Estimates now indicate that children spend an average of five-and-one-half hours a day using media (television, the Internet, radio, etc.) and see or hear an average of over 40,000 TV commercials a year.

5   Marketing junk to kids has worked. In 1997 alone, kids aged 7–12 spent $2.3 billion (and teenagers spent a whopping $58 billion) of discretionary money on snacks and beverages—mostly unhealthy, high-fat, high-sugar ones. The sad truth is that advertising likely has more influence on what kids eat and drink than parents or schools do. Despite attempts at limiting or disallowing advertisements directly to children, the trend of marketing junk to kids has gained momentum as the modes of marketing have diversified and intensified. One advertising executive summed up their tactics in this manner: "You've got to reach kids throughout the day—in school, as they're shopping in the mall . . . or at the movies. You've got to become part of the fabric of their lives."

6   That's exactly what has happened. Advertising has infiltrated our kids' lives even in supposedly "controlled" environments: at home (through television, the Internet, video games, etc.); at the movies (highlighting unhealthy branded foods in so-called "product placements"); at school (via piped-in advertising through programs such as Channel One, field trips, and others); and even on the way to school (via advertising on the outside and inside of buses, plus listening to BusRadio), directly impacting what our kids eat, drink, do and how much weight they gain.

7   Not surprisingly, there are direct correlations between the amount of time a child spends in front of screen media and the risk and degree of obesity. For every

hour a child watches TV or plays video games, the risk of obesity can double. Watching TV and playing video games also slows down metabolism—burning fewer calories than reading does and almost as few as sleeping does.

8   Companies also pay a lot of money to place their products in movies. Branded foods (mostly soda, followed by candy, chips, and pretzels) average about one to two in a typical movie. And this is only in the movie itself; it does not include all the junk food advertisements prior to the start of the featured flick.

9   Additionally, many school districts struggle to make ends meet and some have come up with a creative way to do so—advertising on school buses. While not all ads are for sugary soft drinks, fast food, or unhealthy snacks, some are, and the buses provide a captive audience to influence our kids' eating and lifestyle habits.

10   So what can be done? We need to talk to our kids and tell them (and model for them) what healthy eating and living is—and why. If we don't get to our kids first, the marketers and advertisers sure won't mind telling them what to buy, eat, and do.

JEFFREY **FRIEDMAN**

The Real Cause of Obesity

Jeffrey Friedman (born 1954), a physician and molecular geneticist who works at Rockefeller University in New York City, has done important research on the role of hormones in regulating body weight. In the following essay, which appeared September 9, 2009, in the *Daily Beast* (an online publication associated with *Newsweek*), he claims that obesity is mostly the result of genetics, not personal choice or weakness.

D espite receiving a MacArthur genius award for her work in Alabama "forging an inspiring model of compassionate and effective medical care in one of the most underserved regions of the United States," Regina Benjamin's qualifications to be surgeon general have been questioned. Why? She is overweight. "It tends to undermine her credibility," Dr. Marcia Angell, former editor of *The New England Journal of Medicine,* said in an interview with ABC News. "I do think at a time when a lot of public-health concern is about the national epidemic of obesity, having a surgeon general who is noticeably overweight raises questions in people's minds."

2   It is not enough, it seems, that the obese must suffer the medical consequences of their weight, consequences that include diabetes, heart disease, and cancer, and that cause nearly 300,000 deaths in the United States each year. They must also suffer the opprobrium heaped on them by people like Angell or Rep. James Sensenbrenner (R-WI), who has advised the obese to "Look in the mirror because you are the one to blame." In our society, perhaps no group is more stigmatized than the obese.

3   The abuse is nothing new, of course. Four hundred years ago, Shakespeare had Prince Hal hurl a barrage of insults at Falstaff, calling him "fat-witted," "horseback-breaker," and a "huge hill of flesh." But Shakespeare had an excuse. In his time essentially nothing was known about the real reasons that people are fat. Today we have no

such excuse. Modern medical science has gone a long way toward explaining the causes of obesity, and the bottom line is clear: obesity is not a personal choice. The obese are so primarily as a result of their genes.

Genetic studies have shown that the particular set of weight-regulating genes that a person has is by far the most important factor in determining how much that person will weigh. The heritability of obesity—a measure of how much obesity is due to genes versus other factors—is about the same as the heritability of height. It's even greater than that for many conditions that people accept as having a genetic basis, including heart disease, breast cancer, and schizophrenia. As nutrition has improved over the past 200 years, Americans have gotten much taller on average, but it is still the genes that determine who is tall or short today. The same is true for weight. Although our high-calorie, sedentary lifestyle contributes to the approximately 10-pound average weight gain of Americans compared to the recent past, some people are more severely affected by this lifestyle than others. That's because they have inherited genes that increase their predisposition for accumulating body fat. Our modern lifestyle is thus a necessary, but not a sufficient, condition for the high prevalence of obesity in our population.

Over the past decade, scientists have identified many of the genes that regulate body weight and have proved that in some instances, different variants of these genes can lead a person to be fat or thin. These genes underlie a weight-regulating system that is remarkably precise. The average person takes in a million or more calories per year, maintaining within a narrow range over the course of decades. This implies that the body balances calorie consumption with calorie expenditure, and does with a precision greater than 99.5 percent. Even the most vigilant calorie counter couldn't compete, if for no other reason than that the calorie counts on food labels are often off by 10 percent or more.

The genes that control food intake and metabolism act to keep weight in a stable range by creating a biological force that resists weight change in either direction. When weight is gained, hunger is reduced. When weight is lost, the unconscious drive to eat is stimulated and acts to return weight to the starting point. Moreover, the greater the amount of weight that is lost, the greater the sense of hunger that develops. Thus, when the obese lose large amounts of weight by conscious effort, their bodies fight back even more strongly by increasing hunger and reducing energy expenditure. If you think it is hard to lose 10 to 20 pounds (and it is), try to imagine what it would feel like to lose many tens or even hundreds of pounds.

Anyone who doubts the power of this biologic system should study the case of a young boy in England a few years back. He had a mutation in a critical gene, the one that produces the hormone leptin. Leptin is made by fat tissue and sends a signal informing the brain that there are adequate stores of energy. When leptin drops, appetite increases. Because of a genetic error, this boy could not make this hormone, which left him ravenously hungry all of the time. At age 4 he ate 1,125 calories at a single meal—about half of what a normal adult eats in an entire day. As a result he already weighed 90 pounds and was well on his way to developing diabetes. At the time, his similarly affected cousin was 8 and weighed 200 pounds. After a few leptin injections, the boy's calorie intake dropped to 180 calories per

The Nanny

You only thought *you lived in the land of the free.*

Bye Bye Venti

Nanny Bloomberg has taken his strange obsession with what you eat one step further. He now wants to make it illegal to serve "sugary drinks" bigger than 16 oz. What's next? Limits on the width of a pizza slice, size of a hamburger or amount of cream cheese on your bagel?

New Yorkers need a Mayor, not a Nanny.

Find out more at ConsumerFreedom.com

In May 2012, New York City's mayor, Michael Bloomberg, proposed banning the sale of super-sized sugary drinks—those larger than 16 fluid ounces—in movie theaters, fast-food restaurants, and sports arenas. Grocery stores would be exempt from the ban. Supporters praised the mayor's aggressive stance, agreeing that excessive consumption of sugary drinks promotes obesity. However, one industry group said sodas have been unfairly targeted while the complex causes of obesity remain unaddressed. Still others see the move as interfering with personal freedom. In the end, the ban was approved by the city's Department of Health. Do the human and monetary costs of obesity-related illnesses such as diabetes justify government regulation? What do these two images—the Consumer Freedom ad (above) and an exhibit at a Department of Health press conference (opposite)— say about how far society should go in regulating people's personal lives to benefit society in general?

meal, and by the time he was 6 his weight had dropped into the normal range. Nothing changed except the hormone levels: his parents weren't more or less permissive, his snacks did not switch from processed to organic, his willpower was not bolstered. Rather this boy was a victim of a malfunctioning weight-regulating system that led to an uncontrollable drive to eat. This example illustrates that feeding behavior is a basic drive, similar to thirst and other life-sustaining drives. The key role of leptin and other molecules to control feeding behavior undercuts the common misconception that food intake is largely under voluntary control.

8   While mutations in the leptin gene like the cases described above are rare, nearly 10 percent of morbidly obese individuals carry defects in genes that regulate food intake, metabolism, and body weight. The evidence further indicates that the rest of the obese population carries genetic alterations in other, as yet unidentified, single genes or combinations of genes (polygenes) interacting with environmental factors.

9   So if you are thin, it might be more appropriate for you to thank your own "lean" genes and refrain from stigmatizing the obese. A broad acceptance of the biologic basis of obesity would not only be fair and right, but would also allow us to collectively focus on what is most important—one's health rather than one's weight. There is no evidence that obese individuals need to "normalize" their weight to reap health benefits.

In fact, it is not even clear whether there are enduring health benefits to weight loss among obese individuals who do not suffer from diabetes, heart disease, hypertension, or liver disease. What is known is that the obese who do suffer from these conditions receive a disproportionately large benefit from even modest weight loss, which together with exercise and a heart-healthy diet can go a long way toward improving health.

10   While research into the biologic system that controls weight is moving toward the development of effective therapies for obesity, we are not there yet. In the meantime we must change our attitudes toward the obese and focus less on appearance and more on health. In their efforts to lose weight they are fighting against their biology. But they also are fighting against a society that wrongly believes that obesity is a personal failing.

PATRICK **JOHNSON**

Obesity: Epidemic or Myth?

Patrick Johnson is a clinical exercise physiologist who writes frequently about health, nutrition, and fitness. He published the following essay in the fall of 2005 in the *Skeptical Inquirer*, a journal committed to dispassionate inquiry and investigation.

Y ou have probably heard that we are in the midst of an obesity epidemic. The Centers for Disease Control and Prevention (CDC) have been fervently warning that we are in imminent danger from our expanding waistlines since the beginning of this decade. However, evidence has recently emerged indicating that the CDC's warnings were based on questionable data that resulted in exaggerated risks.

2   This new evidence has led to a hostile backlash of sorts against the CDC. The editors of the *Baltimore Sun* recently called the earlier estimates the "Chicken Little Scare of 2004." The Center for Consumer Freedom, a group that has long been critical of the CDC, declared unequivocally on its Web site and in print ads in several newspapers around the country that the obesity scare was a myth. Even Jay Leno poked fun at the CDC in one of his *Tonight Show* monologues, making the observation that "not only are we fat. . . . We can't do math either." Not everybody believes the new data, however. Cable talk show host Bill Maher commented during an episode of his show *Real Time with Bill Maher* about it being a shame that lobbyists were able to manipulate the CDC into reducing the estimated risk.

3   So which is it? Are we in imminent danger, or is the whole concept a myth? Looking at the scientific evidence makes it clear that the extreme views on either side of the argument are incorrect. There is no doubt that many of our concerns about obesity are alarmist and exaggerated, but it is also apparent that there is a real health risk associated with it.

THE CONTROVERSY

4   Between 1976 and 1991 the prevalence of overweight and obesity in the United States increased by about 31 percent (Heini and Weinsier 1997); then between 1994 and 2000 it increased by another 24 percent (Flegal et al. 2002). This trend, according to a 2004 analysis, shows little sign of slowing down (Hedley et al. 2004). The fact that more of us are getting fatter all the time raises a significant public health concern. The Centers for Disease Control and Prevention (CDC) began calling the problem an epidemic in the beginning of this decade as the result of research that estimated 280,000 annual deaths as a consequence of obesity (Allison et al. 1999). Since then there has been a strong media campaign devoted to convincing Americans to lose weight. In 2003, Dr. Julie Gerberding, the director of the CDC, made a speech claiming that the health impact of obesity would be worse than the influenza epidemic of the early twentieth century or the black plague of the Middle Ages. In 2004 the campaign reached a fever pitch when a report was released that increased the estimate of obesity-related deaths to 400,000 (Mokdad et al. 2004). Finally, in March of this year, a report appeared in the *New England Journal of Medicine* that predicted a decline in life expectancy in the United States as a direct result of obesity (Olshansky, et al. 2005).

5   Despite the assertions that obesity is causing our society great harm, however, many scientists and activist groups have disputed the level of danger that it actually poses. Indeed, a recent analysis presented in the *Journal of the American Medical Association (JAMA)* by Katherine Flegal of the CDC and her colleagues calls the severity of the dangers of excess body fat into question, indicating that the number of overweight and obesity-related deaths is actually about 26,000—about one-fifteenth the earlier estimate of 400,000 (Flegal et al. 2005).

6   There is little argument about the fact that, as a nation, more of us are fatter than ever before; the disagreement lies in the effect that this has on our health. The campaign to convince us to lose weight gained much of its momentum in 2004; not only were there high-profile public health initiatives devoted to stopping the obesity epidemic, but the idea had pervaded popular culture as well. Movies like Morgan Spurlock's *Super Size Me* were the topic of many a discussion, and there were regular news reports about the dangers of too much fat.

7   During this campaign, however, there were some notable dissenters. Paul Ernsberger, a professor of nutrition at Case Western Reserve University, has been doing research since the 1980s that led him to assert that obesity is not the cause of ill health but rather the effect of sedentary living and poor nutrition, which are the actual causes. Another prominent researcher, Steven Blair, director of the Cooper Institute of Aerobics Research in Dallas, Texas, has been an author on several studies indicating that the risks associated with obesity can be significantly reduced if one engages in regular physical activity, even if weight loss is not present. According to Blair, weight loss should not be ignored, but a greater focus should be placed on physical activity and good nutrition. Both Ernsberger and Blair indicated to me that they thought the new research by Flegal and her colleagues provides a more accurate picture of the mortality risk associated with obesity.

8   While scientists like Ernsberger and Blair have been presenting their conclusions in the scientific forum, others have taken a more inflammatory approach. In his 2004 book, *The Obesity Myth,* Paul Campos argues that the public health problem we have associated with obesity is a myth and further claims that our loathing of fat has damaged our culture. The most antagonistic group, however, is the Center for Consumer Freedom (CCF) (www.consumerfreedom.com), which implies that the obesity epidemic is a conspiracy between the pharmaceutical industries and the public health establishment to create a better market for weight-loss drugs. Numerous articles on the organization's Web site bash several of the most prominent obesity researchers who have disclosed financial ties to the pharmaceutical industries. Paul Ernsberger echoed this sentiment. He told me that the inflated mortality statistics were all based on the work of David Allison, a well-known pharmacoeconomics expert. "These experts create cost-benefit analyses which are part of all drug applications to the FDA. These self-serving analyses start by exaggerating as much as possible the cost to society of the ailment to be treated (obesity in the case of weight-loss drugs). The risks associated with the new drug are severely underestimated, which results in an extremely favorable risk-benefit analysis, which is almost never realized once the drug is on the market. Experts who can produce highly favorable risk-benefit analyses are very much in demand, however."

9   The claims made by the CCF are given some credence by Ernsberger's corroboration; however, there is a noteworthy problem with their own objectivity. On their Web site they present themselves as a consumer-minded libertarian group that exists to "promote personal responsibility and protect consumer choices." Upon closer examination, however, it becomes evident that the CCF is an advocacy group for restaurants and food companies, who have as much to gain by the threat of obesity being a myth as the pharmaceutical industry does by the danger being dire.

10   It is clear that there are agenda-determined interests on both sides of the issue. Therefore, the best way to discern what is necessary for good health is to shift our focus away from the sensational parts of the controversy and look at the science itself.

CURRENT SCIENCE AND OBESITY RISKS

11   In their recent article, Katherine Flegal and her colleagues (2005) point out that the earlier mortality estimates were based on analyses that were methodologically flawed because in their calculations the authors used *adjusted* relative risks in an equation that was developed for *unadjusted* relative risk. This, according to Flegal's group, meant that the old estimates only partially accounted for confounding factors. The older estimates, furthermore "did not account for variation by age in the relation of body weight to mortality, and did not include measures of uncertainty in the form of [standard errors] or confidence intervals." These authors also point out that the previous estimates relied on studies that had notable limitations: "Four of six included only older data (two studies ended follow-up in the 1970s and two in the 1980s), three had only self-reported weight and height, three had data only from small geographic areas, and one study included only women. Only one data set, the National Health and Nutrition Examination Survey I, was nationally representative" (Flegal et al. 2005). In their current

investigation, Flegal's group addressed this problem by using data only from nationally representative samples with measured heights and weights. Further, they accounted for confounding variables and included standard errors for the estimates.

12   Obesity was determined in this analysis using each subject's body mass index, which is a simple height-to-weight ratio. A BMI of 18 to 24 is considered to be the normal weight, 25–29 is considered overweight, and 30 and above is considered obese. The data from this study indicated that people who were underweight experienced 33,746 more deaths than normal-weight people, and that people who were overweight or obese experienced 25,814 more deaths than the normal-weight folks. This estimate is being reported in the popular media as being one-fifteenth the earlier estimate of 400,000. However, conflating the categories of overweight and obesity this way is misleading.

13   At first glance, it appears that underweight poses a bigger threat to our health than overweight and obesity, and that the earlier estimates were profoundly exaggerated. However, in this study the people who fit into the *obese* category actually experienced 111,909 excess deaths compared to normal-weight subjects. In contrast, those who were categorized as *overweight* experienced 86,094 fewer deaths than those who were normal weight. The figure of 25,815 is the difference between the obesity deaths and the overweight survivals. In the original study by David Allison and his colleagues (Allison et al. 1999) it is actually estimated that 280,000 deaths result from overweight and obesity and that 80 percent, or 224,000, of these deaths occurred in people who were in the obese category. However, the study by Mokdad and colleagues (2004), using the same methods developed by Allison et al., estimated 400,000 obesity-related deaths, and subsequently fueled much of the recent fervor surrounding the obesity epidemic. In this study, no distinction was made between overweight and obesity and the authors failed to distinguish between obesity, physical inactivity, and poor diet. All of these variables were simply lumped together.

14   A few things become clearer after examining the data. First, it appears that our categories are mislabeled; being classified as overweight appears to give one an advantage (statistically, anyway) over those who are in the ideal weight range. Moreover, it is inappropriate to consider overweight and obese as one group. Despite the current hype, the initial overestimation by Allison and his group was not as exaggerated as is being publicized; compared to that study, the new estimate is actually about half of the old number. Finally, it is apparent that many at the CDC were simply confirming their own biases when they accepted the estimate by Mokdad et al. The categories in that study—that was, intriguingly, co-authored by CDC director Julie Gerberding, which may provide some insight into why it was so readily accepted—were far too broad to provide useful information. The fact that this flaw was ignored shows how easy it is to accept evidence that supports our preconceived notions or our political agendas.

5   There is another problem inherent in all of the above mortality estimates. They are based on epidemiological data that show correlation but leave us guessing as to causation. Various factors are interrelated with increased mortality—obesity, inactivity, poor nutrition, smoking, etc. Yet, without carefully controlled experiments, it is hard to determine which factors cause—and which are symptoms of—poor health. This is a

difficult limitation to overcome, however, because we can't recruit subjects and have them get fat to see if they get sick and/or die sooner. Most institutional review boards would not approve that sort of research, and furthermore I can't imagine that there would be a large pool of subjects willing to participate. There are, however, observational data that were collected with fitness in mind, which help to clarify the picture somewhat.

16   In 1970 researchers at the Cooper Institute for Aerobics Research in Dallas, Texas, began to gather data for a longitudinal study that was called, pragmatically enough, the Aerobics Center Longitudinal Study (ACLS). This study looked at a variety of different variables to estimate the health risks and benefits of certain behaviors and lifestyle choices. What set this study apart from other large-scale observational studies, however, was that instead of relying on self-reporting for variables like exercise habits, they tested fitness levels directly by way of a graded exercise test (GXT). A GXT requires a person to walk on a treadmill as long as he or she can with increases in speed and incline at regular intervals. This is the most reliable way we know of to assess a person's physical fitness.

17   With an accurate measure of the subjects' fitness levels, researchers at the Cooper Institute have been able to include fitness as a covariate with obesity. Analysis of the data obtained in the ACLS shows that there is a risk associated with obesity, but when you control for physical activity, much of that risk disappears (Church et al. 2004; Katzmarzyk et al. 2004; Katzmarzyk et al. 2004; Lee et al. 1999). One study showed that obese men who performed regular exercise had a lower risk of developing cardiovascular disease than lean men who were out of shape (Lee et al. 1999).

18   Steven Blair, who runs the Cooper Institute and was an author on all four of the above-mentioned studies, however, does not think obesity should be ignored. "I do think obesity is a public health problem, although I also think that the primary cause of the obesity epidemic is a declining level of average daily energy expenditure. . . . It will be unfortunate if it is now assumed that we should ignore obesity. I do not think that the [health] risk of obesity is a myth, although it has been overestimated." Blair believes that a focus on good nutrition and increased physical activity rather than on weight loss will better serve us.

19   In spite of the fact that there are virtually no controlled clinical trials examining the effects of obesity in people, we can make some inferences from animal research. Investigations performed by Ernsberger and his colleagues have shown that, over time, weight cycling (temporary weight loss followed by a regain of that weight, otherwise known as yo-yoing) in obese laboratory animals increases blood pressure, enlarges the heart, damages the kidney, increases abdominal fat deposits, and promotes further weight gain (Ernsberger and Koletsky 1993; Ernsberger et al. 1996; Ernsberger and Koletsky 1999). This indicates that the yo-yo effect of crash dieting may be the cause of many of the problems we attribute to simply being fat.

20   Even though there is a health risk from being too fat, you can eliminate much of the potential risk by exercising. Moreover, it is probably a bad idea to jump from diet to diet given the negative consequences the yo-yo effect can have. According to another study published in *JAMA*, the risk of cardiovascular disease has declined

across all BMI groups over the past forty years as the result of better drugs (Gregg et al. 2005).

21   None of this means, however, that we should simply abandon our attempts to maintain a healthy weight; obese people had twice the incidence of hypertension compared to lean people and, most significantly, there has been (according to the above study) a 55 percent increase in diabetes that corresponds to the increase in obesity. So while we are better at dealing with the problem once it occurs, it is still better to avoid developing the problem in the first place.

CONDEMNING THE CDC

22   Whatever side of the argument you are on, it is apparent that many in the CDC acted irresponsibly. However, despite the fact that the initial, exaggerated estimate came from people at the CDC, we should keep in mind that *so did the corrected number.* While this can be frustrating to the casual observer, it is also a testament to the corrective power of the scientific method.

23   Science is about provisional truths that can be changed when evidence indicates that they should be. The fact that scientific information is available to the public is its greatest strength. Most of us, for whatever reason—whether it's self-interest or self-delusion—don't view our own ideas as critically as we should. The fact that scientific ideas are available for all to see allows those who disagree to disprove them. This is what has happened at the CDC; the most current study has addressed the flaws of the earlier studies. It is true that many of those in power at the CDC uncritically embraced the earlier estimates and overreacted, or worse simply accepted research that was flawed because it bolstered their agendas. But that failure lies with the people involved, not with the CDC as an institution or with the science itself.

24   The evidence still shows that morbid obesity is associated with an increased likelihood of developing disease and suffering from early mortality, but it also shows that those who are a few pounds overweight don't need to panic. What's more, it is clear that everyone, fat or thin, will benefit from regular exercise regardless of whether they lose weight.

25   The lesson to be learned from this controversy is that rational moderation is in order. Disproving one extreme idea does not prove the opposite extreme. As Steven Blair told me, "It is time to focus our attention on the key behaviors of eating a healthful diet (plenty of fruits and veggies, a lot of whole grains, and not too much fat and alcohol) and being physically active every day."

REFERENCES

Allison, D. B., et al. 1999. Annual deaths attributable to obesity in the United States. *Journal of the American Medical Association* 282: 1530–38.

Blair, Steven, and James Morrow, Jr. 2005. Comments on U.S. dietary guidelines. *Journal of Physical Activity and Health* 2: 137–142.

Campos, Paul. 2004. *The Obesity Myth.* New York: Gotham Books.

Church, T., et al. 2004. Exercise capacity and body composition as predictor of mortality among men with diabetes. *Diabetes Care* 27(1): 83–88.

Ernsberger, Paul, and Richard Koletsky. 1993. Biomedical rationale for a wellness approach to obesity: An alternative to a focus on weight loss. *Journal of Social Issues* 55(2): 221–259.

Ernsberger, Paul, and Richard Koletsky. 1999. Weight cycling and mortality: support from animal studies. *Journal of the American Medical Association* 269: 1116.

Ernsberger P., et al. 1994. Refeeding hypertension in obese spontaneously hypertensive rats. *Hypertension* 24: 699–705.

Ernsberger P., et al. 1996. Consequences of weight cycling in obese spontaneously hypertensive rats. *American Journal of Physiology: Regulatory, Integrative and Comparative Physiology* 270: R864–R872.

Flegal, Katherine M., et al. 2000. *Journal of the American Medical Association* 288(14): 1723–1727.

Flegal, K., et al. 2005. Excess deaths associated with underweight, overweight, and obesity. *Journal of the American Medical Association* 293(15): 1861–67.

Gregg, E., et al. 2005. Secular trends in cardiovascular disease risk factors according to body mass index in U.S. adults. *Journal of the American Medical Association* 293(15): 1868–74.

Hedley, A., et al. 2004. Prevalence of overweight and obesity among US children, adolescents, and adults, 1999—2000. *Journal of the American Medical Association* 291: 2847–2850.

Heini, Adrian F., and Roland L. Weinsier. 1997. Divergent trends in obesity and fat intake patterns: The American paradox. *Journal of the American Medical Association* 102(3): 254–264.

Katzmarzyk, Peter, et al. 2004. Metabolic syndrome, obesity, and mortality. *Diabetes Care* 28(2): 391–97.

Katzmarzyk, Peter, Timothy Church, and Steven Blair. 2004. Cardiorespiratory fitness attenuates the effects of the metabolic syndrome on all-cause and cardiovascular disease mortality in men. *Archives of Internal Medicine* 164: 1092–97.

Lee, Chong Do, Steven Blair, and Andrew Jackson. 1999. Cardiorespiratory fitness, body composition, and all-cause and cardiovascular disease mortality in men. *American Journal of Clinical Nutrition* 69: 373–80.

Mark, David. 2005. Deaths attributable to obesity. *Journal of the American Medical Association* 293(15): 1918–19.

Mokdad, A.H., et al. 2004. Actual causes of death in the United States. *Journal of the American Medical Association* 291: 1238–45.

Olshansky, S, Jay., et al. 2005. A potential decline in life expectancy in the United States in the 21st century. *New England Journal of Medicine* 352(11): 1138–45.

ISSUE IN FOCUS

Drinking on College Campuses

You know what The Problem is: On college campuses across the United States, excessive alcohol consumption is causing all kinds of trouble—deaths and serious illnesses related to alcohol poisoning (the result of "binge drinking"); property damage, personal violence, and other crimes; unwanted pregnancies and sexual assaults; academic failures and family breakups and long-term career setbacks. Some statistics dramatize the extent of the damage: A 2009 study conducted by the National Institute on Alcohol Abuse and Alcoholism (NIAAA) found that at least 1,825 drinking-related accidental deaths had occurred among 18- to 24-year-old students in 2005, up from 1,440 in 1998. The proportion of students who report that they had engaged in a recent episode of binge drinking is now at 45 percent. Almost 30 percent of students are saying that they have driven while under the influence of alcohol at least once in the past year. The Harvard School of Public Health estimates that 44 percent of college students are heavy drinkers, and it appears that alcohol abuse is responsible for over half a million injuries each year—not to mention any number of suicides or attempted suicides. NIAAA estimates that 696,000 students between the ages of 18 and 24 are assaulted by another student who has been drinking, and 97,000 students are victims of alcohol-related sexual assault or date rape. (For further details, see http://www .collegedrinkingprevention.gov/1College_Bulletin-508_361C4E.pdf.)

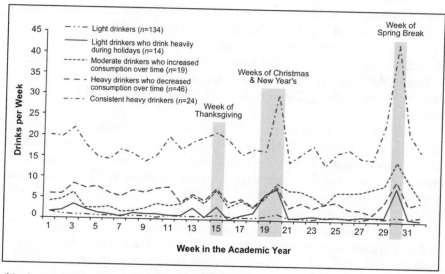

This chart shows trends in alcohol consumption by college freshmen by weeks in the academic year.

2   But what to do about it? That's not so easy to discern. Over the years, universities and partner organizations have developed a wide variety of programs aimed at decreasing the rates of dangerous drinking on college campuses. You have experienced most of them firsthand. Some focus on individuals—such as emphasizing personal responsibility and counseling students with identified drinking problems through Alcohol Awareness Weeks, programs during freshman orientation, or required coursework. Other solutions are centered on creating a safer community through the involvement of campus life personnel, residence hall programs, local law enforcement, and neighboring residents: some campuses ban alcohol in dormitories or offer alcohol-free entertainment options; others have tried vigorous enforcement of alcohol sales and consumption laws; and many others are cracking down on drinking in fraternities.

3   But nothing seems to be working very well. In 1984 President Ronald Reagan signed into law the Uniform Drinking Age Act, which penalized states that did not raise their legal drinking age to 21. By 1988, therefore, all fifty states had modified their laws to reflect this federal legislation. Because of this legislation and because of persistent public advocacy by Mothers Against Drunk Driving (MADD) and other organizations, alcohol-related traffic accidents and arrests for underage drinking have deceased substantially in the general population.

4   Nevertheless, is it wise to criminalize alcohol consumption by those under the age of 21? Are healthy long-term drinking habits promoted when the age limit is 21? Is zero tolerance the best approach? Is the experience of other nations, most of whom have lower legal drinking ages, relevant here? When the legal drinking age was set at 21, many say, colleges became the enforcers of the law. That enforcement subsequently drove drinking out of quads, dorms, and fraternities and into off-campus hiding places where students get smashed before going out on the town or to tailgates or to other places where drinking is policed. In 2009 a group of college presidents began a campaign to reexamine the drinking age. Dubbed "The Amethyst Initiative," after a gemstone that is said to ward off intoxication, the initiative by the presidents has been vigorously supported (e.g., by presidents at Duke, Ohio State, Dartmouth, Johns Hopkins) and loudly opposed (e.g., by MADD, by many other college presidents, and by the International Association of Chiefs of Police).

5   In the Issue in Focus selections that follow, John M. McCardell presents the case for experimenting with a lower drinking age; he is the former president of Middlebury College as well as the founder and president of Choose Responsibility, a nonprofit organization that seeks to engage the public in the debate over the appropriate drinking age. Published on CNN.com in September 2009, McCardell's essay is supported by the next argument, by physician Morris Chafetz, who founded the National Institute for Alcoholism and Alcohol Abuse in 1970 and who argued in the *Huffington Post* in August 2009 that laws setting the minimum drinking age of 21 are ineffective and should be repealed. Chafetz first gained national recognition at the 1984 White House Conference for a Drug-Free America, at which the Uniform Drinking Age Act was signed into law.

ACCOMPLISHMENTS AS...

A CHILD | AN ADULT | A COLLEGE STUDENT

MOMMY, DADDY! I LEARNED HOW TO RIDE A BIKE!

GOOD NEWS, HONEY. I MADE PARTNER!

I CAN'T BELIEVE YOU DID 25 SHOTS LAST NIGHT.

AWESOME.

DUDE, I WAS SOOO DRUNK!

Many college campuses have a culture of binge drinking. What factors explain the pattern of drinking that prevails at your school?

Jeff Keacher/Zoitz.com

6   Then we offer an argument in support of the 21-year-old drinking age. In a commentary published on CNN.com in September 2009, several distinguished health professionals (led by Toben F. Nelson and Traci Toomey) contend that placing the minimum drinking age at 21 has played a pivotal role in reducing alcohol-related deaths. Finally, we conclude this Issue in Focus with a piece by writer James Hibberd, who critiques how large beer manufacturers swell sales by enlisting a corps of "campus representatives." Entitled "Barhopping with the Bud Girls," Hibberd's piece appeared on Salon.com in February 1999. It invites you to go beyond the debate about the legal drinking age to ponder how mixed messages about alcohol permeate college environments, and how you yourself feel about drinking on campus. What is the situation at your college or university? What is being done about it, and what might be done?

John McCardell

A Drinking Age of 21 Doesn't Work

In 2008, a group of college and university presidents and chancellors, eventually totaling 135, issued a statement that garnered national attention.

2   The "Amethyst Initiative" put a debate proposition before the public—"Resolved: That the 21-year-old drinking age is not working." It offered, in much the way that a grand jury performs its du-

ties, sufficient evidence for putting the proposition to the test. It invited informed and dispassionate public debate, and committed the signatory institutions to encouraging that debate. And it called on elected officials not to continue assuming that, after 25 years, the status quo could not be challenged or even improved.

3   One year later, the drinking age debate continues, and new research reinforces the presidential impulse. Just this summer a study published in the *Journal of the American Academy of Child and Adolescent Psychiatry* revealed that, among college-age males, binge drinking is unchanged from its levels of 1979; that among non-college women it has increased by 20 percent; and that among college women it has increased by 40 percent.

4   Remarkably, the counterintuitive conclusion drawn by the investigators, and accepted uncritically by the media, including editorials in *The New York Times* and *The Washington Post*, is that the study proves that raising the drinking age to 21 has been a success.

5   More recently, a study of binge drinking published in the *Journal of the American Medical Association* announced that "despite efforts at prevention, the prevalence of binge drinking among college students is continuing to rise, and so are the harms associated with it." Worse still, a related study has shown that habits formed at 18 die hard: "For each year studied, a greater percentage of 21- to 24-year-olds [those who were of course once 18, 19 and 20] engaged in binge drinking and driving under the influence of alcohol."

6   Yet in the face of mounting evidence that those young adults (age 18 to 20 toward whom the drinking age law has been directed) are routinely—indeed in life- and health-threatening ways—violating it, there remains a belief in the land that a minimum drinking age of 21 has been a "success." And elected officials are periodically reminded of a provision in the 1984 law that continues to stifle any serious public debate in our country's state legislative chambers: Any state that sets its drinking age lower than 21 forfeits 10 percent of its annual federal highway appropriation.

7   But it's not 1984 anymore.

8   This statement may seem obvious, but not necessarily. In 1984 Congress passed and the president signed the National Minimum Drinking Age Act. The Act, which raised the drinking age to 21 under threat of highway fund withholding, sought to address the problem of drunken driving fatalities. And indeed, that problem was serious. States that lowered their ages during the

1970s and did nothing else to prepare young adults to make responsible decisions about alcohol witnessed an alarming increase in alcohol-related traffic fatalities. It was as though the driving age were lowered but no driver's education was provided. The results were predictable.

9   Now, 25 years later, we are in a much different, and better, place. Thanks to the effective public advocacy of organizations like Mothers Against Drunk Driving, we are far more aware of the risks of drinking and driving. Automobiles are much safer. Seatbelts and airbags are mandatory. The "designated driver" is now a part of our vocabulary. And more and more states are mandating ignition interlocks for first-time DUI offenders, perhaps the most effective way to get drunken drivers off the road.

10   And the statistics are encouraging. Alcohol-related fatalities have declined over the last 25 years. Better still, they have declined in all age groups, though the greatest number of deaths still occurs at age 21, followed by 22 and 23. We are well on the way to solving a problem that vexed us 25 years ago.

11   The problem today is different. The problem today is reckless, goal-oriented alcohol consumption that all too often takes place in clandestine locations, where enforcement has proven frustratingly difficult. Alcohol consumption among young adults is not taking place in public places or public view or in the presence of other adults who might help model responsible behavior. But we know it is taking place.

12   If not in public, then where? The college presidents who signed the Amethyst Initiative know where. It happens in "pre-game" sessions in locked dorm rooms where students take multiple shots of hard alcohol in rapid succession, before going to a social event where alcohol is not served. It happens in off-campus apartments beyond college boundaries and thus beyond the presidents' authority; and it happens in remote fields to which young adults must drive.

13   And the Amethyst presidents know the deadly result: Of the 5,000 lives lost to alcohol each year by those under 21, more than 60 percent are lost *off* the roadways, according to the National Institute of Alcoholism and Alcohol Abuse. The principal problem of 2009 is not drunken driving. The principal problem of 2009 is clandestine binge drinking.

14   That is why the Amethyst presidents believe a public debate is so urgent. The law does not say drink responsibly or drink in moderation. It says don't drink. To those affected by it, those who

in the eyes of the law are in every other respect legal adults, it is Prohibition. And it is incomprehensible.

15   The principal impediment to public debate is the 10 percent highway penalty. That penalty should be waived for those states that choose to try something different, which may turn out to be something better. But merely adjusting the age—up or down—is not really the way to make a change.

16   We should prepare young adults to make responsible decisions about alcohol in the same way we prepare them to operate a motor vehicle: by first educating and then licensing, and permitting them to exercise the full privileges of adulthood so long as they demonstrate their ability to observe the law. Licensing would work like driver's education—it would involve a permit, perhaps graduated, allowing the holder the privilege of purchasing, possessing, and consuming alcohol, as each state determined, so long as the holder had passed an alcohol education course and observed the alcohol laws of the issuing state.

17   Most of the rest of the world has come out in a different place on the drinking age. The United States is one of only four countries—the others are Indonesia, Mongolia and Palau—with an age as high as 21. All others either have no minimum age or have a lower age, generally 18, with some at 16. Young adults know that. And, in their heart of hearts, they also know that a law perceived as unjust, a law routinely violated, can over time breed disrespect for law in general.

18   Slowly but surely we may be seeing a change in attitude. This summer, Dr. Morris Chafetz, a distinguished psychiatrist, a member of the presidential commission that recommended raising the drinking age, and the founder of the National Institute for Alcoholism and Alcohol Abuse, admitted that supporting the higher drinking age is "the most regrettable decision of my entire professional career." This remarkable statement did not receive the attention it merited.

19   Alcohol is a reality in the lives of young adults. We can either try to change the reality—which has been our principal focus since 1984, by imposing Prohibition on young adults 18 to 20—or we can create the safest possible environment for the reality.

20   A drinking age minimum of 21 has not changed the reality. It's time to try something different.

21   It's not 1984 anymore.

**Morris
E. Chafetz**

The 21-Year-Old Drinking Age: I Voted for It; It Doesn't Work

In 1982 I accepted appointment to the Presidential Commission on Drunk Driving and agreed to chair its Education and Prevention Committee. The Commission met over the next 18 months and ultimately advanced 39 recommendations to President Reagan, in December 1983. All 39 received unanimous Commission approval.

2 The most conspicuous of those recommendations, and arguably the most controversial, called for raising the minimum legal drinking age to 21 nationwide. I will admit to having had serious reservations about this particular proposal. But in the interest of maintaining unanimity, I reluctantly voted yes. It is the single most regrettable decision of my entire professional career.

3 Legal Age 21 has not worked. To be sure, drunk driving fatalities are lower now than they were in 1982. But they are lower in all age groups. And they have declined just as much in Canada, where the age is 18 or 19, as they have in the United States.

4 It has been argued that "science" convincingly shows a cause-and-effect relationship between the law and the reduction in fatalities. Complicated mathematical formulas, which include subjective estimations (called "imputation") have been devised to demonstrate "proof." But correlation is not cause. We must neither confuse numbers with science nor interpret a lack of numbers as implying an absence of science.

5 But even if we concede that the law has had some effect on our highways, we cannot overlook its collateral, off-road damage. The National Institute for Alcoholism and Alcohol Abuse, which I founded in 1970, estimates that 5,000 lives are lost to alcohol each year by those under 21. More than 3,000 of those fatalities occur off our roadways. If we are seriously to measure the effects of this law, we cannot limit our focus.

6 And if we broaden our look, we see a serious problem of reckless, goal-oriented, drinking to get drunk. Those at whom the law is directed disobey it routinely. Enforcement is frustratingly difficult and usually forces the behavior deeper underground, into places where life and health are put at ever greater risk. The 600,000 assaults reported annually, the date rapes, the property damage, the emergency room calls do not in general occur in

places visible to the public. They are the inevitable result of what happens when laws do not reflect social or cultural reality.

7   The reality is that at age 18 in this country, one is a legal adult. Young people view 21 as utterly arbitrary—which it is. And because the explanation given them is so condescending—that they lack maturity and judgment, these same people who can serve on juries and sign contracts and who turned out in overwhelming numbers to elect our first black president—well, they don't buy it.

8   And neither do I. And neither should the American public.

9   Whether we like it or not, alcohol is woven into the fabric of our world, most of which has determined that the legal drinking age should be 18—or lower. And so far as I can tell, there is no evidence of massive brain impairment, alcohol dependency, or underage alcohol abuse, which the "experts" tell us will be the inevitable result of lowering the age in the United States. It is time to liberate ourselves from the tyranny of "experts," who invoke "science" in order to advance a prohibitionist agenda. Prohibition does not work. It has never worked. It is not working among 18-20 year-olds now.

10   The cult of expertise has made parents feel incapable of raising their children. In many states parents are disenfranchised from helping their sons or daughters learn about responsible alcohol consumption. But as a parent and psychiatrist I trust the instinct of parents more than I do the hubris of "experts."

11   Despite what these latter-day prohibitionists may think, the problem is not the drink—it is the drinker. There should be more emphasis on the person and the surroundings in which alcohol is consumed and less emphasis on alcohol itself. Personal and social responsibility, not the substance, is the real issue. But so long as the age remains a one-size-fits-all, federally-mandated 21, and so long as any state that may want to try something different, in hopes of reversing the dismal trend of binge-drinking that (maybe or maybe not coincidentally) has become more serious in the years since the drinking age was raised, forfeits 10% of its federal highway funds, nothing is likely to change for the better.

12   I do not believe that any state should be forced to adjust its drinking age. But I do believe that the genius of federalism should be allowed to work its will unimpeded, and from that genius, not only better practices, but also safer environments and more responsible consumption, are likely to emerge.

Toben F. Nelson, Traci L. Toomey, and co-authors

The Drinking Age of 21 Saves Lives

The national policy that set a minimum legal drinking age of 21 is being questioned by a group of 135 college and university presidents through an effort called the Amethyst Initiative. In a September 16 commentary on CNN.com, Amethyst Initiative leader John McCardell, a former president of Middlebury College, proposes lowering the drinking age, which he suggests will lead to less drinking and related problems among college students.

2 But history and a comprehensive review of the research tell a much different story. The evidence is clear, consistent, and compelling: A drinking age of 21 has led to less drinking, fewer injuries, and fewer deaths.

3 In the 1970s when many states reduced their drinking ages, drinking-related deaths among young people increased. When the drinking age of 21 was restored, deaths declined. This effect is not simply a historical artifact explained by advances in safety technology and other policies.

4 New Zealand recently lowered the drinking age based on many of the same arguments advanced by the Amethyst Initiative. The result was more alcohol-involved traffic crashes and emergency room visits among 15- to 19-year-olds. New Zealand is now considering raising its drinking age. The National Highway Traffic Safety Administration estimates that setting the drinking age at 21 saves the lives of 900 young people each year and has saved more than 25,000 lives since 1975.

5 It was on the basis of compelling research evidence about its lifesaving benefits that a bipartisan effort created Public Law 98-363, "The National Minimum Legal Drinking Age Act," in the first place. Subsequent research has strengthened the evidence. College students who are underage, for example, binge drink less than students aged 21-23. Underage students who attend colleges that rigorously enforce the drinking age, and who reside in states that have more laws restricting access to alcohol for those under the legal age, are less likely to binge drink.

6 Another myth promulgated by the Amethyst Initiative is that European young people are taught by families to drink responsibly because of the typically lower legal drinking ages there. The reverse is the case. Surveys of youth in multiple European countries show that rates of frequent binge drinking among adolescents are higher in Europe than in the United States. Panels of experts, convened separately by the National Institute on Alcohol Abuse and Alcoholism, the Substance Abuse and Mental Health Services Administration, the National Academy of Sciences Institute of Medicine and the Centers for Disease

Control and Prevention have studied the evidence on the age-21 law and concluded that it is effective public policy. Rather than lowering the drinking age, they recommended bolstering the law by closing loopholes in state law and strengthening enforcement.

7   There is a silver lining to the call for reopening discussion on the minimum legal drinking age. While some college presidents have signed on to the Amethyst Initiative, most have not. College presidents acknowledge that a serious problem exists on their campuses and that something needs to be done. Working effectively with their communities and states to address student drinking is the place to start, not with a discussion about lowering the drinking age.

8   College presidents must show leadership by promoting solutions recommended by a report from the National Institute on Alcohol Abuse and Alcoholism College Drinking Task Force released in 2002. These recommendations for college and community leaders included creating systems for reaching individual students with effective interventions; implementing, publicizing and enforcing laws to prevent alcohol-impaired driving and underage drinking; placing restrictions on alcohol retail outlets; increasing prices and excise taxes on alcoholic beverages; and insisting on responsible beverage service policies at on- and off-campus venues. Few colleges and their communities have even begun the steps needed to enact these efforts.

9   These recommendations will be difficult to implement and significant barriers exist, including resistance from the industries that profit from selling alcohol. College presidents cannot accomplish this alone. They need the support of students, regents, parents, alumni and their communities. State and local legislators need to pass tougher restrictions and provide resources for enforcement. Lobbying legislators to dismantle the effective drinking age law is a step in the wrong direction.

10   So rather than try the approaches advocated by the Amethyst Initiative that have no foundation in research, let's be clear about the issues. College student drinking is a serious problem. Each year more young people are injured, sexually assaulted, and die as the result of drinking. These statistics would be even worse without the age-21 law.

11   Lowering the drinking age will not save lives or make our campuses and communities better places to live. It will increase heavy drinking and the problems that accompany it in college communities and push the problem back into high schools. Real prevention requires constant vigilance, dedication, and the courage to implement difficult solutions.

JAMES **HIBBERD**

Barhopping with the Bud Girls

If you owned a beer company, what would be your ultimate marketing dream?
2   How about placing a beer commercial in every college bar and fraternity organization? There, luscious, tan-line-free women and confident, upper-social-strata jocks would aggressively promote your brands with all the slick enthusiasm of a Madison Avenue production. Imagine these commercials playing in continuous motion throughout the evening without ever resorting to the obvious loops of promotional films. Because this commercial would be live. That's right, real people targeting real college beer drinkers at that crucial moment in their lives when they establish brand loyalty, using no other sales technique than old-fashioned peer pressure.

3   For Anheuser-Busch, the parent company of Budweiser, the dream of student recruitment is real. It wasn't easy or cheap. Or, some argue, anywhere close to ethical. Parenting groups have recently attacked Anheuser-Busch for their animated frog 'n' lizard advertising campaign, but a CNN.com investigation has found that the brewer does more than create cute cartoon characters to court underage drinkers. By hiring popular fraternity members and attractive female students as representatives, Anheuser-Busch distributors directly target the largely underage college market.

4   Considering Harvard's well-publicized 1993 study declaring that 44 percent of American college students and 86 percent of fraternity members qualify as binge drinkers, such a marketing program seems ridiculously ill-advised. Isn't hiring college students a potential PR nightmare? After all, 90 percent of all rapes and most violent crimes on campus are alcohol-related.

5   Such statistics may not have deterred Anheuser-Busch, but they do explain why its college recruiting efforts are managed discreetly. Even the beer industry's most prominent critic, Mothers Against Drunk Driving, was unaware that college reps existed. "Hiring fraternity members as beer distributor reps on university campuses where the majority of students are under the legal drinking age of 21 is frightening and unbelievably irresponsible," said MADD's national president, Karolyn V. Nunnallee, upon hearing the news. "We urge the U.S. beer industry to re-examine its marketing efforts."

6   Last November, midlevel supervisors for Anheuser-Busch wholesaler Brown Distributing allowed me to join their college representatives working a Budweiser parade leading to a University of Texas football game and a night of "bar calls" in Austin. While many alcohol companies hire attractive women to push products in bars and sporting events across the country, these Bud representatives seemed to be recruited predominantly from the college population and assigned to a college beat: They frequent popular college watering holes, sporting events, and other events such as parties at the U.T. alumni center. Of more concern are the existence of fraternity members who work unsupervised in the promotion of their product for college parties. The access was unusual, and the vice president for Brown Distributing later expressed some irritation, commenting that any media inquiries normally require approval from a high-ranking executive.
    In other words: oops.

8   "When we walk into a bar, all we have is ourselves," says 24-year-old Bud Girl Rachel Moore, a recent college graduate. "We may be passing out a key chain or something, but we make the promotion." Brown Distributing Bud Girls (we'll get to the male representatives later) are held to strict standards. A Bud Girl doesn't smoke, swear, use drugs, or have tattoos, non-ear piercings, or a criminal record. Her only permissible vice is drinking Budweiser, and that, of course, is mandatory. If a potential Bud Girl passes the interviews, background checks and drug testing, she's awarded a $15-an-hour part-time position and a Bud Girl wardrobe.

9   Bud Girl clothing isn't simply halter tops and spandex dresses. The wardrobe is Technicolor dream-wear that transforms attractive yet otherwise ordinary girls into a sort of beer-touting Justice League. Once in costume, the Bud Girls are superheroes whose sexual power turns any bar into one of those 1980s beer commercials, where the swimsuit model reduces men to puddles of gratitude and adoration. "I wonder who they think we actually are," says 28-year-old Bud Girl Griselda Mendoza. "[The clothes] change everything. They could see me at a supermarket and I won't get paid much attention. But put on a little Bud vest and all of a sudden guys want everything signed."

10   At one bar promotion I attended, the Bud Girls were asked to sign a promotional banner. They wrote: "This Bud's For You, We Love You." And, in their own way, they do. And men, in their own way, believe it. Bud Girls seem to enjoy their part-time work as hops goddesses as much as men enjoy begging at their feet for key chains and cozies. But just how widespread are these lust-driven promotions?

11   All of the Big Three American labels (Budweiser, Miller and Coors, which constitute nearly 80 percent of the U.S. beer market) practice some college recruiting. But Anheuser-Busch, with nearly 50 percent of the market, has the most extensive program. Miller marketing representative Ann Espey said her company has recently "shied away" from hiring on campus, and agreed that hiring male fraternity representatives is irresponsible. Similarly, Coors spokesman Dave Taylor says his company has "moved away" from such practices. Although "shied away" and "moved away" suggest that Coors and Miller have made significant policy changes, neither representative will say the practice is extinct.

12   "You need to understand the primary consumer target for beer companies is young adult males," Taylor says. "Historically, college programs were very common in the industry when the drinking age was 18. Now at the local level, with 600 independent distributors, does hiring models still occur? Probably, yes."

13   "At the local level" is another key phrase. Because beer girls and college programs are run by independent distributors, parent companies often feign ignorance of the practice. Likewise, while some distributors have never even heard of student recruiting ("College representatives?" asked a shocked receptionist at the Ann Arbor, Michigan, Anheuser-Busch wholesaler. "This is a *beer* distributor, sir"), wholesalers in cities like Tucson, Los Angeles, and Denver have programs in place.

14   To set the stage for the Bud Girls, these distributors pre-pack college bars with streamers, table tents, coasters, inflatable footballs, pool-table lamps, posters, and, of course, neon signs. Add the Bud Girls and the stage is set. The live commercial begins.

15   Two local students, Christi Voigt, 21, and Jaime Franks, 22, enter the Austin BW-3 chicken wing franchise during a Dallas Cowboys football game. They're wearing blue Bud Light halter tops and denim shorts. Bud Girls say they prefer the shorts-and-halter-top ensemble to the classic beer-can-print spandex dress, but noted that the distribution company prefers the tight dress because "It's more visible." (As Mendoza wryly

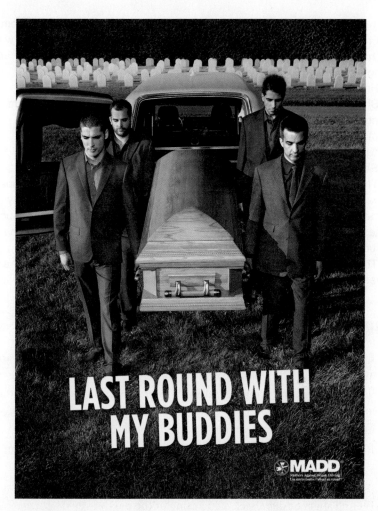

MADD—Mothers Against Drunk Driving—is one of the most respected nonprofit organizations in the United States. For the past 25 years MADD has championed the rights of victims of drunk driving and has promoted public awareness of the consequences of drunk driving. The ad on this page is one of many that were displayed recently on the MADD Web site (www.madd.org).

noted, "A lot of guys have a misconception that if a girl is wearing a dress that looks like a beer can, they can pick us up.")

Although Voigt and Franks give away some free key chains and beers to the rowdy crowd, they mostly distribute charm. Bud Girls have charm on the fly. Once in gear, the beer drinker is the center of attention. The beer drinker is witty and attractive. But if said beer drinker refuses to change brands or asks the nauseatingly common "Can I have you with that beer?" query, the Bud Girl downshifts: The beer drinker is a gnat, an impotent man unworthy of a Bud Girl's slightest concern. They remain professional—the smile never wavers—but the charm is gone and patrons can read "get lost" right through their Colgate teeth.

17   In other words, Bud Girls can really mess with a beer drinker's self-esteem.

18   Franks walks up to a table of four students. She makes eye contact with the tallest male in the group, tilts her head, and slowly asks, "What kind of beer are you drinking?"

19   He guiltily stammers something about Dos Equis.

20   She purposefully lays down a key chain bottle opener in front of him, never breaking eye contact.

21   "What will you drink now?"

22   "Uh, Buh-Bud."

23   She smiles: Good boy.

24   The display is impressive, but Voigt and Franks are rookies. Bud Girl supervisor Eric Bradford sips his Budweiser and wistfully recalls veterans who'd brazenly grab a customers' non-Bud beer and dump it out. Whether sweet or savage, all Bud Girls operate on the same basic principle: their well-endowed bodies become the curvy slates upon which beer slogans and men's horny dreams are projected.

25   The male of the Bud species functions a bit differently. He doesn't wear a spandex dress. He doesn't even need to wear his Budweiser polo shirt. His body is not a

Some Signs that Substance Use Is a Problem

- Being uncomfortable at occasions when alcohol and/or drugs are not available
- When you are not using, regretting things you said or did when you were using
- Arguments with friends or family related to your use
- Being able to handle larger and larger amounts of alcohol and/or drugs over time
- Increased work, family, school, and social problems
- Feeling angry or depressed while using or the next day
- Lying about substance use to friends and loved ones
- Neglecting people and events that don't involve substance use
- "Blackouts" or not remembering what happened when under the influence
- Uncomfortable withdrawal symptoms when not using (e.g., shakiness, fatigue, insomnia, irritability)
- Needing substances to cope with strong feelings, stress, and/or sleeplessness
- Wanting to cut back on use, but not being able to
- Driving a car while under the influence
- Getting in trouble at work or school for using (e.g., showing up late, calling in sick, getting fired)

billboard for Budweiser. It's a double standard straight out of traditional beer commercials, where sexily dressed women wear the product and the cool guys just look like . . . cool guys. Whenever the male rep wishes, he goes unescorted to campus-area bars and buys Bud products for students with his expense account.

26   Corby Ferrell is one of the seven U.T. college reps (or "contemporary marketing representatives," as Budweiser calls them), all of whom are in separate fraternities. Together, the reps keep Budweiser products flowing from local sellers to the frat houses and campus-area parties. Ferrell is the 21-year-old former chairman of Phi Gamma Delta and has blond, anchorman-quality hair. Two or three times a week, Ferrell will go into Cain & Abel's bar located in the heart of Greek territory and approach attractive women drinking Miller or Coors.

27   "Hey, what do you think about switching to Bud Light for the night?" he'll ask. "The first one is on me, and I'll buy you another before I leave." Ferrell admits he has "an awesome job."

28   The second responsibility of male representatives is to arrange beer sales through local vendors. To dispel any confusion about the ethical or legal implications of this practice, Ferrell explains that technically the fraternity organizations do not pay for the beer:

Tips for Safer Drinking

- Drink slowly, don't gulp your drinks, avoid drinking games
- Avoid using alcohol along with other drugs
- Set a limit on how many drinks you are going to have and stick to it
- Eat before you drink, keep in mind that high protein foods help slow alcohol absorption into the bloodstream
- Alternate alcoholic with nonalcoholic drinks
- Don't give in if friends encourage you to drink more than you want to
- Avoid putting your drink down out of sight or accepting drinks from strangers
- Plan ahead! Designate a sober driver in advance, provide transportation at social gatherings where drinking is involved, or use public transportation
- Plan activities that don't involve drinking or drugs

Although these moderation tips are written to apply to the use of alcohol, you can easily adapt these ideas for drug use as well.

In addition, you can also always contact the Counseling Center if you or someone you care about has a problem with drugs and/or alcohol.

Paul Mikowski, PsyD

Postdoctoral Fellow, Counseling and Personal Development Center, Westchester Campus, Pace University

"Members who are at least 21 years old pool their cash to buy beer for parties." When his work with college fraternity members and local vendors leads to a volume sale (five cases of beer, for example), Ferrell is given a commission by Brown Distributing.

29   One sales tactic is for the college rep to establish a relationship with campus-area sellers, then ask who's buying large quantities of competing brands. "Then I'll call the buyer and say, "I can get you 100 cases of [Anheuser-Busch product] Natural Light for at least as cheap as what you're paying for Keystone Light,'" Ferrell says. On average, Ferrell moves 300 cases per week to college buyers. "Fraternities drink the cheapest beer they can find," Bradford, the Bud Girl supervisor, explains. "And his job is to make sure they drink our cheap beer."

30   Neither Ferrell nor Bradford seem reckless or irresponsible, but still—having a Budweiser representative as fraternity chairman is like having Joe Camel as a high school football quarterback. Both popular figureheads not only have a vested interest in which brands are consumed, but the quantity as well. "I think it's better that we do have them out there because of the message that we're bringing," says Laurie Watson, vice president of Brown Distributing. "We're constantly preaching responsibility."

31   Watson was the only senior-level Anheuser-Busch representative willing to comment for this story. A marketing representative for the Anheuser-Busch corporate office at first denied any knowledge of the college program, then agreed only to confirm some facts and produce a copy of the Anheuser-Busch College Marketing Code. The code touts Anheuser-Busch's support of alcohol awareness education and stresses that distributors must limit event sponsorship to venues that check I.D.

32   Bartenders and doormen do check I.D.s, of course. But the Bud Girl handing out free beers doesn't know how much alcohol a patron has consumed. Likewise, frat representatives only card the one individual buying beer for a party. "[Students are] going to have a beer," Watson says. "We just want them to be responsible about it. The representatives always talk to them about responsible drinking." "At least," she adds, "I hope they do. They're supposed to."

33   Imagine a 21-year-old Bud rep arranging a sale of 100 cases of Natural Light, then lecturing to the buyer about responsible drinking. It doesn't click, it doesn't work. The people at Bud must be dreaming. And maybe they are dreaming . . . still. Dreaming of college market saturation, dreaming of young male demographics and dreaming of decades of brand loyalty to come.

34   One week after my Bud barhopping tour, University of Texas junior and Phi Kappa Sigma fraternity member Jack Ivey consumed about 20 drinks, then fell asleep on his apartment couch. He was pronounced dead the next morning of alcohol poisoning, just the latest binge-drinking fatality. Whether Ivey is in the dreams of any beer marketers, no one can say.

FROM READING **TO WRITING**

1. Analyze and compare any two arguments made in this chapter. How is each argument a product of its audience and purpose? What sources of argument are used—ethical appeals, logical appeals, emotional appeals—and what string of "good reasons" are proposed in order to make a case? Why do the composers of those arguments make those particular appeals? (For more on rhetorical analysis, see Chapter 5.)

2. Examine and compare the various visual arguments that appear in this chapter— the photos, ads, and cartoons. What argument, exactly, is being made in each case? How is that argument supported? (See Chapter 6 for information on analyzing visuals.)

3. Write an argument that makes its point by defining a key term related to the regulation of substances like tobacco, high-calorie food, marijuana, alcohol, and so on. You might seek to change people's attitudes by redefining freedom or government regulation or advertising in such a way that your definition supports your views on regulating substances. (See Chapter 8 for more on writing definition arguments.)

4. Propose a particular policy related to the regulation of substances that is important in your community. For example, if binge drinking is an issue at your college or university, you might propose a single measure that might help to ameliorate the situation. Should your institution permit fans to purchase beer at sporting events? What should be the policy of major league baseball toward performance-enhancing drugs? (See Chapter 13 for advice on proposal arguments.)

5. Write a rebuttal of an argument in this chapter concerning the regulation of alcohol, tobacco, steroids, or other substances. (See Chapter 12.) Consider whether you want to show the weaknesses in the argument, or whether you wish to counterargue, or to do both.

6. Write an essay that recounts a personal experience of yours that makes an argument related to the regulation of a particular substance. What exactly does your personal experience lead you to conclude? See Chapter 11 for advice on narrative arguments. Alternatively, consider making your argument based on your observation of another person's experience.

28 | New Media

Personal Space in Cyberspace

Twenty-five years ago, everything seemed so simple and stable. There were a few cable TV stations, but the major networks—NBC, CBS, ABC—still ruled. Radio was delivering comfortable and predictable news, weather, and music to their listeners: Top 40 on one channel, country on another, oldies on a third; talk radio was a late-night-only phenomenon, and sports coverage on the radio was built around familiar voices who were associated with particular teams over many years. The daily local newspaper arrived in the morning or afternoon or both. Every house and office had a central phone line, usually with a few extensions and usually serviced by AT&T.

Is this the future of media? In this publicity still from *Avatar*, all eyes are on the display. What are the consequences of the shift from old to new media?

Then everything changed. Cable television stations multiplied so that the established networks lost market share as well as their monopoly on evening entertainment and news coverage. Even sports coverage changed fundamentally when ESPN began offering its hour-long *SportsCenter* show, and network news gave up market share to the host of news and quasi-news shows that compete so vigorously for an audience today. When Rush Limbaugh created a large audience for his conservative political commentary, many radio stations created or expanded their talk-radio formats. And all that became jumbled still further with the advent of the Internet, which seems to be causing the slow demise of print journalism even as it encourages new, more participatory forms of media in cyberspace. Finally, social networking media and cell phone technologies in the past decade have put a sophisticated communications tool into the pockets and purses of just about everyone.

With these changes have come many concerns and controversies. The effects of new media on our political processes have been particularly criticized. On October 15, 2004, for example, less than three weeks before the presidential elections, popular Comedy Central comedian Jon Stewart, a guest on CNN's political talk show *Crossfire*, got into a celebrated donnybrook with news commentator Tucker Carlson. Stewart, whose hilarious political satire in the form of a mock TV news show sends many Americans to bed with smiles on their faces, took the opportunity of his appearance on *Crossfire* to challenge Carlson about the abysmal level of political commentary in the nation's media. At one point Stewart charged that *Crossfire* and shows like it—he was no doubt thinking of Bill O'Reilly and Rush Limbaugh and Keith Olbermann—are "bad, very bad," for America because they oversimplify and polarize discussion. "It's hurting America," said Stewart. "Stop, stop, stop, stop, stop hurting America." When Carlson protested that *Crossfire* presents intelligent debate from the political left and right, Stewart was outraged: "[Saying *Crossfire* is a debate show is] like saying pro wrestling is a show about athletic competition. You're doing theater when you should be doing debate. . . . What you do is not honest. What you do is partisan hackery . . . just knee-jerk reactionary talk."

While Stewart and his fans were taking their frustrations out on *Crossfire*, they were surely also thinking of much more. In the past decade many Americans have been increasingly concerned about certain trends in the popular media, especially in new media, including Internet news sites, podcasts, and blogs: the development of partisan (rather than "fair and balanced") news coverage; the concentration of news outlets and newspapers into the hands of a few powerful corporations; the impact of sensationalistic and one-sided talk radio and talk TV shows; the effects of the Internet on the political and cultural process; the dubious morality depicted on "reality TV"; attack coverage of events by bloggers and podcasters; and the effects of persistent advertising, violence, graphic sexuality, and cultural stereotyping that are associated now with films, magazines, and television programs. No wonder so many people cringe when they recall the nonstop, no-holds-barred, months-long tabloidization of Tiger Woods's marital infidelities.

Developments in new media—like Wikipedia, avatars, blogs, and Internet social networking sites—are making information and recreation more widely available, but the ease of posting anything on the Internet results in an overwhelming volume of material, a good deal of which is dubious in content. Between the partisanship (both obvious and subtle) of more traditional media and the questionable credibility of new media, many Americans are left wondering where to turn for reliable news and information, and for safe sources of family entertainment. Many, in fact, turn to relentless self-expression via blogs, Twitter, Facebook, and the like—to the personal spaces in cyberspace that may or may not reflect reality. The writers of the selections in this chapter tease out the tensions between freedom and censorship, public and private, in both old and new media; and they ponder the implications of the various new media.

Contemporary Arguments

This chapter opens with four pieces that explore the delicate balance between freedom and restriction on the Internet, as well as the potential consequences of swinging too far in one direction. In "Is Google's Data Grinder Dangerous?" Andrew Keen accuses Google of nefariously plotting for world domination and suggests that the Internet is not (and never will be) the utopian, free intellectual space that John Perry Barlow describes in "A Declaration of the Independence of Cyberspace." Similarly, John Seigenthaler describes a less-than-utopian experience of being the subject of a false Wikipedia biography and the obstacles to finding the identity of the writer. Walt Handelsman's "Information Superhighway" cartoon follows the Internet thread as well; his humorous roadway image shows a strikingly real portrait of priorities on the Internet. All these pieces come together under the broad topic of media and its uses. What is the Internet's purpose? Who should control it? Whose opinions should it publish and validate? And, finally, what are the hidden effects, sacrifices, and benefits when people (and small nonprofit organizations) develop a significant Internet presence?

For many people worldwide, such questions take a backseat to the daily influence of the media in their lives. The balance of the selections in this chapter take up the issue of the Internet, identities, and the burgeoning trend of developing alter egos—and richly detailed alternative worlds—online. In "Where the Avatars Roam," Michael Gerson looks at cyberspace role-playing from a moral perspective: What happens to morality and freedom when we spend so much time in alternative realities where any choice is possible—even criminal or socially undesirable choices? Daniel Okrent follows with a 1999 speech on the future of print media; you will find it highly relevant in the light of what is happening these days to print newspapers, magazine circulation, and e-book technologies such as Kindle and the iPad. (What do you make of the statement by J. K. Rowling, author of the Harry Potter books, that no books about Harry will appear in electronic form?) Then David Carr offers an endorsement of Twitter, and Neil Richards offers a warning about the privacy concerns that are associated with online viewing. Together, these articles tackle the tricky terrain of the private and the public in cyberspace. What kinds of personal expression are meant for public consumption? Should we differentiate between amateur and professional participation online, particularly if amateur expression is so common and so popular? Finally, just what is (and what should be) the purpose of new media—dissemination of information, recreation, commerce, or something else? Are we creating new media, or is it creating us?

The chapter concludes with an Issue in Focus: electronic games. As Chris Kohler indicates in his account of a new fitness game, Nintendo's Wii system actually can provide some exercise for participants, and so he counters concerns that rampant child obesity is the result of all video games. Can other new technologies encourage people to be more active? And what about the other charges against video games—that they undermine learning, encourage teen violence, isolate children socially, and reinforce harmful gender stereotypes? The Issue in Focus takes up all these matters and more. More broadly speaking, to what purposes can we put new media, and how will these technological shifts influence our lives and cultures?

ANDREW **KEEN**

Is Google's Data Grinder Dangerous?

In *The Cult of the Amateur: How Today's Internet Is Killing Our Culture* (2007), Andrew Keen argues that the slew of amateur writing on the Internet—by anyone, about anything—doesn't contribute to knowledge or information, but rather bogs us down with uninformed opinions. Keen's view of the Internet is also evident in the article printed below. First published on July 12, 2007, in the *Los Angeles Times*, "Is Google's Data Grinder Dangerous?" puts a nefarious spin on the most popular Internet search engine—and its seeming quest to know all our private information so it can dominate the world (or at least make billions in advertising).

What does Google want? Having successfully become our personal librarian, Google now wants to be our personal oracle. It wants to learn all about us, know us better than we know ourselves, to transform itself from a search engine into a psychoanalyst's couch or a priest's confessional. Google's search engine is the best place to learn what Google wants. Type "Eric Schmidt London May 22" into Google, and you can read about a May interview the Google chief executive gave to journalists in London. Here is how he described what he hoped the search engine would look like in five years: "The goal is to enable Google users to be able to ask the question such as 'What shall I do tomorrow?' And 'What job shall I take?'"

Schmidt's goal is not inconsiderable: By 2012, he wants Google to be able to tell all of us what we want. This technology, what Google co-founder Larry Page calls the "perfect search engine," might not only replace our shrinks but also all those marketing professionals whose livelihoods are based on predicting—or guessing—consumer desires. Schmidt acknowledges that Google is still far from this goal. As he told the

John Perry Barlow

A Declaration of the Independence of Cyberspace

After seventeen years as a Wyoming rancher who, on the side, wrote songs for the Grateful Dead, John Perry Barlow (born 1947) in the late 1980s began writing about computer-mediated communications. He served on the board of directors of WELL (the Whole Earth Lectronic Link), posts regularly on the WELL Web site, and is a cofounder of the Electronic Frontier Foundation, which advocates keeping government regulations out of the Internet. Since May 1998, he has been a fellow at Harvard Law School's Berkman Center for Internet and Society.

Governments of the Industrial World, you weary giants of flesh and steel, I come from Cyberspace, the new home of Mind. On behalf of the future, I ask you of the past to leave us alone. You are not welcome among us. You have no sovereignty where we gather.

2   We have no elected government, nor are we likely to have one, so I address you with no greater authority than that with which liberty itself always speaks. I declare the global social space we are building to be naturally independent of the tyrannies you seek to impose on us. You have no moral right to rule us nor do you possess any methods of enforcement we have true reason to fear.

3   Governments derive their just powers from the consent of the governed. You have neither solicited nor received ours. We did not invite you. You do not know us, nor do you know our world. Cyberspace does not lie within your borders. Do not think that you can build it, as though it were a public construction project. You cannot. It is an act of nature and it grows itself through our collective actions.

4   You have not engaged in our great and gathering conversation, nor did you create the wealth of our marketplaces. You do not know our culture, our ethics, or the unwritten codes that already provide our society more order than could be obtained by any of your impositions.

5   You claim there are problems among us that you need to solve. You use this claim as an excuse to invade our precincts. Many of these problems don't exist. Where there are real conflicts, where there are wrongs, we will identify them and address them by our means. We are forming our own Social Contract. This governance will arise according to the conditions of our world, not yours. Our world is different.

6   Cyberspace consists of transactions, relationships, and thought itself, arrayed like a standing wave in the web of our communications. Ours is a world that is both everywhere and nowhere, but it is not where bodies live.

7   We are creating a world that all may enter without privilege or prejudice accorded by race, economic power, military force, or station of birth.

8   We are creating a world where anyone, anywhere may express his or her beliefs, no matter how singular, without fear of being coerced into silence or conformity.

9   Your legal concepts of property, expression, identity, movement, and context do not apply to us. They are based on matter. There is no matter here.

10   Our identities have no bodies, so, unlike you, we cannot obtain order by physical coercion. We believe that, from ethics, enlightened self-interest, and the commonweal, our governance will emerge. Our identities may be distributed across many of your jurisdictions. The only law that all our constituent cultures would generally recognize is the Golden Rule. We hope we will be able to build our particular solutions on that basis. But we cannot accept the solutions you are attempting to impose.

11   In the United States, you have today created a law, the Telecommunications Reform Act, which repudiates your own Constitution and insults the dreams of Jefferson, Washington, Mill, Madison, deToqueville, and Brandeis. These dreams must now be born anew in us.

12   You are terrified of your own children, since they are natives in a world where you will always be immigrants. Because you fear them, you entrust your bureaucracies with the parental responsibilities you are too cowardly to confront yourselves. In our world, all the sentiments and expressions of humanity, from the debasing to the angelic, are parts of a seamless whole, the global conversation of bits. We cannot separate the air that chokes from the air upon which wings beat.

13   In China, Germany, France, Russia, Singapore, Italy, and the United States, you are trying to ward off the virus of liberty by erecting guard posts at the frontiers of Cyberspace. These may keep out the contagion for a small time, but they will not work in a world that will soon be blanketed in bit-bearing media.

14   Your increasingly obsolete information industries would perpetuate themselves by proposing laws, in America and elsewhere, that claim to own speech itself throughout the world. These laws would declare ideas to be another industrial product, no more noble than pig iron. In our world, whatever the human mind may create can be reproduced and distributed infinitely at no cost. The global conveyance of thought no longer requires your factories to accomplish.

15   These increasingly hostile and colonial measures place us in the same position as those previous lovers of freedom and self-determination who had to reject the authorities of distant, uninformed powers. We must declare our virtual selves immune to your sovereignty, even as we continue to consent to your rule over our bodies. We will spread ourselves across the Planet so that no one can arrest our thoughts.

16   We will create a civilization of the Mind in Cyberspace. May it be more humane and fair than the world your governments have made before. ▪

London journalists: "We cannot even answer the most basic questions because we don't know enough about you. That is the most important aspect of Google's expansion."

3   So where is Google expanding? How is it planning to know more about us? Many—if not most—users don't read the user agreement and thus aren't aware that Google already stores every query we type in. The next stage is a personalized Web service called iGoogle. Schmidt, who perhaps not coincidentally sits on the board of Apple, regards its success as the key to knowing us better than we know ourselves.

4   iGoogle is growing into a tightly-knit suite of services—personalized homepage, search engine, blog, e-mail system, mini-program gadgets, Web-browsing history, etc.—that together will create the world's most intimate information database. On iGoogle, we all get to aggregate our lives, consciously or not, so artificially intelligent software can sort out our desires. It will piece together our recent blog posts, where we've been online, our e-commerce history and cultural interests. It will amass so much information about each of us that eventually it will be able to logically determine what we want to do tomorrow and what job we want.

5   The real question, of course, is whether what Google wants is what we want too. Do we really want Google digesting so much intimate data about us? Could iGoogle actually be a remix of "1984's" Room 101—that Orwellian dystopia in which our most secret desires and most repressed fears are revealed? Any comparison with 20th century, top-down totalitarianism is, perhaps, a little fanciful. After all, nobody can force us to use iGoogle. And—in contrast to Yahoo and Microsoft (which have no limits on how long they hang on to our personal data)—Google has committed to retaining data for only 18 months. Still, if iGoogle turns out to be half as wise about each of us as Schmidt predicts, then this artificial intelligence will challenge traditional privacy rights as well as provide us with an excuse to deny responsibility for our own actions. What happens, for example, when the government demands access to our iGoogle records? And will we be able to sue iGoogle if it advises us to make an unwise career decision?

6   Schmidt, I suspect, would like us to imagine Google as a public service, thereby affirming the company's "do no evil" credo. But Google is not our friend. Schmidt's iGoogle vision of the future is not altruistic, and his company is not a nonprofit group dedicated to the realization of human self-understanding. Worth more than $150 billion on the public market, Google is by far the dominant Internet advertising outlet—according to Nielsen ratings, it reaches about 70% of the global Internet audience. Just in the first quarter of 2007, Google's revenue from its online properties was up 76% from the previous year. Personal data are Google's most valuable currency, its crown jewels. The more Google knows our desires, the more targeted advertising it can serve up to us and the more revenue it can extract from these advertisers.

7   What does Google really want? Google wants to dominate. Its proposed $3.1-billion acquisition of DoubleClick threatens to make the company utterly dominant in the online advertising business. The $1.65-billion acquisition of YouTube last year made it by far the dominant player in the online video market. And, with a personalized service like iGoogle, the company is seeking to become the algorithmic monopolist of our online behavior. So when Eric Schmidt says Google wants to know us better than we know ourselves, he is talking to his shareholders rather than us. As a Silicon Valley old-timer, trust me on this one. I know Google better than it knows itself.

JOHN **SEIGENTHALER**

A False Wikipedia "Biography"

John Seigenthaler, now retired, is a distinguished journalist who founded the Freedom Forum First Amendment Center at Vanderbilt University—so he is anything but a censor at heart. Nevertheless, in the following essay (published in November 2005 in *USA Today*, a newspaper he helped launch) he expresses grave reservations about *Wikipedia* as he recounts a personal experience. The article printed below generated serious discussion about the reliability, credibility, and ethics of *Wikipedia*, which changed some of its policies subsequently. You can read more about the episode by going to en.wikipedia.org/wiki/ Seigenthaler_controversy. For a writing activity on *Wikipedia*, see page 660.

> John Seigenthaler Sr. was the assistant to Attorney General Robert Kennedy in the early 1960's. For a brief time, he was thought to have been directly involved in the Kennedy assassinations of both John and his brother Bobby. Nothing was ever proven.
>
> —*Wikipedia*

This is a highly personal story about Internet character assassination. It could be your story. I have no idea whose sick mind conceived the false, malicious "biography" that appeared under my name for 132 days on Wikipedia, the popular, online, free encyclopedia whose authors are unknown and virtually untraceable. There was more:

2   "John Seigenthaler moved to the Soviet Union in 1971, and returned to the United States in 1984," Wikipedia said. "He started one of the country's largest public relations firms shortly thereafter."

3   At age 78, I thought I was beyond surprise or hurt at anything negative said about me. I was wrong. One sentence in the biography was true. I was Robert Kennedy's administrative assistant in the early 1960s. I also was his pallbearer. It was mind-boggling when my son, John Seigenthaler, journalist with NBC News, phoned later to say he found the same scurrilous text on Reference.com and Answers.com.

4   I had heard for weeks from teachers, journalists and historians about "the wonderful world of Wikipedia," where millions of people worldwide visit daily for quick reference "facts," composed and posted by people with no special expertise or knowledge—and sometimes by people with malice.

5   At my request, executives of the three websites now have removed the false content about me. But they don't know, and can't find out, who wrote the toxic sentences.

Anonymous Author

6   I phoned Jimmy Wales, Wikipedia's founder and asked, "Do you . . . have any way to know who wrote that?"

7   "No, we don't," he said. Representatives of the other two websites said their computers are programmed to copy data verbatim from Wikipedia, never checking whether it is false or factual. Naturally, I want to unmask my "biographer." And, I am interested in letting many people know that Wikipedia is a flawed and irresponsible research tool.

8   But searching cyberspace for the identity of people who post spurious information can be frustrating. I found on Wikipedia the registered IP (Internet Protocol) number of my "biographer"—65-81-97-208. I traced it to a customer of BellSouth Internet. That company advertises a phone number to report "Abuse Issues." An electronic voice said all complaints must be e-mailed. My two e-mails were answered by identical form letters, advising me that the company would conduct an investigation but might not tell me the results. It was signed "Abuse Team."

9   Wales, Wikipedia's founder, told me that BellSouth would not be helpful. "We have trouble with people posting abusive things over and over and over," he said. "We block their IP numbers, and they sneak in another way. So we contact the service providers, and they are not very responsive."

10   After three weeks, hearing nothing further about the Abuse Team investigation, I phoned BellSouth's Atlanta corporate headquarters, which led to conversations between my lawyer and BellSouth's counsel. My only remote chance of getting the name, I learned, was to file a "John or Jane Doe" lawsuit against my "biographer." Major communications Internet companies are bound by federal privacy laws that protect the identity of their customers, even those who defame online. Only if a lawsuit resulted in a court subpoena would BellSouth give up the name.

Little Legal Recourse

11   Federal law also protects online corporations—BellSouth, AOL, MCI, Wikipedia, etc.— from libel lawsuits. Section 230 of the Communications Decency Act, passed in 1996, specifically states that "no provider or user of an interactive computer service shall be treated as the publisher or speaker." That legalese means that, unlike print and broadcast companies, online service providers cannot be sued for disseminating defamatory attacks on citizens posted by others. Recent low-profile court decisions document that Congress effectively has barred defamation in cyberspace. Wikipedia's website acknowledges that it is not responsible for inaccurate information, but Wales, in a recent C-Span interview with Brian Lamb, insisted that his website is accountable and that his community of thousands of volunteer editors (he said he has only one paid employee) corrects mistakes within minutes.

12   My experience refutes that. My "biography" was posted May 26. On May 29, one of Wales' volunteers "edited" it only by correcting the misspelling of the word "early." For four months, Wikipedia depicted me as a suspected assassin before Wales erased it from his website's history Oct. 5. The falsehoods remained on Answers.com and Reference.com for three more weeks. In the C-Span interview, Wales said Wikipedia has "millions" of daily global visitors and is one of the world's busiest websites. His volunteer community runs the Wikipedia operation, he said. He funds his website through a non-profit foundation and estimated a 2006 budget of "about a million dollars."

13   And so we live in a universe of new media with phenomenal opportunities for worldwide communications and research—but populated by volunteer vandals with poison-pen intellects. Congress has enabled them and protects them.

14   When I was a child, my mother lectured me on the evils of "gossip." She held a feather pillow and said, "If I tear this open, the feathers will fly to the four winds, and I could never get them back in the pillow. That's how it is when you spread mean things about people." For me, that pillow is a metaphor for Wikipedia.

Michael Gerson

Where the Avatars Roam

Michael Gerson, who once worked as a policy analyst and speechwriter under President George W. Bush, is columnist for the *Washington Post* and contributes to *PostPartisan*. His book about the future of conservative politics, *Heroic Conservatism*, was published in 2007. His areas of expertise span democracy and human rights, health and diseases, and religion and politics. Gerson is senior research fellow at the Institute for Global Engagement's Center on Faith and International Affairs. In "Where the Avatars Roam," published in the *Washington Post* July 6, 2007, Gerson asks, what happens to human freedom and human choices in alternative realities constructed online?

I am not usually found at bars during the day, though the state of the Republican Party would justify it. But here I was at a bar talking to this fox—I mean an actual fox, with fluffy tail and whiskers. It turns out that, in the online world of Second Life, many people prefer to take the shape of anthropomorphic animals called "furries," and this one is in a virtual bar talking about her frustrating job at a New York publishing house. But for all I know, she could be a man in outback Montana with a computer, a satellite dish and a vivid imagination.

2　　For a columnist, this is called "research." For millions of Americans, it is an addictive form of entertainment called MMORPGs—massively multiplayer online role-playing games. In this entirely new form of social interaction, people create computer-generated bodies called avatars and mingle with other players in 3-D fantasy worlds.

3　　Some of these worlds parallel a form of literature that J.R.R. Tolkien called "sub-creation"—the Godlike construction of a complex, alternative reality, sometimes with its own mythology and languages. I subscribe along with my two sons (an elf and a dwarf) to The Lord of the Rings Online, based on Tolkien's epic novels, which sends its participants on a series of heroic quests. I'm told that World of Warcraft, which has more than 8 million subscribers, takes a similar approach. Some of the appeal of these games is the controlled release of aggression—cheerful orc killing. But they also represent a conservative longing for medieval ideals of chivalry—for a recovery of honor and adventure in an age dominated by choice and consumption.

4　　Second Life, however, is a different animal. Instead of showing the guiding hand of an author, this universe is created by the choices of its participants, or "residents." They can

If you were to create an avatar, would you want to look like yourself or someone or something else? Why?

build, buy, trade and talk in a world entirely without rules or laws; a pure market where choice and consumption are the highest values. Online entrepreneurs make real money selling virtual clothing, cars and "skins"—the photorealistic faces and bodies of avatars. Companies such as Dell, IBM and Toyota market aggressively within Second Life.

Coca Cola, the marketers from that company have found you on the beach, and for the privilege of getting their message in front of you they have paid the satellite operator a carriage fee. The satellite operator, wanting to guarantee the advertising agency that the impression has been made, credits your master account a few cents. For reading the one-minute message from Coca Cola, you get the first five minutes of tomorrow's electronic newspaper for free. Everyone's happy.

17   As I said, this technology already exists. It's far too expensive today, and the critical elements of payment systems and copyright protection and royalty accounting have not yet been created. But, I guarantee you that such systems are either in development today or soon will be.

18   But, you say, who wants to read a good novel on a computer screen, no matter how clear and snappy and portable it is? Who wants to forgo the tactile engagement with a newspaper or magazine, or even moreso the deeper, more gratifying physical connection with a book, and replace it with this potentially alienating form of modern technology?

19   Well, that brings me to part two of my argument, the part I promised was as obvious as the morning sun. And that is this: last year, Time Inc., spent $1 billion dollars on paper and postage.

20   End of argument.

21   Or, if you'd like, let me put it this way: you may prefer to ride across town in horse-and-carriage, or across a lake in a wind-powered yacht, but no one makes that carriage or that yacht for you anymore, at least not at a reasonable price. So too with the book: in the future that I am imagining with you tonight, the book becomes an elite item for the very few, an *objet,* a collectible—valuable not for the words on the page but for the vessel that contains those words. Will it matter to the book-loving *litterateurs* who stalk Morningside Heights? Probably so, though I can't imagine why. Will it matter to the millions who buy a John Grisham paperback and toss it when it's done? Not a chance.

22   Nor should it. For we—we who work today by accident in paper and ink; who demand, however sheepishly, that vast forests be cut down to make our paper, for vast sums to be invested in hypermodern printing presses and bindery machines that consume megawatts of environment-befouling energy—we should be happy. For we know—we *must* know—that the words and pictures and ideas and images and notions and substance that we produce is what matters—and *not* the vessel that they arrive in.

23   I want to step back for a few moments here to elaborate on business models, consumer prejudices, and what I hope is a somewhat sober-sided consideration of a few of the risks this new world will pose.

24   First, business models. To date, we have seen very few media institutions find a way to charge for their digitally-delivered content: the *Wall Street Journal*, which is as close as one gets in American journalism to being both unique and essential, has been the leader to date. I admire the *Journal* hugely, both in print and online, but I do want to share with you the real reason for its success, the thing that makes it essential. This was explained to by my boss, Norm Pearlstine, several years ago when he was the

Journal's editor: the paper's indispensability, he said, is predicated on the mortal fear, shared by every middle manager in American business, that the boss will say to him or her, "Did you see the piece in the *Journal* this morning about X?"

25   Well, that works online, too, and several hundred thousand people are now paying Dow-Jones for the online paper. But note that they are paying $59 for an annual subscription to the online edition, while the print edition costs $175. That's partly because the physical costs—the nearly $1 billion a year, in our case, that Time Inc. spends on manufacturing and distribution—have evaporated. In other words, savings have been passed on to the reader, and everybody wins. Except, of course, the paper manufacturers, the delivery services, and the US Post Office—so all of you who have been planning careers at International Paper or with the Postal Service, forget it.

26   But the real power of the business model resides in the potential of digital advertising. Except for direct mail, until the Internet came along no advertising medium existed in which the advertiser could be sure his message was received by his targeted audience. We go to the bathroom during commercials, we flip the pages past magazine and newspaper ads, radio and billboards are white noise. But with a truly interactive medium—with say, a question about the advertisement asked next to the button that gives you your thirty cent credit against the cost of reading your *Wall Street Journal*—the effectiveness of media advertising changes radically. And if you don't think advertisers influence the direction of American mass media, you ought to talk to Tom Goldstein about the curriculum here at the J-school.

27   Second digression: consumer prejudices. Inevitably, whenever and wherever I talk about the Death of Print, someone jumps up and says, "But I hate reading on a computer." This is after I have already explained that the technology will change, that economic incentive will create consumer-friendly reading devices, that my father once paid as much for a four-function telephone book-sized calculator as he did for a low-end used car. Or that Oscar Dystel, the former chairman of Bantam Books and one of the founders of the American paperback book industry in the 1940s, once said, "In due course, the word 'paperback' will lose its taint of unpleasantness." And he said that in 1984.

28   No, you won't be reading on a cathode ray tube sitting on your desk. No, the screen won't flicker, and the type won't have visible ragged edges. It won't feel anything like a computer. It won't even feel like those early avatars of the form, the Rocket eBook and the SoftBook Reader, that are already showing up in Christmas catalogs and in consumer electronics stores—not any more than a Model T feels or looks or drives like a 1999 BMW Z3. There's even a guy at MIT, an engineering genius named Jacobson, who's devised something called electronic ink, a palette of digitally changeable molecules that sit on a surface very much like a sheet of paper, and rearrange themselves sequentially into actual sentences and paragraphs.

29   Ah, but you say, who will be able to afford such wonderful devices? In fact, nearly everyone. Because we—the big media companies like Time Warner, the eight or ten major copyright oligarchs, as I like to call them, who control so much of the nation's supply of worthwhile content—we will give them away, for all practical purposes, on the cell phone model. Agree to subscribe to *Time* and *Sports Illustrated* for two years, as well as to listen to a certain amount of, say, Warner Brothers Music, and we'll give you the device. We aren't interested in making money off of hardware; we make money off of what you read and watch and listen to.

30   Last digression: risk. Yes, there are risks. Disaggregated content has already been somewhat socially injurious, and it's only going to get worse, at least insofar as we like to imagine a citizenry that is not only informed, but informed across a range of subjects. The ability to be your own editor—to pick just what news on what topics you wish to read—destroys the potential for serendipity, and the ease with which we achieve balance. I don't know how we'll solve this one, but we must.

31   Similarly, there's a risk in the mutability of digital content. The good news is that if you libel someone at 9 A.M., you can correct it at 9:10 or at noon or whenever it is that you learn of your mistake; it's not like sending out a fleet of trucks with a million copies of the *Times* and then realizing what you did wrong. But by the same token, if the words are never written in stone, or at least in ink, what happens to the notion of historical record?

32   But, of course, that cat is already out of the bag. If great writers are producing their works on computer, as most now do, first drafts no longer exist for the study of future scholars—just as the hurried prose of a daily newspaper, "the first rough draft of history," as it has been called, may disappear to the corrections of lawyers.

33   Yet I think we can live with these things, largely because we must.

34   I will assert once again that The Death of Print is going to happen, far sooner than many of you may think. The word "Internet" was all but unknown in the U.S. six

years ago, and Time Inc., which had not yet even imagined its potential impact, had no one working in the Internet arena. Today, the Internet is inescapable; through the advent of email, it is ubiquitous. In the financial markets, it as essential as dollars. Throughout Time Warner, more than 1,000 people are developing copyrighted internet product, or marketing it to consumers. Someday, we may even make money at it.

35   For now, though, all of this is destabilizing, particularly for those of us who are investing substantially in a future so tantalizingly clear in the ultimate goal, but the path to which is so tangled in thickets of doubt, uncertainty, and confusion. Yet I, for one, take a strange kind of solace in this. What I know to be true is that the human species is hungry for information; that the quality, timeliness, and reliability of information is paramount; and that those of us who grew up in print, who look at the technological future through unconfident eyes, will be asked to do tomorrow exactly what we have done in the past, which is to reach people—intellectually, viscerally, any way we can—on matters they care about. My colleagues and I did not grow up wanting to be in the ink and paper and staples business; we wanted to be in—we *are* in—the business of words and sentences and pictures and ideas. Don't worry about the future of newspapers or magazines or books any more than you would worry about corrugated boxes or shrink-wrap. They are containers; the substance resides elsewhere—for instance, in this room. So thank you for your attention; you may now throw tomatoes at me.

DAVID **CARR**

Why Twitter Will Endure

David Carr is the author of "Media Equation," a column in the *New York Times* that focuses on media issues. His work analyzes the media as they intersect with business, culture, and government. His writing has also appeared in the *Atlantic Monthly* and *New York Magazine.* The following *Times* article was published on January 3, 2010.

I can remember when I first thought seriously about Twitter. Last March, I was at the SXSW conference, a conclave in Austin, Tex., where technology, media, and music are mashed up and re-imagined, and, not so coincidentally, where Twitter first rolled out in 2007. As someone who was oversubscribed on Facebook, overwhelmed by the computer-generated RSS feeds of news that came flying at me, and swamped by incoming e-mail messages, the last thing I wanted was one more Web-borne intrusion into my life.

2   And then there was the name. Twitter. In the pantheon of digital nomenclature—brands within a sector of the economy that grew so fast that all the sensible names were quickly taken—it would be hard to come up with a noun more trite than Twitter. It impugns itself, promising something slight and inconsequential, yet another way to make hours disappear and have nothing to show for it. And just in case the noun is not sufficiently indicting, the verb, "to tweet" is even more embarrassing.

3   Beyond the dippy lingo, the idea that something intelligent, something worthy of mindshare, might occur in the space of 140 characters—Twitter's parameters were set by what would fit in a text message on a phone—seems unlikely.

4   But it was clear that at the conference, the primary news platform was Twitter, with real-time annotation of the panels on stage and critical updates about what was happening elsewhere at a very hectic convention. At 52, I succumbed, partly out of professional necessity.

5   And now, nearly a year later, has Twitter turned my brain to mush? No, I'm in narrative on more things in a given moment than I ever thought possible, and instead of spending a half-hour surfing in search of illumination, I get a sense of the day's news and how people are reacting to it in the time that it takes to wait for coffee at Starbucks. Yes, I worry about my ability to think long thoughts—where was I, anyway?—but the tradeoff has been worth it.

6   Some time soon, the company won't say when, the 100-millionth person will have signed on to Twitter to follow and be followed by friends and strangers. That may sound like a MySpace waiting to happen—remember MySpace?—but I'm convinced Twitter is here to stay.

7   And I'm not alone. "The history of the Internet suggests that there have been cool Web sites that go in and out of fashion and then there have been open standards that become plumbing," said Steven Johnson, the author and technology observer who wrote a seminal piece about Twitter for Time last June. "Twitter is looking more and more like plumbing, and plumbing is eternal."

8   Really? What could anyone possibly find useful in this cacophony of short-burst communication? Well, that depends on whom you ask, but more importantly whom you follow. On Twitter, anyone may follow anyone, but there is very little expectation of reciprocity. By carefully curating the people you follow, Twitter becomes an always-on data stream from really bright people in their respective fields, whose tweets are often full of links to incredibly vital, timely information.

9   The most frequent objection to Twitter is a predictable one: "I don't need to know someone is eating a donut right now." But if that someone is a serious user of Twitter, she or he might actually be eating the curmudgeon's lunch, racing ahead with a clear, up-to-the-second picture of an increasingly connected, busy world. The service has obvious utility for a journalist, but no matter what business you are in, imagine knowing what the thought leaders in your industry were reading and considering. And beyond following specific individuals, Twitter hash tags allow you to go deep into interests and obsession: #rollerderby, #physics, #puppets and #Avatar, to name just a few of many thousands.

10   The act of publishing on Twitter is so friction-free—a few keystrokes and hit send—that you can forget that others are out there listening. I was on a Virgin America cross-country flight, and used its wireless connection to tweet about the fact that the guy next to me seemed to be the leader of a cult involving Axe body spray. A half-hour later, a steward approached me and said he wondered if I would be more comfortable with a seat in the bulkhead. (He turned out to be a great guy, but I was doing a story involving another part of the company, so I had to decline the offer. @VirginAmerica, its corporate Twitter account, sent me a message afterward saying perhaps it should develop a screening process for Axe. It was creepy and comforting all at once.)

11   Like many newbies on Twitter, I vastly overestimated the importance of broadcasting on Twitter; and after a while, I realized that I was not Moses and neither Twitter nor its users were wondering what I thought. Nearly a year in, I've come to understand that the real value of the service is listening to a wired collective voice.

12   Not that long ago, I was at a conference at Yale and looked at the sea of open laptops in the seats in front of me. So why wasn't my laptop open? Because I follow people on Twitter who serve as my Web-crawling proxies, each of them tweeting links that I could examine and read on a Blackberry. Regardless of where I am, I surf far less than I used to.

13   At first, Twitter can be overwhelming, but think of it as a river of data rushing past that I dip a cup into every once in a while. Much of what I need to know is in that cup: if it looks like Apple is going to demo its new tablet, or Amazon sold more Kindles than actual books at Christmas, or the final vote in the Senate gets locked in on health care, I almost always learn about it first on Twitter.

14   The expressive limits of a kind of narrative developed from text messages, with less space to digress or explain than this sentence, has significant upsides. The best people on Twitter communicate with economy and precision, with each element—links, hash tags and comments—freighted with meaning. Professional acquaintances whom I find insufferable on every other platform suddenly become interesting within the confines of Twitter.

15   Twitter is incredibly customizable, with little of the social expectations that go with Facebook. Depending on whom you follow, Twitter can reveal a nation riveted by the last episode of "Jersey Shore" or a short-form conclave of brilliance. There is plenty of nonsense—#Tiger had quite a run—but there are rich threads on the day's news and bravura solo performances from learned autodidacts. And the ethos of Twitter, which is based on self-defining groups, is far more well-mannered than many parts of the Web—more Toastmasters than mosh pit. On Twitter, you are your avatar and your avatar is you, so best not to act like a lout and when people want to flame you for something you said, they are responding to their own followers, not yours, so trolls quickly lose interest.

16   "Anything that is useful to both dissidents in Iran and Martha Stewart has a lot going for it; Twitter has more raw capability for users than anything since e-mail," said Clay Shirky, who wrote "Here Comes Everybody," a book about social media. "It will be hard to wait out Twitter because it is lightweight, endlessly useful and gets better as more people use it. Brands are using it, institutions are using it, and it is becoming a place where a lot of important conversations are being held." Twitter helps define what is important by what Mr. Shirky has called "algorithmic authority," meaning that if all kinds of people are pointing at the same thing at the same instant, it must be a pretty big deal.

17   Beyond the throbbing networked intelligence, there is the possibility of practical magic. Twitter can tell you what kind of netbook you should buy for your wife for Christmas—thanks Twitter!—or call you out when you complain about the long lines it took to buy it, as a tweeter on behalf of the electronics store B & H did when I shared the experience on my Blackberry while in line. I have found transcendent tacos at a car wash in San Antonio, rediscovered a brand of reporter's notepad I adore, uncovered sources for stories, all just by typing a query into Twitter.

18   All those riches do not come at zero cost: If you think e-mail and surfing can make time disappear, wait until you get ahold of Twitter, or more likely, it gets ahold of you. There is always something more interesting on Twitter than whatever you happen to be working on.

19   But in the right circumstance, Twitter can flex some big muscles. Think of last weekend, a heavy travel period marked by a terrorist incident on Friday. As news outlets were scrambling to understand the implications for travelers on Saturday morning, Twitter began lighting up with reports of new security initiatives, including one from @CharleneLi, a consultant who tweeted from the Montreal airport at about 7:30 A.M.: "New security rules for int'l flights into US. 1 bag, no electronics the ENTIRE flight, no getting up last hour of flight." It was far from the whole story and getting ahead of the news by some hours would seem like no big deal, but imagine you or someone you loved was flying later that same day: Twitter might seem very useful.

20   Twitter's growing informational hegemony is not assured. There have been serious outages in recent weeks, leading many business and government users to wonder about the stability of the platform. And this being the Web, many smart folks are plotting ways to turn Twitter into so much pixilated mist. But I don't think so. I can go anywhere I want on the Web, but there is no guarantee that my Twitter gang will come with me. I may have quite a few followers, but that doesn't make me Moses.

NEIL **RICHARDS**

The Perils of Social Reading

Neil M. Richards is a professor of law at Washington University in St. Louis. An expert on privacy law and the First Amendment, he frequently writes about the relationships between civil liberties and technology, and his book *Intellectual Privacy* was recently published by Oxford University Press. Born in England, he holds degrees in law and legal history from the University of Virginia; he was a law clerk for William H. Rehnquist (the late Chief Justice of the U.S. Supreme Court), and he once defended a fantasy baseball company in a lawsuit filed by Major League Baseball. The following item was published as a blog entry in 2012; a much longer version appeared in the *Georgetown Law Journal* in 2013.

Sharing, we are told, is cool. At the urging of Facebook and Netflix, the House of Representatives recently passed a bill to "update" an obscure 1988 law known as the Video Privacy Protection Act ("VPPA").[1] Facebook and Netflix wanted to modernize this law from the VHS era, because its protection of video store records stood in the way of sharing movie recommendations among friends online. The law would have allowed companies to obtain a single consent to automatically share all movies viewed on Facebook and other social networks forever. The bill stalled in the Senate after a feisty hearing[2] before Senator Franken, though some modernization of our video privacy law is inevitable.

2   But the VPPA debate is just the start, merely one part of a much larger trend towards "social reading." The Internet and social media have opened up new vistas for us to share our preferences in films, books, and music. Services like Spotify and the Washington Post Social Reader already integrate our reading and listening into social networks, providing what Facebook CEO Mark Zuckerberg calls "frictionless sharing."[3] Under a regime of frictionless sharing, we don't need to choose to share our activities online. Instead, everything we read or watch automatically gets uploaded to our social media feeds. As Zuckerberg puts it, "Do you want to go to the movies by yourself or do you want to go to the movies with your friends? You want to go with your friends."[4] Music, reading, web-surfing, and Google searches, in this view, would all seem to benefit from being made social.[5]

3   Not so fast. The sharing of book, film, and music recommendations is important, and social networking has certainly made this easier. But a world of automatic, always-on disclosure should give us pause. What we read, watch, and listen to matter, because they are how we make up our minds about important social issues—in a very real sense, they're how we make sense of the world.

4   What's at stake is something I call "intellectual privacy" —the idea that records of our reading and movie watching deserve special protection compared to other kinds of personal information.[6] The films we watch, the books we read, and the web sites we visit are essential to the ways we try to understand the world we live in. Intellectual privacy protects our ability to think for ourselves, without worrying that other people might judge us based on what we read. It allows us to explore ideas that other people might not approve of, and to figure out our politics, sexuality, and personal values, among other things. It lets us watch or read whatever we want without fear of embarrassment or being outed. This is the case whether we're reading communist, gay teen, or anti-globalization books; or visiting web sites about abortion, gun control, or cancer; or watching videos of pornography, or documentaries by Michael Moore, or even "The Hangover 2."

5   I'm not saying we should never share our intellectual preferences. On the contrary, sharing and commenting on books, films, and ideas is the essence of free speech. We need access to the ideas of others so that we can make up our minds for ourselves. Individual liberty has a social component. But when we share —when we speak —we should do so consciously and deliberately, not automatically and unconsciously. Because of the constitutional magnitude of these values, our social, technological, professional, and legal norms should support rather than undermine our intellectual privacy.

6   "Frictionless sharing" isn't really frictionless —it forces on us the new frictions of worrying who knows what we're reading and what our privacy settings are wherever and however we read electronically. It's also not really sharing —real sharing is conscious sharing, a recommendation to read or not to read something rather than a data exhaust pipe of mental activity. At a practical level, then, always-on social sharing of our reader records provides less valuable recommendations than conscious sharing, and it can deter us from exploring ideas that our friends might find distasteful. Rather than "over-sharing," we should share better, which means consciously, and we should expand the limited legal protections for intellectual privacy rather than dismantling them.

7   There is a paradox to reader privacy: we need intellectual privacy to make up our minds, but we often need the assistance and recommendations of others as part of this

A shredder is customarily employed to *safeguard* privacy. What role does irony play in this image? How successful is the image in conveying meaning?

process, be they friends, librarians, or search engines. The work of the ALA and its Office of Intellectual Freedom offers an attractive solution to the problem of reader records. The OIF has argued passionately (and correctly) for the importance of solitary reading as well as the ethical need for those who enable reading —librarians, but also Internet companies —to protect the privacy and confidentiality of reading records. The norms of librarians suggest one successful and proven solution to this paradox. Most relevant here, this means that professionals and companies holding reader records must only disclose them with the express conscious consent of the reader.

8   The stakes in this debate are immense. We are quite literally rewiring the public and private spheres for a new century. Choices we make now about the boundaries between our individual and social selves, between consumers and companies, between citizens and the state, will have massive consequences for the societies our children and grandchildren inherit.

9   Social networking technologies have matured to the point where many new things are possible. But we face a moment of decision. The choice between sharing and privacy is not foreordained; there are many decisions we must make as a society about how our reader records can flow, and under what terms. We've heard from the advocates of "sharing" and "social," but we must also secure a place for the thoughtful, the private, and the eccentric. When it comes to the question of how to regulate our reading records, a world of automatic, constant disclosure is not the answer.

10   The choices we make today will be sticky. They'll have lasting consequences for the kind of networked society we will build, and whether there's a place in that society for intellectual privacy and for confidential, contemplative, and idiosyncratic reading. Sharing might be cool, but some things, like intellectual privacy and our centuries-old culture of solitary reading, are more important. We need to preserve them; we need to choose intellectual privacy.

Notes

1. H.R. 2471, 112th Cong. (2011).
2. *The Video Privacy Protection Act: Protecting Viewer Privacy in the 21st Century: Hearing on H.R. 2471 Before the Subcomm. on Privacy, Technology and the Law of the S. Comm. on the Judiciary*, 112th Cong. (2012).
3. Alexia Tsotsis, *Live from Facebook's 2011 F8 Conference [Video]*, TECHCRUNCH (Feb. 20, 2012, 11:50 PM), http://techcrunch.com/2011/09/22/live-from-facebooks-2011-f8-conference-video/ (Zuckerberg said "[t]hese new apps will focus on 'Frictionless Experiences,' 'Realtime Serendipity' and 'Finding patterns'").
4. Evgeny Morozov, *The Death of the Cyberflâneur*, New York Times , Feb. 5, 2012, at SR2.
5. See also Jeff Jarvis, *Public Parts: How Sharing in the Digital Age Improves the Way We Work and Live* 43–62 (2011) (extolling the values of sharing and "publicness").
6. Neil M. Richards, *Intellectual Privacy*, 87 Tex. L. Rev. 387 (2008). For a partial list of other scholars who have adopted this framework, see, e.g., Julie Cohen, *The Networked Self* (2012); Daniel J. Solove, *Nothing to Hide* (2011); Pauline Kim, *Electronic Privacy and Employee Speech*, 87 Chi.-Kent. L. Rev. (forthcoming 2012); William McGeveran, *Mrs. Mcintyre's Persona: Bringing Privacy Theory to Election Law*, 19 Wm. and Mary Bill Rts. J. 859 (2011); Paul Ohm, *Massive Hard Drives, General Warrants, and the Power of Magistrate Judges*, 97 Va. L. Rev. In Brief 1 (2011); Christopher Slobogin, *Citizens United & Corporate & Human Crime*, 1 Green Bag 2d 77 (2010).

Are Video Games Good for You?

The video game *Tomb Raider,* featuring Lara Croft as its British-archeologist hero-ine, was released in 1996 and soon developed into a pop culture phenomenon. In addition to becoming the most popular video game in history, *Tomb Raider* be-came a movie, and then a second movie (with Angelina Jolie in the starring

Angelina Jolie as Lara Croft in *Lara Croft Tomb Raider: The Cradle of Life* (2003), a film based on a series of bestselling video games.

role)—and then a comic book, a novel, and even a theme park ride. Lara Croft's fans regard her as an ideal female icon—as brave as she is beautiful, strong and daring and smart, resourceful and fiercely independent.

2   But Lara Croft has not been without her critics. Skeptics, noting how Lara Croft's breast size seemed to increase along with her popularity, have contended that she is simply reinforcing traditional stereotypes, that her popularity derives from her starring role in the sexual fantasies of the predominantly male audience that enjoys "playing with her." Almost all teenage boys play video games, but only about half of girls do so, and so no wonder parents worry about the effect of video games on consumers' sex and gender attitudes. For *Tomb Raider* is hardly the only game that depicts women and men in traditional roles, the men as active adventurers, the women as passive victims or sex objects.

3   Critics of video games wonder about other issues as well, just as an earlier generation worried about the effects of television. While many video games depend on social interactions, requiring or permitting multiple players to interact via networked systems and thus bringing people together, many other games can be played individually. Do video games lead to social isolation? Is there an addictive element to gaming that makes their consumers socially inept?

4   And what about the stylized violence that lies at the heart of many video games? If games ask players to abuse women and shoot policemen, is it any wonder that those activities persist in real life? When those who carry out school shootings are shown to be devotees of video games, shouldn't we worry about the effects of prolonged exposure to gaming? True, the games are age-rated, as movies are, but it is easy to evade the rules and obtain adult-rated games illegally. And it is worrisome that adult males are especially eager players of violent video games, particularly when the violence in the games is directed at women. Even though juvenile crime rates actually seem to be down, suggesting that people can usually distinguish the difference between game life and real life, it seems natural to expect that video games are affecting people's values—and actions—negatively. Are video games a kind of propaganda—do the games sensationalize drugs and alcohol and illicit sex, in effect "advertising" a way of life that is socially destructive? Or is it all in good fun?

5   Indeed, people criticize video games irrespective of their content. They contend that video games make people not just socially inept but also sedentary. Is the national obesity epidemic related to the popularity of video gaming? Do games, like television, encourage people to avoid real physical activity in order to perform fantasy deeds in front of a screen? And are children playing video games instead of reading or doing homework? In other words, are video games compromising our educational aspirations? Or do they actually help their users, not only by honing hand-eye coordination and visual perception skills but by improving the analytical and problem-solving abilities of users as well as their creativity and ability to concentrate? It has even been suggested that video games can assist in the treatment of autism and certain other mental health conditions.

6   The selections in this Issue in Focus propose answers to those questions. John Beck and Mitchell Wade blame video games for giving people an unreal sense of reality, while James Paul Gee defends video games for their educational value. Kevin Moss, with a substantial sense of irony, makes a strong case that video games set women back. Finally, Clay Shirky concludes the segment, and the chapter, with a fascinating defense of new media that is based on their ability to bring us together and shake us into becoming our most creative selves. (You should also consult the essay on this topic by student Armadi Tansal in Chapter 9.)

John C. Beck and Mitchell Wade

How the Gamer Revolution Is Reshaping Business Forever

DEFINITELY NOT IN KANSAS ANYMORE

Games are a technology that has been universally adopted by a large, young cohort and ignored by their elders. That's powerful enough to start with. But when you look at the experience that technology delivers—the content and the nature of the gamers' world—things really get interesting. Universally, and almost subliminally, games deliver a "reality" where the rules are quite different from any found out here in the rest of the world. Take a look at this quick overview of the lessons games teach:

The Individual's Role

2
- *You're the star.* You are the center of attention of every game unlike, say, Little League, where most kids will *never* be the star.
- *You're the boss.* The world is very responsive to you. You can choose things about reality, or switch to different experiences, in a way that is literally impossible in real life.
- *You're the customer, and the customer is always right.* Like shopping, the whole experience is designed for your satisfaction and entertainment; the opponents are tough, but never *too* tough.
- *You're an expert.* You have the experience of getting really, really good—especially compared to others who actually see you perform—early and often.
- *You're a tough guy.* You can experience all sorts of crashes, suffering, and death—and it doesn't hurt.

How the World Works

3
- *There's always an answer.* You might be frustrated for a while, you might even never find it, but you know it's there.
- *Everything is possible.* You see yourself or other players consistently do amazing things: defeat hundreds of bad guys singlehandedly, say, or beat the best N.B.A. team ever.
- *The world is a logical, human-friendly place.* Games are basically fair. Events may be random but not inexplicable, and there is not much mystery.
- *Trial-and-error is almost always the best plan.* It's the only way to advance in most games, even if you ultimately break down and buy a strategy guide or copy others on the really hard parts.
- *Things are (unrealistically) simple.* Games are driven by models. Even complex models are a lot simpler than reality. *You can figure a game out, completely.* Try that with real life.

How People Relate

4
- *It's all about competition.* You're always competing; even if you collaborate with other human players, you are competing against some character or score.
- *Relationships are structured.* To make the game work, there are only a few pigeonholes people (real or virtual) can fit into, such as competitor/ally and boss/subordinate.
- *We are all alone.* The gaming experience is basically solitary, even if played in groups. And you don't experience all of the activity, for any sustained time, as part of a group.
- *Young people rule.* Young people dominate gaming. Paying your dues takes a short time, youth actually helps, and there is no attention paid to elders.
- *People are simple.* Most in games are cartoon characters. Their skills may be complex, multidimensional, and user-configurable, but their personality types and behaviors are simple. There's big and strong, wild and crazy, beautiful and sexy, and a few other caricatures. That's it.

What You Should Do

5
- *Rebel.* Edginess and attitude are dominant elements of the culture.
- *Be a hero.* You always get the star's role; that is the only way to succeed or get satisfaction.
- *Bond with people who share your game experience, not your national or cultural background.* It's a very global world, in design, consumption, and characters, and in the phenomenon of the game generation.
- *Make your own way in the world.* Leaders are irrelevant and often evil; ignore them.
- *Tune out and have fun.* The whole experience of gaming is escapist. When reality is boring, you hop into game world. When a game gets boring, you switch to one that isn't.

6
Not exactly like "real life," is it? And remember, this other-worldly experience has been exclusive to gamers. ∎

JAMES PAUL **GEE**

Games, Not Schools, Are Teaching Kids to Think

The US spends almost $50 billion each year on education, so why aren't kids learning? Forty percent of students lack basic reading skills, and their academic performance is dismal compared with that of their foreign counterparts. In response to this crisis, schools are skilling-and-drilling their way "back to basics," moving toward mechanical instruction methods that rely on line-by-line scripting for teachers and endless multiple-choice testing. Consequently, kids aren't learning how to think anymore—they're learning how to memorize. This might be an ideal recipe for the future Babbitts of the world, but it won't produce the kind of agile, analytical minds that will lead the high tech global age. Fortunately, we've got *Grand Theft Auto: Vice City* and *Deus X* for that.

2   After school, kids are devouring new information, concepts, and skills every day, and, like it or not, they're doing it controller in hand, plastered to the TV. The fact is, when kids play videogames they can experience a much more powerful form of learning than when they're in the classroom. Learning isn't about memorizing isolated facts. It's about connecting and manipulating them. Doubt it? Just ask anyone who's beaten *Legend of Zelda* or solved *Morrowind*.

3   The phenomenon of the videogame as an agent of mental training is largely unstudied; more often, games are denigrated for being violent or they're just plain ignored. They shouldn't be. Young gamers today aren't training to be gun-toting carjackers. They're learning how to learn. In *Pikmin*, children manage an army of plantlike aliens and strategize to solve problems. In *Metal Gear Solid 2*, players move stealthily through virtual environments and carry out intricate missions. Even in the notorious *Vice City*, players craft a persona, build a history, and shape a virtual world. In strategy games like *WarCraft III* and *Age of Mythology*, they learn to micromanage an array of elements while simultaneously balancing short- and long-term goals. That sounds like something for their resumes.

4   The secret of a videogame as a teaching machine isn't its immersive 3-D graphics but its underlying architecture. Each level dances around the outer limits of the player's abilities, seeking at every point to be hard enough to be just doable. In cognitive science, this is referred to as the "regime of competence principle," which results in a feeling of simultaneous pleasure and frustration—a sensation as familiar to gamers as sore thumbs. Cognitive scientist Andy diSessa has argued that the best instruction hovers at the boundary of a student's competence. Most schools, however, seek to avoid invoking feelings of both pleasure and frustration, blind to the fact that these emotions can be extremely useful when it comes to teaching kids.

5   Also, good videogames incorporate the principle of expertise. They tend to encourage players to achieve total mastery of one level, only to challenge and undo that mastery in the next, forcing kids to adapt and evolve. This carefully choreographed dialectic has been identified by learning theorists as the best way to achieve expertise in any field. This doesn't happen much in our routine-driven schools, where "good" students are often just good at "doing school."

6   How did videogames become such successful models of effective learning? Game coders aren't trained as cognitive scientists. It's a simple case of free-market economics: If a title doesn't teach players how to play it well, it won't sell well. Game companies don't rake in $6.9 billion a year by dumbing down the material—aficionados condemn short and easy games like *Half Life: Blue Shift* and *Devil May Cry 2*. Designers respond by making harder and more complex games that require mastery of sophisticated worlds and as many as 50 to 100 hours to complete. Schools, meanwhile, respond with more tests, more drills, and more rigidity. They're in the cognitive-science dark ages.

7   We don't often think about videogames as relevant to education reform, but maybe we should. Game designers don't often think of themselves as learning theorists. Maybe they should. Kids often say it doesn't feel like learning when they're gaming—they're much too focused on playing. If kids were to say that about a science lesson, our country's education problems would be solved.

Kevin Moss

Blog Entry: The Enemy of My Irony Is My Friend

I thought I could keep myself away from this kind of thing. Remember when "blogging" used to be called "keeping an online diary"? Yeah, me too. This was one of the most fun things I used to do, back when sites like Diaryland and Xanga ruled the roost. Those were the days. . . . But here we are again, back to those times of endless amounts of typing about nothing of any particular importance. I'm definitely not promising any kind of commitment to this, I just got an itching for typing crazy things again, and I'm willing to indulge myself (with the added justification that I was doing this kind of thing before the blogosphere had reached it's Seventh Day).

2   In any event, what might be appropriate for the first of several Zebra Tales is a rant on a very particular new gaming vehicle that I just became aware of. While on the website I use for all my news, I learned about "GameCrush," a system that sets women back at least 200 years. Now we all know that a lot of the people who game are lonely boys, either very fat or very skinny, who sit in their domestic caves and glue their greasy little eyes to a screen to live out a life where they actually matter. By the light of day these boys are worthless, shunned by almost every caste, from Bro to Awkward-Plain Girl Who Could Be Pretty With Some Make-Up Maybe to Over-Acheiver Kid to Slutty Slut Slut McGee. But when the lights go down and school/work ends, these bepimpled boys can transform into muscle-bound demi gods or elite covert operatives or (in the really creepy department) even hot

slutty girls whose every purpose in-game is to look sexy with the right video card. And so perhaps it was only a matter of time before some idiots like the guys at GameCrush decided to capitalize on the pathetic state of your average gamer boy—and crap all over women in the process.

3   GameCrush is a website that ostensibly encourages boy-girl interactions via games. Boys sign on as "Players" and girls sign on as "PlayDates" (yeah, I'll let you draw your own conclusions). These girls set up a MySpace-like homepage that shows a picture, what games she'd like to pay (currently it allows for Xbox Live support) and several other *vital* statistics. One of these is a Facebook status-like idea which lets the girl set her inclination to either "Flirty" or "Dirty" (and here I thought women were complex). She can include pictures of herself, videos, and an About Me section for showing, I guess, how chaste she is. Now Players (the aforementioned nerdy nerds) select a PlayDate they want to . . . um . . . play with and send her an invite. Now the invite can include anything, from chatting with her to webcamming to actually playing a game with her. But here's the catch: the Players must purchase credits to spend *any* time gaming with the PlayDates in the first place. A certain number of credits get you a certain number of minutes to spend with the girl. The game economics are structured so that you will invariably have credits left over so that, when your session is over, the Players are prompted to spend their remaining credits as a *tip* for the PlayDate.

4   Now whether you tip your PlayDate is open to the Player's discretion, but I have a funny feeling it'll have *something* to do with how flirty or dirty she's been with the Player during their 10 minute rendezvous. . . . But that's just me. Oh, and guess what these lovely ladies can do with these tips? Well they can EXCHANGE THEM FOR CASH. Yes, that's right, cash monies. GameCrush lets their women keep 60% of the money they get from their Johns, I mean Players. And the company keeps the other 40% because, well, Daddy has bills to pay.

5   Then, if this weren't bad enough, the girls are then rated by the Players they interact with on things like hotness and flirtiness. The girls with the highest ratings will not only attract more attention and so make more money for Daddy and themselves but the company behind GameCrush will actually promote their top PlayDates on another website called JaneCrush where these PlayDates will effectively be turned into mini-celebrities. Whether you're looking at this from a Darwinistic view, a Capitalistic view, or a just plain friggin' common sense view, it's clear that the girls who are sluttier on this website will get paid more. Indeed, the girls who are just normal human beings who just want to play a game (god forbid) will be relegated to the unsightly realm of unpopular shunned frag hags. Hey, I like that one, maybe it'll catch on.

6   Now, in some sort of weak preliminary defense for the kind of outcry from certain circles that this company is sure to receive, they claimed in their press release for GameCrush that the game economics are based on the concept and the cost of buying a girl a drink in a bar which, they argue, is not for the purpose of getting to know a new person but really for an ulterior motive. Let me explain to the idiots who made up that ridiculous explanation why the two are *completely* different. When you walk into a bar and see a girl you think is hot, you don't *have* to spend money on her to get her to pay attention to you (maybe you should, but spending money on strange women isn't *built in* to the mechanics of life). You can talk with her, dance with her, even go home with her without being required by the bar owners to liquor her up on your own dime. Now often, a girl *will* broadcast something about her sluttiness in just what she wears so maybe this could be akin to some sort of typed status about how horny she is that everyone can see. Kinda. Oh, and before everyone starts yelling about how sexist it is to even *suggest* that you can infer *anything* from a girl's clothing choice, let me just say that I've known plenty of complete hookers who rarely go out to a social setting looking anything other than complete hookers, and I've known plenty of sweet reserved girls who rarely go out looking like complete hookers. I don't think I've ever seen the innocent, just kisses on the first date, girl next door go out in a microskirt and orange tan.

7   And, as for guys, there's a reason I go to bars in a nice polo and jeans and not a wifebeater, gold necklace, sideways baseball cap, and slicked back hair. Just sayin. But what most bars definitely do *not* have is a system whereby male patrons get to rate these girls on the basis of their flirtiness and hotness. Can you imagine talking to a girl for a little while and then saying, "well I haven't really enjoyed talking to you, bitch, you get a 3 on flirtiness and definitely a 2 on hotness, and forget the tip sweetheart, next time go for the tube top." Damn.

8   Oh yeah, guys tip the *bartender* not the girl they're talking to. Jesus. Should there also be a big bulletin board on the outside of bars that has pictures of all the girls inside with ratings from all the guys they've talked to based on their hotness? Now *that* would be something. Funny how the more you put the GameCrush system in terms of real life it becomes clear that this would be almost completely unacceptable. But for some reason, when it comes to the Internet, here we are.

9   And how did GameCrush get its first batch of PlayDates? Well they opened up an ad on Craigslist. Yeah, no joke. Craigslist. When I think completely consensual and not creepy in any way I think Craigslist. I was reading an article on IGN about it and they actually posted a sample of what one of the PlayDates has on

her page, complete with her picture. Just scroll down to the middle until you see the pic of the sexy blonde. Mmm, must sign up. Damnit GameCrush! The guy who wrote the article actually seems the think GameCrush might be a *good* idea, but I guess when you work with Jessica Chobot you get a slightly warped idea of what the average gamer girl is like.

10   But the worst impact of GameCrush may be its role in further marginalizing women in an everyday environment. Time was, girls were *extremely* rare in online games. As someone who's been gaming online since StarCraft I remember that if ever there was the rarity of seeing a girl in-game it was like throwing a gallon of blood in a kiddie pool filled with vampire sharks. Comments ranged from the more "mild" forms of sexual harassment (are you hot, how old are you, are you single, etc.) to the real depraved and disgusting stuff that most guys would only feel comfortable saying behind the safety of their computer screens. But these days more and more and more girls are taking part in online games, partly because back in the day almost all of the games that had online support were wargames and shooters while today you can play almost anything with friends and also because as games become mainstream acceptable (with things like Wii Fit and RockBand bringing in all sorts) they are becoming more attractive to more than just the super nerds who live off them.

11   Now that we're not only encouraging the vampire sharks but providing the kiddie pool and blood for a small fee, we're saying to girls "sure, you can do what you'd normally do in the privacy of your own home for fun, but you're going to have be slutty and sexy and be ready to pay attention to any asshole who talks to you in the process." I told Dana about this and she raised a good point: why is it necessary to sexualize everything women do? Why can't they just do shit and that's it? Why do I have to pay a girl to play a game with me when I could just go out and friggin ASK one of the tens of thousands to just play?

12   Interestingly enough, I think I actually pissed off one of my feminst-inclined Oberlin friends when I posted something about this as my fb status. Because the system is outlined by gender roles (as far as I can tell, guys can't be PlayDates), I suggested that the sexist part about this system is the fact that GameCrush discriminates against *men* because they can't play both parts and get paid. It should be obvious why this is *not* the main problem with GameCrush, but ironically it seems as though I pissed off one of the many people I was trying to speak up for.

13   But then there's just something deliciously funny about that.

Clay Shirky

Gin, Television, and Social Surplus: A Speech—April 26, 2008

I was recently reminded of some reading I did in college, way back in the last century, by a British historian arguing that the critical technology, for the early phase of the industrial revolution, was gin. The transformation from rural to urban life was so sudden, and so wrenching, that the only thing society could do to manage was to drink itself into a stupor for a generation. The stories from that era are amazing—there were gin pushcarts working their way through the streets of London.

2 And it wasn't until society woke up from that collective bender that we actually started to get the institutional structures that we associate with the industrial revolution today. Things like public libraries and museums, increasingly broad education for children, elected leaders—a lot of things we like—didn't happen until having all of those people together stopped seeming like a crisis and started seeming like an asset. It wasn't until people started thinking of this as a vast civic surplus, one they could design for rather than just dissipate, that we started to get what we think of now as an industrial society.

3 If I had to pick the critical technology for the 20th century, the bit of social lubricant without which the wheels would've come off the whole enterprise, I'd say it was the sitcom. Starting with the Second World War a whole series of things happened—rising GDP per capita, rising educational attainment, rising life expectancy and, critically, a rising number of people who were working five-day work weeks. For the first time, society forced onto an enormous number of its citizens the requirement to manage something they had never had to manage before—free time.

4 And what did we do with that free time? Well, mostly we spent it watching TV.

5 We did that for decades. We watched "I Love Lucy." We watched "Gilligan's Island." We watch "Malcolm in the Middle." We watch "Desperate Housewives." "Desperate Housewives" essentially functioned as a kind of cognitive heat sink, dissipating thinking that might otherwise have built up and caused society to overheat. And it's only now, as we're waking up from that collective bender, that we're starting to see the cognitive surplus as an asset rather than as a crisis. We're seeing things being designed to take advantage of that surplus, to deploy it in ways more engaging than just having a TV in everybody's basement.

6 This hit me in a conversation I had about two months ago. I've finished a book called *Here Comes Everybody*, which has recently come out, and this recognition came out of a conversation I had about the book. I was being interviewed by a TV producer to see whether I should be on their show, and she asked me, "What are you seeing out there that's interesting?" I started telling her about the Wikipedia article on Pluto. You may remember that Pluto got kicked out of the planet club a couple of years ago, so all of a sudden there was all of this activity on Wikipedia. The talk pages light up, people are editing the article like mad, and the whole community is in

an ruckus—"How should we characterize this change in Pluto's status?" And a little bit at a time they move the article—fighting offstage all the while—from, "Pluto is the ninth planet," to "Pluto is an odd-shaped rock with an odd-shaped orbit at the edge of the solar system."

7 So I tell her all this stuff, and I think, "Okay, we're going to have a conversation about authority or social construction or whatever." That wasn't her question. She heard this story and she shook her head and said, "Where do people find the time?" That was her question. And I just kind of snapped. And I said, "No one who works in TV gets to ask that question. You know where the time comes from. It comes from the cognitive surplus you've been masking for 50 years."

8 So how big is that surplus? If you take Wikipedia as a kind of unit, all of Wikipedia, the whole project—every page, every edit, every talk page, every line of code, in every language that Wikipedia exists in—that represents something like the cumulation of 100 million hours of human thought. I worked this out with Martin Wattenberg at IBM; it's a back-of-the-envelope calculation, but it's the right order of magnitude, about 100 million hours of thought.

9 And television watching? Two hundred billion hours, in the U.S. alone, every year. Put another way, now that we have a unit, that's 2,000 Wikipedia projects a year spent watching television. Or put still another way, in the U.S., we spend 100 million hours every weekend, just watching the ads. This is a pretty big surplus. People asking, "Where do they find the time?" when they're looking at things like Wikipedia don't understand how tiny that entire project is, as a carve-out of this asset that's finally being dragged into what Tim calls an architecture of participation.

10 Now, the interesting thing about a surplus like that is that society doesn't know what to do with it at first—hence the gin, hence the sitcoms. Because if people knew what to do with a surplus with reference to the existing social institutions, then it wouldn't be a surplus, would it? It's precisely when no one has any idea how to deploy something that people have to start experimenting with it, in order for the surplus to get integrated, and the course of that integration can transform society.

11 The early phase for taking advantage of this cognitive surplus, the phase I think we're still in, is all special cases. The physics of participation is much more like the physics of weather than it is like the physics of gravity. We know all the forces that combine to make these kinds of things work: there's an interesting community over here, there's an interesting sharing model over there, those people are collaborating on open source software. But despite knowing the inputs, we can't predict the outputs yet because there's so much complexity. The way you explore complex ecosystems is you just try lots and lots and lots of things, and you hope that everybody who fails fails informatively so that you can at least find a skull on a pikestaff near where you're going. That's the phase we're in now.

12 Just to pick one example, one I'm in love with, but it's tiny. A couple of weeks one of my students forwarded me a project started by a professor in Brazil, in Fortaleza, named Vasco Furtado. It's a Wiki Map for crime in Brazil. If there's an assault, if there's a burglary, if there's a mugging, a robbery, a rape, a murder, you can go and put a push-pin on a Google Map, and you can characterize the assault, and you start to see a map of where these crimes are occurring.

13   Now, this already exists as tacit information. Anybody who knows a town has some sense of, "Don't go there. That street corner is dangerous. Don't go in this neighborhood. Be careful there after dark." But it's something society knows without society really knowing it, which is to say there's no public source where you can take advantage of it. And the cops, if they have that information, they're certainly not sharing. In fact, one of the things Furtado says in starting the Wiki crime map was, "This information may or may not exist some place in society, but it's actually easier for me to try to rebuild it from scratch than to try and get it from the authorities who might have it now."

14   Maybe this will succeed or maybe it will fail. The normal case of social software is still failure; most of these experiments don't pan out. But the ones that do are quite incredible, and I hope that this one succeeds, obviously. But even if it doesn't, it's illustrated the point already, which is that someone working alone, with really cheap tools, has a reasonable hope of carving out enough of the cognitive surplus, enough of the desire to participate, enough of the collective goodwill of the citizens, to create a resource you couldn't have imagined existing even five years ago.

15   So that's the answer to the question, "Where do they find the time?" Or, rather, that's the numerical answer. But beneath that question was another thought, this one not a question but an observation. In this same conversation with the TV producer I was talking about World of Warcraft guilds, and as I was talking, I could sort of see what she was thinking: "Losers. Grown men sitting in their basement pretending to be elves."

16   At least they're doing something.

17   Did you ever see that episode of "Gilligan's Island" where they almost get off the island and then Gilligan messes up and then they don't? I saw that one. I saw that one a lot when I was growing up. And every half-hour that I watched that was a half an hour I wasn't posting at my blog or editing Wikipedia or contributing to a mailing list. Now I had an ironclad excuse for not doing those things, which is that none of those things existed then. I was forced into the channel of media the way it was because it was the only option. Now it's not, and that's the big surprise. However lousy it is to sit in your basement and pretend to be an elf, I can tell you from personal experience it's worse to sit in your basement and try to figure if Ginger or Mary Ann is cuter.

18   And I'm willing to raise that to a general principle. It's better to do something than to do nothing. Even lolcats, even cute pictures of kittens made even cuter with the addition of cute captions, hold out an invitation to participation. When you see a lolcat, one of the things it says to the viewer is, "If you have some sans-serif fonts on your computer, you can play this game, too." And that's message—I can do that, too—is a big change.

19   This is something that people in the media world don't understand. Media in the 20th century was run as a single race—consumption. How much can we produce? How much can you consume? Can we produce more and you'll consume more? And the answer to that question has generally been yes. But media is actually a triathlon, it's three different events. People like to consume, but they also like to produce, and they like to share. And what's astonished people who were committed to the structure of the previous society, prior to trying to take this surplus and do something interesting, is that they're discovering that when you offer people the opportunity to produce and to share, they'll take you up on that offer. It doesn't mean that we'll never sit around mindlessly watching "Scrubs" on the couch. It just means we'll do it less.

20   And this is the other thing about the size of the cognitive surplus we're talking about. It's so large that even a small change could have huge ramifications. Let's say that everything stays 99 percent the same, that people watch 99 percent as much television as they used to, but 1 percent of that is carved out for producing and for sharing. The Internet-connected population watches roughly a *trillion* hours of TV a year. That's about five times the size of the annual U.S. consumption. One per cent of that is 100 Wikipedia projects per year worth of participation.

21   I think that's going to be a big deal. Don't you?

22   Well, the TV producer did not think this was going to be a big deal; she was not digging this line of thought. And her final question to me was essentially, "Isn't this all just a fad?" You know, sort of the flagpole-sitting of the early early 21st century? It's fun to go out and produce and share a little bit, but then people are going to eventually realize, "This isn't as good as doing what I was doing before, and settle down. And I made a spirited argument that no, this wasn't the case, that this was in fact a big one-time shift, more analogous to the industrial revolution than to flagpole-sitting. I was arguing that this isn't the sort of thing society grows out of. It's the sort of thing that society grows into. But I'm not sure she believed me, in part because she didn't want to believe me, but also in part because I didn't have the right story yet. And now I do.

23   I was having dinner with a group of friends about a month ago, and one of them was talking about sitting with his four-year-old daughter watching a DVD. And in the middle of the movie, apropos nothing, she jumps up off the couch and runs around behind the screen. That seems like a cute moment. Maybe she's going back there to see if Dora is really back there or whatever. But that wasn't what she was doing. She started rooting around in the cables. And her dad said, "What you doing?" And she stuck her head out from behind the screen and said, "Looking for the mouse."

24   Here's something four-year-olds know: A screen that ships without a mouse ships broken. Here's something four-year-olds know: Media that's targeted at you but doesn't include you may not be worth sitting still for. Those are things that make me believe that this is a one-way change. Because four-year-olds, the people who are soaking most deeply in the current environment, who won't have to go through the trauma that I have to go through of trying to unlearn a childhood spent watching "Gilligan's Island," they just assume that media includes consuming, producing and sharing.

25   It's also become my motto, when people ask me what we're doing—and when I say "we" I mean the larger society trying to figure out how to deploy this cognitive surplus, but I also mean we, especially, the people who are working hammer and tongs at figuring out the next good idea. From now on, that's what I'm going to tell them: We're looking for the mouse. We're going to look at every place that a reader or a listener or a viewer or a user has been locked out, has been served up passive or a fixed or a canned experience, and ask ourselves, "If we carve out a little bit of the cognitive surplus and deploy it here, could we make a good thing happen?" And I'm betting the answer is yes.

26   Thank you very much.

FROM READING TO WRITING

1. Analyze the arguments by Michael Gerson and Daniel Okrent: How is each argument the product of its audience and purpose? What sources of argument (ethical appeals, emotional appeals, and logical appeals) does each author choose and why? (See Chapter 5 for more on rhetorical analysis.)

2. Write an argument that makes its point by defining a key term related to new media. You might choose to change someone's attitude toward a particular technology or concept in order to defend or challenge it, for instance, by defining it in a certain way. For example, you might start with the claim that "Facebook is just a marketing ploy based on the same principles that define high school yearbooks" or "Second Life is actually a blessing for people who are shy by nature." (See Chapter 8 for strategies for writing definition arguments.)

3. Write a humorous story about your own experience with a particular new media technology—but write your story in order to make a point. (See Chapter 11 for advice on writing narrative arguments.) For example, you could report on your unfortunate experience with a new cell phone or video game in order to convince people to avoid making the same mistake.

4. Propose a change in policy related to a technology issue in your community. Are there regulations that would improve the social impact of video games, for example, or *Wikipedia*? (See Chapter 13 for help with writing a proposal argument.)

5. Write a rebuttal of an article related to the new media in your local or school newspaper. Are there misperceptions that you want to correct? (See Chapter 12 for advice on rebuttals.) Consider whether you wish to show the weaknesses in the article, whether you wish to counterargue, or both.

6. Write an essay that argues for the existence of a particular social effect that has resulted from a new media technology. For example, you might argue that the success of a particular local charity derives from its ability to connect with people despite a small staff. Or you might write about the effects of new technology on your local library's internal architecture. Or you could argue that new technologies have actually created a range of new jobs at your university. (For more on cause and effect arguments, see Chapter 9.)

7. Many new media technologies permit people to participate anonymously. Wikipedians, for example, are notoriously anonymous, video games networked through the Internet permit people to play with anonymous others, and people are able to make anonymous comments in response to online news sources. Analyze the effects of this anonymity: reflect on the impact of anonymity on your own participation, or your own consumption, of online media.

Handlbook

1 | Fragments, Run-Ons, and Comma Splices

1a Fragments

Fragments are incomplete sentences. They are punctuated to look like sentences, but they lack a key element—often a subject or a verb—or else they are subordinate clauses or phrases. Consider this example of a full sentence followed by a fragment:

> The university's enrollment rose unexpectedly during the fall semester. Because the percentage of students who accepted offers of admission was much higher than in previous years and fewer students than usual dropped out or transferred.

When a sentence starts with *because,* we expect to find a main clause later. Instead, the *because* clause refers back to the previous sentence. The writer no doubt knew that the fragment gave the reasons why enrollment rose, but a reader must stop to determine the connection.

In formal writing you should avoid fragments. Readers expect words punctuated as a sentence to be a complete sentence. They expect writers to complete their thoughts rather than force readers to guess the missing element.

Basic strategies for turning fragments into sentences

Incorporate the fragment into an adjoining sentence.

In many cases you can incorporate the fragment into an adjoining sentence.

I was hooked on the ~~game. Playing~~ *game, playing* day and night.

Add the missing element.

If you cannot incorporate a fragment into another sentence, add the missing element.

When aiming for the highest returns, ~~and also thinking~~ *investors should think* about the possible losses.

COMMON ERRORS

Recognizing fragments

If you can spot fragments, you can fix them. Grammar checkers can find some of them, but they miss many fragments and may identify other sentences wrongly as fragments. Ask these questions when you are checking for sentence fragments.

- **Does the sentence have a subject?** Except for commands, sentences need subjects:

  Incorrect　　Jane spent every cent of credit she had available. And then applied for more cards.

- **Does the sentence have a complete verb?** Sentences require complete verbs. Verbs that end in *-ing* must have an auxiliary verb to be complete.

  Incorrect　　Ralph keeps changing majors. He trying to figure out what he really wants to do after college.

- **If the sentence begins with a subordinate clause, is there a main clause in the same sentence?**

  Incorrect　　Even though Seattle is cloudy much of the year, no American city is more beautiful when the sun shines. Which is one reason people continue to move there.

Remember:
1. A sentence must have a subject and a complete verb.
2. A subordinate clause cannot stand alone as a sentence.

1b Run-On Sentences

While fragments are incomplete sentences, run-ons (also called "fused sentences") jam together two or more sentences, failing to separate them with appropriate punctuation.

Fixing run-on sentences

Take three steps to fix run-on sentences: (1) identify the problem, (2) determine where the run-on sentence needs to be divided, and (3) choose the punctuation that best indicates the relationship between the main clauses.

COMMON ERRORS

Recognizing run-on sentences

When you read this sentence, you realize something is wrong.

Incorrect　　I do not recall what kind of printer it was all I remember is that it could sort, staple, and print a packet at the same time.

The problem is that two main clauses are not separated by punctuation. The reader must look carefully to determine where one main clause stops and the next one begins.

> I do not recall what kind of printer it was | all I remember is that it could sort, staple, and print a packet at the same time.

A period should be placed after *was*, and the next sentence should begin with a capital letter:

Correct   I do not recall what kind of printer it was. All I remember is that it could sort, staple, and print a packet at the same time.

Run-on sentences are major errors.

Remember: Two main clauses must be separated by correct punctuation.

1. Identify the problem.

When you read your writing aloud, run-on sentences will often trip you up, just as they confuse readers. If you find two main clauses with no punctuation separating them, you have a run-on sentence. You can also search for subject and verb pairs to check for run-ons.

> ┌────── SUBJ ──────┐ ┌── VERB ──┐
> **Internet businesses are** not **bound** to specific locations or old ways of
> ┌S┐┌V┐
> running a business **they are** more flexible in allowing employees to telecommute and to determine the hours they work.

2. Determine where the run-on sentence needs to be divided.

> Internet businesses are not bound to specific locations or old ways of running a business | they are more flexible in allowing employees to telecommute and to determine the hours they work.

3. Determine the relationship between the main clauses.

You will revise a run-on more effectively if you first determine the relationship between the main clauses and understand the effect or point you are trying to make. There are several punctuation strategies for fixing run-ons.

■ **Insert a period.** This is the simplest way to fix a run-on sentence.

> Internet businesses are not bound to specific locations or old ways of running a business. They are more flexible in allowing employees to telecommute and to determine the hours they work.

However, if you want to indicate more clearly a closer relationship between the two main clauses, you may want to choose one of the following strategies.

- ■ **Insert a semicolon (and possibly a transitional word specifying the relationship between the two main clauses).**

  Internet businesses are not bound to specific locations or old ways of running a business; therefore, they are more flexible in allowing employees to telecommute and to determine the hours they work.

- ■ **Insert a comma and a coordinating conjunction (and, but, or, nor, for, so, yet).**

  Internet businesses are not bound to specific locations or old ways of running a business, so they are more flexible in allowing employees to telecommute and to determine the hours they work.

- ■ **Make one of the clauses subordinate.**

  Because Internet businesses are not bound to specific locations or old ways of running a business, they are more flexible in allowing employees to telecommute and to determine the hours they work.

1c Comma Splices

Comma splices occur when two or more sentences are incorrectly joined by a comma: A comma should not be used to link two clauses that could stand on their own. In this example, the comma following "classes" should be a period.

> Most of us were taking the same classes, if someone had a question, we would all help out.

Such sentences include a punctuation mark—a comma—separating two main clauses. However, a comma is not a strong enough punctuation mark to separate two main clauses.

COMMON ERRORS

e Edit Help

Recognizing comma splices

When you edit your writing, look carefully at sentences that contain commas. Does the sentence contain two main clauses? If so, are the main clauses joined by a comma and a coordinating conjunction (*and, but, for, or, not, so, yet*)?

Incorrect The ⌐SUBJ⌐ concept of "nature" ⌐VERB⌐ depends on the concept of human "culture," the ⌐SUBJ⌐ problem ⌐V⌐ is that "culture" is itself shaped by "nature." [Two main clauses joined by only a comma]

Correct Even though the concept of "nature" depends on the concept of human "culture," "culture" is itself shaped by "nature." [Subordinate clause plus a main clause]

Correct	The concept of "nature" depends on the concept of human "culture," but "culture" is itself shaped by "nature." [Two main clauses joined by a comma and a coordinating conjunction]

The word *however* produces some of the most common comma splice errors. When *however* begins a main clause, it should be preceded by a semicolon or a period, not a comma.

Incorrect	The White House press secretary repeatedly vowed the Administration was not choosing a side between the two countries embroiled in conflict, however the developing foreign policy suggested otherwise.
Correct	The White House press secretary repeatedly vowed the Administration was not choosing a side between the two countries embroiled in conflict; however, the developing foreign policy suggested otherwise. [Two main clauses joined by a semicolon]

Remember: Do not use a comma as a period.

Fixing comma splices

You have several options for fixing comma splices. Select the one that best fits where the sentence is located and the effect you are trying to achieve.

1. Change the comma to a period.

Most comma splices can be fixed by changing the comma to a period.

It didn't matter that I worked in a windowless room for 40 hours a ~~week, on~~ *week. On* the Web I was exploring and learning more about distant people and places than I ever had before.

2. Change the comma to a semicolon.

A semicolon indicates a close connection between two main clauses.

It didn't matter that I worked in a windowless room for 40 hours a ~~week,~~ *week;* on the Web I was exploring and learning more about distant people and places than I ever had before.

3. Insert a coordinating conjunction.

Other comma splices can be repaired by inserting a coordinating conjunction (*and, but, or, nor, so, yet, for*) to indicate the relationship of the two main clauses. The coordinating conjunction must be preceded by a comma.

Digital technologies have intensified a global culture that affects us daily in large and small ways, **yet** their impact remains poorly understood.

4. Make one of the main clauses a subordinate clause.

If a comma splice includes one main clause that is subordinate to the other, rewrite the sentence using a subordinating conjunction (such as *after, although, because, if*).

Because community
~~Community~~ is the vision of a great society trimmed down to the size of a small town, it is a powerful metaphor for real estate developers who sell a mini-utopia along with a house or condo.

5. Make one of the main clauses a phrase.

You can also rewrite one of the main clauses as a phrase.

Community—the vision of a great society trimmed down to the size of a small town—is a powerful metaphor for real estate developers who sell a mini-utopia along with a house or condo.

2 | Subject-Verb Agreement

2a Agreement in the Present Tense

When your verb is in the present tense, agreement in number is straightforward: The subject takes the base form of the verb in all but the third person singular. For example, the verb *walk*, in the present tense, agrees in number with most subjects in its base form:

First person singular	I walk
Second person singular	You walk
First person plural	We walk
Second person plural	You walk
Third person plural	They walk

Third person singular subjects are the exception to this rule. When your subject is in the third person singular (*he, it, Fido, Lucy, Mr. Jones*), you need to add *s* or *es* to the base form of the verb.

Third person singular (add *s*)	He walks. It walks. Fido walks.
Third person singular (add *es*)	Lucy goes. Mr. Jones goes.

2b Singular and Plural Subjects

Follow these rules when you have trouble determining whether to use a singular or plural verb form.

Subjects joined by *and*

When two subjects are joined by *and,* treat them as a compound (plural) subject.

> **Mary and Jane** are leaving for New York in the morning.

Some compound subjects work together as a single noun and are treated as singular. Although they appear to be compound and therefore plural, these subjects take the singular form of the verb:

> **Rock and roll** remains the devil's music, even in the twenty-first century.

When two nouns linked by *and* are modified by *every* or *each,* these two nouns are likewise treated as one singular subject:

> **Each night and day** brings no new news of you.

An exception to this rule arises when the word *each* follows a compound subject. In these cases, usage varies depending on the number of the direct object.

> **The army and the navy each** have their own airplanes.

> **The owl and the pussycat each** has a personal claim to fame.

Subjects joined by *or, either ... or,* or *neither ... nor*

When a subject is joined by *or, either ... or,* or *neither ... nor,* make sure the verb agrees with the subject closest to the verb.

> ⌐ SING ⌐ ⌐ PLURAL ⌐ ⌐PL⌐
> Is it **the sky or the mountains** that are blue?
> ⌐ PLURAL ⌐ ⌐ SING ⌐ ⌐ SING ⌐
> Is it **the mountains or the sky** that surrounds us?
> ⌐ PLURAL ⌐ ⌐ SING ⌐⌐ SING ⌐
> **Neither the animals nor the zookeeper** knows how to relock the gate.
> ⌐ SING ⌐ ⌐ PLURAL ⌐ ⌐PL⌐
> **Either a coyote or several dogs** were howling last night.

Subjects along with another noun

Verbs agree with the subject of a sentence, even when a subject is linked to another noun with a phrase like *as well as, along with,* or *alongside.* These modifying phrases are usually set off from the main subject with commas.

> ⌐ IGNORE THIS PHRASE ⌐
> **Chicken,** alongside various steamed vegetables, is my favorite meal.
> ⌐ IGNORE THIS PHRASE ⌐
> Besides B. B. King, **John Lee Hooker and Muddy Waters** are my favorite blues artists of all time.

COMMON ERRORS

Subjects separated from verbs

The most common agreement errors occur when words come between the subject and verb. These intervening words do not affect subject-verb agreement. To ensure that you use the correct verb form, identify the subject and the verb. Ignore any phrases that come between them.

┌──────── IGNORE THIS PHRASE ────────┐

Incorrect   **Students** at inner-city Washington High reads more than suburban students.

Correct   **Students** at inner-city Washington High read more than suburban students.

Students is plural and *read* is plural; subject and verb agree.

Incorrect   **The whale shark,** the largest of all sharks, feed on plankton.

Correct   **The whale shark,** the largest of all sharks, feeds on plankton.

The plural noun *sharks* that appears between the subject *the whale shark* and the verb *feeds* does not change the number of the subject. The subject is singular and the verb is singular. Subject and verb agree.

Remember: When you check for subject-verb agreement, identify the subject and the verb. Ignore any words that come between them.

2c Indefinite Pronouns as Subjects

The choice of a singular or plural pronoun is determined by the **antecedent**—the noun that pronoun refers to. Indefinite pronouns, such as *some, few, all, someone, everyone,* and *each,* often do not refer to identifiable subjects; hence they have no antecedents. Most indefinite pronouns are singular and agree with the singular forms of verbs. Some, like *both* and *many,* are always plural and agree with the plural forms of verbs. Other indefinite pronouns are variable and can agree with either singular or plural verb forms, depending on the context of the sentence.

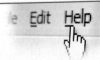

COMMON ERRORS

Agreement errors using each

When a pronoun is singular, its verb must be singular. A common stumbling block to this rule is the pronoun *each*. *Each* is always treated as a singular pronoun in college writing. When *each* stands alone, the choice is easy to make:

Incorrect   Each are an outstanding student.

Correct   Each is an outstanding student.

But when *each* is modified by a phrase that includes a plural noun, the choice of a singular verb form becomes less obvious:

Incorrect	**Each** of the girls are fit.
Correct	**Each** of the girls is fit.
Incorrect	**Each** of our dogs get a present.
Correct	**Each** of our dogs gets a present.

Remember: *Each* is always singular.

2d Collective Nouns as Subjects

Collective nouns refer to groups (*audience, class, committee, crowd, family, government, group, jury, public, team*). When members of a group are considered as a unit, use singular verbs and singular pronouns.

The **crowd** is unusually quiet at the moment, but it will get noisy soon.

When members of a group are considered as individuals, use plural verbs and plural pronouns.

The **faculty** have their differing opinions on how to address the problems caused by reduced state support.

Sometimes collective nouns can be singular in one context and plural in another. Writers must decide which verb form to use based on sentence context.

The **number** of people who live downtown is increasing.

A **number** of people are moving downtown from the suburbs.

2e Inverted Word Order

Writers use inverted word order most often in forming questions. The statement *Cats are friendly* becomes a question when you invert the subject and the verb: *Are cats friendly?* Writers also use inverted word order for added emphasis or for style considerations.

Do not be confused by inverted word order. Locate the subject of your sentence, and then make sure your verb agrees with that subject.

2f Amounts, Numbers, and Pairs

Subjects that describe amounts of money, time, distance, or measurement are singular and require singular verbs.

Three days is never long enough to unwind.

Some subjects, such as courses of study, academic specializations, illnesses, and even some nations, are treated as singular subjects even though their names end in -s or -es. For example, *economics, news, ethics, measles,* and *the United States* all end in -s but are all singular subjects.

Economics is a rich field of study.

Other subjects require a plural verb form even though they refer to single items such as *jeans, slacks, glasses, scissors,* and *tweezers.* These items are all treated as pairs.

My **glasses** are scratched.

3 | Verbs

3a Basic Verb Forms

Almost all verbs in English have five possible forms. The exception is the verb *be.* Regular verbs follow this basic pattern:

Base form	Third-person singular	Past tense	Past participle	Present participle
jump	jumps	jumped	jumped	jumping
like	likes	liked	liked	liking
talk	talks	talked	talked	talking
wish	wishes	wished	wished	wishing

Base form

The base form of the verb is the one you find listed in the dictionary. This form indicates an action or condition in the present.

I **like** New York in June.

Third person singular

Third person singular subjects include *he, she, it,* and the nouns they replace, as well as other pronouns, including *someone, anybody,* and *everything.* Present tense verbs in the third person singular end with *s* or *es.*

Ms. Nessan **speaks** in riddles.

Past tense

The past tense describes an action or condition that occurred in the past. For most verbs, the past tense is formed by adding *d* or *ed* to the base form of the verb.

> She inhaled the night air.

Many verbs, however, have irregular past tense forms. (See Section 3b.)

Past participle

The past participle is used with *have* to form verbs in the perfect tense, with *be* to form verbs in the passive voice, and to form adjectives derived from verbs.

Past perfect	They **had** gone to the grocery store prematurely.
Passive	The book **was** written thirty years before it **was** published.
Adjective	In the eighties, teased hair was all the rage.

COMMON ERRORS

e Edit Help

Missing verb endings

Verb endings are not always pronounced in speech, especially in some dialects of English. It's also easy to omit these endings when you are writing quickly. Spelling checkers will not mark these errors, so you have to find them while proofreading.

Incorrect	Jeremy feel as if he's catching a cold.
Correct	Jeremy feels as if he's catching a cold.
Incorrect	Sheila hope she would get the day off.
Correct	Sheila hoped she would get the day off.

Remember: Check verbs carefully for missing *s* or *es* endings in the present tense and missing *d* or *ed* endings in the past tense.

Present participle

The present participle functions in one of three ways. Used with an auxiliary verb, it can describe a continuing action. The present participle can also function as a noun, known as a **gerund**, or as an adjective. The present participle is formed by adding *ing* to the base form of a verb.

Present participle	Wild elks **are** competing for limited food resources.
Gerund	Sailing around the Cape of Good Hope is rumored to bring good luck.
Adjective	We looked for shells in the ebbing tide.

3b Irregular Verbs

A verb is **regular** when its past and past participle forms are created by adding *ed* or *d* to the base form. If this rule does not apply, the verb is considered an **irregular** verb. Here are selected common irregular verbs and their basic forms.

Common irregular verbs

Base form	Past tense	Past participle
be (is, am, are)	was, were	been
become	became	become
bring	brought	brought
come	came	come
do	did	done
get	got	got or gotten
have	had	had
go	went	gone
know	knew	known
see	saw	seen

COMMON ERRORS

Past tense forms of irregular verbs
The past tense and past participle forms of irregular verbs are often confused. The most frequent error is using a past tense form instead of the past participle with *had.*

	PAST TENSE
Incorrect	She had never rode a horse before.

	PAST PARTICIPLE
Correct	She had never ridden a horse before.

	PAST TENSE
Incorrect	He had saw many alligators in Louisiana.

	PAST PARTICIPLE
Correct	He had seen many alligators in Louisiana.

Remember: Change any past tense verbs preceded by *had* to past participles.

3c Transitive and Intransitive Verbs
Lay/lie, set/sit, and *raise/rise*

Do your house keys lay or lie on the kitchen table? Does a book set or sit on the shelf? *Raise/rise, lay/lie,* and *set/sit* are transitive/intransitive verb pairs that writers frequently confuse. **Transitive verbs** take direct objects—nouns that receive the action of the verb. **Intransitive verbs** act in sentences that lack direct objects.

The following charts list the trickiest pairs of transitive and intransitive verbs and the correct forms for each verb tense. Pay special attention to *lay* and *lie,* which are irregular.

	lay (put something down)	**lie (recline)**
Present	lay, lays	lie, lies
Present participle	laying	lying
Past	laid	lay
Past participle	laid	lain

Transitive	When you complete your test, please lay your pencil [direct object, the thing being laid down] on the desk.
Intransitive	The *Titanic* lies upright in two pieces at a depth of 13,000 feet.

	raise (elevate something)	**rise (get up)**
Present	raise, raises	rise, rises
Present participle	raising	rising
Past	raised	rose
Past participle	raised	risen

Transitive	We raise our glasses [direct object, the things being raised] to toast Uncle Han.
Intransitive	The sun rises over the bay.

	set (place something)	**sit (take a seat)**
Present	set, sets	sit, sits
Present participle	setting	sitting
Past	set	sat
Past participle	set	sat

Transitive	Every morning Stanley sets two dollars [direct object, the amount being set] on the table to tip the waiter.
Intransitive	I sit in the front seat if it's available.

4 | Pronouns

4a Pronoun Case

Subjective pronouns function as the subjects of sentences. **Objective pronouns** function as direct or indirect objects. **Possessive pronouns** indicate ownership.

Subjective pronouns	Objective pronouns	Possessive pronouns
I	me	my, mine
we	us	our, ours
you	you	your, yours
he	him	his
she	her	her, hers
it	it	its
they	them	their, theirs
who	whom	whose

Pronouns in compound phrases

Picking the right pronoun can sometimes be confusing when the pronoun appears in a compound phrase.

> If we work together, you and **me** can get the job done quickly.

> If we work together, you and **I** can get the job done quickly.

Which is correct—*me* or *I*? Removing the other pronoun usually makes the choice clear.

Incorrect	Me can get the job done quickly.
Correct	I can get the job done quickly.

We and *us* before nouns

Another pair of pronouns that can cause difficulty is *we* and *us* before nouns.

> **Us** friends must stick together.

> **We** friends must stick together.

Which is correct—*us* or *we*? Removing the noun indicates the correct choice.

Incorrect   Us must stick together.

Correct   We must stick together.

Who versus whom

Choosing between *who* and *whom* is often difficult, even for experienced writers. The distinction between *who* and *whom* is disappearing from spoken language. *Who* is more often used in spoken language, even when *whom* is correct.

COMMON ERRORS   e Edit Help

Who or whom

In writing, the distinction between *who* and *whom* is still often observed. *Who* and *whom* follow the same rules as other pronouns: *Who* is the subject pronoun; *whom* is the object pronoun. If you are dealing with an object, *whom* is the correct choice.

Incorrect   Who did you send the letter to?

              Who did you give the present to?

Correct   To whom did you send the letter?

              Whom did you give the present to?

Who is always the right choice for the subject pronoun.

Correct   Who gave you the present?

              Who brought the cookies?

If you are uncertain of which one to use, try substituting *she* and *her* or *he* and *him*.

Incorrect   You sent the letter to she **[who]**?

Correct   You sent the letter to her **[whom]**?

Incorrect   Him **[Whom]** gave you the present?

Correct   He **[Who]** gave you the present?

Remember: *Who* = subject
         Whom = object

Whoever versus whomever

With the rule regarding *who* and *whom* in mind, you can distinguish between *whoever* and *whomever*. Which is correct?

Her warmth touched **whoever** she met.

Her warmth touched **whomever** she met.

In this sentence the pronoun functions as the direct object in its own clause: she met whomever. Thus *whomever* is the correct choice.

Pronouns in comparisons

When you write a sentence using a comparison that includes *than* or *as* followed by a pronoun, usually you will have to think about which pronoun is correct. Which of the following is correct?

> Vimala is a faster swimmer than **him**.

> Vimala is a faster swimmer than **he**.

The test that will give you the correct answer is to add the verb that finishes the sentence—in this case, *is*.

| Incorrect | Vimala is a faster swimmer than him is. |
| Correct | Vimala is a faster swimmer than he is. |

Adding the verb makes the correct choice evident.

Possessive pronouns

Possessive pronouns are confusing at times because possessive nouns are formed with apostrophes, but possessive pronouns do not require apostrophes. Pronouns that use apostrophes are always **contractions**.

It's	=	It is
Who's	=	Who is
They're	=	They are

The test for whether to use an apostrophe is to determine if the pronoun is possessive or a contraction. The most confusing pair is *its* and *it's*.

Incorrect	Its a sure thing she will be elected. [Contraction needed]
Correct	It's a sure thing she will be elected. [**It is** a sure thing.]
Incorrect	The dog lost it's collar. [Possessive needed]
Correct	The dog lost its collar.

Possessive pronouns before *-ing* verbs

Pronouns that modify an *-ing* verb (called a *gerund*) or an *-ing* verb phrase (*gerund phrase*) should appear in the possessive.

| Incorrect | The odds of you making the team are excellent. |
| Correct | The odds of your making the team are excellent. |

4b Pronoun Agreement

Because pronouns usually replace or refer to other nouns, they must match those nouns in number and gender. The noun that the pronoun replaces is called its **antecedent**. If pronoun and antecedent match, they are in **agreement**. When a pronoun is close to the antecedent, usually there is no problem.

> **Maria** forgot her coat.

> The band **members** collected their uniforms.

Pronoun agreement errors often happen when pronouns and the nouns they replace are separated by several words.

Incorrect

> The **players**, exhausted from the double-overtime game, picked up his sweats and walked toward the locker rooms.

Correct

> The **players**, exhausted from the double-overtime game, picked up their sweats and walked toward the locker rooms.

Careful writers make sure that pronouns match their antecedents.

COMMON ERRORS   e Edit Help

Indefinite pronouns

Indefinite pronouns (such as *anybody, anything, each, either, everybody, everything, neither, none, somebody, something*) refer to unspecified people or things. Most take singular pronouns.

Incorrect	Everybody can choose their roommates.
Correct	Everybody can choose his or her roommate.
Correct alternative	All students can choose their roommates.

A few indefinite pronouns (*all, any, either, more, most, neither, none, some*) can take either singular or plural pronouns.

Correct	**Some** of the shipment was damaged when it became overheated.
Correct	**All** thought they should have a good seat at the concert.

A few pronouns are always plural (*few, many, several*).

Correct	**Several** want refunds.

Remember: Words that begin with *any, some,* and *every* are usually singular.

Collective nouns

Collective nouns (such as *audience, class, committee, crowd, family, herd, jury, team*) can be singular or plural depending on whether the emphasis is on the group or on its individual members.

Correct   The **committee** was unanimous in its decision.

Correct   The **committee** put their opinions ahead of the goals of the unit.

---

e   Edit   Help

COMMON ERRORS

Pronoun agreement with compound antecedents

Antecedents joined by *and* take plural pronouns.

Correct   *Moncef and Driss* practiced their music.

Exception: When compound antecedents are preceded by *each* or *every,* use a singular pronoun.

Correct   **Every male cardinal and warbler** arrives before the female to define its territory.

When compound antecedents are connected by *or* or *nor,* the pronoun agrees with the antecedent closer to it.

Incorrect   **Either the Ross twins or Angela** should bring their CDs.

Correct   **Either the Ross twins or Angela** should bring her CDs.

Better   **Either Angela or the Ross twins** should bring their CDs.

When you put the plural *twins* last, the correct choice becomes the plural pronoun *their.*

Remember:

1. Use plural pronouns for antecedents joined by *and.*
2. Use singular pronouns for antecedents preceded by *each* or *every.*
3. Use a pronoun that agrees with the nearest antecedent when compound antecedents are joined by *or* or *nor.*

4c Avoid Sexist Pronouns

English does not have a neutral singular pronoun for a group of mixed genders or a person of unknown gender. Referring to a group of mixed genders using male pronouns is unacceptable to many people. Unless the school in the following example is all male, many readers would object to the use of *his.*

Sexist   **Each student** must select his courses using the online registration system.

One strategy is to use *her or his* or *his or her* instead of *his*.

Correct   **Each student** must select his or her courses using the online registration system.

Often you can avoid using *his or her* by changing the noun to the plural form.

Better   **All students** must select their courses using the online registration system.

In some cases, however, using *his or her* is necessary.

4d Vague Reference

Pronouns can sometimes refer to more than one noun, thus confusing readers.

The **coach** rushed past the injured **player** to yell at the **referee**. She was hit in the face by a stray elbow.

You have to guess which person *she* refers to—the coach, the player, or the referee. Sometimes you cannot even guess the antecedent of a pronoun.

The new subdivision destroyed the last remaining habitat for wildlife within the city limits. They have ruined our city with their unchecked greed.

Whom does *they* refer to? the mayor and city council? the developers? the people who live in the subdivision? or all of the above?

    Pronouns should never leave the reader guessing about antecedents. If different nouns can be confused as the antecedent, then the ambiguity should be clarified.

Vague   Mafalda's pet boa constrictor crawled across Tonya's foot. She was mortified.

Better   When Mafalda's pet boa constrictor crawled across Tonya's foot, Mafalda was mortified.

COMMON ERRORS   e Edit Help

Vague use of this

Always use a noun immediately after *this, that, these, those,* and *some*.

Vague   Enrique asked Meg to remove the viruses on his computer. This was a bad idea.

Was it a bad idea for Enrique to ask Meg because she was insulted? Because she didn't know how? Because removing viruses would destroy some of Enrique's files?

Better   Enrique asked Meg to remove the viruses on his computer. This imposition on Meg's time was a bad idea.

Remember: Ask yourself "this *what?*" and add the noun that *this* refers to.

5 | Shifts

5a Shifts in Tense

Appropriate shifts in verb tense

Changes in verb tense are sometimes necessary to indicate a shift in time.

Past to future   Because Oda **won** [PAST TENSE] the lottery, she **will quit** [FUTURE TENSE] her job at the hospital as soon as her supervisor **finds** [PRESENT TENSE] a qualified replacement.

Inappropriate shifts in verb tense

Be careful to avoid confusing your reader with shifts in verb tense.

Incorrect   While Brazil **looks** [PRESENT TENSE] to ecotourism to fund rain forest
preservation, other South American nations **relied** [PAST TENSE] on foreign

aid and conservation efforts.

The shift from present tense (*looks*) to past tense (*relied*) is confusing. Correct the
mistake by putting both verbs in the present tense.

Correct   While Brazil **looks** [PRESENT TENSE] to ecotourism to fund rain forest
preservation, other South American nations **rely** [PRESENT TENSE] on foreign aid

and conservation efforts.

COMMON ERRORS

Unnecessary tense shift

Notice the tense shift in the following example.

Incorrect   In May of 2000 the "I Love You" virus **crippled** [PAST TENSE] the computer
systems of major American companies and **irritated** [PAST TENSE] millions of private computer users. As the virus **generates** [PRESENT TENSE] millions of e-mails and
erases [PRESENT TENSE] millions of computer files, companies such as Ford and Time
Warner **are** [PRESENT TENSE] forced to shut down their clogged e-mail systems.

The second sentence shifts unnecessarily to the present tense, confusing the reader. Did the "I Love You" virus have its heyday several years ago, or is it still wreaking havoc now? Changing the verbs in the second sentence to the past tense eliminates the confusion.

Correct
    In May of 2000 the "I Love You" virus **PAST TENSE** crippled the computer systems of major American companies and **PAST TENSE** irritated millions of private computer users. As the virus **PAST TENSE** generated millions of e-mails and **PAST TENSE** erased millions of computer files, companies such as Ford and Time Warner **PAST TENSE** were forced to shut down their clogged e-mail systems.

Remember: Shift verb tense only when you are referring to different time periods.

5b Shifts in Mood

Verbs can be categorized into three moods—indicative, imperative, and subjunctive—defined by the functions they serve.

    Indicative verbs state facts, opinions, and questions.

Fact
    Many same-sex couples in the United States are fighting for the right to marry.

    Imperative verbs make commands, give advice, and make requests.

Command
    Tell me why you support same-sex marriage.

    Subjunctive verbs express wishes, unlikely or untrue situations, hypothetical situations, requests with *that* clauses, and suggestions.

Unlikely or
untrue situation
    If heterosexual marriage were as sacred as some pundits would have us believe, there would be no divorce.

Be careful not to shift from one mood to another in mid-sentence.

Incorrect
    If the government **were** to shift funding priorities away from earthquake research, scientists lose even more time in understanding how to predict earthquakes.

The sudden shift from subjunctive to indicative mood in this sentence is confusing. Are the scientists losing time now, or is losing time a likely result of a government funding shift? Revise the sentence to keep both verbs in the subjunctive.

Correct
    If the government **were** to shift funding priorities away from earthquake research, scientists would lose even more time in understanding how to predict earthquakes.

5c Shifts in Voice

Watch for unintended shifts from active (*I ate the cookies*) to passive voice (*the cookies were eaten*).

Incorrect   The sudden storm toppled several trees, and numerous windows were shattered.

The unexpected shift from active voice (*toppled*) to passive (*were shattered*) forces readers to wonder whether it was the sudden storm, or something else, that broke the windows.

Correct   The sudden storm toppled several trees and shattered numerous windows.

5d Shifts in Person and Number

Sudden shifts from third person (*he, she, it, one*) to first (*I, we*) or second (*you*) are confusing to readers and often indicate a writer's uncertainty about how to address a reader. We often make such shifts in spoken English, but in formal writing shifts in person need to be recognized and corrected.

Incorrect   When one is reading a magazine, you often see several different type fonts used on a single page.

The shift from third person to second person in this sentence is confusing.

Correct   When reading a magazine, you often see several different type fonts used on a single page.

Similarly, shifts from singular to plural subjects (see Section 2b) within a single sentence confuse readers.

Incorrect   Administrators often make more money than professors, but only a professor has frequent contact with students.

Correct   Administrators often make more money than professors, but only professors have frequent contact with students.

The revised sentence eliminates a distracting and unnecessary shift from plural to singular.

6 | Modifiers

6a Choose the Correct Modifier

Modifiers come in two varieties: adjectives and adverbs. The same words can function as adjectives or adverbs, depending on what they modify.

Adjectives modify

nouns—*iced* tea, *power* forward
pronouns—He is *brash.*

Adverbs modify

verbs—*barely* reach, drive *carefully*
adjectives—*truly* brave activist, *shockingly* red lipstick
other adverbs—*not* soon forget, *very* well
clauses—*Honestly,* I find ballet boring.

Adjectives answer the questions *Which one? How many?* and *What kind?* Adverbs answer the questions *How often? To what extent? When? Where? How?* and *Why?*

Use the correct forms of comparatives and superlatives

Comparative modifiers weigh one thing against another. They either end in *er* or are preceded by *more.*

Road bikes are faster on pavement than mountain bikes.

The more courageous juggler tossed flaming torches.

Superlative modifiers compare three or more items. They either end in *est* or are preceded by *most.*

April is the hottest month in New Delhi.

Wounded animals are the most ferocious.

Some frequently used comparatives and superlatives are irregular. The following list can help you become familiar with them.

Adjective	Comparative	Superlative
good	better	best
bad	worse	worst
little (amount)	less	least
many, much	more	most

Adverb	Comparative	Superlative
well	better	best
badly	worse	worst

Do not use both a suffix (*er* or *est*) and *more* or *most*.

Incorrect	The service at Jane's Restaurant is more slower than the service at Alphonso's.
Correct	The service at Jane's Restaurant is slower than the service at Alphonso's.

Absolute modifiers are words that represent an unvarying condition and thus aren't subject to the degrees that comparative and superlative constructions convey. Common absolute modifiers include *complete, ultimate,* and *unique. Unique,* for example, means "one of a kind." There's nothing else like it. Thus something cannot be *very unique* or *totally unique.* It is either unique or it isn't. Absolute modifiers should not be modified by comparatives (*more* + modifier or modifier + *er*) or superlatives (*most* + modifier or modifier + *est*).

Double negatives

In English, as in mathematics, two negatives equal a positive. Avoid using two negative words in one sentence, or you'll end up saying the opposite of what you mean. The following are negative words that you should avoid doubling up:

barely	nobody	nothing
hardly	none	scarcely
neither	no one	

Incorrect, double negative	Barely no one noticed that the pop star lip-synched during the whole performance.
Correct, single negative	Barely anyone noticed that the pop star lip-synched during the whole performance.

Incorrect, double negative	When the pastor asked if anyone had objections to the marriage, nobody said nothing.
Correct, single negative	When the pastor asked if anyone had objections to the marriage, nobody said anything.

6b Place Adjectives Carefully

As a general rule, the closer you place a modifier to the word it modifies, the less the chance you will confuse your reader.

Confusing	Watching from the ground below, the kettle of broadwing hawks circled high above the observers.

Is the kettle of hawks watching from the ground below? You can fix the problem by putting the modified subject immediately after the modifier or placing the modifier next to the modified subject.

Better	The kettle of broadwing hawks circled high above the **observers** who were watching from the ground below.
Better	Watching from the ground below, the **observers** saw a kettle of broadwing hawks circle high above them.

6c Place Adverbs Carefully

Single-word adverbs and adverbial clauses and phrases can usually sit comfortably either before or after the words they modify.

Dimitri quietly **walked** down the hall.

Dimitri **walked** quietly down the hall.

Conjunctive adverbs—*also, however, instead, likewise, then, therefore, thus,* and others—are adverbs that show how ideas relate to one another. They prepare a reader for contrasts, exceptions, additions, conclusions, and other shifts in an argument. Conjunctive adverbs can usually fit well into more than one place in the sentence. In the following example, *however* could fit in three different places.

Between two main clauses

Professional football players earn exorbitant salaries; however, they pay for their wealth with lifetimes of chronic pain and debilitating injuries.

Within second main clause

Professional football players earn exorbitant salaries; they pay for their wealth, however, with lifetimes of chronic pain and debilitating injuries.

At end of second main clause

Professional football players earn exorbitant salaries; they pay for their wealth with lifetimes of chronic pain and debilitating injuries however.

Subordinating conjunctions—words such as *after, although, because, if, since, than, that, though, when,* and *where*—often begin **adverb clauses.** Notice that we can place adverb clauses with subordinating conjunctions either before or after the word(s) being modified:

After someone in the audience yelled, he **forgot** the lyrics.

He **forgot** the lyrics after someone in the audience yelled.

COMMON ERRORS

e Edit Help

Placement of limiting modifiers

Words such as *almost, even, hardly, just, merely, nearly, not, only,* and *simply* are called limiting modifiers. Although people often play fast and loose with their placement in everyday speech, limiting modifiers should always go immediately before the word or words they modify in your writing. Like other limiting modifiers, *only* should be placed immediately before the word it modifies.

Incorrect	The Gross National Product only gives one indicator of economic growth.
Correct	The Gross National Product gives only one indicator of economic growth.

The word *only* modifies *one* in this sentence, not *Gross National Product.*

Remember: Place limiting modifiers immediately before the word(s) they modify.

6d Hyphens with Compound Modifiers

When to hyphenate

Hyphenate a compound modifier that precedes a noun.

When a compound modifier precedes a noun, you should usually hyphenate the modifier. A **compound modifier** consists of words that join together as a unit to modify a noun.

middle-class values   self-fulfilling prophecy

Hyphenate a phrase when it is used as a modifier that precedes a noun.

all-you-can-eat buffet   step-by-step instructions

Hyphenate the prefixes *pro-, anti-, post-, pre-, neo-,* and *mid-* before proper nouns.

neo-Nazi racism   mid-Atlantic states

Hyphenate a compound modifier with a number when it precedes a noun.

eighteenth-century drama   one-way street

When not to hyphenate

Do not hyphenate a compound modifier that follows a noun.

The instructor's approach is student-centered.

Do not hyphenate compound modifiers when the first word is *very* or ends in *ly*.

newly recorded data   very cold day

6e Revise Dangling Modifiers

Some modifiers are ambiguous because they could apply to more than one word or clause. Dangling modifiers are ambiguous for the opposite reason; they don't have a word to modify. In such cases the modifier is usually an introductory clause or phrase. What is being modified should immediately follow the phrase, but in the following sentence it is absent.

After bowling a perfect game, Surfside Lanes hung Marco's photo on the wall.

You can eliminate a dangling modifier in two ways:

1. Insert the noun or pronoun being modified immediately after the introductory modifying phrase.

   After bowling a perfect game, Marco was honored by having his photo hung on the wall at Surfside Lanes.

2. Rewrite the introductory phrase as an introductory clause to include the noun or pronoun.

   After Marco bowled a perfect game, Surfside Lanes hung his photo on the wall.

COMMON ERRORS

Dangling modifiers

A dangling modifier does not seem to modify anything in a sentence; it dangles, unconnected to the word or words it presumably is intended to modify. Frequently, it produces funny results:

Incorrect   When still a girl, my father joined the army.

It sounds like *father* was once a girl. The problem is that the subject, *I*, is missing:

Correct   When I was still a girl, my father joined the army.

Remember: Modifiers should be clearly connected to the words they modify, especially at the beginning of sentences.

---

7 | Grammar for Multilingual Writers

7a Nouns

Perhaps the most troublesome conventions for nonnative speakers are those that guide usage of the common articles *the*, *a*, and *an*. To understand how articles work in English, you must first understand how the language uses **nouns**.

Kinds of nouns

There are two basic kinds of nouns. A **proper noun** begins with a capital letter and names a unique person, place, or thing: *Theodore Roosevelt, Russia, Eiffel Tower*.

The other basic kind of noun is called a **common noun**. Common nouns do not name a unique person, place, or thing: *man, country, tower*.

Count and noncount nouns

Common nouns can be classified as either *count* or *noncount*. **Count nouns** can be made plural, usually by adding *-s* (*finger, fingers*) or by using their plural forms (*person, people; datum, data*). **Noncount nouns** cannot be counted directly and cannot take the plural form (*information*, but not *informations; garbage*, but not *garbages*). Some nouns can be either count or noncount, depending on how they are used. *Hair* can refer to either a strand of hair, where it serves as a count noun, or a mass of hair, where it becomes a noncount noun.

COMMON ESL ERRORS

Singular and plural forms of count nouns

Count nouns are simpler to quantify than noncount nouns. But remember that English requires you to state both singular and plural forms of nouns explicitly. Look at the following sentences.

Incorrect The three bicyclist shaved their leg before the big race.

Correct The three bicyclists shaved their legs before the big race.

Remember: English requires you to use plural forms of count nouns even if a plural number is otherwise indicated.

7b Articles

Articles indicate that a noun is about to appear, and they clarify what the noun refers to. There are only two kinds of articles in English, definite and indefinite:

1. **the:** *The* is a **definite article**, meaning that it refers to (1) a specific object already known to the reader, (2) one about to be made known to the reader, or (3) a unique object.

2. **a, an:** The **indefinite articles** *a* and *an* refer to an object whose specific identity is not known to the reader. The only difference between *a* and *an* is that *a* is used before a consonant sound (*man, friend, yellow*), while *an* is used before a vowel sound (*animal, enemy, orange*).

COMMON ESL ERRORS

Articles with count and noncount nouns

Knowing how to distinguish between count and noncount nouns can help you decide which article to use. Noncount nouns are never used with the indefinite articles *a* or *an*.

Incorrect Maria jumped into a water.

Correct Maria jumped into the water.

No articles are used with noncount and plural count nouns when you wish to state something that has a general application.

Incorrect The water is a precious natural resource.

Correct Water is a precious natural resource.

Remember:
1. Noncount nouns are never used with *a* and *an*.
2. Noncount and plural nouns used to make general statements do not take articles.

7c Verbs

The verb system in English can be divided between simple verbs like *run, speak,* and *look,* and verb phrases like *may have run, have spoken,* and *will be looking.* In these examples, the words that appear before the main verbs—*may, have, will,* and *be*—are called **auxiliary verbs** (also called **helping verbs**).

Indicating tense and voice with *be* verbs

Like the other auxiliary verbs *have* and *do, be* changes form to signal tense. In addition to *be* itself, the **be verbs** are *is, am, are, was, were,* and *been.* To show ongoing action, *be* verbs are followed by the present participle, which is a verb with an *-ing* ending:

Incorrect	I am think of all the things I'd rather be do.
Correct	I am thinking of all the things I'd rather be doing.

To show that an action is being done to, rather than by, the subject, follow *be* verbs with the past participle (a verb usually ending in *-ed, -en,* or *-t*):

Incorrect	The movie was direct by John Woo.
Correct	The movie was directed by John Woo.

Modal auxiliary verbs

Modal auxiliary verbs *will, would, can, could, may, might, shall, must,* and *should* express conditions like possibility, permission, speculation, expectation, obligation, and necessity. Unlike the auxiliary verbs *be, have,* and *do,* modal verbs do not change form based on the grammatical subject of the sentence (*I, you, she, he, it, we, they*).

Two basic rules apply to all uses of modal verbs. First, modal verbs are always followed by the simple form of the verb. The simple form is the verb by itself, in the present tense, such as *have* but not *had, having,* or *to have.*

Incorrect	She should studies harder to pass the exam.
Correct	She should study harder to pass the exam.

The second rule is that you should not use modals consecutively.

Incorrect	If you work harder at writing, you might could improve.
Correct	If you work harder at writing, you might improve.

Phrasal verbs

The liveliest and most colorful feature of the English language, its numerous idiomatic verbal phrases, gives many multilingual speakers the greatest difficulty.

Phrasal verbs consist of a verb and one or two **particles:** either a preposition, an adverb, or both. The verb and particles combine to form a phrase with a particular meaning that is often quite distinct from the meaning of the verb itself. Consider the following sentence.

I need to go over the chapter once more before the test.

Here, the meaning of *go over*—a verb and a preposition that, taken together, suggest casual study—is only weakly related to the meaning of either *go* or *over* by itself. English has hundreds of such idiomatic constructions, and the best way to familiarize yourself with them is to listen to and read as much informal English as you can.

Like regular verbs, phrasal verbs can be either transitive (they take a direct object) or intransitive. In the preceding example, *go over* is transitive. *Quiet down*—as in *Please quiet down*—is intransitive. Some phrases, like *wake up*, can be both: *Wake up!* is intransitive, while *Jenny, wake up the children* is transitive.

In some transitive phrasal verbs, the particles can be separated from the verb without affecting the meaning: *I made up a song* is equivalent to *I made a song up.* In others, the particles cannot be separated from the verb.

Incorrect   You shouldn't play with love around.

Correct   You shouldn't play around with love.

Unfortunately, there are no shortcuts for learning which verbal phrases are separable and which are not. As you become increasingly familiar with English, you will grow more confident in your ability to use phrasal verbs.

8 | Commas

8a Commas with Introductory Elements

Introductory elements usually need to be set off by commas. Introductory words or phrases signal a shift in ideas or a particular arrangement of ideas; they help direct the reader's attention to the writer's most important points.

When a conjunctive adverb (see Section 6c) or introductory phrase begins a sentence, the comma follows.

Therefore, the suspect could not have been at the scene of the crime.

Above all, remember to let water drip from the faucets if the temperature drops below freezing.

When a conjunctive adverb comes in the middle of a sentence, set it off with commas preceding and following.

> If you really want to prevent your pipes from freezing, *however,* you should insulate them before the winter comes.

Occasionally the conjunctive adverb or phrase blends into a sentence so smoothly that a pause would sound awkward.

Awkward   Even if you take every precaution, the pipes in your home may freeze, *nevertheless.*

Better   Even if you take every precaution, the pipes in your home may freeze *nevertheless.*

COMMON ERRORS

e Edit Help

Commas with long introductory modifiers

Long subordinate clauses or phrases that begin sentences should be followed by a comma. The following sentence lacks the needed comma.

Incorrect   Because teens and younger adults are so comfortable with and reliant on cell phone devices texting while driving does not immediately seem like an irresponsible and possibly deadly act.

When you read this sentence, you likely had to go back to sort it out. The words *cell phone devices* and *texting* tend to run together. When the comma is added, the sentence is easier to understand because the reader knows where the subordinate clause ends and where the main clause begins:

Correct   Because teens and younger adults are so comfortable with and reliant on cell phone devices, texting while driving does not immediately seem like an irresponsible and possibly deadly act.

How long is a long introductory modifier? Short introductory adverbial phrases and clauses of five words or fewer can get by without the comma if the omission does not mislead the reader. Using the comma is still correct after short introductory adverbial phrases and clauses:

Correct   In the long run stocks have always done better than bonds.

Correct   In the long run, stocks have always done better than bonds.

Remember: Put commas after long introductory modifiers.

8b Commas with Compound Clauses

Two main clauses joined by a coordinating conjunction (*and, or, so, yet, but, nor, for*) form a compound sentence. Writers sometimes get confused about when to insert a comma before a coordinating conjunction.

Use a comma and a coordinating conjunction to separate main clauses

Main clauses carry enough grammatical weight to be punctuated as sentences. When two main clauses are joined by a coordinating conjunction, place a comma before the coordinating conjunction in order to distinguish them.

> Sandy borrowed Martin's iPad on Tuesday, and she returned it on Friday.

Very short main clauses joined by a coordinating conjunction do not need commas.

> She called and she called, but no one answered.

Do not use a comma to separate two verbs with the same subject

> Incorrect   Sandy borrowed Martin's video camera on Tuesday, and returned it on Friday.

Sandy is the subject of both *borrowed* and *returned*. This sentence has only one main clause; it should not be punctuated as a compound sentence.

> Correct   Sandy borrowed Martin's video camera on Tuesday and returned it on Friday.

Do not use a comma to separate a main clause from a restrictive clause or phrase

When clauses and phrases that follow the main clause are essential to the meaning of a sentence, they should not be set off with a comma.

> Incorrect   Sandy plans to borrow Felicia's DVD collection, while Felicia is on vacation.

> Correct   Sandy plans to borrow Felicia's DVD collection while Felicia is on vacation.

COMMON ERRORS

Commas in compound sentences

The easiest way to distinguish between compound sentences and sentences with phrases that follow the main clause is to isolate the part that comes after the conjunction. If the part that follows the conjunction can stand on its own as a complete sentence, insert a comma. If it cannot, omit the comma.

Main clause plus phrases

Mario thinks he lost his passport while riding the bus or by absentmindedly leaving it on the counter when he checked into the hostel.

Look at what comes after the coordinating conjunction *or:*

by absentmindedly leaving it on the counter when he checked into the hostel

This group of words is not a main clause and cannot stand on its own as a complete sentence. Do not set it off with a comma.

Main clauses joined with a conjunction

On Saturday Mario went to the American consulate to get a new passport, but the officer told him that replacement passports could not be issued on weekends.

Read the clause after the coordinating conjunction *but:*

the officer told him that replacement passports could not be issued on weekends

This group of words can stand on its own as a complete sentence. Thus, it is a main clause; place a comma before *but.*

Remember:

1. Place a comma before the coordinating conjunction (*and, but, for, or, nor, so, yet*) when there are two main clauses.

2. Do not use a comma before the coordinating conjunction when there is only one main clause.

COMMON ERRORS

e Edit Help

Do not use a comma to set off a *because* clause that follows a main clause

Writers frequently place unnecessary commas before *because* and similar subordinate conjunctions that follow a main clause. *Because* is not a coordinating conjunction; thus it should not be set off by a comma unless the comma improves readability.

Incorrect I struggled to complete my term papers last year, because I worked at two jobs.

Correct I struggled to complete my term papers last year because I worked at two jobs.

But do use a comma after an introductory *because* clause.

Incorrect Because Danny left his red jersey at home Coach Russell benched him.

Correct Because Danny left his red jersey at home, Coach Russell benched him.

Remember: Use a comma after a *because* clause that begins a sentence. Do not use a comma to set off a *because* clause that follows a main clause.

8c Commas with Nonrestrictive Modifiers

Imagine that you are sending a friend a group photo that includes your aunt. Which sentence is correct?

> In the back row the woman wearing the pink hat is my aunt.
>
> In the back row the woman, wearing the pink hat, is my aunt.

Both sentences can be correct depending on what is in the photo. If there are three women standing in the back row and only one is wearing a pink hat, this piece of information is necessary for identifying your aunt. In this case the sentence without commas is correct because it identifies your aunt as the woman wearing the pink hat. Such necessary modifiers are **restrictive** and do not require commas.

If only one woman is standing in the back row, *wearing the pink hat* is extra information and not necessary to identify your aunt. The modifier in this case is **nonrestrictive** and is set off by commas.

Distinguish restrictive and nonrestrictive modifiers

You can distinguish between restrictive and nonrestrictive modifiers by deleting the modifier and then deciding whether the essential meaning of the sentence is changed. For example, delete the modifier *still stained by its bloody Tianamen Square crackdown* from the following sentence:

> Some members of the Olympic Site Selection Committee wanted to prevent China, still stained by its bloody Tianamen Square crackdown, from hosting the 2008 games.

The result leaves the meaning of the main clause unchanged.

> Some members of the Olympic Site Selection Committee wanted to prevent China from hosting the 2008 games.

The modifier is nonrestrictive and should be set off by commas.

Pay special attention to appositives

Clauses and phrases can be restrictive or nonrestrictive, depending on the context. Often the difference is obvious, but some modifiers require close consideration, especially appositives. An **appositive** is a noun or noun phrase that identifies or adds information to the noun preceding it.

Consider the following pair.

1 Apple's tablet computer the iPad introduced a class of devices between smartphones and laptops.
2 Apple's tablet computer, the iPad, introduced a class of devices between smartphones and laptops.

Which is correct? The appositive *the iPad* is not essential to the meaning of the sentence and simply offers additional information. Sentence 2 is correct.

Use commas to mark off parenthetical expressions

A **parenthetical expression** provides information or commentary that usually is not essential to the sentence's meaning.

Incorrect	My mother much to my surprise didn't say anything when she saw my pierced nose.
Correct	My mother, much to my surprise, didn't say anything when she saw my pierced nose.

8d Commas with Items in a Series

In a series of three or more items, place a comma after each item except the last one. The comma between the last two items goes before the conjunction (*and, or*).

> Health officials in Trenton, Manhattan, and the Bronx have all reported new cases of the West Nile virus.

8e Commas with Coordinate Adjectives

Coordinate adjectives are two or more adjectives that modify the same noun independently. Coordinate adjectives that are not linked by *and* must be separated by a comma.

> After the financial crisis of 2007–2010, the creators of credit-default swaps and other risky investments are no longer the **fresh-faced, giddy** kids of Wall Street.

You can recognize coordinate adjectives by reversing their order; if their meaning remains the same, the adjectives are coordinate and must be linked by *and* or separated by a comma.

Commas are not used between **cumulative adjectives**. Cumulative adjectives are two or more adjectives that work together to modify a noun: *deep blue sea, inexpensive mountain bike*. If reversing their order changes the description of the noun (or violates the order of English, such as *mountain inexpensive bike*), the adjectives are cumulative and should not be separated by a comma.

The following example doesn't require a comma in the cumulative adjective series *massive Corinthian*.

> Visitors to Rome's Pantheon pass between the **massive Corinthian** columns flanking the front door.

We know they are cumulative because reversing their order to read *Corinthian massive* would alter the way they modify *columns*—in this case, so much so that they no longer make sense.

8f Commas with Quotations

Properly punctuating quotations with commas can be tricky unless you know a few rules about when and where to use commas.

When to use commas with quotations

Commas set off signal phrases that attribute quotations to a speaker or writer, such as *he argues, they said,* and *she writes.*

> "When you come to a fork in the road," said Yogi Berra, "take it!"

If the signal phrase follows a quotation that is a complete sentence, replace the period that would normally come at the end of the quotation with a comma.

Incorrect	"Simplicity of language is not only reputable but perhaps even sacred." writes Kurt Vonnegut.
Correct	"Simplicity of language is not only reputable but perhaps even sacred," writes Kurt Vonnegut.

When not to use commas with quotations

Do not replace a question mark or exclamation point with a comma.

Incorrect	"Who's on first," Costello asked Abbott.
Correct	"Who's on first?" Costello asked Abbott.

Not all phrases that mention the author's name are signal phrases. When quoting a term or using a quotation within a subordinate clause, do not set off the quotation with commas.

> "Stonewall" Jackson gained his nickname at the First Battle of Bull Run when General Barnard Bee shouted to his men that Jackson was "standing like a stone wall."

8g Commas with Dates, Numbers, Titles, and Addresses

Some of the easiest comma rules to remember are the ones we use every day in dates, numbers, personal titles, place names, direct address, and brief interjections.

Commas with dates

Use commas to separate the day of the week from the month and to set off a year from the rest of the sentence.

> Monday, November 14, 2011

> On July 27, 2014, the opening ceremony of the World Scout Jamboree will be televised.

Do not use a comma when the month immediately precedes the year.

April 2013

Commas with numbers

Commas mark off thousands, millions, billions, and so on.

16,500,000

However, do not use commas in street addresses or page numbers.

page 1542

7602 Elm Street

Commas with personal titles

When a title follows a person's name, set the title off with commas.

Gregory House, MD

Commas with place names

Place a comma between street addresses, city names, state names, and countries but not before zip codes.

Write to the president at 1600 Pennsylvania Avenue, Washington, DC 20500.

Commas in direct address

When addressing someone directly, set off that person's name in commas.

I was happy to get your letter yesterday, Jamie.

Commas with brief interjections

Use commas to set off brief interjections like *yes* and *no,* as well as short questions that fall at the ends of sentences.

Have another piece of pie, won't you?

8h Commas to Avoid Confusion

Certain sentences can be confusing if you do not indicate where readers should pause within the sentence. Use a comma to guide a reader through these usually compact constructions.

> **Unclear** With supplies low prices of gasoline and fuel oil will increase.

This sentence could be read as meaning *With supplies, low prices will increase.*

> **Clear** With supplies low, prices of gasoline and fuel oil will increase.

8i Unnecessary Commas

Do not place a comma between a subject and the main verb.

> **Incorrect** American children of immigrant parents, often do not speak their parents' native language.

> **Correct** American children of immigrant parents often do not speak their parents' native language.

However, you do use commas to set off modifying phrases that separate subjects from verbs.

> **Correct** Steven Pinker, author of *The Language Instinct,* argues that the ability to speak and understand language is an evolutionary adaptive trait.

Do not use a comma with a coordinating conjunction unless it joins two main clauses. (See the Common Errors box on page 696.)

> **Incorrect** Susana thought finishing her first novel was hard, but soon learned that getting a publisher to buy it was much harder.

> **Correct** Susana thought finishing her first novel was hard but soon learned that getting a publisher to buy it was much harder.

> **Correct** Susana thought finishing her first novel was hard, but she soon learned that getting a publisher to buy it was much harder.

Do not use a comma after a subordinating conjunction such as *although, despite,* or *while.*

> **Incorrect** Although, soccer is gaining popularity in the States, it will never be as popular as football or baseball.

> **Correct** Although soccer is gaining popularity in the States, it will never be as popular as football or baseball.

Some writers mistakenly use a comma with *than* to try to heighten the contrast in a comparison.

Incorrect   Any teacher will tell you that acquiring critical thinking skills is more important, than simply memorizing information.

Correct   Any teacher will tell you that acquiring critical thinking skills is more important than simply memorizing information.

A common mistake is to place a comma after *such as* or *like* before introducing a list.

Incorrect   Many hourly workers, such as, waiters, dishwashers, and cashiers, do not receive health benefits from their employers.

Correct   Many hourly workers, such as waiters, dishwashers, and cashiers, do not receive health benefits from their employers.

9 | Semicolons and Colons

9a Semicolons with Closely Related Main Clauses

Why use semicolons? Sometimes we want to join two main clauses to form a complete sentence in order to indicate a relationship and avoid wordiness. We can connect them with a comma and a coordinating conjunction like *or, but,* or *and.* To create variation in sentence style and show a closer relationship, we can omit the comma and coordinating conjunction and insert a semicolon between the two clauses.

Semicolons can join only clauses that are grammatically equal. In other words, they join main clauses only to other main clauses, not to phrases or subordinate clauses. Look at the following examples:

Incorrect
———MAIN CLAUSE———
Gloria's new weightlifting program will help her recover from

——— PHRASE ———
knee surgery; doing a series of squats and presses with a physical

therapist.

Correct
———MAIN CLAUSE———
Gloria's new weightlifting program will help her recover from knee

———MAIN CLAUSE———
surgery; a physical therapist leads her through a series of squats

and presses.

COMMON ERRORS

e Edit Help

Semicolons with transitional words and phrases

Closely related main clauses sometimes use a conjunctive adverb (such as *however, therefore, moreover, furthermore, thus, meanwhile, nonetheless, otherwise*) or a transitional phrase (*in fact, for example, that is, for instance, in addition, in other words, on the other hand, even so*) to indicate the relationship between them. When the second clause begins with a conjunctive adverb or a transitional phrase, a semicolon is needed to join the two clauses. This sentence pattern is frequently used; therefore, it pays to learn how to punctuate it correctly.

Incorrect (comma splice)	No one doubts that exercise burns calories, however, few people can lose weight by exercise alone.
Correct	No one doubts that exercise burns calories; however, few people can lose weight by exercise alone.

Remember: Two main clauses joined by a conjunctive adverb or a transitional phrase require a semicolon.

Do not use a semicolon to introduce quotations

Use a comma or colon instead.

Incorrect	Robert Frost's poem "Mending Wall" contains this line; "Good fences make good neighbors."
Correct	Robert Frost's poem "Mending Wall" contains this line: "Good fences make good neighbors."

Do not use a semicolon to introduce lists

Incorrect	William Shakespeare wrote four romance plays at the end of his career; *The Tempest, The Winter's Tale, Cymbeline,* and *Pericles.*
Correct	William Shakespeare wrote four romance plays at the end of his career: *The Tempest, The Winter's Tale, Cymbeline,* and *Pericles.*

9b Semicolons Together with Commas

When an item in a series already includes a comma, adding more commas to separate it from the other items will only confuse the reader. Use semicolons instead of commas between items in a series that has internal punctuation.

Confusing	The church's design competition drew entries from as far away as Gothenberg, Sweden, Caracas, Venezuela, and Athens, Greece.
Clearer	The church's design competition drew entries from as far away as Gothenberg, Sweden; Caracas, Venezuela; and Athens, Greece.

9c Colons in Sentences

Like semicolons, colons can join two closely related main clauses (complete sentences). A colon indicates that what follows will explain or expand on what comes before the colon. Use a colon in cases where the second main clause interprets or sums up the first.

> Anthrozoology, the study of how animals and people relate to one another, sheds light on larger issues in human psychology: people's interactions with animals illustrate concepts of altruism, ethics, and taboo.

You may choose to capitalize the first word of the main clause following the colon or leave it lowercase. Either is correct as long as you are consistent throughout your text.

Colons linking main clauses with appositives

A colon calls attention to an appositive, a noun, or a noun phrase that renames the noun preceding it. If you're not certain whether a colon would be appropriate, put *namely* in its place. If *namely* makes sense when you read the main clause followed by the appositive, you probably need to insert a colon instead of a comma. Remember, the clause that precedes the colon must be a complete sentence.

> I know the perfect person for the job, namely me.

The sentence makes sense with *namely* placed before the appositive. Thus, a colon is appropriate.

> I know the perfect person for the job: me.

Never capitalize a word following a colon unless the word starts a complete sentence or is normally capitalized.

Colons joining main clauses with quotations

Use a colon to link a main clause and a quotation that interprets or sums up the clause. Be careful not to use a colon to link a phrase with a quotation.

Incorrect: phrase–colon–quotation

> President Roosevelt's strategy to change the nation's panicky attitude during the Great Depression: "[T]he only thing we have to fear," he said, "is fear itself."

Correct: main clause–colon–quotation

President Roosevelt's strategy to end the Great Depression was to change the nation's panicky attitude: "[T]he only thing we have to fear," he said, "is fear itself."

The first example is incorrect because there is no main verb in the first part of the sentence and thus it is a phrase rather than a main clause. The second example adds the verb (*was*), making the first part of the sentence a main clause.

9d Colons with Lists

Use a colon to join a main clause to a list. The main clauses in these cases sometimes include the phrase *the following* or *as follows*. Remember that a colon cannot join a phrase or an incomplete clause to a list.

Incorrect: phrase–colon–list

Three ingredients for soup: chicken stock, peeled shrimp, and chopped tomatoes.

Correct: main clause–colon–list

You can make a tasty soup with just three ingredients: chicken stock, peeled shrimp, and chopped tomatoes.

COMMON ERRORS

e **E**dit **H**elp

Colons misused with lists

Some writers think that anytime they introduce a list, they should insert a colon. Colons are used correctly only when a complete sentence precedes the colon.

Incorrect   Jessica's entire wardrobe for her trip to Cancun included: two swimsuits, one pair of shorts, two T-shirts, a party dress, and a pair of sandals.

Correct   Jessica's entire wardrobe for her trip to Cancun included two swimsuits, one pair of shorts, two T-shirts, a party dress, and a pair of sandals.

Correct   Jessica jotted down what she would need for her trip: two swimsuits, one pair of shorts, two T-shirts, a party dress, and a pair of sandals.

Remember: A colon should be placed only after a clause that can stand by itself as a sentence.

10 | Dashes and Parentheses

10a Dashes and Parentheses to Set Off Information

Dashes and parentheses call attention to groups of words. In effect, they tell the reader that a group of words is not part of the main clause and should be given special attention. If you want to make an element stand out, especially in the middle of a sentence, use parentheses or dashes instead of commas.

Dashes with final elements

A dash is often used to set off a phrase or subordinate clause at the end of a sentence to offer a significant comment about the main clause. Dashes can also anticipate a shift in tone at the end of a sentence.

> A full-sized SUV can take you wherever you want to go in style—
> if your idea of style is a gas-guzzling tank.

Parentheses with additional information

Parentheses are more often used for identifying information, afterthoughts or asides, examples, and clarifications. You can place full sentences, fragments, or brief terms within parentheses.

> Some argue that ethanol **(**the pet solution of politicians for achieving energy independence**)** costs more energy to manufacture and ship than it produces.

COMMON ERRORS

Do not use dashes as periods

Do not use dashes to separate two main clauses (clauses that can stand as complete sentences). Use dashes to separate main clauses from subordinate clauses and phrases when you want to emphasize the subordinate clause or phrase.

Incorrect: main clause–dash–main clause
I was one of the few women in my computer science classes—most of the students majoring in computer science at that time were men.

Correct: main clause–dash–phrase
I was one of the few women in computer science—a field then dominated by men.

Remember: Dashes are not periods and should not be used as periods.

10b Dashes and Parentheses versus Commas

Like commas, parentheses and dashes enclose material that adds, explains, or digresses. However, the three punctuation marks are not interchangeable. The mark you choose depends on how much emphasis you want to place on the material. Dashes indicate the most emphasis. Parentheses offer somewhat less, and commas offer less still.

Commas indicate a moderate level of emphasis

Bill covered the new tattoo on his bicep, a pouncing tiger, because he thought it might upset our mother.

Parentheses lend a greater level of emphasis

I'm afraid to go bungee jumping (though my brother tells me it's less frightening than a roller coaster).

Dashes indicate the highest level of emphasis and, sometimes, surprise and drama

Christina felt as though she had been punched in the gut; she could hardly believe the stranger at her door was really who he claimed to be—the brother she hadn't seen in twenty years.

COMMON ERRORS

The art of typing a dash

Although dashes and hyphens may look similar, they are actually different marks. The distinction is small but important because dashes and hyphens serve different purposes. A dash is a line much longer than a hyphen. Most word processors will create a dash automatically when you type two hyphens together. Or you can type a special character to make a dash. Your manual will tell you which keys to press to make a dash.

Do not leave a space between a dash or a hyphen and the words that come before and after them. Likewise, if you are using two hyphens to indicate a dash, do not leave a space between the hyphens.

Incorrect   A well - timed effort at conserving water may prevent long - term damage to drought - stricken farms - - if it's not already too late.

Correct   A well-timed effort at conserving water may prevent long-term damage to drought-stricken farms—if it's not already too late.

Remember: Do not put spaces before or after hyphens and dashes.

10c Other Punctuation with Parentheses

Parentheses around letters or numbers that order a series within a sentence make the list easier to read.

> Angela Creider's recipe for becoming a great novelist is to **(1)** set aside an hour during the morning to write, **(2)** read what you've written out loud, **(3)** revise your prose, and **(4)** repeat every morning for the next thirty years.

Abbreviations made from the first letters of words are often used in place of the unwieldy names of institutions, departments, organizations, or terms. To show readers what the abbreviation stands for, the writer must state the complete name, followed by the abbreviation in parentheses, the first time the organization is mentioned in the text.

> The University of California, Santa Cruz **(UCSC)** supports its mascot, the banana slug, with pride and a sense of humor. And although the nickname sounds strange to outsiders, UCSC students are even referred to as "the banana slugs."

COMMON ERRORS   e Edit Help

Using periods, commas, colons, and semicolons with parentheses

When an entire sentence is enclosed in parentheses, place the period before the closing parenthesis.

Incorrect   Our fear of sharks, heightened by movies like *Jaws*, is vastly out of proportion with the minor threat sharks actually pose. **(**Dying from a dog attack, in fact, is much more likely than dying from a shark attack**)**.

Correct   Our fear of sharks, heightened by movies like *Jaws*, is vastly out of proportion with the minor threat sharks actually pose. **(**Dying from a dog attack, in fact, is much more likely than dying from a shark attack.**)**

When the material in parentheses is part of the sentence and the parentheses fall at the end of the sentence, place the period outside the closing parenthesis.

Incorrect   Reports of sharks attacking people are rare **(**much rarer than dog attacks.**)**

Correct   Reports of sharks attacking people are rare **(**much rarer than dog attacks**)**.

Place commas, colons, and semicolons after the closing parenthesis.

Remember: When an entire sentence is enclosed in parentheses, place the period inside the closing parenthesis. (Otherwise, put the punctuation outside the closing parenthesis.)

11 | Apostrophes

11a Possessives

Nouns and indefinite pronouns (for example, *everyone, anyone*) that indicate possession or ownership are marked by attaching an apostrophe and *-s* or an apostrophe only to the end of the word.

Singular nouns and indefinite pronouns

For singular nouns and indefinite pronouns, add an apostrophe plus *-s: -'s.* Even singular nouns that end in *-s* usually follow this principle.

> Iris's coat
>
> everyone's favorite
>
> a woman's choice

There are a few exceptions to adding *-'s* for singular nouns:

- **Nouns plural in form, singular in meaning** *politics' influence, United States' power*
- **Official names of certain places, institutions, companies** *Governors Island, Teachers College of Columbia University, Mothers Café, Saks Fifth Avenue, Walgreens Pharmacy.* Note, however, that many companies do include the apostrophe: *Denny's Restaurant, Macy's, McDonald's, Wendy's Old Fashioned Hamburgers.*

Plural nouns

For plural nouns that do not end in *-s*, add an apostrophe plus *-s: -'s.*

> media's responsibility
>
> children's section

For plural nouns that end in *-s*, add only an apostrophe at the end.

> attorneys' briefs
>
> the Kennedys' legacy

Compound nouns

For compound nouns, add an apostrophe plus *-s* to the last word of the compound noun: *-'s*.

> mayor of Cleveland's speech

Two or more nouns

For joint possession, add an apostrophe plus *-s* to the final noun: *-'s*.

> mother and dad's yard

When people possess or own things separately, add an apostrophe plus *-s* to each noun: *-'s*.

> Roberto's and Edward's views are totally opposed.

COMMON ERRORS

e <u>Edit</u> <u>Help</u>

Possessive forms of personal pronouns never take the apostrophe

Incorrect	*her's, it's, our's, your's, their's*
	The bird sang in **it's** cage.
Correct	*hers, its, ours, yours, theirs*
	The bird sang in **its** cage.

Remember: *It's = It is*

11b Contractions and Omitted Letters

In speech we often leave out sounds and syllables of familiar words. These omissions are noted with apostrophes.

Contractions

Contractions combine two words into one, using the apostrophe to mark what is left out.

I am ⟶ I'm   we are ⟶ we're
I would ⟶ I'd   they are ⟶ they're
you are ⟶ you're   cannot ⟶ can't
you will ⟶ you'll   do not ⟶ don't
he is ⟶ he's   does not ⟶ doesn't
she is ⟶ she's   will not ⟶ won't
it is ⟶ it's

Omissions

Using apostrophes to signal omitted letters is a way of approximating speech in writing. They can make your writing look informal and slangy, but overuse can quickly become annoying.

rock and roll ⟶ rock 'n' roll

the 1960s ⟶ the '60s

neighborhood ⟶ 'hood

11c Plurals of Letters, Symbols, and Words Referred to as Words

When to use apostrophes to make plurals

The trend is away from using apostrophes to form plurals of letters, symbols, and words referred to as words. In a few cases adding the apostrophe and *s* is still used, as in this old saying:

Mind your p's and q's.

Words used as words are italicized, and their plural is formed by adding an *s* not in italics, not an apostrophe and *s*.

Take a few of the *and*s out of your writing.

Words in quotation marks, however, typically use apostrophe and *s*.

She had too many "probably's" in her letter for me to be confident that the remodeling will be finished on schedule.

When not to use apostrophes to make plurals

Do not use an apostrophe to make family names plural.

Incorrect	You've heard of keeping up with the Jones's.
Correct	You've heard of keeping up with the Joneses.

12 | Quotation Marks

12a Direct Quotations

Use quotation marks to enclose direct quotations

Enclose direct quotations—someone else's words repeated verbatim—in quotation marks.

> Michael Pollan, the author of *Food Rules* and *The Omnivore's Dilemma*, argues that industrial agriculture uses too much fossil fuel to grow food: "We need to reduce the dependence of modern agriculture on oil, an eminently feasible goal—after all, agriculture is the original solar technology."

Do not use quotation marks with indirect quotations

Do not enclose an indirect quotation—a paraphrase of someone else's words—in quotation marks. However, do remember that you need to cite your source not only when you quote directly but also when you paraphrase or borrow ideas.

> Dan Glickman of the MPAA thinks that because parents don't want their children to start smoking, they should be warned when movies contain scenes where characters smoke (98).

Do not use quotation marks with block quotations

When a quotation is long enough to be set off as a block quotation, do not use quotation marks. MLA style defines long quotations as more than four lines of prose or poetry. APA style defines a long quotation as one of more than forty words.

In the following example in MLA format, notice that the long quotation is indented and quotation marks are omitted. Also notice that the parenthetical citation for a long quotation comes after the period.

> Complaints about maintenance in the dorms have been on the rise ever since the physical plant reorganized its crews into teams in August. One student's experience is typical:
>
>> When our ceiling started dripping, my roommate and I went to our resident director right away to file an emergency maintenance request. Apparently the physical plant felt that "emergency" meant they could get around to it in a week or two. By the fourth day without any word from a maintenance person, the ceiling tiles began to fall and puddles began to pool on our carpet. (Trillo)
>
> The physical plant could have avoided expensive ceiling tile and carpet repairs if it had responded to the student's request promptly.

12b Titles of Short Works

While the titles of longer works such as books, magazines, and newspapers are italicized or underlined, titles of shorter works should be set off with quotation marks. Use quotation marks with the following kinds of titles:

Short stories	"Light Is Like Water," by Gabriel García Márquez
Magazine articles	"Race against Death," by Erin West
Newspaper articles	"Cincinnati Mayor Declares Emergency," by Liz Sidoti
Short poems	"We Real Cool," by Gwendolyn Brooks
Essays	"Self-Reliance," by Ralph Waldo Emerson

The exception.

Don't put the title of your own paper in quotation marks. If the title of another short work appears within the title of your paper, retain the quotation marks around the short work.

12c Other Uses of Quotation Marks

Quotation marks around a term can indicate that the writer is using the term in a novel way, often with skepticism, irony, or sarcasm. The quotation marks indicate that the writer is questioning the term's conventional definition.

Italics are usually used to indicate that a word is being used as a word, rather than standing for its conventional meaning. However, quotation marks are correct in these cases as well.

Beginning writers sometimes confuse "their," "they're," and "there."

12d Other Punctuation with Quotation Marks

The rules for placing punctuation with quotation marks fall into three general categories.

Periods and commas with quotation marks

Place periods and commas inside closing quotation marks.

Incorrect "The smartest people", Dr. Geisler pointed out, "tell themselves the most convincing rationalizations".

Correct "The smartest people," Dr. Geisler pointed out, "tell themselves the most convincing rationalizations."

Colons and semicolons with quotation marks

Place colons and semicolons outside closing quotation marks.

Incorrect "From Stettin in the Baltic to Trieste in the Adriatic, an iron curtain has descended across the Continent;" Churchill's statement rang through Cold War politics for the next fifty years.

Correct "From Stettin in the Baltic to Trieste in the Adriatic, an iron curtain has descended across the Continent"; Churchill's statement rang through Cold War politics for the next fifty years.

Exclamation points, question marks, and dashes with quotation marks

When an exclamation point, question mark, or dash belongs to the original quotation, place it inside the closing quotation mark. When it applies to the entire sentence, place it outside the closing quotation mark.

In the original quotation

"Are we there yet?" came the whine from the back seat.

Applied to the entire sentence

Did the driver in the front seat respond, "Not even close"?

COMMON ERRORS

e **Edit Help**

Quotations within quotations

Single quotation marks are used to indicate a quotation within a quotation. In the following example single quotation marks clarify who is speaking. The rules for placing punctuation with single quotation marks are the same as the rules for placing punctuation with double quotation marks.

Incorrect   When he showed the report to Paul Probius, Michener reported that Probius "took vigorous exception to the sentence "He wanted to close down the university," insisting that we add the clarifying phrase "as it then existed"" (Michener 145).

Correct   When he showed the report to Paul Probius, Michener reported that Probius "took vigorous exception to the sentence 'He wanted to close down the university,' insisting that we add the clarifying phrase 'as it then existed'" (Michener 145).

Remember: Single quotation marks are used for quotations within quotations.

12e Misuses of Quotation Marks

It's becoming more and more common to see quotation marks used to emphasize a word or phrase. Resist the temptation in your own writing; the usage is incorrect. In fact, because quotation marks indicate that a writer is using a term with skepticism or irony, adding quotation marks for emphasis will highlight unintended connotations of the term.

Incorrect   "fresh" seafood

By using quotation marks here, the writer seems to call into question whether the seafood is really fresh.

| Correct | fresh seafood |
| Incorrect | Enjoy our "live" music every Saturday night. |

Again, the quotation marks unintentionally indicate that the writer is skeptical that the music is live.

| Correct | Enjoy our live music every Saturday night. |

You have better ways of creating emphasis using your word processing program: **boldfacing**, underlining, *italicizing*, and using color.

13 | Other Punctuation Marks

13a Periods

Periods at the ends of sentences

Place a period at the end of a complete sentence that is not a direct question or an exclamatory statement.

Periods with quotation marks and parentheses

When a quotation falls at the end of a sentence, place the period inside the closing quotation marks.

> Although he devoted decades to a wide range of artistic and political projects, Allen Ginsberg is best known as the author of the poem "Howl."

When a parenthetical phrase falls at the end of a sentence, place the period outside the closing parenthesis. When parentheses enclose a whole sentence, place the period inside the closing parenthesis.

Periods with abbreviations

Many abbreviations require periods; however, there are few set rules. The rules for punctuating two types of abbreviations do remain consistent: Postal abbreviations for states and most abbreviations for organizations do not require periods. When an abbreviation with a period falls at the end of a sentence, do not add a second period to conclude the sentence.

Incorrect	Her flight arrives at 6:22 p.m..
Correct	Her flight arrives at 6:22 p.m.

Periods as decimal points

Decimal points are periods that separate integers from tenths, hundredths, and so on.

99.98% pure silver	98.6° Fahrenheit
on sale for $399.97	2.6-liter engine

Since large numbers with long strings of zeros can be difficult to read accurately, writers sometimes clarify them by using words and decimal points. In this way, 16,600,000 can be written as 16.6 million.

13b Question Marks

Question marks with direct questions

Place a question mark at the end of a direct question. A direct question is one that the questioner puts to someone outright. In contrast, an indirect question merely reports the asking of a question. Question marks give readers a cue to read the end of the sentence with rising inflection. Read the following sentences aloud. Hear how your inflection rises in the second sentence to convey the direct question.

Indirect question

Desirée asked whether Dan rides his motorcycle without a helmet.

Direct question

Desirée asked, "Does Dan ride his motorcycle without a helmet?"

Question marks with quotations

When a quotation falls at the end of a direct question, place the question mark outside the closing quotation mark.

Did Abraham Lincoln really call Harriet Beecher Stowe "the little lady who started this big war"?

Place the question mark inside the closing quotation when only the quoted material is a direct question.

> Slowly scientists are beginning to answer the question "Is cancer a genetic disease?"

When quoting a direct question in the middle of a sentence, place a question mark inside the closing quotation mark and place a period at the end of the sentence.

> Market researchers estimate that asking Burger World's customers "Do you want fries with that?" was responsible for a 15% boost in french fries sales.

13c Exclamation Points

Exclamation points to convey strong emotion

Exclamation points conclude sentences and, like question marks, tell the reader how a sentence should sound. They indicate strong emotion. Use exclamation points sparingly in formal writing; they are seldom appropriate in academic and professional prose.

Exclamation points with emphatic interjections

Exclamation points can convey a sense of urgency with brief interjections. Interjections can be incorporated into sentences or stand on their own.

> Run! They're about to close the doors to the jetway.

Exclamation points with quotation marks

In quotations, exclamation points follow the same rules as question marks. If a quotation falls at the end of an exclamatory statement, place the exclamation point outside the closing quotation mark.

> The singer forgot the words to "America the Beautiful"!

When quoting an exclamatory statement at the end of a sentence that is not itself exclamatory, place the exclamation point inside the closing quotation mark.

> Jerry thought his car would be washed away in the flood, but Anna jumped into action, declaring, "Not if I can help it!"

13d Brackets

While brackets (sometimes called *square brackets*) look quite similar to parentheses, the two perform different functions. Brackets have a narrow set of uses.

Brackets to provide clarification within quotation marks

Use brackets if you are interjecting a comment of your own or clarifying information within a direct quotation. In the following example the writer quotes a sentence with the pronoun *they*, which refers to a noun in a previous, unquoted sentence. The material in brackets clarifies to whom the pronoun refers.

> The Harris study found that "In the last three years, they [Gonzales Junior High students] averaged 15% higher on their mathematics assessment tests than their peers in Northridge County."

Brackets within parentheses

Since parentheses within parentheses might confuse readers, use brackets to enclose parenthetical information within a parenthetical phrase.

> Representative Patel's most controversial legislation (including a version of the hate crimes bill [HR 99-108] the house rejected two years ago) has a slim chance of being enacted this session.

13e Ellipses

Ellipses let a reader know that a portion of a passage is missing. You can use ellipses to keep quotations concise and direct readers' attention to what is important to the point you are making. An ellipsis is a string of three periods with spaces separating the periods.

Ellipses to indicate an omission from a quotation

When you quote only a phrase or a short clause from a sentence, you usually do not need to use an ellipsis.

> Mao Zedong first used "let a hundred flowers blossom" in a Beijing speech in 1957.

Except at the beginning of a quotation, indicate omitted words with an ellipsis.

The original source

> "The female praying mantis, so named for the way it holds its front legs together as if in prayer, tears off her male partner's head during mating. Remarkably, the headless male will continue the act of mating. This brutal dance is a stark example of the innate evolutionary drive to pass genes onto offspring; the male praying mantis seems to live and die only for this moment."

An ellipsis indicates omitted words

"The female praying mantis . . . ~~tears off her male partner's head~~ during mating."

When the ellipsis is at the end of a sentence, place the period or question mark after the ellipsis and follow with the closing quotation mark.

Words omitted at the end of a sentence

"This brutal dance is a stark example of the innate evolutionary drive to pass genes onto offspring . . . ."

13f Slashes

Slashes to indicate alternative words

Slashes are used to indicate the concept of *or*. When using slashes for this purpose, do not put a space between the slash and the words.

Incorrect	Maya was such an energetic baby that her exhausted parents wished she had come with an on / off switch.
Correct	Maya was such an energetic baby that her exhausted parents wished she had come with an on/off switch.

Slashes with fractions

Place a slash between the numerator and the denominator in a fraction. Do not put any spaces around the slash.

Incorrect	3 / 4
Correct	3/4

14 Capitalization, Italics, Abbreviations, Numbers

14a Capital Letters

Capitalize the initial letters of proper nouns (nouns that name particular people, places, and things). Capitalize the initial letters of proper adjectives (adjectives based on the names of people, places, and things).

African American bookstore   Avogadro's number   Irish music

Do not capitalize the names of seasons, academic disciplines (unless they are languages), or job titles used without a proper noun.

14b Italics

Italicize the titles of entire works (books, magazines, newspapers, films), but place the titles of parts of those works within quotation marks. Also italicize or underline the names of ships and aircraft.

> I am fond of reading *USA Today* in the morning.

The exceptions.
Do not italicize or underline the names of sacred texts.

Italicize unfamiliar foreign words

Italicize foreign words that are not part of common English usage. Do not italicize words that have become a common word or phrase in the English vocabulary. How do you decide which words are common? If a word appears in a standard English dictionary, it can be considered as adopted into English.

Use italics to clarify your use of a word, letter, or number

In everyday speech, we often use cues—a pause, a louder or different tone—to communicate how we are using a word. In writing, italics help clarify when you use words in a referential manner, or letters and numbers as letters and numbers.

14c Abbreviations

Abbreviations are shortened forms of words. Because abbreviations vary widely, you will need to look in the dictionary to determine how to abbreviate words on a case-by-case basis. Nonetheless, there are a few patterns that abbreviations follow.

Abbreviate titles before and degrees after full names

> Ms. Ella Fitzgerald
>
> Prof. Vijay Aggarwal

Write out the professional title when it is used with only a last name.

> Professor Chin
>
> Reverend Ames

° Conventions for using abbreviations with years and times

BCE (before the common era) and CE (common era) are now preferred for indicating years, replacing BC (before Christ) and AD (*anno Domini* ["the year of our Lord"]). Note that all are now used without periods.

479 **BCE** (or BC)   1610 **CE** (or AD, but AD is placed before the number)

The preferred written conventions for times are a.m. (*ante meridiem*) and p.m. (*post meridiem*).

9:03 a.m.   3:30 p.m.

Latin abbreviations

Some writers sprinkle Latin abbreviations throughout their writing, apparently thinking that they are a mark of learning. Frequently these abbreviations are used inappropriately. If you use these, make sure you know what they stand for.

e.g. (*exempli gratia*) for example   i.e. (*id est*) that is

et al. (*et alia*) and others   N.B. (*nota bene*) note well

etc. (*et cetera*) and so forth

In particular, avoid using *etc.* to fill out a list of items. Use of *etc.* announces that you haven't taken the time to finish a thought.

Lazy   The contents of his grocery cart described his eating habits: a big bag of chips, hot sauce, frozen pizza, etc.

Better   The contents of his grocery cart described his eating habits: a big bag of chips, a large jar of hot sauce, two frozen pizzas, a twelve-pack of cola, three Mars bars, and a package of Twinkies.

Conventions for using abbreviations in formal writing

Most abbreviations are inappropriate in formal writing except when the reader would be more familiar with the abbreviation than with the words it represents. When your reader is unlikely to be familiar with an abbreviation, spell out the term, followed by the abbreviation in parentheses, the first time you use it in a paper.

The **Office of Civil Rights (OCR)** is the agency that enforces Title IX regulations. In 1979 **OCR** set out three options for schools to comply with Title IX.

14d Acronyms

Acronyms are abbreviations formed from the first letter of each word. Acronyms are pronounced as words.

AIDS   NASA

Initial-letter abbreviations are commonly pronounced as letters.

ACLU   HIV   rpm

Familiar acronyms and initial-letter abbreviations such as CBS, CIA, FBI, IQ, and UN are rarely spelled out. Unfamiliar acronyms and abbreviations should always be spelled out. Acronyms and abbreviations frequent in particular fields should be spelled out on first use. For example, MMPI (Minnesota Multiphasic Personality Inventory) is familiar in psychology but unfamiliar outside that discipline.

14e Numbers

In formal writing spell out any number that can be expressed in one or two words, as well as any number, regardless of length, at the beginning of a sentence. Also, hyphenate two-word numbers from twenty-one to ninety-nine. When a sentence begins with a number that requires more than two words, revise it if possible.

The exceptions.

Most scientific reports and some business writing use numerals consistently. Most styles do not write out in words a year, a date, an address, a page number, the time of day, decimals, sums of money, phone numbers, rates of speed, or the scene and act of a play. Use numerals instead.

> In 2001 only 33% of respondents said they were satisfied with the City Council's proposals to help the homeless.

> The 17 trials were conducted at temperatures 12–14°C with results ranging from 2.43 to 2.89 mg/dl.

When one number modifies another number, write one out and express the other in numeral form.

> Only after Meryl had run in 12 fifty-mile ultramarathons did she finally win first place in her age group.

Glossary of Grammatical Terms and Usage

This glossary gives the definitions of grammatical terms and items of usage. The grammatical terms are shown in blue. Some of the explanations of usage that follow are not rules, but guidelines to keep in mind for academic and professional writing. In these formal contexts, the safest course is to avoid words that are described as *nonstandard, informal,* or *colloquial.*

A

a/an   Use *a* before words that begin with a consonant sound *(a train, a house).* Use *an* before words that begin with a vowel sound *(an airplane, an hour).*

a lot/alot   *A lot* is generally regarded as informal; *alot* is nonstandard.

accept/except   *Accept* is a verb meaning "receive" or "approve." *Except* is sometimes a verb meaning "leave out," but much more often it's used as a conjunction or preposition meaning "other than."

active   A clause with a transitive verb in which the subject is the doer of the action. In the sentence *Leonardo da Vinci painted Mona Lisa,* the verb *painted* is active. See also **passive**.

adjective   A modifier that qualifies or describes the qualities of a noun or pronoun (see Sections 6a and 6b).

adjective clause   A subordinate clause that modifies a noun or pronoun and is usually introduced by a relative pronoun (see Section 6b). Sometimes called a *relative clause.*

adverb   A word that modifies a verb, another modifier, or a clause (see Sections 6a and 6c).

adverb clause   A subordinate clause that functions as an adverb by modifying a verb, another modifier, or a clause (see Section 6c).

advice/advise   The noun *advice* means a "suggestion"; the verb *advise* means to "recommend" or "give advice."

affect/effect   Usually, *affect* is a verb (to "influence") and *effect* is a noun (a "result"). Less commonly, *affect* is used as a noun and *effect* as a verb.

agreement   The number and person of a subject and verb must match—singular subjects with singular verbs, plural subjects with plural verbs (see Sections 2a to 2f). Likewise, the number and gender of a pronoun and its antecedent must match (see Section 4b).

all ready/already   The adjective phrase *all ready* means "completely prepared"; the adverb *already* means " previously."

all right/alright   *All right,* meaning "acceptable," is the correct spelling. *Alright* is nonstandard.

allude/elude   *Allude* means "refer to indirectly." *Elude* means "evade."

allusion/illusion   An *allusion* is an indirect reference; an *illusion* is a false impression.

among/between   *Between* refers to precisely two people or things; *among refers* to three or more.

amount/number   Use *amount* with things that cannot be counted; use *number* with things that can be counted.

an   See **a/an.**

antecedent   The noun (or pronoun) that a pronoun refers to (see Section 4b).

anybody/any body; anyone/any one   *Anybody* and *anyone* are indefinite pronouns and have the same meaning. In *any body, body* is a noun modified by *any,* and in *any one, one* is a pronoun or adjective modified by *any.*

anymore/any more *Anymore* means "now," while *any more* means "no more." Both are used in negative constructions.

anyway/anyways *Anyway* is correct. *Anyways* is nonstandard.

articles The words *a, an,* and *the* (see Section 7b).

as/as if/as though/like Use *as* instead of *like* before dependent clauses (which include a subject and verb). Use *like* before a noun or a pronoun.

assure/ensure/insure *Assure* means "promise," *ensure* means "make certain," and *insure* means to "make certain in either a legal or financial sense."

auxiliary verb Forms of *be, do,* and *have* combine with verbs to indicate tense and mood (see Section 7c). The modal verbs *can, could, may, might, must, shall, should, will,* and *would* are a subset of auxiliaries.

B

bad/badly Use *bad* only as an adjective. *Badly* is the adverb.

being as/being that Both constructions are colloquial and awkward substitutes for *because.* Don't use them in formal writing.

beside/besides *Beside* means "next to." *Besides* means "in addition to" or "except."

between See **among/between.**

bring/take *Bring* describes movement from a more distant location to a nearer one. *Take* describes movement away.

C

can/may In formal writing, *can* indicates ability or capacity, while *may* indicates permission.

case The form of a noun or pronoun that indicates its function. Nouns change case only to show possession: the **dog,** the **dog's** bowl. See pronoun case (Section 4a).

censor/censure To *censor* is to edit or ban on moral or political grounds. To *censure* is to reprimand publicly.

cite/sight/site To *cite* is to "mention specifically"; *sight* as a verb means to "observe" and as a noun refers to "vision";

site is most commonly used as a noun that means "location," but it is also used as a verb to mean "situate."

clause A group of words with a subject and a predicate. A main or independent clause can stand as a sentence. A subordinate or dependent clause must be attached to a main clause to form a sentence (see Section 1a).

collective noun A noun that refers to a group or a plurality, such as *team, army,* or *committee* (see Section 2d).

comma splice Two independent clauses joined incorrectly by a comma (see Section 1c).

common noun A noun that names a general group, person, place, or thing (see Section 7a). Common nouns are not capitalized unless they begin a sentence.

complement A word or group of words that completes the predicate. See also linking verb.

complement/compliment To *complement* something is to complete it or make it perfect; to *compliment* is to flatter.

complex sentence A sentence that contains at least one subordinate clause attached to a main clause.

compound sentence A sentence that contains at least two main clauses.

compound-complex sentence A sentence that contains at least two main clauses and one subordinate clause.

conjunction See coordinating conjunction and subordinating conjunction.

conjunctive adverb An adverb that often modifies entire clauses and sentences, such as *also, consequently, however, indeed, instead, moreover, nevertheless, otherwise, similarly,* and *therefore* (see Section 6c).

continual/continuous *Continual* refers to a repeated activity; *continuous* refers to an ongoing, unceasing activity.

coordinate A relationship of equal importance, in terms of either grammar or meaning. In *The dog barks, and the cat meows,* the two clauses joined by *and* are coordinate.

coordinating conjunction A word that links two equivalent grammatical elements, such as *and, but, or, yet, nor, for,* and *so.*

could of Nonstandard. See **have/of.**

count noun A noun that names things that can be counted, such as *block, cat,* and *toy* (see Section 7a).

cumulative adjective Two or more adjectives not separated by a comma because they do not make sense if the order is changed. For example, an *enormous dump truck* cannot be changed to a *dump enormous truck* (see Section 8e).

D

dangling modifier A modifier that is not clearly attached to what it modifies (see Section 6e).

data The plural form of *datum;* it takes plural verb forms.

declarative A sentence that makes a statement.

dependent clause See **subordinate clause.**

determiners Words that initiate noun phrases, including possessive nouns *(Pedro's);* possessive pronouns *(my, your);* demonstrative pronouns *(this, that);* and indefinite pronouns *(all, both, many).*

differ from/differ with To *differ from* means to "be unlike"; to *differ with* means to "disagree."

different from/different than Use *different from* where possible.

Dark French roast is different from ordinary coffee.

direct object A noun, pronoun, or noun clause that names who or what receives the action of a transitive verb.

discreet/discrete Both are adjectives. *Discreet* means "prudent" or "tactful"; *discrete* means "separate."

disinterested/uninterested *Disinterested* is often misused to mean *uninterested.* Disinterested means "impartial." A judge can be interested in a case but disinterested in the outcome.

double negative The incorrect use of two negatives to signal the same negative meaning.

due to the fact that Avoid this wordy substitute for *because.*

E

each other/one another Use *each other* for two; use *one another* for more than two.

effect See **affect/effect.**

elicit/illicit The verb *elicit* means to "draw out." The adjective *illicit* means "unlawful."

emigrate from/immigrate to *Emigrate* means to "leave one's country"; *immigrate* means to "settle in another country."

ensure See **assure/ensure/insure.**

enthused Nonstandard in academic and professional writing. Use *enthusiastic* instead.

etc. Avoid this abbreviation for the Latin *et cetera* in formal writing. Either list all the items or use an English phrase such as *and so forth.*

every body/everybody; every one/everyone *Everybody* and *everyone* are indefinite pronouns referring to all people under discussion. *Every one* and *every body* are adjective-noun combinations referring to all members of a group.

except See **accept/except.**

except for the fact that Avoid this wordy substitute for *except that.*

expletive The dummy subjects *it* and *there* used to fill a grammatical slot in a sentence. *It is raining outside. There should be a law against it.*

explicit/implicit Both are adjectives; *explicit* means "stated outright," while *implicit* means just the opposite, "unstated."

F

farther/further *Farther* refers to physical distance; *further* refers to time or other abstract concepts.

fewer/less Use *fewer* with what can be counted and *less* with what cannot be counted.

flunk In formal writing, avoid this colloquial substitute for *fail.*

fragment A group of words beginning with a capital letter and ending with a period that looks like a sentence but lacks a subject or a predicate or both (see Section 1a).

further See **farther/further.**

G

gerund An *-ing* form of a verb used as a noun, such as *running, skiing,* or *laughing.*

good/well *Good* is an adjective and is not interchangeable with the adverb *well.* The one exception is health. Both she feels *good* and she feels *well* are correct.

H

hanged/hung Use *hanged* to refer only to executions; *hung* is used for all other instances.

have/of *Have,* not *of,* follows *should, could, would, may, must,* and *might.*

he/she; s/he Try to avoid language that appears to exclude either gender (unless this is intended, of course) and awkward compromises such as *he/she* or *s/he.* The best solution is to make pronouns plural (the gender-neutral *they)* wherever possible (see Section 4c).

helping verb See **auxiliary verb.**

hopefully This adverb is commonly used as a sentence modifier, but many readers object to it.

I

illusion See **allusion/illusion.**

immigrate See **emigrate from/immigrate to.**

imperative A sentence that expresses a command. Usually the subject is implied rather than stated.

implicit See **explicit/implicit.**

imply/infer *Imply* means to "suggest"; *infer* means to "draw a conclusion."

in regards to Avoid this wordy substitute for *regarding.*

incredible/incredulous *Incredible* means "unbelievable"; *incredulous* means "not believing."

independent clause See **main clause.**

indirect object A noun, pronoun, or noun clause that names who or what is affected by the action of a transitive verb.

infinitive The word *to* plus the base verb form: *to believe, to feel, to act.* See also **split infinitive.**

infinitive phrase A phrase that uses the infinitive form of a verb.

interjection A word expressing feeling that is grammatically unconnected to a sentence, such as *cool, wow, ouch,* or *yikes.*

interrogative A sentence that asks a question.

intransitive verb A verb that does not take an object, such as *sleep, appear,* or *laugh* (see Sections 3c and 7c).

irregardless Nonstandard for *regardless.*

irregular verb A verb that does not use either *-d* or *-ed* to form the past tense and past participle (see Section 3b).

it is my opinion that Avoid this wordy substitute for *I believe that.*

its/it's *Its* is the possessive of *it* and does not take an apostrophe; *it's* is the contraction for *it is.*

-ize/-wise The suffix *-ize* changes a noun or adjective into a verb *(harmony, harmonize).* The suffix *-wise* changes a noun or adjective into an adverb *(clock, clockwise).* Some writers are tempted to use these suffixes to convert almost any word into an adverb or verb form. Unless the word appears in a dictionary, don't use it.

K

kind of/sort of/type of Avoid using these colloquial expressions if you mean *somewhat* or *rather.* It's *kind of hot* is nonstandard. Each is permissible, however, when it refers to a classification of an object. Be sure that it agrees in number with the object it is modifying.

L

lay/lie *Lay* means "place" or "put" and generally takes a direct object (see Section 3c). Its main forms are *lay, laid, laid. Lie* means "recline" or "be positioned" and does not take an object. Its main forms are *lie, lay, lain*.

less See **fewer.**

lie See **lay/lie.**

linking verb   A verb that connects the subject to the complement, such as *appear, be, feel, look, seem,* or *taste.*

lots/lots of Nonstandard in formal writing; use *many* or *much* instead.

M

main clause   A group of words with a subject and a predicate that can stand alone as a sentence. Also called an *independent clause.*

mankind This term offends some readers and is outdated. Use *humans, humanity,* or *people* instead.

may/can See **can/may.**

may be/maybe *May be* is a verb phrase; *maybe* is an adverb.

media This noun is the plural form of *medium* and requires a plural verb.

might of See **have/of.**

modal   A kind of auxiliary verb that indicates ability, permission, intention, obligation, or probability, such as *can, could, may, might, must, shall, should, will,* or *would.*

modifier   A general term for adjectives, adverbs, phrases, and clauses that describe other words (see Sections 6a to 6e).

must of See **have/of.**

N

noncount noun   A noun that names things that cannot be counted, such as *air, energy,* or *water* (see Section 7a).

nonrestrictive modifier   A modifier that is not essential to the meaning of the word, phrase, or clause it modifies and should be set off by commas or other punctuation (see Section 8c).

noun   The name of a person, place, thing, concept, or action. See also common noun and proper noun (see Section 7a).

noun clause   A subordinate clause that functions as a noun.

number See **amount/number.**

O

object   Receiver of the action within the clause or phrase.

OK, O.K., okay Informal; avoid using in academic and professional writing. Each spelling is accepted in informal usage.

owing to the fact that Avoid this wordy, colloquial substitute for *because.*

P

parallelism   The principle of putting similar elements or ideas in similar grammatical form. In this sentence, the grammatical elements following *not only* and *but also* are parallel: *Purchasing the undeveloped land not only will give our city a new park but also will leave our children a lasting inheritance.*

participle   A form of a verb that uses *-ing* in the present (*laughing, playing*) and usually *-ed* or *-en* in the past (*laughed, played*). See Section 3a. Participles are either part of the verb phrase (*She had played the game before*) or used as adjectives (*the laughing girl*).

participial phrase   A phrase formed either by a present participle (for example, *racing*) or by a past participle (for example, *taken*).

parts of speech   The eight classes of words according to their grammatical function: nouns, pronouns, verbs, adjectives, adverbs, prepositions, conjunctions, and interjections.

passive   A clause with a transitive verb in which the subject is being acted upon. In the sentence *Mona Lisa was painted by Leonardo da Vinci*, the verb *was painted* is passive. See also **active.**

people/persons *People* refers to a general group; *persons* refers to a collection of individuals. Use *people* over *persons* except when you're emphasizing the idea of separate persons within the group.

per   Try not to use the English equivalent of this Latin word except in technical writing or familiar usages like *miles per gallon*.

phenomena   This noun is the plural form of *phenomenon* ("observable fact" or "unusual event") and takes plural verbs.

phrase   A group of words that does not contain both a subject and predicate.

plenty   In academic and professional writing, avoid this colloquial substitute for *very*.

plus   Do not use *plus* to join clauses or sentences. Use *and* or use a conjunctive adverb such as *also, moreover, furthermore*.

precede/proceed   Both are verbs but they have different meanings: *precede* means "come before," and *proceed* means "go ahead" or "continue."

predicate   The part of the clause that expresses the action or tells something about the subject. The predicate includes the verb and all its complements, objects, and modifiers.

prejudice/prejudiced   *Prejudice* is a noun; *prejudiced* is an adjective.

preposition   A class of words that indicate relationships and qualities.

prepositional phrase   A phrase formed by a preposition and its object, including the modifiers of its object.

principal/principle   *Principal* means first in importance (*school principal, principal reason*). *Principle* applies to beliefs or understandings (*It goes against my principles*).

pronoun   A word that stands for other nouns or pronouns. Pronouns have several subclasses, including personal pronouns, possessive pronouns, demonstrative pronouns, indefinite pronouns, relative pronouns, interrogative pronouns, reflexive pronouns, and reciprocal pronouns (Sections 4a to 4d).

pronoun case   Pronouns that function as the subjects of sentences are in the **subjective** case (*I, you, he, she, it, we, they*). Pronouns that function as direct or indirect objects are in the **objective** case (*me, you, him, her, it, us, them*). Pronouns that indicate ownership are in the

possessive case (*my, your, his, her, its, our, their*) (see Section 4a).

proper noun   A noun that names a particular person, place, thing, or group (see Section 7a). Proper nouns are capitalized.

Q

question as to whether/question of whether   Avoid these wordy substitutes for *whether*.

R

raise/rise   The verb *raise* means "lift up" and takes a direct object. Its main forms are *raise, raised, raised*. The verb *rise* means "get up" and does not take a direct object. Its main forms are *rise, rose, risen*.

real/really   Avoid using *real* as if it were an adverb. *Really* is an adverb; *real* is an adjective.

reason is because   Omit either *reason is* or *because* when explaining causality.

reason why   Avoid using this redundant combination.

relative pronoun   A pronoun that initiates clauses, such as *that, which, what, who, whom*, or *whose*.

restrictive modifier   A modifier that is essential to the meaning of the word, phrase, or clause it modifies (see Section 8c). Restrictive modifiers are usually not set off by punctuation.

rise/raise   See **raise/rise**.

run-on sentence   Two main clauses fused together without punctuation or a conjunction, appearing as one sentence (see Section 1b).

S

sentence   A grammatically independent group of words that contains at least one main clause.

sentence fragment   See fragment.

set/sit   *Set* means "put" and takes a direct object; its main forms are *set, set, set*. *Sit* means "be seated" and does not take a direct object; its main forms are *sit, sat, sat*. *Sit* should not be used as a synonym for *set*.

shall/will *Shall* is used most often in first person questions, while *will is* a future tense helping verb for all persons. British English consistently uses *shall* with first person: *I shall, we shall.*

should of See **have/of.**

sit/set See **set/sit.**

some time/sometime/sometimes *Some time* means "a span of time," *sometime* means "at some unspecified time," and *sometimes* means "occasionally."

somebody/some body; someone/some one *Somebody* and *someone* are indefinite pronouns and have the same meaning. In *some body, body* is a noun modified by *some,* and in *some one, one* is a pronoun or adjective modified by *some.*

sort of See **kind of/sort of/type of.**

split infinitive An infinitive with a word or words between *to* and the base verb form, such as *to boldly go, to better appreciate.*

stationary/stationery *Stationary* means "motionless"; *stationery* means "writing paper."

subject A noun, pronoun, or noun phrase that identifies what the clause is about and connects with the predicate.

subject-verb agreement See **agreement.**

subordinate A relationship of unequal importance, in terms of either grammar or meaning. In this sentence, the element starting with *after* is a subordinate clause: *Because of the stop-loss policy, many soldiers must stay in the military after their commitment ends.*

subordinate clause A clause that cannot stand alone but must be attached to a main clause. Also called a *dependent clause.*

subordinating conjunction A word that introduces a subordinate clause. Common subordinating conjunctions are *after, although, as, because, before, if, since, that, unless, until, when, where,* and *while.*

sure A colloquial term used as an adverb to mean "certainly." Avoid using it this way in formal writing.

sure and/sure to; try and/try to *Sure to* and *try to* are correct; do not use *and* after *sure* or *try.*

T

take See **bring/take.**

that/which *That* introduces a restrictive or essential clause. Restrictive clauses describe an object that must be that particular object and no other. Though some writers occasionally use *which* with restrictive clauses, it is most often used to introduce nonrestrictive clauses. These are clauses that contain additional nonessential information about the object (see Section 8c).

transition A word or phrase that notes movement from one unit of writing to another.

transitive verb A verb that takes a direct object (see Section 3c).

U

unique *Unique* means "one of a kind." Things cannot be "very unique" or "more unique." They are either unique or not.

V

verb A word that expresses action or characterizes the subject in some way. Verbs can show tense and mood (see Sections 3a to 3c and 7c).

verbal A form of a verb used as an adjective, adverb, or noun. See also **gerund, infinitive, participle.**

W

well/good See **good/well.**

which/that See **that/which.**

who/whom *Who* and *whom* follow the same rules as other pronouns: *Who* is the subject pronoun; *whom* is the object pronoun (see Section 4a).

will/shall See **shall/will.**

-wise/-ize See **-ize/-wise.**

would of See **have/of.**

Y

you Avoid indefinite uses of *you.* It should only be used to mean "you, the reader."

your/you're The two are not interchangeable. *Your* is the possessive form of "you"; *you're* is the contraction of "you are."

Glossary

A

abstract A summary of an article or book

aesthetic criteria Evaluative criteria based on perceptions of beauty and good taste

analogy An extended comparison of one situation or item to another

APA American Psychological Association

APA documentation Documentation style commonly used in social-science and education disciplines

argument A claim supported by at least one reason

assumption An unstated belief or knowledge that connects a claim with evidence

audience Real or assumed individuals or groups to whom a verbal or written communication is directed

B

bandwagon appeal A fallacy of argument based on the assumption that something is true or correct because "everyone" believes it to be so

bar chart Visual depiction of data created by the use of horizontal or vertical bars that comparatively represent rates or frequencies

because clause A statement that begins with the word *because* and provides a supporting reason for a claim

begging the question A fallacy of argument that uses the claim as evidence for its own validity

bias A personal belief that may skew one's perspective or presentation of information

bibliography List of books and articles about a specific subject

blog A Web-based journal or diary featuring regular entries about a particular subject or daily experiences (also known as a Web log)

brainstorming A method of finding ideas by writing a list of questions or statements about a subject

C

causal argument An argument that seeks to identify the reasons behind a certain event or phenomenon

claim A declaration or assertion made about any given topic

claim of comparison A claim that argues something is like or not like something else

common factor method A method used by scientists to identify a recurring factor present in a given cause–effect relationship

consequence The cause–effect result of a given action

context The combination of author, subject, and audience and the broader social, cultural, and economic influences surrounding a text

contextual analysis A type of rhetorical analysis that focuses on the author, the audience, the time, and the circumstances of an argument

counterargument An argument offering an opposing point of view with the goal of demonstrating that it is the stronger of two or more arguments

criteria Standards used to establish a definition or an evaluation

critical reading A process of reading that surpasses an initial understanding or impression of basic content and proceeds with the goal of answering specific questions or examining particular elements

cropping In photography, the process of deleting unwanted parts of an image

cultural assumptions Widely held beliefs that are considered common sense in a particular culture

D

database Large collection of digital information organized for efficient search and retrieval

debate A contest or game in which two or more individuals attempt to use arguments to persuade others to support their opinion

definition argument An argument made by specifying that something does or does not possess certain criteria

diction The choice and use of words in writing and speech

E

either–or A fallacy of argument that presents only two choices in a complex situation

emotional appeal An argumentation strategy that attempts to persuade by stirring the emotions of the audience

empirical research Research that collects data from observation or experiment

ethos An appeal to the audience based on the character and trustworthiness of the speaker or writer

evaluation argument An argument that judges something based on ethical, aesthetic, and/or practical criteria

evaluation of sources The assessment of the relevance and reliability of sources used in supporting claims

evidence Data, examples, or statistics used to support a claim

experimental research Research based on obtaining data under controlled conditions, usually by isolating one variable while holding other variables constant

F

fallacy of argument Failure to provide adequate evidence to support a claim. See *bandwagon appeal, begging the question, false analogy, hasty generalization, name calling, non sequitur, oversimplification, polarization, post hoc fallacy, rationalization, slippery slope, straw man*

false analogy A fallacy of argument that compares two unlike things as if they were similar

feasibility The ability of a proposed solution to be implemented

figurative language The symbolic transference of meaning from one word or phrase to another, such as with the use of metaphor, synecdoche, and metonymy

firsthand evidence Evidence such as interviews, observations, and surveys collected by the writer

font The specific size and weight of a typeface

freewriting A method of finding ideas by writing as fast as possible about a subject for a set length of time

G

generalization A conclusion drawn from knowledge based on past occurrences of the phenomenon in question

good reason A reason that an audience accepts as valid

H

hasty generalization A fallacy of argument resulting from making broad claims based on a few occurrences

I

idea map A brainstorming tool that visually depicts connections among different aspects of an issue

image editor Software that allows you to create and manipulate images

intellectual property Any property produced by the intellect, including copyrights for literary, musical, photographic, and cinematic works; patents for inventions and industrial processes; and trademarks

J

journal A general category of publications that includes popular, trade, and scholarly periodicals

K

keyword search A Web-based search that uses a robot and indexer to produce results based on a chosen word or words

L

line graph A visual presentation of data represented by a continuous line or lines plotted at specific intervals

logos An appeal to the audience based on reasoning and evidence

M

metaphor A figure of speech using a word or phrase that commonly designates one thing to represent another, thus making a comparison

metonymy A type of figurative language that uses one object to represent another that embodies its defining quality

MLA Modern Language Association

MLA documentation Documentation style commonly used in humanities and fine-arts disciplines

multimedia The use of multiple content forms including text, voice and music audio, video, still images, animation, and interactivity

N

name calling A fallacy of argument resulting from the use of undefined, and therefore meaningless, names

narrative arguments A form of argument based on telling stories that suggest the writer's position rather than explicitly making claims

non sequitur A fallacy of argument resulting from connecting two or more unrelated ideas

O

oversimplification A fallacy in argument caused by neglecting to account for the complexity of a subject

P

pathos An appeal based on the audience's emotions or deeply held values

periodical A journal, magazine, or newspaper published at standard intervals, usually daily, weekly, monthly, or quarterly

periodical index Paper or electronic resource that catalogs the contents of journals, magazines, and newspapers

pie chart A circular chart resembling a pie that illustrates percentages of the whole through the use of delineated wedge shapes

plagiarism The improper use of the unauthorized and unattributed words or ideas of another author

podcast Digital media files available on the Internet for playback on a portable media player, such as an iPod

polarization A fallacy of argument based on exaggerating the characteristics of opposing groups to highlight division and extremism

popular journal A magazine aimed at the general public; usually includes illustrations, short articles, and advertisements

position argument A general kind of argument in which a claim is made for an idea or way of thinking about a subject

post hoc fallacy A fallacy of argument based on the assumption that events that follow each other have a causal relationship

practical criteria Evaluative criteria based on usefulness or likely results

primary research Information collected directly by the writer through observations, interviews, surveys, and experiments

process of elimination method A means of finding a cause by systematically ruling out all other possible causes

proposal argument An argument that either advocates or opposes a specific course of action

R

rationalization A fallacy of argument based on using weak explanations to avoid dealing with the actual causes

reason In an argument, the justification for a claim

rebuttal argument An argument that challenges or rejects the claims of another argument

reference librarian Library staff member who is familiar with information resources and who can show you how to use them (you can find a reference librarian at the reference desk in your library)

refutation A rebuttal argument that points out the flaws in an opposing argument

rhetorical analysis Careful study of a written argument or other types of persuasion aimed at understanding how the components work or fail to work

rhetorical situation Factors present at the time of writing or speaking, including the writer or speaker, the audience, the purpose of communicating, and the context

S

sans serif type A style of type recognized by blunt ends and a consistency in thickness

scholarly journals Journals containing articles written by experts in a particular field; also called peer-reviewed or academic journals

secondary research Information obtained from existing knowledge, such as research in the library

secondhand evidence Evidence from the work of others found in the library, on the Web, and elsewhere

serif type A style of type developed to resemble the strokes of an ink pen and recognized by wedge-shaped ends on letter forms

single difference method A method of finding a cause for differing phenomena in very similar situations by identifying the one element that varies

slippery slope A fallacy of argument based on the assumption that if a first step is taken, additional steps will inevitably follow

straw man A fallacy of argument based on the use of the diversionary tactic of setting up the opposing position in such a manner that it can be easily rejected

sufficiency The adequacy of evidence supporting a claim

synecdoche A type of figurative language in which a part is used to represent the whole

T

textual analysis A type of rhetorical analysis that focuses exclusively on the text itself

thesis One or more sentences that state the main idea of an argument

typeface A style of type, such as serif, sans serif, or decorative

U

URL (Universal Resource Locator) An address on the Web

V

visual argument A type of persuasion using images, graphics, or objects

voice In writing, the distinctive style of a writer that provides a sense of the writer as a person

W

Web directory A subject guide to Web pages grouped by topic and subtopic

Web editors Programs that allow you to compose Web pages

wiki A Web-based application designed to let multiple authors write, edit, and review content, such as Wikipedia

working thesis A preliminary statement of the main claim of an argument, subject to revision

Credits

Photo Credits

Text Credits

Handbook Index

Index